Lecture Notes in Computer Science 9164

Commenced Publication in 1973
Founding and Former Series Editors:
Gerhard Goos, Juris Hartmanis, and Jan van Leeuwen

More information about this series at http://www.springer.com/series/7412

Mohamed Kamel · Aurélio Campilho (Eds.)

Image Analysis and Recognition

12th International Conference, ICIAR 2015
Niagara Falls, ON, Canada, July 22–24, 2015
Proceedings

 Springer

Editors
Mohamed Kamel
University of Waterloo
Waterloo, ON
Canada

Aurélio Campilho
University of Porto
Porto
Portugal

ISSN 0302-9743 ISSN 1611-3349 (electronic)
Lecture Notes in Computer Science
ISBN 978-3-319-20800-8 ISBN 978-3-319-20801-5 (eBook)
DOI 10.1007/978-3-319-20801-5

Library of Congress Control Number: 2015942241

LNCS Sublibrary: SL6 – Image Processing, Computer Vision, Pattern Recognition, and Graphics

Springer Cham Heidelberg New York Dordrecht London

Printed on acid-free paper

Springer International Publishing AG Switzerland is part of Springer Science+Business Media
(www.springer.com)

Preface

These are the proceedings of the 12th edition of ICIAR. This series of annual conferences offers an opportunity for the participants to interact and present their latest research in theory, methodology, and applications of image analysis and recognition. ICIAR 2015, the International Conference on Image Analysis and Recognition, was held in Niagara Falls, Canada, July 22–24, 2015. ICIAR is organized by AIMI — Association for Image and Machine Intelligence — a not-for-profit organization registered in Ontario, Canada.

For ICIAR 2015, we received a total of 80 papers, 69 regular and 11 short papers, from 24 countries. Before the review process all the papers were checked for similarity using a comparison database of scholarly work. The review process was carried out by members of the Program Committee and other reviewers. Each paper was reviewed by at least two reviewers, and checked by the conference chairs. A total of 60 papers (55 regular and five short) were finally accepted and appear in these proceedings. We would like to sincerely thank the authors for responding to our call, and we thank the reviewers for the careful evaluation and feedback provided to the authors. It is this collective effort that resulted in the strong conference program and high-quality proceedings.

We were very pleased to include three outstanding keynote talks: "Computational Inference of Emotion in Images: A Final Frontier and a Data-Intensive Approach" by Jiebo Luo, University of Rochester, USA; "Relating Retinal Anatomy, Pathology, Function, and Therapy Guidance: Precision Medicine via Analysis of Ophthalmic 3D OCT" by Milan Sonka, University of Iowa, USA; and "Objective Image Quality Assessment ? Current Status and What's Beyond" by Zhou Wang, University of Waterloo, Canada. We would like to express our gratitude to the keynote speakers for accepting our invitation to share their vision and recent advances in their areas of expertise.

We would like to thank Khaled Hammouda, the webmaster of the conference, for maintaining the website, interacting with the authors, and preparing the proceedings.

We are also grateful to Springer's editorial staff, for supporting this publication in the LNCS series. We would also like to acknowledge the professional service of Cathie Lowell in taking care of the registration process and the special events of the conference.

Finally, we were very pleased to welcome all the participants to ICIAR 2015. For those who were not able to attend, we hope this publication provides a good view into the research presented at the conference, and we look forward to meeting you at the next ICIAR conference.

July 2015

Mohamed Kamel
Aurélio Campilho

Organization

General Chairs

Mohamed Kamel   University of Waterloo, Canada
Aurélio Campilho   University of Porto, Portugal

Conference Secretariat

Cathie Lowell   Dundas, Ontario, Canada

Webmaster

Khaled Hammouda   Waterloo, Ontario, Canada

Supported by

AIMI – Association for Image and Machine Intelligence

CPAMI – Centre for Pattern Analysis and Machine Intelligence
University of Waterloo
Canada

Center for Biomedical Engineering Research
INESC TEC - INESC Technology and Science
Portugal

U.PORTO
FEUP **FACULDADE DE ENGENHARIA**
UNIVERSIDADE DO PORTO

Department of Electrical and Computer Engineering
Faculty of Engineering
University of Porto
Portugal

Advisory Committee

M. Ahmadi	University of Windsor, Canada
P. Bhattacharya	Concordia University, Canada
T.D. Bui	Concordia University, Canada
M. Cheriet	University of Quebec, Canada
E. Dubois	University of Ottawa, Canada
Z. Duric	George Mason University, USA
G. Granlund	Linköping University, Sweden
L. Guan	Ryerson University, Canada
M. Haindl	Institute of Information Theory and Automation, Czech Republic
E. Hancock	The University of York, UK
J. Kovacevic	Carnegie Mellon University, USA
M. Kunt	Swiss Federal Institute of Technology (EPFL), Switzerland
K.N. Plataniotis	University of Toronto, Canada
A. Sanfeliu	Technical University of Catalonia, Spain
M. Shah	University of Central Florida, USA
M. Sid-Ahmed	University of Windsor, Canada
C.Y. Suen	Concordia University, Canada
A.N. Venetsanopoulos	University of Toronto, Canada
M. Viergever	University of Utrecht, The Netherlands
B. Vijayakumar	Carnegie Mellon University, USA
R. Ward	University of British Columbia, Canada
D. Zhang	The Hong Kong Polytechnic University, Hong Kong, SAR China

Program Committee

A. Abate	University of Salerno, Italy
L. Alexandre	University of Beira Interior, Portugal
H. Araujo	University of Coimbra, Portugal
E. Balaguer-Ballester	Bournmouth University, UK
T. Barata	Centro de Geofísica da Universidade de Coimbra, Portugal
J. Barbosa	University of Porto, Portugal

A. Monteiro	University of Porto, Portugal
M. Nappi	University of Salerno, Italy
H. Ogul	Helsinki University of Technology, Turkey
V. Palazon-Gonzalez	Universitat Jaume I, Spain
M. Penedo	University of Coruña, Spain
F. Perales	Universitat de les Illes Balears, Spain
E. Petrakis	Technical University of Crete, Greece
P. Pina	Instituto Superior Técnico, Portugal
A. Pinheiro	UBI - University of Beira Interior, Portugal
A. Pinho	University of Aveiro, Portugal
J. Pinto	Instituto Superior Técnico, Portugal
H. Proença	University of Beira Interior, Portugal
P. Quelhas	Instituto de Engenharia Biomédica, Portugal
P. Radeva	Universitat de Barcelona, CVC, Spain
S. Rahnamayan	University of Waterloo, Canada
E. Ricci	University of Perugia, Italy
S. Rota Bulò	Fondazione Bruno Kessler, Italy
K. Roy	North Carolina A&T State University, USA
A. Ruano	University of Algarve, Portugal
M. Ruano	University of Algarve, Portugal
J. Sanches	Instituto Superior Técnico, Portugal
J. Sánchez	University of Las Palmas de Gran Canaria, Spain
A. Sappa	Computer Vision Center, Spain
F. Sattar	University of Waterloo, Canada
G. Schaefer	Loughborough University, UK
P. Scheunders	University of Antwerp, Belgium
J. Sequeira	Ecole Supérieure d'Ingénieurs de Luminy, France
J. Silva	University of Porto, Portugal
B. Smolka	Silesian University of Technology, Poland
S. Sural	Indian Institute of Technology, India
A. Taboada-Crispi	Universidad Central "Marta Abreu" de Las Villas, Cuba
L. Teixeira	University of Porto, Portugal
O. Terrades	Universitat Autonoma de Barcelona - Computer Vision Center, Spain
R. Torres	University of Campinas (UNICAMP), Brazil
A. Torsello	Università Ca' Foscari Venezia, Italy
A. Uhl	University of Salzburg, Austria
M. Vento	Università di Salerno, Italy
R. Vigário	Aalto University School of Science, Finland
Y. Voisin	Université de Bourgogne, France
E. Vrscay	University of Waterloo, Canada
M. Wirth	University of Guelph, Canada
J. Wu	University of Windsor, Canada
X. Xie	Swansea University, UK
J. Xue	University College London, UK
P. Zemcik	Brno University of Technology, Czech Republic

Q. Zhang	Waseda University, Japan
H. Zhou	Queen's University Belfast, UK
R. Zwiggelaar	Aberystwyth University, UK

Additional Reviewers

M. Camplani	University of Bristol, UK
C. Caridade	Instituto Politécnico de Coimbre/Instituto Superior de Engenharia de Coimbra, Portugal
J. Chen	Lehigh University, USA
L. Fernandez	University of León, Spain
M. Gangeh	University of Toronto, Canada
V. Gonzalez	The University of Edinburgh, UK
H. Haberdar	University of Houston, USA
M. Hortas	Universidade de Coruña, Spain
V. Kaul	Facebook, USA
S. Mahmoud	University of Waterloo, Canada
Y. Miao	University of Waterloo, Canada
F. Monteiro	IPB, Portugal
P. Moreno	Instituto Superior Tecnico, Portugal
J. Novo	Universidade do Porto, Portugal
H. Oliveira	INESC TEC, Portugal
R. Rocha	INEB, Portugal
J. Rodrigues	University of the Algarve, Portugal
N. Rodriguez	Universidade de Coruña, Spain
J. Rouco	INESC TEC, Portugal

Contents

Image Quality Assessment

Modelling of Subjective Radiological Assessments with Objective Image
Quality Measures of Brain and Body CT Images 3
  Ilona A. Kowalik-Urbaniak, Jane Castelli, Nasim Hemmati,
  David Koff, Nadine Smolarski-Koff, Edward R. Vrscay,
  Jiheng Wang, and Zhou Wang

Blind Image Quality Assessment Through Wakeby Statistics Model 14
  Mohsen Jenadeleh and Mohsen Ebrahimi Moghaddam

Improving Image Quality of Tiled Displays 22
  Steven B. McFadden and Paul A.S. Ward

Image Enhancement

Structural Similarity-Based Optimization Problems with L^1-Regularization:
Smoothing Using Mollifiers 33
  Daniel Otero, Davide La Torre, and Edward R. Vrscay

Improved Non-Local Means Algorithm Based on Dimensionality
Reduction 43
  Golam M. Maruf and Mahmoud R. El-Sakka

Non-local Means for Stereo Image Denoising Using Structural Similarity.... 51
  Monagi H. Alkinani and Mahmoud R. El-Sakka

Structural Similarity Optimized Wiener Filter: A Way to Fight
Image Noise.. 60
  Mahmud Hasan and Mahmoud R. El-Sakka

Image Segmentation, Registration and Analysis

A Real-Time Framework for Detection of Long Linear Infrastructural
Objects in Aerial Imagery 71
  Hrishikesh Sharma, Tanima Dutta, V. Adithya, and P. Balamuralidhar

Structural Representations for Multi-modal Image Registration Based
on Modified Entropy 82
  Keyvan Kasiri, Paul Fieguth, and David A. Clausi

Attributed Relational Graph-Based Learning of Object Models for Object
Segmentation   90
   Nasreen Akter and Iker Gondra

Label Fusion for Multi-atlas Segmentation Based on Majority Voting   100
   Jie Huo, Guanghui Wang, Q.M. Jonathan Wu, and Akilan Thangarajah

Image Coding, Compression and Encryption

An Optimized Selective Encryption for Video Confidentiality   109
   Khalfan Almarashda, Ali Dawood, Thomas Martin,
   Mohammed Al-Mualla, and Harish Bhaskar

Near-Lossless PCA-Based Compression of Seabed Surface with Prediction . . .   119
   Paweł Forczmański and Wojciech Maleika

Adaptive Weighted Neighbors Lossless Image Coding   129
   AbdulWahab Kabani and Mahmoud R. El-Sakka

Dimensionality Reduction and Classification

Dimensionality Reduction of Proportional Data Through Data Separation
Using Dirichlet Distribution   141
   Walid Masoudimansour and Nizar Bouguila

Image Categorization Using a Heuristic Automatic Clustering Method
Based on Hierarchical Clustering   150
   François LaPlante, Mustapha Kardouchi, and Nabil Belacel

Semantic Scene Classification with Generalized Gaussian Mixture Models . . .   159
   Tarek Elguebaly and Nizar Bouguila

Biometrics

Classification of Tooth Shapes for Human Identification Purposes–An
Experimental Comparison of Selected Simple Shape Descriptors   169
   Katarzyna Gościewska and Dariusz Frejlichowski

Micro Genetic and Evolutionary Feature Extraction: An Exploratory
Data Analysis Approach for Multispectral Iris Recognition   178
   Pablo A. Arias, Joseph Shelton, Kaushik Roy, Foysal Ahmad,
   and Gerry V. Dozier

Biometric Analysis of Human Ear Matching Using Scale and Rotation
Invariant Feature Detectors   186
   Soumyajit Sarkar, Jizhong Liu, and Guanghui Wang

Mutibiometric System Based on Game Theory 194
Nawaf Aljohani, Foysal Ahmad, Kaushik Roy, and Joseph Shelton

Face Description, Detection and Recognition

Head Pose Classification Using a Bidimensional Correlation Filter 203
*Djemel Ziou, Dayron Rizo-Rodriguez, Antoine Tabbone,
and Nafaa Nacereddine*

Illumination Robust Facial Feature Detection via Decoupled Illumination
and Texture Features 210
Brendan Chwyl, Alexander Wong, and David A. Clausi

Posed Facial Expression Detection Using Reflection Symmetry
and Structural Similarity 218
Harish Bhaskar, Davide La Torre, and Mohammed Al-Mualla

Improving the Recognition of Occluded Faces by Means
of Two-dimensional Orthogonal Projection into Local Subspaces 229
Paweł Forczmański and Piotr Łabędź

Hybrid Age Estimation Using Facial Images. 239
Simon Reade and Serestina Viriri

Unsupervised Sub-graph Selection and Its Application in Face Recognition
Techniques. 247
Ahmed ElSayed, Ausif Mahmood, and Tarek Sobh

Human Activity Recognition

Dynamic Perceptual Attribute-Based Hidden Conditional Random Fields
for Gesture Recognition. 259
Gang Hu and Qigang Gao

The Bag of Micro-Movements for Human Activity Recognition 269
Pejman Habashi, Boubakeur Boufama, and Imran Shafiq Ahmad

An Efficient Method for Extracting Key-Frames from 3D Human Joint
Locations for Action Recognition 277
Md. Hasanul Kabir, Ferdous Ahmed, and Abdullah-Al-Tariq

Robotics and 3D Vision

A Simple View-Based Software Architecture for an Autonomous Robot
Navigation System 287
*Salvador E. Ayala-Raggi, Pedro de Jesús González,
Susana Sánchez-Urrieta, and Aldrin Barreto-Flores*

A Comparison of Feature Detectors and Descriptors in RGB-D SLAM
Methods.   297
    Oguzhan Guclu and Ahmet Burak Can

Accuracy Improvement for Depth from Small Irregular Camera Motions
and Its Performance Evaluation.   306
    Syouta Tsukada, Yishin Ho, Norio Tagawa, and Kan Okubo

Fast and Robust Algorithm for Fundamental Matrix Estimation   316
    Ming Zhang, Guanghui Wang, Haiyang Chao, and Fuchao Wu

Medical Image Analysis

Biologically-Inspired Supervised Vasculature Segmentation in SLO Retinal
Fundus Images   325
    Samaneh Abbasi-Sureshjani, Iris Smit-Ockeloen, Jiong Zhang,
    and Bart Ter Haar Romeny

Assessment of Retinal Vascular Changes Through Arteriolar-to-Venular
Ratio Calculation   335
    Behdad Dashtbozorg, Ana Maria Mendonça, and Aurélio Campilho

Automatic Segmentation of Vertebrae in Ultrasound Images.   344
    Florian Berton, Wassim Azzabi, Farida Cheriet, and Catherine Laporte

Towards an Automatic Clinical Classification of Age-Related Macular
Degeneration   352
    Thanh Vân Phan, Lama Seoud, and Farida Cheriet

Optical Flow Based Approach for Automatic Cardiac Cycle Estimation in
Ultrasound Images of the Carotid   360
    Teresa Araújo, Guilherme Aresta, José Rouco, Carmen Ferreira,
    Elsa Azevedo, and Aurélio Campilho

Statistical Textural Distinctiveness in Multi-Parametric Prostate MRI
for Suspicious Region Detection   368
    Audrey G. Chung, Christian Scharfenberger, Farzad Khalvati,
    Alexander Wong, and Masoom A. Haider

Automatic Detection of Immunogold Particles from Electron Microscopy
Images.   377
    Ricardo Gamelas Sousa, Tiago Esteves, Sara Rocha,
    Francisco Figueiredo, Pedro Quelhas, and Luís M. Silva

Specular Reflectance Suppression in Endoscopic Imagery via Stochastic
Bayesian Estimation   385
    Brendan Chwyl, Audrey G. Chung, Alexander Wong,
    and David A. Clausi

Characterization of Medical Images Using Edge Density and Local
Directional Pattern (LDP)................................... 394
   Serestina Viriri

Automated Detection of Aortic Root Landmarks in Preprocedure CT
Angiography Images for Transcatheter Aortic Valve Implantation Patients . . . 402
   Mustafa Elattar, Esther Wiegerinck, Floortje van Kesteren,
   Lucile Dubois, Nils Planken, Ed vanbavel, Jan Baan,
   and Henk Marquering

Retinal Blood Vessels Differentiation for Calculation of Arterio-Venous
Ratio.. 411
   Samra Irshad, M. Usman Akram, Sara Ayub, and Anaum Ayaz

Graph Structuring of Skeleton Object for Its High-Level Exploitation 419
   Rabaa Youssef, Anis Kacem, Sylvie Sevestre-Ghalila,
   and Christine Chappard

Applications

Vehicle Detection Using Approximation of Feature Pyramids in the DFT
Domain 429
   Mohamed A. Naiel, M. Omair Ahmad, and M.N.S. Swamy

Real-Time Speed-Limit Sign Detection and Recognition Using Spatial
Pyramid Feature and Boosted Random Forest...................... 437
   JaWon Gim, MinCheol Hwang, Byoung Chul Ko, and Jae-Yeal Nam

Automatic Nacre Thickness Measurement of Tahitian Pearls............. 446
   Martin Loesdau, Sébastien Chabrier, and Alban Gabillon

Automated Wheat Disease Classification Under Controlled and
Uncontrolled Image Acquisition 456
   Punnarai Siricharoen, Bryan Scotney, Philip Morrow, and Gerard Parr

Color Space Identification for Image Display 465
   Martin Vezina, Djemel Ziou, and Fatma Kerouh

Application of the General Shape Analysis in Determining the Class
of Binary Object Silhouettes in the Video Surveillance System........... 473
   Katarzyna Gościewska, Dariusz Frejlichowski, and Radosław Hofman

Speedy Character Line Detection Algorithm Using Image Block-Based
Histogram Analysis... 481
   Chinthaka Premachandra, Katsunari Goto, Shinji Tsuruoka,
   Hiroharu Kawanaka, and Haruhiko Takase

Detecting Parked Vehicles in Static Images Using Simple Spectral Features
in the 'SM4Public' System.   489
    Dariusz Frejlichowski, Katarzyna Gościewska, Adam Nowosielski,
    Paweł Forczmański, and Radosław Hofman

Road Detection in Urban Areas Using Random Forest Tree-Based
Ensemble Classification   499
    Safaa M. Bedawi and Mohamed S. Kamel

Application of the Polar–Fourier Greyscale Descriptor to the Automatic
Traffic Sign Recognition   506
    Dariusz Frejlichowski

Camera-Based Lane Marking Detection for ADAS and Autonomous
Driving   514
    Yasamin Alkhorshid, Kamelia Aryafar, Gerd Wanielik,
    and Ali Shokoufandeh

Handling Inter-object Occlusion for Multi-object Tracking Based
on Attraction Force Constraint   520
    Yuke Li, Isabelle Bloch, and Weiming Shen

Indian Sign Language Recognition Using Kinect Sensor   528
    Kapil Mehrotra, Atul Godbole, and Swapnil Belhe

Automatic Planning of Minimally Invasive Aortic Valve Replacement
Surgery   536
    Mustafa Elattar, Floortje van Kesteren, Esther Wiegerinck,
    Ed van Bavel, Jan Baan, Riccardo Cocchieri, Nils Planken,
    and Henk Marquering

Author Index   541

Image Quality Assessment

Modelling of Subjective Radiological Assessments with Objective Image Quality Measures of Brain and Body CT Images

Ilona A. Kowalik-Urbaniak[1]([✉]), Jane Castelli[3], Nasim Hemmati[4], David Koff[3],
Nadine Smolarski-Koff[3], Edward R. Vrscay[1], Jiheng Wang[2], and Zhou Wang[2]

[1] Department of Applied Mathematics, Faculty of Mathematics,
University of Waterloo, Waterloo, ON N2L 3G1, Canada
{iakowali@uwaterloo.ca,ervrscay,jiheng.wang}@uwaterloo.ca
[2] Department of Electrical and Computer Engineering, Faculty of Engineering,
University of Waterloo, Waterloo, ON N2L 3G1, Canada
zhouwang@ieee.org
[3] Department of Radiology, McMaster University,
Hamilton, ON L8S 4L8, Canada
jane.castelli@miircam.ca, koff@hhsc.ca, nadine.koff@realtimemedical.com
[4] Department of Diagnostic Imaging, Hamilton Health Sciences,
McMaster University, Hamilton, ON L8S 4L8, Canada
nasim.hemmati@medportal.ca

Abstract. In this work we determine how well the common objective image quality measures (Mean Squared Error (MSE), local MSE, Signal-to-Noise Ratio (SNR), Structural Similarity Index (SSIM), Visual Signal-to-Noise Ratio (VSNR) and Visual Information Fidelity (VIF)) predict subjective radiologists' assessments for brain and body computed tomography (CT) images.

A subjective experiment was designed where radiologists were asked to rate the quality of compressed medical images in a setting similar to clinical. We propose a modified Receiver Operating Characteristic (ROC) analysis method for comparison of the image quality measures where the "ground truth" is considered to be given by subjective scores. The best performance was achieved by the SSIM index and VIF for brain and body CT images. The worst results were observed for VSNR.

We have utilized a logistic curve model which can be used to predict the subjective assessments with an objective criteria. This is a practical tool that can be used to determine the quality of medical images.

1 Introduction

Speed limitations of existing networks along with the explosive growth of image modalities with extremely high volume outputs have combined to make the issue of irreversible medical image coding one of the key considerations in the design of future PACS systems. Existing lossy image compression techniques are well suited for images where the only concern is visual quality.

© Springer International Publishing Switzerland 2015
M. Kamel and A. Campilho (Eds.): ICIAR 2015, LNCS 9164, pp. 3–13, 2015.
DOI: 10.1007/978-3-319-20801-5_1

As expected, increasing the degree of compression of an image leads to decreasing fidelity. The extent of allowable irreversible compression is dependent on the imaging modality and the nature of the image pathology and anatomy. Image compression often results in the distortion of the images and therefore creates the risk of losing or altering relevant diagnostic information.

If not implemented properly, distortions resulting from lossy compression can impede the ability of radiologists to make confident diagnoses from compressed medical images. However, defining the amount of accepted distortion is a complex task. For this reason, reliable image quality assessment methods are needed in order to achieve "Diagnostically Acceptable Irreversible Compression (DAIC)", defined in [13], which refers to an irreversible compression that has no effect on diagnostic task.

2   Image Quality Assessment

Many objective image quality metrics have been proposed in the last decade. Due to the wide variety of image types and applications, image quality assessment is not (yet) fully automatic and subjective approaches are still predominant [12]. How do we measure diagnostic quality?

There is no standard method to measure the quality of compressed medical images, however, three approaches are usually considered [3]:

1. Subjective image quality rating using psychovisual tests or questionnaires with numerical ratings.
2. Diagnostic accuracy is measured by simulating a clinical environment with the use of statistical analysis (e.g. Receiver Operating Characteristic (ROC)).
3. Objective quality measures such as the Mean Squared Error (MSE) and Structural Similarity (SSIM).

2.1   Objective Image Quality Methods

The existing objective image quality measures are not necessarily reliable measures of diagnostic quality for medical images. Moreover, compression ratios, generally used as pre-compression quality predictors, indicate a poor correlation with image quality and are image dependent [4]. According to Marmolin [10]: "MSE is not very valid as a quality criterion for pictures reproduced for human viewing and the improved measures could be derived by weighting the error in accordance with assumed properties of the visual system." Although MSE is shown to poorly correlate with visual quality, it should not be taken for granted that any perceptual object quality measure must be better. According to the relevant literature, SSIM and other objective measures show better performance than MSE for natural image/video content for consumer electronics applications based on subjective tests [16,17]. It cannot be assumed that an objective quality metric that performs well for natural images will ensure a superior diagnostic quality for medical images. In spite of these pitfalls, MSE and other objective methods have been used in medical image quality assessment. Moreover, no objective model has been yet "established" for medical images, especially when using radiologists as subjects.

There are many full reference image quality assessment algorithms proposed in the literature. A lengthy review of objective image quality was presented in [5]. Full reference methods are based on comparison between the original image and its distorted version. Among the most common ones are Mean Squared Error (MSE), Signal-to-Noise Ratio (SNR), Structural Similarity (SSIM) [15], Visual Signal-to-Noise Ratio (VSNR) [1] and Visual Information Fidelity (VIF) [14].

MSE is related to the L^2 distance between image functions. The MSE between the compressed image g and the original image f is given by

$$\text{MSE}(f, g) = \frac{1}{MN} \sum_{i=1}^{M} \sum_{j=1}^{N} \left(f(i,j) - g(i,j) \right)^2. \tag{1}$$

The SSIM index, introduced by Wang and Bovik [16], assumes that the HVS is highly sensitive to structural information/distortions (e.g. JPEG blockiness, "salt-and-pepper" noise, ringing effect, blurring) in an image and automatically adjusts to the non-structural (e.g. luminance or spatial shift, contrast change) ones [15]. Another assumption of the SSIM index is that images are highly structured and there exist strong neighbouring dependencies among the pixels, which the MSE totally ignores. The SSIM index measures the difference/similarity between two images by combining three components of the human visual system: luminance, $l(f,g)$, contrast, $c(f,g)$ and structure, $s(f,g)$.

The (local) SSIM is given by:

$$SSIM(f,g) = \left(\frac{2\mu_f\mu_g + C_1}{\mu_f^2 + \mu_g^2 + C_1} \right) \cdot \left(\frac{2\sigma_f\sigma_g + C_2}{\sigma_f^2 + \sigma_g^2 + C_2} \right) \cdot \left(\frac{\sigma_{fg} + C_3}{\sigma_f\sigma_g + C_3} \right). \tag{2}$$

where μ is the mean, σ_f^2 is the variance, and σ_{fg} is the covariance. SSIM is computed over $m \times n$ pixel neighbourhoods. The (non-negative) parameters C_1, C_2 and C_3 are stability constants of relatively small magnitude, which are designed to avoid numerical "blowups", which could occur in the case of small denominators. In the special case $C_3 = C_2/2$, the following simplified, two-term version of the SSIM index is obtained:

$$SSIM(f,g) = \left(\frac{2\mu_f\mu_g + C_1}{\mu_f^2 + \mu_g^2 + C_1} \right) \left(\frac{2\sigma_{fg} + C_2}{\sigma_f^2 + \sigma_g^2 + C_2} \right). \tag{3}$$

For natural images there are recommended default values for these parameters [15]. On the other hand, the question of optimal values for these stability constants for medical images is still an open one. The smaller the values of these constants, the more sensitive the SSIM index is to small image textures such as noise. In our study the constants were adopted from our previous work [8,9], where we examined a range of stability constants in order to determine the value(s) which are optimal for the assessment of diagnostic quality of medical images.

In this study, we also employ the local MSE. This score is computed in a similar manner as the SSIM index, i.e. for a local $m \times n$ pixel neighbourhood. The quality score is computed by averaging the local MSE scores. In this work we use 11×11 pixel neighbourhoods for the computation of SSIM and local MSE measures, which is the default parameter in the computation of the SSIM index [15].

SNR is a measure of quality that considers the MSE and the variance of the original signal. It is defined as follows,

$$SNR(f,g) = 10 \log_{10} \frac{\sigma_f^2}{MSE(f,g).} \tag{4}$$

The result is measured in decibels. SNR is considered in the literature as a valid quality measure [3].

Another image fidelity measure that we consider in our work is the VSNR [2]. The VSNR is a low complexity method that considers near-threshold and suprathreshold properties of the HVS. There are two stages in the algorithm. In the first one, wavelet-based models for the computation of contrast thresholds for distortions detection are used in order to determine whether distortions are visible. Based on the outcome of the first step, if the distortions are below the threshold of detection, then no further computation is required and the distorted image is of perfect visual fidelity. In the case where distortions are "suprathreshold", a second step of the algorithm is applied. In the second step, two properties are computed: the perceived contrast of the distortions and the disruption of global precedence. Finally, VSNR is computed as follows,

$$VSNR(f,g) = 20 \log_{10} \left(\frac{C(f)}{\alpha d_{pc} + (1-\alpha)(d_{gp}/\sqrt{2})} \right) \tag{5}$$

where $C(f)$ denotes the contrast of the original image f, $d_{pc} = C(E)$ is the perceived contrast of the distortions, $E = f - g$ is the distortion, d_{gp} is the global precedence and $\alpha \in [0,1]$ determines the relative contribution of d_{pc} and d_{gp}. A detailed explanation and equations required to compute the VSNR are presented in [2]. According to the author, the VSNR metric has relatively low computational complexity.

VIF is based on visual information fidelity that considers natural scene statistical information of images. A detailed description can be found in [14]. The idea is to quantify the statistical information that is shared between the original and distorted images using conditional mutual information.

$$VIF(f,g) = \text{Distorted Image Information / Reference Image Information.} \tag{6}$$

3   Design of the Subjective Experiment

A subjective experiment was designed in order to assess the global prediction of the image quality assessments being examined. The experiment employed sixty CT slices - thirty neurological and thirty upper body images- obtained from Medical Informatics Research Centre at McMaster (MIIRC@M), Hamilton, Canada. These images were first windowed according to their default viewing parameters (window width and window centre) in order to reduce their bit-depth from 16 to 8 bits per pixel (bpp). The resulting 512×512 pixel, 8 bpp images were compressed at five different compression levels using both the JPEG and JPEG2000 compression algorithms. Preliminary visual observations were used to select the compression levels employed in the experiment. The range of compression ratios was intended to represent a wide variety of visual qualities, from no and barely noticeable to fairly noticeable distortion.

An image viewer was developed specifically for this study in order to provide an easy-to-use graphical interface for the radiologists. The viewer displayed a compressed image beside its uncompressed counterpart without zoom. The compressed images were presented randomly and independently to each subject. During the course of the experiment, each compressed image was presented to each radiologist with some repetitions, but without the radiologists' knowledge. The subjects were not made aware of the compression ratios or quality factors of the compressed images. Three buttons were placed at the bottom of the user interface: (1) not noticeable and acceptable, (2) noticeable and acceptable and (3) noticeable and not acceptable. A confirmation was requested before passing to the next stimulus. The experiment can be summarized as follows,

- The subjects were six radiologists including experienced radiologists as well as residents (McMaster University, Hamilton, ON, Canada).
- Types of pathologies: Based on previous findings by Koff *et al.* [6,7], the pathologies include subtle lesions in the liver for the body, and parenchyma and posterior fossa for brain. Subtle lesions include the following two types:
  • Very small lesions, limit in size, of less than 2 mm, but high contrast (calcifications) or low density (tiny cysts);
  • Subtle parenchymal alterations translating into subtle differences in density such as cerebral infarcts.
- The brain CT and body CT images used in the experiment were carefully chosen with the help of radiologists and contain pathological and normal cases (about 1/3 of images represented normal cases).
- Working environment: MIIRC@M office (Hamilton, ON, Canada); Eizo Radiforce monitor, 54 cm (21.3") display, with a 1200×1600 native resolution (3:4 aspect ratio) and a viewing size of 324.0×432.0 mm. Capable of displaying 10-bit colors.
- Compression levels: Five quality factors (JPEG input parameters) were chosen:
  • $[90, 65, 45, 20, 5]$ for brain CT images, $[90, 75, 55, 35, 10]$ for body CT images. First the images were compressed using JPEG algorithm, then using JPEG2000 with the corresponding compression ratios.
- Trial and main experiments:
  • Trial experiment included 6 images from each brain CT and body CT sets. These images were repetitions of images that were included in the main part of the experiment.

- Main experiment: Number of images: 306 brain CT, 306 body images (30 different images compressed at five compression ratios using JPEG and JPEG2000 algorithms including 6 repetitions added at the end of the sequence).
- Repetitions were included in the trial experiment as well as at the end of the first part of the main experiment.
- Duration of the experiment: The number of images was adjusted to the time limitation of the experiment. Expected duration of the experiment: 60 min.
- Trial experiment including explanation of the task: 10 min.
- Main experiment, Part 1:
  * brain CT: 25 min, body CT: 25 min.

4 Data Analysis

4.1 Modified ROC Analysis

The Receiver Operating Characteristic (ROC) curve is a common tool for visually assessing the performance of a classifier in medical decision making [11]. ROC curves illustrate the trade-off of benefit (true positives, TP) versus cost (false positives, FP) as the discriminating threshold is varied. In our experiment, we employed a three-level subjective rating of image quality by radiologists: (1) not noticeable and acceptable, (2) noticeable and acceptable and (3) noticeable and not acceptable. Since we are concerned about diagnostic quality, we combine the images that fell into the two classes during subjective assessments: (1) not noticeable (distortions) and acceptable, (2) noticeable (distortions) and acceptable. By doing so, we now have a binary rating scale: acceptable and unacceptable images. At this point, we must clarify that due to the nature of the problem we are investigating, our definitions of FP and TP differ from those normally applied for the purposes of medical diagnosis. In this study, we wish to examine how well different "image quality indicators" compare to the subjective assessments of image quality by radiologists. As such, we must assume that the "ground truth" for a particular experiment, i.e., whether or not a compressed image is acceptable or unacceptable, is defined by the radiologist(s). From this ground truth, we measure the effectiveness of each image quality indicator in terms of FP, TP, etc. This leads to the following definitions of P, N, TP, FP, etc.:

P= FP+TP total positives (acceptables) and **N= TN+FN** total negatives (unacceptables): these refer to radiologists' subjective opinions, which represent the True Class. On the other hand, **P'** and **N'** belong to the Hypothesis Class which, in our experiment, corresponds to a given objective image quality assessment method.

TP (true positives): images that are acceptable to both radiologists and a given quality assessment method.
TN (true negatives): images that are unacceptable to both radiologists and a given quality assessment method.

FN (false negatives): images that are acceptable to radiologists but unacceptable to a given quality assessment method.
FP (false positives): images that are unacceptable to radiologists but acceptable to a given quality assessment method.

The Acceptability/unacceptability of a given quality measure is defined with respect to the discrimination threshold s' associated with the method, where $0 \le s' \le 1$. Using this threshold value s', FPR and TPR are computed. Each threshold value s' generates a point on the ROC curve which corresponds to the pair of values **(FPR, TPR) = (1-SP, SE)**, where SP denotes specificity and SE denotes sensitivity, i.e.,

FPR (false positive rate) $= FP/N = 1 - SP$ (specificity)
TPR (true positive rate) $= TP/P = SE$ (sensitivity)
FNR (false negative rage) $= FN/N = 1 - SE$
TNR (true negative rate) $= TN/N = SP.$

4.2   ROC Analysis Results

ROC curves were computed corresponding to SSIM, MSE, SNR, VIF, VSNR for body and brain CT images; they are shown in Fig. 1 and 2. Table 1 shows the Area Under the (ROC) Curve (AUC) scores corresponding to each of the objective measures studied. The largest AUC corresponds to the SSIM index. The second best method is the VIF measure. We observed that MSE, MSE local, SNR and VSNR have smaller AUC. Moreover, the AUC scores from ROC analysis are larger for brain CT images than for body CT images with respect to all objective image quality measures considered. This indicates that the studied objective measures can predict the subjective assessments of radiologists of brain CT images with better accuracy than those corresponding to body CT images.

According to the presented modified ROC analysis, SSIM index provides the closest match with radiologists' subjective assessments. The second best measure is the VIF. A worse performance is observed for MSE, local MSE, SNR and

Table 1. AUC scores resulting from ROC analysis corresponding to objective quality measures and subjective radiologists' assessments for brain and body CT images.

Objective quality measure	AUC (brain CT)	AUC (body CT)
SSIM	0.9924	0.9618
MSE (local)	0.9899	0.9326
MSE	0.9892	0.9366
SNR	0.9896	0.9351
VNSR	0.9662	0.9400
VIF	0.9916	0.9571

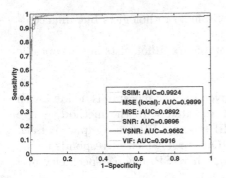

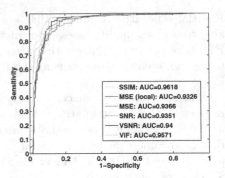

Fig. 1. ROC curves corresponding to SSIM, MSE, local MSE, SNR, VSNR and VIF for brain CT images(Color figure online).

Fig. 2. ROC curves corresponding to SSIM, MSE, local MSE, SNR, VSNR and VIF for body CT images(Color figure online).

VSNR. According to our previous work, where we studied both local and global image quality [9], SSIM also showed a better correspondence with subjective assessments of image quality.

4.3 Logistic Curve Model

For medical images, the goal is to find an objective image quality measure that can best predict the subjective radiologists' assessments. The performance of an objective quality measure to predict subjective scores is usually measured by means of a curve-fitting model. First MSE values are plotted against mean scores of subjective assessments, then a curve (e.g. polynomial spline, quadratic, exponential, logistic) is fitted to the resulting points [3].

In this study we used a logistic curve model as a proposed predictor of subjective radiologists' assessments corresponding to the studied objective quality measures. In order to take into account the variability in the subjective quality assessment of compressed medical images, a logistic cumulative probability distribution is assumed to model the decision of a radiologist to either accept or not accept an image at a given objective score. A robust curve-fitting is performed on the plot of the average subjective score over all the radiologists as a function of the objective score.

Given x_1, the predicted value (SSIM, VIF) and y_1, the average subjective score, we determine the parameters a and b of the logistic function

$$y = 1/(1 + \exp(-a * x + b))$$

that produce the least weighted square error, with weighting according to the bisquare method.

A threshold can be selected so that the cumulative probability distribution model represents the desired level of confidence that the quality of the compressed

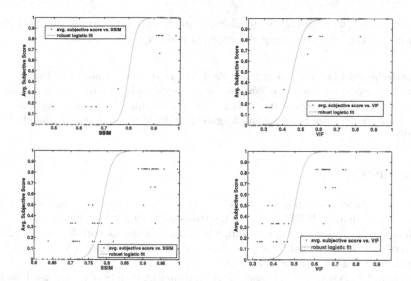

Fig. 3. Logistic curves corresponding to SSIM for (top left) brain, (bottom left) body CT images and VIF for (top right) brain, (bottom right) body CT images.

image is diagnostically acceptable. For example, if one requires a 99 % confidence, the recommended threshold has to be selected at the value for which the fitted logistic curve is at 0.99. Figure 3 shows logistic curves fitted with LAD Regression corresponding to SSIM and VIF for brain and body CT images.

5 Conclusions

The task of achieving Diagnostically Acceptable Irreversible Compression (DAIC) of medical images is a complex one. It involves tuning technology with radiological subjective responses/preferences. In this work, we compared the performances of some of the most popular image quality measures (MSE, SNR, SSIM, VSNR, VIF) based on experimental data collected in an experiment involving radiologists' subjective assessment of image quality. The experiment involved a global quality assessments of brain and body CT images at several compression ratios. Six radiologists evaluated compressed images as acceptable (with and without noticeable distortions) or unacceptable as compared to their uncompressed counterparts. An ROC analysis indicates that SSIM demonstrated the best performance, i.e., it provides the closest match to the radiologists' assessments. The worst performance was observed for the VSNR quality measure.

We have utilized a logistic curve model, which can be used to predict the subjective assessments with an objective criteria. This is a practical tool that can be used to determine the quality of medical images. The optimal quality score can be selected so that the cumulative probability distribution model represents the desired level of confidence that the quality of the compressed image is diagnostically acceptable.

Our current work involves developing advanced techniques of choosing a threshold for compression using the most popular quality measures.

Acknowledgements. We thank Prof. Paul Marriott, Department of Statistics and Actuarial Sciences, University of Waterloo for valuable advice with regard to the statistical design of our experiments. This research was supported in part by Discovery Grants from the Natural Sciences and Engineering Research Council of Canada (ERV and ZW).

References

1. Chandler, D.M., Hemami, S.S.: VSNR: A wavelet-based visual signal-to-noise ratio for natural images. IEEE Trans. Image Process. **16**(9), 2284–2298 (2007)
2. Chandler, D.M., Lim, K.H., Hemami, S.S.: Effects of spatial correlations and global precedence on the visual fidelity of distorted images. In: Human Vision and Electronic Imaging XI, vol. 6057, February 2006
3. Cosman, P.C., Gray, R.M., Olshen, R.A.: Evaluating quality of compressed medical images: Snr, subjective rating, and diagnostic accuracy. In: 82 (ed.) Proceedings of the IEEE, vol. 6, pp. 919–932, June 1994
4. Fidler, A., Likar, B.: What is wrong with compression ratio in lossy image compression? Radiology **245**(1), 299 (2007)
5. A. George and S. J. Livingston. A survey on full reference image quality assessment algorithms. IJRET: Int. J. Research Eng. Technol. 2(12), December 2013
6. Koff, D., Bak, P., Brownrigg, P., Hosseinzadeh, D., Khademi, A., Kiss, A., Lepanto, L., Michalak, T., Shulman, H., Volkening, A.: Pan-canadian evaluation of irreversible compression ratios (lossy compression) for development of national guidelines. J. Digit. Imaging **22**(6), 569–578 (2009)
7. Koff, D., Shulman, H.: An overview of digital compression of medical images: Can we use lossy image compression in radiology? CARJ **57**(4), 211–217 (2006)
8. Kowalik-Urbaniak, I.A.: The quest for 'diagnostically lossless' medical image compression using objective image quality measures. Ph.D. thesis, University of Waterloo, 200 University Ave W, Waterloo, ON N2L 3G1 (2014)
9. Kowalik-Urbaniak, I.A., Brunet, D., Wang, J., Vrscay, E., Wang, Z., Koff, D., Koff, N., Wallace, B.: The quest for 'diagnostically lossless' medical image compression: a comparative study of objective quality metrics for compressed medical images. In: Medical Imaging : Image Perception. Observer Performance, and Technology Assessment **9037**, 2014 (2014)
10. Marmolin, H.: Subjective MSE measures. IEEE Trans. Syst. Man and Cybern., SMC **16**(3), 486–489 (1986)
11. Metz, C.E.: Basic principles of ROC analysis. Semin. Nucl. Med. **8**, 282–298 (1978)
12. Nait-Ali, A., Cavaro-Menard, C.: Compression of Biomedical Images and Signals. Wiley, London (2008)
13. European Society of Radiology: (ESR). Usability of irreversible image compression in radiological imaging. Insights into. Imaging **2**(2), 103–115 (2011)
14. Sheikh, H.R., Bovik, A.C., de Veciana, S.G.: An information fidelity criterion for image quality assessment using natural scene statistics. IEEE Trans. Image Proces. **14**(12), 2117–2128 (2005)
15. Wang, Z., Bovik, A.C.: Mean squared error: love it or leave it? - a new look at signal fidelity measures. IEEE Signal Proc. Mag. **26**(1), 98–117 (2009)

16. Wang, Z., Bovik, A.C., Sheikh, H.R., Simoncelli, E.P.: Image quality assessment: from error visibility to structural similarity. IEEE Trans. Image Proces. **13**(4), 600–612 (2004)
17. Wang, Z., Li, Q.: Information content weighting for perceptual image quality assessment. IEEE Trans. Image Proces. **20**(5), 1185–1198 (2011)

Blind Image Quality Assessment Through Wakeby Statistics Model

Mohsen Jenadeleh$^{(\boxtimes)}$ and Mohsen Ebrahimi Moghaddam

Faculty of Computer Science and Engineering,
Shahid Beheshti University G.C, Tehran, Iran
{m_jenadeleh, m_moghadam}@sbu.ac.ir

Abstract. In this paper, a new universal blind image quality assessment algorithm is proposed that works in presence of various distortions. The proposed algorithm uses natural scene statistics in spatial domain for generating Wakeby distribution statistical model to extract quality aware features. The features are fed to an SVM (support vector machine) regression model to predict quality score of input image without any information about the distortions type or reference image. Experimental results show that the image quality score obtained by the proposed method has higher correlation with respect to human perceptual opinions and it's superior in some distortions comparing to some full-reference and other blind image quality methods.

Keywords: Blind image quality assessment · Natural scene statistics of special domain · Wakeby distribution model · Support vector machine

1 Introduction

Image quality assessment (IQA) algorithms are widely used in many image processing and video applications, such as watermarking, ton mapping, compression and enhancement. Today, the most trustworthy way of evaluating an algorithm is subjective human perception [1]. Subjective IQA is the most reliable approach because the end user always would be a human. Thus, subjective assessments offer high correlation with human vision system. Subjective methods are time consuming, expensive, and cannot be performed in real-time applications [2]. It is therefore necessary to define an objective criterion that can calculate the human-like judgment score difference between a reference image and its distorted version. Ideally, such an objective metric should be highly correlated by the perceived difference between distorted and reference images and should be varied linearly with the subjective quality assessment. Based on the availability of the reference image, the objective image quality methods are categorized into three classes [1]: full-reference methods that need both original and distorted images to compute quality of input image [3], reduced reference methods that besides the input image, need an access to some of the information from original image to calculate quality score [4] and finally, no-reference or blind methods are those which designed to compute the quality metric of a distorted image without any kind of need to access the original image's data [5]. The point is, reference image or its extracted features-information may not be always available. For instance, think of shared images

M. Kamel and A. Campilho (Eds.): ICIAR 2015, LNCS 9164, pp. 14–21, 2015.
DOI: 10.1007/978-3-319-20801-5_2

in social networks on the internet. As the original image would not be accessible, the only way to assess quality of them is using blind image quality assessment approaches.

2 Related Works

Most of no-reference image quality assessment (NR-IQA) methods are based on prior knowledge of the distortion type, called distortion-specifics [6, 7]. This constraint limits the algorithm applications. For example, in the real world, images are usually corrupted by more than one distortion, and the distortion type is usually unknown. Recently, some methods proposed to overcome this problem. Such methods make no assumption about the type of distortions. In [8] a NR-IQA algorithm which operates in DCT domain is proposed. In this method, features are computed from natural scene statistics (NSS) of block DCT coefficients. Then quality aware features based on modeling these NSS are calculated and fed to a regression SVM to predict quality of the input image. This method is a good achievement but requires nonlinear sorting of the block based natural scene statistic features which makes it slow for real time applications. BRIS-QUE [5] is another recent state of the art method using suitable quality-aware NSS features in the spatial domain to learn human opinion scores on databases including some sort of distortions, even large ones [9]. Saad et al. [10] Proposed BLIINDS-II image quality method which extracts NSS of discrete cosine transform (DCT) using a single-stage framework. Liu et al. [11] proposed dubbed spatial–spectral entropy based quality metric (SSEQ) to predict image quality blindly. SSEQ utilizes local spatial and spectral entropy features of distorted images to form quality aware features. The features then feed to a regression machine to predict image quality. The problem of these methods is the limitation of possible applications caused by limited range of distortion types they have been trained on. Consider their performance is directly affected by the ability of distortions that they are familiar with.

In this work, Wakeby distribution –also known as advanced distribution- is used to modeling the NSS coefficients and extracting quality aware feature vectors. This distribution has a couple of scale and shape parameters (four parameters), which makes it more flexible in comparison to the other distribution models used in the state of the art methods. These parameters let us form a feature vector that is very sensitive to changes in an NSS coefficient's empirical distribution which causes more accurate model fitting and better prediction of image quality score.

3 Proposed Method

A novel method to assess quality of natural images based on NSS modeling is proposed in the presented model, the natural features are extracted from input images that would be a composition of the local mean subtraction and contrast divisive normalization (MSCN) coefficients. Additionally, the product of MSCN coefficients in four directions (horizontal, vertical and two diagonals) is calculated and used as a part of the feature vector. Wakeby distribution has been adapted for modeling of the MSCN coefficients and their relative products. This model is achieved by estimating the distribution parameters obtained by the best fitting trials of MSCN coefficients. Then the estimated parameters of Wakeby distribution has been used to form the quality aware feature vector. Since the range of raw data values vary widely, in order to obtain faster converges, the range of all features should be normalized between [-1, 1] so we make a fair deal between each feature's contribution. The feature vectors of the training samples are fed to an SVM to form the model. Then the SVM model and feature vector of each testing sample is being used as a prediction module to find a blind approximation of quality score for the test image.

3.1 Natural Scene Statistics Extraction

The statistics of natural images, have been studied for more than 50 years by vision scientists and television engineers. The idea is simple: All natural images share some common statistical behaviors regularities related to the real world. One of the best examples of NSS is MSCN coefficients where its histogram is approximately Gaussian like for a natural image [12]. Figure 1 shows the behavior of these statistics in presence of different distortions is predictable. It helps the reader to have a better imagination of the relation between NSS and severity of distortions. As it is shown in Fig. 1 each distortion affects each image distribution in a distinguishable way and all the behaviors are independent of image contents. For example, presence of JPEG2000 and JPEG distortions, makes the distributions highly picked but JPEG makes it sharper and when it comes to white noise, we see the distribution is more Gaussian like. By generating models based on these regular behaviors, presence and severity of the distortions are objectively sensible. To model the statistical regularities observed in natural images, the local mean subtraction and contrast divisive normalization (MSCN) coefficients are calculate by the Eq. (1):

$$\hat{I}(i,j) = \frac{I(i,j) - \mu(i,j)}{\sigma(i,j) + d} \tag{1}$$

Where $i \in (1, 2, .., M)$ and $J \in (1, 2, .., N)$ are spatial indices of a natural image's pixels with size of, $M \times N$ and d is a small value to prevent division by zero. μ and σ can be calculated by Eqs. (2) and (3) respectively:

$$\mu(i,j) = \sum_{k=-K}^{K} \sum_{l=L}^{L} \omega_{k,l} I_{k,l}(i,j) \tag{2}$$

$$\sigma(i,j) = \sqrt{\sum_{k=-K}^{K} \sum_{l=L}^{L} \omega_{k,l} [I_{k,l}(i,j) - \mu(i,j)]^2} \tag{3}$$

Where is $\omega_{k,l} | k = -K, \ldots, K, l = -L, \ldots, L$ is a 2D circularly symmetric Gaussian weighting function.

3.2 Wakeby Distribution Model

The MSCN coefficients can be modeled by different statistical distributions, in [5], zero-mean general Gaussian distribution (GGD) with two parameters and in [13] Weibull distribution with three parameters is used to model the MSCN coefficients. Both of these distributions have some inabilities to fit the coefficients efficiently, and it encouraged us to use a more flexible distribution with more degree of freedom to model MSCN coefficients. Therefore, our choice comes to the advanced continuous Wakeby distribution [20] with five parameters for modeling and extract quality aware features. The Wakeby distribution's mathematic definition is shown in Eq. (4):

$$x(F) = \zeta + \frac{\alpha}{\beta}(1 - (1 - F)^{\beta}) - \frac{\gamma}{\delta}(1 - (1 - F)^{-\delta}) \qquad (4)$$

$x(F)$ represents Wakeby distribution with shape parameters β and δ, scale parameters α and γ, and location parameter ζ. Where $F = F(x) = P(X \le x)$ is non-exceedance probability and $x(F)$ is F corresponding quantile value. Also the following conditions are necessary to satisfy:

$$\alpha \neq 0 \ or \ \gamma \neq 0$$

$$\beta + \delta > 0 \ or \ \beta = \lambda = \delta = 0$$

$$if \ \alpha = 0 \ then \ \beta = 0$$

$$if \ \gamma = 0 \ then \ \delta = 0$$

$$\gamma \ge 0 \ and \ \alpha + \gamma \ge 0$$

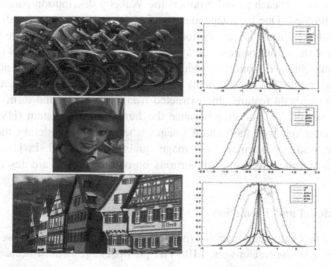

Fig. 1. Empirical histograms of the MSCN coefficients of three random reference images from LIVE database and their distorted versions.

An analytical technique based on probability-weighted moments [21] is used to estimate $(\beta, \delta, \alpha, \gamma, \zeta)$ parameters of the Wakeby distribution. Also, mean and variance (m, v) of best Wakeby distribution fitted of MSCN coefficients are calculated and used for the Wakeby distribution modeling.

3.3 Quality Aware Feature Extraction

In addition to the MSCN coefficients that have been modeled in previous section, the statistical relationships between adjacent pixels are also modeled. A study [5] shows that the MSCN coefficients are more homogenous for original natural images, and the product values of adjacent coefficients exhibit a regular structure that changes in presence of different distortions. Same to BRISQUE [5], To model this regular structure between neighbor coefficients, pairwise products on a distance of one pixel along four orientations (horizontal, vertical, main diagonal and secondary diagonal) between adjacent MSCN coefficients, are calculated by Eqs. (5), (6), (7) and (8) respectively. Figure 2 shows the neighboring MSCN coefficients which are computed along four directions and their horizontal (i,j) histograms for a sample image and its distorted versions.

$$\text{Horizontal } (i,j) = \hat{I}(i,j) \times \hat{I}(i,j+1) \tag{5}$$

$$\text{Vertical } (i,j) = \hat{I}(i,j) \times \hat{I}(i+1,j) \tag{6}$$

$$\text{Main diagonal } (i,j) = \hat{I}(i,j) \times \hat{I}(i+1,j+1) \tag{7}$$

$$\text{Secondary diagonal } (i,j) = \hat{I}(i,j) \times \hat{I}(i+1,j-1) \tag{8}$$

In each orientation, for each paired products the Wakeby distribution parameters (β, δ, α, γ, ζ) are estimated. Due to independency of position parameter to distortions, this parameter is not used in the feature vector. Therefore, the 22 quality aware features are a composition of these four parameters: $(\beta, \delta, \alpha, \gamma)$ (from modeling MSCN coefficients) and 16 elements obtained from the products of adjacent MSCN coefficients along the four directions, and the last two elements are (μ, v). The features are extracted over two scales and this yields 44 features that extracted from each image and forms the quality aware feature vector. This is done because the human visual system (HVS) extracts structural information from the natural images, therefore by modeling the structural similarities, a good approximation of image quality is obtained. In [14] multiscale nature of HVS and the affection of distortions on natural images are described.

3.4 SVM Model and Prediction

In this paper, a support vector machine (SVM) regression (SVR) [15] is used to predict the quality score of the test images. LIBSVM [16] package is used beside the implementation of this algorithm as the regression machine, implementing SVR with radial basis function (RBF) kernel that makes the suggested SVM model. The feature vectors

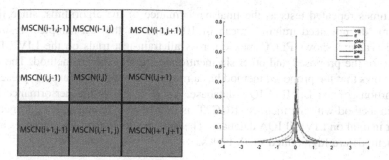

Fig. 2. Left: Pairwise products of MSCN coefficients are computed along four directions, Right: Horizontal(i,j) histograms of buildings reference image and its five distorted versions from LIVE II database that shows the product values of adjacent coefficients exhibit a regular structure.

of training samples (described in previous section), and corresponding differential mean opinion score (DMOS) (described in Sect. 4.1) are fed to the SVR to generate the suggested SVM model. Then the prediction module uses the SVM model and the test image feature vector to estimate quality score. The prediction module is also implemented in the LIBSVM package.

4   Experimental Results

4.1   Database

LIVE II IQA database [17] consists of images with five types of distortions including JPEG2000, JPEG, white noise (WN), Gaussian blur (Blur) and fast fading channel distortion (FF). All of them derived from 29 reference images. In this database the differential mean opinion score (DMOS) of each distorted image is included. DMOS scores are in range [0, 100], where lower DMOS indicates higher quality.

4.2   Performance Evaluation

Two commonly used performance metrics, Pearson Linear Correlation Coefficient (PLCC) and Spearman Rank-Order Correlation Coefficient (SRCC) as suggested in [18] are employed to evaluate the proposed algorithm. First, 80 % of LIVE database are randomly selected as training samples. To prove method's content independency, we made sure there is no content overlap between train and test samples. We conducted performance comparisons between the proposed method and six other state of the art image quality assessment methods: Three full reference algorithms including (PSNR [19], SSIM [3], MS-SSIM [14]), and other three no-reference (blind) algorithms including (SSEQ [11], BRISQUE [5], BLIINDS-II [10]). All of them tested via the mentioned performance evaluation metrics. To make a fair comparison, we performed random 20 % test and 80 % training samples for 100 times. Then we employed mean of all 100 times repeated tests as the final performance of the algorithms, since the FR algorithms do not need training, mean of 100 runs on the test samples' results are reported. Table 1 shows PLCC metric across all train-test trials on the LIVE II IQA database for the proposed and other six mentioned state of the art method. The PLCC metric shows that the proposed method has a more accurate performance in presence of all distortions of the LIVE II IQA database. Table 2 shows the performance of the proposed method with the metrics SRCC. This metric also demonstrates our method is superior in total on LIVE II IQA database. The best results in the full references and the blind methods are highlighted in all tables.

Table 1. PLCC metric across 100 train-test trials on the LIVE II IQA database.

Methods	JPEG2k	JPEG	WN	Blur	FF	ALL
PSNR	0.8814	0. 9112	0.9221	0.8134	0.8933	0.8781
SSIM	0.9555	0.9531	**0.9832**	0.9143	0.9518	0.9165
MS-SSIM	**0.9689**	**0.9733**	**0.9832**	**0.9592**	**0.9501**	**0.9573**
SSEQ	0.9492	**0.9595**	0.9709	0.9445	0.9033	0.9310
BRISQUE	0.9486	0.9407	**0.9891**	**0.9450**	0.9101	0.9239
BLIINDS-II	0.9358	0.9399	0.9637	0.9102	0.8994	0.9198
Proposed method	**0.9540**	0.9330	0.9716	0.9219	**0.9186**	**0.9414**

Table 2. SRCC metric across 100 train-test trials on the LIVE II IQA database

Methods	JPEG2k	JPEG	WN	Blur	FF	ALL
PSNR	0.8577	0.9014	0.9398	0.7776	0.8803	0.8665
SSIM	0.9399	0.9500	0.9601	0.9112	0.9369	0.9088
MS-SSIM	**0.9665**	**0.9801**	**0.9760**	**0.9502**	**0.9411**	**0.9533**
SSEQ	0.9443	0.9454	0.9770	**0.9443**	0.9104	0.9358
BRISQUE	0.9246	**0.9699**	**0.9803**	0.9433	0.8888	0.9370
BLIINDS-II	0.9519	0.9220	0.9655	0.9207	0.9021	0.9359
Proposed method	**0.9575**	0.9410	0.9737	0.9406	**0.9135**	**0.9437**

5   Conclusion

In this paper a novel general purpose blind image quality assessment model is presented, which uses MSCN spatial natural scene statistics of the input images. A feature vector with 44 dimensions is then extracted based on the Wakeby distribution modeling. Then an SVM is trained to predict image quality scores from these feature vectors. We then evaluated performance of the proposed method in terms of correlation with human perception. The experimental results have shown this method is statistically better than the full reference PSNR and SSIM metrics as well as highly competitive to all state of the art blind image quality methods.

References

1. Narvekar, N.D., Karam, L.J.: A no-reference image blur metric based on the cumulative probability of blur detection (CPBD). IEEE Trans. Image Process. **20**, 2678–2683 (2011)
2. Zaric, A., Loncaric, M., Tralic, D., Brzica, M., Dumic, E., Grgic, S.: Image quality assessment - comparison of objective measures with results of subjective test. In: ELMAR, 2010 proceedings, pp. 113–118 (2010)
3. Zhou, W., Bovik, A.C., Sheikh, H.R., Simoncelli, E.P.: Image quality assessment: from error visibility to structural similarity. IEEE Trans. Image Process. **13**, 600–612 (2004)
4. Dacheng, T., Xuelong, L., Wen, L., Xinbo, G.: Reduced-reference IQA in contourlet domain. IEEE Trans. Syst. Man Cybern. Part B Cybern. **39**, 1623–1627 (2009)
5. Mittal, A., Moorthy, A.K., Bovik, A.C.: No-reference image quality assessment in the spatial domain. IEEE Trans. Image Process. **21**, 4695–4708 (2012)
6. Li, L., Lin, W., Wang, X., Yang, G., Bahrami, K., Kot, A.C.: No–reference image blur assessment based on discrete orthogonal moments. IEEE Trans. Cybern. **PP**, 1–1 (2015)
7. Ji, S., Qin, L., Erlebacher, G.: Hybrid no-reference natural image quality assessment of noisy, blurry, jpeg2000, and jpeg images. IEEE Trans. Image Process. **20**, 2089–2098 (2011)
8. Saad, M.A., Bovik, A.C., Charrier, C.: Model-based blind image quality assessment using natural DCT statistics. IEEE Trans. Image Process. **21**, 3339–3352 (2011)
9. Ponomarenko, N., Ieremeiev, O., Lukin, V., Egiazarian, K., Jin, L., Astola, J., et al., Color image database TID2013: peculiarities and preliminary results. In: 2013 4th European Workshop on Visual Information Processing (EUVIP), pp. 106–111 (2013)
10. Saad, M.A., Bovik, A.C., Charrier, C.: Blind image quality assessment: a natural scene statistics approach in the DCT domain. IEEE Trans. Image Process. **21**, 3339–3352 (2012)
11. Liu, L., Liu, B., Huang, H., Bovik, A.C.: No-reference image quality assessment based on spatial and spectral entropies. Sig. Process. Image Commun. **29**, 856–863 (2014)
12. Moorthy, A.K., Bovik, A.C.: Statistics of natural image distortions. In: IEEE International Conference on Acoustics Speech and Signal Processing (ICASSP), pp. 962–965 (2010)
13. Shuhong, J., Abdalmajeed, S., Wei, L., Ruxuan, W.: Totally blind image quality assessment algorithm based on weibull statistics of natural scenes. Inf. Technol. J. **13**, 1548–1554 (2014)
14. Wang, Z., Simoncelli, E.P., Bovik, A.C.: Multiscale structural similarity for image quality assessment. In: 2004. Conference Record of the Thirty-Seventh Asilomar Conference on Signals, Systems and Computers, pp. 1398–1402 (2003)
15. Schölkopf, B., Smola, A.J., Williamson, R.C., Bartlett, P.L.: New support vector algorithms. Neural Comput. **12**, 1207–1245 (2000)
16. Chang, C.-C., Lin, C.-J.: LIBSVM: A library for support vector machines. ACM Trans. Intell. Syst. Technol. **2**, 1–27 (2011)
17. Sheikh, H.R., Sabir, M.F., Bovik, A.C.: A statistical evaluation of recent full reference image quality assessment algorithms. IEEE Trans. Image Process. **15**, 3440–3451 (2006)
18. Rohaly, A.M., Libert, J., Corriveau, P., Webster, A.: Final report from the video quality experts group on the validation of objective models of video quality assessment, ITU-T Standards Contribution COM, pp. 9–80 (2000)
19. Huynh-Thu, Q., Ghanbari, M.: Scope of validity of PSNR in image/video quality assessment. Electron. Lett. **44**, 800–801 (2008)
20. Griffiths, G.A.: A theoretically based Wakeby distribution for annual flood series. Hydrol. Sci. J. **34**, 231–248 (1989)
21. Öztekin, T.: Estimation of the parameters of wakeby distribution by a numerical least squares method and applying it to the annual peak flows of Turkish rivers. Water Resour. Manage. **25**, 1299–1313 (2011)

Improving Image Quality of Tiled Displays

Steven B. McFadden$^{(\boxtimes)}$ and Paul A.S. Ward

Department of Electrical and Computer Engineering, University of Waterloo,
200 University Avenue West, Waterloo, ON, Canada
steve.mcfadden@uwaterloo.ca

Abstract. Tiled displays provide an effective means of displaying very
large images but suffer from a grid distortion caused by gaps between
individual tiles. This paper introduces new image correction algorithms
that use elements of the human visual system to improve perceived quality of the displayed images without directly modifying the static grid distortion. These correction techniques, validated through use of a formal
user study, provide statistically significant improvements over unmodified grid-distorted images.

Keywords: Image quality · Image tiling · Image enhancement

1 Introduction

Tiled displays allow for visualization of images that cannot be practically viewed
on individual displays. They support sizes that are orders of magnitude greater
than the largest individual display, with equivalent or superior pixel densities,
and they offer this support with the option of different shapes and configurations
that are infeasible using individual displays.

These advantages come at the cost of certain distortions that are unique
to tiled displays such as non-uniformity, inter-tile brightness or colour mismatch, and misaligned tiles [2, 4], but these distortions can generally be managed
through careful design and manufacturing.

Another distortion inherent to tiled displays, caused by the gaps between each
active region, creates the appearance of a grid overtop of any image displayed.
This grid distortion is not correctable with current manufacturing techniques,
making it an objectionable artifact on every tiled display. The image quality
impact of this grid distortion has been largely unresearched; [6] and [7] have
investigated the grid distortion's quality *measurement* and *impact*, but there
has thus far been no work done for *improvement* of this distortion.

Improving the quality of grid-distorted images is a problem requiring *perceptual* image processing where the goal is to modify pixels in the image "active
areas" such that the grid (i.e., "pixels" that cannot be modified) appears less
objectionable. We address this problem by developing new image correction algorithms that use characteristics of the human visual system (HVS) to *perceptually*
improve the quality of grid-distorted images. Formal verification of these correction algorithms shows that viewers clearly and consistently prefer the corrected
images over unmodified grid-distorted images.

© Springer International Publishing Switzerland 2015
M. Kamel and A. Campilho (Eds.): ICIAR 2015, LNCS 9164, pp. 22–29, 2015.
DOI: 10.1007/978-3-319-20801-5_3

2 Theory

This section describes the theory behind the algorithms used to improve tiled image quality without directly modifying the grid.

2.1 Edge Brightening

Brightening pixels near the grid distortion can reduce its perception due to the point spread function (PSF) of the human eye. The PSF describes the effect of passing a point source of light through an imperfect lens [3]. The diffraction-limited PSF (i.e., ignoring effects of defocus, aberrations, and scatter), provides the luminance distribution in the resulting image according to Eq. 1,

$$L(\zeta) = \frac{[2J_1(\zeta)]^2}{\zeta^2} , \qquad (1)$$

where $L(\zeta)$ represents the relative light level at distance ζ from the center of the PSF, $J_1(\zeta)$ is a Bessel function, and

$$\zeta = \frac{\pi\theta D}{\lambda} , \qquad (2)$$

where θ is the angular distance (in radians), D is the pupil diameter, and λ is the light wavelength. An example of a point-spread function is shown in Fig. 1.

Fig. 1. PSF example; *(Left)* Input point source; *(Right)* Output image.

The application of the PSF to improving tiled image quality relies on the effect shown in Fig. 1. At sufficient viewing distances, the "spread" of any point source of light (i.e., pixels) overlaps with one or more adjacent points (Fig. 2). We can therefore affect the *perceived* values of unmodifiable "grid pixels" by changing the values of nearby pixels. A similar procedure has been used to hide individual defective display pixels [5] but this procedure aims only to hide a single pixel. Hiding a large supra-threshold distortion such as a grid is more difficult because each "grid pixel" has fewer adjacent "compensation pixels" and the grid is a global distortion that spreads across the entire image (Fig. 3).

Corner Brightening. Corner brightening is a special case of edge brightening that must be accounted for. As illustrated in Fig. 4, corner "grid pixels" have fewer adjacent "correction pixels". Therefore, any correction applied to these pixels must be greater than that of a typical grid correction pixel.

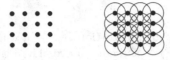

Fig. 2. PSF illustration; *(Left)* Input point grid (i.e., pixels); *(Right)* Perceived image.

Fig. 3. PSF illustration with Grid Line; *(Left)* Input point grid (i.e., pixels); *(Right)* Perceived image; squares represent "grid pixels". Note that each "grid pixel" has a minimum of three adjacent "correction pixels".

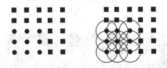

Fig. 4. PSF illustration with Grid Corner; *(Left)* Input point grid (i.e., pixels); *(Right)* Perceived image; squares represent "grid pixels". Note that "grid pixels" have fewer adjacent "correction pixels" as they approach a corner.

2.2   Global Darkening

Edge brightening cannot be applied when pixels are near their maximum values and the display is operating at maximum brightness. In these cases, contrast compression can be applied to the entire image, mapping the original pixel intensities to a smaller range. This darkens the image as a whole but enables image correction through brightening of pixels near the grid.

3   Image Correction Algorithms

We used the concepts presented in Sect. 2 to develop six[1] image correction algorithms for comparison:

---

[1] Arguably *five* new algorithms; Algorithm 0 is a "do nothing" reference case.

Algorithm 0. This "algorithm" leaves the grid-distorted reference image unchanged, applying no edge brightening and no global darkening. These images represent typical uncorrected images as viewed on a tiled display.

Algorithm 1. This algorithm performs no edge brightening but applies global darkening ("contrast reduction") of 40 % by scaling the pixel range of [0,255] to [0,182]. These images represent a common reference for comparing edge brightening independent of any potential clipping.

Algorithm 2. This algorithm performs 40 % global darkening of the images, followed by a 40 % "step correction" edge brightening. Step correction brightens only the rows and columns immediately adjacent to the grid and is the simplest form of edge brightening.

Algorithm 3. Algorithm 3 applies a "sinc correction" brightening with no global darkening. This correction applies 40 % brightening to the first row/column, 20 % darkening to the second, and 10 % brightening to the third. With no global darkening, immediately adjacent pixels above the level of 182 will clip at 255.

Algorithm 4. This algorithm applies the same sinc correction as Algorithm 3 (40/-20/10), but does so after a 20 % global darkening (i.e., [0,255] scaled to [0,212]). This algorithm represents a trade-off between global darkening and potential clipping during edge brightening.

Algorithm 5. Algorithm 5 applies the same sinc correction as Algorithm 3 and Algorithm 4 (40/-20/10), but applies global darkening of 40 % (i.e., [0,255] scaled to [0,182]), allowing for full edge brightening with no clipping.

Corner Correction. All algorithms with edge brightening (i.e., Algorithms 2-5) apply an extra corner brightening of 20 %.

4 Validation

We tested the effectiveness of our image correction algorithms with a formal user study roughly based on the TID2008 image database [8].

4.1 Methodology

Each session consisted of an instruction and training phase, where subjects were familiarized with the study, followed by the experiment phase. For the experiment, we used a forced-choice side-by-side image presentation similar to that used for the TID2008 database, but we elected not to show reference images in the user interface (Fig. 5) and we added extra options for subjects to select.

We excluded reference images because we were more interested in each subject's preference between the two distorted images than in the fidelity to the original undistorted image. We felt inclusion of the "perfect" reference image would skew results by making both grid-distorted images look relatively "bad". The extra options ("Certainly Better" and "Probably Better") were added to distinguish strong preferences from weak.

We used a round-robin comparison instead of the Swiss tournament principle used for TID2008 to gain a higher granularity in scoring results (i.e., every image was directly compared against every other image). This came at the expense of efficiency with round-robin requiring $\mathcal{O}(N^2)$ image comparisons while Swiss tournament only requires $\mathcal{O}(N \log_2(N))$ comparisons (to determine a distinct "winner" and "loser"; the rankings of intermediate images are much less defined for Swiss tournament). The use of round-robin limited the number of source images and correction algorithms that could be included in the study without exceeding the recommended maximum session time ([1]) of 30 minutes.

User Interface. Figure 5 shows our user study interface. Subjects selected between four possible options: "Certainly Better" for left image, "Probably Better" for left image, "Probably Better" for right image, and "Certainly Better" for right image. The image ordering was reversed for roughly half of the user subjects to account for potential bias in left/right vs. right/left placement.

Scoring. User selections were converted to opinion scores by assigning "points" to an image each time it was preferred: 2 points for "Certainly Better" and 1

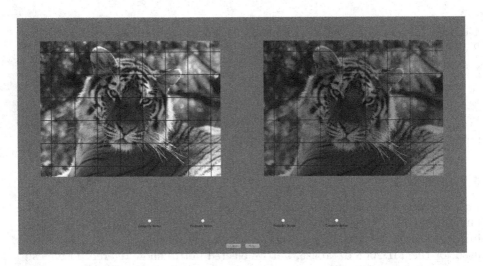

Fig. 5. The image-correction user study interface. The 'Next' button is shown inactive because the subject must select a score before moving to the next image. Left/right ordering of images is reversed between viewing sessions.

point for "Probably Better". With 6 algorithms, each image ended with a score in the range [0,10].

Subjects. The study recruited 31 subjects from undergraduate engineering and various graduate university programs. The male-to-female ratio of subjects was 22:9 and average subject age was 26.4 years with a standard deviation of 5.1 years. Average session duration was 17:39 minutes with a standard deviation of 3:45 minutes.

Images. Use of the round-robin method (with $\mathcal{O}(N^2)$ image comparisons) required a reduction in the number of images used compared to earlier tiled display quality studies [6,7] and only the 16 images shown in Fig. 6 were used.

Fig. 6. Source images used in the image-correction user study.

Equipment. All images were displayed on a 23″ IPS LCD monitor set to its native resolution of 1920×1080 and factory default settings. Subjects were seated at a fixed distance of 1.5 metres from the display in a windowless room with typical office lighting.[2]

4.2 Results

Results from our user study are shown in Fig. 7. Notches on each box plot indicate 95 % confidence intervals.

---

[2] This distance was greater than the typical recommended viewing distance of 3–4 times the image height because the image correction algorithms require a minimum viewing distance to be effective (as described in Sect. 2).

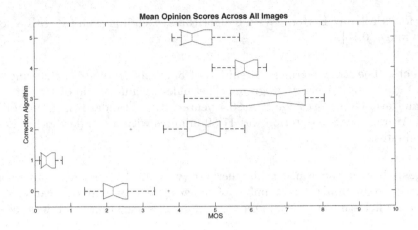

Fig. 7. Mean opinion scores across all images.

5 Discussion and Conclusions

Based on the results of Sect. 4, we note the following key points:[3]

1. The "darken-only" algorithm ("Correction 1") is statistically worse than the "no-modification" algorithm ("Correction 0").
2. All other correction algorithms result in statistically better quality images than the unmodified grid-distorted image ("Correction 0").
3. Algorithms with significant darkening (i.e., Algorithms "2" and "5") are statistically worse than those without (i.e., Algorithms "3" and "4").
4. Corrections "3" and "4" show similar performance; "Correction 3" has a higher average score, but also a much higher spread of scores.

5.1 Conclusions

1. Global Darkening is always[4] undesirable.
2. Edge Brightening is always desirable, even at the expense of a darker image.
3. The "best" image correction algorithm studied here is either "Correction 3" or "Correction 4", subject to preference and interpretation:
   (a) Correction 4 is best if consistency is more highly valued.
   (b) Correction 3 is best if maximum potential quality is prioritized.
   (c) If "the majority of cases" is considered, Correction 3 is best; preferred over Correction 4 by a ratio of nearly 2:1 when directly compared.

---

[3] All statements of "statistically better" or "statistically worse" refer to a 95 % confidence interval).

[4] True for our user study; may not hold true for darker environments.

5.2 Future Work

Future work is required to determine the optimal tradeoff between edge brightening correction and global darkening, allowing development of a dynamic algorithm that darkens by the minimal amount required for optimal edge brightening.

References

1. Methodology for the subjective assessment of the quality of television pictures, ITU-R Rec. BT. 500–13 January 2012
2. Alphonse, G., Lubin, J.: Psychophysical requirements for tiled large-screen displays. In: SPIE/IS&T 1992 Symposium on Electronic Imaging: Science and Technology, International Society for Optics and Photonics. pp. 230–240 (1992)
3. Atchison, D.A., Smith, G.: Optics of the human eye. ch. 18. Butterworth-Heinemann, Boston (2000)
4. Hereld, M., Judson, I.R., Paris, J., Stevens, R.L.: Developing tiled projection display systems. In: Proceedings IPT 2000 (Immersive Projection Technology Workshop) (2000)
5. Kimpe, T.: Defective pixels in medical lcd displays: problem analysis and fundamental solution. J. Digit. Imaging 19(1), 76–84 (2006)
6. McFadden, S., Ward, P.: A new image quality assessment database for tiled images. In: Image Quality and System Performance XI, Proceedings SPIE (Feb. 2014), vol. 9016, pp. 90160X1-90160X10
7. McFadden, S.B., Ward, P.: A Towards a new image quality metric for evaluating the effects of tiled displays. In: 2014 IEEE International Conference on Image Processing (ICIP). pp. 561–565. IEEE (2014)
8. Ponomarenko, N., Lukin, V., Zelensky, A., Egiazarian, K., Carli, M., Battisti, F.: TID2008 - a database for evaluation of full-reference visual quality assessment metrics. Adv. Mod. Radioelectronics 10, 30–45 (2009)

Image Enhancement

Structural Similarity-Based Optimization Problems with L^1-Regularization: Smoothing Using Mollifiers

Daniel Otero[1]([✉]), Davide La Torre[2,3], and Edward R. Vrscay[1]

[1] Department of Applied Mathematics, Faculty of Mathematics,
University of Waterloo, Waterloo, ON N2L 3G1, Canada
{dotero,ervrscay}@uwaterloo.ca
[2] Department of Economics, Management, and Quantitative Methods,
University of Milan, Milan, Italy
[3] Department of Applied Mathematics and Sciences, Khalifa University,
Abu Dhabi, UAE
davide.latorre@unimi.it, davide.latorre@kustar.ac.ae

Abstract. In this paper we propose a new method of solving optimization problems involving the structural similarity image quality measure with L^1-regularization. The regularization term $\|x\|_1$ is approximated by a sequence of smooth functions $\|x\|_1^\varepsilon$ by means of C_0^∞ functions known as mollifiers. Because the functions $\|x\|_1^\varepsilon$ epi-converge to $\|x\|_1$, the sequence of minimizers of the smooth objective functions converges to a minimizer of the non-smooth problem. This approach permits the use of gradient-based methods to solve the minimization problems as opposed to methods based on subdifferentials.

1 Introduction

Many problems in image processing may be cast into the following form: Given a $y \in \mathbb{R}^m$ and a compact subset $D \subset \mathbb{R}^n$, find

$$\min_{x \in D} \frac{1}{2} \|Ax - y\|_2^2 + \gamma \|x\|_1, \tag{1}$$

where A is an $m \times n$ transformation matrix (e.g., wavelet, Fourier, random matrix, etc.). Such a functional is known as the *Lasso problem*, whose L^1 regularizing term induces sparseness in its solution [1,16,23]. The quadratic term, which is usually called the "fidelity term", keeps the solution close to the observation y.

A great variety of algorithms have been proposed to solve the Lasso problem, e.g., Fast Iterative Soft-Thresholding Algorithm (FISTA) [1] and the Least Angle Regression [16]. These specialized methods usually rely on techniques from subdifferential calculus to overcome the non-differentiability of the regularizing term of (1). Nevertheless, classical methods can be employed by either casting (1) as a Quadratic Program (QP) [16] or by approximating the L^1 norm with a family of smooth functions $\varphi_\varepsilon \in C_c^\infty(\mathbb{R}^n)$ known as *mollifiers* [12].

© Springer International Publishing Switzerland 2015
M. Kamel and A. Campilho (Eds.): ICIAR 2015, LNCS 9164, pp. 33–42, 2015.
DOI: 10.1007/978-3-319-20801-5_4

In particular, in [24], the Gaussian distribution is used as an approximate mollifier to solve a smooth version of (1), which is obtained by convolving each component of the L^1 norm with a standard one-dimensional Gaussian density function of variance ε^2. This technique allows the usage of gradient-based methods for approximating the optimal solution $x^\star$ of (1). In this case, the smooth approximation of the original problem is given by

$$\min_{x \in D} \frac{1}{2} \|Ax - y\|_2^2 + \gamma \|x\|_1^\varepsilon, \tag{2}$$

where $\|x\|_1^\varepsilon$ is equal to

$$\|x\|_1^\varepsilon = \sum_{i=1}^n \int_{\mathbb{R}} |x_i - z_i| \hat{\phi}_\varepsilon \left(\frac{z_i}{\varepsilon}\right) \, dz. \tag{3}$$

Here, $\hat{\phi}(x)$ is the standard normal distribution in one dimension.

In an imaging context, the main drawback of these approaches is that they employ the square of the Euclidian distance as a fitting term, which is not the best choice when it comes to measure visual closeness [28, 29]. To overcome this difficulty, many authors have incorporated the Structural Similarity Index Measure (SSIM) as a fidelity term in different types of optimization problems [6,7,17–20]. The SSIM is one of the most popular measures of visual quality, which was introduced in [28], and it has been shown to outperform the square of the Euclidian distance as a measure of visual quality.

Nevertheless, mathematical treatment of the SSIM is difficult, thus simpler versions of the SSIM are desirable. In particular, the definition of this measure as a normalized metric has been employed in [6,17,18]. This simplified version of the SSIM has nice properties such as quasi-convexity [4,18], which allows the use of quasi-convex techniques to solve optimization problems that employ the SSIM as a fidelity term [18].

In [18], several imaging tasks are carried out by solving different types of quasi-convex optimization problems in which the SSIM is minimized subject to a set of convex constraints. One of the problems that is addressed is

$$\min_x \ T(Ax, y) \tag{4}$$

$$\text{subject to } \|x\|_1 \le \lambda.$$

Here, the fidelity term is given by $T(Ax, y) = 1 - S(Ax, y)$, where $S(\cdot, \cdot)$ is the simplified version of the SSIM as a normalized metric [6,17,18]. The unconstrained counterpart of (4) was studied in [17]. In this case, an algorithm that uses a generalization of the soft-thresholding operator [11,23] is employed for solving the following optimization problem:

$$\min_{x \in D} \ T(Ax, y) + \gamma \|x\|_1. \tag{5}$$

The advantage of these formulations is that the concepts of similarity and sparsity are combined into a single optimization problem; therefore, solutions of this problem are similar to the observation y in the SSIM sense and also sparse.

In this paper, we extend the work of [17] by solving (5) via mollifiers. This approach allows us to use gradient-based methods for solving the non-smooth problem (5). In this case, the following smooth version of (4) is solved:

$$\min_{x \in D} T(Ax, y) + \gamma \|x\|_1^\varepsilon, \tag{6}$$

where $\|x\|_1^\varepsilon$ is obtained by convolving the L^1 norm with a multivariate Gaussian distribution of variance ε^2. As expected, the sequence of minimizers x_ε^* of (6) converges to an optimal solution x^* of (5) when $\varepsilon \to 0$. Numerical results that show the performance of the gradient-based method presented in this paper are also included.

2   Smoothing via Mollifiers

In this section we recall some basic notions and properties of mollifiers and introduce a smoothing approach. For each $\varepsilon > 0$, let us consider a family of functions $\varphi_\varepsilon \in C_0^\infty(\mathbb{R}^n)$ that satisfies the following properties:

1. $\varphi_\varepsilon(x) \geq 0$, for all $x \in \mathbb{R}^n$,
2. $support(\varphi_\varepsilon) \subseteq \{x \in \mathbb{R}^n : \|x\| \leq \varepsilon\}$,
3. $\int_{\mathbb{R}^n} \varphi_\varepsilon(x) dx = 1$.

Such functions are called *mollifiers* [12].

We now provide a way to construct a family of smooth functions approximating any function f in L_{loc}^1 (locally integrable functions). Given a family of mollifiers $\{\varphi_\varepsilon : \mathbb{R}^n \to \mathbb{R}_+ | \varepsilon \in \mathbb{R}_+\}$, we can define a smooth function approximation f^ε of f through the convolution

$$(f * \varphi_\varepsilon)(x) := \int_{\mathbb{R}^n} f(x - z)\varphi_\varepsilon(z) dz = \int_{\mathbb{R}^n} f(z)\varphi_\varepsilon(x - z) dz.$$

The sequence $f * \varphi_\varepsilon$ is said to be a sequence of mollified functions. Some properties of mollified functions can be considered classical. From a computational perspective let us notice that if $Y_\varepsilon(x, \cdot)$ is a random vector with density defined by $z \to \varphi_\varepsilon(x - z)$, the above definition can be written as

$$(f * \varphi_\varepsilon)(x) := \mathbb{E}(f(Y_\varepsilon(x, \cdot))),$$

where $\mathbb{E}$ is the expected value of the random variable $f(Y_\varepsilon(x, \cdot))$. This stochastic interpretation allows us to avoid the calculation of the above integral by estimating the expected valued of $f(Y_\varepsilon(x, \cdot))$ instead.

Theorem 1. *[2] Let $f \in C(\mathbb{R}^n)$. Then $f * \varphi_\varepsilon$ converges continuosly to f, i.e. $f * \varphi_{\varepsilon_m}(x_m) \to f(x)$ for all $x_m \to x$. In fact, $f * \varphi_\varepsilon$ converges uniformly to f on every compact subset of $\mathbb{R}^n$ as $\varepsilon_m \to 0$.*

The previous convergence property can be generalized.

Definition 1. *[2] A sequence of functions $f_m : \mathbb{R}^n \to \mathbb{R}$ epi-converges to $f : \mathbb{R}^n \to \mathbb{R}$ at x if:*

1. $\liminf_{m \to +\infty} f_m(x_m) \geq f(x)$ *for all $x_m \to x$;*
2. $\lim_{m \to +\infty} f_m(x_m) = f(x)$ *for some sequence $x_m \to x$.*

The sequence f_m epi-converges to f if this holds for all $x \in \mathbb{R}^n$. In this case we say that f is the epi-limit of f_m.

It can be easily checked that when f is the epi-limit of some sequence f_m, then f is lower semicontinuous. Moreover if f_m converges continuously, then it also epi-converges. The notion of epi-convergence ensures the convergence of mimimizers of f_m to the minimizers of f (see [22]).

Definition 2. *[12] A function $f : \mathbb{R}^n \to \mathbb{R}$ is strongly lower semicontinuous (s.l.s.c.) at x if it is lower semicontinuous at x and there exists a sequence $x_m \to x$ with f continuous at x_m (for all m) such that $f(x_m) \to f(x)$. The function f is strongly lower semicontinuous if this holds at all x.*

Theorem 2. *[12] Let $\varepsilon_m \to 0$ if $m \to +\infty$. For any s.l.s.c. function $f : \mathbb{R}^n \to \mathbb{R}$, and any associated sequence f_{ε_m} of mollified functions we have that f is the epi-limit of f_{ε_m}.*

Lemma 1. *The mollified norm $\|x\|_1^\varepsilon$ is greater or equal than its non-smooth counterpart $\|x\|_1$ for any $x \in \mathbb{R}^n$.*

Proof. Let $f(z) = \|x - z\|_1$. Then, by convexity of f and using Jensen's inequality, we have that

$$\|x - \mathbb{E}(z)\|_1 \leq \int_{\mathbb{R}^n} \|x - z\|_1 \varphi_\varepsilon(z) dz. \tag{7}$$

Given that $\mathbb{E}(z) = 0$, we immediately obtain that $\|x\|_1 \leq \|x\|_1^\varepsilon$ for all $x \in \mathbb{R}^n$.

Theorem 3. *Let $g : \mathbb{R}^n \to \mathbb{R}$ and (ε_m) be a sequence of positive real numbers such that $\varepsilon_m \to 0$. The function $g(x) + \gamma\|x\|_1$ is the epi-limit of the sequence of functions $h_m : \mathbb{R}^n \to \mathbb{R}$ defined as*

$$h_m(x) := g(x) + \gamma\|x\|_1^{\varepsilon_m}. \tag{8}$$

Proof. Let (x_m) be a sequence in $\mathbb{R}^n$ such that $x_m \to x$. Since $\|x\|_1^{\varepsilon_m}$ converges to $\|x\|_1$ as m tends to infinity, we have that

$$\lim_{m \to \infty} h_m(x_m) = g(x) + \gamma\|x\|_1. \tag{9}$$

Also, by lemma 1, it follows that for any $x_m \in \mathbb{R}^n$ and any $\varepsilon_m \in \mathbb{R}_+$

$$g(x_m) + \gamma\|x_m\|_1^{\varepsilon_m} \geq g(x_m) + \gamma\|x_m\|_1. \tag{10}$$

Taking $\liminf$ at both sides over all sequences $x_m \to x$ we obtain that

$$\liminf_{m \to \infty} g(x_m) + \gamma\|x_m\|_1^{\varepsilon_m} \geq g(x) + \gamma\|x\|_1. \tag{11}$$

This completes the proof.

By means of mollified functions it is possible to define generalized directional derivatives for a non-smooth function f, which, under suitable regularity of f, coincide with Clarke's subdifferential. In [12] (see also [8,9,15] for alternative definitions of generalized derivatives through mollified functions), a generalized gradient w.r.t. the mollifier sequence $f_{\varepsilon m}$ has also been defined in the following way:

$$\partial_\varepsilon f(x) := \left\{ \limsup_{m \to +\infty} \nabla f_{\varepsilon m}(x_m), x_m \to x \right\}. \tag{12}$$

Theorem 4. *[12] Let $f : \mathbb{R}^n \to \mathbb{R}$ be locally Lipschitz at x; then $\partial_\varepsilon f(x)$ coincides with Clarke's subdifferential at x.*

Theorem 5. *Let $g : \mathbb{R}^n \to \mathbb{R}$ be differentiable and locally Lipschitz at x. Also, let $h(x) = g(x) + \gamma\|x\|_1$. Then, $\partial_\varepsilon h(x)$ coincides with Clarke's subdifferential at x.*

Proof. Clearly, $\|x\|_1$ is Lipschitz continuous with Lipschitz constant one since

$$|\|x\|_1 - \|y\|_1| \leq \|x - y\|_1. \tag{13}$$

Moreover, since g is locally Lipschitz at x, it follows that h is locally Lipschitz at x as well. Also, by definition of $\partial_\varepsilon(\cdot)$ one has that

$$\partial_\varepsilon h(x) := \left\{ \limsup_{m \to +\infty} \nabla(g(x_m) + \gamma\|x_m\|_1^{\varepsilon m}), x_m \to x \right\} \tag{14}$$

$$:= \left\{ \limsup_{m \to +\infty} \nabla g(x_m) + \gamma\nabla(\|x_m\|_1^{\varepsilon m}), x_m \to x \right\} \tag{15}$$

$$:= \nabla g(x) + \gamma \left\{ \limsup_{n \to +\infty} \nabla(\|x_m\|_1^{\varepsilon m}), x_m \to x \right\}, \tag{16}$$

where the last equation is indeed the set of Clarke's subgradients of h at x.

In the sequel we will use the following family of smoothing Gaussian functions:

$$\hat{\phi}_\varepsilon(x) = \frac{1}{\varepsilon^n} \hat{\phi}\left(\frac{x}{\varepsilon}\right), \tag{17}$$

where

$$\hat{\phi}(x) = \frac{1}{\sqrt{2\pi}} e^{-\frac{\|x\|_2^2}{2}}. \tag{18}$$

It is well known that ϕ_ε is a density function, so its integral over $\mathbb{R}^n$ is equal to one, it is smooth, and ϕ_ε goes to zero when $\|x\| \to +\infty$. However, this sequence is not a proper family of mollifiers as each element $\hat{\phi}_\varepsilon$ does not have a compact support. Nevertheless, it can be proved that, given a function f, the family of smooth functions

$$\hat{f}_\varepsilon(x) = (f * \hat{\phi}_\varepsilon)(x) = \frac{1}{\varepsilon^n} \int_{\mathbb{R}^n} f(x - z) \hat{\phi}\left(\frac{z}{\varepsilon}\right) dz \tag{19}$$

epi-converges to f when $\varepsilon \to 0$. This easily follows by taking a sequence of mollifiers φ_δ with compact support converging to $\hat\phi$ when $\delta \to 0$, and then use the convergence properties of mollifiers.

Furthermore, Theorems 3 and 5 guarantee that the sequence of minimizers x_ε^* of (6) converges to a minimizer x^* of (5) when ε tends to zero. In other words, $x_\varepsilon^* \to x^*$ as $\varepsilon \to 0$.

3   SSIM-Based Optimization with Sparsity

The Structural Similarity Index Measure (SSIM) between x and y, where $x, y \in \mathbb{R}^n$, is defined as [28]

$$\text{SSIM}(x,y) = \left(\frac{2\mu_x\mu_y + C_1}{\mu_x^2 + \mu_y^2 + C_1} \right) \left(\frac{2\sigma_x\sigma_y + C_2}{\sigma_x^2 + \sigma_y^2 + C_2} \right) \left(\frac{\sigma_{xy} + C_3}{\sigma_x\sigma_y + C_3} \right). \tag{20}$$

Here, μ_x and μ_y denote the mean values of x and y, respectively, and σ_{xy} denotes the cross correlation between x and y, from which all other definitions follow. The small positive constants, C_1, C_2 and C_3 provide numerical stability and can be adjusted to accommodate the Human Visual System (HVS) [28,29].

Under the assumption that the vectors x and y have zero mean, the latter expression can be simplified:

$$S(x,y) = \frac{2x^T y + C}{\|x\|_2^2 + \|y\|_2^2 + C}, \tag{21}$$

where $C = (n-1)C_2$. Reformulation of the SSIM as a normalized metric comes out from the definition of the following distance-dissimilarity function $T(x,y)$ [6,17,18]:

$$T(x,y) = 1 - S(x,y) = \frac{\|x - y\|_2^2}{\|x\|_2^2 + \|y\|_2^2 + C}. \tag{22}$$

Note that $0 \leq T(x,y) \leq 2$. Furthermore, $T(x,y) = 0$ if and only if $x = y$.

Algorithms for solving (6) can be developed by first computing its gradient. To do this, we define the following non-linear functional:

$$f(x) = T(x,y) + \gamma\|x\|_1^\varepsilon. \tag{23}$$

Its gradient is given by

$$\nabla f_\varepsilon(x) = \frac{2S(x,y)A^T Ax - 2A^T y}{\|Ax\|_2^2 + \|y\|_2^2 + C} + \gamma \int_{\mathbb{R}^n} \|z\|_1 \nabla\hat\phi_\varepsilon \left(\frac{x-z}{\varepsilon} \right) dz, \tag{24}$$

where $\nabla\hat\phi_\varepsilon(x)$ is equal to

$$\nabla\hat\phi_\varepsilon \left(\frac{x}{\varepsilon} \right) = \frac{-x}{\sqrt{(2\pi)^n}\varepsilon^{n+2}} e^{-\frac{\|x\|_2^2}{2\varepsilon^2}}. \tag{25}$$

By using (24), and defining $\mathbf{1} = [1, \cdots, 1]^T \in \mathbb{R}^m$, we propose the following algorithm for solving (6):

Algorithm 1. Gradient descent for unconstrained SSIM-L^1 optimization via mollifiers

---

initialize Choose $x = x_0$, λ;
data preprocessing $\bar{y} = \frac{1}{n}\mathbf{1}^T y$, $y = y - \bar{y}\mathbf{1}$;
repeat
 $x = x - \lambda \nabla f_\varepsilon(x)$;
until stopping criterion is met (e.g., $\|x^{(new)} - x^{(old)}\|_\infty < \delta$);
return x, $y = y + \bar{y}\mathbf{1}$.

Notice that this algorithm will return an optimal x^* such that the mean of Ax^* is zero. Nevertheless, it is possible to obtain the non-zero mean optimal x^* by means of the following equation:

$$x^* = x^* + \bar{y}(A^T A)^{-1} A^T \mathbf{1}, \tag{26}$$

provided that the inverse of $A^T A$ exists (see [17] and [18] for more details).

4 Experiments

In these experiments we solve the approximate sparse reconstruction problem (6) with the proposed gradient-descent algorithm. Its performance is measured by comparing its recovered solutions with the solutions obtained by the algorithm introduced in [17] for solving (5) and the solutions of problem (1). In all computations a set of Discrete Cosine Transform (DCT) coefficients is to be recovered; therefore, problem (1) was solved by means of the soft-thresholding (ST) operator [16,23].

In all the experiments images were divided into non-overlapping 8×8 pixel blocks. As expected, the means of each block are subtracted prior to processing, which are added after the non-overlapping blocks have been processed. This is also done when problem (1) is solved at each pixel block for the sake of a fair comparison between the different methods.

It is worthwhile to mention that for computing the integral of the gradient of (23) we performed a Monte Carlo integration (see Eq. (24)). This can be done by noticing the fact that calculating

$$\int_{\mathbb{R}^n} \|z\|_1 \nabla \hat{\phi}_\varepsilon \left(\frac{x - z}{\varepsilon} \right) dz \tag{27}$$

is equivalent to compute the expected value $\mathbb{E}(\|z\|_1(x - z))$, where z follows a Gaussian distribution of variance ε^2 and mean equal to x.

In Fig. 1, in the left plot it can be observed an example of the optimal DCT coefficients that are obtained by the different methods that are being compared. Plots in red and green correspond to the solutions obtained by the algorithm introduced in [17] and ST respectively. The blue plot is the optimal solution that was obtained by the proposed method when $\varepsilon = 0.001$. True sparsity in the solution is not achieved since this occurs in the limit when $\varepsilon \to 0$; nevertheless, it can be seen that the proposed method gives a good non-sparse approximation of the solution of the non-smooth problem (5). This in fact can be useful for providing a good initial guess of a thresholding method that solves (5) [24]. In the plot on the right it can be seen how a sequence of optimal solutions of (6) gets closer to a solution of (5) as ε tends to zero. In this case, the plot in magenta corresponds to the set of optimal DCT coefficients that is obtained by solving problem (5).

As for visual results, these are shown in Fig. 2. In the presented example, a sub-image of the test image *Lena* was employed. In the bottom row the original sub-image and its recovered counterparts can be observed. Regularization was carried out at all non-overlapping pixel blocks in such a way that the number of non-zero DCT coefficients obtained by the algorithm introduced in [17] and the ST operator is always 19. As for the regularization of the proposed algorithm, the values of the regularization parameter that were used were the same that were employed for the algorithm that solves the non-smooth problem (5).

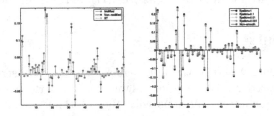

Fig. 1. The plot on the left shows an example of the different solutions that were obtained by the three methods that were compared. The plot on the right shows how a sequence of minimizers x_ε^* of the mollified SSIM-based optimization problem (6) converges to a minimizer x^* of the non-smooth problem (5).

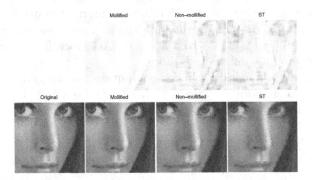

Fig. 2. Visual results for a sub-image from the test image *Lena*. In all cases, regularization is carried out to induce the same degree of sparsity for all methods at each non-overlapping pixel block. In the bottom row the original image and its reconstructions are shown. The corresponding SSIM maps can be seen in the top row.

This was done in this way since in the limit when $\varepsilon \to 0$, both problems (5) and (6) are equivalent. In other words, the strength of the regularization tends to be the same for these two methods. Along with the images of the bottom row, the SSIM maps that depict the similarity between the original sub-image and its reconstructions are shown in the top row. The higher the brightness of these maps at a given location, the higher the SSIM at that particular point [28]. As mentioned in [17], performance of the ST approach and their algorithm is very similar, however, the average $T(Ax, y)$ of the non-mollified SSIM-based optimization problem (0.9156) is higher than the average $T(Ax, y)$ of the L^2 counterpart (0.9117). As for the proposed approach, the recovered image is visually more appealing than the other two methods, and as expected, the average $T(Ax, y)$ is the highest of the three approaches that are being compared (0.9629). This should not be surprising since several recovered DCT coefficients are not set to zero by the proposed algorithm, which is not always the case for the other two methods.

Acknowledgements. We gratefully acknowledge that this research has been supported in part by the Natural Sciences and Engineering Research Council of Canada (NSERC) in the form of a Discovery Grant (ERV).

References

1. Beck, A.A., Teboulle, M.: A fast iterative shrinkage-thresholding algorithm for linear inverse problems. SIAM J. Imaging Sci. Arch. **2**(1), 183–202 (2009)
2. Brezis, H.: Analyse Fonctionelle Theorie et Applications. Masson editeur, Paris (1963)
3. Bruckstein, A., Donoho, D., Elad, M.: From sparse solutions of systems of equations to sparse modeling of signals and images. SIAM Rev. **51**(1), 34–81 (2009)
4. Brunet, D.: A Study of the Structural Similarity Image Quality Measure with Applications to Image Processing, Ph.D. thesis, University of Waterloo (2010)
5. Brunet, D., Vrscay, E.R., Wang, Z.: On the mathematical properties of the structural similarity index. IEEE Trans. Image Proc. **21**(4), 1488–1499 (2012)
6. Brunet, D., Vrscay, E.R., Wang, Z.: Structural similarity-based approximation of signals and images using orthogonal bases. In: Campilho, A., Kamel, M. (eds.) ICIAR 2010. LNCS, vol. 6111, pp. 11–22. Springer, Heidelberg (2010)
7. Channappayya, S.S., Bovik, A.C., Caramanis, C., Heath Jr, R.W.: Design of linear equalizers optimized for the structural similarity index. IEEE Trans. Image Process. **17**(6), 857–872 (2008)
8. Crespi, G.P., La Torre, D., Rocca, M.: Second-order mollified derivatives and optimization. Rendiconti del Circolo Matematico di Palermo **52**(2), 251–262 (2003)
9. Crespi, G.P., La Torre, D., Rocca, M.: Mollified derivatives and second-order optimality conditions. J. Nonlinear Convex Anal. **4**(3), 437–454 (2003)
10. Donoho, D., Elad, M.: Optimality sparse representation in general (non-orthogonal) dictionaries via L^1-minimization. Proc. Nat. Acad. Sci. **100**, 2197–2202 (2003)
11. Donoho, D.: Denoising by soft-thresholding. IEEE Trans. Inf. Theory **41**(3), 613–627 (1995)

12. Ermoliev, Y.M., Norkin, V.I., Wets, R.J.B.: The minimization of semicontinuous functions: mollifier subgradients. SIAM J. Control Optim. **33**, 149–167 (1995)
13. Jongen, H.T., Stein, O.: Smoothing by mollifiers. Part I: semi-infinite optimization. J. Global Optim. **41**(3), 319–334 (2008)
14. Jongen, H.T., Stein, O.: Smoothing by mollifiers. Part II: nonlinear optimization. J. Global Optim. **41**(3), 335–350 (2008)
15. La Torre, D., Rocca, M.: Remarks on second order generalized derivatives for differentiable functions with Lipschitzian Jacobian. Appl. Math. E - Notes **3**, 130–137 (2003)
16. Mairal, J., Bach, F., Jenatton, R., Obozinski, G.: Convex Optimization with Sparsity-Inducing Norms. Optimization for Machine Learning. MIT Press, Cambridge (2011)
17. Otero, D., Vrscay, E.R.: Unconstrained structural similarity-based optimization. In: Campilho, A., Kamel, M. (eds.) ICIAR 2014, Part I. LNCS, vol. 8814, pp. 167–176. Springer, Heidelberg (2014)
18. Otero, D., Vrscay, E.R.: Solving problems that employ structural similarity as the fidelity measure. In: Proceedings of the Internartional Conference on Image Processing, Computer Vision and Patter Recognition IPCV 2014, pp. 474–479. Springer, Heidelberg (2014)
19. Rehman, A., Rostami, M., Wang, Z., Brunet, D., Vrscay, E.R.: SSIM-inspired image restoration using sparse representation. EURASIP J. Adv. Sig. Proc. (2012)
20. Rehman, A., Gao, Y., Wang, J., Wang, Z.: Image classification based on complex wavelet structural similarity. Sig. Proc. Image Comm. **28**(8), 984–992 (2013)
21. Richter, T., Kim. K.J.: A MS-SSIM optimal JPEG 2000 encoder. In: Data Compression Conference, pp. 401–410, Snowbird, Utah, March 2009
22. Rockafellar, R.T., Wets, R.J.-B.: Variational Analysis. Springer Verlag, Berlin (1998)
23. Turlach, B.A.: On algorithms for solving least squares problems under an L^1 penalty or an L^1 constraint. In: Proceedings of the American Statistical Association, Statistical Computing Section, pp. 2572–2577 (2005)
24. Voronin, S., Yoshida, D.: Gradient Based Methods for Non-Smooth Regularization Via Convolution Smoothing http://arxiv.org/pdf/1408.6795.pdf
25. Wainwright, M.J., Schwartz, O., Simoncelli, E.P.: Natural image statistics and divisive normalization: modeling nonlinearity and adaptation in cortical neurons. In: Rao, R., Olshausen, B., Lewicki, M. (eds.) Probabilistic Models of the Brain: Perception and Neural Function, pp. 203–222. MIT Press, Cambridge (2002)
26. Wandell, B.A.: Foundations of Vision. Sinauer Publishers, Sunderland (1995)
27. Wang, Z., Bovik, A.C.: Mean squared error: love it or leave it? a new look at signal fidelity measures. IEEE Signal Proc. Mag. **26**(1), 98–117 (2009)
28. Wang, Z., Bovik, A.C., Sheikh, H.R., Simoncelli, E.P.: Image quality assessment: from error visibility to structural similarity. IEEE Trans. Image Proc. **13**(4), 600–612 (2004)
29. Wang, Z., Bovik, A.C.: A universal image quality index. IEEE Signal Process. Lett. **9**(3), 81–84 (2002)

Improved Non-Local Means Algorithm
Based on Dimensionality Reduction

Golam M. Maruf and Mahmoud R. El-Sakka$^{(\boxtimes)}$

Department of Computer Science, University of Western Ontario, London,
Ontario, Canada
{gmaruf,melsakka}@uwo.ca

Abstract. Non-Local Means is an image denoising algorithm based on patch similarity. It compares a reference patch with the neighboring patches to find similar patches. Such similar patches participate in the weighted averaging process. Most of the computational time for Non-Local Means scheme is consumed to measure patch similarities. In this paper, we have proposed an improvement where the image patches are projected into a global feature space. Then we have performed a statistical t-test to reduce the dimensionality of this feature space. Denoising is achieved based on this reduced feature space. The proposed modification exploits an improvement in terms of denoising performance and computational time.

Keywords: Non-Local Means algorithm · Image denoising · Image smoothing · Image enhancement · Additive white Gaussian noise · Spatial domain filtering

1 Introduction

An image may be numerically represented as a two dimensional discrete function u, in the spatial coordinates x and y. Intensity or gray level is the amplitude of u at any pair of coordinates. A digital image is composed of finite number of elements called pixels. An image may be contaminated with noise during acquisition, transmission or transformation. Noise is a variation of pixel intensity. Such noise can be additive or multiplicative. Additive noise is generally independent of image data whereas multiplicative noise is dependent on image data. Additive noise can be formularized as,

$$v(i) = u(i) + n(i), \tag{1}$$

whereas, multiplicative noise is formularized as,

$$v(i) = u(i) \times n(i). \tag{2}$$

Here, u(i) is the original value, n(i) is the noise value and v(i) is the observed value at pixel i. Despite the good quality of acquisition devices, an image denoising

M. Kamel and A. Campilho (Eds.): ICIAR 2015, LNCS 9164, pp. 43–50, 2015.
DOI: 10.1007/978-3-319-20801-5_5

method is always required to reduce unwanted noise signals. An image denoising scheme is used to find the best estimate of the original image from its noisy version.

Some of the basic filtering such as Gaussian and average filtering have a drawback of over-smoothing on edges and losing image details. Wavelet based denoising method [1], anisotropic diffusion [2], and bilateral filtering [3] try to overcome this drawback and preserve the image quality by preserving edges. But they may introduce a staircase effect or false edges. Recently, Buades et al. [4] proposed a denoising algorithm called Non-Local Means (NLM) which allows neighboring patches in the search window to participate in the denoising process for a certain reference patch in the noisy image. Most of the computational time for NLM is allocated to the similarity assessments between patches. In a general case, NLM needs to search the entire image for similar patches and performs weighted average based on the similarities. However, searching in a fixed area around the pixel of interest (POI) can reduce this computational time. Our main focus is to further reduce this computational time and improve denoising performance over the original Non-Local Means algorithm.

Many improvements have been suggested on the Non-Local Means algorithm in recent years. Bhujle et al. [5] proposed a dictionary based denoising in which patches with similar photometric structures are clustered together to create groups. Mahmoudi et al. [6] accelerate the NLM algorithm by pre-classifying neighborhood patches based on average gray values, gradient orientation, or both. Chaudhury et al. [7] claimed that the denoising performance of the Non-Local Means algorithm can be improved by replacing the mean operation by a median operation. Vignesh et al. [8] proposed a speed up technique for the Non-Local Means algorithm based on a probabilistic early termination (PET). Tasdizen et al. [9] proposed principal component based Non-Local Means algorithm where a global feature space is created to select important features. Brox et al. [10] proposed a technique to improve the performance of the NLM method using a clustering tree.

In this paper, we have proposed to created feature vectors for the noisy image. Then we have implemented a statistical *t-test* on these feature vectors to reduce their dimensionality. Our proposed method reduces the computational time and improves the overall performance of the original NLM algorithm.

2 Methods

The Non-Local Means algorithm searches neighboring patches to match with the reference patch. The original algorithm requires an extensive amount of time to select patches similar to the reference patch. These similar patches contribute to the weighted averaging process to denoise the center pixel of the reference patch. The computation time for the NLM algorithm can be reduced by improving this searching process.

We have formalized our proposed work into three steps. In the first step (pre-processing), we have created a global feature space and stored all possible neighborhood pixels. Then in the second step, we have performed a statistical *t-test* to reduce the dimensionality of the feature space on the previous feature points. Finally, we implement the non-local means algorithm, where we have used the selected feature points for calculating similarity measures of image neighborhood.

2.1 Preprocessing

In this step, we have created a feature vector space for the noisy image. An image patch is linearized and represented as a row vector of size j. Thus the dimension of this feature vector space will be j × N, where N is the total number of image pixels. Feature vectors can be represented as matrix C,

$$
C = \begin{bmatrix} c(1,1) & \cdots & c(1,j) \\ \vdots & \ddots & \vdots \\ c(N,1) & \cdots & c(N,j) \end{bmatrix} \tag{3}
$$

Here, for example if we have a patch size of 7 × 7 then j will be equal to 49. This matrix will be used during the dimensionality reduction process.

2.2 t-Testing

We have implemented a paired *t-test* of the null hypothesis. This test is performed on the matrix C. For each test case (i.e., each column in the matrix C), once the t value is determined, the students t-distribution lookup table is used to find the value of p. When the calculated p value is below a given threshold value, then the null hypothesis is rejected. In our denoising problem, we have considered each patch as a feature vector. The hypothesis tries to accept or reject a feature (i.e. an entire column in the matrix C). Here, the null hypothesis is whether a feature is significant or not. In calculating the null hypothesis, one uses the following normalization equation

$$
T = \frac{\bar{x} - \mu_0}{s/\sqrt{n}} \tag{4}
$$

Where, $\bar{x}$ is the sample mean, μ_0 is the population mean, s is the sample standard deviation and n is the sample size. When the null hypothesis is accepted, it concludes that the feature is significant. Otherwise, this feature is not significant. Thus the entire column is deleted and hence reduces the size of matrix C.

2.3   Non-Local Means Algorithm

In the Non-Local Means algorithm a discrete noisy image $v = \{v(j) \mid j \in I\}$, where I is the input image, can be denoised by the estimated value NL[v](i) for a pixel i. It is computed as a weighted average for all of the pixels in the image,

$$NL[v](i) = \sum_{j \in I} w(i, j) v(j) \tag{5}$$

where, the weight w(i, j) depends on the similarity between the pixel i and the pixel j of the intensity gray level vectors $v(N_i)$ and $v(N_j)$. Here, N_k is the square patch around the center pixel k. The weight is then assigned to value v(j) to denoise pixel i. The summation of all weight is equal 1 and each weight value w(i, j) has a range between [0, 1]. To measure similarity between patches, the Euclidean distance between patches is calculated,

$$\left\| v(N_i) - v(N_j) \right\|^2_{2,\sigma} \tag{6}$$

where, $\sigma > 0$ is the standard deviation of the Gaussian kernel. The weight w(i, j) are computed as follows,

$$w(i,j) = \frac{1}{z(i)} e^{-\frac{\left\| v(N_i) - v(N_j) \right\|^2_{2,\sigma}}{h^2}} \tag{7}$$

where, Z(i) is a normalization constant such that,

$$Z(i) = \sum_j e^{-\frac{\left\| v(N_i) - v(N_j) \right\|^2_{2,\sigma}}{h^2}} \tag{8}$$

Here, h is a smoothing kernel width which controls decay of the exponential function and therefore controls the decay of the weights as a function of the Euclidean distances. In our proposed method N_k is replaced by f_k, where f_k is the reduced feature vector. Then we have selected similar patches and calculated weights based on this reduced feature vector.

Our proposed algorithm is summarized as follows.

Algorithm Improved Non-Local Means

Input I: Image with additive white Gaussian noise
Output NL(I): Denoised image
1. Crate a global feature matrix C (as shown in Equation 3).
2. Perform the *t-test* on matrix C to produce the reduced row matrix f_k.
3. For each pixel i, where $i \in [1, N]$,
4. Do
4.1. For each pixel in N_k , i.e., the square patches around the center pixel k
4.2. Do

4.2.1. Evaluate the normalization constant $Z(i) \leftarrow \sum_j e^{-\frac{\left\|v(f_i)-v(f_j)\right\|_2^2}{h^2}}$,
    where j refers to the N_k patches.

4.2.2. Calculate the weight matrix $W(i, j) \leftarrow \frac{1}{Z(i)} e^{-\frac{\left\|v(f_i)-v(f_j)\right\|_2^2}{h^2}}$

4.2.3. Done

4.3. Denoise pixel i: $NL[v](i) \leftarrow \sum_{j \in I} w(i, j)v(j)$

4.4. Done

---

3 Results

The performance of our proposed method is compared in terms of PSNR with other denoising schemes, namely the original NLM method, the principal component analysis based NLM method (PCA-NLM), the patch regression based NLM method (NLM-Patch) and the BM3D method. Eight 512×512 test images (Bridge, Columbia, Lake, Lax, Milk drop, Plane, Woman1 and Woman2) are utilized to assess the performance of these schemes. See Fig. 1.

Tables 1 and 2 show the average PSNR and SSIM comparative performance, respectively, for all test images. The bolded values in Tables 1 and 2 represent the highest PSNR and SSIM values, respectively, among all of the algorithms for a given noise level.

Fig. 1. The set of the test images (512 × 512) for performance analysis.

For noise level $\sigma < 50$, the proposed method performs better than any other denoising scheme, including the BM3D method. Yet, for noise level $\sigma > 50$ the proposed method performs better than the original NLM and its variants. Yet, the BM3D method performs better at higher noise levels.

Table 3 compares the average running time performance for all test images for the proposed method and the other denoising schemes. It has been found that our proposed method outperforms the NLM method, variants of the NLM method and the BM3D method at all noise levels, as it requires fewer features to compare and calculate weights. Thus the computational time is dramatically reduced while keeping the denoising performance in an acceptable range.

Table 1. Average PSNR(dB) comparison for all test images among the proposed method, the NLM method, variants of the NLM method and the BM3D method for various noise levels.

Noise level	NLM	PCA-NLM	NLM-patch	Proposed method	BM3D
10	32.52	32.94	31.47	**33.94**	33.84
20	29.87	29.95	29.04	**31.0**	30.50
30	28.13	28.26	27.45	**28.96**	28.38
40	26.69	26.43	25.87	**27.72**	27.70
50	25.49	25.38	24.61	26.49	**26.86**
60	23.85	23.87	22.75	24.30	**25.94**
70	22.90	22.81	22.31	23.22	**25.29**
80	22.32	22.32	21.92	22.60	**24.75**
90	21.73	21.57	20.89	21.86	**24.18**
100	21.13	20.94	20.14	21.19	**23.68**
Average	25.46	25.45	24.64	26.15	**27.11**

Table 2. Average SSIM comparison for all test images among the proposed method, the NLM method, variants of the NLM method and the BM3D method for various noise levels.

Noise level	NLM	PCA-NLM	NLM-patch	Proposed method	BM3D
10	0.9078	0.9015	0.9051	0.9201	0.9124
20	0.8625	0.8605	0.8610	0.8785	0.8711
30	0.8389	0.8341	0.8291	0.8469	0.8415
40	0.8071	0.8065	0.8017	0.8202	0.8201
50	0.7689	0.7597	0.7659	0.7810	0.7841
60	0.7487	0.7491	0.7412	0.7524	0.7617
70	0.7059	0.7032	0.7015	0.7195	0.7217
80	0.6925	0.6912	0.6907	0.7079	0.7138
90	0.6857	0.6815	0.6851	0.6992	0.7051
100	0.6711	0.6504	0.6522	0.6975	0.7004
Average	0.7878	0.7819	0.7823	0.8022	0.8099

Table 3. Running time (in milliseconds) for Lena image among the proposed method, the NLM method, variants of the NLM method and the BM3D method for different noise levels.

Noise level	NLM	PCA-NLM	NLM-patch	Proposed method	BM3D
10	209.5	195.1	208.1	**161.2**	223.2
20	210.7	196.7	210.6	**164.5**	224.2
30	212.3	197.4	210.0	**165.7**	225.1
40	212.6	198.8	211.5	**169.9**	229.3
50	212.4	200.3	211.0	**173.9**	230.2
60	213.0	204.4	212.8	**181.2**	230.8
70	214.5	207.9	213.1	**182.5**	231.3
80	214.9	208.6	213.9	**184.0**	231.6
90	216.0	209.9	214.0	**185.2**	232.9
100	217.1	210.1	216.4	**185.9**	233.1
Average	213.3	202.9	212.1	**175.4**	229.8

4 Conclusions

Non-Local Means is a popular image denoising algorithm implemented in the spatial domain. In this research, we have proposed a statistics based improvement for the Non-Local Means algorithm. The key of this improvement is to reduce the size of the feature space, which reduces the patch similarity measurement time and increases the overall denoising performance. We have utilized a statistical *t-test* to reduce the dimensionality of the feature space Experimental results show that our proposed method provides the best running time among all other algorithms in all test cases at various noise levels. It also provides a good denoising improvement in terms of the PSNR and the SSIM values. In addition, it performs better than the NLM method and its variants at all noise levels and perform better than the BM3D method for lower noise levels.

References

1. Portilla, G., Strela, J., Wainwright, V., Simoncelli, M.: Image denoising using scale mixtures of gaussians in the wavelet domain. IEEE Trans. Image Process. **12**(11), 1338–1351 (2003)
2. Perona, P., Malik, J.: Scale-space and edge detection using anisotropic diffusion. IEEE Trans. Pattern Anal. Mach. Intell. **12**(7), 629–639 (1990)
3. Tomasi C., Manduchi, R.: Bilateral filtering for gray and color images. In: IEEE Sixth International Conference on Computer Vision, pp. 839–846 (1998)
4. Buades, A., Coll, B., Morel, J-M.: A non-local algorithm for image denoising. In: IEEE Computer Society Conference on Computer Vision and Pattern Recognition, pp. 60–65 (2005)
5. Bhujle, H., Chaudhuri, S.: Novel speed-up strategies for non-local means denoising with patch and edge patch based dictionaries. IEEE Trans. Image Process. **23**(1), 356–365 (2014)
6. Mahmoudi, M., Sapiro, G.: Fast image and video denoising via nonlocal means of similar neighborhoods. IEEE Signal Process. Lett. **12**(12), 839–842 (2005)
7. Chaudhury, K., Singer, A.: Non-local Euclidean medians. IEEE Signal Process. Lett. **19**(11), 745–748 (2012)
8. Vignesh, R., Oh, B., Kuo, C.-C.: Fast non-local means (NLM) computation with probabilistic early termination. IEEE Signal Process. Lett. **17**(3), 277–280 (2010)
9. Tasdizen, T.: Principal components for non-local means image denoising. In: 15th IEEE International Conference on Image Processing, pp.1728–1731 (2008)
10. Brox, T., Kleinschmidt, O., Cremers, D.: Efficient nonlocal means for denoising of textural patterns. IEEE Trans. Image Process. **17**(7), 1083–1092 (2008)

Non-local Means for Stereo Image Denoising Using Structural Similarity

Monagi H. Alkinani and Mahmoud R. El-Sakka$^{(\boxtimes)}$

Computer Science Department, University of Western Ontario,
London, ON N6A 5B7, Canada
{malkinan,melsakka}@uwo.ca

Abstract. We present a novel stereo image denoising algorithm. Our algorithm takes as an input a pair of noisy images of an object captured form two different directions. We use the structural similarity index as a similarity metric for identifying locations of similar patches in the input images. We adapt the Non-Local Means algorithm for denoising collected patches from the input images. We validate our algorithm on various stereo images at various noise levels. Experimental results show that the denoising performance of our algorithm is better than the original Non-Local Means and Stereo-MSE methods at low noise level ($\sigma \leqslant 20$).

Keywords: Non-local means · Patch-based image filtering · Stereo imaging · Structural similarity index · Additive noise reduction · Disparity map

1 Introduction

Digital images are captured using sensors during the data acquisition phase, where they are often contaminated with an undesired random noise. Such noise can also be produced during image transmission or image compression. Additive noise is generally modelled as:

$$v(x) = u(x) + n(x)_d, x \in \Omega \tag{1}$$

where $v(x)$ is the noisy component of the image, $u(x)$ is the true image, $n(x)_d$ is the random additive noise, and Ω denotes the set of all pixels in the image. In particular, if $n(x)_d$ is a Gaussian random process, then the noise is identified as a Gaussian noise. The noise level in digital images vary from being almost imperceptible to being very noticeable. Image denoising schemes attempt to produce a new image that has less noise, i.e., closer to the noise-free image $u(x)$.

Denoising techniques can be grouped into two main approaches: pixel-based image filtering and patch-based image filtering. A pixel-based image filtering scheme is mainly a proximity operation used for manipulating one pixel at a time based on its spatial neighbouring pixels. Such methods include low-pass filtering using Gaussian filter [1], Yaroslavsky filter [2], bilateral filter [3], total variation filter [4], and anisotropic diffusion filter [5]. On the other hand, in patch-based image filtering, the noisy image is divided into patches, or "blocks",

© Springer International Publishing Switzerland 2015
M. Kamel and A. Campilho (Eds.): ICIAR 2015, LNCS 9164, pp. 51–59, 2015.
DOI: 10.1007/978-3-319-20801-5_6

which are then manipulated separately in order to provide an estimate of the true pixel values based on similar patches located within a searching window. Such methods include Non-Local Means [6], patch-based PCA [7], K-SVD [8], and BM3D [9]. Patch-based image filtering approach utilizes the redundancy and the similarity among the various parts of the input image.

Non-Local Means (NL-Means) is a patch-based image filter proposed by Buades *et al.* [6] as a modification to the pixel-based bilateral filter. Like the bilateral filter, it blurs the homogeneous areas and preserves edges.

As a new application for NL-Means filter, we would like to adapt it for denoising stereo images in order to improve the extracted depth information coming from noisy stereo images. A stereo image uses two or more images generated from cameras at different locations. By computing the differences between the images, the depth information can be extracted. Noisy stereo images would give disappointing results when they are used for extracting depth information. In this work, NL-Means is utilized for denoising stereo images. Our proposed method extends the searching window to search the two images when seeking similar patches.

Using multi-view images for noise reduction has a unique advantage over using only one-view image. In multi-view images, a pixel in one image is estimated based on the corresponding pixels from all other images. This approach is popular in video denoising where multi-frames are used for noise reduction [10,11]. Recently, great progress has been made to break the limits of using one input image when denoising 3D images. Zhang *et al.* extended the idea of using patch-based PCA for denoising single image to multi-view images [12]. While patch-based PCA collects similar patches locally and globally from single image before applying the PCA algorithm, Zhang *et al.* algorithm collects similar patches from multiple images. Heo *et al.* use Maximum A Posteriori-Markov Random Field (MAP-MRF) as a model for energy minimization in order to find the disparity maps from stereo image [13]. In order to find the disparity maps, they proposed an algorithm that consists of two terms: the first term is the restored intensity difference, and the second term is the dissimilarity of support pixel distribution. They adapted NL-Means algorithm for the restoration of intensity values of the first term. They extended the NL-Means algorithm for denoising stereo images by grouping similar patches by using MSE from two similar windows in left and right images, we called this method Stereo-MSE.

The rest of the paper is organized as follow. Section 2 introduces the NL-Means filter and its mathematical formulation. Section 3 describes our proposed method. In Sect. 4, we compare the performance of the proposed method with other denoising filters. Section 5 offers concluding comments, and future works.

2   NL-Means Algorithm

The NL-Means filter divides the input image into sub-images and then filters each sub-image separately in a technique that is referred to as being patch-based. Each sub-image contains several patches. As in the bilateral filter, the similarity in NL-Means filter is assessed based on two measurements: (1) the Euclidean distance between the centres of the patches, and (2) the luminance distance between the patches. In contrast to the bilateral filter, NL-Means filter uses patches from a searching window instead of using single neighbouring pixels when assigning weights and averaging. This is why it is called a non-local method. Patches with similar grey levels are assigned larger weights when averaging. Similar to bilateral filter, NL-Means filter preserves edges regardless of their directions.

Equation 2 is used to estimate a pixel i using NL-Means filter,

$$NLMeans\,[v]_i = \sum_{j \in I} \omega(i,j)\,[v]_j \tag{2}$$

where $[v]_i$ and $[v]_j$ are pixels intensities at location i and j, respectively, and $\omega(i,j)$ is a similarity measure between pixels i and j. The similarity weight, $\omega(i,j)$, satisfies the condition $0 \le \omega(i,j) \le 1$ and $\sum_j \omega(i,j) = 1$. It depends on the grey level similarity and the Euclidean distance between vectors $N\,[v]_i$ and $N\,[v]_j$, where $N\,[v]_k$ denotes a square neighbourhood of fixed size and centred at a pixel k. The weights are described as,

$$\omega(i,j) = \frac{1}{Z(i)} e^{-\frac{\|(N[v]_i)-(N[v]_j)\|^2}{h^2}} \tag{3}$$

where $Z(i)$ is a normalization factor and h is a filtering parameter set depending on the noise level.

The level of noise determines the sizes needed for the searching window and patches. For a robust comparison between patches, the size of the patches increases when the noise level is high. Accordingly, the value of the filtering parameter h increases as the size of the patch is increased. Meanwhile, the size of the searching window must be increased in order to find more similar patches.

3 Proposed Algorithm

In this section, we describe a new algorithm for solving the problem of denoising stereo images. The novelty of this algorithm is the use of the NL-Means algorithm to denoise multi-view images. We increase the number of similar patches by grouping similar patches from left and right images of a stereo image. Figure 1 shows the way of collecting similar patches.

3.1 Algorithm Outline

Our algorithm is illustrated in Fig. 2. The left stereo image is processed in a raster scan. At each pixel, the following procedure is performed:

1. Obtain from the left image a fixed-size square patch "reference patch" $N\,[vl]_k$ centred at location k.
2. Use the structural similarity (SSIM) index [14] to find from the right image the best patch $N\,[vr]_q$ centred at location q that is similar to the reference patch and identify its window location.

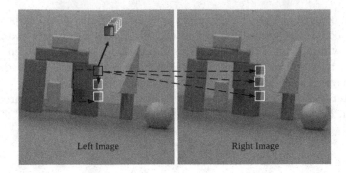

Fig. 1. Collecting similar patches from a stereo image: the patch with a black border is the reference patch, and the patches with white borders are similar patches

3. Collect patches from the two windows (using MSE) and assign weights ω to each patch. Similar patches to the reference patch are assigned high weights. The weights are assigned as described in Eq. 3.
4. Calculate the weighted average of patches, in order to estimate the true pixel of the left image. The estimated value $NLMeans\,[vl]_i$, for a pixel i located in the left image, is computed as:

$$NLMeans\,[vl]_i = \sum_{j \in I} \omega(i,j)\,[v]_j \qquad (4)$$

where $[vl]_i$ and $[v]_j$ are pixel intensities at location i in the left image and j from the left or right image, and $\omega(i,j)$ is a similarity weight between pixels i and j.

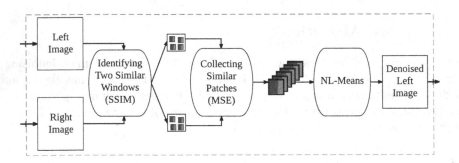

Fig. 2. A block digram of the proposed denoising method for stereo image denoising

3.2   Structural Similarity Index

Patch-based denoising methods achieve better results when there are enough similar patches that are accurately grouped before starting the actual denoising process. Choosing an accurate similarity metric would improve the whole denoising process. The main contribution of our method is to use the structural similarity index as a similarity metric for extending the search area, which makes our algorithm groups better similar patches from left and right images.

SSIM index is a metric for measuring the similarity between two images. Unlike the traditional approaches, e.g., peak signal-to-noise ratio (PSNR) and mean squared error (MSE), SSIM has been proven to be consistent with human perception. SSIM considers image degradation as perceived change in structural information, traditional approaches estimate perceived errors in image data. The SSIM metric between two patches of size $n \times n$ is calculated as:

$$SSIM(N\,[vl]_k, N\,[vr]_q) = \frac{(2\mu_L\mu_R + C_1)\,(2\sigma_{LR} + C_2)}{(\mu_L^2 + \mu_R^2 + C_1)\,(\sigma_L^2 + \sigma_R^2 + C_2)} \tag{5}$$

where $N\,[vl]_k$ is a reference patch from the left image, $N\,[vr]_q$ is a corresponding patch from the right image, μ_L and μ_R are the mean of the reference and corresponding patches, respectively. σ_L^2 and σ_R^2 are the variance of the reference and corresponding patches, respectively. σ_{LR} is the covariance between the reference and the corresponding patches. C_1 and C_2 are constants used to avoid instability.

4 Experimental Results

The objective of this section is to experimentally study the performance of the proposed method at various noise levels. The complexity of our algorithm is linear with respect to the size of stereo input image. We use a fixed 5×5 patch size and a fixed 11×11 searching window size. Four stereo images are used to perform this experiment. The four images are grey-scale images, they are shown in Fig. 3. MatLab is used for this experiment. The computer's processor is Intel® Core^{TM} i7 (2.5 GHz). In Subsects. 4.1 and 4.2, the methods are evaluated both quantitatively and qualitatively, respectively.

4.1 Quantitative Evaluation

Image Similarity Metrics. Two image similarity metrics are used for objective comparison between the results: (1) SSIM, and (2) peak signal-to-noise ratio (PSNR). The best result for SSIM is 1, while the PSNR has good result when its value is high. Equations 5 and 6 show the formulas for these two quality metrics. The peak signal-to-noise ratio is defined as:

$$PSNR = 10 \log \left(\frac{(2^n - 1)^2}{MSE} \right) \tag{6}$$

where n is an integer number representing the number of bits per pixel. When $n = 8$, i.e., in case of grey-scale images.

It is worth mentioning that a study conducted by Horé et al. [15] has revealed that SSIM is less sensitive to additive noise than PSNR. They used F-score test to compare between SSIM and PSNR performances with additive Gaussian white noise.

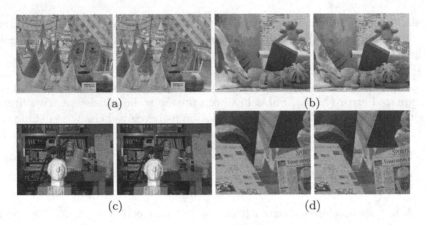

(a)   (b)

(c)   (d)

Fig. 3. The four used images in the experiment: (a) *cones* images 450 × 375, (b) *teddy* image 450 × 375, (c) *tsukuba* image 384 × 288, and (d) *venus* image 434 × 383.

Experimental Results. The experimental results of our proposed method are shown in Table 1, which compares the performance of our method with two other denoising methods: the original NL-Means [6] and Stereo-MSE [13]. The highest values of SSIM are highlighted by a bold font with a wavy under-bar, while the highest values of PSNR are highlighted with a bold font. The results in Table 1 are computed by measuring the differences between the true original images and the denoised images. At low noise level ($\sigma \leqslant 20$) our method performs better than the original NL-Means and Stereo-MSE (from both SSIM and PSNR point of views).

Table 1. The performance of the denoising algorithms at various noise levels (σ).

σ		σ = 10		σ = 20		σ = 40		σ = 60	
	Method	SSIM	PSNR	SSIM	PSNR	SSIM	PSNR	SSIM	PSNR
Cones	Noisy	0.5726	25.067	0.3538	21.138	0.1651	15.914	0.0973	12.914
	NLMeans	0.7208	26.648	0.6111	25.254	0.4385	23.083	0.3462	**21.768**
	Stereo-MSE	0.7204	26.620	0.6168	25.321	0.4356	23.052	0.3162	21.198
	Our Meth	**0.7273**	**26.754**	**0.6397**	**25.555**	**0.4758**	**23.395**	**0.3553**	21.490
Teddy	Noisy	0.5430	25.681	0.3170	21.42	0.1472	16.160	0.0870	13.191
	NLMeans	0.7763	27.886	0.6686	26.471	0.4958	24.155	**0.4000**	**22.62**
	Stereo-MSE	0.7813	27.927	0.6670	26.524	0.4586	23.884	0.3323	21.805
	Our Meth	**0.7924**	**28.070**	**0.7058**	**26.870**	**0.5284**	**24.487**	0.3970	22.255
Tsukuby	Noisy	0.5884	25.635	0.3673	21.670	0.1830	16.792	0.1067	13.823
	NLMeans	0.8009	27.658	0.7028	26.180	**0.5374**	23.654	**0.4289**	**21.743**
	Stereo-MSE	0.8105	27.862	0.7051	26.402	0.5084	23.693	0.3727	21.559
	Our Meth	**0.8216**	**28.023**	**0.7308**	**26.571**	0.5115	**24.123**	0.4043	21.726
Venus	Noisy	0.4941	24.901	0.2850	21.138	0.1401	16.235	0.0845	13.275
	NLMeans	0.7572	26.779	0.6523	25.681	0.5069	23.745	**0.4119**	**22.165**
	Stereo-MSE	0.7575	26.783	0.6396	25.658	0.4523	23.589	0.3324	21.651
	Our Meth	**0.7707**	**26.929**	**0.6725**	**25.907**	**0.5424**	**23.789**	0.3913	22.153

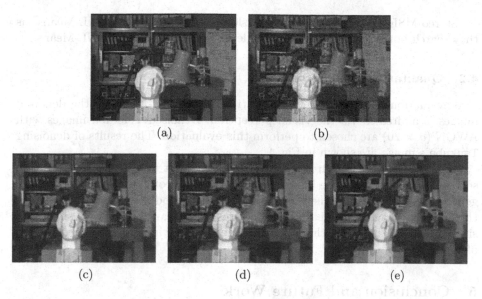

(a)   (b)

(c)   (d)   (e)

Fig. 4. The results of the denoising methods when denoising Tsukuba image at noise levels ($\sigma = 20$): (a) *Tsukuba* image 384×288, (b) AWGN image, ($\sigma = 20$), (c) NL-Means, (d) Stereo-MSE, and (e) Our method

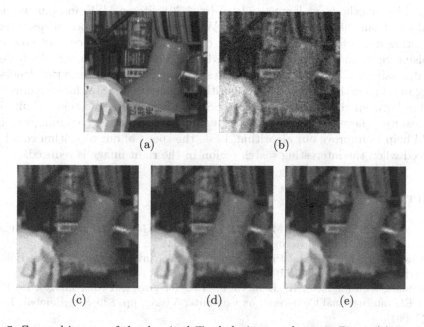

(a)   (b)

(c)   (d)   (e)

Fig. 5. Zoomed images of the denoised *Tsukuba* images shown in Fig. 4: (a) *Tsukuba* image, (b) AWGN image ($\sigma = 20$), (c) NL-Means, (d) Stereo-MSE and (e) Our method

Stereo-MSE and our algorithm are slower than the original NL-Means, as they search both images, not just a single image like the original NL-Means.

4.2 Qualitative Evaluation

The evaluation in this section is subjective, where the quality of the denoised images is addressed via the visual perception. Denoised Tsukuba images with AWGN ($\sigma = 20$) are chosen to perform this evaluation. The results of denoising Tsukuba's image are shown in Fig. 4.

Figure 4e shows that our method achieved the best results. Our method preserves sharp edges; i.e., the books in the background of Tsukuba image. Homogeneous regions are smoothed properly by our method; i.e., head and lamp in the Tsukuba image. Our method does not restored clearly words with small font size written on the board that shown in the Tsukuba image. A zoomed version of Fig. 4 is shown in Fig. 5.

5   Conclusion and Future Work

In this paper, we looked at stereo image as a multi-view image and sought to restore left image by using SSIM and NL-Means approaches. Empirical results show that our method achieved better denoising than the original NL-Means and Stereo-MSE methods, at low noise level ($\sigma \leqslant 20$). Stereo-MSE and our method are slower than the original NL-Means. We believe that our work opens several interesting doors for future work. First, our current method does not consider denoising right image at the same time when it denoising left image. We believe that denoising left and right image at the same time would produce two denoised image in shortest time. Second, our algorithm does not use SSIM for assigning the weights between similar patches. Since SSIM combats the traditional similarity metrics, we believe that using SSIM as a similarity metric for assigning weights would help to improve our algorithm. Last, the speed of our algorithm could be reduced when the interesting search region in the right image is reduced.

References

1. Lindenbaum, M., Fischer, M., Bruckstein, A.: On Gabor's contribution to image enhancement. Pattern Recogn. **27**(1), 1–8 (1994)
2. Yaroslavsky, L.P.: Digital Picture Processing: An Introduction. Springer, Heidelberg (1985). ISBN 3-540-11934-5
3. Tomasi, C., Manduchi, R.: Bilateral filtering for gray and color images. In: 1998 IEEE International Conference on Computer Vision, pp. 839–846, Bombay, India (1998)
4. Rudin, L.I., Osher, S., Fatemi, E.: Nonlinear total variation based noise removal algorithms. In: 11th Annual international Conference of the Center for Nonlinear Studies on Experimental Mathematics, vol. 60(1–4), pp. 259–268. Elsevier North-Holland Inc., Amsterdam (1992)

5. Perona, P., Malik, J.: Scale-space and edge detection using anisotropic diffusion. IEEE Trans. Pattern Analysis Mach. Intel. **12**, 629–639 (1990)
6. Buades, A., Coll, B., Morel, J.: A non-local algorithm for image denoising. In: IEEE Conference on Computer Vision and Pattern Recognition, CVPR 2005, vol. 2, pp. 60–65 (2005)
7. Deledalle, C., Salmon, J., Dalalyan, A.: Image denoising with patch based PCA: local versus global. In: Hoey, J., McKenna, S., Trucco, E. (eds.) Proceedings of the British Machine Vision Conference, pp. 25.1–25.10. BMVA Press, Durham (2011)
8. Aharon, M., Elad, M., Bruckstein, A.: K-SVD: an algorithm for designing overcomplete dictionaries for sparse representation. IEEE Trans. Signal Process. **54**(11), 4311–4322 (2006)
9. Dabov, K., Foi, A., Katkovnik, V., Egiazarian, K.: Image denoising by sparse 3-D transform-domain collaborative filtering. IEEE Trans. Image Process. **16**, 2080–2095 (2007)
10. Bennett, E.P., McMillan, L.: Video enhancement using per-pixel virtual exposures. ACM Trans. Graph. **24**(3), 845–852 (2005)
11. Danielyan, A., Foi, A., Katkovnik, V., Egiazarian, K.: Image and video super-resolution via spatially adaptive blockmatching filtering. In: SPIE Electronic Imaging, 2008, no. 6812-07, San Jose, California, USA (2008)
12. Zhang, L., Vaddadi, S., Jin, H., Nayar, S.K.: Multiple view image denoising. In: IEEE Conference on Computer Vision and Pattern Recognition, CVPR 2009, pp. 1542–1549 (2009)
13. Heo, Y., Lee, K., Lee, S.: Simultaneous depth reconstruction and restoration of noisy stereo images using non-local pixel distribution. In: IEEE Conference on Computer Vision and Pattern Recognition, CVPR 2007, pp. 1–8 (2007)
14. Wang, Z., Bovik, A.C., Sheikh, H.R., Simoncelli, E.P.: Image quality assessment: from error visibility to structural similarity. IEEE Trans. Image Process. **13**, 600–612 (2004)
15. Hore, A., Ziou, D.: Image quality metrics: PSNR vs. SSIM. In: 20th International Conference on Pattern Recognition (ICPR), pp. 2366–2369 (2010)

Structural Similarity Optimized Wiener Filter: A Way to Fight Image Noise

Mahmud Hasan and Mahmoud R. El-Sakka[✉]

Department of Computer Science, University of Western Ontario,
London, ON, Canada
{mhasan62,melsakka}@uwo.ca

Abstract. Wiener filter is widely used for image denoising and restoration. It is alternatively known as the *minimum mean square error filter* or the *least square error filter*, since the objective function used in Wiener filter is an age-old benchmark called the Mean Square Error (MSE). Wiener filter tries to approximate the degraded image so that its objective function is optimized. Although MSE is considered to be a robust measurement metric to assess the closeness between two images, recent studies show that MSE can sometimes be misleading whereas the Structural Similarity (SSIM) can be an acceptable alternative. In spite of having this misleading natured objective function, Wiener filter is being heavily used as a fundamental component in many image denoising and restoration algorithms such as in current state-of-the-art of image denoising- *BM3D*. In this study, we explored the problem with the objective function of Wiener filter. We then improved the Wiener filter by optimizing it for SSIM. Our proposed method is tested using the standard performance evaluation methods. Experimental results show that the proposed SSIM optimized Wiener filter can achieve significantly better denoising (and restoration) as compared to its original MSE optimized counterpart. Finally, we discussed the potentials of using our improved Wiener filter inside *BM3D* in order to eventually improve *BM3D*'s denoising performance.

Keywords: Wiener filter · Structural similarity · Mean square error · Image denoising · Image restoration · BM3D

1 Introduction

Image denoising is a salient image pre-processing step in sophisticated imaging applications like medical and satellite imaging. There are a number of mechanisms proposed over years for reducing noises from digital images. These mechanisms vary with the type of noise introduced during image acquisition. Wiener filter is one such popular mechanism which works in frequency domain for image denoising/restoration [1]. This filter assumes that the noise and the image are random processes (i.e., they are uncorrelated) and either of the two has zero mean. Based on these assumptions, Wiener filter is used for image denoising

© Springer International Publishing Switzerland 2015
M. Kamel and A. Campilho (Eds.): ICIAR 2015, LNCS 9164, pp. 60–68, 2015.
DOI: 10.1007/978-3-319-20801-5_7

as well as for image restoration [1,2]. Throughout this paper, we will assume *zero-mean Additive White Gaussian Noise (AWGN)* whenever the term *noise* is used.

For experimental purposes, we start Wiener filter with an uncorrupted image I and add noise to it in order to degrade it. Then the objective of Wiener filter is to estimate a denoised version of this noisy image so that the mean square error between original image I and the estimated image $\hat{I}$ is minimized. This error measure is given by Eq. 1.

$$e^2 = E\{(I - \hat{I})^2\} \tag{1}$$

Wang et al. [3] showed that the MSE can generate higher error despite the similarity of the overall structure between two images are same. For instance, if we just increase the brightness of an image by adding a constant to all intensity levels, MSE still generates huge errors, although both the images are visually same. To deal with such misleading measures, Wang et al. proposed a new error measurement metric called the Structural Similarity (SSIM) that takes the *similarity* between two images into consideration rather than the *distance* between them. The SSIM is given by Eq. 2.

$$SSIM(x,y) = \frac{(2\mu_x\mu_y + c_1)(2\sigma_{xy} + c_2)}{(\mu_x^2 + \mu_y^2 + c_1)(\sigma_x^2 + \sigma_y^2 + c_2)} \tag{2}$$

In Eq. 2, x and y are considered two image blocks taken from exactly same locations of I and $\hat{I}$, respectively. SSIM is calculated block by block in order to take advantages of local similarity and a *mean* of those blocks is calculated for representing the SSIM value for the whole estimated image $\hat{I}$. For a detailed explanation of Eq. 2, we refer the reader to original article [3].

In this study, we attempted to answer the question- *can we improve the Wiener filter that performs significantly better than the MSE optimized one?* With much detailed experiments, we discovered that the age-old MSE optimized Wiener filter can be modified in such a way that the overall denoising and restoration performance is improved.

The rest of the paper is organized as follows. In Sect. 2, we will discuss the related background and the motivation for this work. In Sect. 3, we will discuss the improvement we propose. We will discuss our performance analysis in detail in Sect. 4. We discuss the potentials of our proposed method to eventually improve the performance of *BM3D* in Sect. 5. Finally we conclude in Sect. 6 by briefly discussing the future work of this study.

2   Background

2.1   Wiener Filter

Wiener filter was designed based on a popular restoration filter called the *Inverse filter*. The inverse filter is used for image restoration only. In contrast, Wiener filter is capable of both image denoising and restoration. If there is no noise (i.e., zero noise) in the degraded image, Wiener filter simply reduces to Inverse filter and performs only restoration. This is one of the unique properties of the Wiener filter [2].

Wiener filter works in frequency domain, meaning that it does not directly take into consideration the pixel intensities of the degraded image; instead, it works with the Fourier Transform of the degraded image. This filter also requires a degradation function for performing denoising/restoration. The degradation function is usually unknown but can be estimated by a number of ways [2]. For experimental purposes, although we can have a well-suited degradation function, in practical cases, it is a tough job to find a suitable one. The response of Wiener filter largely depends on the choice of the degradation function. Since estimating the degradation function is beyond the scope of our study, we assume that a suitable degradation function is available.

Wiener filter is defined by Eq. 3 where $H(u,v)$ is the degradation function. $H^*(u,v)$ is the conjugate complex of $H(u,v)$, and $G(u,v)$ is the Fourier Transform of the degraded image. S_n and S_f are power spectrum of noise and power spectrum of the undegraded image, respectively. The term $\frac{S_n}{S_f}$ can also be replaced by a constant K and a suitable value for K can easily be obtained.

$$\hat{F}(u,v) = \frac{H^*(u,v)}{H^2(u,v) + \frac{S_n}{S_f}} G(u,v) \tag{3}$$

The filter produces an output $\hat{F}(u,v)$ which is the Fourier Transform version of the denoised image. Using Inverse Fourier Transform, we can have $\hat{f}$ (or $\hat{I}$ as we defined in Sect. 1). Finally, our target is to minimize Eq. 1. Since a suitable K is found, it is guaranteed that Eq. 1 will be minimized.

2.2   Recent Advances and Usage of Wiener Filter

Over the past few decades, there have been numerous modifications suggested to improve the performance of Wiener filter. Also, many of its usages are currently outlined in the literature. To report its usage in this section, We do not consider any area of signal processing other than image denoising and restoration.

Sandeep et al. [4] suggested an empirical Wiener filter specially designed for Wavelet domain. They could achieve better denoising performance than the original Wiener filter, however, they re-designed the Wiener filter for Wavelet domain instead of trying to improve it in Fourier domain. Peng Shui [5] proposed a doubly local Wiener filter that also works in Wavelet domain. Similar to BM3D [10], their strategy is to use the Wiener filter twice in Wavelet domain, one for generating a pilot image and the other is for generating the final denoised/restored image based on the pilot image or degradation function. There are other good usage and improvements of Wiener filter available in Wavelet domain as in [6].

Some studies tried to use Wiener filter adaptively to improve its performance as in [7,13]. Some studies tried to use a hybrid Wiener filtering technique by combining 1D and 2D Wiener filters [8,9]. There are other studies that focused on improving the denoising performance by some modified usage of Wiener filter, but they did not focus on improving the Wiener filter itself.

Perhaps BM3D (Block Matching and 3D Filtering) discussed in [10] is the best usage of Wiener filter presented so far in image denoising/restoration literature. Although it is similar in nature with [5], BM3D is current state-of-the-art of image denoising. BM3D has an excellent way of estimating the degradation function and then denoising the image by Wiener filter with the help of previously estimated degradation function. As stated earlier, Wiener response largely depends on how perfect the degradation function is; Wiener filter responses really great with BM3D since BM3D provides a nearly perfect degradation function to Wiener.

2.3 Motivation

Our study is motivated by some interesting findings that suggest that MSE based linear estimators and optimizers can be optimized for SSIM [11,12]. The linear SSIM optimized denoising filters in [11,12] was compared with MSE optimized Wiener filter. Reported results show that they were able to achieve higher SSIM than MSE optimized Wiener filter. However, the PSNR achieved by MSE optimized Wiener was still high. So, there is much scope to improve Wiener filter to achieve high quality denoising of noisy images (and restoration of degraded images), which is demanding for any image denoising method that uses Wiener filter.

Unlike achieving only higher SSIM as in [11] and [12], we focused on achieving both higher PSNR and SSIM for our proposed method. Experimental results will show that we have been able to do so.

3   Proposed Improvement

We wanted to record Wiener filter's response when it is optimized for SSIM, not for MSE. We modified the Wiener filter's objective function so that it can now assess the *similarity* between the degraded image and undegraded image, instead of assessing the *distance*. For doing so, we changed the objective function of Wiener filter from Eq. 1 to Eq. 2 considering that x and y are I and $\hat{I}$ respectively. As before, we will still get $\hat{F}(u,v)$ as the output of Wiener filter, however, $\hat{I}$ will no longer be used in Eq. 1. Instead, it will be used in Eq. 2.

Generally, x and y used in Eq. 2 are two image blocks of same size from undegraded and denoised images and the SSIM calculated by Eq. 2 provides the similarity between *two blocks*, not between *two images*. What is done to measure the similarity between two images is to apply Eq. 2 on images in a sliding window manner and keep the SSIM values from each block. Finally a mean of all obtained SSIM values is calculated which gives the mean similarity between the images in a 0 to 1 scale, where 1 is possible only if both the images are exactly same. A higher SSIM value (close to 1) indicates more closeness than a lower SSIM value. An SSIM optimized Wiener filter should yield better visual results.

This is because, in MSE optimized Wiener, the whole image was considered as one single signal while in our proposed method, the optimization is done in block by block, dividing it into many signals and hence yielding better results.

While it is guaranteed that (see Sect. 2) a suitable value for K should be found, there are many ways to find the K. One such way is to solve the Eq. 3 over a range of K and take the K for which the error is minimum. Likewise, in our case of SSIM optimization, we can find a K for which the error is maximum. For the results presented in this paper, we obtained the K empirically.

4   Performance Analysis

We used eight standard gray scale test images for our experiment. For all these images, we recorded the responses of MSE optimized Wiener filter and our proposed SSIM optimized Wiener filter. All plots used in this paper are based on the average output of these eight test images for each noise level.

We assumed the Gaussian Blur function as our degradation function as given by Eq. 4. However, in practical cases the degradation function is often unknown. For many image denoising applications, the degradation function is usually estimated prior starting denoising.

$$G(x,y) = \frac{1}{2\pi\sigma^2} e^{-\frac{x^2+y^2}{2\sigma^2}} \tag{4}$$

We added noise to the test images in different levels using the variance of Gaussian noise function. We re-scaled the variance of Gaussian function in 0.0 to 1.0 range. However, for the experiments presented in this paper, we used noise variance from 0.01 to 0.25 only.

We considered two types of degraded images for our experiment. First, the images are contaminated by only noise. Second, the images are contaminated by noise and further degraded by Gaussian blur. Since the Wiener filter is capable of dealing with both denoising and restoration, these two types of degraded images will represent the Wiener response for denoising and restoration, respectively.

We used standard quality measurement metrics for our performance evaluation. We measured Peak Signal to Noise Ratio (PSNR) which is given by Eq. 5 and is based on MSE. A higher value indicates a better restored/denoised image. Note that, since the MSE measure is the core of the PSNR measure, we do not separately report the responses of MSE measures in this paper.

$$PSNR = 10\log_{10}\left(\frac{MAX_I^2}{MSE}\right) \tag{5}$$

We also measured the mean SSIM between our denoised/restored image and the original undegraded image. The mean SSIM is basically the mean value from all the blocks obtained from Eq. 2. For SSIM, higher value means better or close approximation.

Our obtained result is promising. For all the performance measurement metrics, we obtained better results as compared to original Wiener filter.

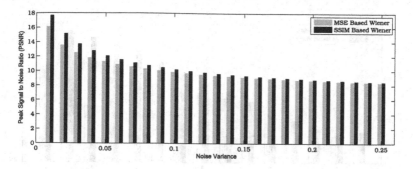

Fig. 1. Average PSNR comparison for denoising

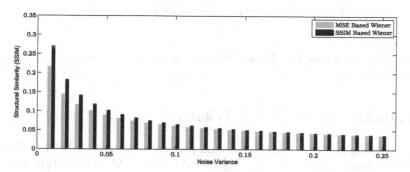

Fig. 2. Average SSIM comparison for denoising

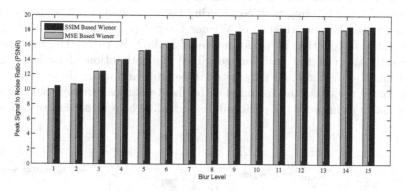

Fig. 3. Average PSNR comparison for restoration

Figures 1 and 2 respectively show the average PSNR and SSIM comparison of our proposed SSIM optimized Wiener filter with the MSE optimized Wiener filter. Clearly, the proposed method achieves consistent improvement. These results are given for our first degradation environment i.e., for image denoising only.

To observe the SSIM optimized Wiener response for restoration, we take into consideration the images that are noisy as well as Gaussian blurred (degraded).

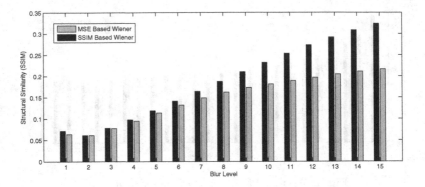

Fig. 4. Average SSIM comparison for restoration

We present the average PSNR and SSIM comparison for them in Fig. 3 and in Fig. 4, respectively.

5   Potentials of Proposed Wiener Filter in BM3D

Block Matching and 3D (BM3D) filtering proposed in [10] can be described by the block diagram shown in Fig. 5. As stated earlier, BM3D algorithm works in two identical steps. In first step, it generates a basic estimate from the noisy image, and in second step, it performs denoising on the noisy image by collaborative Wiener filtering with considering the basic image as the degradation function. Since the performance of Wiener filter depends largely on how good the degradation function is, performance of BM3D, in turns, largely depends on the estimation of the basic image. Since the estimation of basic image is defined based on some fixed parameters (see [10]) and since these parameters are rigorously reviewed and assumed to be fixed [14], we can say that the only scope remains to improve the performance of BM3D is in its second step. Again,

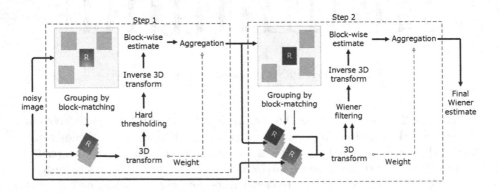

Fig. 5. Block diagram of BM3D [10]

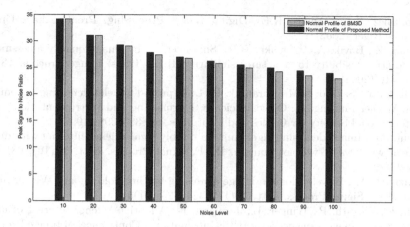

Fig. 6. Performance comparison of original BM3D and BM3D with our improved Wiener filter

components in second step except Wiener filter are either fixed or largely influenced by first step. Therefore, visibly, the only possibility to improve BM3D is to improve Wiener filter.

Having improved the performance of Wiener filter by optimizing it for SSIM, we can simply replace the existing Wiener filter of BM3D by our improved one. Experimental results show that (in Fig. 6) this idea essentially improves the performance of BM3D.

6 Future Work and Conclusion

We explored the core of Wiener filter in this study. We reported the recent attempts for Wiener filter improvements. We also reported how these studies are case dependent. We then proposed an SSIM optimized Wiener filter. Our experimental results showed that our proposed method can achieve consistent improvement over MSE optimized Wiener Filter for all perceptual noise levels in terms of standard quality measurement metrics. We conducted more experiments and comparisons to prove the superiority of our proposed method over Wiener filter, however, due to the page limitation, we only discussed partial outcomes. Moreover, we briefly discussed the potential of using our improved Wiener filter in the current state-of-the-art image denoising- BM3D. In future, we will report in detail how our proposed Wiener filter helps us achieve better denoising performance for all profiles of the state-of-the-art image denoising technique- BM3D.

References

1. Wiener, N.: The Interpolation, Extrapolation and Smoothing of Stationary Time Series, vol. 19. MIT press, New York (1949)

2. Gonzalez, R.C., Woods, R.E.: Digital Image Processing. Prentice hall, Upper Saddle River (2002)
3. Wang, Z., Bovik, A.C., Sheikh, H.R., Simoncelli, E.P.: Image quality assessment: from error visibility to structural similarity. IEEE Trans. Image Process. **13**(4), 600–612 (2004)
4. Ghael, S.P., Sayeed, A.M., Baraniuk, R.G.: Improved wavelet denoising via empirical Wiener filtering. In: Optical Science, Engineering and Instrumentation 1997. International Society for Optics and Photonics, pp. 389–399 (1997)
5. Shui, P.L.: Image denoising algorithm via doubly local Wiener filtering with directional windows in wavelet domain. IEEE Signal Process. Lett. **12**(10), 681–684 (2005)
6. Kazubek, M.: Wavelet domain image denoising by thresholding and Wiener filtering. IEEE Signal Process. Lett. **10**(11), 324–326 (2003)
7. Jin, F., Fieguth, P., Winger, L., Jernigan, E.: Adaptive Wiener filtering of noisy images and image sequences. In: IEEE International Conference on Image Processing. vol. 3, pp. III-349 (2003)
8. Malik, M.B., Deller, J.J.R.: Hybrid Wiener filter. In: IEEE International Conference on Acoustics, Speech, and Signal Processing, vol. 4, pp. IV-229 (2005)
9. Hung, K.W., Siu, W.C.: Hybrid DCT-Wiener-based interpolation via learnt Wiener filter. In: IEEE International Conference on Acoustics, Speech, and Signal Processing, pp. 1419–1423 (2013)
10. Dabov, K., Foi, A., Katkovnik, V., Egiazarian, K.: Image denoising by sparse 3-D transform-domain collaborative filtering. IEEE Trans. Image Process. **16**(8), 2080–2095 (2007)
11. Channappayya, S.S., Bovik, A.C., Heath, R.W.: A linear estimator optimized for the structural similarity index and its application to image denoising. In: IEEE International Conference on Image Processing, pp. 2637–2640 (2006)
12. Channappayya, S.S., Bovik, A.C., Caramanis, C., Heath, R.W.: Design of linear equalizers optimized for the structural similarity index. IEEE Trans. Image Process. **17**(6), 857–872 (2008)
13. Lim, J.S.: Two-dimensional Signal and Image Processing, vol. 1. Prentice Hall, Englewood (1990)
14. Lebrun, M.: An analysis and implementation of the BM3D image denoising method. Image Processing On Line, pp. 175–213 (2012)

Image Segmentation, Registration and Analysis

A Real-Time Framework for Detection of Long Linear Infrastructural Objects in Aerial Imagery

Hrishikesh Sharma[1]($\boxtimes$), Tanima Dutta[2], V. Adithya[1], and P. Balamuralidhar[1]

[1] TCS Innovation Labs, Bangalore, India
{hrishikesh.sharma,adithya.v,balamurali.p}@tcs.com
[2] Department of Computer Science, IIT Indore, Indore, India
tanimad@iiti.ac.in

Abstract. In any nation, many long linear infrastructures exist, which need to be periodically inspected for faults and subsequent maintenance. These include power grid, pipelines, railway corridor etc. Most of these infrastructures support critical utilities, and hence operated 24 x 7 throughout the year. The length of these infrastructures can be in tens of kilometers. Hence maintenance inspections via acquisition of aerial imagery is gaining popularity. Since such video can have thousands of frames, it is imperative that its analysis be automated. Such infrastructure detection is against a background that is quite heterogeneous and complex. In this paper, we propose an algorithmic framework that can be used for automatic, real-time detection of different linear infrastructural objects in outdoor aerial images. The five-stage algorithm focuses on minimization of false positives. The algorithm was tested against video data captured for two different power grids in outskirts of Bangalore. The results show seldom false positives, and false negatives in certain frames occur sparsely enough that we are able to do a continuous video tracking. We believe that this framework will be useful in real deployments as well.

1 Introduction

Almost all countries have certain critical utility infrastructures that have the characteristic of being long and linear. These infrastructural systems are **vast**, running into hundreds of kilometers. Maintenance, both preventive and breakdown, of all such systems is an obvious must, and typically a costly legal responsibility towards public safety. Usage of UAVs for maintenance inspections, especially of long linear infrastructures, is rapidly emerging as a popular option [6,11]. However, the amount of video or image data acquired is typically huge, due to vastness of infrastructures. Hence automated analysis of such images/video is being increasingly sought. Such analysis entails detection of *elongated foreground objects*, commonly subjected as **linear feature detection**.

So far, for automated linear feature detection, most researchers have used Hough space for clustering of lines [16–18]. However, the Hough Transform has a computational complexity of the order of $O(n^3)$ *i.e.* very high. Some researchers use Gabor filters for edge detection stage [8] or canny edge detection [6], but

© Springer International Publishing Switzerland 2015
M. Kamel and A. Campilho (Eds.): ICIAR 2015, LNCS 9164, pp. 71–81, 2015.
DOI: 10.1007/978-3-319-20801-5_8

both approaches have high complexity of the order of $O(n^2 \log n)$. In [7], detection of linear structure is followed by region filtration. With similar objective, [1] designed a near-real time algorithm that uses geometric relationships to detect line segments in aerial images using canny and steerable filters. In [11], a 3-stage algorithm for automatic detection of power lines in aerial images is described. However, the method is not much robust against false positives, and also higher complexity, $O(n^2 \log n)$. The literature of medical image analysis is replete with linear feature extraction [4,12]. However, the background is not as heterogeneous/complex as is the case with **outdoor** video of infrastructures. Hence the methods are not directly applicable to this class of application.

To summarize, to the best of authors' knowledge, there is no vision- or learning-based framework that is publicly known and targets *near-real-time* automatic detection of multiple linear infrastructural objects, especially against highly varying and complex background using color images (RGB) till date. The background is complex since in aerial imagery, multiple different artefacts on the ground get imaged as well, e.g. trees, barren patches, unpaved roads, occasional hutment etc. Further, most of these background artefacts are texture-rich, while the foreground objects of consideration are almost texture-less (other than being fairly thin), which makes the detection problem very challenging. For this requirement, we propose a five-stage algorithm, having following properties.

- As a novelty, at the core stage of edge-based segmentation, we mark a seed point pair along the linear feature boundary instead of traditional seed segments. From such pairs, we "grow" the boundary/contour of the desired elongated foreground, again in a novel way.
- The gradient magnitudes, gradient orientations and pixel value in HSV space are selected as key features for our algorithm. It is expected that gradient will always be a common feature for detection of *any* linear infrastructure, and pixel value for *most* infrastructures since they have mostly metallic surface.
- Complexity of our algorithm is shown to be O(N).
- The proposed algorithm aims to minimize false negatives in detecting linear structures like power line in UAV based color images (RGB) and guarantees a minimum tracking of linear feature across all frames.
- We also minimize mis-classification of random linear feature i.e. false positive, by using a novel feature, **rigidity**.

The rest of the paper is organized as follows. We first describe our detection algorithm in Sect. 2. We then describe the nature of our experiments in Sect. 3, which is followed by the main Sect. 4 on results and analysis. We conclude the paper finally in Sect. 5.

2   Proposed Detection Algorithm

Various long linear infrastructures, when imaged aerially, exhibit following characteristics that are similar, if not same.

- Objects such as railway lines being rigid metal-based structures, are close to a straight thick line, *i.e.*, with a very small curvature in the aerial image.
- During monitoring of infrastructures using down-looking camera, the UAVs can fly at a height, yet in relative proximity. Hence there is no occlusion over the linear image objects.
- Typically being constructed using metals/alloys which reflect brightly, the corresponding linear artefacts in the aerial image exhibit high pixel intensity.
- High gradients are found at least along the contour of the infrastructure.

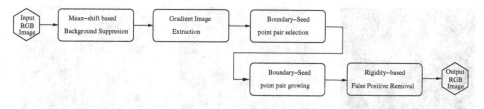

Fig. 1. Functional block diagram of detection algorithm

Using these properties, we construct a **3-dimensional feature space** to locate required conductors with high fidelity. The value component in HSV space of pixels corresponding to *interior* of infrastructural objects shows prominent peaks. This is the **first** distinguishing feature that we consider. The **second** distinguishing feature we consider is a set of **paired** gradients within a short vertical window of configurable pixel width. The pairing happens because both boundaries are approximately at the same distance, and same tangential slant with respect to camera optical center. The **third** distinguishing feature is a novel feature called **rigidity**, which we introduce later.

The proposed detection algorithm consists of five stages for detection of linear structures, especially power lines in aerial images, as shown in Fig. 1. We describe relevance and other details of each stage over next few sections. The overall algorithm is summarized in Algorithm 1.

Algorithm 1. Detection of infrastructural linear features

For Each Frame in the Video

Mean shift filtering to find the peak of a confidence map using the color histogram of the image.

Gradient image generation that retains all linear features.

Based on camera position, the medial strip is considered, and seed point pairs for contour growing selected based on gradient magnitude and pixel value as features.

Detection of contour of infrastructural linear features in Image Space using contour growing approach.

Removal of false positives using rigidity feature, as represented by total sum of gradient orientations.

End For

(a) Sample Video Frame

(b) Mean-shift Background Suppression

(c) Gradient Image Generation

(d) Candidate Seed Point Pair Selection

(e) Output with False Positives

(f) Output post Rigidity Considerations

Fig. 2. Stage-wise output of detection algorithm for typical frame

2.1 Mean Shift Filtering

Due to vastness and complexity of background as discussed earlier, almost all edge detection algorithms give a number of edges in the background, along with those in the foreground. Therefore, to reduce background clutter and simultaneously accentuate the foreground, we first filter the images. The comparison in [15], as well as our prior research [2] concur in the fact that mean shift procedure outperforms other popular segmentation schemes for outdoor images. The **typical** output of this filtering for single frame is shown in Figs. 2a and 2b.

2.2 Gradient Vector Image Generation

After background suppression, the gradient magnitudes for all edges of the segmented image is estimated as first feature, using Sobel function [13]. The **typical** gradient profile for a background-suppressed frame of Fig. 2b is shown in Fig. 2c.

2.3 Context-Based Potential Seed Point Selection

Our algorithm detects linear features by tracking the prominent boundary of such objects in the gradient image. Since the objects are linear, the boundary contour is open in some sense, and occurs in a pair of approximately parallel lines. Due to perspective projection in image via side-looking camera, the lines are thickest near the middle of the frame. To extract such open contour with two boundaries [9], we use a novel method for boundary growing. We focus on having just a (boundary) seed point pair along the prominent middle vertical cut. We use the first two features to identify the boundary seed point pairs.

The construction of set of seed point pairs is done via construction of another set of candidate seed points. Let us define the set of gradient magnitudes of the pixels along medial vertical line as $\mathbb{G}_{w/2}$, and set of values from HSV space as $\mathbb{V}_{w/2}$, for a $w \times h$-sized image. Every seed point which is part of any pair can be represented by $\mathbf{s}(g, v)$, where $\mathbf{g}$ and $\mathbf{v}$ are appropriate gradient and HSV value, respectively. Conversely, let $\mathbf{g}(s)$ and $\mathbf{v}(s)$ represent the gradient and HSV value of a seed point. Also, let $\mathbf{L}(s)$ represent pixel location of a seed point, and $v(l) : l \in L$ be value at a pixel location. First, the set of candidate seed points $\mathbb{C}$ is prepared by taking high gradient pixels on the medial vertical line as follows.

$$\mathbb{C} = \left\{ \exists\, \mathbf{s}(g, v) : \left\{ \mathbf{g}(s) > (\text{mean}(\mathbb{G}_{\frac{w}{2}}) + \text{var}(\mathbb{G}_{\frac{w}{2}})) \right\} \wedge \right.$$
$$\left. \mathbf{L}(s) \in \left\{ (\frac{w}{2}, 0), (\frac{w}{2}, 1), \cdots, (\frac{w}{2}, (h-1)) \right\} \right\} \qquad (1)$$

where $\text{mean}(\mathbb{G}_{\frac{w}{2}})$ and $\text{var}(\mathbb{G}_{w/2})$ are mean and variance of gradient magnitudes respectively. From this candidate set $\mathbb{C}$, the set of **paired** seed points, $\mathbb{S}$, is constructed as follows.

$$\mathbb{S} \subset \mathbb{C} = \{ \exists s_1, s_2 : \{ |s_1 - s_2| < 10 \} \wedge \{ |\mathbf{g}(s_1) - \mathbf{g}(s_2)| < 15\% \times \max(\mathbf{g}(s_1), \mathbf{g}(s_2)) \} \wedge$$
$$\{ \exists\, l : \{ \mathbf{L}(s_1) < l < \mathbf{L}(s_2) \} \wedge \{ v(l) > 85\% \times \max(\mathbb{V}_{w/2}) \} \} \} \qquad (2)$$

Seed point pairs such extracted for a typical gradient profile shown in Fig. 2c are illustrated in Fig. 2d. One may also note that if the camera position is front-facing, the seed points will be detected from the bottom horizontal line. Such context based sensory information is assumed to be provided as prior knowledge.

2.4 Contour Growing Approach

After selection of seed points, a novel iterative contour growing approach is initiated to detect the boundaries of linear features. The method is derived from *non-maximum suppression* method for thinning of boundaries detected by Sobel operator [13]. The image is scanned along the gradient direction from each seed point. The local maxima of a pixel (x, y) is estimated in the current neighborhood window including the orientation, i.e. 3 pixels $\{ (y+0, x+1), (y+1, x+1), (y-1, x+1) \}$, notionally represented by $GO_{0,1}$, $GO_{1,1}$ and $GO_{-1,1}$. Here, 1 represents the gradient direction. After comparison, new seed points that are local maxima in both the left- and right 3-neighborhoods are located, and simultaneously considered for growing the boundary, in the next iteration. Boundary pairs thus grown from various seed point pairs for a typical frame shown in Fig. 2d are shown back-annotated on original frame as in Fig. 2e. If we represent a seed point at a particular location as $\mathbf{s}(\mathbf{x}, \mathbf{y})$, location of the seed as $\mathbb{L}(s)$, (second) feature value of the seed as $\mathbb{V}(s)$, then

$$\mathbf{s}(\mathbf{x}, \mathbf{y}) \equiv \{ \mathbb{L}, \mathbb{V} \}$$

By this definition, it is easy to conjure a bijective mapping and its inverse between a L-V pair, which we can denote as $\mathbb{L} \leftrightarrow \mathbb{V}$ and $\mathbb{V} \leftrightarrow \mathbb{L}$ respectively. If $\mathbb{N}(\mathbf{s})$ is the next location of boundary seed point that is computed in an iteration, then

$$\mathbb{N}(\mathbf{s}) = \{\mathbb{V} \leftrightarrow \mathbb{L}\} \left[\mathbf{max}\left\{\mathbb{V}(\mathbb{L}(\mathbf{s}) + \mathbf{GO}_{0,1}), \mathbb{V}(\mathbb{L}(\mathbf{s}) + \mathbf{GO}_{1,1}), \mathbb{V}(\mathbb{L}(\mathbf{s}) + \mathbf{GO}_{-1,1})\right\}\right] \tag{3}$$

2.5   Rigidity-Based Removal of False Positives

All linear infrastructures are thick metallic objects, and hence have a limited degree of elasticity. Due to high rigidity, their curvature, if any, manifests itself as a very gradual change in gradient orientation across a sequence of boundary pixels, thus limiting them into a narrow band of orientation values. As a byproduct, the range of orientations is also limited, somewhat influenced by the camera pose as well as distance of object from camera optical center (c.f. Fig. 3a).

On the other hand, most of the false positives occurring in the heterogeneous background exhibit certain degree of randomness in gradient orientations. Unlike rigid infrastructures, such false positives do not have spatial correlation and banding of gradient orientations in a narrow band, but a spread out function (c.f. Fig. 3b). We use this observation to weed out false positives in the final, fifth stage. We use newly defined **third** distinguishing feature called **rigidity** of the linear infrastructural object for this purpose. It is hard to parameterize band shape and size, which in turn defines rigidity. This is because mechanical bends (e.g. sag in power line, slow turn in railway line) can be purposefully introduced in the infrastructure, and the amount of such bend differs in various conditions. However, to compensate for the somewhat dependency of band size on camera pose and distance, we use the metric of **total orientation sum** to threshold and identify/remove false positives. The sum of all orientations along each of the grown boundary pair sequence, is defined as the *total orientation sum* for that object. The threshold for total sum is taken as 90 % of maximum total gradient sum for all the boundary pairs identified **after** fourth stage. This is because the maximum total sum, for a true positive, will be dominated by spatially correlated angles, clustered around a mean, while total sum for a false positive is expected to a sum of random angles as per some spread function, thus having lesser mean

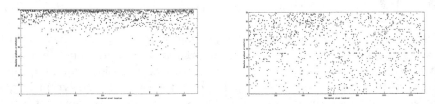

(a) Banding of Rigidity Feature in True (b) High Dispersion of Rigidity in False
Positive   Positive

Fig. 3. Rigidity distribution for true and false detection

value. Many times, usage of this feature also removes a linear feature whose boundary tracking strays away from actual boundary during iterations till a late stage (up to almost complete tracking). This occurs because once strayed, the gradient orientation of remaining part of tracked boundary becomes random, and hence total sum becomes less than expected threshold for most of the times.

2.6 Computational Complexity

Mean Shift. The computational cost of mean shift is $O(N)$ by the use of the volume integral to compute the mean in a constant manner, where N is the number of image pixels and the mean is directly computed via only few additions without any search for neighboring colors samples in the Parzen window [5].

Sobel Operation. If there are N pixels and k discrete values are used for estimating first derivative, then complexity is $O(kN)$. To reduce the computational complexity, we might make k smaller or constant. In this case, time complexity for n pixels is $O(n)$ [3].

Other Operations and Final Complexity. It can be argued in a straightforward manner that the complexity of seed selection, which is along one vertical line, is $O(N)$. Similarly, for each of the pair of seed points, the complexity of contour growing, by considering 3-neighborhood each time, is also at maximum $O(N)$. The number of paired up seed points is a finite constant. Hence the overall cost of contour growing is in the order of $\leq O(N)$. Finally, the complexity of using rigidity feature to remove false positives is $O(N)$, since calculation of total sum, the dominant computation, is $O(N)$.

In summary, by taking the maximum of above complexity orders, the overall complexity of infrastructural linear feature detection is $O(N)$. It is an **improvement** over complexity of some of the recent works on fast linear detector, including [10,11,14], all of which have complexity in order of $O(N^2)$.

3 Experiments and Data Collection

A 11 MP f/2.8 120° FOV wide-lens RGB camera, GoPro Hero3, was mounted on a mini-UAV and used for imaging. The frame rate chosen was 10 fps (low value). This is because the UAV speed is high enough and higher frame rates lead to significant overlap between successive frames. Test sites provided by *Hot Line Training Center*, outside Bangalore, were used for collection of power line video data. The legal permission to fly atop railway corridors has just been granted, and data collection will be done soon. For other national utilities of long linear nature, permission to capture video is still awaited. Hence we have so far evaluated our algorithm against power line data only. A quadcopter provided by our collaborators was flown at a speed of around 40 km/hour, while having a sideways view of the power grids, having approximately 8 meter separation from the grid. For such view, the pitch of the camera mount was fixed to around 60°, while yaw was azimuth-facing and roll angle towards horizon. Given the typical separation between conductors of a power grid so as to avoid unnecessary harmonics due to induction, quick modeling revealed that such angle provides the best view while avoiding occlusion by one near conductor of a far conductor to a good extent. The length captured was around 380 meters for each of the two sites, which resulted in around 420 frames per flight. While the testing and analysis has been carried out on entire video, we only show results from sample frames for the sake of brevity.

4 Results and Performance Analysis

The proposed algorithm was implemented using OpenCV. Due to high degree of scene overlap between two successive frames, we downsample the frame rate, pick every 4th frame, and test our algorithm over 209 representative frames, out of 837 frames captured. To *showcase* our algorithm's effectiveness, we show suggestive tracking of power line in two specific frames in this paper, in Figs. 2 and 4. The two images have been chosen with different enough background.

Given the average speed of UAV, frame size, frame rate, camera FOV and average distance of UAV from the grid, all provided in previous section, it can be easily calculated that per frame, we need to just track around 51 pixels (26 pixels on either side of the medial vertical cut) in **each frame**, so that we do not miss out tracking any segment of any line, *across all frames*. The reason being that we want to cover as much segment length in terms of automated tracking, as does the UAV move between successive frames at a certain speed. In such a case, we can claim that segment-by-segment, we have tracked entire linear feature. More specifically, this tantamounts to continuous video tracking of linear feature with no segment-wise false negatives.

(a) Sample Video Frame 1   (b) Frame Overlaid with Detected Power Lines

Fig. 4. Detection of linear features in sample frame 1

Due to nature of iterations during boundary growing, the boundary grows unbounded to both left/right sides of each frame. There are times when the tracking strays away from actual boundary especially in late iterations (c.f. Fig. 4). From the tracking statistics generated after manual inspection of all output frames, we have found that up to 78 % of the detected lines do not stray away, and hence are detected fully i.e. around 1280 pixels. Such detection caters to **more than 25×** amount of required pixels to be tracked per frame, i.e. 51 pixels.

From the inspection, we also found that only up to around 20 % frames have shown false negatives. In these frames, most of the time 1 conductor out of 5 or 6 conductors have missed detection. On observation, we have found that such missed detections are either due to power lines that have got imaged from so close that their curvilinear image does not cross the medial vertical cut in the wide-angle image at all, or there is another closeby power grid whose lines, being somewhat far away, do not have reflected luminance within 85 % of maximum which is governed by the closest conductor of the closest grid. Degeneracy in latter case can also happen when UAV drifts away sometimes to such distance from the grid that the reflected luminance in a frame falls beyond the required threshold for all conductors. In the former case, since we are covering more than 20 times the required amount of pixels for all detected conductors, we clearly expect that we cover the segment that is un-imaged around middle cut to get imaged around left/right sides of some prior or later frame. In the latter case, the objective of tracking is to track one power grid corridor at a time, so any missed detection in another nearby but distant corridor has no practical implications.

Similarly, while analyzing manually for false positives, we have again found that upto around 20 % of the frames have typically 1 false positive detected. In around 3 % of frames where the *maximum* of 2 false positives were detected, it was found that tracked conductors had strayed near left/right boundaries of the image, mostly due to barren patches beneath, or finding similar linear feature in the beams of the pylon truss. However, as mentioned in Sect. 2.5, the last stage tends to omit a partially detected line many a times. Hence partially true detection has got misclassified into false positive in around 3 % of frames.

For a comparison, we also ran the program corresponding to our earlier work [11] on the same videos. It was observed that a) in many frames, previous algorithm detects true positive linear features almost partially, while the current one detects almost full length, and b) Few false positives are detected in many frames using previous algorithm, while current one barely detects any false positive.

To summarize, our detection algorithm not only improves on our earlier work, but also exhibits very limited false positives per frame. False negatives do occur in around 20 % of the frames. But since the typical detected lengths are long (around 960 pixels), across the video, we are able to detect each possible conductor segment, and hence are able to have **continuous** video tracking.

5   Conclusion

Automatic detection of linear infrastructure in aerial images is a practically useful field of research for the community of computer vision. The usage of aerial platform such as UAV is the most feasible solution to inspect tens of kilometers of infrastructure installation. The challenge of detection and tracking problem in corresponding aerial imagery is that we are looking to detect thin linear structure against highly complex and vast background, due to usage of aerial sensing platform. However, so far, certain algorithms to detect specific infrastructures have been proposed, with most of them being at maximum near-real-time. A real-time framework for detection of this important class of objects is expected to be of high importance, in a variety of surveillance and maintenance applications. In this paper, we have proposed one such real-time framework. The framework uses a 3-D feature space, including a novel feature to represent rigidity. The way of growing boundary from seed points is also novel. The entire algorithm was tested on data acquired from 2 sites, of around 380 m length infrastructure. The results show seldom false positives, and false negatives in certain frames (upto 20 %) occur sparsely enough that we are able to do a continuous video tracking. We believe that our framework is robust enough with good performance, and hence can be scalably used in real deployment scenarios.

Acknowledgments. We thank Prof. Omkar and his research group from Dept. of Aerospace, Indian Institute of Science, Bangalore for collaborating and providing us with video data to test our algorithm.

References

1. Ceron, A., Mondragon, B., Prieto, F.: Power line detection using a circle based search with UAV images. In: International Conference on Unmanned Aircraft Systems, pp. 632–639 (2014)
2. Dutta, T., Sharma, H., Adithya, V., Balamurali, P.: Image analysis-based automatic detection of transmission towers using aerial imagery. In: 7th Iberian Conference on Pattern Recognition and Image Analysis. Springer Verlag (2015)
3. Ercal, F.: Image Processing Algorithms. Lecture Notes. http://web.mst.edu/~ercal/387/Suppl/class.11.txt
4. Lagerstrom, R., Sun, C., Pascal, V.: Boundary extraction of linear features using dual paths through gradient profiles. Elsevier J. Pat. Rec. Lett. **29**(12), 1753–1757 (2008)
5. Lebourgeois, F., Drira, F., Gaceb, D., Duong, J.: Fast Integral MeanShift: Application to Color Segmentation of Document Images. In: International Conference on Document Analysis and Recognition, pp. 52–56, August 2013
6. Li, Z., Liu, Y., Hayward, R., Zhang, J., Cai, J.: Knowledge-based power line detection for uav surveillance and inspection systems. In: IEEE International Conference on Image and Vision Computing (2008)
7. Luo, X., Zhang, J., Cao, X., Yan, P., Li, X.: Object-aware power line detection using color and near-infrared images. IEEE Trans. Aerosp. Electron. Syst. **50**(2), 1374–1389 (2014)
8. Mu, C., Yu, J., Feng, Y., Cai, J.: Power lines extraction from aerial images based on gabor filter. In: International Symposium on Spatial Analysis, Spatial-temporal Data Modeling, and Data Mining (2009)

9. Sargin, M., Altinok, A., Manjunath, B., Rose, K.: Variable length open contour tracking using a deformable trellis. IEEE Trans. Image Process. **20**(4), 1023–1035 (2011)
10. Shao, Y., Guo, B., Hu, X., Di, L.: Application of a fast linear feature detector to road extraction from remotely sensed imagery. IEEE J. Sel. Top. Appl. Earth Obs. Remote Sens. **4**(3), 626–631 (2011)
11. Sharma, H., Bhujade, R., Adithya, V., Balamurali, P.: Vision-based Detection of Power Distribution Lines in Complex Remote Surroundings. In: National Conference on Communications, pp. 1–6 (February 2014)
12. Sonka, M., Winniford, M., Collins, S.M.: Robust simultaneous detection of coronary borders in complex images. IEEE Trans. Med. Imaging **14**(1), 151–161 (1995)
13. Sonka, M., Hlavac, V., Boyle, R.: Image Processing, Analysis, and Machine Vision. Thomson-Engineering, Birchmount Road, Toranto, Ontario, CA (2007)
14. Sun, C., Vallotton, P.: Fast linear feature detection using multiple directional non-maximum suppression. In: IEEE International Conference on Pattern Recognition, pp. 288–291 (2006)
15. Unnikrishnan, R., Pantofaru, C., Hebert, M.: Toward objective evaluation of image segmentation algorithms. IEEE Trans. Pattern Anal. Mach. Intell. **29**(6), 929–944 (2007)
16. Yan, G., Li, C., Zhou, G., Zhang, W., Li, X.: Automatic extraction of power lines from aerial images. IEEE Geosci. Remote Sens. Lett. **4**(3), 387–391 (2007)
17. Yang, T.W., Yin, H., Ruan, Q.Q., Han, J.D., Qi, J.T., Yong, Q., Wang, Z.T., Sun, Z.Q.: Overhead power line detection from uav video images. In: IEEE International Conference on Mechatronics and Machine Vision in Practice, pp. 74–79 (2012)
18. Zhang, J., Liu, L., Wang, B., Chen, X., Wang, Q., Zheng, T.: High speed automatic power line detection and tracking for a UAV-based inspection. In: IEEE International Conference on Industrial Control and Electronics Engineering, pp. 266–269 (2012)

Structural Representations for Multi-modal Image Registration Based on Modified Entropy

Keyvan Kasiri$^{(\boxtimes)}$, Paul Fieguth, and David A. Clausi

Vision and Image Processing (VIP) Lab, Systems Design Engineering,
University of Waterloo, Waterloo, ON N2L 3G1, Canada
{kkasiri,pfieguth,dclausi}@uwaterloo.ca

Abstract. Registration of multi-modal images has been a challenging task due to the complex intensity relationship between images. The standard multi-modal approach tends to use sophisticated similarity measures, such as mutual information, to assess the accuracy of the alignment. Employing such measures imply the increase in the computational time and complexity, and makes it highly difficult for the optimization process to converge. A new registration method is proposed based on introducing a structural representation of images captured from different modalities, in order to convert the multi-modal problem into a mono-modal one. Structural features are extracted by utilizing a modified version of entropy images in a patch-based manner. Experiments are performed on simulated and real brain images from different modalities. Quantitative assessments demonstrate that better accuracy can be achieved compared to the conventional multi-modal registration method.

Keywords: Multi-modal registration · Structural features · Entropy

1 Introduction

Image registration is the process of aligning images by finding the correct spatial transformation between corresponding elements and structures in images. In medical imaging applications, registration of images acquired from different sensors or imaging protocols helps clinicians in diagnosis and computer-aided surgery by using complementary information obtained from different modalities [1]. Because of the intensity variations originated from illumination changes, inhomogeneities, or simply different imaging techniques, the registration task is becoming more difficult.

To deal with this problem, a key issue is to define an appropriate similarity measure robust to those intensity variations. Traditionally, multi-modal registration is carried out by measuring statistical dependency using similarity measures, such as mutual information (MI)[10], assuming a functional or statistical relationship between image intensities [1]. However, these measures would be problematic in those cases with complex and spatially dependent intensity relations [7]. Conditional mutual information (cMI) [9], contextual conditioned

© Springer International Publishing Switzerland 2015
M. Kamel and A. Campilho (Eds.): ICIAR 2015, LNCS 9164, pp. 82–89, 2015.
DOI: 10.1007/978-3-319-20801-5_9

mutual information (CoCoMI) [12] and self-similarity weighted mutual information (α-MI) [11] are further works that try to overcome this problem by integrating spatial and contextual information in the MI formulation in expense of higher computational time and complexity.

Structural information has been used in the literature of multi-modality problem for improving the robustness of similarity measures to image intensity variations [3,6,8,18]. Edge and intensity information was utilized in [8] to register visible and infra-red (IR) images. Employing the dual-tree complex wavelet transform (DT-CWT) for registering IR and visible images in a multi-resolution approach was proposed in [3]. Complex phase order has been used as a similarity measure in registering magnetic resonance (MR) with computed tomography (CT) images in [18]. A structural similarity measure relying on un-decimated wavelet transform coefficients was proposed in previous work for cross-modality label fusion [6].

Structural information has been recently utilized to transform multi-modal to mono-modal registration. Reducing the multi-modal problem to a mono-modal one results in using simple L1 or L2 distance metrics that are computationally less expensive than statistical or structural similarity measures. Usage of gradient intensity, ridge, and estimation of cross correlating gradient directions are examples of creating a structural representation of input images for registration [4]. Structural representation based on entropy images followed by measuring sum of squared distances (SSD) was proposed in [16]. In our previous work, we have proposed a method based on a combination of phase congruency and gradient information to form a structural representation of different MR modes [5].

In this paper, a registration method is proposed based on converting the multi-modal problem into a mono-modal one by using a new structural representation of multi-modal images. Structural features, which are invariant to the image intensity, are obtained from modified version of entropy images in a patch-based paradigm. Simple measure based on intensity difference is used that will lead to faster evaluation of the image similarity and efficient optimization. In our experiments, the application of proposed structural representation is evaluated for registration. Simulated and real brain images of different modalities are used to assess the accuracy of the registration.

2   Methodology

The problem of registering two images $I_m, I_f : \Omega \longrightarrow \mathcal{I}$, as the moving and fixed image, defined on the grid Ω and the intensity values $\mathcal{I} = \{1, \cdots, n\}$ is formulated as:

$$\hat{T} = \underset{T}{\operatorname{argmin}} \, D\big(I_f, T(I_m)\big), \tag{1}$$

where T represents the space transformation and D stands for the dissimilarity (distance) measure to evaluate the degree of alignment. For images being represented with the same intensity values, sum of absolute differences (SAD) or SSD can be good choices for the distance measure. Registration of images with complex intensity relationships requires more complicated similarity/dissimilarity

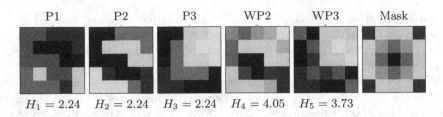

P1   P2   P3   WP2   WP3   Mask

$H_1 = 2.24$ $H_2 = 2.24$ $H_3 = 2.24$ $H_4 = 4.05$ $H_5 = 3.73$

Fig. 1. Applying a location dependent weighting to differentiate patches with different structures and the same entropy: P1 and P2, with the same structure and entropy, are encoded in two different intensity mappings. P3 has different structure and the same entropy, encoded with the same intensity mapping as P2. Applying a Gaussian kernel (Mask) to P2 and P3 results in WP1 and WP2 with different entropy values.

measures. Correlation coefficient (CC), correlation ratio (CR), and MI are widely used in this case [1]. In this paper, we aim to find a new structural representation, R, of different modalities and therefore, reduce the problem of multi-modal registration to a mono-modal one, so that a simple measure can effectively be employed to assess the degree of alignment. For the representation R, the registration problem stated in (1) will be reformulated as

$$\hat{T} = \underset{T}{\operatorname{argmin}} D\big(R_f, T(R_m)\big), \qquad (2)$$

where R_f and R_m stand for the structural representation of images I_f and I_m, respectively.

Consider patches P_x defined on the local neighborhood N_x centered at x. To form the new representations, the idea is to extract structural information of each patch based on the amount of information content in the patch. The bound for patch information can be represented by Shannon's entropy which is defined as

$$H\big(I(x)\big) = - \sum_{x \in P_x} p(I = I(x)) \log \big(p(I = I(x))\big), \qquad (3)$$

where the random variable I gets the pixel intensity values in P_x with possible values in $\mathcal{I}$ characterized by the patch histogram p. However, it is possible that patches with different structures can end up with the same histogram and therefore the same entropy. Figure 1 shows how entropy value differentiates patches with different structures. In this figure, patches P1 and P2, which are encoded in two different intensity mappings but the same structure, take the same value as entropy. Patch P3, encoded with the same intensity mapping as P2, have different structure than P1 and P2 but the same entropy value. Weighting patch histogram based on spatial information can differentiate different patches with the same information content. A Gaussian weighting kernel defined as follows is employed for this purpose

$$G(x) = G_\sigma(\|x - x_0\|), \qquad (4)$$

where $G(x)$ is centered at x_0 with variance σ. Therefore, the entropy for the patch P_x will be modified to

$$\tilde{H}\big(I(P_x)\big) = - \sum_{x \in P_x} G(x)p\big(I = I(x)\big) \log\big(p(I = i)\big). \tag{5}$$

Patches WP2 and WP3 in Fig. 1 illustrate how weighting two 5×5 patches with the same entropy by using a Gaussian Mask helps to differentiate them.

Patch information is mainly concentrated on structures and edges, whereas smooth areas contain less information in the patch. Edges and structures are mostly pixels with lower probability and smooth areas are represented with the higher probability values in the patch histogram. To extract patch structural information, we propose to focus on structures and highlight the pixels with higher uncertainty while decreasing the contribution of those pixels in the patch that are located in smooth areas.

Let's define

$$h(y) = -y \log(y) \tag{6}$$

as the weighted pixel information, where $y = p\big(I = I(x)\big)$ for calculating patch entropy in (5). In Fig. 2.a, $h(y)$ is shown by the blue curve. When y represents the histogram for the patch intensity, smoother areas will take larger values of y, and edges and structures will take smaller ones. To lessen the contribution of smoother areas and highlight edges and structures, one way is to use the function f to map the probability values of the patch histogram such that $f(y) > y$ for large ys, and $f(y) < y$ for small ys. Therefore, the weighted pixel information in (6) will be modified to

$$h(y) = -y \log(f(y)). \tag{7}$$

The green curve in Fig. 2.a is the result of applying such function on the patch histogram. As is illustrated in this figure, applying f increases the contribution of pixels with lower probability and highly weakens the pixel contribution in the smooth areas compared to calculating the conventional entropy. Finally, the modified entropy with respect to P_x will be defined as

$$\tilde{H}\big(I(P_x)\big) = - \sum_{i \in \mathcal{I}} G(x)p\big(I(x) = i\big) \log\big(f(p(I(x) = i))\big), \tag{8}$$

which is used as the new representation, $R(x)$, for the pixel located at x.

$$H_x = -p(x) \log\big(p(x)\big). \tag{9}$$

Having these characteristics for the function $f(.)$, it should be an ascending function defined in the range of $[0, 1]$ with lower derivatives on the two endpoints of the range $[-1, 1]$ and a linear behavior in the middle of the range. The function f, which is able to satisfy those characteristics, can simply be chosen as an m–th order polynomial function with symmetry property:

$$f(y) = \sum_{i=0}^{m} a_i y^i. \tag{10}$$

As an example of such function, we chose a polynomial function with order $m = 5$. The resulting polynomial function, which is shown in Fig. 2.b, will be:

$$f(y) = 6y^5 - 15y^4 + 10y^3. \tag{11}$$

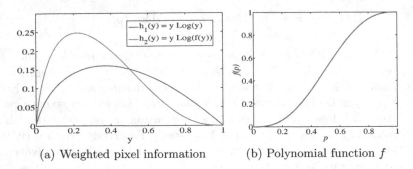

(a) Weighted pixel information   (b) Polynomial function f

Fig. 2. Applying function f on the patch histogram. (a) Weighted pixel-information before and after applying the function f on the patch histogram. Applying f makes the curve tilt towards the vertical axis and highly attenuates its value around $y = 1$, where we have higher intensity probabilities. (b) Function f to apply on the patch histogram, which has almost linear behaviour around center and a smooth slope around boundaries.

Structural features will be calculated by applying the proposed function, f, and weighting kernel, G. Figure 3 shows structural representation of different MR modes for a slice of a brain scan from simulated BrainWeb MR data [13]. As indicated in this figure, structural representation changes the problem of multi-modal registration to a mono-modal one. Therefore, SSD can be used to measure the alignment accuracy:

$$D(R_m, R_f) = \sum_n \left| T_n(R_m(n)) - R_f(n) \right|^2. \tag{12}$$

3   Experimental Results

3.1   Experimental Setup

In order to evaluate the performance of the proposed method, experiments are conducted on the BrainWeb simulated database [13] and a real dataset from the Retrospective Image Registration Evaluation (RIRE) [15] that are provided by ground truth alignment. BrainWeb simulated database contains simulated MR brain scans in T1, T2, and PD modes with different levels of noise and intensity non-uniformity. In the following experiments, scans with 3 % noise and 20 % intensity non-uniformity are chosen. Real brain scans that are used from the RIRE dataset are in different modes of T1, T2, PD, and CT images.

In the experiments, the registration accuracy is quantitatively assessed using the target registration error (TRE), which measures the Euclidean distance between the pixel positions in the transformed image and their corresponding position in the ground truth [2].

$$TRE = \frac{1}{|\Omega|} \sum_{i=1}^{|\Omega|} (x_i - x_i')^2, \tag{13}$$

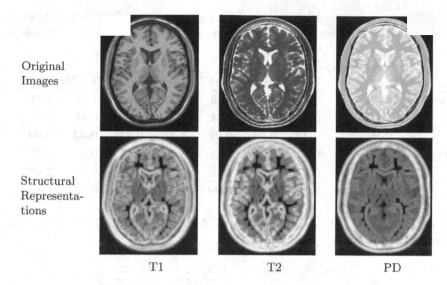

Fig. 3. Structural representation for different MR modes. The first row shows a slice of brain scans in T1, T2, and PD modes from BrainWeb database. Second row shows the structural features associated with the first row images.

where x_i and x'_i are respectively the position of the i-th pixel in the ground truth and aligned image.

The proposed method, which is represented as Reg in the following tables, is compared with the MI-based registration (MI) [17] and SSD on entropy images (eSSD) [16]. The optimization for the rigid registration is carried out by MAT-LAB tools based on gradient descent optimizer for the SSD based mono-modal, and one-plus-one evolutionary optimizer for the MI-based multi-modal regis-tration. Both rigid and deformable registration scenarios are considered for the evaluation procedure. The deformable registration is performed by free-from deformation (FFD) based on cubic B-Splines using Image Registration and Seg-mentation Toolkit (ITK) [14]. In our simulations, the patch size and number of bins in the histogram are empirically chosen to be 7×7 pixels and 64 bins.

3.2 Rigid and Deformable Registration

For rigid registration, the proposed method is evaluated by using MI and eSSD for the alignment, when translation is in the range of $[-20, 20]$ mm with $0°$ rotation, and maximum rotation of $\pm 20°$ with zero translation. Table 1 reports the average results for 100 multi-modal rigid registration over different rotations and translations in terms of TRE in mm.

For deformable registration, a set of training data was generated from the dataset using artificial deformations by the thin-plate spline (TPS). The defor-mation field is normalized such that the maximum displacement is limited to 15 mm. The results of deformable registration is given in Table 2 for different combinations of image modalities. Similar to Table 1, the proposed method is

Table 1. Multi-modal rigid registration (translation T and rotation R) for RIRE and BrainWeb datasets. Registration errors are represented in average pixel displacement.

	Similarity	BrainWeb			RIRE			
		T1-T2	T1-PD	T2-PD	T1-T2	T1-PD	T2-PD	T1-CT
Rotation	MI	0.83	0.76	0.32	3.02	1.14	1.15	3.62
	eSSD	0.65	0.54	0.14	2.03	0.83	0.64	2.87
	Reg	**0.44**	**0.38**	**0.08**	**1.74**	**0.61**	**0.43**	**2.64**
Translation	MI	**0.41**	0.52	0.29	1.58	0.87	0.93	2.53
	eSSD	0.72	0.64	0.18	0.35	0.44	0.48	**1.69**
	Reg	0.51	**0.48**	**0.24**	**0.28**	**0.33**	**0.31**	1.73

Table 2. Multi-modal deformable registration for RIRE dataset. Registration errors are represented in average pixel displacement.

Similarity	T1-T2	T1-PD	T2-PD	T1-CT
MI	1.83	2.12	2.87	**3.12**
eSSD	0.67	**0.61**	**0.55**	7.32
Reg	**0.61**	0.68	0.81	6.43

compared with eSSD and MI-based registration results. Quantities in this table are obtained by averaging the results of aligning ten randomly deformed images to a fixed image.

As can be seen, the proposed method in most cases outperforms the eSSD and MI-based registration. Since the proposed method tends to extract structural features and structural features are mainly located in the rigid body of the image, the improvement in the alignment accuracy for the rigid registration is more significant. It can be seen that for non-rigid registration, the method is not able to outperform the eSSD method in all of the cases, however, the results are still comparable.

4   Conclusions

We proposed a method based on introducing a structural representation for the purpose of registering multi-modal images. Unlike common multi-modal registration techniques that utilize sophisticated similarity measures, the new structural representation helps to map different intensity mappings to a common intensity space, so that a simple similarity measure can be employed to assess the alignment accuracy. The statistical representation is generated in a patch-based framework by modifying the patch entropy. To validate the merit of the method, experiments were carried out on different brain image modalities. Based on the results presented in this paper, the proposed method improved the registration accuracy compared to the eSSD and conventional MI registration methods.

References

1. Crum, W.R., Hartkens, T., Hill, D.L.G.: Non-rigid image registration: theory and practice. Br. J. Radiol. **2**, S140–S153 (2004)
2. Fitzpatrick, J.M., West, J.B., Maurer Jr, C.R.: Predicting error in rigid-body point-based registration. IEEE Trans. Med. Imag. **17**(5), 694–702 (1998)
3. Ghantous, M., Ghosh, S., Bayoumi, M.: A multi-modal automatic image registration technique based on complex wavelets. In: IEEE International Conference on Image Processing (ICIP), pp. 173–176 (2009)
4. Haber, E., Modersitzki, J.: Intensity gradient based registration and fusion of multimodal images. In: Larsen, R., Nielsen, M., Sporring, J. (eds.) MICCAI 2006. LNCS, vol. 4191, pp. 726–733. Springer, Heidelberg (2006)
5. Kasiri, K., Clausi, D.A., Fieguth, P.: Multi-modal image registration using structural features. In: International Conference on Engineering in Medicine and Biology Society (EMBC), pp. 5550–5553 (2014)
6. Kasiri, K., Fieguth, P., Clausi, D.A.: Cross modality label fusion in multi-atlas segmentation. In: IEEE International Conference on Image Processing (ICIP), pp. 16–20 (2014)
7. Keller, Y., Averbuch, A.: Multisensor image registration via implicit similarity. IEEE Trans. Pattern Anal. Machine Intell. **28**(5), 794–801 (2006)
8. Kim, Y.S., Lee, J.H., Ra, J.B.: Multi-sensor image registration based on intensity and edge orientation information. Pattern Recogn. **41**(11), 3356–3365 (2008)
9. Loeckx, D., Slagmolen, P., Maes, F., Vandermeulen, D., Suetens, P.: Nonrigid image registration using conditional mutual information. IEEE Trans. Med. Imag. **29**(1), 19–29 (2010)
10. Pluim, J.P.W., Maintz, J.B.A., Viergever, M.A.: Mutual-information-based registration of medical images: a survey. IEEE Trans. Med. Imag. **22**(8), 986–1004 (2003)
11. Rivaz, H., Karimaghaloo, Z., Collins, D.L.: Self-similarity weighted mutual information: a new nonrigid image registration metric. Med. Image Anal. **18**(2), 343–358 (2014)
12. Rivaz, H., Karimaghaloo, Z., Fonov, V.S., Collins, D.L.: Nonrigid registration of ultrasound and mri using contextual conditioned mutual information. IEEE Trans. Med. Imag. **33**(3), 708–725 (2014)
13. BrainWeb: simulated brain database. http://www.bic.mni.mcgill.ca/brainweb/
14. ITK: Image Registration and Segmentation Toolkit. www.itk.org
15. RIRE: Retrospective Image Registration Evaluation. http://www.insight-journal.org/rire/
16. Wachinger, C., Navab, N.: Structural image representation for image registration. In: Computer Vision and Pattern Recognition Workshops (CVPRW), pp. 23–30 (2010)
17. Wells, W.M., Viola, P., Atsumi, H., Nakajima, S., Kikinis, R.: Multi-modal volume registration by maximization of mutual information. Med. Image Anal. **1**(1), 35–51 (1996)
18. Wong, A., Clausi, D.A., Fieguth, P.: CPOL: complex phase order likelihood as a similarity measure for MR- CT registration. Med. Image Anal. **14**(1), 50–57 (2010)

Attributed Relational Graph-Based Learning of Object Models for Object Segmentation

Nasreen Akter and Iker Gondra[✉]

Department of Mathematics, Statistics and Computer Science,
St. Francis Xavier University, Antigonish, NS, Canada
{x2012tvh,igondra}@stfx.ca

Abstract. In object recognition accurate segmentation of a particular object of interest (OOI) is critical. The OOI usually consists of a set of homogeneous regions with spatial relations among them. Thus, class-specific knowledge on the visual appearance and spatial arrangement of the regions can be useful in discriminating among objects from different classes. In this paper, we propose the use of the Attributed Relational Graph (ARG)-based formalism as a means of representing both visual and spatial information in a single structure. In the proposed framework, a training set of images, each of which contains an instance of the OOI, is given. Afterwards, each image is over-segmented into a set of visually homogeneous regions and the corresponding ARG is constructed. Given such graph representations, OOI model learning reduces to a subgraph matching problem.

1 Introduction

Automatic extraction of objects of interest (OOI) from an image is an important problem that remains unsolved in computer vision applications like object-specific segmentation and recognition. Traditional image segmentation techniques, e.g., [2,4,5,13,17], generally use low-level visual features, e.g., color, texture, to segment an image into a set of homogeneous regions, which do not necessarily correspond to semantically meaningful objects.

In order to improve segmentation accuracy, several methods [1,3,6–8,10–12, 16] employ machine learning. In [3], an object recognition framework is presented that adapts the segmentation parameters based on the quality of segmentation achieved by comparing the segmentation results with a target model. This algorithm is restricted by the fact that the object model and position of the target object are assumed to be known. The work proposed in [11] continued along this direction by using reinforcement learning as part of the evaluation function to relax the assumption of known position of the target object. However, the object model still has to be provided in advance. In [10] an interactive model based graph matching approach is proposed where the object model is defined by the user according to traces drawn over the input image. This approach also needs significant user intervention.

In [1,6–8], Multiple Instance Learning (MIL) [9] is used to determine which regions in an oversegmented image are part of an OOI and, in turn, learn a model

© Springer International Publishing Switzerland 2015
M. Kamel and A. Campilho (Eds.): ICIAR 2015, LNCS 9164, pp. 90–99, 2015.
DOI: 10.1007/978-3-319-20801-5_10

of it. In MIL each training sample consists of a "bag" (set) of instances, which is labeled positive if at least one instance in the bag is positive, or negative otherwise. Different from standard supervised learning, we are only given the labels of the bags, but not the labels of the instance(s). The goal of MIL is to find a representation of the instance(s) that the positive bags have in common. In [6], a regional directional spatial template is proposed where the object segmentation algorithm learns a model which includes both visual and spatial information. Although templates are an effective way of including visual and spatial relations into the model they are not invariant to scaling, rotation and translation.

In traditional MIL, instances in a bag have been treated as independently and identically distributed. However, it is often the case that they are related. For example, in the case of object segmentation, objects have inherent structures. An OOI in an image is usually composed of homogeneous regions, i.e., "instances", with (spatial) relations among them. Such relations and their overall structure can be modeled with, e.g., a graph (see Fig. 1(a)–(c)). The work by Zhou et. al. [18] on MIL treats instances in a bag as non-i.i.d. samples. They propose the use of an undirected graph to represent the instances in a bag. In the graph, each instance is a node. They compute the distance (based on visual similarity) of every pair of nodes and, if smaller than a predefined threshold, an edge with weight equal to the inverse of the distance is added connecting the two nodes. After extracting the graphs of a set of training images, a subgraph matching algorithm can then be used to find a common subgraph, i.e., what the positive bags have in common, which can then serve as a model of the common object. An undirected graph used in [18] can only represent a single type of relation, i.e., visual similarity, among the regions. In this paper, we extend the work in [18] by employing an attributed relational graph [14] that can represent visual as well as multiple (spatial) relations in a single structure (see Fig. 1(d)).

2   ARG-Based Learning of OOI Model

2.1   Attributed Relational Graph Representation

The attributed relational graph (ARG) [14] is a directed, weighted and multi-relational graph defined as $G = (V, E, \mu, \nu)$, where V stands for its set of vertices, E its set of (directed) edges, μ represents the vertex attributes, i.e., $\mu(v)$ denotes the attributes of $v \in V$, and ν represents the edge attributes, i.e., $\nu((u, v))$ denotes the attributes of $(u, v) \in E$. In this paper, vertices represent image regions and edges represent spatial relations among these regions. Each edge has a weight which represents the connectivity between two regions with respect to a particular spatial relation between them. Subscripts are used to denote the corresponding graph generated from an image, e.g., $u_i \in V_i$ denotes a vertex of $G_i = (V_i, E_i, \mu_i, \nu_i)$ generated from an image I_i, similarly $(u_i, v_i) \in E_i$ denotes an edge of G_i.

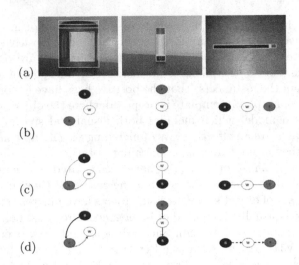

Fig. 1. Modeling relations among instances in a bag: (a) sample "bags", with marked "instances" of the OOI; (b) if we do not consider relations among instances the three bags are similar as they all have a black, a red and a white region; (c) simple graph can represent one relation, e.g., adjacency. Middle and rightmost graphs are similar; model cannot distinguish the two objects; (d) multi-relational graph: bold, dotted and dashed edges mean *below*, *surrounded* and *right* spatial relations respectively. Graphs are all different.

2.2   OOI Model Learning

Let I_i denote an image (or "bag") for a given training set $T = \{I_1, I_2, \ldots\}$ of images which contain OOI instance(s). A pixel $p_i = (p_i^x, p_i^y, p_i^R, p_i^G, p_i^B)$ in I_i is represented by its x and y coordinates and R,G,B color components. A set of visually homogeneous regions $\{R_{i,1}, R_{i,2}, \ldots\}$ is extracted, where $R_{i,j} \subset I_i$ and $\mathbf{x}_{i,j}$ is the visual feature vector which represents the color and shape of $R_{i,j}$,

$$\mathbf{x}_{i,j} = \frac{1}{|R_{i,j}|} \left(\sum_{p_k \in R_{i,j}} p_k^R, \sum_{p_k \in R_{i,j}} p_k^G, \sum_{p_k \in R_{i,j}} p_k^B, |B_{R_{i,j}}| \right) \tag{1}$$

where $|\cdot|$ denotes set cardinality and $B_{R_{i,j}}$ is the set of pixels on the border of $R_{i,j}$,

$$B_{R_{i,j}} = \left\{ p_k \big| (p_k \in R_{i,j}) \wedge (p_l \in N) \wedge border(p_k, p_l) == 1 \right\}$$

where

$$N = \left\{ p_l \big| p_l^x \in \{p_k^x, p_k^{x-1}, p_k^{x+1}\} \wedge p_l^y \in \{p_k^y, p_k^{y-1}, p_k^{y+1}\} \wedge (p_l \in I_i) \wedge (p_l \neq p_k) \right\}$$

$$border(p_k, p_l) = \begin{cases} 1 & if \ \| (p_k^R, p_k^G, p_k^B) - (p_l^R, p_l^G, p_l^B) \|^2 \geq \delta \\ 0 & otherwise \end{cases}$$

where δ, $0 \leq \delta \leq 255$ is a color feature threshold.

We consider four binary directional relations: *above(A)*, *right(R)*, *below(B)* and *surrounded(S)*. The regions are sorted in ascending order with respect to the top leftmost coordinates of their corresponding minimum bounding boxes (see Fig. 2). In the sorted order, if $R_{i,j}$ is to the *right* of $R_{i,k}$, it is obvious that $R_{i,k}$ must be to the *left* of $R_{i,j}$. Thus, we can ignore the *left* spatial relation. Region $R_{i,j}$ is surrounded by region $R_{i,k}$ if $R_{i,k}$ is *above*, *below*, to the *right* of $R_{i,j}$ and $R_{i,j}$ is to the *right* of $R_{i,k}$. Region $R_{i,j}$ is connected to region $R_{i,k}$ with respect to a directional relation d if $B_{R_{i,j}} \cap B_{R_{i,k}} \neq \emptyset$ and $R_{i,k}$ is in direction d of $R_{i,j}$. The set of regions with which $R_{i,j}$ is connected with respect to d is denoted by $C_{R_{i,j}}^{d}$, where $d \in \{A, R, B, S\}$. Algorithm 2 is used to construct an ARG $G_i(V_i, E_i, \mu_i, \nu_i)$ for each $I_i \in T$. The visual appearance information of a vertex v_i, i.e., region R_{v_i}, is denoted by $\mu(v_i) = \mathbf{x}_{v_i}$. Similarly, the spatial relational attributes of an edge $(u_i, v_i) \in E_i$, denoted by $\nu((u_i, v_i))$, correspond to the following weight and directional label attributes,

$$\nu((u_i, v_i)) = \left(\frac{\displaystyle\sum_{p_j \in R_{u_i} ; p_k \in R_{v_i} \in C_{R_{u_i}}^{d}} adj(p_j, p_k)}{|B_{R_{u_i}}|}, d \right)$$

where

$$adj(p_j, p_k) = \begin{cases} 1 & if \ (p_j \neq p_k) \wedge p_k^x \in \{p_j^x, p_j^{x-1}, p_j^{x+1}\} \wedge p_k^y \in \{p_j^y, p_j^{y-1}, p_j^{y+1}\} \\ 0 & otherwise \end{cases}$$

After constructing ARG (see Fig. 2) for each $I_i \in T$, a graph matching algorithm Algorithm 3 is applied to find a best-matching smallest common (sub)graph G_m from the ARG set $D = \{G_1, G_2, \ldots\}$. The "model" ARG $G_m(V_m, E_m, \mu_m, \nu_m)$ represents the visual and structural pattern of the particular OOI. In Algorithm 3, two (sub)graphs G_i and G_j are considered equal when $|V_i| = |V_j|$, $|E_i| = |E_j|$ and structural and appearance dissimilarities are smaller than a color $0 \leq \delta \leq 255$, shape $0 \leq \beta \leq 1$ and edge weight $0 \leq \gamma \leq 1$ threshold. In Algorithm 3, $E_i(u_i)$ denotes the set of edges that originate from u_i such that $(u_i, v_i) \in E_i, v_i \in V_i$. A 1-edge (u, v) subgraph G' of graph G is a graph with $V' = \{u, v\}, E' = \{(u, v)\}, \mu'(u) = \mu(u), \mu'(v) = \mu(v), \nu'((u, v)) = \nu((u, v))$. The union of two graphs $G_i(V_i, E_i, \mu_i, \nu_i)$ and $G_j(V_j, E_j, \mu_j, \nu_j)$, denoted by $G_i \cup G_j$, is the graph $G_k(V_k, E_k, \mu_k, \nu_k)$ where $V_k = V_i \cup V_j$, $E_k = E_i \cup E_j$, $\mu_k(u) = \mu_i(u)$ if $u \in V_i$ and $\mu_k(u) = \mu_j(u)$ otherwise, $\nu_k((u, v)) = \nu_i((u, v))$ if $(u, v) \in E_i$ and $\nu_k((u, v)) = \nu_j((u, v))$ otherwise. Algorithm 1 summarizes the learning process.

3   ARG-Based Segmentation

Given a new image I, it is over-segmented into a set of visually homogeneous regions $\{R_1, R_2, \ldots\}$, where $R_i \subset I$ and $\mathbf{x}_i$ is the visual feature vector of R_i, as defined in Eq. (1). The ARG $G(V, E, \mu, \nu)$ of I is constructed using Algorithm 2. Afterwards, Algorithm 3 with input $D = \{G_m, G\}$ is used to find a subgraph of G

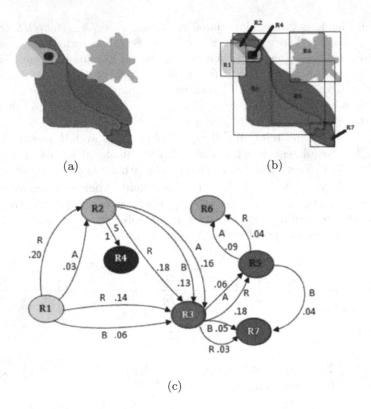

(a)   (b)

(c)

Fig. 2. Sample ARG construction; (a) image; (b) regions with corresponding minimum bounding box; (c) corresponding ARG.

Algorithm 1. OOI model learning

Inputs: $T = \{I_1, I_2, \ldots\}$, δ, β, γ
Output: frequent subgraph G_m
   for each $I_i \in T$ **do**
      Generate G_i using Algorithm 2 with inputs I, δ
      Generate G_m using Algorithm 3 with inputs $D = \{G_1, G_2, \ldots\}$, δ, β, γ

Algorithm 2. ARG construction

Inputs: I_i, δ
Output: G_i
   Oversegment I_i to generate $\{R_{i,1}, R_{i,2}, \ldots\}$
   for each region $R_{i,j}$ **do**
      Compute visual features $\mathbf{x}_{i,j}$ and minimum bounding box (MBB) of $R_{i,j}$
   Sort regions in ascending order of top leftmost coordinates of MBB
   for each region $R_{i,j}$ **do**
      for each spatial relation d **do**
         Compute $C_{R_{i,j}}^d$
   Form $G_i(V_i, E_i, \mu_i, \nu_i)$

Algorithm 3. Frequent sub-graph mining

Inputs: $D = \{G_1, G_2, \ldots\}$, δ, β, γ
Output: frequent subgraph G_f

  $G_s \leftarrow$ smallest graph in D
  $D \leftarrow D - \{G_s\}$
  $minSup \leftarrow |D| - 1$
  $G_f \leftarrow \phi$
  for each vertex $u_s \in V_s$ **do**
    for each edge $(u_s, v_s) \in E_s(u_s)$ **do**
      $G' \leftarrow$ 1-edge (u_s, v_s) subgraph of G_s
      $support \leftarrow 0$
      for each graph $G_i \in D$ **do**
        if G' is a subgraph of G_i **then**
          $support = support + 1$
      if $support = minSup$ **then**
        $G_f \leftarrow G_f \bigcup G'$

---

that matches the model G_m. If such subgraph G_f is found the final segmentation S is generated by keeping only the pixels of I that appear in regions represented by G_f. Algorithm 4 summarizes the segmentation process.

Algorithm 4. OOI segmentation

Inputs: I, model ARG G_m, δ, β, γ
Output: S

  $S \leftarrow I$
  Generate G using Algorithm 2 with inputs I, δ
  Generate G_f using Algorithm 3 with inputs $D = \{G_m, G\}$, δ, β, γ
  if $G_f = G_m$ **then**
    Remove pixels in S that do not appear in any of the regions represented by G_f

---

4 Results

We experimented with both an artificial dataset of JPEG-format images of a parrot (see Fig. 3(a)) and with a real image dataset of JPEG-format images of a computer mouse (see Fig. 4(a)). The artificial dataset consists of a training set and a test set containing 10 and 5 images respectively of the OOI in a variety of settings. The real image dataset consists of 15 images, 10 images were used for training and 5 images for testing. In both cases Algorithm 1 runs with input: training set T, $\delta = 20$, $\beta = .2$ and $\gamma = .05$.

Let S be the final set of OOI pixels generated by the segmentation algorithm Algorithm 4. The segmentation quality measure is,

$$Q = \left| \frac{S \cap G}{G} \right| \times \left| \frac{S \cap G}{S} \right|$$

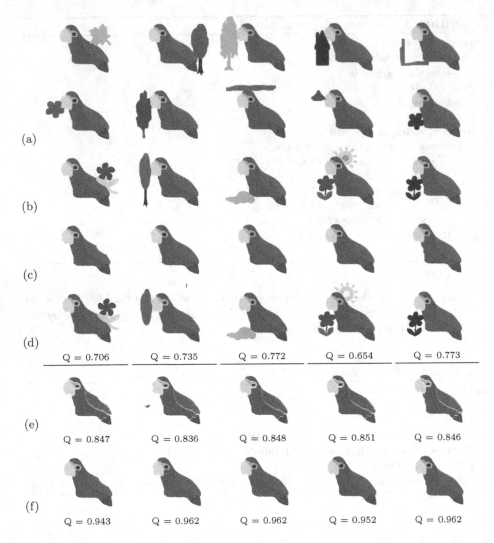

(a)

(b)

(c)

(d)

| Q = 0.706 | Q = 0.735 | Q = 0.772 | Q = 0.654 | Q = 0.773 |

(e)

| Q = 0.847 | Q = 0.836 | Q = 0.848 | Q = 0.851 | Q = 0.846 |

(f)

| Q = 0.943 | Q = 0.962 | Q = 0.962 | Q = 0.952 | Q = 0.962 |

Fig. 3. Segmentation comparison: (a) training images; (b) test images; (c) ground truth images; (d) VIS segmentations; (e) TEM segmentations; (f) ARG segmentations

where G is the set of pixels corresponding to the OOI in the ground-truth segmentation. Hence, Q is the percentage of pixels in agreement with the ground-truth segmentation over the OOI. Thus, Q is to be maximized. Figs. 3 and 4 show the segmentations and their Q values obtained with our proposed method Algorithm 4 (ARG) and with three other methods. The first method (VIS) uses the standard MIL formulation in which relations among instances in a bag are not considered. Thus, the resulting OOI model consists of a description of the visual appearances of the OOI regions (see Fig. 1(b)). To segment a new image, every pixel whose color is sufficiently similar (threshold $\delta = 20$) to that of the

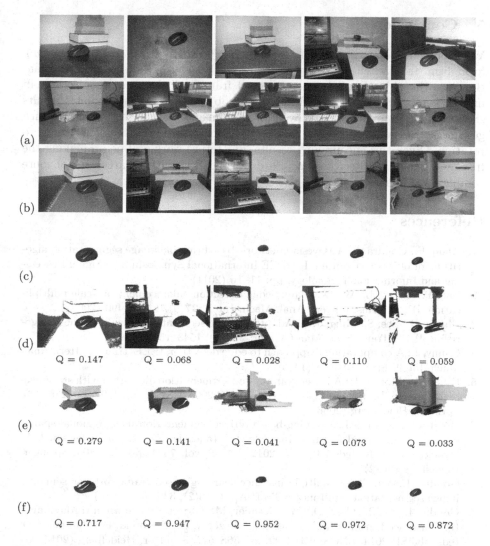

Fig. 4. Segmentation comparison: (a) training images; (b) test images; (c) ground truth images; (d) VIS segmentations; (e) WAT segmentations; (f) ARG segmentations

colors in the OOI model is included as part of the OOI. The second method is the regional directional spatial template approach [6] (TEM). The third method is the Watershed segmentation algorithm [15] (WAT).

The average Q values in the artificial dataset are 0.956, 0.728, 0.845 for ARG, VIS, TEM respectively. The average Q values in the real image dataset are 0.892, 0.082, 0.113 for ARG, VIS and WAT respectively. These results clearly show that the proposed ARG-based MIL formalism is capable of learning a more accurate model of the OOI which in turn results in a more accurate segmentation. Also, differently from our method, the regional directional spatial template approach presented in [6] is not invariant to geometric transformations of the OOI such as scaling and translation.

5 Conclusion

We proposed the attributed relational graph based multiple instance learning formalism. It is an effective way of including both visual and spatial information into the object model. The proposed framework does not require human interaction or preexisting knowledge of the object model. Experimental results show that the framework works well for real images. Although it is robust with geometric transformations such as scaling and translation, it is not invariant to rotation. Given this encouraging results, our future work will be on making the framework invariant to rotation and experimenting with a larger set of more complex real images.

References

1. Alam, F., Gondra, I.: A Bayesian network-based tunable image segmentation algorithm for object recognition. In: IEEE International Symposium on Signal Processing and Information Technology, pp. 11–16 (2011)
2. Bao, P., Zhang, L., Wu, X.: Canny edge detection enhancement by scale multiplication. IEEE Trans. Pattern Anal. Mach. Intell. **27**(9), 1485–1490 (2005)
3. Bhanu, B., Lee, S., Ming, J.C.: Adaptive image segmentation using a genetic algorithm. IEEE Trans. Syst. Man Cybern. **25**(12), 1543–1567 (1995)
4. Canny, J.: A computational approach to edge detection. IEEE Trans. Pattern Anal. Mach. Intell. **8**(6), 679–698 (1986)
5. Fahad, A., Morris, T.: A faster graph-based segmentation algorithm with statistical region merge. In: Bebis, G., et al. (eds.) ISVC 2006. LNCS, vol. 4292, pp. 286–293. Springer, Heidelberg (2006)
6. Gondra, I., Alam, F.I.: Learning-based object segmentation using regional spatial templates and visual features. In: Bolc, L., Tadeusiewicz, R., Chmielewski, L.J., Wojciechowski, K. (eds.) ICCVG 2012. LNCS, vol. 7594, pp. 397–406. Springer, Heidelberg (2012)
7. Gondra, I., Xu, T.: A multiple instance learning based framework for semantic image segmentation. Multimedia Tools Appl. **48**(2), 339–365 (2010)
8. Gondra, I., Xu, T., Chiu, D.K.Y., Cormier, M.: Object segmentation through multiple instance learning. In: Elmoataz, A., Lezoray, O., Nouboud, F., Mammass, D. (eds.) ICISP 2014. LNCS, vol. 8509, pp. 568–577. Springer, Heidelberg (2014)
9. Maron, O., Lozano-Pérez, T.: A framework for multiple-instance learning. In: Jordan, M.I., Kearns, M.J., Solla, S.A. (eds.) Advances in Neural Information Processing Systems, vol. 10, pp. 570–576. MIT Press, Cambridge (1998)
10. Noma, A., Graciano, A.B.V., Cesar, J.R.M., Consularo, L.A., Bloch, I.: Interactive image segmentation by matching attributed relational graphs. Pattern Recogn. **45**(3), 1159–1179 (2012)
11. Peng, J., Bhanu, B.: Closed-loop object recognition using reinforcement learning. IEEE Trans. Pattern Anal. Mach. Intell. **20**(2), 139–154 (1998)
12. Qi, Z., Xu, Y., Wang, L., Song, Y.: Online multiple instance boosting for object detection. Neurocomputing **74**(10), 1769–1775 (2011)
13. Shi, J., Malik, J.: Normalized cuts and image segmentation. IEEE Trans. Pattern Anal. Mach. Intell. **22**(8), 888–905 (2000)
14. Tsai, W.H., Fu, K.S.: Error-correcting isomorphisms of attributed relational graphs for pattern analysis. IEEE Trans. Syst. Man Cybern. **9**(12), 757–768 (1979)

15. Vincent, L., Soille, P.: Watersheds in digital spaces: an efficient algorithm based on immersion simulations. IEEE Trans. Pattern Anal. Mach. Intell. **13**(6), 583–598 (1991)
16. Viola, P.A., Platt, J.C., Zhang, C.: Multiple instance boosting for object detection. Adv. Neural Inf. Process.Syst. **18**, 1417–1424 (2005)
17. Wu, Z., Leahy, R.: An optimal graph theoretic approach to data clustering: theory and its application to image segmentation. IEEE Trans. Pattern Anal. Mach. Intell. **15**(11), 1101–1113 (1993)
18. Zhou, Z.H., Sun, Y.Y., Li, Y.F.: Multi-instance learning by treating instances as non-i.i.d. samples. In: Proceedings of International Conference on Machine Learning, pp. 1249–1256 (2009)

Label Fusion for Multi-atlas Segmentation Based on Majority Voting

Jie Huo[1], Guanghui Wang[2]([✉]), Q.M. Jonathan Wu[1],
and Akilan Thangarajah[1]

[1] Department of ECE, University of Windsor,
Windsor, ON N9B 3P4, Canada
[2] Department of EECS, University of Kansas,
Lawrence, KS 66045, USA
ghwang@ku.edu

Abstract. Multi-atlas based segmentation is a popular approach in medical image analysis. Majority voting, as the simplest label fusion method in multi-atlas based segmentation, is a powerful tool for segmentation. In this paper, a novel majority voting-based label fusion algorithm is proposed by introducing a patch-based analysis for automatic segmentation of brain MR images. The proposed approach, by comparing the similarity between patches, avoids the over-segmentation problem of the majority fusion. The approach is successfully applied to the segmentation of hippocampus, and the experimental results demonstrate significant improvement over three state-of-the-art approaches in the literature.

Keywords: Multi-atlas segmentation · Majority voting · Label fusion

1 Introduction

Segmentation of anatomical structures in medical images is essential for scientific inquiry into the complex relationships between biological structure and clinical diagnosis, treatment and assessment. As a method of incorporating the prior knowledge and the anatomical structure similarity between target image and atlases, multi-atlas segmentation has been successfully applied in segmenting a variety of medical images, including brain, cardiac, and abdominal images [1–3]. Motivated by the observation that segmentation strongly correlates with image appearance, atlas segmentation transfers spatial information from an existing dataset (labeled atlas) to a target image via deformable registration based on image similarity. In multi-atlases segmentation, multiple atlases are separately registered to the target image, and voxelwise label conflicts between the registered atlases are resolved by using label fusion.

The label of the voxel in target image is determined by fusing the labels of corresponding voxels in each atlas. Weighted voting is the most popular method for label fusion, where the label of each atlas voxel contributes to the final result with a weight. One approach to obtaining the optimal weight is to compute the similarity between the image patch centered at the target voxel and the image

© Springer International Publishing Switzerland 2015
M. Kamel and A. Campilho (Eds.): ICIAR 2015, LNCS 9164, pp. 100–106, 2015.
DOI: 10.1007/978-3-319-20801-5_11

patch centered at the corresponding atlas voxel, and this forms the patch-based segmentation [4]. Other methods of considering correlated labelling errors [1] or employing sparse representation [5] are also used to determine the weight. In addition to weighted voting, another type of label fusion method is statistical label fusion, such as STAPLE [6], or non-local STAPLE [7].

Although weighted fusion and statistical fusion yield good results in segmentation of magnetic resonance (MR) image [1,2,7], the estimation of the weight and the EM estimation, which play important roles in weighted fusion and statistical fusion, is very computationally intensive. In contrast, majority voting, which is probably the simplest label fusion method, has been demonstrated to yield powerful segmentation results with less computation. Majority voting method, however, may yield over-segmentation since it does not utilize image intensity information. Patch-based method, which compares the similarity of intensity between patches, can be combined with majority voting multi-atlases segmentation to avoid such over-segmentation errors.

Motivated by this idea, we propose a novel label fusion method which combines majority voting with patch-based method to achieve automatic segmentation in brain MR images. The proposed method is successfully applied to the segmentation of hippocampus. In addition, the influences of different parameters are studied empirically, and a comparison with three closely related methods is performed to demonstrate the effectiveness of the proposed approach.

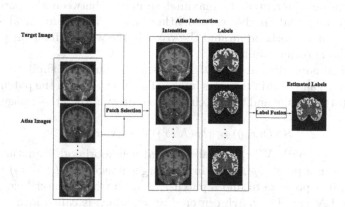

Fig. 1. Illustration of label generation for the target patch. Where red square in target image denotes the target patch; the blue, pink and green squares in atlas image denote patches in a searching window; and the best matched patch in each atlas is shown as red squares (Color figure online).

2   The Proposed Method

Consider an image $I = \{I(x)|x \in \Omega\}$, where x denotes the voxel; and $\Omega \subset \mathbb{R}^3$ denotes the lattice on which the image is defined. The goal of segmentation is to estimate a label map L associated with the image I, in which each voxel is assigned a discrete label l. The label l takes discrete values from 1 to $\mathcal{L}$ for all the possible labels for the voxels in the image. In multi-atlas segmentation, I_T is a target image and $A_1, \cdots, A_n$ are n atlases with $A_i = (I_i, S_i)$, where I_i is the atlas image which has aligned to the target image (I_i is also called warped atlas image); and S_i is the corresponding manual segmentation of this atlas image. After combing the warped atlas images, a fused label map is generated which can be considered as the segmentation of the target image.

Figure 1 illustrates the generation of labels for the target patch of the proposed method. First, the atlases (intensity and label image) are pairwisely registered to the target image. Then, for each atlas image, a patch selection scheme is performed to choose the patch in each atlas with the highest similarity with the target patch. Finally, by applying label fusion algorithm to the patches with corresponding location of the patches in atlas images, we obtain the estimated label of each patch. The approach is applied for every voxel in the target image so as to obtain the labels for the entire target image.

2.1 Patch Selection

The performance of atlas-based segmentation can be moderately improved by applying a local searching technique [4]. Although deformable registration has been performed before label fusion, the correspondence obtained from the registration may not guarantee the maximal similarity between the patch in the target image and that in the warped atlas image. Therefore, local searching within a small neighborhood around the voxel in the warped image is performed to achieve the maximal similarity.

Summed squared distance (SSD) is used to measure the similarity between the target patch and that in the atlas image. The SSD between the patch centered at x in the target image and the patch centered at x' in the atlas image is shown below.

$$SSD(x, y) = \|I_T(\mathcal{N}(x)) - I_i(\mathcal{N}(x'))\|^2 \tag{1}$$

where $x' \in \mathcal{N}'(x)$ with $\mathcal{N}'(x)$ a local searched neighborhood. Equation (1) indicates that given a patch $I_T(\mathcal{N}(x))$ in the target image and $I_i(\mathcal{N}(x))$ in the ith atlas image, it is possible to find a patch $I_i(\mathcal{N}(x'))$ whose center belongs to the neighborhood $\mathcal{N}'(x)$. The patch centered at x^i, which is called locally searched optimal correspondence, has higher similarity with the target patch than other patches with centers inside the neighborhood $\mathcal{N}'(x)$. Thus, the locally searched optimal correspondence is

$$x^i = argmin_{x' \in \mathcal{N}'(x)}[SSD(I_T(\mathcal{N}(x)), I_i(\mathcal{N}(x')))] \tag{2}$$

where $I_i(\mathcal{N}(x'))$ is the patch in the ith atlas image centered at x' with a radius r, and $I_T(\mathcal{N}(x))$ is the target patch centered at x with a radius r. x' is the voxel in the local neighborhood $\mathcal{N}'(x)$ with a radius r_s. By calculating the SSD between the patches in the target and the atlas images, we obtain x^i, which is the location from the ith atlas with the best image matching for the location x in the target image.

2.2   Label Fusion and Validation

Majority Voting: After label fusion, n patches are selected as the candidate of voting for the target patch. The probability of that the label of x is l can be computed by counting the number of occurrence for l from x_i, $i \in 1, 2, \ldots, n$. Then, the label for x in the target image can be determined by choosing the label with the highest probability. The final label $\widehat{L}(x)$ is obtained by

$$\widehat{L}(x) = argmax_{l \in \{1, \ldots, \mathcal{L}\}} p_x(l) = argmax_{l \in \{1, \ldots, \mathcal{L}\}} \frac{1}{n} \sum_{i=1}^{n} p(l|A^i, x) \qquad (3)$$

where x indexes through image voxels; $p(l|A^i, x)$ is the posterior probability that A^i votes for the label l at x. Typically, deterministic atlases have unique label for every location, which means $p(l|A^i, x) = 1$ if $S_i(x) = l$, and 0, otherwise.

Improvement on Majority Voting: The label of the center voxel of the target patch can be produced using majority voting. However, since we have chosen the most similar patch to the target patch from each atlas images based on the intensity information, these selected patches can be considered to have similar segmentation to the target patch. For each voxel in the target patch, we can find a candidate voxel from the corresponding position in each selected patch, and thus, the label of each voxel in target patch can be determined by performing (1) from its n candidate voxels. Given a three-dimensional image, for every patch with a radius r in the target image, $(2r+1)^3$ voxels within the patch will be labeled by performing the above majority voting scheme. Assuming that there are N voxels in the target image, $(2r+1)^3 \times N$ labels will be produced and each voxel in the target image have $(2r+1)^3$ candidates. Therefore, the majority voting is performed twice to generate the final label for the target voxel.

Validation: The kappa index (Dice coefficient or similarity index) [9] was computed by comparing the manual segmentations with those obtained with our method. For two binary segmentations A and B, the kappa index was computed as

$$\kappa(A, B) = \frac{2|A \cap B|}{|A| + |B|} \qquad (4)$$

In quantitative MR analysis, manual segmentation is usually considered as a gold standard. The segmentation quality was estimated with the Dice coefficient by comparing the expert-based segmentations with the automatic segmentations.

3   Experimental Evaluation

The proposed approach is applied to segment the hippocampus using T1-weighted MR images. The dataset used in the experiment includes 35 brain MR imaging scans obtained from the OASIS project. The manual brain segmentations of these images were produced by Neuromorphometrics, Inc., using the brain-COLOR labeling protocol. The dataset was applied in the MICCAI 2012

Multi-Atlas Labeling Challenge, where 15 subjects were used at the atlases and the remaining 20 images were used for testing.

In the experiment, we perform pairwise registered transformations between the atlas and the target images, as well as between each pair of the atlas images. The ANTs registration tool was used in this study to implement pairwise registration [10]. The antsApplyTransforms with linear interpolation was applied to generate the warped images, and the antsApplyTransforms with nearest neighbor interpolation was applied to generate the warped segmentations.

In order to improve computation efficiency, we select a region of interest (ROI) before computing. First, for every atlas image, a 3D binary image which segment the hippocampus region is generated. Then, OR operator is applied in these 3D binary images, and a new 3D binary image is obtained which fuses all the hippocampus segmentation of the atlas images. The resulted image is dilated by a $(2(r + r_s) + 1)$-dimensional cubic structuring element to produce the ROI of computation. In order to increase the robustness of image matching, instead of using the raw image intensities, we normalize the intensity vector obtained from each local image intensity patch such that the normalized vector has zero mean and a constant norm for each label fusion method.

3.1 Impact of the Size of 3D Patch and Search Volume

The proposed method has two parameters, r for the local patch radius and r_s for the local searched neighborhood. The influence of these parameters are studied by evaluating a range of values $r \in \{1, 2, 3\}$; $r_s \in \{1, 2, 3, 4, 5\}$ in the experiment. First, we studied the impact of the patch radius on segmentation accuracy. The mean dice overlap coefficient results are shown in Fig. 2 (left). Using the patch radius of $r = 1$, the algorithm performs much better than using larger patch radius. The segmentation accuracy also improves with the increase of the searched radius r_s. However, the dice overlap decreases when the searched radius $r_s > 4$. Larger searched radius improves the probability to find a similar patch with target patch, however, it also leads to an increase of mismatches. Figure 3 shows the segmentation results for different sizes of local patch and searched patch.

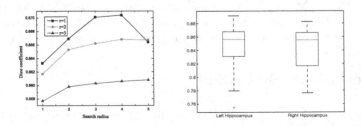

Fig. 2. (left) Hippocampus segmentation performance using different patch radius and searched patch radius. (right) The dice overlap coefficient of the left and right hippocampi.

3.2 Comparison Results in Hippocampus Segmentation

The average Dice overlap between automatic segmentation and manual segmentation for testing data is measure in the experiment. We compared our results with three popular benchmark approaches, i.e. majority voting, global weighted fusion, and STAPLE [8]. The dice overlap coefficient of the left and the right hippocampi by the proposed approach is 0.8473 ± 0.0325 and 0.8447 ± 0.0370, respectively, and the average overlap is 0.846 ± 0.03. The box plot is shown in Fig. 2 (right), where the central mark is the median, the edges of the box are the 25th and 75th percentiles. The whiskers extend to 2.7 standard deviations around the mean, and the outliers are marked individually as a '+'. As a comparison, the average Dice overlap obtained by majority voting, global weighted fusion, and STAPLE are 0.821, 0.807, and 0.836, respectively [8]. It is clear that the propose technique yields more than 1.2 % Dice overlap improvement. In addition, the results of other three approaches were obtained by conducting the experiments in a leave-one-out strategy on a data set containing 39 subjects, while our approach use only 15 subjects as atlas set. Overall, the proposed method yields better segmentation accuracy while using significantly fewer atlases than other reported methods.

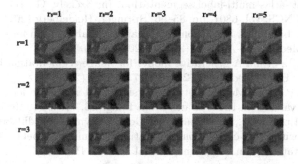

Fig. 3. Sagittal views of the segmentations produced by different patch radius and searched patch radius. Where the red region shows the overlap between the automatic and the manual segmentation; the green region is the manual segmentation; and the blue region is automatic segmentation using the proposed method (Color figure online).

4 Conclusion

In this paper, we have proposed a novel approach to automatically segment anatomical structures based on the majority voting method. A patch selection strategy is proposed to ensure that the patch in the atlas with the highest similarity to the target patch is selected as the voting candidate. The proposed approach is verified by experimental evaluations on a standard dataset. Compared with three benchmark techniques, the segmentation results are significantly improved by the proposed method.

Acknowledgment. The work is partly supported by the NSERC, Kansas NASA EPSCoR Program, and the NSFC (61273282).

References

1. Wang, H., Sun, J., Pluta, J., Craige, J., Yushkevich, P.: Multiatlas segmentation with joint label fusion. IEEE Trans. Pattern Anal. Mach. Intell. **35**(3), 311–623 (2013)
2. Bai, W., et al.: A probabilistic patch-based label fusion model for multi-atlas segmentation with registration refinement: application to cardiac MR images. IEEE Trans. Med. Imag. **32**(7), 1302–1315 (2013)
3. Wolz, R., et al.: Automated abdominal multi-organ segmentation with subject-specific atlas generation. IEEE Trans. Med. Imag. **32**(9), 1723–1730 (2013)
4. Coupé, P., Manjón, J.V., Fonov, V., Pruessner, J., Robles, M., Collins, D.L.: Nonlocal patch-based label fusion for hippocampus segmentation. In: Jiang, T., Navab, N., Pluim, J.P.W., Viergever, M.A. (eds.) MICCAI 2010, Part III. LNCS, vol. 6363, pp. 129–136. Springer, Heidelberg (2010)
5. Wu, G., et al.: Hierarchical multi-atlas label fusion with multi-scale feature representation and label-specific patch partition. NeroImage **103**, 34–46 (2015)
6. Asman, A.J., Landman, B.A.: Characterizing spatially varying performance to improve multi-atlas multi-label segmentation. In: Székely, G., Hahn, H.K. (eds.) IPMI 2011. LNCS, vol. 6801, pp. 85–96. Springer, Heidelberg (2011)
7. Asman, A.J., Landman, B.A.: Non-local statistical label fusion for multi-atlas segmentation. Med. Image Anal. **17**(2), 194–208 (2013)
8. Sabuncu, M.R., et al.: A generative model for image segmentation based on label fusion. IEEE Trans. Med. Imag. **29**(10), 1714–1729 (2010)
9. Zijdenbos, A.P., et al.: Morphometric analysis of whitematter lesions in MR images: method and validation. IEEE Trans. Med. Imag. **13**, 716–724 (1994)
10. Avants, B., Epstein, C., Grossman, M., Gee, J.: Symmetric diffeomorphic image registration with cross-correlation: evaluating automated labeling of elderly and neurodegenerative brain. Med. Image Anal. **12**, 26–41 (2008)

Image Coding, Compression
and Encryption

An Optimized Selective Encryption for Video Confidentiality

Khalfan Almarashda$^{(\boxtimes)}$, Ali Dawood, Thomas Martin,
Mohammed Al-Mualla, and Harish Bhaskar

Electrical and Computer Engineering Department,
Khalifa University of Science, Technology and Research,
P. O. Box 127788, Abu Dhabi, UAE
{khalfan.almarashda,dawood,thomas.martin,almualla,
harish.bhaskar}@kustar.ac.ae

Abstract. Selective Encryption (SE) offers effective and efficient protection of visual content for assuring video confidentiality. However, it is challenging to optimize SE's computational overhead while maintaining encryption effectiveness. This paper suggests the study of classifying the targeted sign-flip Quantized Coefficients (QC) so as to minimize the Encryption Computation Overhead (ECO), while maximizing Perceptual Encryption Effectiveness (PEE) both across the H.264/AVC and the HEVC video coding standards. The evaluation of this min-max optimization is based on the number of encryption bits used to flip the targeted QC sign and the Peak Signal to Noise Ratio (PSNR) estimated post encryption for quantifying ECO and PEE respectively. Results of simulation on different video sequences indicate that the derived set of QC's can reduce ECO cost by up to 78 % without affecting the video confidentiality when compared to state-of-the-art approaches.

1 Introduction

The wide use of visual analytical systems in video surveillance has raised the threat of the information being accessed by non-authorized users [1]. Therefore, providing video confidentiality is critical and various approaches such as: raw video encryption [2], compressed video stream encryption [3] and selective encryption(SE) [4] have become popular. Among these approaches, SE is well known for its scalability and format compliance features [5]. As the name suggests, the SE technique targets a selected portion of the video signal, such as a region-of-interest [6] or motion vector difference or Quantized Coefficients (QC) [7,8] for encryption. This targeted part of the signal could be scrambled randomly using a pseudo random number generator [8], or based on chaotic sources [1], or even more commonly using the Advanced Encryption Standard (AES) algorithm [5].

One of the earliest SE schemes based on sign flipping QC was proposed by Dufaux et al. in [9], where SE targeted all QC. Although well known, this scheme was inefficient as it considered all QC equivalently. Therefore, many optimization techniques have been proposed in order to minimize the computational overhead

© Springer International Publishing Switzerland 2015
M. Kamel and A. Campilho (Eds.): ICIAR 2015, LNCS 9164, pp. 109–118, 2015.
DOI: 10.1007/978-3-319-20801-5_12

of the encryption process. For example, in [10], Tong et al. proposed a scheme that excluded the DC QC, while in contrast, the scheme proposed in [11] targeted the DC QC exclusively. Despite improving the Encryption Computation Overhead (ECO), both methods were restricted by their inability to maximize the perceptual encryption effectiveness (PEE). In contrast, Shahid et al. [12] proposed targeting all non-zero (NZ) QC to achieve better trade-off between ECO and PEE. In this paper, this method of [12] has been treated as a benchmark due to its superior performance in minimizing ECO while not compromising on maximal PEE when compared with other state of the art schemes.

This paper studies the impact that different classes of QC have on SE, particularly optimized against constraints of ECO and PEE, have been proven to exceed the benchmark SE of [12], by saving nearly 60 %-78 % of computational overhead with small improvements (0.18-2.51 dB) in PEE.

This paper is divided into four sections. In Sect. 2 the background of SE is introduced. Section 3 covers the methodology, experimental framework, and details of the experimental results for Classification and Optimization. Section 4 concludes with recommendations and some highlights of future work.

2   Background

Fundamentally, the SE scheme generates bits to be used in an Exclusive-OR operations with the encoded bit stream. A state-of-the-art SE approach [12] uses encryption bits to flip the signs of targeted QC; QC_x, where $x = \{1, 2, \ldots, 16\}$ for a $4x4$ block [5]. This approach uses the encryption Sign Flip (SF) bit-stream bits $(SF_{B_i} = \{1, 0\}, i = 1, 2, ..., S$, where S is the size of the $SF_{B_i})$ to flip the sign values of selected or targeted QC, (QC_x), based on the following simple condition:

$$SF(QC_x) = \begin{cases} -QC_x & \text{if } SF_{B_i} = 1 \\ QC_x & \text{if } SF_{B_i} = 0 \end{cases}$$

Figure 1 shows a general overview of a SE scheme based on sign flip for a set of targeted QC. In this study, this category of SE has been adapted and its effectiveness based on specifically chosen (QC) has been investigated.

The criteria for optimizing the performance of the SE strategy based on targeted QC can be based on many indicators including performance overhead (memory and computation), coding efficiency (bit-rate) and even security (encryption algorithm or key size). In this paper, since the assessment methodology is focused on evaluating performance optimization within the bounds of acceptable confidentiality. The two metrics that have been considered are a) PEE for confidentiality and b) ECO for performance. The objective is to minimize ECO without compromising on video content confidentiality measured through maximizing PEE.

In order to quantitatively estimate PEE, the Peak Signal to Noise Ratio (PSNR) metric has been used. PSNR assesses the gap in quality between the authorized and non-authorized video retrieval (decoding), while ECO uses S_{QC_x}

(size of the sign flip bits) as the performance overhead indicator. S_{QC_x} reflects the number of encryption operations to be generated in order to sign flip the targeted QC_x. The choice of QC chosen by different SE scheme vary, for example in [9] $QC_{x=[1-16]}$ are used, while in [10] $QC_{x=[2-15]}$ is chosen by ignoring the DC QC. The PEE metric based on PSNR measures the gap in quality between the 'secured' and 'intercepted' videos using Eq. 1.

$$PSNR(X,Y) = 10\log \frac{h.w.n.255^2}{\sum_{k=1}^{n} \sum_{j=1}^{w} \sum_{i=1}^{h}(X_{i,j,k} - Y_{i,j,k})^2} \tag{1}$$

where h, w and n represent the height, width and number of the video frame respectively. $X_{i,j,k}$ represents a pixel in i and j coordinates at k frame. X and Y are 'secured' and 'intercepted' decoded video frame. Furthermore, a target PEE value (PEE_τ) has been considered as a benchmark to ensure that the derived approach does not compromise on video confidentiality beyond the baseline counterpart. In other words, any scheme that at the least does not achieve the benchmarked PEE, PEE_τ, was marked unacceptable. Beyond achieving, PEE_τ, high ECO is preferred to guarantee bounded computational overhead.

The ECO indicator has been based on the number of encryption operation required to encrypt the QC_x. For simplicity, this indicator has to be normalized to a percentage amount of encryption performed in [12]. Equation 2 illustrates ECO_{QC_x} reflecting percentage saving based on the optimized selection of QC, where S_{BM} denotes the size of the encryption stream used in [12].

$$ECO_{QC_x} = 100 \times (1 - \frac{S_{QC_x}}{S_{BM}}) \tag{2}$$

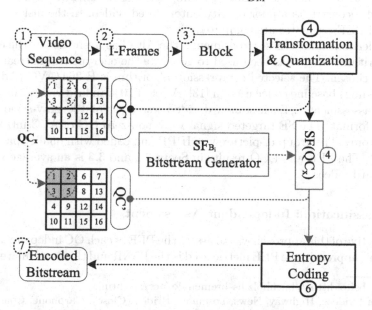

Fig. 1. An overview of the SE based on SF approach. QC_x represent selected (targeted) QC to be encrypted using SF bitstream

3   SE Optimization

One outcome of this paper was to study the impact of targeted QC (independently and when combined) on the performance of the SE. In other words, a specific combination of QC's can provide better trade-off between quality of encryption and encryption cost saving. In order to systematically verify this hypothesis, targeted QC assessment has been undertaken in 3 stages: a) *Classification* through independent QC_x assessment, b) *Optimization* through combined class (groups of QC_x) assessments and c) *Validation* of extended optimization over other standards.

During the classification stage Sect. 3.2, the individual QC_x are assessed based on the quality of encryption using the H.264/AVC coding standard. Further, in the optimization phase Sect. 3.3, combinations of specific classes and targeted QC_x have been explored for investigation on the performance based on encryption cost and quality. Finally, in the validation step, the chosen combination of targeted QC_x has been applied on the HEVC coding standard and evaluations reported in Sect. 3.4.

3.1   Experimental Framework

In the first stage, the SF_B bitstream is used to encrypt the targeted QC (QC_x) and generate an encrypted bit stream. During the second stage, two decoding schemes are used to retrieve each video sequence. The first decoding scheme undergoes the SF effect using symmetric SF_B to reconstruct a high quality 'secured' video, while, the second decoding scheme decodes the QC_x with SF effect and reconstructs a poor quality 'intercepted' video. In the last stage, the ECO and PEE estimates are computed.

In order to conduct these experiments, the AES has been used as the encryption algorithm[1] which has been used to generate the encryption bitstream SF_B, has been chosen. The selected compression algorithm is H.264/AVC (Advanced Video Coding) baseline codec used in [13]. A set of 10 standard videos[2] have been used for assessments[3]. Each standard video was a set of 100 gray-scale frames in QCIF format. The SE targeted signal were non-zero QC of AVC intra-coded I-Frames only. The group-of-picture was IPPP and coded with quality parameter (QP=27). The PEE and ECO results in Sects. 3.2 and 3.3 is an average value of all standard videos.

3.2   Classification: Independent Assessment

The objective of this approach was to assess the PEE of each QC independently. As part of this approach, the PEE metric used is the PSNR and this is calculated using

---

[1] AES website: http://buchholz.hs-bremen.de/aes/aes.html.
[2] Standard videos: Highway, News, Foreman, Bridge (Close), Carphone, Coastguard, Container, Hall Monitor, Highway and Mobile.
[3] Standard Video Website: http://trace.eas.asu.edu/yuv/.

Eq. 1. In order to show the independent QC_x assessment, this paper considered the case study of the H.264/AVC video codec. This codec has 16 (4 x 4) QC_x per block which are accessed in a zig-zag order. To assess each QC_x independently, 16 experiments have been conducted and in each experiment a single QC was encrypted. Subsequently, measurement of ECO_{QC_x} and PSNR were calculated using Eqs. 1 and 2 respectively. This approach of optimization can be extended to other standards and an example of how this has been applied to HEVC standard is presented in Sect. 3.4.

Figure 2 represents the histogram of calculated PEE (PSNR, dB) values for each QC_x. The normalized ECO_{QC_x} value depicted over each bar represents the share (percentage) of each QC_x as compared to the bitstream size (Eq. 2) of the benchmark algorithm [12]. For example, $QC_{x=1}$ (number 1 in zig-zag order) shows maximum PEE indicator with PSNR value of almost 30 dB. However, this improved confidentiality raises the ECO by up to 12 % of the total QC as obtained from the benchmark [12].

It can be observed in Fig. 2 that the PEE and ECO values decrease when assessed the QC_x in zig-zag order. We desire higher PEE values with minimum corresponding ECO costs. Furthermore, as shown in the same Fig. 2, the quality of encryption (PEE) varies for different QC_x while the encryption cost (ECO) remains equivalent. For example, (a) $QC_{x=2}$ and $QC_{x=4}$ have a PEE value of 12.45 dB and 16.11 dB respectively while their ECO value is 9 % (b) $QC_{x=7}$ and $QC_{x=11}$ have a PEE value of 12 dB and 10 dB respectively while their ECO value is 5 %. This indicates that some QC_x can achieve higher quality of encryption while maintaining low encryption cost. It also helped to understand which QC_x

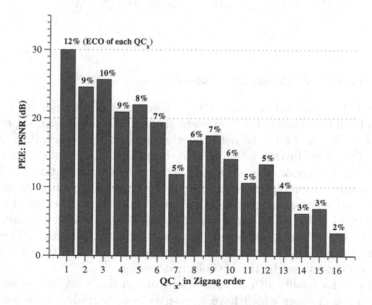

Fig. 2. Classification model results based on PEE (PSNR) and ECO_{QC_x} of QC_x in Zigzag order

can be targeted for better quality of encryption than others. This led to propose a classification model of QC_x based on PEE indicators.

Since the performance of any individual QC_x did not reach the optimal PEE, and remained ineffective against the benchmark results, there was a need to seek for combinations of QC_x to accomplish this target. However, exploring all possible combinations of 16 $QC_{x=1-16}$ can often be impractical, a smaller subsets of these individual coefficients were first chosen. Here, based on the study of the performance of individual QC_x, 4 classes (or groups) were defined across the entire PEE range. The details of these classes are shown in the Table 1. The class that has the highest quality of encryption (25-30 dB), with $QC_{x=1}$ has alone been categorized into Class 1. Class 2 and Class 3 include the $QC_{x=2}$ - $QC_{x=5}$ and $QC_{x=6}$ - $QC_{x=12}$ respectively. These 2 classes have a mid level of quality of encryption (10-25 dB). Class 4 includes the $QC_{x=13}$ - $QC_{x=16}$ which have the least quality of encryption (¡10 dB) QC_x.

Table 1. Classification model outcomes, classified QC_x based on the PEE indicator (PSNR) range.

Classification (Classes)	PEE (PSNR)	ECO (ECO_{QC_x})
Class 1: $QC_{x=1}$	(25-30) dB	12 %
Class 2: $QC_{x=2}$ - $QC_{x=5}$	(20-25) dB	(8-10) %
Class 3: $QC_{x=6}$ - $QC_{x=12}$	(10-20) dB	(5-7) %
Class 4: $QC_{x=13}$ - $QC_{x=16}$	(5-10) dB	(2-4) %

3.3   Optimization: Combined Assessment

In the second step of assessments, the performances of the individual classes generated from the classification step were studied. In this context, experiments on individual classes of QC_x did not reach the targeted benchmark PEE (PEE_τ) of 31 dB. Therefore, further fusion of QC_x between the pairs of classes of QC_x in a hierarchical manner were explored such that the combination yielded significant savings in encryption cost and improvement in quality. A subset of these proposed schemes assessed is summarized in Table 2. The first 4 schemes are examples of accepted SE proposals ($Case_{A1}$-$Case_{A4}$), while the following 4 schemes ($Case_{R1}$-$Case_{R4}$) represent the unaccepted SE proposals. These proposed schemes are a product of fewer combinations that can be accomplished using the constraints set by the optimization model.

Based on the quality of encryption and encryption cost indicators shown in Fig. 3, a set of cases which have a positive confidentiality level have been identified. This set of cases have high encryption cost saving of nearly (60 % - 78 %). One observation that can be highlighted from Table 2 is that, all accepted

Table 2. Optimization model outcomes: 8 proposed schemes (4 accepted and 4 unaccepted)

SE (Cases)	Class	Accepted (SE)	PEE (Gaining)	ECO (Saving)	QC_x (Zigzag order)
$Case_{A1}$	1-2	Yes	+0.18 dB	78 %	$x = 1, 3$
$Case_{A2}$	1-2	Yes	+0.35 dB	69 %	$x = 1 - 3$
$Case_{A3}$	1-2	Yes	+0.63 dB	61 %	$x = 1 - 3, 5$
$Case_{A4}$	1-2	Yes	+2.51 dB	60 %	$x = 1 - 4$
$Case_{R1}$	4	No	-23.37 dB	88 %	$x = 13 - 16$
$Case_{R2}$	1	No	-0.8 dB	88 %	$x = 1$
$Case_{R3}$	3-4	No	-15.20 dB	77 %	$x = 9 - 12$
$Case_{R4}$	2-3	No	-13.12 dB	75 %	$x = 5 - 8$

proposals are based on the combination of QC_x from Class 1 and Class 2. As an example, the SE designer could save 60 % of the encryption cost by targeting the first 4 QC ($Case_{A4}$) only, as opposed to targeting all QC (as in [12]). Moreover, the scheme will also yield higher quality of encryption (PEE gaining is 2.5 dB on average). In another example, the designer could gain more than 75 % of encryption cost saving by implementing the $Case_{A1}$ (with $QC_{x=1}$ and $QC_{x=3}$).

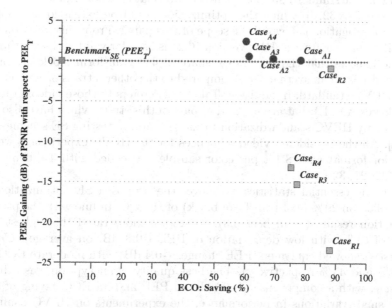

Fig. 3. The proposed SE optimization results compared to the $Benchmark_{SE}$: The accepted optimization (circles) and the unaccepted optimization (squares)

Table 3. The set of benchmark video sequences used to study the performance of the proposed optimizations in HEVC video codec

Sequences		Frames			Transform	Cases (ECO saving)			
Class	Name	Resolution	Number	Rate	4 x 4 Share	$Case_{A1}$	$Case_{A2}$	$Case_{A3}$	$Case_{A4}$
A	People On Street	2560 x 1600	150	30	28 %	56 %	38 %	20 %	37 %
	Traffic		150	30	23 %	55 %	39 %	20 %	38 %
B	BQ Terrace	1920 x 1080	600	60	28 %	69 %	57 %	42 %	55 %
	Kimono 1		240	24	6 %	49 %	35 %	17 %	34 %
	Park Scene		240	24	25 %	59 %	43 %	26 %	43 %
C	Basketball Drill	832 x 480	500	50	40 %	66 %	52 %	39 %	49 %
	BQ Mall		600	60	34 %	63 %	49 %	36 %	46 %
	Race Horses		300	30	26 %	66 %	52 %	39 %	50 %
D	Basketball Pass	416 x 240	500	50	31 %	65 %	51 %	37 %	47 %
	Blowing Bubbles		500	50	61 %	69 %	55 %	45 %	51 %
	BQ Square		600	60	56 %	78 %	68 %	59 %	63 %
E	Four People	1280 x 720	600	60	23 %	58 %	36 %	21 %	33 %
	Johnny		600	60	12 %	49 %	33 %	19 %	29 %
	Kristen And Sara		600	60	14 %	58 %	40 %	27 %	35 %
Average					**29 %**	**61 %**	**46 %**	**32 %**	**43 %**

3.4 HEVC Case Study

The combined assessment of the targeted QC_x classes revealed superior performance of 4 schemes. In this section, these 4 acceptable schemes are validated using the HEVC standard on the 4 x 4 transform block size only. However, HEVC being the latest standard supports three additional transform block sizes: 8 x 8, 16 x 16, and 32 x 32, to which the optimization could be extended and applied to. This investigation is beyond the scope of this paper. From this point onward, HEVC Reference Software (HM) version 16.2[4] is used for validation experiments.

Table 3 shows that the percentage share of 4x4 transform block size on the HEVC codec is on an average 29 % compared to the other 3 transform block sizes for the HEVC standard. In addition, Table 3 also refers to those video sequences (from classes A to E) that are selected as part of this study, which have also been used in many HEVC standardization tasks [14] and in testing SE schemes such as in [4]. All the considered video sequences for the HEVC experiments were in 4:2:0 color format with 8 bit per color sample and coded with 4 different QP values (22, 27, 32 and 37).

Using the essential statistics as above, the proposed SE optimization has been applied on 29 % (4x4 transform block) of the QC. In line with the previous optimization results (as in Sect. 3.3), $Case_{A1}$ demonstrated the highest ECO savings of 61 % with low depreciation of PEE (-0.8 dB, on average). $Case_{A2}$ and $Case_{A4}$ showed equivalent PEE changes (-0.4 dB) with moderate ECO saving (46 % and 43 % respectively). The best quality of encryption was achieved by $Case_{A3}$ with a compromise of -0.1 dB in PEE and an ECO saving of 32 %. Despite small variations in performance, the experiments on HEVC confirmed

---

[4] HEVC software repository (main at HHI), http://hevc.hhi.fraunhofer.de.

that the judicious choice of targeted QC_x needs to be made for achieving favorable trade-off between encryption cost and quality.

4 Conclusion

In this paper, the classification, optimization and validation stages of applying selective encryption for video confidentiality has been introduced. The classification model assesses and groups the targeted QC independently. The optimization model proposes the schemes (with combined QC) with acceptable quality of encryption (PEE) above the targeted quality of encryption (PEE_τ), then sorts them based on the encryption cost saving (ECO). The optimized selection of QC for selective encryption indicates an enhancement in PEE of up to 2.5 dB (PSNR) and an ECO saving between 60% and 78%. An adaptive system may trade-off 18% ECO to enhance PEE with more than 2 dB (PSNR) by utilizing $Case_{A4}$ which guarantees the minimum PEE.

References

1. Pande, A., Zambreno, J.: Securing Multimedia Content Using Joint Compression and Encryption, Embedded Multimedia Security Systems, vol. Part 1, pp. 23–30. Springer, London (2013)
2. Yang, S., Sun, S.: A video encryption method based on chaotic maps in DCT domain. Prog. Nat. Sci. **18**(10), 1299–1304 (2008)
3. Wei, Z., Wu, Y., Ding, X., Deng, R.H.: A scalable and format-compliant encryption scheme for H.264/SVC bitstreams. Sig. Process. Image Commun. **27**(9), 1011–1024 (2012)
4. Shahid, Z., Puech, W.: Visual Protection of HEVC Video by Selective Encryption of CABAC Binstrings. IEEE Trans. Multimedia **16**(1), 24–36 (2014)
5. Stutz, T., Uhl, A.: A survey of H.264 AVC/SVC encryption. IEEE Trans. Circuits Syst. Video Technol. **22**(3), 325–339 (2012)
6. Saini, M., Atrey, P., Mehrotra, S., Kankanhalli, M.: Anonymous surveillance. In: 2011 IEEE International Conference on Multimedia and Expo (ICME), pp. 1–60 July 2011
7. Boho, A., Van Wallendael, G., Dooms, A., De Cock, J., Braeckman, G., Schelkens, P., Preneel, B., Van de Walle, R.: End-to-end security for video distribution: the combination of encryption, watermarking, and video adaptation. IEEE Signal Process. Mag. **30**(2), 97–107 (2013)
8. Wang, Y., O'Neill, M., Kurugollu, F.: Adaptive binary mask for privacy region protection. In: 2012 IEEE International Symposium on Circuits and Systems (ISCAS), pp. 1127–1130 May 2012
9. Dufaux, F., Ebrahimi, T.: Scrambling for privacy protection in video surveillance systems. IEEE Trans. Circuits Syst. Video Technol. **18**(8), 1168–1174 (2008)
10. Tong, L., Dai, F., Zhang, Y., Li, J.: Restricted H.264/AVC video coding for privacy region scrambling. In: 2010 17th IEEE International Conference on Image Processing (ICIP), pp. 2089–2092 September 2010
11. Yeung, S.-K.A., Zhu, S., Zeng, B.: Partial video encryption based on alternating transforms. IEEE Signal Process. Lett. **16**(10), 893–896 (2009)

12. Shahid, Z., Chaumont, M., Puech, W.: Fast protection of H.264/AVC by selective encryption of CABAC. In: IEEE International Conference on Multimedia and Expo, 2009. ICME 2009, pp. 1038–1041 July 2009
13. Muhit, A., Pickering, M., Frater, M., Arnold, J.: Video coding using elastic motion model and larger blocks. IEEE Trans. Circuits Syst. Video Technol. **20**(5), 661–672 (2010)
14. Sullivan, G., Ohm, J., Han, W.-J., Wiegand, T.: Overview of the High Efficiency Video Coding (HEVC) standard. IEEE Trans. Circuits Syst. Video Technol. **22**(12), 1649–1668 (2012)

Near-Lossless PCA-Based Compression of Seabed Surface with Prediction

Paweł Forczmański[(✉)] and Wojciech Maleika

Faculty of Computer Science and Information Technology,
West Pomeranian University of Technology, Żołnierska Str. 52,
71–210 Szczecin, Poland
{pforczmanski,wmaleika}@wi.zut.edu.pl

Abstract. The paper presents a compression method based on Principal Component Analysis applied to reduce the volume of data in seabed Digital Terrain Model. Such data have to be processed in a manner very different from typical digital images because of practical aspects of analysed problem. Hence, the developed algorithm features a variable compression ratio and a possibility to control a maximal reconstruction error. The main objective is to build an orthogonal base and find a number of PCA coefficients representing analysed surface with an acceptable reconstruction accuracy. We present two variants of processing: an iterative compression approach and an approach predicting a number of coefficients before compression starts. It yields much lower computational demand and is faster. The later algorithm employs several statistical measures of an input surface describing its complexity at the prediction stage. Employed, simple classifier based on Classification and Regression Tree do not introduce high additional time overhead. Performed experiments on real data showed high compression ratios, better than for typical DCT-based methods. The possible application of developed method is modern data management system employed in maritime industry.

1 Introduction

Most of bodies of water (in terms of large accumulations of water, such as oceans, seas, and lakes) have a specific structure, created by common physical phenomena, mainly from tectonic movement, and sediment from various sources. Their main areas are abyssal plains featuring variable forms and structures. The knowledge of such forms is crucial in many different application areas, e.g. maritime cartography, deep-sea exploration, hydrography, environmental protection and natural resources exploitation.

The use of water areas in most cases requires the knowledge of detailed bathymetric data. This type of information is more and more frequently visualized and processed with geo-information tools, so that more profound and comprehensive analyses can be made. At present, sounding by a multibeam echosounder (MBES) is one of the most effective and most accurate methods of depth measurements, yielding a set of measured points covering the entire seabed. As a rule, multibeam

M. Kamel and A. Campilho (Eds.): ICIAR 2015, LNCS 9164, pp. 119–128, 2015.
DOI: 10.1007/978-3-319-20801-5_13

echosounder data recordings consist of a huge collection of measurement points, characterized by irregular spatial distribution. Such data, due to their large quantity and irregular distribution are not suitable for direct processing, such as visualization or analysis. For these reasons sounding data are processed into more ordered structures, such as grid (regular square network), that describes a digital terrain model (DTM) [9,10,17]. Grid structures are often created through interpolation of measurement data [9,16,18].

Thanks to advanced equipment (multibeam echosounders, precise positioning systems) and complex numerical algorithms, we get high quality output data. However, the constant increase in their volume and the need of retaining their quality makes a problem of compression very up-to-date [22]. The proposed algorithm of compression should meet specific requirements such as high compression ratio and accurate reconstruction. Hence, it will make the measurements of larger areas possible. Input data characteristics and their amount determine the most important features of compression method. For practical application, it should be a lossy compression (giving higher compression ratios), incorporate predefined, maximal reconstruction error in any grid node (difference between original and reconstructed depth), involve adaptive and variable compression ratio in small sub regions (maximal compression for requested accuracy), implement fast retrieval and reconstruction for small sub areas.

1.1   Previous Works

Despite the fact that the problem of handling measurement data is present in scientific literature [1,3,13], it seems that a particular issue of seabed data compression has not been solved in an acceptable way. Although certain approaches have been proposed, they only work in limited cases [7,12] or are insufficient for modern applications [2,23,26,27]. Even the sophisticated software known to the authors of this work and used in maritime business does not provide any satisfactory data compression.

On the other hand, there are many scientific works addressing general compression of elevation (depth) data. Most of them describe the compression of land surfaces, often gathered using the Light Detection and Ranging technology (LIDAR) and stored as grayscale images. The authors of [20] proposed the Triangulated irregular network DEM (TIN DEM) compression using second-generation wavelet transform (SGWT). In [24] the Over-determined Laplacian Partial Differential Equation solver (ODETLAP) method was presented, applied to the compression and reconstruction of terrain data used in GIS systems. In [8] different methods of DEM images compression were proposed. In [28] authors described surface data compression by means of overdetermined Laplacian approximation. In [21] compression of elevation data based on general JPEG-LS was presented. In [1] an application of 3-D DCT and hybrid DPCM/DCT for compression of hyperspectral imagery was presented.

Above literature survey shows, that, most of the works in this area deals with compression of elevation data stored in images (bitmaps). The assumption about regular structure of depth measurements was also taken in this work.

It is extremely difficult to compare the results of different research performed on various datasets (mainly DEMs and DTMs). Most of the works related to the compression are devoted to land data, which is gathered and processed in a different manner. Moreover, such data have different characteristics than seabed, i.e. rapid changes of shape, often faults versus smooth forms, large areas of constant depth (in case of seabed).

Hence, the article is focused on two aspects of the presented problem. The first one is near-lossless compression of seabed data by means of two-dimensional analysis and projection based on two-dimensional Principal Component Analysis. It is an advancement over the method presented in [19]. The second one is the increase in computations speed thanks to predicting an initial number of compression coefficients. The idea of using a set of simple statistical measures and a simple classifier learned on ground-truth surfaces and compression coefficients is inspired by a more general approach applied to natural images, which was described in [5]. In this case, however, the features are slightly different and the classification is no longer based on a linear model.

2 Algorithm Description

2.1 Assumptions

During the compression of DTM-based measurements we have to cope with data denoted with real values (representing depth). Such an approach is very different from typical digital image processing techniques where pixels are denoted with integer numbers. The main objective of compression is therefore to obtain the highest compression factor while not exceeding pre-defined reconstruction error. Both assumptions should be fulfilled in order to satisfy IHO standards [11]. During compression involving PCA we have to select the minimal number of transform coefficients satisfying criteria related to compression factor and reconstruction accuracy.

2.2 Base Algorithm

The compression algorithm (see Fig. 1) is divided into two stages, namely offline processing of reference surfaces (based on two-dimensional Principal Component Analysis) in order to create a set of eigensurfaces (similar to eigenfaces [25]) and online compression of actual measurement data based on two-dimensional Karhunen-Loeve Transform. We intentionally distinguish PCA from KLT, since the first one is used for analysis and the later - for transformation [14]. Hence, the compression consists of the following steps:

1. Decompose data matrix into non-overlapping, square blocks D of $N \times N$ elements,
2. For each block D:
   (a) perform two-dimensional Karhunen-Loeve Transform;
   (b) set components number M in each direction to 1;

(c) extract a square submatrix of $M \times M$ form upper-left corner of 2DKLT spectrum of D;

(d) perform inverse two-dimensional Karhunen-Loeve Transform for spectrum with $M \times M$ components (the rest is set to zero);

(e) evaluate the difference (reconstruction error E between original block D and reconstructed one);

(f) if error E is greater than a set threshold (according to given IHO norm) increment M (while $M < N$) and go to (2c);

(g) otherwise store $M \times M$ components of 2DKLT spectrum for analysed block D,

3. Save all 2DKLT components for all blocks describing whole surface.

We applied 2DPCA/2DKLT as it has some advantages over typical Discrete Cosine Transform, namely it creates an optimal base for any specific class of images (in this case - seabed surface) and captures most of energy in few first components of its spectrum. In comparison to the classical PCA/KLT where we have to create large covariance and transformation matrices of $N^2 \times N^2$ elements, we create two transformation matrices, one for row and one for column representations of data block of $N \times N$ elements [14]. It makes handling large blocks easier and requires less memory space.

If we assume a seabed surface being an image, then the application of 2DPCA/ 2DKLT is rather straightforward. This approach to the surface compression assumes also that data are placed in a regular grid and from this point of view differs from other "geometrical" approaches [15]. The reconstruction error is calculated on a basis of maximum absolute difference and verified according to appropriate surface class [11] (in terms of threshold). In order to achieve adequate accuracy, data were stored on real (double precision) values.

2.3   Predicting the Number of Coefficients

Proposed algorithm, in its basic form, is rather straightforward in terms of looking for final M value for each block, hence the steps (2c,2d,2e) are executed many times, making the search for optimal compression factor a typical linear search problem. During experiments, those steps were often repeated more than 10 times, which is far from optimum. The obvious solution is a binary search, that halves the number of items to check with each iteration, so locating proper M value takes logarithmic time. For example, if $N = 32$ then we perform $log_2(N) = 5$ searches for each block.

In order to further increase the speed of computations (in terms of decreasing the number of reconstruction/error estimation stages) we propose to predict M value on a base of surface characteristics. It is clear than the more complex the surface is, the less it can be compressed (hence the number of 2DPCA components is larger). Therefore, we calculate a set of characteristics for each block as an input to the classifier and get the value of M. Since the prediction of M is not 100 % error-free, we introduce a stage of local search in the neighborhood of predicted M to find its final value. Full algorithm is presented in Fig. 1.

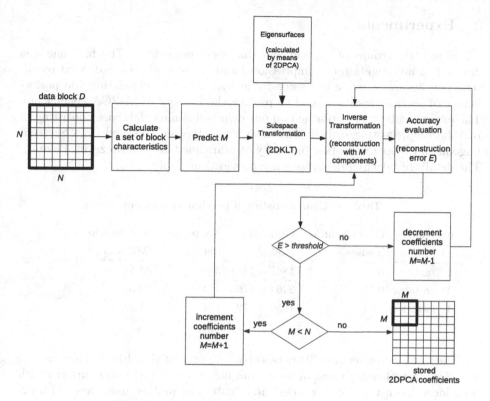

Fig. 1. Compression algorithm with prediction

2.4   Surface Characteristics in Blocks

We investigated several typical scalar measures that describe the complexity level of surface under compression. In our investigations we assumed, that there is a link between surface complexity (seen as a grayscale image) and reconstruction accuracy (in terms of compression quality). Hence we propose to use the following measures calculated for each block being compressed, independently: variance, standard deviation, entropy, contrast, autocorrelation, features derived from Gray-Level Coocurrence Matrix (contrast, correlation, energy, homogenity) calculated for horizontal and vertical directions in two-pixel neighborhood. Such selection was inspired by our previous works aimed at graphical objects detection and classification [4,6].

Hence, we create a 13-element vector for each block and on its base predict compression ratio. The further analysis leads to the conclusion that not all values are equally important, hence we investigated an additional variant of feature vectors - a reduced one, containing only standard deviation, entropy, contrast, and autocorrelation. They were selected as a compromise between calculation complexity and their discrimination ability.

3   Experiments

There are two groups of experiments that were performed. The first one was devoted to investigation of compression factor in respect to pre-defined reconstruction accuracy, while the second one was aimed at evaluating the performance of several classifiers used to predict the number of 2DPCA coefficients. The experiments were performed on our own benchmark database consisting of real data representing seabed. The measurements were collected from Szczecin Lagoon and Pomeranian Bay (courtesy of Maritime Office in Szczecin, Poland). The details of benchmark surfaces are provided in Table 1.

Table 1. Characteristics of benchmark surfaces

No	Name	Grid resolution [meters]	Grid size [nodes]	No. points [thousands]	Raw filesize [MBytes]
1	gate	0.5	1888 × 1888	3081	23.51
2	rotator	0.75	2464 × 1760	4336	33.09
3	wrecks	0.01	1856 × 672	1247	9.52

The surfaces rendered in 3D perspective are presented in Fig. 2. They include a surface of rather high and uniform complexity ("rotator") and surfaces with high local depth variance ("wrecks" and "gate") as well as many areas of near-constant depth. The "gate" is a visualization of a route gate, "wrecks" presents an area with car wrecks, and "rotator" is a place where ships can rotate. They have been intentionally chosen to cover most representative types of seabed. While the seabed in most areas in the world is not so variable the results of the experiments should give good approximation of projected efficiency of the method. The measurements are given in meters. Hence, after decomposition, the benchmark database consists of three above surfaces decomposed (in total) in 3875 blocks of 32 × 32 elements. We investigated four accuracies, namely 0.01, 0.05, 0.1 and 0.3 m, which are much more strict than IHO-suggested accuracies for that kind of areas (more than 0.3 m).

The results of compression experiment on all benchmark surfaces for 2DPCA are provided in Fig. 3. As for comparison, we investigated the same procedure, but using classical 2DDCT approach (the results are also provided). It should be noted that the compression ratio does not take into consideration the size of eigenvectors which are common for all surfaces. If they are calculated for a representative set of seabed surfaces, they can be taken as a constant for the algorithm.

As it can be seen, the compression ratio is, in general, much higher for 2DPCA-based approach. It increases with the decrease of reconstruction error and increase of block size. For small acceptable errors and small block size, the difference between methods is less visible. Due to practical aspects of implementation (see previous research [19]), block size of 32 × 32 pixels is advisable.

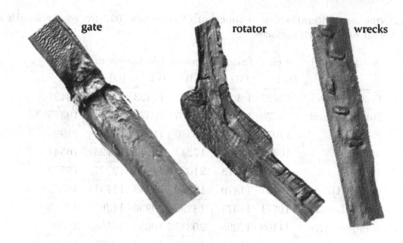

Fig. 2. Benchmark surfaces

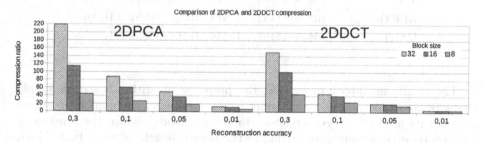

Fig. 3. Compression efficiency for 2DPCA/2DKLT and 2DDCT approaches as a function of block size and reconstruction error

At the prediction stage we selected several state-of-the-art classifiers, namely: Decision Trees (Random Tree, Random Forest, CART, REPTree, J48), Naive Bayes Classifier (NBC), Multi-Layer Perceptron (MLP), Nearest Neighbor with $k = 1$ (1NN), Support Vector Machine (both with RBF and linear kernels). We employed typical 10-fold cross validation technique to make the results objective.

As a ground truth, we took values of M (the number of iterations) calculated for each test block using above mentioned linear search (brute-force strategy). As for the comparison, we included the number of iterations using binary search (also described above). The performance was evaluated on a basis of the number of correctly predicted M values and the number of additional reconstruction/error estimation iterations in case of failure (consisting of increment/decrement stages in algorithm presented in Fig. 1).

Based to the results, we selected CART classifier as a compromise between accuracy and computational overhead. It was slightly worse than MLP, but much more efficient (especially at the stage of learning). Using prediction, for the most strict 0.01 m accuracy, we are able to reduce the number of compression iterations (in case of $N = 32$) from 32421 (linear search, for those particular benchmark data) and 19375 (binary search, theoretical value) to just 16773.

Table 2. Number of iterations as a function of accuracy, feature vector length and classifier for all benchmark surfaces

Accuracy [m]	4-el.	feature	vector	13-el.	feature	vector
	0.1	0.05	0.01	0.1	0.05	0.01
Linear Search	15423	18934	32421	15423	18934	32421
Binary Search	19375	19375	19375	19375	19375	19375
NBC	11077	12035	19380	11611	13237	21926
MLP	10414	11006	17243	10111	10723	16544
1NN	11175	12278	21024	11295	12247	19552
SVM (RBF)	10797	11470	18060	10936	11741	18346
SVM (Linear)	10771	11371	18292	10936	11308	17905
Random Tree	11109	12098	20347	10609	11508	18560
Random Forest	10495	11207	17952	10061	10778	16655
J48	10678	11503	18327	10290	11124	17059
REPTree	10498	11144	17513	10224	10981	16780
CART	10439	11101	17344	10166	10892	16773

The results in Table 2 prove that the proposed algorithm based on simple image (surface) features and a classifier is able to predict the number of stored components used at the compression stage and, hence, reduce the number of computations (in average, comparing to the binary search, of more than 34 %). As it can be seen, the usage of full, 13-element feature vector is not justified. In most cases, the best results gave the Multi-Layer Perceptron, hoverer it is complex in training. When we forget the computational overhead associated with calculating four simple features and an appropriate, unsophisticated classifier (in most cases tree-based, e.g. CART or J48), it leads to the real improvement in performance.

It is important for the proposed algorithm, that a total computational overhead depends not only on the number of reconstruction/error estimation iterations but also on the features calculation and classification. However, those operations are rather fast and do not influence much the total computations time. It should be also noted that the algorithm's efficiency (in terms of a gain in computations speed in comparison to binary search) depends on the requested accuracy. For example, it gives 46 % less reconstruction/error estimation operations for accuracy of 0.1 m, while 43 % for 0.05 m and 11 % for 0.01 m, respectively.

4   Summary

A novel approach for compression of seabed data was presented. It consists of data processing stage employing Principal Component Analysis and some elements from digital image processing together with data-mining algorithms.

It has been tested on real data and proved its efficiency. In a comparison to typical Discrete Cosine Transform it gives significantly higher compression ratio and a significant decrease in computational overhead (in comparison to direct method of searching the coefficients number). Another important practical aspect of the proposed method is that in comparison to the classical one-dimensional PCA/KLT, developed algorithm requires less memory and processing power. The performed experiments showed also that when we employ much lower number of surface features (4 out of 13), we will be able to significantly reduce the number of operations needed while retaining high reconstruction accuracy and compression rate.

References

1. Abousleman, G.P., Marcellin, M.W., Hunt, B.R.: Compression of hyperspectral imagery using the 3-D DCT and hybrid DPCM/DCT. IEEE Trans. Geosci. Remote Sens. **33**(1), 26–34 (1995)
2. Bruun, B.T., Nilsen, S.: Wavelet representation of large digital terrain models. Comput. Geosci. **29**, 695–703 (2003)
3. Cao, W., Li, B., Zhang, Y.: A remote sensing image fusion method based on PCA transform and wavelet packet transform. Neural Netw. Sig. Process. **2**, 976–981 (2003)
4. Forczmański, P., Markiewicz, A.: Low-Level image features for stamps detection and classification. Adv. Intell. Syst. Comput. **226**, 383–392 (2013)
5. Forczmański, P., Mantiuk, R.: Adaptive and quality-aware storage of JPEG files in the web environment. In: Chmielewski, L.J., Kozera, R., Shin, B.-S., Wojciechowski, K. (eds.) ICCVG 2014. LNCS, vol. 8671, pp. 212–219. Springer, Heidelberg (2014)
6. Forczmański, P., Markiewicz, A.: Stamps detection and classification using simple features ensemble. Math. Prob. Eng. Article ID 367879 (2014) (in press)
7. Fowler, J.E., Fox, D.N.: Wavelet based coding of three dimensional oceanographic images around land masses. In: Proceedings of the IEEE International Conference on Image Processing, Vancouver, pp. 431–434 (2000)
8. Franklin, W.R., Said, A.: Lossy compression of elevation data. In: Seventh International Symposium on Spatial Data Handling, Delft, pp. 29–41(1996)
9. Gaboardi, C., Mitishita, E.A., Firkowski, H.: Digital terrain modeling generalization with base in wavelet transform. Bol. de Cienc. Geodesicas **17**(1), 115–129 (2011)
10. Hamilton, E.L.: Geoacoustic modeling of the sea floor. J. Acoust. Soc. Am. **68**(5), 1313–1340 (1980)
11. IHO standards for hydrographic surveys, Publication No. 44 of International Hydrographic Organization, 5th Edition (2008). http://www.iho.int/iho_pubs/standard/S-44_5E.pdf
12. Kazimierski, W., Zaniewicz, G.: Analysis of the possibility of using radar tracking method based on GRNN for processing sonar spatial data. In: Kryszkiewicz, M., Cornelis, C., Ciucci, D., Medina-Moreno, J., Motoda, H., Raś, Z.W. (eds.) RSEISP 2014. LNCS, vol. 8537, pp. 319–326. Springer, Heidelberg (2014)
13. Klimesh, M.: Compression of Multispectral Images. TDA Progress Report. 42–129 (1997)
14. Kukharev, G., Forczmański, P.: Facial images dimensionality reduction and recognition by means of 2DKLT. Mach. Graph. Vis. **16**(3/4), 401–425 (2007)

15. Maes, J., Bultheel, A.: Surface compression with hierarchical powell-sabin B-Splines. Int. J. Wavelets Multiresolut. Inf. Process. **4**(1), 177–196 (2004)
16. Maleika, W., Palczynski, M., Frejlichowski, D.: Interpolation methods and the accuracy of bathymetric seabed models based on multibeam echosounder data. In: Pan, J.-S., Chen, S.-M., Nguyen, N.T. (eds.) ACIIDS 2012, Part III. LNCS, vol. 7198, pp. 466–475. Springer, Heidelberg (2012)
17. Maleika, W.: The influence of track configuration and multibeam echosounder parameters on the accuracy of seabed DTMs obtained in shallow water. Earth Sci. Inform. **6**(2), 47–69 (2013)
18. Maleika, W.: Moving average optimization in digital terrain model generation based on test multibeam echosounder data. Geo-Mar. Lett. **35**(1), 61–68 (2015)
19. Maleika, W., Czapiewski, P.: Evaluation of KLT method for controlled lossy compression of high-resolution seabeds DTM. Earth Science Informatics (in press). doi:10.1007/S12145-014-0191-1
20. Pradhan, B., Mansor, S.: Three dimensional terrain data compression using second generation wavelets. In: 8th International Conference on Data, Text and Web Mining and Their Business Applications. WIT Transactions on Information and Communication Technologies 38 (2007)
21. Rane, S.D., Sapiro, G.: Evaluation of JPEG-LS, the new lossless and controlled-lossy still image compression standard, for compression of high-resolution elevation data. IEEE Trans. Geosci. Remote Sens. **39**(1), 2298–2306 (2001)
22. Stateczny, A., Wlodarczyk-Sielicka, M.: Self-organizing artificial neural networks into hydrographic big data reduction process. In: Kryszkiewicz, M., Cornelis, C., Ciucci, D., Medina-Moreno, J., Motoda, H., Raś, Z.W. (eds.) RSEISP 2014. LNCS, vol. 8537, pp. 335–342. Springer, Heidelberg (2014)
23. Stateczny, A., Łubczonek J.: Radar sensors implementation in river information services in poland. In: Proceedings of 15th International Radar Symposium (IRS), pp. 1–5 (2014)
24. Stookey, J., Xie, Z., Cutler, B., Franklin, W., Tracy, D., Andrade, M.: Parallel ODETLAP for terrain compression and reconstruction. In: GIS 2008: Proceedings of the 16th ACM SIGSPATIAL International Conference on Advances in Geographic Information Systems, pp. 1–9 (2008)
25. Turk, M., Pentland, A.: Eigenfaces for recognition. J. Cogn. Neurosci. **3**(1), 71–86 (1991)
26. Wessel, P.: Compression of large data grids for Internet transmission. Comput. Geosci. **29**, 665–671 (2003)
27. Wright, D.J., Goodchild, M.F.: Data from the deep: implications for the GIS community. Int. J. Geograph. Inf. Sci. **11**(6), 523–528 (1997)
28. Xie, Z., Franklin, W., Cutler, B., Andrade, M., Inanc, M., Tracy, D.: Surface compression using over-determined Laplacian approximation. In: Proceedings of SPIE, vol. 6697. Advanced Signal Processing Algorithms, Architectures, and Implementations XVII, San Diego CA. International Society for Optical Engineering (2007)

Adaptive Weighted Neighbors Lossless Image Coding

AbdulWahab Kabani and Mahmoud R. El-Sakka$^{(\boxtimes)}$

Department of Computer Science,
The University of Western Ontario, London, ON, Canada
{akabani5,melsakka}@uwo.ca

Abstract. Adaptive Weighted Neighbors Lossless Image Coding *AWN* is a symmetric lossless image compression algorithm. *AWN* makes two initial predictions, creates a weighted combination of the initial predictions before adjusting the prediction to end up with the final prediction. In order to achieve more compression, we encode the error in multiple bins depending on the expected error magnitude. Also, instead of encoding the signed error, the algorithm attempts to guess the sign and encodes the error magnitude and whether guessing the sign was successful or not.

Keywords: Image compression · Lossless compression · Context modeling · Adaptive prediction · Entropy coding

1 Introduction

Data compression is the process of representing information using fewer bits than the original representation would use. The main objective of data compression is to reduce the size of the information being encoded. As the size of different kinds of data (text, audio, and video) is growing, the need to have better compression techniques is increasing [5,7].

In general, compression can be broken down into two major fields, namely: lossy compression and lossless compression. Lossy compression usually achieves excellent compression rates at the expense of information loss. In other words, the reconstructed information after compression and decompression is not an exact replica of the original information before compression. On the other hand, lossless compression achieves less compression than lossy. The main advantage of lossless compression is that the reconstructed information matches the original information exactly. This is very important for legal and medical applications. The research presented in this paper is a lossless image compression. Therefore, the reconstructed image is exactly the same as the original image.

There are many methods that are used on image to achieve compression. These methods include statistical methods (Huffman encoding [3] and Arithmetic encoding [9]), dictionary methods (Lempel-Ziv-77 (LZ77) scheme [11] and Lempel-Ziv-78 (LZ78) scheme [12]), prediction methods (Differential pulse-code modulation

© Springer International Publishing Switzerland 2015
M. Kamel and A. Campilho (Eds.): ICIAR 2015, LNCS 9164, pp. 129–138, 2015.
DOI: 10.1007/978-3-319-20801-5_14

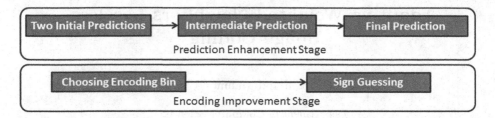

Fig. 1. Algorithm Overview: AWN consists of two main stages. The first stage is the *Prediction Enhancement Stage*, which consists of three steps that starts with two *initial predictions* and ends with a *final prediction*. The second stage aims to improve the entropy to achieve a better compression. This is achieved by grouping the errors in different encoding bins and attempting to guess the sign of the error.

(DPCM) scheme [2]), and context methods (Context-based Adaptive Lossless Image Codec (CALIC) scheme [10], LOw COmplexity LOssless COmpression for Images (LOCO-I) scheme [8], Prediction by Partial Matching (PPM) scheme [1], and Weighted Ratio-based Adaptive Lossless Image Coding [4]).

In this paper, we introduce Adaptive Weighted Neighbors (AWN) Lossless Image Coding. AWN is a lossless image codec. It combines statistical-based, prediction-based, and context-based techniques to achieve an excellent compression rate. The rest of the paper is organized as follows. Section 2 provides a general overview about the proposed algorithm. Sections 3 to 6 explain each component of the codec in more details. Section 7 presents our experimental works by showing the bit rates we achieved along with a comparison with other lossless compression algorithms. Finally, Sect. 8 concludes this work.

2   General Overview

The system can be broken down into 6 major steps. These steps are: calculating two initial predictions, combining the two predictions, prediction adjustment, error sign guessing, choosing an encoding bin and entropy encoding.

Figure 1 shows how these steps can be broken down into two stages: *prediction enhancement* stage and *encoding improvement* stage. In the *prediction enhancement* stage, we start with two *initial predictions*. Then, we combine them into an *intermediate prediction*. After that, the prediction is adjusted through an *error context feedback*. The aim of this stage is to come up a prediction of the pixel being encoded.

Better compression can be achieved when encoding the error in an effective way. This is done in the *encoding improvement* stage. In this stage, we choose the encoding bin that promises to yield the lowest entropy. In addition, we do not encode the sign of the error. Instead, we try to guess the sign. Finally, we perform entropy encoding such as: arithmetic encoding.

3   Predictors: Calculating Initial Predictions

Statistical redundancy in a set of pixels is the smoothness of the intensity function. In other words, pixels spatially close to each other tend to have similar values. The predictor of AWN views the prediction as depending on the direction of the small changes. There are four directions that we use to calculate the prediction. These directions are: horizontal, diagonal (45 degrees), vertical, diagonal (135 degrees). The direction with the smallest absolute change tends to give the best prediction.

Based on this notion, we designed our predictor. The predictor gives more weight to predictions that are inferred from the directions with the least changes. Equations 1–4 define the gradient magnitude estimates in the four directions:

$$GM_h = ||I_W - I_{WW}|| + ||I_{NW} - I_{NWW}|| + ||I_N - I_{NW}|| + ||I_{NE} - I_N|| \quad (1)$$

$$GM_{D1} = ||I_W - I_{NWW}|| + ||I_{NW} - I_{NNWW}|| + ||I_N - I_{NNW}|| + ||I_{NE} - I_{NN}|| \quad (2)$$

$$GM_v = ||I_W - I_{NW}|| + ||I_{NW} - I_{NNW}|| + ||I_N - I_{NN}|| + ||I_{NE} - I_{NNE}|| \quad (3)$$

$$GM_{D2} = ||I_W - I_N|| + ||I_{NW} - I_{NN}|| + ||I_N - I_{NNE}|| + ||I_{NE} - I_{NNEE}|| \quad (4)$$

where $I_W, I_{WW}, ..., I_{NNEE}$ are the values of the neighbours of the pixel. For example, I_W is the pixel to the west of the current pixel and I_{NW} is the north-west neighbour of the pixel.

Figure 2 shows how we calculate the gradient magnitude estimates in the four directions. The gradient magnitude estimate in each direction is the summation of the absolute differences of the neighboring pixels. The lower the value of the magnitude, the more likely a prediction based on the corresponding direction can yield better results.

The less the magnitude of absolute changes in one direction, the higher the weight of the corresponding pixel should be. In other words, the weight of each pixel is determined by dividing the total absolute changes in all directions by the directional absolute changes.

$$\delta = GM_h + GM_{d1} + GM_v + GM_{d2} \quad (5)$$

$$w_h = \frac{\delta}{GM_h}, w_{d1} = \frac{\delta}{GM_{d1}}, w_v = \frac{\delta}{GM_v}, w_{d2} = \frac{\delta}{GM_{d2}} \quad (6)$$

We define two initial predictions. The first initial prediction is a weighted combination of the neighboring pixels: W, NW, N, and NE. The *Horizontal, Diagonal 1, Horizontal,* and *Diagonal 2* directions correspond to W, NW, N, and NE, respectively. The resulting weights are normalized. We need to normalize them when we calculate the predictions.

$$w_{total1} = w_h + w_{d1} + w_v + w_{d2} \quad (7)$$

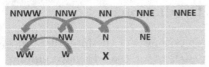

(a) Horizontal Gradient Magnitude

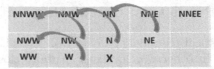

(b) Diagonal (135 degrees) Gradient Magnitude

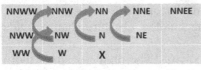

(c) Vertical Gradient Magnitude

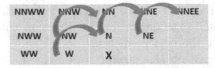

(d) Diagonal (45 degrees) Gradient Magnitude

Fig. 2. Gradient magnitude estimation: (a) The estimation of the horizontal gradient magnitude, which is performed by taking the absolute values of the differences indicated by the arrows. (c),(b) and (d) are the gradient magnitude estimations in the vertical directions and the diagonals respectively.

$$w_{h,norm} = \frac{w_h}{w_{total1}}, w_{d1,norm} = \frac{w_{d1}}{w_{total1}}, w_{v,norm} = \frac{w_v}{w_{total1}}, w_{d2,norm} = \frac{w_{d2}}{w_{total1}} \tag{8}$$

After normalizing the weights for the initial prediction 1, we can now calculate the initial prediction 1. The weights play a significant role in computing the first initial prediction. If the gradient magnitude estimation in one of the four directions is low, the corresponding neighbor will have higher contribution to the first initial prediction.

$$I_{initial1} = w_{h,norm} \times I_W + w_{d1,norm} \times I_{NW} + w_{v,norm} \times I_N + w_{d2,norm} \times I_{NE} \tag{9}$$

The second initial prediction uses only the pixels that correspond to the directions with the least changes and the second least changes (lowest and second lowest gradient magnitude estimations). More weight is given to the pixel that corresponds to the direction with the least change. To do that, we boost the original weight of the pixel with the minimum change. The boosting value will always be larger than 1 because the nominator is always larger than the denominator.

$$w_{LowestBoosted} = \frac{w_{lowest}}{w_{2ndLowest}} \times w_{lowest} \tag{10}$$

In order to use these weights, we should normalize them first. The normalization process is similar to the one we did for the initial prediction 1. We first get the total of the 2 weights. Then, we divide these weights by the total.

$$w_{total2} = w_{LowestBoosted} + w_{2ndLowest} \tag{11}$$

$$w_{LowestBoosted,Norm} = \frac{w_{LowestBoosted}}{w_{total2}} \tag{12}$$

$$w_{2ndSmoothest,Norm} = \frac{w_{2ndSmoothest}}{w_{total2}} \tag{13}$$

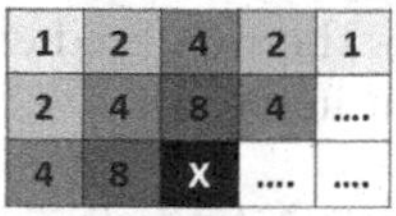

Fig. 3. This figure shows the weights of the neighbours of the pixel being encoded.

Using the normalized weights, we can compute the second initial prediction (Eq. 14). The contribution of the neighbor that corresponds to the best prediction is always more than the one with the second best. For example, if the lowest and second lowest gradient magnitude estimations were in the horizontal and the vertical directions, the best and second neighbors that we use to compute the second initial prediction are the W and N pixels.

$$I_{initial2} = w_{LowestBoosted,Norm} \times I_{best} + w_{2ndSmoothest,Norm} \times I_{2ndbest} \quad (14)$$

4 Combining the Two Predictions

Using the two *initial predictions* we calculated, we compute the *intermediate prediction*. The *intermediate prediction* is a weighted combination of the two initial predictions. We have found that creating a weighted combination of the two initial predictions yields a better compression rate. In order to determine the weight of the two *initial predictions*, we examine their errors for pixels that are spatially close to the pixel being encoded. Pixels closer to the pixel we are encoding are much more important than pixels that are far away. Figure 3 shows the weights of the neighbours surrounding the pixel being encoded.

Using the weights shown in Fig. 3, we can now compute the spatial sum of errors that correspond for the initial prediction 1 and 2 as shown in Eqs. 15 and 16:

$$E_{initial1} = \sum_{n \in Neighbours} w_n \|I_{initial1,n} - I_n\| \quad (15)$$

$$E_{initial2} = \sum_{n \in Neighbours} w_n \|I_{initial2,n} - I_n\| \quad (16)$$

In order to speed up the computation in Eqs. 15 and 16, a shift left operation may be performed instead of the multiplication since all weights are multiples of 2.

To get the *intermediate prediction*, we combine the *initial predictions* for this block. The weight of each initial prediction depends on the value of the sum of *absolute error* E for each prediction. The prediction with the higher *sum of absolute error* E will contribute less to the *intermediate prediction*. On the other hand, the prediction with the lower *sum of absolute error* E will contribute more to the *intermediate prediction*. Equation 17 show how we calculate the weights of each prediction using the spatial error of each:

$$w_{initial1} = 1 - \frac{E_{initial1}}{E_{initial1} + E_{initial2}} \quad (17)$$

$$w_{initial2} = 1 - w_{initial1}$$

The *intermediate prediction* is the weighted combination of the 2 initial predictions. It is calculated as shown in Eq. 18:

$$I_{intermediate} = w_{initial1} \times I_{initial1} + w_{initial2} \times I_{initial2} \qquad (18)$$

5 Contexts

In order to improve the compression performance, we quantize the blocks into a set of contexts based on different features such as: comparisons between the prediction to other pixels in the block, the magnitude of the gradient, the direction of the gradient, and the quantization of the average prediction error in the block. Using contexts helps us to:

- Adjust prediction through error context feedback (Sect. 5.1)
- Guess the sign of the error (Sect. 5.2)
- Choose an Encoding Bin (Sect. 5.3)

5.1 Prediction Adjustment Through Error Context Feedback

After we calculated the intermediate prediction, we adjust the prediction to end up with the final prediction. Adjusting the intermediate prediction to get the final prediction is a very important step. This step removes any redundancy in predicting pixels that belong to the same context. In other words, this step allows the algorithm to improve the quality of the prediction for each context. Equation 19 shows how we calculate the adjustment value. The adjustment value is the result of dividing the running sum of the error for a context by the running count of the pixels that belong to this context.

$$e_C = \frac{sum(C)}{count(C)} \qquad (19)$$

$$I_{final} = I_{intermediate} + e_C$$

5.2 Sign Guessing

When encoding an image, it is expected that the number of positive and the number of negative errors to be almost the same. For example, the total number of $+2$ errors is expected to be similar to -2. Therefore, instead of encoding the sign, we can encode our success or failure in guessing the sign. For example, when the encoder receives the error -2, it knows that the absolute error 2 and we were not successful at guessing the sign. Since both the encoder and decoder use the same method to guess the sign, the sign can be inferred.

In order to guess the sign, we collect the above features about the block and keep track of the number of positive and negative errors for each context. When encoding a pixel, we check its context, if the number of negative error is more than the positive, it is more likely that the sign of error is negative. Therefore, the error magnitude is encoded and in case the guess was not successful, a negative error is encoded.

5.3   Choosing Encoding Bin

Instead of encoding all errors as one sequence of numbers, the performance can be enhanced by grouping the pixels into different bins. Ideally, if all errors in a bin have the same values, the entropy is 0 (for the bin). Of course, this is very unlikely to happen. However, having similar errors in each bin tends to yield better compression.

In order to determine the best bin to add the error to, we examine both the spatial neighbors of the pixel and the context of the pixel.

$$Bin = round(W_{spatial} \times E_{spatial} + W_{context} \times E_{context}) \qquad (20)$$

where $E_{Spatial}$ is the average absolute error of the neighbours surrounding the pixel and $E_{Context}$ is the average absolute error of the context.

In other words, the bin is a weighted combination of the spatial absolute error and the context absolute error. The weights in this equation are calculated as shown in Eqs. 21. If the weighted average of the absolute errors of the encoding block is higher than the context average absolute error, the spatial weight will be low. On the other hand, if it is lower than the context average absolute error, the spatial weight will be high. The values of the spatial weight and the context weight add up to 1.

$$W_{spatial} = 1 - \frac{E_{Spatial}}{E_{Spatial} + E_{Context}}$$

$$W_{context} = 1 - W_{Spatial} \qquad (21)$$

The outcome of this process is an integer that determines the bin number that we will add the error to encode. This number is a weighted combination of the spatial weighted average of the absolute error of the block and the average context error.

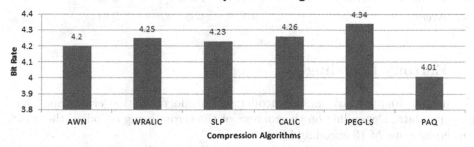

Fig. 4. This figures shows the bit rate (lower values are better) of our algorithm along with other algorithms. *AWN* achieves good results than many well known algorithms.

Table 1. Table showing the compressed size, compression rates, and encoding/decoding times (in seconds) achieved for each image in the Kodak image set. The original size for all images is 393,231 bytes.

Image name	Compressed (Bytes)	Bit rate	Encoding time	Decoding time
Kodim01	251,815	5.12	1.417	0.997
Kodim02	190,330	3.87	1.401	0.919
Kodim03	161,017	3.28	1.308	0.872
Kodim04	194,411	3.96	1.307	0.919
Kodim05	237,627	4.83	1.479	0.981
Kodim06	220,010	4.48	1.416	0.967
Kodim07	166,452	3.39	1.337	0.889
Kodim08	253,493	5.16	1.556	0.982
Kodim09	185,926	3.78	1.323	0.903
Kodim10	187,353	3.81	1.339	0.903
Kodim11	210,567	4.28	1.354	0.936
Kodim12	181,273	3.69	1.274	0.887
Kodim13	288,567	5.87	1.604	1.043
Kodim14	234,230	4.77	1.417	0.965
Kodim15	181,350	3.69	1.34	0.935
Kodim16	194,952	3.97	1.307	0.903
Kodim17	191,591	3.9	1.339	0.919
Kodim18	244,072	4.97	1.432	0.982
Kodim19	213,896	4.35	1.369	0.919
Kodim20	149,730	3.05	1.229	0.889
Kodim21	217,703	4.43	1.4	1.013
Kodim22	217,811	4.43	1.386	0.966
Kodim23	164,854	3.35	1.277	0.888
Kodim24	217,589	4.43	1.386	0.951
Average	-	4.2	1.38	0.94

6   Entropy Encoding

We use an adaptive arithmetic encoder to encode prediction errors and sign guessing data. Depending on the context of the errors being encoded, the error can go into one of 16 encoding bins.

In a similar manner to the entropy encoding in [10], each encoding bin is further split into 2 bins. In other words, the total number of encoding bins is 32. Depending on the value of the error and the bin, the encoder may encode an escape symbol and encode the error in an extended bin. The values of the bins are: $\{5, 9, 12, 13, 15, 17, 21, 25, 29, 33, 37, 41, 46, 57, 93, 128\}$. If the absolute value of an error being encoding is higher than the boundary, an escape symbol is encoded and the error is encoded in a separate bin.

7 Results and Experiments

We tested *AWN* on the well known Kodak image set, which is comprised of 24 gray-scale images. The total size of the images is 9437544 bytes. The overall bit rate we achieved for the whole set is 4.2, which is comparable to many state of the art algorithms.

Figure 4 shows a comparison between our algorithm with other algorithms. *AWN* achieves better results than our older proposed algorithm *WRALIC* [4]. In addition, *AWN* outperforms JPEG-LS [8] and CALIC [10]. On the other hand, PAQ [6] achieved better results than our proposed algorithm. However, because PAQ uses neural nets, the execution time is very high. Table 1 shows the compression rates and encoding/decoding times for each image in the Kodak set. As shown in Table 1, the average encoding and decoding times is 1.38 s and 0.94 s, respectively, on a machine with 2.2 GHz processor.

8 Conclusion and Future Work

We have presented a symmetric lossless image compression algorithm. The algorithm makes two initial predictions, creates a weighted combination of the initial predictions before adjusting the prediction to end up with the final prediction. In order to achieve more compression, we encode the error in multiple bins depending on the expected error magnitude. Also, instead of encoding the signed error, the algorithm attempts to guess the sign and encodes the error magnitude and whether guessing the sign was successful or not.

While developing our solution, we noticed that using multiple predictions enhances the compression rate. Therefore, we intend to build on this observation in the future and make more initial predictions. We can create a ensemble (weighted combination) of these initial predictions by using an on-line stochastic gradient descent *SGD*. The objective of the *SGD* is to give more weights to predictions that are closer to the real pixel values in a certain image.

Acknowledgment. This research is partially funded by the Natural Sciences and Engineering Research Council of Canada (NSERC). This support is greatly appreciated.

References

1. Cleary, J.G., Witten, I.: Data compression using adaptive coding and partial string matching. IEEE Trans. Commun. **32**(4), 396–402 (1984)
2. Cutler, C.C.: Cutler (July 29 1952), uS Patent 2,605,361
3. Huffman, D.A., et al.: A method for the construction of minimum redundancy codes. Proc. IRE **40**(9), 1098–1101 (1952)

4. Kabani, A., El-Sakka, M.R.: Weighted ratio-based adaptive lossless image coding. In: 2014 IEEE 27th Canadian Conference on Electrical and Computer Engineering (CCECE), pp. 1–6. IEEE (2014)
5. Salomon, D.: Data Compression: The Complete Reference. Springer, New York (2004)
6. Salomon, D., Motta, G.: Handbook of Data Compression. Springer Science & Business Media, London (2009)
7. Sayood, K.: Introduction to Data Compression. Newnes, Amsterdam (2012)
8. Weinberger, M.J., Seroussi, G., Sapiro, G.: The loco-i lossless image compression algorithm: principles and standardization into jpeg-ls. IEEE Trans. Image Process. 9(8), 1309–1324 (2000)
9. Witten, I.H., Neal, R.M., Cleary, J.G.: Arithmetic coding for data compression. Commun. ACM 30(6), 520–540 (1987)
10. Wu, X., Memon, N.: Context-based, adaptive, lossless image coding. IEEE Trans. Commun. 45(4), 437–444 (1997)
11. Ziv, J., Lempel, A.: A universal algorithm for sequential data compression. IEEE Trans. Inf. Theory 23(3), 337–343 (1977)
12. Ziv, J., Lempel, A.: Compression of individual sequences via variable-rate coding. IEEE Trans. Inf. Theory 24(5), 530–536 (1978)

Dimensionality Reduction
and Classification

Dimensionality Reduction of Proportional Data Through Data Separation Using Dirichlet Distribution

Walid Masoudimansour[1]([⊠]) and Nizar Bouguila[2]

[1] Department of Electrical and Computer Engineering, Concordia University,
Montreal, QC, Canada
w_masou@encs.concordia.ca
[2] Concordia Institute for Information Systems Engineering, Concordia University,
Montreal, QC, Canada
nizar.bouguila@ciise.concordia.ca

Abstract. In this paper, a novel method is proposed for dimensionality reduction of proportional data. Non-negative, unit-sum data, namely, proportional data emerges in many applications such as document classification, image classification using visual bag of words, etc. The introduced method is supervised and can be used for classification of data into binary classes. In the proposed method, the intra-class correlation is maximized while minimizing the interclass correlation, using a linear transform. Design of this transform is formulated as an optimization problem with proper cost function. The projected data is matched to two Dirichlet distributions with careful parameter selection which allows to separate the classes in the Dirichlet parameter space. Finally, simulations are performed to demonstrate the effectiveness of the algorithm.

Keywords: Dimensionality reduction · Supervised learning · Data classification · Dirichlet distribution

1 Introduction

With the advancements in manufacturing techniques which made cheap sensors and storage devices possible, the amount of acquired and stored data grew exponentially. This enormous amount of data which is used in different fields of science and engineering for several purposes such as analysis, classification and clustering demands strong processing power and large storage devices along with unaffordable processing time [1]. Therefore, the problem of high dimensionality has been tackled by researcher in different fields, and considerable amounts of investigation have focused to solve this problem [2,3]. The main purpose of dimensionality reduction (DR) is to find a lower dimensional manifold on which the data lie, and to eliminate highly correlated data.

DR techniques are divided into two major categories of Linear and Non-Linear, where the former uses a linear transform to project the data into a low

© Springer International Publishing Switzerland 2015
M. Kamel and A. Campilho (Eds.): ICIAR 2015, LNCS 9164, pp. 141–149, 2015.
DOI: 10.1007/978-3-319-20801-5_15

dimensional space. Any technique that does not use such a linear transform is called a Non-Liner method. Among various linear methods, PCA and Factor Analysis are the most known [4–6] in both which the second statistics of the data is used. Also, non-linear techniques such as kernel PCA [7,8], MDS [9], MVU [10] and LLE [11] have been proven to be efficient on some real data. Non-linear methods can capture more complex structures in the data, however, due to faster and more efficient transformation, easier implementation and strong tendency for maintaining the topology of the original data [12], linear methods are better candidates for DR. Furthermore, exploiting some general properties of the data, one can design methods that exhibit improved performance compared to general methods. For example, considering the consistency of the positive, unit-sum property of proportional data with Dirichlet distribution support, this distribution has been proven to be effective in modeling such data [13,14]. In this paper, a novel method is introduced for dimensionality reduction of proportional data. The method is especially designed for classification, and can be used along with SVM classifier to result in high detection rates. Through a supervised learning process using very few training samples, the algorithm will find a proper model for the projected data, and optimize the projection to separate the data efficiently. Since Dirichlet distribution is a proper fit for proportional data, the algorithm exploits this model to fit each class of data to one Dirichlet distribution after projection. The projection matrix is designed such that the parameters of the resulting model make the data separable easily using a standard classifier. Unlike PCA, this method considers nonlinear correlation between the data, and thus, results in better detection rates. The parameters of the fitted distributions are used to define a proper objective function with a high cost for the case where projected data lie on similar models. Therefore, using a constrained optimization technique, the algorithm is able to find the projection matrix that makes this separation possible.

The rest of this paper is organized as follows. In Sect. 2, the proposed method is explained in details, and a proper objective function is introduced. An optimization problem is formulated to find the optimum separating transform in Sect. 3. In Sect. 4, the effectiveness of the algorithm is demonstrated through comparison with the method proposed in [14] (which will be called Dirichlet Component Analysis, *DCA* hereafter) as well as the standard PCA. Finally, in Sect. 5 some concluding remarks are drawn.

2   Proposed Method

2.1   Projection Matrix Properties

Consider M samples of proportional data in the form of N dimensional column vectors $\mathbf{x}_i$ such that

$$\sum_{k=1}^{N} x_{i,k} = 1, \quad x_{i,j} \geq 0, \quad \forall i \in \{1, 2, \ldots, M\}, j \in \{1, 2, \ldots, N\} \tag{1}$$

where $x_{i,j}$ is the j-th element of the i-th vector (sample) $\mathbf{x}_i$. This set of data is on an (N-1)-simplex which will be denoted by Δ^{N-1}. The first step in the proposed algorithm is a linear projection from the high dimensional space to the low dimensional space. Let this projection be performed by the matrix Π consisting of elements $\pi_{r,s}$ where $r \in \{1, 2, \ldots, K\}$ and $s \in \{1, 2, \ldots, N\}$. Also, assume that the matrix X denotes the complete set of data consisting of $\mathbf{x}_i$s as its columns. Therefore, the projected data can be obtained as follows

$$Y = \Pi X \tag{2}$$

where Y is a K by M matrix of the projected data in the new K dimensional space and $K < N$. Note that, to keep the proportional data on a simplex after projection, and making Y a mapping from Δ^{N-1} to Δ^{K-1}, elements of Π must satisfy the following properties

$$\sum_{t=1}^{K} \pi_{t,s} = 1, \quad \pi_{r,s} \geq 0, \quad \forall r \in \{1, 2, \ldots, K\}, \; \forall s \in \{1, 2, \ldots, N\} \tag{3}$$

It also can be shown that the above conditions are necessary and sufficient for the projected data to be in Δ^{K-1} for any $\mathbf{x}$ in Δ^{N-1}. Moreover, considering all the possible projections that satisfy (3), it can be seen that there is $N(K - 1)$ free parameters in Π to be determined.

2.2 Data Separation

The Dirichlet distribution, which is the multivariate generalization of the beta distribution, is also the conjugate prior of the multinomial distribution

$$\text{Dir}_\alpha(\mathbf{y}) = \frac{\Gamma(\sum_{i=1}^{N} \alpha_i)}{\prod_{i=1}^{N} \Gamma(\alpha_i)} \prod_{i=1}^{N} y_i^{\alpha_i - 1} \tag{4}$$

where $\Gamma(.)$ is the Gamma function, and the parameter α is a vector of the same size of the vector $\mathbf{y}$ with non-negative elements. The density and concentration of the samples drawn from a Dirichlet distribution depend on the elements of the parameter vector α. In fact, if $\alpha_i < 1$, the data tend to be concentrated around the corresponding axis, and, on the contrary, for $\alpha_i > 1$ the corresponding dimension of the data is concentrated around the central point. This property of the Dirichlet distribution is exploited in the proposed algorithm to separate the projected data.

Assume the projected training data of each class consists of samples of a Dirichlet distribution with parameters $\alpha^{(0)}$ for class 0 and $\alpha^{(1)}$ for class 1. Note that with no prior knowledge of the data, the elements of $\alpha^{(0)}$ and $\alpha^{(1)}$ are considered to be equal and will be denoted by α_0 and α_1, respectively. The principal idea of the proposed algorithm is that if the projection matrix Π is designed such that the projected samples from classes 0 and 1 come from two Dirichlet distributions with distant parameters α_0 and α_1, the projected data will be easily separable. To quantify this main idea, a proper objective function must be defined along with an optimization problem. Solving this problem, one can obtain a projection matrix to separate the data for efficient classification.

2.3   Objective Function

To define a proper objective function, one needs to find a family of functions of two variables (namely α_0 and α_1) for which the value of the function is minimum for distant parameters. Considering the previously mentioned property of Dirichlet distribution choosing $\alpha_0 \ll 1$ and $\alpha_1 \gg 1$ (or vice versa) will serve the model most efficiently. On the other hand, considering the numerical method used for calculating the derivative of the objective function, the following function proves to be efficient in resulting two separate distributions.

$$J_Y(\alpha_0, \alpha_1) = \frac{1 + \alpha_0\alpha_1}{\alpha_0 + \alpha_1} + \frac{1}{(\alpha_0 - \alpha_1)^2} \tag{5}$$

3   Optimization Algorithm

In this section, we formulate the optimization problem to find a proper projection to separate the data in Δ^{K-1}. Note that as mentioned before, based on (3), we have $N(K-1)$ variables to solve. Let the training samples from classes 0 and 1 be shown by the sets C_0 and C_1, respectively, such that $|C_0| = M_0$ and $|C_1| = M_1$. In the first step, the EM algorithm is used to estimate $\alpha_\kappa, \kappa \in \{0, 1\}$. The likelihood of α_κ is obtained as follows

$$L(\alpha_\kappa; Y) = \prod_{i=1}^{M_\kappa} f_{\mathbf{y}|\boldsymbol{\alpha_\kappa}}(\mathbf{y}_i|\boldsymbol{\alpha_\kappa}), \quad \kappa \in \{0, 1\} \tag{6}$$

Note that, all the samples of one class are assumed to be from the same distribution and independent. Now, replacing the distribution function with Dirichlet distribution we obtain

$$L(\alpha_\kappa; Y) = \prod_{i=1}^{M_\kappa} \mathrm{Dir}_{\alpha_\kappa}(\mathbf{y}_i) = \frac{\Gamma^{M_\kappa}(K\alpha_\kappa)}{\Gamma^{KM_\kappa}(\alpha_\kappa)} \prod_{i=1}^{M_\kappa} \prod_{j=1}^{K} y_{i,j}^{\alpha_\kappa - 1} \tag{7}$$

Finally, using the log-likelihood, and replacing the projected data by the original data from (2), we obtain

$$\ln(L(\alpha_\kappa; Y)) = M_\kappa \ln(\Gamma(K\alpha_\kappa)) - KM_\kappa \ln(\Gamma(\alpha_\kappa)) + (\alpha_\kappa - 1) \sum_{i=1}^{M_\kappa} \sum_{j=1}^{K} y_{i,j} =$$

$$M_\kappa \ln(\Gamma(K\alpha_\kappa)) - KM_\kappa \ln(\Gamma(\alpha_\kappa)) + (\alpha_\kappa - 1) \sum_{i=1}^{M_\kappa} \sum_{j=1}^{K} \sum_{r=1}^{N} \pi_{j,r} x_{i,r} \tag{8}$$

To maximize (8), the derivative is calculated and is set to 0. Therefore

$$\frac{d\ln(L(\alpha_\kappa; Y))}{d\alpha_\kappa} = KM\psi(K\alpha_\kappa) - KM\psi(\alpha_\kappa) + \sum_{i=1}^{M_\kappa}\sum_{j=1}^{K}\sum_{r=1}^{N}\pi_{j,r}x_{i,r} = 0 \tag{9}$$

where $\psi(.) = \frac{\Gamma'(.)}{\Gamma(.)}$ is the Digamma function. Assuming that α_κ^* satisfies (9), this equation can be solved using a numerical method such as Newton-Raphson to estimate α_κ^* for $\kappa = 0, 1$, and then, these values can be used to evaluate the objective function and its numerical gradient.

Using the above results, one can formulate the following optimization problem

$$\underset{\pi_{r,s}}{\text{minimize}}\ J_Y(\alpha_0^*, \alpha_1^*)$$

$$\text{subject to}\ \sum_{r=1}^{K}\pi_{r,s} = 1$$

$$\pi_{r,s} \geq 0 \tag{10}$$

where $r \in \{1, 2, \ldots, K\}$ and $s \in \{1, 2, \ldots, N\}$. To optimize the proposed objective function, we use a gradient descent method [15]. The value of the objective function is calculated by first estimating α_κ^* from (9) and then substituting the values in (5). The gradient is also evaluated through small steps in $\pi_{r,s}$ using the following two point formula

$$\frac{\partial J_Y(\alpha_0^*, \alpha_1^*)}{\partial \pi_{r,s}} \approx \frac{J_Y(\alpha_0^*, \alpha_1^*)|_{\pi_{r,s}+\delta} - J_Y(\alpha_0^*, \alpha_1^*)|_{\pi_{r,s}-\delta}}{2\delta} \tag{11}$$

where δ is a small variation in $\pi_{r,s}$. In each iteration, a small step is taken toward the opposite direction of the gradient. If the resulting Π satisfied the constraints, its values are used for the next iteration; otherwise, the elements of this Π are projected into the constraint space and the resulting values are used for the next iteration. Note that projection into the constraint space can be solved defining a standard quadratic programming problem. Eventually, the standard SVM classifier with a linear kernel is used to classify the data.

4   Experimental Results

To evaluate the efficiency of the proposed algorithm, it has been tested for classification in different real world applications against DCA and PCA. The SVM classifier with linear kernel is used in each experiment, and equal number of samples are chosen randomly from each class. Then, the remaining samples are used as test data. To cancel the effect of outliers in each random selection of training data, especially for the case of small number of training samples, every test is performed several times and the average of the detection rates is reported in each case.

4.1   Image Classification

The Caltech 101 is one of the well known image datasets, and it is used in this scenario for evaluating the detection rate of the introduced method. There are images from 101 object categories in the dataset. Two of the image classes, namely `Airplanes` and `Motorbikes`, are used as classes 0 and 1. In each test, after choosing the training samples, SIFT features are extracted from each image, and a vocabulary of 100 words is built from all the features of the training set using `kmeans` algorithm. Then, the bag of visual words is built for the training set and is fed to the algorithm. This test has been repeated 100 times for each case, and the results are average detection rates. Figure 1 shows the detection rate for different values of target dimension and training samples.

From this figure, it can be seen that the proposed method almost always results in comparable detection rates with the original data which is highly efficient considering the low value of the projection space dimension. Moreover, it outperforms DCA and PCA, especially for small numbers of training data. Particularly, Fig. 1a shows that with only 10 samples (5 from each class), the proposed method is still able to produce results as good as the original data.

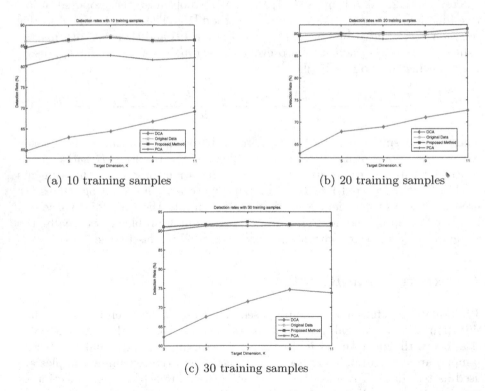

(a) 10 training samples   (b) 20 training samples

(c) 30 training samples

Fig. 1. Detection rates vs. target dimension for different numbers of training samples. The data are two image classes from Caltech 101.

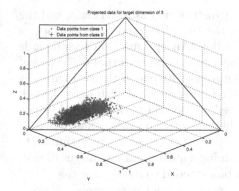 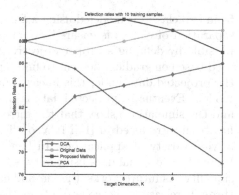

Fig. 2. Visualization of the projected data on a 2-simplex for image samples from Caltech 101.

Fig. 3. Detection rates vs. target dimension for 10 training samples. The data are two tumor types from Wisconsin Breast Cancer Diagnostic Dataset.

To illustrate proper data separation, Fig. 2 shows a visualization of the projected test data using a target dimension of 3 (K=3) with 10 total training samples. In this figure, points from classes 1 and 0 are shown using red dots and blue crosses, respectively. Also, the 2-simplex is shown as a triangle with black solid lines. As it can be seen, the data are properly separated and the interclass variance is higher. Note that by looking at the figure, one can deduce that the Dirichlet parameter of class 1, α_1^*, must be higher than the Dirichlet parameter of class 0, α_0^*. In fact, in this case, $\alpha_1^* = 4.39$ and $\alpha_0^* = 0.23$.

4.2 Tumor Classification

In this experiment, we use Wisconsin Breast Cancer Diagnostic Dataset which is available in UCI Machine Learning Repository. This dataset contains 569 samples with 30 features where the features are physical properties of the cells such as radius, compactness and perimeter of the nucleus. The tumors are categorized to Malignant and Benign classes. After a preprocessing step consisting of normalizing each sample to unit-sum, 10 training samples have been used for each test, and it has been repeated 20 times. The average resulting detection rates are shown in Fig. 3. As it can be seen, the proposed algorithm detects the tumor type more efficiently compared to both DCA and PCA. It is also worth mentioning that, PCA starts to fail in higher target dimensions which can be due to redundancy of the features. Note that the change in detection rate of the original data is due to random choice of a relatively small number of training data.

5   Conclusion and Future Work

In this paper, a novel supervised linear algorithm is introduced for dimensionality reduction of proportional data. The projected data which is assumed to be from two classes is modeled using a Dirichlet distribution for each class, and the separation of classes is ensured by making the two class models as distinct as possible by defining a proper objective function. An optimization technique is used based on gradient descent to find a proper projection such that each class of the projected data under this linear transform best fits one of the two Dirichlet models. Eventually, projected data is classified using an SVM with linear kernel, and the simulations show that the introduced method outperforms DCA which has been introduced in [14]. It also offers higher detection rates than PCA for a wide variety of applications. In fact, the detection rates are very similar to those of the original data using very few training samples and low target dimensionality. As future works, the method can be extended to multi-class cases, and through releasing the constraint on the Dirichlet model parameters, allowing parameter vectors with non-equal elements. This, along with new definition of a cost function, can result in better separation of the data.

References

1. Donoho, D.L., et al.: High-dimensional data analysis: The curses and blessings of dimensionality. In: AMS Math Challenges Lecture, pp. 1–32 (2000)
2. Lu, X., Yuan, Y.: Hybrid structure for robust dimensionality reduction. J. Neurocomput. **124**, 131–138 (2014)
3. Wang, S.J., Yan, S., Yang, J., Zhou, C.G., Fu, X.: A general exponential framework for dimensionality reduction. IEEE Trans. Image Proces. **23**(2), 920–930 (2014)
4. Jolliffe, I.: Principal Component Analysis. Springer Series in Statistics. Springer, Heidelberg (2002)
5. Abdi, H., Williams, L.J.: Principal component analysis. Wiley Interdisc. Rev.: Comput. Statis. **2**(4), 433–459 (2010)
6. Mulaik, S.A.: The foundations of factor analysis, vol. 88. McGraw-Hill, New York (1972)
7. Kokiopoulou, E., Saad, Y.: Orthogonal neighborhood preserving projections: a projection-based dimensionality reduction technique. IEEE Trans. Pattern Anal. Mach. Intel. **29**(12), 2143–2156 (2007)
8. Mika, S., Schölkopf, B., Smola, A.J., Müller, K.R., Scholz, M., Rätsch, G.: Kernel PCA and de-noising in feature spaces. Proc. Neural Inform. Proces. Syst. **11**, 536–542 (1998)
9. Verbeek, J.: Learning nonlinear image manifolds by global alignment of local linear models. IEEE Trans. Pattern Anal. Mach. Intel. **28**(8), 1236–1250 (2006)
10. Welling, M., Rosen-Zvi, M., Hinton, G.E.: Exponential family harmoniums with an application to information retrieval. Proc. Neural Inform. Proces. Syst. **17**, 1481–1488 (2004)
11. Chang, H., Yeung, D.Y., Xiong, Y.: Super-resolution through neighbor embedding. In: Proceedings of the 2004 IEEE Computer Society Conference on Computer Vision and Pattern Recognition, vol. 1, June 2004
12. Koren, Y., Carmel, L.: Robust linear dimensionality reduction. IEEE Trans. Vis. Comput. Graph. **10**(4), 459–470 (2004)

13. Bouguila, N., Ziou, D.: A dirichlet process mixture of generalized dirichlet distributions for proportional data modeling. IEEE Trans. Neural Netw. **21**(1), 107–122 (2010)
14. Wang, H.Y., Yang, Q., Qin, H., Zha, H.: Dirichlet component analysis: Feature extraction for compositional data. In: Proceedings of the 25th International Conference on Machine Learning (ICML), pp. 1128–1135. ACM (2008)
15. Bertsekas, D.P.: Nonlinear Programming, 2nd edn. Athena Scientific, September 1999

Image Categorization Using a Heuristic Automatic Clustering Method Based on Hierarchical Clustering

François LaPlante[1]([✉]), Mustapha Kardouchi[1], and Nabil Belacel[2]

[1] Université de Moncton, Moncton, NB, Canada
`francois.laplante@umoncton.ca, mustapha.kardouchi@umoncton.ca`
[2] National Research Council-Information and Communication Technologies,
Moncton, NB, Canada
`nabil.belacel@nrc-cnrc.gc.ca`

Abstract. One approach to image categorization is the use of clustering algorithms to sets of images represented by various image descriptors. We propose the use of an automatic clustering algorithm to categorize an image-set represented by color moments. Using this clustering algorithm based on hierarchical clustering, this approach produced adequate results with only minimal user input when applied to a restricted image-set.

Keywords: Image classification · Image processing · Clustering

1 Introduction

Image categorization, or the separation of image sets into significant subgroups, can be simplified by the use of meta-data containing relevant information about said images. However there are cases where meta-data is unavailable or simply not relevant to the desired categorization, in which case only the data present in the image itself must be used. We represent images by their color moments as described by Stricker and Orengo in (Stricker and Orengo, 1995) and apply the automatic clustering method presented in (LaPlante et al., 2014) to categorize an image set.

2 Related Works

2.1 Image Classification

In this paper, we use the terms image categorization or image classification to refer to the grouping of multiple images together to form meaningful classes. This is opposed to the grouping of regions within an image into meaningful classes, for which the term is also used in (Vailaya et al., 2001) but we will refer to it as image segmentation (Sathya and Manavalan, 2011).

In order to classify images, an appropriate representation of the images must be used. These can vary from simple colour histograms to more complex features

M. Kamel and A. Campilho (Eds.): ICIAR 2015, LNCS 9164, pp. 150–158, 2015.
DOI: 10.1007/978-3-319-20801-5_16

such as the bag of features presented in (Bouachir et al., 2010) or color indexing proposed in (Deng et al., 2001). The method we have chosen to use is color moments as described in (Stricker and Orengo, 1995). These representations can vary in both time and space complexity, and suitability to a given dataset.

2.2   Clustering

Clustering methods can be categorized in many ways such as hard or fuzzy, hierarchical or partitional, and as combinations of these types.

Hard vs. Fuzzy Clustering. Hard clustering is a type of clustering where every datum belongs to one and only one cluster. In contrast, fuzzy clustering is a form of clustering where data belong to multiple clusters according to a membership function (Gan, 2011). Hard clustering is generally simpler to implement and has lower time complexity. It performs well with linearly separable data but tends to not perform as well with non linearly separable data, outliers, or noise. Fuzzy clustering often has a larger memory footprint as it often requires a $c \times n$ matrix to store memberships, where c is the number of clusters and n is the number of data points. Fuzzy clustering is generally able to handle non-linearly separable data as well as outliers, and noise better than hard clustering.

Hierarchical vs. Partitional Clustering. A hierarchical clustering method yields a dendrogram representing the nested grouping of patterns and similarity levels at which groupings change (Jain et al., 1999). A partitional clustering method yields a single partition of the data instead of a clustering structure, such as the dendrogram produced by a hierarchical method (Gan, 2011).

Automatic Clustering. Automatic clustering is a form of clustering where the number of clusters c is unknown and determining its optimal value is left up to the clustering method. Some automatic clustering methods may require an initial number of clusters, from which clusters will be split and merged until a pseudo-optimal number of clusters is achieved. Other methods require no initial value or additional information regarding the number of clusters and will determine a pseudo-optimal value without any user input. Other parameters, such as a fuzzy constant (for fuzzy clustering algorithms) or thresholds, may still be required, but are generally kept to minimum or are optional with good default values.

3   Clustering Method

The proposed clustering method, Heuristic Divisive Analysis (HDA), consists of two phases: splitting and merging. The first phase splits the data set into a number of clusters, often leading to more cluster than optimal. The second phase merges (or links) clusters, leading to a more optimal clustering. The reason for this two-step approach is to address one of the larger drawbacks of many hard clustering methods; poor performance when dealing with data which is not linearly separable. Both steps use different approaches to computing the dissimilarity between clusters, which allows for the creation of non-elliptical clusters which may be nested or interlocked.

3.1 Splitting

The splitting algorithm is a divisive hierarchical method based on the DIANA clustering algorithm (Kaufman and Rousseeuw, 1990). However, the proposed method employs a heuristic function to interrupt the hierarchical division of the data set once an "adequate" clustering for this step has been reached.

DIANA. DIANA (DIvisive ANAlysis) is a divisive hierarchical clustering algorithm based on the idea of MacNaughton-Smith et al. (MacNaughton-Smith, 1964). Given $X = x_1, x_2, \ldots, x_n$ a data set consisting of n records and beginning with all points being in one cluster, the algorithm will alternate between separating the cluster in two and selecting the next cluster to split until every point has become its own cluster. To split a cluster in two, the algorithm must first find the point with the greatest average dissimilarity to the rest of the records. The average dissimilarity of a record x_i with regards to X is defined as

$$D_i = \frac{1}{n-1} \sum_{j=1, j \neq i}^{n} D(x_i, xj) \tag{1}$$

where $D(x, y)$ is a dissimilarity metric (in this case, we use Euclidean distance). Given $D_{max} = max_{0 \leq i \leq n-1} D_i$, x_{max} is the point with the greatest average dissimilarity which is then split from the cluster. We then have two clusters: $C_1 = \{x_{max}\}$ and $C_2 = X \backslash C_1$. Next, the algorithm checks every point in C_2 to determine whether or not it should be moved to C_1. To accomplish this, the algorithm must compute the dissimilarity between x and C_1 as well as the dissimilarity between x and $C_2 \backslash x$. The dissimilarity between x and C_1 is defined as

$$D_{C_1}(x) = \frac{1}{|C_1|} \sum_{y \in C_1} D(x, y), x \in C_{/1} \tag{2}$$

where $|C_1|$ denotes the number of records in C_1. The dissimilarity between x and $C_2 \backslash x$ is defined as

$$D_{C_2}(x) = \frac{1}{|C_2 - 1|} \sum_{y \in C_2, y \neq x} D(x, y), x \in C_2 \tag{3}$$

If $D_{C_1} < D_{C_2}$, then x is moved from C_2 to C_1. This process is repeated until there are no more records in C_2 which should be moved to C_1.

To select the next cluster to separate, the algorithm will chose the cluster with the greatest diameter. The diameter of a cluster is defined as

$$Diam(C) = \max_{x, y \in C} D(x, y) \tag{4}$$

Heuristic Stopping Function. The first phase in our method consists of running the DIANA algorithm with a heuristic function in order to stop it once an "adequate" clustering has been reached. This function consists of first calculating the average intra-cluster dissimilarity (again, we use Euclidean distance) of each cluster, defined as

$$AvgIntraClusterDistance(C) = \frac{\sum\limits_{x \in C} D(x, \bar{x})}{|C|} \tag{5}$$

where $\bar{x}$ denotes the mean of all points in cluster C. The heuristic index for this clustering is the average of all the average intra-cluster dissimilarities. If the heuristic index for this clustering is lower than that of the previous clustering, the current clustering is considered the most optimal to date. Otherwise, we have reached our "adequate" clustering at the previous step, but we will continue running the DIANA algorithm for a set number of iterations as a preventative measure against falling into a local optimum. We chose this rather simple heuristic instead of one of the many known validity indices because it allowed us to decrease the complexity (as it uses values which our implementation had already calculated) and still produced good results.

3.2   Merging

The splitting phase's result can be non-optimal, especially when data sets contain clusters which are not linearly separable or have irregular shapes. In these cases, the "adequate" clustering will usually contain instances where multiple clusters should be one and the same. These clusters will be very close to each other in relation to the other clusters and it is the goal of this merging phase to collect them into optimal clusters.

For each pair of clusters, we calculate the *average nearest neighbor* dissimilarity, defined as

$$AvgNearestNeighbor(C) = \frac{\sum\limits_{x \in C} \min\limits_{y \in C, y \neq x} D(x, y)}{|C|} \tag{6}$$

for both clusters and keep the greater of both values as our merging dissimilarity threshold M_T. We then go through each pair of objects with one object from each cluster and if we find a pair where the dissimilarity between the two objects is less than the merging dissimilarity threshold (multiplied by a constant), then the two clusters would be merged. We express the test for merging as

$$CanMerge(C_1, C_2) = \begin{cases} true, & \exists x \in C_1, \exists y \in C_2 | D(x, y) < M_T \cdot K \\ false, & otherwise \end{cases} \tag{7}$$

where K is a merging constant. Our approach differs from that of (LaPlante et al., 2014) in that pairs of candidate clusters are not merged as they are found but in order of increasing *average nearest neighbor dissimilarity*. Additionally, because single-object clusters have an *average nearest neighbor dissimilarity* of 0, any pair of clusters where one contains a single object will use the other cluster's *average nearest neighbor dissimilarity* as M_T. In the case of two single-object clusters, M_T will be the average standard deviation across all clusters.

Once all merges are completed, we are left with the final clustering. The value of the merging constant can be adjusted depending on the data set and we have found experimentally that a value of 2 generally produces good results.

We have also tested an alternative merging method based on the Y-means approach to merging. Because the Y-means algorithm uses dissimilarities between cluster centroids, merging clusters will relocate the centroids in such a way that is detrimental to our method. To avoid this drawback, we link clusters by attributing them labels instead of merging them until all pairs are linked, after which we merge all linked clusters. We express the test for linking as

$$CanLink(C_1, C_2) = \begin{cases} true & D(C_1, C_2) \leq (\sigma_{C_1} \cdot \sigma_{C_2}) \cdot L \\ false & otherwise \end{cases} \tag{8}$$

where σ_{C_i} is the standard deviation of the dissimilarity between the objects in a cluster C_i to the centroid of that cluster and L is a linking constant. The value of the linking constant can be adjusted depending on the data set and we have found that a value of 0.5 generally produces good results with our method.

4 Data

The dataset used is a subset of the COIL-100 dataset (Nayar et al., 1996). The subset consists of 72 images each of 9 objects, taken in rotation around the objects at 5° of rotation intervals for a total of 648 of the 7200 images in the dataset. The objects in question are:

#4 A red tomato
#17 A yellow plastic cat figurine
#19 A red toy fire truck
#23 A red toy sports car
#24 A white and orange plastic bottle
#34 A green yo-yo
#36 A blue plastic wall hook
#37 A white and grey toy tank
#41 A wood block

We represent each image using the three central color moments defined by Stricker and Orengo in (Stricker and Orengo, 1995). These three moments, calculated on each of the three RGB channels of the images, produce our nine-dimensional vector representation of the image. Given the value of the ith color channel at the jth image pixel being defined as p_{ij}, the three color moments are defined as:

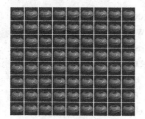

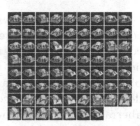

Fig. 1. Cluster 0.   **Fig. 2.** Cluster 1.   **Fig. 3.** Cluster 2.

1 - Average

$$E_i = \frac{1}{N} \sum_{j=1}^{N} p_{ij} \tag{9}$$

2 - Variance

$$E_i = \sqrt{\frac{1}{N} \sum_{j=1}^{N} (p_{ij} - E_i)^2} \tag{10}$$

3 - Skewness

$$E_i = \sqrt[3]{\frac{1}{N} \sum_{j=1}^{N} (p_{ij} - E_i)^3} \tag{11}$$

5 Results

Adjusting the merging constant K to a value of 3.0 produced the best results for this dataset. With this value, ten clusters were produced. clusters 0, 1, 4, 5, 8, and 9 correspond to all pictures of objects objects #34, #24, #4, #41, #36, and #17 respectively and no images of other objects (Figs. 1, 2, 7, 8, 9 and 10). Cluster 2 contains the majority of images of object #37, cluster 3 contains three images of object #19 and four of object #23, cluster 6 contains the remaining two images of object #37, and cluster 7 contains the remaining majority of images of both object #19 and #23 (Figs. 3, 4, 5 and 6).

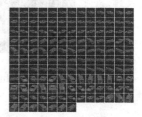

Fig. 4. Cluster 3.   **Fig. 5.** Cluster 6.   **Fig. 6.** Cluster 7.

In clusters 3 and 7, within which images of different objects occur, the objects confused as the same are visually rather similar, more so when considering that color is primary factor used in comparison. Both are a similar shade of red, occupy a similar space (leave a similar amount of background color), have a black rectangular shape near the center, and have white areas (stripes or ladder). Clusters 3 and 6 contain relatively very few objects and could be seen as aberrations. Table 1 shows the results of clustering with different values of K, outlining the total number of cluster produced, the number of clusters considered aberrations (clusters with a small enough number of objects to be negligible), and the number of conjoined clusters (clusters containing images of more than one object, i.e. which should be separate clusters) including the numbers of clusters which were conjoined into one. Table 2 shows the results of calculating validity indices on the same clustering results using some of the same indices as (LaPlante et al., 2014), namely: Xie & Beni index (Xie and Beni, 1991), Kwon Index (Kwon, 1998), and Compose Within and Between Scattering (Rezaee et al., 1998), for which a lower value represents a better clustering, as well as PBM index (Pakhira et al., 2004) and Silhouettes index (Rousseeuw, 1987), for which higher values represent a better clustering.

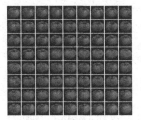

Fig. 7. Cluster 4.

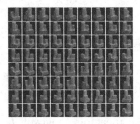

Fig. 8. Cluster 5.

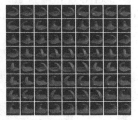

Fig. 9. Cluster 8.

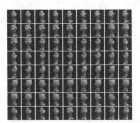

Fig. 10. Cluster 9.

An attempt was made to cluster the entirety of the COIL-100 dataset, however the results were not as ideal. As we have seen with the 9 object subset, some

Table 1. Results of clustering the 9-object subset of COIL-100 using HDA clustering algorithm with different merging constants K

Merging constant K	Total # of clusters	# of aberration clusters	# of instances of conjoined clusters (# of clusters conjoined)
2.0	16	7	1(2)
2.5	16	7	1(2)
2.75	13	5	1(2)
3.0	10	2	1(2)
3.25	8	1	1(3)
3.5	8	1	1(3)
4.0	8	1	1(3)
5.0	6	1	1(5)

Table 2. Cluster validation results of the 9-object subset of COIL-100 using HDA clustering algorithm with different merging constants K

Merging constant K	Xie & Beni	Kwon	CWB	PBM	Silhouettes
2.0	0.294688	201.069	0.0699704	6118.08	0.695539
2.5	0.294688	201.069	0.0699704	6118.08	0.695539
2.75	0.349674	235.375	0.0939078	7104.66	0.688336
3.0	0.146937	98.1284	0.0449371	8307.76	0.678347
3.25	0.441257	289.001	0.0505758	4663.42	0.540493
3.5	0.441257	289.001	0.0505758	4663.42	0.540493
4.0	0.441257	289.001	0.0505758	4663.42	0.540493
5.0	1.16144	756.173	0.0572099	3694.55	0.30045

similar images end up being grouped together whether or not this is desired as well as some images of the same object may not end up in the same cluster. In our subset, these issues are minor, the aberrant clusters are small and the different objects being clustered together are quite similar. In the full dataset, these effects can be amplified. Seeing as the method relies on evolving averages and standard deviations, the complete dataset has a less pronounced overall variation between objects. The level of difference which may be allowed in a same cluster to address this would be so strict as to likely break up adequate clusters.

6   Conclusion

The chosen clustering method's two-step approach provides very similar results as some better known algorithms with the added benefit of being able to identify non-linear data. The potential disadvantage is that inadequate initial parameters can lead to poor results. We used a single color descriptor to represent the image data, it is possible that better results (also for the complete COIL-100 dataset) could be obtained with a different representation of the images, such as alternate color descriptors or adding form descriptors, and with more fine tuning of the parameters. However, an adequate result was obtained with a fairly simple data representation and very few and minor adjustments to the clustering algorithm's initial parameters. This adequate result with minimal user input was our primary objective, and as such we consider this application of the clustering method successful in its goal.

Acknowledgements. We gratefully acknowledge the support from NBIF's (RAI 2012-047) New Brunswick Innovation Funding granted to Dr. Nabil Belacel.

References

Bouachir, W., Kardouchi, M., Belacel, N.: Fuzzy indexing for bag of features scene categorization. In: 5th International Symposium on I/V Communications and Mobile Network (ISVC), 2010, pp. 1–4 (2010)

Deng, Y., Manjunath, B., Kenney, C., Moore, M.S., Shin, H.: An efficient color representation for image retrieval. IEEE Trans. Image Process. **10**(1), 140–147 (2001)

Gan, G.: Data Clustering in C++: An Object-Oriented Approach. Chapman and Hall/CRC, Boca Raton (2011)

Jain, A.K., Murty, M.N., Flynn, P.J.: Data clustering: a review. ACM Comput. Surv. **31**(3), 264–323 (1999)

Kaufman, L.R., Rousseeuw, P.: Finding Groups in Data: An Introduction to Cluster Analysis. Wiley, New York (1990)

Kwon, S.: Cluster validity index for fuzzy clustering. Electron. Lett. **34**(22), 2176–2177 (1998)

LaPlante, F., Belacel, N., Kardouchi, M.: A hierarchical clustering heuristic for automatic clustering. In: Proceedings of the 6th International Conference on Agents and Artificial Intelligence, pp. 201–210 (2014)

MacNaughton-Smith, P.: Dissimilarity analysis: a new technique of hierarchical subdivision. Nature **202**, 1034–1035 (1964)

Nayar, S.K., Nene, S.A., Murase, H.: Columbia object image library (coil 100). Department of Computer Science, Columbia University, Technical report, CUCS-006-96 (1996)

Pakhira, M.K., Bandyopadhyay, S., Maulik, U.: Validity index for crisp and fuzzy clusters. Pattern Recogn. **37**(3), 487–501 (2004)

Rezaee, M.R., Lelieveldt, B., Reiber, J.: A new clustervalidity index for the fuzzy c-mean. Pattern Recogn. Lett. **19**(34), 237–246 (1998)

Rousseeuw, P.J.: Silhouettes: a graphical aid to the interpretation and validation of cluster analysis. J. Comput. Appl. Math. **20**, 53–65 (1987)

Sathya, B., Manavalan, R.: Image segmentation by clustering methods: performance analysis. Int. J. Comput. Appl. **29**(11), 27–32 (2011)

Stricker, M.A., Orengo, M.: Similarity of color images. In: Proceedings of the SPIE, vol. 2420, pp. 381–392 (1995)

Vailaya, A., Figueiredo, M.A., Jain, A.K., Zhang, H.-J.: Image classification for content-based indexing. IEEE Trans. Image Process. **10**(1), 117–130 (2001)

Xie, X., Beni, G.: A validity measure for fuzzy clustering. IEEE Trans. Pattern Anal. Mach. Intell. **13**(8), 841–847 (1991)

Semantic Scene Classification with Generalized Gaussian Mixture Models

Tarek Elguebaly and Nizar Bouguila[(✉)]

Concordia Institute for Information Systems Engineering,
Concordia University, Montreal, QC H3G 2W1, Canada
t_elgue@encs.concordia.ca, nizar.bouguila@concordia.ca

Abstract. The work proposed in this paper is motivated by the need to develop powerful approaches for scene classification which is a challenging problem mainly due to varying conditions. In this paper, we are mostly interested in automatically assigning a scene image to a semantic category when RGB channels and near infrared information are simultaneously available. We represent images by a collection of local image patches that we use to learn a global generalized Gaussian mixture (GGM) using the split and merge expectation-maximization (SMEM) algorithm. Using this approach, we built an effective scene classification system capable of handling outliers and noise level in the data. Extensive experiments show the merits of the proposed framework.

1 Introduction

Recently, scene understanding and classification has gained a lot of interest. The goal of scene classification is to automatically classify a scene image to a semantic category based on analyzing the visual content of the image. Most of existing computer vision approaches are applied on visible (RGB) images due to their wide availability. However, lighting condition represents one of the most challenging problem when dealing with RGB images. Hence, researchers were encouraged to employ thermal infrared sensors. Despite its robustness to illumination changes, infrared has various drawbacks such as its sensitivity to ambient temperature and its higher cost compared to RGB cameras. Thus, some researchers decided to look beyond the conventional visible band and into the near-infrared (NIR) part of the electromagnetic spectrum (700–1100 nm). NIR has three main advantages: 1- robust to variation in ambient lighting compared to visible images, 2- less affected by ambient temperature relative to infrared, 3- can work in both daytime and nighttime. Furthermore, NIR images can be easily obtained by removing the NIR blocking filter affixed to digital cameras. Moreover, RGB and NIR cues have been successfully combined in many applications [1,2]. In this paper, we examine whether fusion of visual and NIR images can increase the overall performance of scene classification systems.

Most existing scene classification approaches differ by: the image representation method, the learning algorithm, and the classification method. In [3],

© Springer International Publishing Switzerland 2015
M. Kamel and A. Campilho (Eds.): ICIAR 2015, LNCS 9164, pp. 159–166, 2015.
DOI: 10.1007/978-3-319-20801-5_17

the authors built a scene classification system without the need for segmenting and processing individual objects or regions. The work in [4] presented an approach to find intermediate semantic models of natural scenes using region-based information. Firstly, the scene images are divided into local regions, which are represented by a combination of a color and a texture feature. Secondly, through so-called concept classifiers (k-NN or SVM), the local regions are classified. Thirdly, each image is represented by a concept occurrence vector (COV) computed as the histogram of the semantic concepts. Finally, in order to classify a novel image, its COV representation is used as input to an additional SVM. However, a large number of local regions of training images need to be annotated manually with the above semantic concepts which is not effective. In [5], the authors presented an approach based on local invariant features and probabilistic latent semantic analysis (pLSA). Motivated by this work we try to model the semantic of the image in an unsupervised manner. In the training process, we represent an image by a collection of local image patches from which we extract local features that we quantize into a visual codebook using a global mixture model. Next, we use the posterior to distribute each patch in the image to the best component in the mixture (codeword) in order to represent each image with a histogram of codeword occurrences. Then, we use these bag-of-words (BoW) histograms as feature vectors to discover "Z" latent topics using pLSA. Finally, we use the topics representation of the training images to learn an SVM classifier. In the testing phase, each input image is partitioned into patches and local features are extracted from each patch. Next, it is represented by a BOW histogram and then its topic distribution vector is determined. Finally, SVM is used to choose the best category to the image. A complete diagram of our approach is shown in Fig. 1. Generally, the Gaussian is used, but is not the best choice in real life applications. Therefore, we consider the generalized Gaussian density (GGD) has been widely used recently for its flexibility. Moreover, we use the split and merge EM (SMEM) for the parameters estimation.

The rest of this paper is organized as follows. Section 2 introduces the GGM and its parameters estimation algorithm. In Sect. 3, we present the method used for scene classification. We assess the performance of the new approach on RGB and NIR images; while comparing it to other model in Sect. 4. Our last section is devoted to the conclusion.

2   The GGM and Its Parameters Estimation Algorithm

In this paper, we break all training images down into orderless N patches. Then we select a 40 dimensional feature vector for each patch ($D=40$). Thus, the input for our GGM is a set of N i.i.d vectors $\mathcal{X} = (\boldsymbol{X}_1,\ldots, \boldsymbol{X}_N)$, each of D-dimensions $\boldsymbol{X}_i = [X_{i1},\ldots, X_{iD}]^T$. If we assume that $\mathcal{X}$ arise from a finite generalized Gaussian mixture model with K components then:

$$p(\mathcal{X}|\Theta) = \prod_{i=1}^{N}\sum_{j=1}^{K} p(\boldsymbol{X}_i|\xi_j)p_j \qquad (1)$$

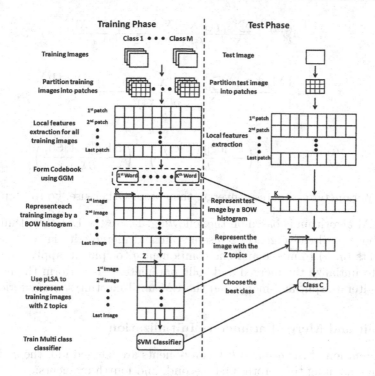

Fig. 1. Complete diagram of our approach

where $p(\boldsymbol{X}_i|\xi_j)$ is a generalized Gaussian probability distribution given by:

$$p(\boldsymbol{X}_i|\xi_j) = \prod_{d=1}^{D} \frac{\lambda_{jd} \left[\frac{\Gamma(3/\lambda_{jd})}{\Gamma(1/\lambda_{jd})}\right]^{1/2}}{2\sigma_{jd}\Gamma(1/\lambda_{jd})} \exp\left[-A(\lambda_{jd})\left|\frac{X_{id}-\mu_{jd}}{\sigma_{jd}}\right|^{\lambda_{jd}}\right] \qquad (2)$$

where $A(\lambda_{jd}) = \left[\frac{\Gamma(3/\lambda_{jd})}{\Gamma(1/\lambda_{jd})}\right]^{\lambda_{jd}/2}$; ξ_j is the set of the parameters of the j component given by $\xi_j=(\boldsymbol{\mu}_j, \boldsymbol{\sigma}_j, \boldsymbol{\lambda}_j)$ where $\boldsymbol{\mu}_j = (\mu_{j1},\ldots,\mu_{jD})$, $\boldsymbol{\sigma}_j = (\sigma_{j1},\ldots,\sigma_{jD})$,
$\boldsymbol{\lambda}_j = (\lambda_{j1},\ldots, \lambda_{jD})$ are the mean, the standard deviation, and the shape para-
meters of the D-dimensional GGD, respectively. Note that p_j are the mixing
proportions which must be positive and sum to one and Θ the set of parameters
of the mixture with K classes is defined by $\Theta = (\boldsymbol{\mu}_1,\ldots, \boldsymbol{\mu}_K, \boldsymbol{\sigma}_1,\ldots, \boldsymbol{\sigma}_K, \boldsymbol{\lambda}_1,\ldots,$
$\boldsymbol{\lambda}_K, p_1,\ldots,p_K)$. The EM algorithm for the GGM can be summarized as [6]

1. Start with an initialized parameter set $\Theta^{(0)}$
2. Compute the posterior probabilities: $p(j|\boldsymbol{X}_i) = \frac{p(\boldsymbol{X}_i|\xi_j^{(l)})p_j^{(l)}}{\sum_{j=1}^{K} p(\boldsymbol{X}_i|\xi_j^{(l)})p_j^{(l)}}$
3. Compute a new set of parameters:

$$\hat{p}_j^{(l+1)} = \frac{1}{N} \sum_{i=1}^{N} p(j|\boldsymbol{X}_i) \qquad (3)$$

$$\hat{\mu}_{jd}^{(l+1)} = \frac{\sum_{i=1}^{N} p(j|X_i)|X_{id} - \mu_{jd}|^{\lambda_{jd}-2} X_{id}}{\sum_{i=1}^{N} p(j|X_i)|X_{id} - \mu_{jd}|^{\lambda_{jd}-2}} \tag{4}$$

$$\hat{\sigma}_{jd}^{(l+1)} = \left[\frac{\lambda_{jd} A(\lambda_{jd}) \sum_{i=1}^{N} p(j|X_i)|X_{id} - \mu_{jd}|^{\lambda_{jd}}}{\sum_{i=1}^{N} p(j|X_i)} \right]^{1/\lambda_{jd}} \tag{5}$$

$$\hat{\lambda}_{jd}^{(l+1)} \simeq \lambda_{jd} - \left[\left(\frac{\partial^2 \log[p(\mathcal{X}|\Theta)]}{\partial \lambda_{jd}^2} \right)^{-1} \left(\frac{\partial \log[p(\mathcal{X}|\Theta)]}{\partial \lambda_{jd}} \right) \right] \tag{6}$$

4. If the parameter estimates converge, then stop. Otherwise, go to Step 2.

The SMEM algorithm is based on the following: 1- use the EM algorithm represented above until convergence; 2- use a split and merge criteria to choose two components (g, h) to merge and one component q to split; 3- apply an efficient method to initialize the merged and split parameters; 4- perform the next EM round; 5- iterate split-and-merge and the EM until meeting some criterion.

2.1   Split and Merge Parameters Initialization

The combination of the gth and hth components are merged into the $g*$th component by matching the zeroth, first, second, and fourth moments:

$$p_{g*} = p_g + p_h \tag{7}$$

$$p_{g*} \mu_{g*d} = p_g \mu_{gd} + p_h \mu_{hd} \tag{8}$$

$$p_{g*}(\mu_{g*d}^2 + \sigma_{g*d}^2) = p_g(\mu_{gd}^2 + \sigma_{gd}^2) + p_h(\mu_{hd}^2 + \sigma_{hd}^2) \tag{9}$$

$$p_{g*}\left(\sigma_{g*d}^4 \frac{\Gamma(5/\lambda_{g*d})\Gamma(1/\lambda_{g*d})}{\Gamma^2(3/\lambda_{g*d})} + 6\mu_{g*d}^2 \sigma_{g*d}^2 + \mu_{g*d}^4 \right) =$$
$$p_g\left(\sigma_{gd}^4 \frac{\Gamma(5/\lambda_{gd})\Gamma(1/\lambda_{gd})}{\Gamma^2(3/\lambda_{gd})} + 6\mu_{gd}^2 \sigma_{gd}^2 + \mu_{gd}^4 \right) +$$
$$p_h\left(\sigma_{hd}^4 \frac{\Gamma(5/\lambda_{hd})\Gamma(1/\lambda_{hd})}{\Gamma^2(3/\lambda_{hd})} + 6\mu_{hd}^2 \sigma_{hd}^2 + \mu_{hd}^4 \right) \tag{10}$$

Suppose that we want to split the qth component in the mixture to two components g and h. Thus, we construct a set of solutions for this problem:

$$p_g = u_1 p_q \qquad p_h = (1 - u_1) p_q \tag{11}$$

$$\mu_{gd} = \mu_{qd} - u_2 \sigma_{qd} \sqrt{\frac{p_h}{p_g}} \qquad \mu_{hd} = \mu_{qd} + u_2 \sigma_{qd} \sqrt{\frac{p_g}{p_h}} \tag{12}$$

$$\sigma_{gd}^2 = u_3(1 - u_2^2)\sigma_{qd}^2 \frac{p_q}{p_g} \qquad \sigma_{hd}^2 = (1 - u_3)(1 - u_2^2)\sigma_{qd}^2 \frac{p_q}{p_h} \tag{13}$$

where u_1, u_2, and u_3 are randomly sampled from the Beta distribution $\beta(2,2)$, $\beta(2,2)$, $\beta(1,1)$, respectively. For λ_g and λ_h we set them equal to λ_q.

Country Field Forest Mountain Indoor Old Building Street Urban Water

Fig. 2. Sample images from the EPFL scene classification data set.

2.2 Split and Merge Criteria

We define the following merge criterion:

$$J_{merge}(g,h,\Theta) = \frac{P_g(\Theta)^T P_h(\Theta)}{||P_g(\Theta)||\,||P_h(\Theta)||} \tag{14}$$

where $P_j(\Theta) = (p(j|\boldsymbol{X}_1),\dots,p(j|\boldsymbol{X}_N))$, T denotes the transpose operation, and $||.||$ denotes the Euclidean vector norm. If the two components g and h have large J_{merge} (g,h,Θ) then they are a good candidate for the merge. For the split criterion, we adopt the local Kullback divergence as:

$$J_{split}(q,\Theta) = \int f_q(\mathcal{X}|\Theta) \log \frac{f_q(\mathcal{X}|\Theta)}{p(\mathcal{X}|\xi_q)} dx \tag{15}$$

where $f_q(\mathcal{X},\Theta)$ is an empirical distribution weighted by the posterior probability [7]. Thus, if the component q has the largest $J_{split}(q,\Theta)$ this means that it has the worst estimate and we should try to split it. Therefore, the SMEM algorithm can be summarized by:

1. Run EM algorithm from initial parameters $\Theta^{(0)}$ until convergence Θ^*
2. Sort the Split and Merge candidates using Θ^* (described in 2.2). Let $(g,h,q)_c$ denotes the cth candidate.
3. For $c = 1,\dots,C_{max}$ initialize the split and merge parameters (See 2.1).
4. Perform the full EM algorithm until convergence Θ^{**}
5. If $\log[p(\mathcal{X}|\Theta^{**})] > \log[p(\mathcal{X}|\Theta^*)]$ then set $\Theta^* \leftarrow \Theta^{**}$, $\log[p(\mathcal{X}|\Theta^*)] \leftarrow \log[p(\mathcal{X}|\Theta^{**})]$, and go to step 2

3 Experimental Results: Scene Classification

In our approach, an image is represented as a number of 5×5 patches. Our next step is feature extraction. For RGB images, experimental evaluation of several color models has indicated significant correlations between the colour bands and that the luminance component amounts to around 90 % of the signal energy, thus, we consider only the luminance channel. On the other hand, NIR has only one channel that has a much weaker dependence on R, G and B than they do to each other. Moreover, we consider the Haralick texture measurements [8] derived from the Gray-Tone Spatial Dependency Matrix (GLCM). Following [9], we calculate four angular Gray-Tone Spatial Dependency Matrices with 1 or 2 pixel offsets for each patch. Therefore we end up with

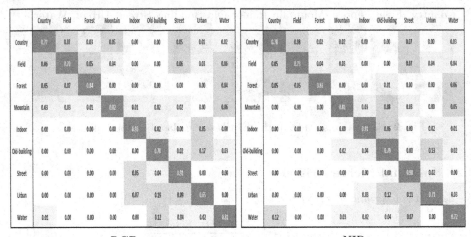

RGB   NIR

RGB+NIR

Fig. 3. Confusion tables for scene classification.

8 GLCMs for any image patch. Using these matrices, we extract 5 features namely: dissimilarity, Angular Second Moment (ASM), mean, standard deviation (STD) and correction. Thus, we end up with 40 component feature vector measures for each image patch. The next step is to use the global GGM introduced above to build a codebook for the data set, where each component in the mixture represents a codeword. Knowing, the different codewords we can deduce the BoW histogram for each image by classifying each patch to the component that gives the highest posterior probability. Later, we apply the pLSA model to the bag of visual words representation which allows the description of each image as a Z-dimensional vector, where Z is the number of aspects (or learnt topics) [10]. Finally, SVM classifier is used via LIBSVM package [11].

Our experimental study is applied on the EPFL scene classification data set (EPFL) [12]. This dataset consists of 477 images in 9 categories, (Country (52), Field (51), Forest

Table 1. Classification accuracy.

	RGB	NIR	RGB+NIR
GGM	80.1±(2.4)	80.7±(3.2)	82.9±(2.1)
Kmeans	77.2±(2.7)	77.5±(4.2)	79.3±(3.2)

(53), Mountain (55), Indoor (56), Old Building (51), Street (50), Urban (58), Water (51)), captured in RGB and NIR. As described in [12], the NIR images in this data set were captured by removing the NIR blocking filter in the digital camera. Sample images of different categories from the EPFL data set are displayed in Fig. 2. The major challenge in this data set is the overlap between object categories. For example urban and old building classes can be confused with each others also country can be confused with water class. For evaluation, we followed the same protocol as in [2] where we randomly selected, 10 times, 11 images per class for testing and trained the classifier using the remaining images. Firstly, we experiment with various different sizes of the visual vocabulary or in our case GGM components (80–512). We found that starting from K = 125 the classification accuracy did not changed as compared to difference in computational time. Thus, we have chosen to use K=125 in our approach. Concerning the number of latent topics used in the pLSA model we have used Z = 25. In order to assess if NIR can be a good alternative for RGB in classification, we applied our approach on the RGB images as well as the NIR images. In the case of using both RGB and NIR information together, we have built two codebooks: one for the luminance channel and one for NIR channel. Then, in order to fuse both information, we concatenated both BOW histograms together as input to the pLSA model. Figure 3 shows the confusion matrix of the EPFL data set for RGB, NIR, and RGB+NIR, respectively. In order to validate our method, we have compared it with the same method when K-means and Euclidean distance are used for codebook construction and BOW histogram calculation. From Table 1 we can conclude that our approach outperformed the K-means method. In addition, NIR performs better than RGB in case of scene classification, and fusing both the RGB and NIR cues together shows a small improvement over both individual results which confirms that both cues contain complementary information.

4   Conclusion

This paper makes three contributions. First, we implement a SMEM approach for the estimation of the GGM parameters. This approach can overcome the EM problem related to local maxima. Second, we use a global GGM to build a codebook for the image data set. This approach overcome the different problems of using K-means due to its robustness to outliers and noise level. Finally, we explore the idea that near-infrared (NIR) information, captured from an ordinary digital camera, can be useful in scene recognition. The obtained results show the merits of the approach.

Acknowledgment. The completion of this research was made possible thanks to the Natural Sciences and Engineering Research Council of Canada (NSERC).

References

1. Schaul, L., Fredembach, C., Süsstrunk, S.: Color image dehazing using the near-infrared. In: Proceedings of the IEEE International Conference on Image Processing (ICIP), pp. 1629–1632 (2009)
2. Salamati, N., Larlus, D., Csurka, G.: Combining visible and near-infrared cues for image categorisation. In: Proceedings of the British Machine Vision Conference (BMVC) (2011)
3. Oliva, A., Torralba, A.: Modeling the shape of the scene: a holistic representation of the spatial envelope. Int. J. Comput. Vis. **42**(3), 145–175 (2001)
4. Vogel, J., Schiele, B.: Natural scene retrieval based on a semantic modeling step. In: Enser, P.G.B., Kompatsiaris, Y., O'Connor, N.E., Smeaton, A.F., Smeulders, A.W.M. (eds.) CIVR 2004. LNCS, vol. 3115, pp. 207–215. Springer, Heidelberg (2004)
5. Quelhas, P., Monay, F., Odobez, J.M., Gatica-Perex, D., Tuytelaars, T., Van Gool, L.: Modeling Scenes with local descriptors and latent aspects. In: Proceedings of the International Conference on Computer Vision (ICCV), pp. 883–890 (2005)
6. Allili, M.S., Bouguila, N., Ziou, D.: Finite general Gaussian mixture modeling and application to image and video foreground segmentation. J. Electron. Imaging **17**(1), 1–13 (2008)
7. Ueda, N., Nakano, R., Ghahramani, Z., Hinton, G.E.: SMEM algorithm for mixture models. Neural Comput. **12**(9), 2109–2128 (2000)
8. Haralick, R., Shanmugam, K., Dinstein, I.: Texture features for image classification. IEEE Trans. Syst., Man, Cybern., SMC **3**(6), 610–621 (1973)
9. Lu, L., Toyama, K., Hager, G.D.: A two level approach for scene recognition. In: Proceedings of the IEEE Computer Society Conference on Computer Vision and Pattern Recognition (CVPR), pp. 688–695 (2005)
10. Hofmann, T.: Unsupervised learning by probabilistic latent semantic analysis. Mach. Learn. **42**(1/2), 177–196 (2001)
11. Chang, C.-C., Li, C.-J.: LIBSVM: a library for support vector machines. ACM Trans. Intel. Syst. Technol. **2**(27), 1–27 (2011)
12. Brown, M., Süsstrunk, S.: Multispectral SIFT for scene category recognition. In: Proceedings of the IEEE Computer Society Conference on Computer Vision and Pattern Recognition (CVPR), pp. 177–184 (2011)

Biometrics

Classification of Tooth Shapes for Human Identification Purposes–An Experimental Comparison of Selected Simple Shape Descriptors

Katarzyna Gościewska and Dariusz Frejlichowski[✉]

Faculty of Computer Science and Information Technology, West Pomeranian University of Technology, Szczecin, Żołnierska 52, 71-210 Szczecin, Poland
{kgosciewska,dfrejlichowski}@wi.zut.edu.pl

Abstract. The application of teeth as biometric features for human identification purposes is widely known thanks to their durability and distinguishability. Nowadays, due to both improved dental care and dental filling materials that are invisible on dental radiographs, the identification should focus on the analysis of tooth shapes, both crown and root, alongside their positions in the mouth. Such an approach requires the automation of digital radiograph processing methods, including: image enhancement, tooth contour extraction, tooth classification and numbering. This paper considers and examines the problem of tooth shape classification using simple shape descriptors and a template matching approach. An attempt is made to establish which simple shape descriptor gives the best classification results.

Keywords: Human identification · Teeth classification · Dental biometrics · Dental radiographs · Forensic odontology

1 Introduction

Over the past decades, the use of dental biometrics has systematically increased, and presently is commonly acceptable and appreciated thanks to a characteristic tooth's resistance to high temperatures and decomposition as well as its durability and distinguishability [1]. Dental data is frequently analysed by forensic odontology specialists, who are responsible for the proper handling, evaluation and examination of dental evidence that is to be further presented in the interest of justice. Odontology aims to identify unique features of human dentition [2]. This identification could concern the recognition of both suspects and victims and include age estimations or lesion detections.

In order to establish the identity of a dead person, post-mortem (PM) and ante-mortem (AM) data must be compared. This comparison uses dental records and/or dental radiographs [3]. Tooth features, fillings and other dental modifications and restorations can make identification possible without the need for

M. Kamel and A. Campilho (Eds.): ICIAR 2015, LNCS 9164, pp. 169–177, 2015.
DOI: 10.1007/978-3-319-20801-5_18

additional evidence [4]. Recent advances in dentistry have resulted in several obstacles that need to be dealt with during the identification process. Better oral hygiene has caused some people to have never undergone dental treatment. Additionally, during dental radiograph analysis, modern filling materials are barely distinguishable from natural tooth tissue. These changes have led to a greater focus on other dental characteristics, such as the shapes of crowns and roots, the size of the teeth, and the gaps between the teeth [5]. This, alongside the increasing amount of dental records and advances in image processing, created a need for the automation of the dental radiograph matching process and ultimately caused the creation of the Automated Dental Identification System (ADIS, e.g. [6]). ADIS comprises three main modules: i.e. feature extraction, dental atlas registration and feature matching. All of these stages aim to improve the dental radiograph comparison process through its automation and eliminating the need for human involvement. For the identification to be handled properly, it is crucial to select an appropriate description algorithm that can extract the most distinguishable tooth features.

This paper focuses on finding a suitable simple shape descriptor for tooth shape classification. Such a classification can act as a stage of the automated human identification process, which might occur before dental atlas registration or could be used to reduce the database before a more detailed shape matching process takes place. The rest of the paper is organized as follows: the second section presents some applications of dental data and examples of tooth classification. The third section describes some selected simple shape descriptors and the fourth section presents the experimental conditions and some results. The final section summarises and concludes the paper.

2   Example Applications of Dental Data

Teeth are built of different tissues whose hardnesses and densities and thereby visibilities on dental radiographs vary. There are a few types of dental radiographic images: i.e. periapical, bitewing and panoramic. The last one, whose images are called orthopantomograms (see Fig. 1 for examples), makes the visibility of all teeth and adjacent structures possible. Therefore, panoramic radiographs are considered a valuable source of data to determine the condition of teeth and their relative positions in the mouth, and the presence of other tissues [6]. For example, in [7–9], orthopantomograms were utilized as input data for methods proposed for an automatic forensic human identification process.

There are situations, such as plane crashes or natural disasters, when identification of victims becomes complicated and time-consuming, especially when a human body is severely damaged, or when there are a large number of victims and difficult conditions within the crash site or affected area. In these cases, dental data can be utilised to increase the accuracy of the identification process. In the past, certain catastrophic events have proven the efficiency of this approach and confirmed the need for dental identification systems. The Asian tsunami of 26th December 2004 left over 5000 people from 44 countries dead in Thailand.

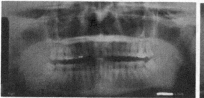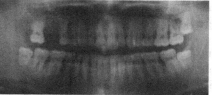

Fig. 1. Sample panoramic dental radiographs [6,10].

By 11th May 2005, 1474 bodies had been successfully identified and in general, dental features helped in 87 % of the identifications [11]. An earthquake in the Christchurch region of New Zealand on 22nd February 2011 caused the deaths of 181 people from 22 nations. 117 victims were successfully identified, among which 33 % of identifications were attributed to odontology alone and a further 14 % to odontology combined with fingerprint and DNA analysis. Moreover, for fragmented remains alone, odontology was either the primary identifier or participated to a total of 85 % of identifications [12].

The dental data can be considered as a group of images, each representing a tooth contour. In this case, the problem becomes one of a two-class classification of the tooth's type. There are several applications in which this approach is valuable. Firstly, it can be applied as a coarse classification in an attempt to reduce the size of the data space that will be further recognized using more sophisticated algorithms. Segmenting this data by tooth type should increase the degree of similarity within the class and of dissimilarity between the classes. Secondly, such pre-processing could simplify tooth numbering, i.e. dental atlas registration. Furthermore, only corresponding teeth of the same number would be matched during the identification process, hence decreasing computation time and increasing matching accuracy.

There are several examples of tooth classification found in the literature. In [13] a classification into molars and premolars based on bitewing radiographs is suggested as a step to precede tooth numbering. Teeth were classified using the Support Vector Machine (SVM) method and the classification accuracy was 89.07 % [13]. The authors of [14] proposed the use of Bayesian classification and tooth contour analysis to classify teeth into molars and premolars for bitewing radiographs. Contours were represented by Fourier descriptors calculated using a complex coordinate signature and the centroid distance function. For the pre-classification stage, the teeth were divided into molars and premolars. Final classification was then performed by considering the arrangement of the teeth and correcting any misclassifications. The pre-classification performance ratios varied from 72 % to 95.5 % depending on the type and position of each tooth, i.e. molars or premolars in the maxilla or the mandible [14]. Another way of classifying teeth into molars and premolars for dental bitewing radiographs was described in [15]. The authors of this paper proposed a binary linear SVM using three features: relative length to width ratios of both teeth and pulps, and relative crown size. The percentage classification accuracy was 95.1 % [15].

3   A Description of Selected Simple Shape Descriptors and a Shape Matching Approach

An automated dental identification process requires a selection of effective methods and algorithms to extract distinctive features from dental radiographs and for feature matching. Here the problem of tooth classification using simple shape descriptors is considered. The template matching approach was selected for shape matching. The purpose of this approach is to represent all shapes in the same way and to calculate the dissimilarities between every test object and every template representations in order to indicate a template that least differs from a particular test object. Then the template that has the smallest dissimilarity indicates the test object's class.

Simple shape descriptors are basic shape measurements or shape factors that represent specific shape characteristics by a single number. Basic shape measurements are for example the area A or perimeter P, which might be the number of pixels within a shape's region or contour respectively. In turn, shape factors are dimensionless quantities based on at least two shape measurements, which makes them invariant to scaling and translation of the shape within an image plane. Some selected shape descriptors are presented below.

There are three basic Feret measures (or Feret diameters): the X Feret—i.e. the distance between the minimal and maximal horizontal coordinates of a contour; the Y Feret—i.e. the distance between the minimal and maximal vertical coordinates of a contour; and the Max Feret—i.e. the maximum distance between any two points of a contour. A fourth measure, the X/Y Feret, is the ratio of the X Feret measure to the Y Feret measure [16].

A minimum bounding rectangle (MBR) is the smallest rectangular region that can contain every single point of a shape. The area, perimeter, length, and width of an MBR can be used as shape measurements. Moreover, they can be combined either with the area of an original shape or with each other to create three different shape factors—rectangularity, eccentricity and elongation. Rectangularity is the ratio of the area of a shape to the area of its MBR. Eccentricity is calculated as the ratio of width to length of the MBR, whereby length represents the longer side of the MBR and width the shorter one. Elongation is then the value of eccentricity subtracted from 1 [17].

A convex hull is the smallest convex region that contains all points of the original shape. The concept of this approach is similar to that of the MBR method, except the convex hull is better fitted to the shape. Two basic measurements of the convex hull are area and perimeter, from which two shape factors can be calculated, i.e. convexity as the ratio of the convex hull's perimeter to the original shape's perimeter [17] and solidity as the ratio of the area of a shape to the area of its convex hull. The solidity value is equal 1 for convex shapes [18].

The elongation and eccentricity measures can also be computed using the principal axes method (PAM). Principal axes are two unique line segments that cross each other orthogonally within the centroid of a shape [19]. The computation of eccentricity and elongation comprises several steps. Firstly, the covariance matrix C of the contour shape is calculated. Secondly, the lengths of the principal axes are equivalent to the eigenvalues λ_1 and λ_2 of the matrix C. Furthermore, the eccentricity is the ratio of λ_2 to λ_1, and the elongation is the eccentricity value multiplied by 2.

Another six shape factors are also taken into consideration, i.e. compactness, roundness, circularity ratio, circle variance, ellipse variance and the ratio of width to length. Compactness can be computed as the ratio of the square of the shape's perimeter to its area. The most compact shape is a circle. The roundness is a measure of a shape's sharpness and is based on two basic shape features, i.e. the area and perimeter. The circularity ratio defines the degree of similarity between an original shape and a perfect circle. It can be calculated as the ratio of the shape's area to the square of the shape's perimeter. The ellipse variance is defined as the mapping error of a shape fitting an ellipse that has an equal covariance matrix as the shape [17]. The ratio of width to length is based on the distance between the shape's centroid and its contour points. It is computed as a ratio of the maximal distance between the centroid and the contour points to the minimal distance [16].

4   Experimental Conditions and Results

The main goal of the experiments was to choose the best simple shape descriptor for two-class tooth classification. The test database consisted of 903 images (586 non-molars and 317 molars), each with a single tooth contour (which included both roots and crowns), extracted from panoramic radiographs of 30 different people. The template database consisted of ten other tooth contour images (see Fig. 2) and only one template set was used. Five of these images, with sample molar contours, represented the molar class. The rest represented the non-molar class (i.e. premolars, canines and incisors). Since the original tooth classes were known, it was possible to obtain a percentage classification accuracy.

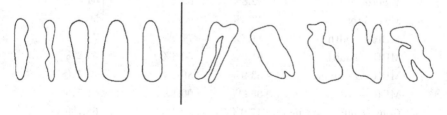

Fig. 2. Templates used in the experiments: non-molar class representatives are on the left, and molar class representatives are on the right.

The appearance of templates and test objects results from the type of the images and their low quality, which influence the teeth contour extraction. All teeth contours were automatically extracted from pantomograms using methods described in [7–9]. The general steps of contour extraction process include: pantomogram enhancement using Laplacian pyramid, separation of the upper and lower jaws, localization of the areas between the necks of teeth, removing the areas below the roots of teeth, extracting areas possibly containing a tooth based on separation lines, image morphological opening, image entropy filtration, calculation of each segment's features based on original image (segment's centroid, normalized mean value of the intensities of its pixels and the normalized vertical distance from the centroid to the curve separating the upper and lower jaw), determination of a tooth existence in a given segment using a fitness function and threshold value depending on the type of the tooth, morphological dilation on segments containing a tooth, tracing exterior objects boundaries, selection of the longest contour lying closest to the jaws separating line, Gaussian filtration of border pixels and ultimately the generation of final contour as a list of points.

Twenty-five experiments were performed in an attempt to ascertain the classification accuracy of the simple shape descriptors. Each experiment was carried out in the same way—all templates and test objects were represented using the same shape description algorithm. Each test object was then compared with each template using the template matching approach. The template that was the least different from a corresponding test object indicated the object's class. The classification results were compared with the original tooth classes in order to calculate the final classification accuracy. The percentage accuracy values obtained in the experiments using shape measurements and shape factors are provided in Tables 1 and 2 respectively.

Table 1. Percentage classification accuracy of the experiments using shape measurements.

Shape measurements	Percentage classification accuracy		
	Molar class	Non-molar class	In total
Shape – area	58.7%	91.5%	80.0%
Shape – perimeter	52.7%	79.0%	69.8%
X Feret	**82.6%**	**91.8%**	**88.6%**
Y Feret	32.8%	66.2%	54.5%
Max Feret	43.2%	68.1%	59.4%
MBR – width	81.7%	71.2%	74.9%
MBR – length	61.2%	50.3%	54.2%
MBR – perimeter	53.9%	86.5%	75.1%
MBR – area	65.6%	90.1%	81.5%
Convex hull – perimeter	47.0%	80.4%	68.7%
Convex hull – area	61.2%	91.0%	80.5%

In the experiments utilizing shape measurements (see Table 1) the best classification results were obtained for the X Feret measure and equal 88.6 % in total, where the accuracy of non-molar classification was 91.8 % and of molar—82.6 %. The shape's area, the area of the shape's convex hull and the MBR's area are also good solutions for non-molar classification—the accuracy values for these were 91.5 %, 91.0 % and 90.1 % respectively. Among the shape factors the best was the X/Y Feret measure—the total classification accuracy equal 87.2 %.

Table 2. Percentage classification accuracy of the experiments using shape factors.

Shape factors	Percentage classification accuracy		
	Molar class	Non-molar class	In total
Roundness	49.5%	55.3%	53.3%
Compactness	47.6%	56.8%	53.6%
Eccentricity (PAM)	80.1%	69.8%	73.4%
Circularity ratio	49.5%	55.3%	53.2%
Ellipse variance	52.7%	78.5%	69.4%
Elongation (PAM)	80.1%	69.7%	73.4%
Ratio of width to length	54.6%	56.6%	55.9%
Circle variance	65.9%	63.8%	64.6%
X/Y Feret	**94.0%**	**83.4%**	**87.2%**
Eccentricity (MBR)	88.0%	64.1%	72.5%
Elongation (MBR)	88.6%	76.1%	80.5%
Rectangularity	58.0%	40.1%	46.4%
Convexity	63.7%	67.4%	66.1%
Solidity	59.3%	59.7%	59.6%

The second best result can be attributed to the elongation measure and equal 80.5 % in total. Test objects were best classified to molar class using X/Y Feret, elongation, and eccentricity measures, the latter two being both based on MBRs. The percentage classification accuracy for these was 94.0 %, 88.6 % and 88.0 % respectively. Exemplary shapes that were correctly or incorrectly classified are presented in Fig. 3. Miscalssifications result from the image quality (noise, blur), quality of tooth contours extraction and the dentition type—dental implants or dental bridges give contours that differ from the selected templates.

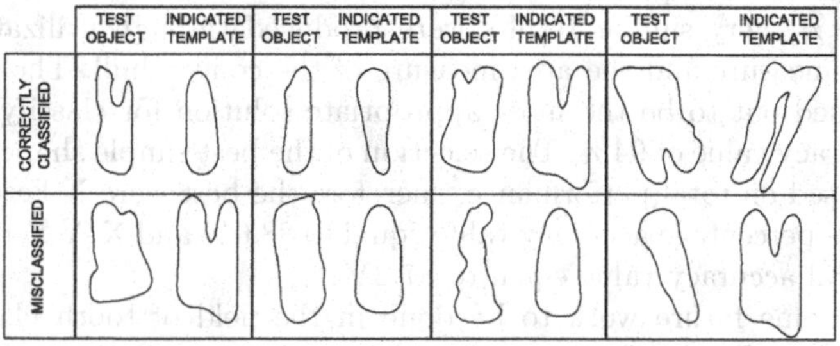

Fig. 3. Exemplary results showing correct and incorrect classifications for the experiment using X Feret measure.

The experimental results led to a significant conclusion. Taking into consideration the highest results obtained for individual classes it turned out that the shape measurements provided better solutions for the classification of non-molars while the shape factors were more suitable for molar classification. However, during the classification we process unknown tooth contours and the applied solution should be equally efficient for the classification to both classes. Therefore, based on the total percentage accuracy the most effective simple shape descriptors are the X Feret and the X/Y Feret measures. Surprisingly, such simple features were sufficient to distinguish between the two types of teeth and to obtain high classification performance ratios. The compact forms of the simple shape descriptors and the possibility of fast and easy matching are additional advantages, especially in the case of large databases. For the classification of molars, the results were similar to those presented in [13–15] despite the fact that here all human teeth extracted from orthopantomograms were taken into consideration, not only a dentition segment from bitewing radiograph images, such as in the above cited papers. The exact comparison of the results cannot be performed due to the mentioned differences in the input data used in the experiments.

5   Summary and Conclusions

This paper discussed the problem of teeth classification based on simple shape features. Such a classification can precede the teeth numbering process in automated dental identification systems or can be utilized to reduce the number of objects in large databases. Teeth are able to maintain their properties even in the cases of fire, water soaking, drying and decomposition. A high resistance to unfavourable conditions and the diversity of human dentition has resulted in the extensive use of teeth as biometric features for human identification in the field of odontology.

The main goal of the experiments was to find the best method for tooth classification. 903 test objects were classified into molar and non-molar classes across twenty-five experiments. Each of these was performed using different simple shape descriptors and a template matching approach. The experimental results were compared to the original tooth classes and the percentage classification accuracy was calculated. The best classification results for the non-molar class were obtained in the experiment using the X Feret measure, with an accuracy value of 91.8 %. Very similar results were produced through utilization of the shape's area measure and the area measure of the convex hull. The X/Y Feret measure turned out to be the most appropriate solution for classifying molars with an accuracy value of 94 %. The selection of the best simple shape descriptor should be based on total performance, therefore the best were X Feret measure with the total percentage accuracy value equal to 88.6 % and X/Y Feret measure for which total accuracy value equal to 87.2 %.

There is some future work to be done in the field of tooth classification. Obviously, other shape descriptors should be experimentally tested as well as different shape matching techniques wherever possible. Moreover, an attempt could be made to perform teeth classification over more than two classes.

References

1. Marana, A.N., Barboza, E.B., Papa, J.P., Hofer, M., Oliveira, D.T.: Dental Biometrics for Human Identification. In: Midori, A. (ed.) Biometrics – Unique and Diverse Applications in Nature, Science, and Technology, pp. 41–56. InTech (2011)

2. Parvathi, D., Thimmarada, V.B., Vishal, M., Vikas, S.: Automated dental identification system: an aid to forensic odontology. J. Indian Academy Oral Med. Radiol. 23(3), 360–364 (2011)
3. Chen, H., Jain, A.K.: Automatic forensic dental identification. In: Jain, A.K., Flynn, P., Ross, A.A. (eds.) Handbook of Biometrics, pp. 231–251 (2008)
4. Pushparaj, V., Gurunathan, U., Arumugam, B.: An effective dental shape extraction algorithm using contour information and matching by mahalanobis distance. J. Digit. Imaging, 1–10 (2012)
5. Nassar, D., Ammar, H.H.: A neural network system for matching dental radiographs. Pattern Recog. 40(1), 65–79 (2007)
6. Chen, H., Jain, A.K.: Dental biometrics. In: Li, S.Z., Jain, A.K. (eds.) Encyclopedia of Biometrics, pp. 216–223. Springer, US (2009)
7. Frejlichowski, D., Wanat, R.: Application of the Laplacian pyramid decomposition to the enhancement of digital dental radiographic images for the automatic person identification. In: Campilho, A., Kamel, M. (eds.) ICIAR 2010, Part II. LNCS, vol. 6112, pp. 151–160. Springer, Heidelberg (2010)
8. Frejlichowski, D., Wanat, R.: Extraction of teeth shapes from orthopantomograms for forensic human identification. In: Real, P., Diaz-Pernil, D., Molina-Abril, H., Berciano, A., Kropatsch, W. (eds.) CAIP 2011, Part II. LNCS, vol. 6855, pp. 65–72. Springer, Heidelberg (2011)
9. Frejlichowski, D., Wanat, R.: Automatic segmentation of digital orthopantomograms for forensic human identification. In: Maino, G., Foresti, G.L. (eds.) ICIAP 2011, Part II. LNCS, vol. 6979, pp. 294–302. Springer, Heidelberg (2011)
10. Jain, A.K., Chen, H.: Registration of dental atlas to radiographs for human identification. In: Proceedings of SPIE Conference on Biometric Technology for Human Identification II, vol. 5179, pp. 292–298 (2005)
11. James, H. (ed.): Thai tsunami victim identification – overview to date. J. Forensic Sci. 23(1), 1–18 (2005)
12. Trengrove, H.: Operation earthquake 2011: Christchurch earth-quake disaster victim identification. J. Forensic Odonto-Stomatology 29(2), 1–7 (2011)
13. Yuniarti, A., Nugroho, A.S., Amaliah, B., Arifin, A.Z.: Classification and numbering of dental radiographs for an automated human identification system. TELKOMNIKA 10(1), 137–146 (2012)
14. Mahoor, M.H., Abdel-Mottaleb, M.: Classification and numbering of teeth in dental bitewing images. Pattern Recog. 38, 517–586 (2005)
15. Lin, P.L., Lai, Y.H., Huang, P.W.: An effective classification and numbering system for dental bitewing radiographs using teeth region and contour information. Pattern Recog. 43, 1380–1392 (2010)
16. Frejlichowski, D.: An analysis of general shape of objects extracted from digital images using simple shape descriptors. Metody Informatyki Stosowanej 4, 23–29 (2009). (in Polish)
17. Yang, M., Kpalma, K., Ronsin, J.: A survey of shape feature extraction techniques. In: Yin, P.Y. (ed.) Pattern Recognition, pp. 43–90 (2008)
18. Rosin, P.L.: Computing global shape measures. In: Chen, C.H., Wang, P.S.P. (eds.) Handbook of Pattern Recognition and Computer Vision, 3rd edn., pp. 177–196 (2005)
19. Peura, M., Iivarinen, J.: Efficiency of simple shape descriptors. In: Aspects of Visual Form, pp. 443–451. World Scientific (1997)

Micro Genetic and Evolutionary Feature Extraction: An Exploratory Data Analysis Approach for Multispectral Iris Recognition

Pablo A. Arias, Joseph Shelton, Kaushik Roy$^{(\boxtimes)}$, Foysal Ahmad, and Gerry V. Dozier

North Carolina A&T State University, Greensboro, NC, USA
{parias,jasheltl,fahmad}@aggies.ncat.edu,
{kroy,gvdozier}@ncat.edu

Abstract. Most of the current iris recognition methods utilize the iris images that are captured between the 700 and 900 nm range for verification and identification purposes. However, iris images acquired beyond this narrow range have shown to uncover identifiable information not previously available within the 700 − 900 nm near-infrared range (NIR). In this work, we will employ a feature extraction technique on iris images from 450 nm to 1550 nm to elicit iris information on a wider electromagnetic spectrum. We will employ the use of a Genetic and Evolutionary Feature Extraction technique (GEFE) and compare the performance against an exploratory data analytic approach, referred to as mGEFE. The mGEFE technique discovers salient pixel regions in iris images. We also perform cross spectral analysis among the wavelengths. Results show that GEFE outperforms mGEFE and LBP in regards to recognition accuracy, but mGEFE produces FEs that show salient areas of iris images to explore for optimal recognition.

Keywords: Iris recognition · Exploratory data analysis · Genetic and evolutionary feature extraction · Genetic and evolutionary computation

1 Introduction

Iris recognition technologies are becoming more renown due to the ease at which iris samples can be obtained as well as their recognition accuracy. The iris as a form of identification and verification has the advantages of not being easy to forget or steal, unlike traditional text based or token based artifacts. The iris image is normally captured in the 700-900 nm range [1, 2]. However, more information can be captured using different ranges outside of the norm. More specifically, a multispectral image contains information across multiple wavelengths (or wavelength bands) of the electromagnetic spectrum [2].

In this work, we are focused on texture based feature extraction. Some popular iris texture based extraction techniques include Gabor filters [3], HAAR transforms [4], and the Local Binary Patterns (LBP) technique [5–7]. It is the LBP technique that our focus is on, due to its simplistic nature and resistance to illumination invariance.

© Springer International Publishing Switzerland 2015
M. Kamel and A. Campilho (Eds.): ICIAR 2015, LNCS 9164, pp. 178–185, 2015.
DOI: 10.1007/978-3-319-20801-5_19

This technique divides an image into even sided grids and extracts features from each grid, or patch.

Previous research has been done on hybridizing the LBP technique with Genetic and Evolutionary Computation (GEC) for iris recognition [8, 9]. This hybrid technique, Genetic and Evolutionary Feature Extraction (GEFE), evolves the locations, number, and dimensions of patches in order to extract features from the most discriminatory regions of an image. GEFE has been shown to outperform the traditional LBP approach on facial datasets [9]. Other research has been conducted using GEFE at the Center for Advanced Studies in Identity Science (CASIS) involving iris recognition [10, 11].

In this work, we will use a variation of GEFE that reduces the patch size to its smallest possible dimensions. By constraining the patches to this degree, patches will discover the most salient pixels within iris images. This variation will be known as micro-GEFE (mGEFE), and we can consider this to be an exploratory data analysis approach for biometric data.

Exploratory data analysis is an approach that employs techniques in order to identify the key features of a data set, its uses ranging from age distribution of Vietnamese population to regional per capita GDP in Europe [12–16]. Exploratory data analysis can be characterized by putting emphasis on "substantive understanding of data that address the broad question of 'what is going on here' [16]." In our experiments, we apply exploratory techniques in order to discover the highest discriminating pixels within an iris image. This will result in not only a reduction of the amount of time for feature extraction, but an increase in recognition accuracy.

The remainder of this paper is as follows. In Sect. 2, we will discuss the feature extraction techniques used. In Sect. 3, we will describe the process used to execute our experiment. Section 4 will contain the results of the experiments and Sect. 5 concludes the manuscript.

2 Feature Extraction Methods

2.1 Local Binary Patterns

One of the more popular texture based feature extraction techniques is the LBP technique [6]. This technique can locate texture patterns within an image and form a feature vector (FV). The LBP technique is effective in the field of biometric recognition for extracting texture features. The LBP technique will create a unique FV for each uniquely textured image, and FVs can be enrolled in the biometric system for future comparisons.

The LBP technique divides images using a user specified grid-based scheme. This scheme, or group of patches, is referred to as a feature extractor (FE). Within each partition, or patch, the pixels are compared to one another. Each pixel that is surrounded by neighboring pixels is associated with a texture pattern. The surrounded pixel is referred to as the center pixel. The number of neighboring pixels and the distance between neighboring pixels and center pixels is user specified. We use the 8 closest neighboring pixels for each center pixel. A texture pattern is then represented as a binary string, which is formed by taking the differences between neighboring pixels and the corresponding center pixel. If the difference is less than zero, a 0 bit is placed in the texture pattern; else a 1 bit is used.

Each patch has a histogram associated with it, where the bins within the histogram represent a texture pattern. The number of bins is equivalent to the number of possible texture patterns given the specification of the binary string length as well as any other specifications. For example, using 8 neighboring pixels will result in $2^8 = 256$ possible texture patterns, and 256 bins in the histogram. The histograms are filled in and concatenated together to form the FV for the input image.

2.2   GEFE$_{ML}$ and MGEFE$_{ML}$

The feature extraction technique we are using is a hybrid between the LBP technique and GECs. GECs are an artificial intelligence technique that simulates Darwinian principles to evolve solutions for problems. Important components within a GEC include candidate solutions (CSs) and a fitness function. The CSs are possible solutions to the problem, and the fitness function is a function that evaluates the effectiveness of CSs.

In the case of GEFE, a CS consists of the locations, dimensions and numbers of patches in a LBP based FE. The fitness function is the representation of how accurate a FE is on a biometric system. The resulting fitness is the number of errors that occurs on the simulated system plus the percentage of patches being used for extraction.

GEFE will create patches within the range of 3 by 3 to the entire image dimensions. These patch areas encompass enough of an area to extract salient information. However, by restricting the size of the patches to a dimension of 5 by 5, the patches will focus on the most salient pixels in an image. This variation will be known as mGEFE. The fitness function for mGEFE is based on recognition accuracy, so patches that extract from the most salient pixels will be strongly considered. Apart from the patch dimensions, mGEFE functions exactly like GEFE.

In the original implementation of GEFE, a set of FEs is evolved on a training set to produce FEs that could correctly identify subjects in that particular data set. To produce FEs that could generalize well on unseen subjects, cross validation concepts are incorporated into GEFE.

Cross validation in Genetic and Evolutionary Feature Extraction – Machine Learning (GEFE$_{ML}$) is done by initially generating a population of random FEs. Every candidate FE is then evaluated on the training set and additionally evaluated on a validation set. The results of the FEs on the validation set do not affect the training of FEs. While a stopping condition has not been met, FEs are selected to breed, and offspring FEs are created. The offspring are evaluated on the training set, but they are also applied on the validation set.

The FE with the best results on the validation set is stored as FE*. FE* is only updated when a new candidate FE performs better on the validation set than the currently stored FE*. The offspring are used to create the new population and this process repeats until the stopping condition has been met. Under this design, FE* should generalize better on unseen subjects opposed to the best performing FE on the training set. The mGEFE technique with cross validation is simply referred to as mGEFE$_{ML}$.

3   Experiments

In this paper, we conducted our experiments on 38,129 iris images [17]. These images were divided into 13 sections, each section approximating roughly 3000 images. Each section corresponded to spectral band used to capture each image, ranging from 405 nm to 1550 nm. For our first experiment, we conducted pair-wise comparisons for each band. We divided the set into three sections: training, validation, and testing. The training, validation, and testing have a total of 44, 18, and 29 subjects respectively. For both $GEFE_{ML}$ and $mGEFE_{ML}$, we ran it for 30 runs and for each run; we ran it through 1000 generations. For cross-spectral analysis, we used the FEs evolved from the pair-wise comparisons and applied them to each of the opposing spectral bands in our dataset. FEs were evolved based on iris identification performance, while verification performance is shown in the form of the Receiver Operating Characteristic (ROC) curve. The LBP variation that we used uses all 256 possible texture patterns; this variation proved to have the best performance on the face and iris datasets [10, 11]. Previous research has shown similar results, where using 256 patterns has shown to be the best variation [10]. We tested different partitions of LBP and found that 7 columns by 10 rows was the best performing partition. This 70 patch LBP partition is compared to $GEFE_{ML}$ & $mGEFE_{ML}$ in the results.

4   Results

In Table 1, the performances of LBP and $mGEFE_{ML}$ are shown. The performance includes not only the identification accuracy but the percentage of patches activated as well. The purpose of $GEFE_{ML}$ and $mGEFE_{ML}$ is to evolve FEs that will accurately match subjects that they were not trained on. With this in mind, all performances are of the feature extraction techniques on the test set. Please note that $GEFE_{ML}$ evolves a set of FEs that were optimized on the training set and FEs that performed best on the validation set. We refer to each set as <opt> or <val> .

The first column shows the spectrum in which the performances are based on. The second column shows the spectrum from which the FEs were evolved. For each spectrum, the cross spectrum chosen was the spectrum that the spectrum FEs had the best performance on. Because LBP is deterministic, there is only a single accuracy associated with each spectrum. The columns below $mGEFE_{ML}$ are the accuracies of <Opt> $mGEFE_{ML}$ and <Val> $mGEFE_{ML}$. The last two columns are the average numbers of patches used from the 30 FEs for both <Opt> FEs and <Val> FEs.

The results of $mGEFE_{ML}$ are varied by spectrum. In every case, mGEFE outperformed LBP in respect to number of patches used. However, in certain spectrums LBP outperformed $mGEFE_{ML}$ in regards to recognition accuracy. $GEFE_{ML}$ was run and had a statistically significant performance over $mGEFE_{ML}$ and LBP in regards to accuracy. To determine statistical significance, a t-test was used to compare the performances of <opt> and <val> for each spectrum. A confidence value of 0.05 was used to determine significance. The 800-1300 nm cross spectral range had the best recognition accuracies for GEFE overall, with the 800 nm spectrum being the best for $GEFE_{ML}$. It should be noted that the <Val> FEs had an average fewer amount of patches used.

Table 1. Comparison of mGEFE$_{ML}$ and LBP.

Spectrum	Cross Spectrum	Accuracy			Patches	
		LBP	mGEFE$_{ML}$		Opt	Val
			\<Opt\>	\<Val\>		
405	405	7.02	7.02(2.57)	8.77(3.16)	30.17	31.22
	1300	n/a	10.53(3.68)	8.77(3.68)	39.90	40.42
505	505	45.61	59.65(46.32)	54.39(44.15)	36.91	35.16
	1300	n/a	61.40(48.95)	61.40(47.84)	39.90	40.42
620	620	64.91	68.42(60.35)	71.93(59.59)	37.92	38.94
	1300	n/a	75.44(61.40)	75.44(59.82)	39.90	40.42
700	700	50.87	35.09(27.60)	36.84(27.72)	44.30	42.33
	1300	n/a	52.63(34.97)	52.63(37.87)	39.90	40.42
800	800	91.23	96.49(89.24)	91.23(86.84)	39.53	39.57
	970	n/a	96.49(90.76)	96.49(89.82)	39.77	39.93
910	910	89.66	77.19(66.55)	75.44(63.27)	46.80	45.48
	970	n/a	87.82(70.58)	87.72(65.79)	39.77	39.93
911	911	87.93	75.44(55.15)	77.19(51.58)	39.53	37.96
	1300	n/a	84.21(61.46)	84.21(59.18)	39.90	40.42
970	970	84.48	78.95(59.01)	78.95(54.85)	39.77	39.93
	1300	n/a	73.68(58.13)	75.44(54.80)	39.90	40.42
1070	1070	89.66	70.18(58.30)	68.42(51.99)	49.23	45.45
	505	n/a	80.70(48.83)	71.93(39.82)	36.91	35.16
1200	1200	93.10	70.18(61.17)	68.42(55.96)	40.36	40.46
	1300	n/a	82.46(64.68)	82.46(60.29)	39.90	40.42
1300	1300	82.76	70.18(51.36)	66.67(47.95	39.90	40.42
	911	n/a	70.18(48.25)	70.18(42.75)	39.54	37.96
1450	1450	36.21	14.04(3.98)	8.77(3.45)	34.97	32.93
	910	n/a	8.77(4.04)	17.54(5.79)	46.80	45.48
1550	1550	31.03	8.77(3.68)	8.77(2.81)	35.36	33.92
	1300	n/a	14.04(5.32)	12.28(4.74)	39.90	40.42

Though mGEFE$_{ML}$ had the worse accuracy than LBP in the 910-1550 nm range, in the 405-620 nm spectrum range mGEFE$_{ML}$ had a better accuracy.

Figures 1, 2, 3 and 4 show the ROC curves for both GEFE$_{ML}$ and mGEFE$_{ML}$. ROC curve plots the rate of impostor attempts accepted on the x-axis, against the corresponding rate of genuine attempts accepted on the y-axis along a rising threshold. Figure 1 shows that the pair wise matching achieved 48 % true accept rate (TAR) at 1 % false accept rate (FAR) in the 800 nm spectrum using GEFE$_{ML}$. Figure 2 shows that the cross spectral matching reached 54 % TAR at 1 % FAR in the 800 nm spectrum using GEFE$_{ML}$. Figure 3 shows that the pair wise matching obtained 48 % TAR at 1 % FAR in the 800 nm spectrum using mGEFE$_{ML}$. In Fig. 4, the cross spectral performance reached 40 % TAR at 1 % FAR in the 800 nm spectrum using mGEFE$_{ML}$. The 800 nm spectrum seems to show the best performance whereas the 450 spectrum has the worst performing FEs for both GEFE$_{ML}$ and mGEFE$_{ML}$. Figures 5 and 6 show

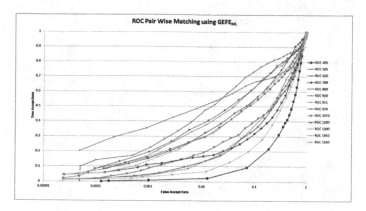

Fig. 1. ROC curve for pair wise matching using GEFE

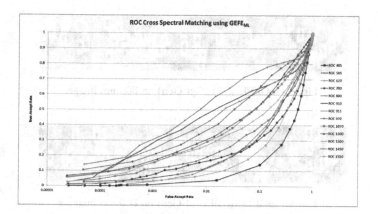

Fig. 2. ROC curve for cross spectral matching using GEFE$_{ML}$

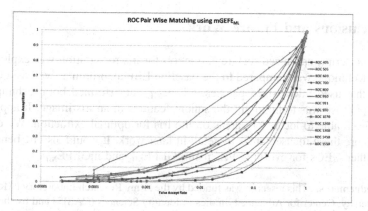

Fig. 3. ROC curve for pair wise matching using mGEFE$_{ML}$

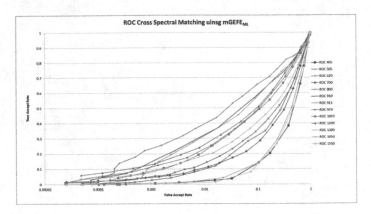

Fig. 4. ROC curve for cross spectral matching using mGEFE$_{ML}$

Fig. 5. mGEFE$_{ML}$ FE(Opt Gen) on 800 nm image

Fig. 6. mGEFE$_{ML}$ FE(Val Gen) on 800 nm image

the best mGEFE$_{ML}$ FEs on the 800 nm dataset. It appears that the right area is the preferred area of extraction for distinguishing between different individuals.

5   Conclusions and Future Work

In this manuscript, optimized feature extraction for iris recognition was explored. The GEFE$_{ML}$ technique was compared to the baseline LBP algorithm as well as a GEFE$_{ML}$ variation that used micro sized patches. GEFE$_{ML}$ outperformed both techniques, but the main purpose was to highlight the salient features in an iris image. It appears that we have been able to locate key areas on the iris for optimal extraction. We can most likely explore these focused areas in detail in later work. It would also be beneficial to explore other GECs for evolving FEs using GEFE$_{ML}$ and mGEFE$_{ML}$.

Acknowledgements. This research was funded by the Army Research Laboratory (ARL) for the multi-university, Center for Advanced Studies in Identity Sciences (CASIS) and by the National Science Foundation (NSF), Science & Technology Center: Bio/Computational Evolution in

Action Consortium (BEACON). The authors would like to thank the ARL, NSF, and BEACON for their support of this research.

References

1. Popplewell, K., Roy, K., Ahmad, F., Shelton, J.: Multispectral iris recognition utilizing Hough transform and modified LBP, pp. 1396–1399. Proc. in IEEE Intl. Conf. on Systems, Man and Cybernetics (2014)
2. Boyce, C., Ross, A., Monaco, M., Hornak, L., Li, X.: Multispectral iris analysis: a preliminary study. In: Proceedings of Computer Vision and Pattern Recognition Workshop, pp. 51–59 (2006)
3. Grigorescu, S.E., Petkov, N., Kruizinga, P.: Comparison of texture features based on Gabor filters. IEEE Trans. on Image Process. **11**, 1160–1167 (2002)
4. Pang, Y., Li, X., Yuan, Y., Tao, D., Pan, J.: Fast Haar transform based feature extraction for face representation and recognition. IEEE Trans. Inf. Forensics Secur. **4**(3), 441–450 (2009)
5. Ahonen, T., Hadid, A., Pietikainen, M.: Face description with local binary patterns: application to face recognition. IEEE Trans. Pattern Anal. Mach. Intell **28**(12), 2037–2041 (2006)
6. Ojala, T., Pietikainen, M.: Unsupervised texture segmentation using feature distributions. Pattern Recogn. **32**(3), 477–486 (1999)
7. Mäenpää, T.: The Local binary pattern approach to texture analysis: Extensions and applications. Oulun yliopisto (2003)
8. Shelton, J., Dozier, G., Bryant, K., Adams, J., Popplewell, K., Abegaz, T., Ricanek, K.: Genetic based LBP feature extraction and selection for facial recognition. In: Proceedings of ACM Annual Southeast Regional Conference, pp. 197–200 (2011)
9. Shelton, J., Dozier, G., Bryant, K., Small, L., Adams, J., Leflore, D., Alford, A., Woodard, D., Ricanek, K.: Genetic and Evolutionary Feature Extraction via X-TOOLSS. In: Proceedings of International Conference on Genetic and Evolutionary Methods (2011)
10. Shelton, J., Roy, K., O'Connor, B., Dozier, G.: Mitigating iris-based replay attacks. Intl. J. Mach. Learn. Comput. **4**(3), 204–209 (2014)
11. O'Connor, B., Roy, K., Shelton, J., Dozier, G.: Iris recognition using fuzzy level set and GEFE. Intl. J. Mach. Learn. Comput. **4**(3), 204–209 (2014)
12. Jones, K.: Exploratory Data Analysis. National Physical Laboratory (2004)
13. 1.1.1. What Is EDA? 1.1.1. What Is EDA? National Institute of Science and Technology, n.d. Web, 19 February (2015)
14. Le Gallo, J., Ertur, C.: Exploratory spatial data analysis of the distribution of regional per capita GDP in Europe, 1980–1995. Pap. Reg. sci. **82**(2), 175–201 (2003)
15. Tukey, J.W.: Exploratory data analysis (1977)
16. Behrens, J.T.: Principles and procedures of exploratory data analysis. Psychol. Methods **2**(2), 131 (1997)
17. Multispectral Iris Dataset: Portions of the research in this paper use the Consolidated Multispectral Iris Dataset of iris images collected under the Consolidated Multispectral Iris Dataset Program, sponsored by the US Government

Biometric Analysis of Human Ear Matching Using Scale and Rotation Invariant Feature Detectors

Soumyajit Sarkar[1], Jizhong Liu[2], and Guanghui Wang[1(✉)]

[1] Department of EECS, University of Kansas, Lawrence, Kansas 66045, USA
ghwang@ku.edu
[2] Institute of Robotics, Nanchang University, Nanchang 330031, China

Abstract. Biometric ear authentication has received enormous popularity in recent years due to its uniqueness for each and every individual, even for identical twins. In this paper, two scale and rotation invariant feature detectors, SIFT and SURF, are adopted for recognition and authentication of ear images; an extensive analysis has been made on how these two descriptors work under certain real-life conditions; and a performance measure has been given. The proposed technique is evaluated and compared with other approaches on two data sets. Extensive experimental study demonstrates the effectiveness of the proposed strategy.

Keywords: Biometrics · Image matching · SIFT · SURF · Ear recognition

1 Introduction

Biometric authentication of people based on various anatomical characteristics, like eye, ear, face, iris, and fingerprint have attracted lots of attention during the past few decades, and some of these techniques have already been successfully applied for recognition and authentication. However, many systems are not very robust and may fail to work under certain conditions. Biometric ear recognition is a relatively new technique that may surpass the existing systems due to several significant reasons. For example, the acquisition of ear images is relatively easy and, unlike iris, can be captured without the co-operation of individuals [1].

Human ear contains rich and stable features which are more reliable than face features, as the structure of the ear is not subject to change with age. It has also been found out that no two ears are exactly the same even for identical twins [3]. The detailed structure of ear is not only very unique but also permanent, since the shape of a human ear never shows drastic changes over the course of life. The research on ear identification was first conducted by Bertillon, a French criminologist, in 1890. The process was refined by American police officer, Iannarelli [6], who divided the ear based on various distinctive features of seven parts: i.e. helix, concha, antihelix, crux of helix, intertragic notch, tragus, and antitragus [3].

In this Paper, we propose to use two scale and rotation invariant feature detectors, i.e. SIFT (scale invariant feature transform) and SURF (speed up robust features), for

© Springer International Publishing Switzerland 2015
M. Kamel and A. Campilho (Eds.): ICIAR 2015, LNCS 9164, pp. 186–193, 2015.
DOI: 10.1007/978-3-319-20801-5_20

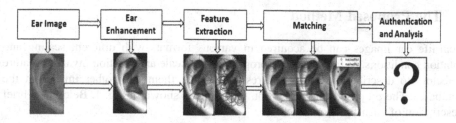

Fig. 1. The pipeline of the propose ear recognition system

ear recognition. Both SIFT and SURF extract specific interest points from an image and generate descriptors for the feature points to a form a reliable matching results. Extensive experiments have been carried out on two different sets of databases to evaluate their performance with respect to various rotations and scales. One of the most important feature of ear images is its easiness in acquisition, however, the acquired images may be in different scales, rotations, and illumination. The scale and rotation invariant property of the SIFT and SURF algorithms makes them perfect for ear authentication under various circumstances.

The rest of the paper is organized as follows. Some background and related research are discussed in Sect. 2; the proposed method is presented in details in Sect. 3; some experimental results and analysis are given in Sect. 4; and the paper is concluded in Sect. 5.

2   Background and Related Research

Human ears start to develop between fifth and seventh weeks of pregnancy. At this stage, the embryo face takes on more definition as mouth perforation, nostrils and ear indentations become visible. Forensic science literature reports that ear growth after the first four months of birth is highly linear [6]. The rate of stretching is five times greater than normal during the period from 4 months to the age of 8, after which, it is constant until the age of seventy when it again increases. Thus it can be said that ear remains almost unchanged during a substantial period of 62 years and, thus, it is one of the strong points of considering ear for biometric authentication.

An ear biometric system can be viewed as a typical pattern recognition problem, where the input image is reduced to a set of features that are subsequently used to compare against the feature sets of the other images in the database in order to find a best match to determine identity [2]. Based on this finding, a good amount of research has been done on ear recognition [5, 8].

Haar-based methods have given fairly better results for face detection as it is robust and fast. The different types of ear recognition systems include those of intensity-based, force-field based, 2D curves geometry, wavelet transformation, Gabor filters, SIFT, and 3D features. The force-field transforms gained popularity due to its uniqueness and efficiency [10]. Similar methods have also been implemented on other kinds of ear recognition systems [8].

3 The Proposed Method

Real-life ear images can be acquired in various formats with different scaling and rotation conditions. In this paper, we propose to use scale and rotation invariant feature detectors to describe interested features and match them with other images in the databases. The proposed ear recognition technique is shown in Fig. 1. Below is a brief description of each function block.

3.1   Ear Image Enhancement

The ear enhancement process starts with contrast enhancement, where we apply histogram equalization to improve the contrast in an image in order to stretch out its intensity range, from which, we get an enhanced version of the original image by maximizing the contrast level of an image, as shown in Fig. 2.

It has been experimentally found that after contrast stretching, both the SIFT and SURF detectors are able to find more feature points. Thus, image enhancement is an

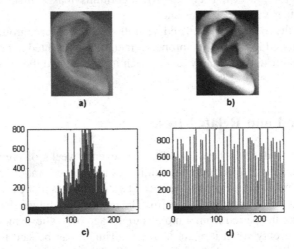

Fig. 2. Image enhancement result.(a) Original image;(b) enhanced image; (c) histogram distribution of the original image;d) histogram distribution of the enhanced image

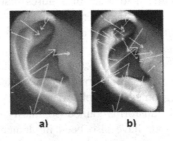

Fig. 3. (a) 10 SIFT features detected in the original image; (b) 32 SIFT features detected in the enhanced image.

essential step of the entire process. As shown in Fig. 3, 10 SIFT keypoints were detected in the original image, while 32 features were detected in the enhanced image.

3.2 Feature Extraction and Matching

Feature Extraction is the process of extracting salient features from the image, and each feature is described by a vector which summarizes the required information for that point [2]. Features are extracted exclusively in order for the image to be matched with the features of the input image to authenticate the ear so that a decision can be made. In this paper, two rotation and scale invariant features are studied.

Speed Up Robust Features (SURF): SURF is a high performance, fast scale and rotation invariant point detector and descriptor. It outperforms previously proposed schemes with respect to repeatability, distinctiveness and robustness [9]. The detector is based on the Hessian matrix and uses a very basic Laplacian-based detector, called difference of Gaussian (DoG). The implementation of SURF can be divided into three main steps. First, interest points are selected at distinctive locations in the image, such as corners, blobs, and T-junctions. Then, the neighborhood of every interest point is represented by a feature vector. This descriptor has to be distinctive and robust to noise, detection errors, and geometric and photometric deformations. Finally, the descriptor vectors are matched between different images. When working with local features, the issue that needs to be settled is the required level of invariance. Here the rotation and scale invariant descriptors seem to offer a good compromise between feature complexity and robustness to commonly occurring deformations, skew, anisotropic scaling, and perspective effects [9].

Given a point in an Image, the Hessian matrix is defined as follows:

$$H(x, \sigma) = \begin{bmatrix} L_{XX}(x, \sigma) & L_{Xy}(x, \sigma) \\ L_{Xy}(x, \sigma) & L_{yy}(x, \sigma) \end{bmatrix} \tag{1}$$

where $L_{XX}(x, \sigma)$ is the convolution of the Gaussian second order derivative $\frac{\partial^2}{\partial x^2} g(\sigma)$ at the point. This method leads to a novel detection, description and subsequent matching steps. Using relative strengths and orientations of gradient reduces the effect of photometric changes. Figure 4 shows the detection results with respect to rotation and scale change. As shown in Sect. 4, it has been found that though SURF is rotation invariant,

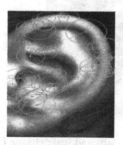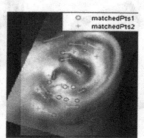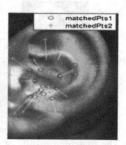

Fig. 4. The detected SURF features (left), matching result under rotation (middle) and scale change (right).

its performance in matching, i.e. matching score, decreases sharply when the images are rotated or scaled. The SURF features are not stable over various rotation angles and scale changes.

Scale Invariant Feature Transform (SIFT): The SIFT features are invariant to image scaling and rotation and shown to provide robust matching across a substantial range of affine distortion, change in 3D viewpoint, addition of noise, and change in illumination. The computation stages of SIFT are as follows.

Step 1. Scale space extrema detection: The first step is to construct a Gaussian scale over all the locations. It is implemented efficiently by using a difference of Gaussian (DoG) to identify potential interest points. The 2D Gaussian operator $G(x,y,\sigma)$ is convolved with the input image $I(x,y)$:

$$L(x, y, \sigma) = G(x, y, \sigma) * I(x, y) \tag{2}$$

where the DoG images are obtained by subtracting the subsequent scales in each octave.

$$G(x, y, \sigma) = L(x, y, k\sigma) - L(x, y, \sigma) \tag{3}$$

Step 2. Accurate keypoint localization: Once a keypoint has been detected, a detailed model is fitted to determine its location and scale. The keypoints are selected based on measures of their stability. Further details can be found in [4].

Step 3. Orientation assignment: One or more orientations are assigned to each keypoint location based on local image gradient directions. All future operations are performed on image data that has been transformed relative to the assigned orientation, scale, and location for each feature.

Step 4. Keypoint descriptor: The local image gradients are measured at selected scale in the region around each keypoint. They are transformed into a certain representation that allows for significant levels of local shape distortion and shape illumination.

Figure 5 shows an evaluation of the SIFT detector. It is evident the SIFT keypoints are very stable when the images are rotated and scaled. The scaling results are much better compared to the rotation results in our experiments.

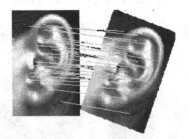 

Fig. 5. The matching results of SIFT detectors under rotation (left) and scale change (right).

Matching of Ear Images: Image matching is the process by which the features extracted from the SIFT and the SURF descriptors of the input image are being matched with the features already computed and stored in the database. Figure 6 shows the matching results using the SURF and SIFT detectors, where the nearest neighbor is defined as the keypoint with the minimum Euclidean distance for the invariant descriptor vector.

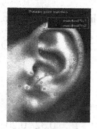
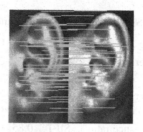

Fig. 6. The matching results of SURF detector (left) and SIFT detector (right).

4 Experimental Results and Analysis

The proposed approach has been evaluated on two data sets. One is the AMI database [7], which consists of 175 ear images; and the other is the IIT Delhi database [5], which consists of 494 images of 125 distinct persons. The images were all converted to grayscale images for ease of work. It has also been found out that contrast enhancement is an important factor for feature detection and matching, because it makes the feature detectors find better set of keypoints and increase the effectiveness of matching.

According to the experiments performed, it has been found that upper helix, antihelix, and tragus are the most important regions for feature selection compared to others. These regions contribute to about 64 % of the feature points.

Figure 7 shows the average number of keypoints found and matched by the SIFT and SURF detectors when the images are rotated from 0 to 180°. The results suggest that the SIFT detector is fairly stable over a variation from 20° to 160°, whereas the SURF detector, though faster and rotation invariant, is not very stable.

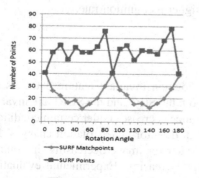
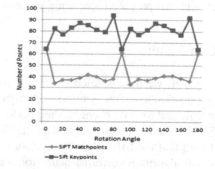

Fig. 7. The detected and matched keypoints by SURF and SIFT

Table 1 shows the keypoints detected and matched by the SIFT and SURF detectors, where the performance ratio is the ratio of the number of matched points to that of detected features. It is obvious that the SIFT algorithm performs better when the sizes of images are decreased, while the SURF algorithm performs better when the image sizes are increased. However, the amount of detected keypoints by the SIFT detector is always higher than that by the SURF detector.

Table 1. SIFT and SURF detection and matching results at different scales

Scaling		0.25	0.5	0.75	1.0	2.0	3.0	4.0
Number of features	SIFT	28	53	58	64	170	247	233
	SURF	3	12	30	41	39	41	44
Number of matches	SIFT	24	45	52	64	53	47	51
	SURF	2	9	23	41	20	21	16
Performance ratio	SIFT	0.85	0.85	0.89	1	0.32	0.20	0.22
	SURF	0.67	0.75	0.75	1	0.51	0.51	0.30

Table 2. Experimental results on the IIT Delhi database

Method	Number of images	Matched images	Unmatched images	Time for matching (s)	Recognition rate (%)
SIFT	125	121	4	0.21	96.8
SURF	125	118	7	0.183	94.4

Table 2 shows an overview of how the two detectors work in real-life conditions where some images are not matched due to illumination changes as those images were mostly taken at night and at different angles. Thus, the descriptors fail to find enough feature keypoints for matching. The overall recognition rates of the SIFT and SURF algorithms on the IIT Delhi database are 96.8 % and 94.4 %, respectively. As a comparison, we also implemented other methods for ear recognition. The template matching technique yields a recognition rate of 93 % for [12], and 92.6 % for [11], whereas the recognition rate by the contour extraction technique [13] is 85 %. It is evident that the proposed technique yields a higher recognition rate.

5 Conclusion

In this paper, we have studied two scale and rotation invariant feature detectors and their application to ear recognition. Although both the SIFT and the SURF are invariant under scale and rotation changes, their performance decreases under certain conditions. The SIFT detector is more stable than the SURF detector under rotation changes. It is also found that the SIFT algorithm performs better for image decreasing, in contrast, the SURF algorithm performs better for image increasing. Experimental evaluations have demonstrated the effectiveness of the proposed techniques in ear recognition.

In future study, we will further investigate how to increase the performance and reliability of the proposed approach.

Acknowledgment. The work is partly supported by Kansas NASA EPSCoR Program (NNX13AB11A) and the National Natural Science Foundation of China (61273282).

References

1. Pflug, A., Busch, C.: Ear Biometrics: A survey of detection, feature extraction and recognition methods. IET Biometrics **1**(2), 114–129 (2012)
2. Abaza, A., Ross, A., Hebert, C., Harrison, M.A.F., Nixon, M.S.: A survey on ear biometrics. ACM Computing Surveys (CSUR) **45**(2), 22 (2013)
3. Tariq, A., Akram, M.U.: Personal identification using ear recognition. Telkomnika **10**(2), 321–326 2012
4. Lowe, D.G.: Distinctive image features from scale-invariant keypoints. Int. J. Comput. Vision **60**(2), 91–110 (2004)
5. Kumar, A., Wu, C.: Automated human identification using ear imaging. Pattern Recognition **45**(3), 956–968 (2012)
6. Iannarelli, A.: Ear identification, forensic identification series, Paramount Publishing Company. Fremont, CA (1989)
7. Gonzalez, E., Alvarez, L., Morazza, L.: AMI Ear Database, Centro de I + D de Tecnologias de la Imagen
8. Mu, Z., Yuan, L., Xu, Z., Xi, D., Qi, S.: Shape and structural feature based ear recognition. In: Li, S.Z., Lai, J.-H., Tan, T., Feng, G.-C., Wang, Y. (eds.) SINOBIOMETRICS 2004. LNCS, vol. 3338, pp. 663–670. Springer, Heidelberg (2004)
9. Bay, H., Ess, A., Tuytelaars, T., Van Gool, L.: SURF: speeded up robust features. Comput. Vis. Image Underst. **110**(3), 346–359 (2008)
10. Hurley, D., Nixon, M., Carter, J.: Automatic ear recognition by force field transformations. In: Proceedings of the IEEE Colloquium on Visual Biometrics, pp. 7/1–7/5
11. Chen, H., Bhanu, B.: Human ear detection from side face range images. In: Proceedings of International Conference on Pattern Recognition, ICPR 3, 574–577 (2004)
12. Ansari, S., Gupta, P.: Localization of ear using outer helix curve of the ear. In: Proceedings of the IEEE International Conference on Computing: Theory and Applications. pp. 688–692
13. Yan, P., Bowyer, K.: Biometric recognition using 3D ear shape. IEEE Trans. Pattern Anal. Mach. Intell. **29**(8), 1297–1308 (2007)

Mutibiometric System Based on Game Theory

Nawaf Aljohani, Foysal Ahmad, Kaushik Roy[✉], and Joseph Shelton

Department of Computer Science, North Carolina A&T State University,
Greensboro, NC 27411, USA
{naaljoh, fahmad, jasheltl}@aggies.ncat.edu,
kroy@ncat.edu

Abstract. Biometric systems based on a single biometric trait have drawbacks that are alleviated by multibiometric systems, which combine multiple sources of information. The novelty of this research effort is that Coalition Game Theory (CGT) is applied to improve the performance of the iris and face based multibiometric system. The CGT technique selects the most salient patches obtained using the Local Binary Patterns (LBP) and modified LBP (mLBP) feature extraction techniques. The CGT chooses patches that have better individual importance along with a strong interaction with other patches based on the Shapely value. Results show that CGT model maintains impressive recognition accuracy while using smaller image areas for recognition. More specifically, CGT outperforms the LBP and mLBP techniques.

Keywords: Multibiometric system · Coalition game theory · Modified local binary pattern · Patch selection

1 Introduction

Researchers have been conducting extensive investigations on biometrics. Most of the state-of-the-art biometric systems focus on a single biometric modality. However, systems using a single biometric trait have drawbacks due to lack of uniqueness, non-universality and noisy data. Multibiometric systems overcome these drawbacks by using multiple sources of information [1]. Face and iris traits are commonly implemented and studied due to the popularity of the individual traits. In addition, both face and iris features can be extracted from facial images. Although there is research based on face and iris traits, a very small amount of research has been conducted on combined facial and iris biometrics [2].

The face is one of the most broadly used biometric traits, and iris is one of the most accurate and stable. Face and iris traits have been combined to improve overall performance in several applications [2, 3]. Face and iris identification have been used in many biometric applications in an effort to improve the verification and identification performance. However, there are some practical issues that need to be resolved in both systems. For example, face recognition accuracy is influenced by illumination, pose, and facial expression [3]. In the case of iris recognition, the quality of the image may affect the iris identification systems. Eye disease may also alter the iris, resulting in poor performance on an iris based system. Multibiometric identification systems can overcome or reduce the influence of these issues [3].

© Springer International Publishing Switzerland 2015
M. Kamel and A. Campilho (Eds.): ICIAR 2015, LNCS 9164, pp. 194–199, 2015.
DOI: 10.1007/978-3-319-20801-5_21

In this research effort, the Local Binary Patterns (LBP) and modified LBP (mLBP) techniques are used to extract features from different patches of normalized iris and face images [4]. Both techniques divides an image into a grid of patches and extracts features from each patch. The mLBP technique combines both the sign and magnitude features to improve feature extraction and enhance the accuracy whereas with traditional LBP, only the signed difference information is used [5].

An important aspect in machine learning and pattern recognition is the feature selection step. In this research, a Coalition Game Theory (CGT) model is deployed to select only important iris and face patches over the entire image. The CGT evaluates each patch based on its influence to the intricate and intrinsic interrelations among all patches by using the Shapley value [6]. Each patch is considered as a player in CGT model and the selected patches have the most significant contributions in the coalition's outcome. We have applied the CGT based approach previously for multispectral iris recognition [7] and face recognition [8].

The remainder of this paper is organized as follows. Section 2 briefly describes the preprocessing steps of iris and face images and patch based CGT. Section 3 reports the experimental results and Sect. 4 provides our conclusions.

2 Proposed Approach

2.1 Prepossessing

In this experiment, we segment the iris from eye images using the fuzzy level set method [3]. We divide the iris and face image samples into a multitude of different patch combinations. We then apply the LBP and mLBP techniques on each patch to feed into the CGT methods. Iris and face image samples are shown in Fig. 1.

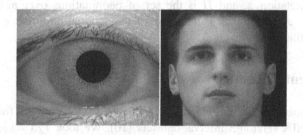

Fig. 1. Samples of iris and facial images.

2.2 Patch Based Coalition Game Theory (CGT)

The process of CGT is as follows: the decision makers communicate with each other and the reward for each participant in the coalition depends not just on its own decisions but on the decisions made by every participant. Coalition games involve a set of players and an associated reward based on different groups or coalitions of players. As a result, the reward of a certain coalition is based on individual contributions of players composing this coalition to the game where the larger the contribution of a player is, the greater the benefit of having this player in a coalition [6]. Coalitions with high reward are selected over those with small reward. This perspective yields an iterative algorithm, called contribution selection algorithm (CSA), for patch selection on unseen data classifier. Each patch in CGT is obtained using a LBP/mLBP based feature extractor and is considered as a player. The CSA algorithm ranks each patch on each step. The ranking is based on the Shapley value, a well-known concept from game theory. The purpose of that is to estimate the importance of each patch by considering the interactions between patches [6]. In our previous research efforts, we applied CGT for multispectral iris recognition [7] and facial recognition [8].

The Shapley value is computed by measuring the distribution of the power among the players in the voting game that can be transformed into the arena of patch selection where the importance of each patch can be estimated. Every subset of patches can be considered as a candidate subset for the final selected optimal subset. Each patch's power can be measured by averaging the contributions that it makes to each - subset it belongs to.

The Shapley value is defined as follows [6]. Let the marginal importance of player i to a coalition S $(i \notin S)$ be

$$\Delta_i = v(S \cup \{i\}) - v(S) \tag{1}$$

where $v(S)$ is the reward associated with coalition S. The reward can be negative, zero, or positive. Negative or zero reward means no benefits of inclusion of player i into the current coalition. The Shapley value is then defined as

$$\phi_i(v) = \frac{1}{n!} \sum_{\pi \in \Pi} \Delta_i(S_i(\pi)) \tag{2}$$

where n is the total number of players, $S_i(\pi)$ is the set of players appearing before player i in permutation π, and Π is the set of permutations over n. Therefore, the Shapley value of a given player is the mean of its marginal importance averaged over all possible coalitions of players.

3 Experimental Results

To build the datasets for the multimodal experiments, we took images from the FERET [9] and the CASIA version 3 interval datasets [10]. We took 175 subjects from each dataset, and for each subject, we took 6 samples from each dataset. We divide the dataset into training and test sets. In the multimodal dataset, we include 2 random samples from each of the 175 subjects in the test set and rest of the samples in the training set. We divide each sample image into a multitude of different patch variations and generate LBP/mLBP feature vectors for each patch. While each LBP patch provides 256 features (only sign components), each mLBP patch produces 512 features as it utilizes both the sign and magnitude components for experiments. CGT methods select patches that have strong individual contribution along with strong interaction with other patches, as shown in Figs. 2 and 3. Then these selected patches are used to verify samples in the test set. The results of this approach are included in Table 1.

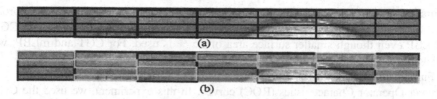

Fig. 2. Sample patch combination of iris images. (a) 28 patches given input to CGT model. (b) CGT model selects only 10 important patches.

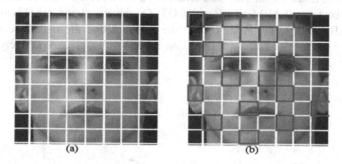

Fig. 3. Sample patch combination of face images. (a) 72 patches given input to CGT model. (b) CGT model selects only 16 important patches.

Table 1. Recognition results of the proposed scheme

Patches (R × C)	Accuracy with LBP	Accuracy with LBP and CGT (% area used)	Accuracy with mLBP	Accuracy with mLBP and CGT (% area used)
4 × 5	0.8857	0.9257 (50 %)	0.9143	0.9257 (50 %)
5 × 5	0.8800	0.9086 (40 %)	0.8971	0.9200 (40 %)
5 × 7	0.8914	0.9486 (28 %)	0.9029	0.9200 (28 %)
5 × 8	0.8629	0.9200 (25 %)	0.8571	0.9371 (25 %)
6 × 5	0.9200	0.9257 (28 %)	0.8800	0.9371 (33 %)
6 × 7	0.9143	0.9314 (47 %)	0.9257	0.9200 (24 %)
6 × 9	0.8743	0.9200 (37 %)	0.9029	0.9200 (27 %)

In Table 1, the number of patches are represented in the first column where R is the number of rows and C is the number of column. The second and forth columns include the accuracies without CGT model, and third and the fifth column represent the accuracies with CGT model including percentage of surface area used in this experiment in parenthesis. The second and the third columns correspond to the LBP technique, where the fourth and fifth columns show results using the mLBP technique. The results in Table 1 indicates that CGT based approach maintains better accuracies and exploits less surface area than the LBP and mLBP approaches on the face and iris images. The results of Table 1 states that CGT based approach achieves better accuracies and uses less surface area than the regular LBP and mLBP based approaches. For 5 × 8 patches combination, we achieve the best accuracy of 94 % with CGT and LBP even though smaller surface area of 25 % is used. For CGT and mLBP, we achieved 93 % accuracy with 5 × 8 combinations.

Further analysis is shown using the Cumulative Match Characteristics (CMC) and Receiver Operator Characteristics (ROC) curves. In this experiment, we used the CGT model with LBP and mLBP techniques for 5 × 8 patch combination. We also compared CGT based approaches with regular LBP and mLBP. In Fig. 4, the ROC curve shows the verification performance of the multibiometric system. The CMC curve (see Fig. 5) shows the identification results of the proposed scheme. Genuine Accept Rate (GAR) is 35 % at 1 % False Accept rate (FAR) for LBP with CGT. On the other hand, GAR is 36 % at 1 % FAR for mLBP with CGT. From Fig. 5, we can find that the rank-1 accuracies are 89.15 % and 90.85 % for LBP with CGT and mLBP with CGT, respectively.

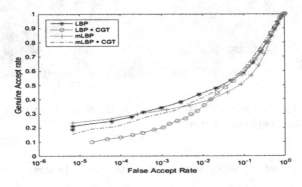

Fig. 4. ROC curve

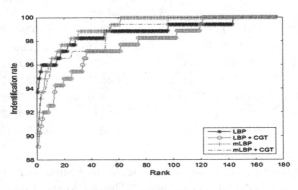

Fig. 5. CMC curve

4   Conclusions

In this research effort, a CGT based patch selection model is deployed on iris and face images. The results of this research show that CGT based approach achieves better accuracies than the regular LBP/mLBP. The CGT based path selection model yields not only the individual importance of a patch but also its interactions with other patches based on the Shapley value. The CGT model also achieves better accuracy and reduces the amount of surface area required for matching. In future research, we will apply an evolutionary game theory based approach with LBP and mLBP in an effort to improve the performance.

Acknowledgements. This research was funded by the National Science Foundation (NSF) and Science & Technology Center: Bio/Computational Evolution in Action Consortium (BEACON).

References

1. Wang, Y., Tan, T., Jain, A.: Combining face and iris biometrics for identity verification. In: Proceedings in International Conference on Audio- and Video-based Biometric Person Authentication, pp. 805–813 (2003)
2. Rattani, A., Tistarelli, M.: Robust multi-modal and multi-unit feature level fusion of face and iris biometrics. In: Tistarelli, M., Nixon, M.S. (eds.) ICB 2009. LNCS, vol. 5558, pp. 960–969. Springer, Heidelberg (2009)
3. Roy, K., Shelton, J., O'Connor, B., Kamel, M.S.: Multibiometric system using fuzzy level set, and genetic and evolutionary feature extraction. IET Biometrics, p. 11 (2015)
4. Ojala, T., Pietikäinen, M., Mäenpää, T.: Multiresolution gray-scale and rotation invariant texture classification with local binary pattern. IEEE Trans. Pattern Anal. Mach. Intell. **24**(7), 971–987 (2002)
5. Guo, Z., Zhang, L., Zhang, D.: A completed modeling of local binary pattern operator for texture classification. IEEE Trans. Image Process. **19**(6), 1657–1663 (2010)
6. Cohen, S., Dror, G., Ruppin, E.: Feature selection via coalition game theory. Neural Comput. **19**(7), 1939–1961 (2007)
7. Ahmad, F., Roy, K., Popplewell, K.: Multispectral iris recognition using patch based game theory. In: Campilho, A., Kamel, M. (eds.) ICIAR 2014, Part II. LNCS, vol. 8815, pp. 112–120. Springer, Heidelberg (2014)
8. Ahmad, F., Roy, K., O'Connor, B., Shelton, J., Arias, P., Esterline, A., Dozier, G.: Facial recognition utilizing patch based game theory. Intl. J. Mach. Learn. Comput. **5**(4), 334–338 (2015)
9. Phillips, P., Wechslerb, H., Huangb, J., Raussa, P.: The FERET database and evaluation procedure for face-recognition algorithms. Image Vis. Comput. **16**, 295–306 (1997)
10. CASIA-Iris Version 3 interval dataset. http://www.cbsr.ia.ac.cn/IrisDatabase.htm

Face Description, Detection and Recognition

Head Pose Classification Using a Bidimensional Correlation Filter

Djemel Ziou[1]([✉]), Dayron Rizo-Rodriguez[1], Antoine Tabbone[2],
and Nafaa Nacereddine[3]

[1] Départment d'Informatique, Université de Sherbrooke,
Sherbrooke, QC J1K 2R1, Canada
djemel.ziou@usherbrooke.ca
[2] LORIA UMR 7503, Université de Lorraine,
BP 239, 54506 Vandoeuvre-les-nancy, France
[3] Centre de Recherche Scientifique et Technique en Soudage et
Controle Chéraga, 16002 Algiers, Algeria

Abstract. Correlation filters have been extensively used in face recognition but surprisingly underused in head pose classification. In this paper, we present a correlation filter that ensures the tradeoff between three criteria: peak distinctiveness, discrimination power and noise robustness. Such a filter is derived through a variational formulation of these three criteria. The closed form obtained intrinsically considers multiclass information and preserves the bidimensional structure of the image. The filter proposed is combined with a face image descriptor in order to deal with pose classification problem. It is shown that our approach improves pose classification accuracy, especially for non-frontal poses, when compared with other methods.

Keywords: Head pose classification · Bidimensional correlation filter

1 Introduction

The orientation of a subject's head relative to a given coordinate systems is commonly referred as head pose in computer vision [11]. The pose of a human head in such a system depends on the muscular movement of the neck as well as the orientation of the body. Pose estimation can be useful in multiple practical applications including face recognition, gaze direction estimation and hands-free human computer interaction. Taking into account the level of precision, we can carry out either a fine or a coarse pose estimation. In the first case, we aim at determining the pitch, roll and yaw rotation angles by assuming that human head is limited to three degrees of freedom [11]. In the second case, a finite number of poses are modeled so that pose estimation becomes a classification problem.

Pose estimation problem from both perspectives has been tackled using different types of approaches. The reader can find further details about the taxonomy

© Springer International Publishing Switzerland 2015
M. Kamel and A. Campilho (Eds.): ICIAR 2015, LNCS 9164, pp. 203–209, 2015.
DOI: 10.1007/978-3-319-20801-5_22

of these methods in [11]. In this work, we address in particular the appearance-based category for coarse pose classification [1,2,9,16–18]. Appearance-based approaches extract facial features assuming that such features are related to the pose of the head [9]. As a result, a statistical learning technique is used from the features extracted in order to infer each pose class. According to [11], these methods are advantageous because they do not require facial points to be detected. However, their most significant drawback is the fact that a different identity can produce more dissimilarity than a change in pose classification.

An interesting technique that has not been widely exploited for pose classification are correlation filters, especially considering that they are quite popular in face recognition [4,7,8]. A correlation filter represents a template for recognizing a specific pattern. Thus, a sharp peak is expected to indicate the presence of the such a pattern when correlating the filter with a target image. Such a technique allow us to operate in frequency domain, beneficial for recognition problems, while providing shift-invariance, noise robustness and a closed form solution [7]. Consequently, a correlation filter can be advantageous for coping with the problem of appearance-based pose classification.

A well-know filter is the Optimal Trade-off Filter (OTF) [13], which is derived from the constrained optimization of two criteria: Signal-to-Noise Ratio (SNR) and the Peak-to-Correlation Energy (PCE). Other filters (MVSDF [6], ECPSDF [12], MACE [10], and POUMACE [8]) are special cases of the OTF. However, most of these correlation filters are designed by transforming the image into a one-dimensional vector. It means that the spatial structure of the image is somehow neglected. In this work, a correlation filter is derived from three criteria through a variational formulation. As a result, we obtain a close form preserving image spatial structure unlike existing correlation filters. The correlation filter proposed is compared with state-of-the-art approaches for face pose classification. The rest of the paper is structured as follows. In Sect. 2, the derivation of the filter is presented. Experimental results are shown in Sect. 3. Finally, the conclusions are drawn in Sect. 4.

2 Derivation of 2D Correlation Filter

In this section, we propose a new correlation filter $h_k(X)$ where $X = (x, y)$ represents space domain coordinates. For this purpose, we assume that common features are mostly shared within the same class k and not with other classes. Firstly, we define the three criteria to be fulfilled by our correlation filter. Secondly, a closed form is obtained by using variational calculus.

The first criteria represents that a correlation filter should deliver a sharp peak at the origin for an image belonging to the correct class. For this reason, we force the correlation space to resemble a known function $g_k(X)$ having the maximal energy in the origin such as: Gaussian function or a Dirac distribution. It would be then defined as follows:

$$min_{h_k} \oint_{-\infty}^{+\infty} ((v_{ik} © h_k)(X) - g_k(X))^2 dX \tag{1}$$

where the correlation space $(v \copyright h)(X)$ represents an inner product of the image $v(X)$ and the shifted correlation filter $h(X)$.

The second criteria imposes that the correlation energy between a filter and an image of the same class should be maximal while being minimal otherwise. Then, it can be simply expressed as the minimization of the correlation energy with respect to other classes:

$$min_{h_k} \sum_{l \neq k}^{M} \sum_{j=1}^{N_l} \oint_{-\infty}^{+\infty} (v_{jl} \copyright h_k)^2 (X) dX \tag{2}$$

The third requirement focuses on the effects of noise in filter performance. According to Rice [14], noise produces several maxima in the correlation surface. Setting the distance between maxima to a specific constant reduces the number of maxima in the correlation space. It has been shown in [3], that such a requirement is equivalent to derive a filter that ensures a smooth correlation space. Then, the smoothness can be measured through the norm of the field produced by a differentiation operator applied to the correlation space:

$$min_{h_k} \oint_{-\infty}^{+\infty} ||\nabla (v_{ik} \copyright h_k)(X)||^2 dX \tag{3}$$

Therefore, the variational problem can be formulated as the minimization of the weighted sum of the three criteria. Taking into account all images of the kth class, it can be written as:

$$h_k = argmin_{h_k} \oint_{-\infty}^{+\infty} (\sum_{i=1}^{N_k} ((v_{ik} \copyright h_k)(X) - g_k(X))^2$$

$$+ \lambda_2 \sum_{i=1}^{N_k} ((v_{ik} \copyright h_{xk})(X)^2 + (v_{ik} \copyright h_{yk})(X)^2)$$

$$+ \lambda_1 (\sum_{l \neq k}^{M} \sum_{j=1}^{N_l} (v_{jl} \copyright h_k)^2 (X))) dX \tag{4}$$

where λ_1 and λ_2 are Lagrangian multipliers, N_k is the number of samples for the kth class, and $h_{kx}(X)$ and $h_{ky}(X)$ are the first order derivatives of $h_k(X)$. In this variational formulation, we notice the multiclass nature of this correlation filter, i.e., it depends on both the images of the kth class and those of the other classes. Moreover, the bidimensional structure of the images is preserved because they are never transformed into a column vector. This is a distinctive point of our proposal when compared to traditional correlation filters.

In order to derive the closed form of the filter $h_k(X)$ solving the variational problem, Gateaux derivatives are used to find the Euler-Lagrange partial differential equation (PDE). A straightforward manipulation of the PDE in Fourier domain results in the following closed form (see Appendix):

$$\hat{h}_k(W) = \frac{\hat{g}_k(W)}{\sum_{i=1}^{N_k} ||\hat{v}_{ik}(W)||^2 (1 + \lambda_2 ||W||^2) + \lambda_1 \sum_{l \neq k}^{M} \sum_{j=1}^{N_l} ||\hat{v}_{jl}(W)||^2} \sum_{i=1}^{N_k} \hat{v}_{ik}^*(W)$$

Fig. 1. Pose classes in CMU PIE database (Left:-90° to Right: 90°)

where $\hat{}$ denotes the Fourier Transform, $*$ the complex conjugate and $W = (w_x, w_y)$ represents the frequency domain coordinates.

3   Experimental Results

In the experiments, the CMU PIE database [15] is employed for comparing the correlation filter proposed with state-of-the-art approaches in pose classification. This database was constructed from 68 individuals, each one captured under 9 different horizontal poses (yaw) and 21 illumination conditions. Since we are evaluating pose variations, only the 612 images frontally illuminated will be used in our experiments. Those poses range from -90° to 90° using a 22.5° step, see Fig. 1. From all these images, the faces were automatically detected and cropped to a 32 x 32 resolution based on the position of the eyes. Then, a half of the images per each pose class are randomly selected for training, 306 in total, and the other 306 are used for testing. This two-fold cross-validation is the same experimental setup used for testing the other three methods to which we will compare our approach. Additionally, we use the Local Binary Patterns (LBP) descriptor of the face images for designing the corresponding correlation filter because LBP has been effective in face recognition [5]. It should be noticed that we refer to the LBP descriptor as an image, i.e. we do not compute the histogram, so that the bidimensional structure is preserved. This idea of using a face descriptor instead of the raw image is also exploited in [2] but employing Gabor features.

Table 1. Pose estimation accuracy (%) per Class for 32 x 32 resolution.

	Mean	Per pose class								
		-90°	-67.5°	-45°	-22.5°	0°	22.5°	45°	67.5°	90°
Brown(Probabilistic) [2]	91	–	–	–	–	–	–	–	–	–
Brown(Neural Network) [2]	91	–	–	–	–	–	–	–	–	–
Takallou [16]	90.1	85	87	91	87	94	97	89	**93**	88
LBP+2DCorrFilter	**94.38**	**91.18**	**91.18**	**95.88**	**95.29**	**95.88**	**100**	**94.71**	89.41	**95.88**

In Table 1, we present the performance delivered by pose estimation approaches in CMU PIE database. The first column shows the mean score, i.e. considering all pose classes, and the other columns the specific score per class if provided. In the case of the state-of-the-art methods, we simply display the percentages reported by each of them. For this reason, we limit our comparison to those pose classification approaches that has been tested in CMU PIE database following the experimental setup described above. For our proposal, the average pose estimation accuracy computed from 10 different two-fold cross-validation configurations is reported.

On one hand, it can be seen in the first column that the LBP+2DCorrFilter approach improves the other methods in more than 3 % in terms of the mean score. The best performance of the 2D correlation filter is obtained by setting $\lambda_1 = \lambda_2 = 0.5$ and using a Gaussian function as $g_k(X)$. On the other hand, we appreciate that our method is superior to Takallou's approach in 8 out of the 9 pose classes considered. For frontal pose, $0°$, both of them deliver comparable percentages. In the case of $67.5°$ pose, Takallou's method overcomes LBP+2DCorrFilter in about 4 %. However, in the remaining pose classes the difference in favour of LBP+2DCorrFilter combination is clearly observed reaching a maximal gap of about 8 % for the $90°$ pose class.

Overall, we can see that the LBP+2DCorrFilter method delivers the top mean pose classification score among the approaches compared. More importantly, our approach is capable of overcoming Takallou's approach for most of the pose classes deviated from the frontal pose. It means that preserving bidimensional image structure actually contributes to improve pose estimation when dealing with non-frontal head orientations. In terms of computational complexity, the design of the correlation filters representing each class is $O(Nd(1+\log d))$ where N the total number of training images and d the dimension of one image. It means that the complexity of our proposal is based on the computation of N Fourier Transforms which can be executed in $O(d \log d)$. If we consider that the correlation filters can be derived off-line, such a cost is reduced to computing one Fourier Transform for the target image in recognition phase.

4   Conclusions

In this work, a bidimensional correlation filter is presented. It is derived from three criteria which take into account the peak at the origin, the discrimination power and the robustness to noise of the filter. The closed form obtained through variational calculus has a multiclass nature and preserves the bidimensional structure of an image representation. In the experimental evaluation, we combine the effective LBP descriptor with the correlation filter proposed for head pose classification. When compared with other state-of-the-art methods, our approach delivers the top performance in terms of the mean percentage as well as for most of the nine pose classes evaluated.

5   Appendix

Let us now compute Gateaux derivative of the variational problem in Eq. (4).

$$\frac{\partial}{\partial \varepsilon} E^k(h_k + \varepsilon \varphi_k))|_{\varepsilon=0} = \oint_{-\infty}^{\infty} (\sum_{i=1}^{N_k}((v_{ik}©h_k)(X) - g_k(X))(v_{ik}©\varphi_k(X))$$

$$+\lambda_2 \sum_{i=1}^{N_k}((v_{ik}©h_{xk})(X)(v_{ik}©\varphi_{xk})(X) + (v_{ik}©h_{yk})(X)(v_{ik}©\varphi_{yk})(X))$$

$$+\lambda_1 \sum_{l \neq k}^{M} 2 \sum_{j=1}^{N_l} (v_{jl} \copyright h_k)(X)(v_{jl} \copyright \varphi_k)(X))dX = 0$$

The first term of this equation can be rewritten as:

$$\oint_{-\infty}^{\infty} \sum_{i=1}^{N_k} ((v_{ik} \copyright h_k)(X) - g_k(X))(v_{ik} \copyright \varphi_k)(X)dX$$

$$= \oint_{-\infty}^{\infty} \varphi_k(t) \sum_{i=1}^{N_k} (v_{ik} \copyright ((v_{ik} \copyright h_k) - g_k)(t)dt$$

We apply the same analysis for second and third terms. Then, the result of the second term is integrated by parts. As a result, we get the following Euler-Lagrange equation:

$$\sum_{i=1}^{N_k} (v_{ik} \copyright v_{ik} \copyright h_k)(X) + \lambda_2 \sum_{i=1}^{N_k} ((v_{ik} \copyright v_{ik} \copyright h_{xk})_x(X) + (v_{ik} \copyright v_{ik} \copyright h_{yk})_y(X))$$

$$+ \lambda_1 \sum_{l \neq k}^{M} \sum_{j=1}^{N_l} (v_{jl} \copyright v_{jl} \copyright h_k)(X) = \sum_{i=1}^{N_k} (v_{ik} \copyright g_k)(X)$$

A straightforward manipulation allows to write:

$$\sum_{i=1}^{N_k} (v_{ik} \copyright v_{ik} \copyright h_k)(X) + \lambda_2 \sum_{i=1}^{N_k} ((v_{xik} \copyright v_{xik} \copyright h_k)(X) + (v_{yik} \copyright v_{yik} \copyright h_k)(X))$$

$$+ \lambda_1 \sum_{l \neq k}^{M} \sum_{j=1}^{N_l} (v_{jl} \copyright v_{jl} \copyright h_k)(X) = \sum_{i=1}^{N_k} (v_{ik} \copyright g_k)(X)$$

This equation is solved in the Fourier domain by using the properties $\hat{a}\hat{a}^* = ||\hat{a}||^2$ and $\widehat{f_x(X)}(W) = jw_x \hat{f}(W)$, the resulting filter is given by:

$$\hat{h}_k(W) = \frac{\sum_{i=1}^{N_k} \hat{v}_{ik}^*(W)\hat{g}_k(W)}{\sum_{i=1}^{N_k} ||\hat{v}_{ik}(W)||^2(1 + \lambda_2||W||^2) + \lambda_1 \sum_{l \neq k}^{M} \sum_{j=1}^{N_l} ||\hat{v}_{jl}(W)||^2}$$

where * denotes the complex conjugate.

References

1. Ba, S.O., Odobez, J.M.: A probabilistic framework for joint head tracking and pose estimation. In: Proceedings of ICPR 2004. vol. 4, pp. 264–267. IEEE (2004)
2. Brown, L.M., Tian, Y.L.: Comparative study of coarse head pose estimation. In: Proceedings Workshop on Motion and Video Computing, 2002. pp. 125–130. IEEE (2002)

3. Canny, J.: A computational approach to edge detection. IEEE TPAMI PAMI 8(6), 679–698 (1986)
4. Heo, J., Savvides, M., Vijayakumar, B.V.K.: Advanced correlation filters for face recognition using low-resolution visual and thermal imagery. In: Kamel, M.S., Campilho, A.C. (eds.) ICIAR 2005. LNCS, vol. 3656, pp. 1089–1097. Springer, Heidelberg (2005)
5. Huang, D., Shan, C., Ardabilian, M., Wang, Y., Chen, L.: Local binary patterns and its application to facial image analysis: a survey. IEEE Trans. Syst. Man Cybern. 41(6), 765–781 (2011)
6. Kumar, B.V.K.V.: Minimum-variance synthetic discriminant functions. J. Opt. Soc. Am. A 3(10), 1579–1584 (1986)
7. Kumar, B.V., Savvides, M., Xie, C.: Correlation pattern recognition for face recognition. Proc. IEEE 94(11), 1963–1976 (2006)
8. Levine, M.D., Yu, Y.: Face recognition subject to variations in facial expression, illumination and pose using correlation filters. CVIU 104(1), 1–15 (2006)
9. Ma, B., Chai, X., Wang, T.: A novel feature descriptor based on biologically inspired feature for head pose estimation. Neurocomputing 115, 1–10 (2013)
10. Mahalanobis, A., Kumar, B.V.K.V., Casasent, D.: Minimum average correlation energy filters. Appl. Opt. 26(17), 3633–3640 (1987)
11. Murphy-Chutorian, E., Trivedi, M.M.: Head pose estimation in computer vision: a survey. IEEE Trans. Pattern Anal. Mach. Intell. 31(4), 607–626 (2009)
12. Ng, C.: PDA Face Recognition System Using Advanced Correlation Filters. Master thesis, Carnegie Mellon University (2005)
13. Refregier, P.: Optimal trade-off filters for noise robustness, sharpness of the correlation peak, and horner efficiency. Opt. Lett. 16(11), 829–831 (1991)
14. Rice, S.O.: Mathematical analysis of random noise. Bell Syst. Tech. J. 23, 282–332 (1944)
15. Sim, T., Baker, S., Bsat, M.: The cmu pose, illumination, and expression (pie) database. In: IEEE International Conference on Automatic Face and Gesture Recognition, pp. 46–51 May 2002
16. Takallou, H.M., Kasaei, S.: Head pose estimation and face recognition using a non-linear tensor-based model. IET Comput. Vision 8(1), 54–65 (2014)
17. Tian, Y., Brown, L., Connell, J., Pankanti, S., Hampapur, A., Senior, A., Bolle, R.: Absolute head pose estimation from overhead wide-angle cameras. In: IEEE International Workshop on Analysis and Modeling of Faces and Gestures, AMFG 2003, pp. 92–99. IEEE (2003)
18. Yan, D., Yan, Y., Wang, H.: Robust head pose estimation with a new principal optimal tradeoff filter. In: Sun, C., Fang, F., Zhou, Z.-H., Yang, W., Liu, Z.-Y. (eds.) IScIDE 2013. LNCS, vol. 8261, pp. 320–327. Springer, Heidelberg (2013)

Illumination Robust Facial Feature Detection via Decoupled Illumination and Texture Features

Brendan Chwyl[✉], Alexander Wong, and David A. Clausi

University of Waterloo, Waterloo, ON N2L 3G1, Canada
{bchwyl,a28wong,dclausi}@uwaterloo.ca
http://vip.uwaterloo.ca/

Abstract. A method for illumination robust facial feature detection on frontal images of the human face is proposed. Illumination robust features are produced from weighted contributions of the texture and illumination components of an image where the illumination is estimated via Bayesian least-squares minimization with the required posterior probability inferred using an adaptive Monte-Carlo sampling approach. This estimate is used to decouple the illumination and texture components, from which Haar-like features are extracted. A weighted aggregate of each component's features is then compared with a cascade of pre-trained classifiers for the face, eyes, nose, and mouth. Experimental results against the Yale Face Database B suggest higher sensitivity and F_1 score values than current methods while maintaining comparable specificity and accuracy in the presence of non-ideal illumination conditions.

Keywords: Illumination robust · Object detection · Image processing

1 Introduction

The detection of facial features such as the eyes, nose, or mouth on human faces is useful in a wide variety of applications. Examples of such applications include biometric authentication [7], gaze tracking [16], and human-computer interaction [2]. Methods exist to address the problem of facial feature detection in controlled environments, however, their performance suffers when non-ideal illumination conditions are present.

Viola and Jones [22] suggest a method for object detection using a cascade of simple features and apply this method specifically to face and facial feature detection. By cascading a collection of Haar-like features over an image at different scales, strong and weak classifiers can be trained. Weak classifiers determine regions of likely facial features in order to narrow the search area and progressively stronger classifiers are used to positively identify objects of interest. This results in a fast and scale-invariant method for object detection.

We would like to thank the Natural Sciences and Engineering Research Council of Canada (NSERC), the Canada Research Chairs Program, and the Ontario Ministry of Research and Innovation for their sponsorship of this research.

© Springer International Publishing Switzerland 2015
M. Kamel and A. Campilho (Eds.): ICIAR 2015, LNCS 9164, pp. 210–217, 2015.
DOI: 10.1007/978-3-319-20801-5_23

Various improvements to speed and accuracy [4, 23, 24] have made this method widely used. Naruniec [17] compiled a comprehensive survey of facial feature detection methods and while this survey recognizes the accuracy and speed of appearance-based methods, it notes that trained classifiers are unreliable when recognizing features not well represented in the training data, such as facial hair, face orientation, or illumination conditions.

Methods exist to address the problem of inconsistent illumination of human faces. Gourier *et al.* [9] present a method to extract features from a face which are robust to pose and illumination using linear combinations of Gaussian derivatives. Hu *et al.* [12] detect faces under varying illumination conditions by using a YCbCr skin-colour model. Local binary patterns (LBPs) [18] have been used with success for the purpose of face recognition [1, 13, 21] and have been extended to general object detection tasks [26, 27] as well as face detection in particular [10, 11, 20]. One other possible alternative is to first employ Retinex approaches [5, 14, 25] prior to feature extraction.

This paper will be organized as follows: the proposed method is first presented, followed by a description of the experimental setup, a discussion of the experimental results, and conclusions.

2   Proposed Method

The proposed method aims to build upon the framework established by Viola and Jones [22] by extracting illumination robust features for comparison against trained classifiers to compensate for non-ideal illumination conditions. This is achieved by decoupling the illumination and texture components of an image through Bayesian least-squares estimation with Monte Carlo posterior sampling [25]. Weighted contributions from each of these aspects are then used to produce robust features for comparison against trained classifiers. A flow chart illustrating the steps used in this method can be seen in Fig. 1.

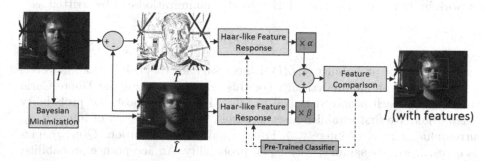

Fig. 1. General illustration of the proposed method. A weighted combination of features extracted from the texture and illumination components is obtained for each classifier in a cascade. This feature is then compared based on methods described by Viola and Jones [22].

2.1   Illumination Robust Features

Since the texture component of an image is both useful in quantifying local distinctiveness and relatively insensitive to spatially-varying illumination changes, contributions from texture are helpful in producing illumination robust features. However, texture alone fails to encapsulate sufficient geometric information, leading to the need to also incorporate the information from the illumination aspect of an image. We model the image I as an additive relation of the texture, T, and illumination, L, components:

$$I = T + L. \tag{1}$$

Let f_T and f_L denote sets of Haar-like features [19] extracted from T and L respectively. A weighted combination of these feature sets can be produced as

$$f_{I'} = \alpha f_T + \beta f_L, \tag{2}$$

where α and β are weighting factors and $f_{I'}$ represents the set of illumination compensated features.

2.2   Texture Illumination Decoupling

To produce these features, the texture (T) and illumination (L) aspects of an image are required. We aim to disassociate T and L by first producing an approximation of L (denoted as $\hat{L}$) and calculating an estimate of T (denoted as $\hat{T}$) based off of the model described in Eq. 1 as $\hat{T} = I - \hat{L}$. To obtain $\hat{L}$, a Bayesian least-squares minimization approach is used. This minimization can be formulated as

$$\hat{L} = \arg\min_{\hat{L}} E((L - \hat{L})^2 | I), \tag{3}$$

where $E(.)$ denotes the expectation and $\hat{L}$ represents the estimate of L. Based on work by Lui *et al.* [15], the solution to the minimization can be written as

$$\hat{L} = \int L p(L|I) dL \tag{4}$$

The posterior probability, $p(L|I)$, is necessary for this calculation; however, it is difficult to obtain analytically. For this reason, we adapt the Monte Carlo sampling approach proposed in [25] to infer the required posterior probability distribution. We first establish a set of pixels, Ω, from a region of interest, $\eta_{\bar{q}}$, surrounding a pixel of interest, $\bar{q}$. From a uniform distribution, $Q(q_k, \bar{q})$, pixels $q_1, q_2, ..., q_M$ are sampled with equal probability. An acceptance probability, $\alpha(q_k|\bar{q})$, is calculated for each sampled pixel, q_k, based on its regional similarity to the center pixel, $\bar{q}$, as follows:

$$\alpha(q_k|\bar{q}) = \exp\left(\sigma - \frac{1}{N}\sum_{i=1}^{N}(\aleph_{q_k}(i) - \aleph_{\bar{q}}(i))^2\right) \tag{5}$$

where $\aleph_{q_k}$ and $\aleph_{\bar{q}}$ are regions of equal size surrounding q_k and $\bar{q}$ respectively, σ is a constant, and N represents the number of pixels in each region. The likelihood that q_k is added to Ω is determined by $\alpha(q_k|\bar{q})$. The sampling process is repeated until M sample pixels are acquired, at which point, the posterior probability can be estimated as

$$\hat{p}(L|I) = \frac{\sum_{k=0}^{M} \alpha(q_k|\bar{q})\delta(L - I(q_k))}{Z},\tag{6}$$

where Z is a normalization factor such that $\sum \hat{p}(L|I) = 1$ and $\delta(.)$ represents the Dirac function.

2.3 Feature Cascade Object Detection

Feature cascade object detection [22] relies on many classifiers trained over a large number of positive and negative sample images. These classifiers are trained by applying Haar-like features to each training image at various position and scale to produce many classification features. AdaBoost [6] is used to select the features which best classify the objects and combine these features into weak classifiers. By iteratively comparing analogous features from the input image with those in the weak classifiers, areas of unimportance can be quickly discarded. Weak classifiers alone cannot classify an image, however, a strong classifier consisting of the weighted summation of weak classifiers is sufficient to detect objects of interest.

3 Experimental Setup

For the purpose of testing the performance of the proposed method under drastic lighting conditions, the Yale Face Database B was used [8]. This database provides images of human faces for 39 different subjects facing various angles under 64 different illumination conditions per subject. For this project, only the frontal view of each face was used. Each image is 256 bits, 480 × 640, and grayscale. The various illumination conditions include combinations of lighting angles ranging from $-130°$ to $+130°$ horizontally and $-40°$ to $+90°$ degrees vertically. In addition, one image taken with ambient lighting is included for each subject. Example images from the database can be viewed in Fig. 2. It should be noted that subject 14 was not available for download and subject 16 had no corresponding frontal view and were therefore omitted from testing.

Ground truth was obtained for each subject by performing detection under ideal lighting conditions. These results were visually verified and manually corrected. Because each of the 64 different illumination condition images were taken in rapid succession, it was assumed that the location of facial features for each subject did not vary. For this reason, the ground truth acquired for each subject under ideal lighting conditions was used as the ground truth across all lighting scenarios for the same subject.

For every subject and lighting condition, the method proposed by Viola and Jones [22] as well as our method were applied. For comparison purposes, we also tested two Retinex-based methods for improving illumination robustness in facial feature detection: (i) Gaussian Retinex as described by Jobson *et al.* [14], and (ii) Bilateral Retinex as proposed by Elad [5]. To increase computation speed, illumination estimation for all decoupling methods was performed on images which were down sampled by a factor of four. In addition, the α and β values used throughout this project are 0.85 and 0.15 respectively.

Pre-trained classifiers available through the OpenCV library [3] were used throughout this paper. Because multiple instances of faces, eye pairs, noses, and mouths may be returned, automatic selection of the most probable true features is performed based on logical assumptions regarding the face. Such assumptions include: each face contains only one eye pair, one nose, and one mouth, and each eye pair, nose, and mouth feature is approximately horizontally centered on the face.

From the detected regions, areas of true positive (TP), true negative (TN), false positive (FP), and false negative (FN) were calculated based on areas of overlap with the ground truth data. The resulting values were then used to calculate four metrics for analysis: sensitivity, specificity, accuracy, and F_1 score. The equations for these metrics are defined as follows:

$$Sensitivity = \frac{TP}{TP+FN}, \qquad Specificity = \frac{TN}{TN+FP},$$
$$Accuracy = \frac{TP+TN}{TP+TN+FP+FN}, \quad F_1 \; Score = \frac{2TP}{2TP+FP+FN}, \quad (7)$$

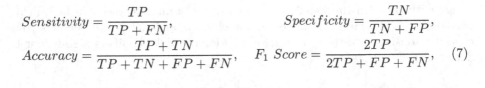

(a) Ambient lighting (b) Light shone at (c) Light shone at (d) Light shone at
+45° vertically   +90° horizontally   +35°   horizontally
and +40° vertically

Fig. 2. Selection from Yale Face Database B

4 Experimental Results

The average sensitivity, specificity, accuracy, and F_1 score across all subjects and lighting conditions can be seen in Table 1. Our method achieves sensitivity values and F_1 scores which are generally higher than those achieved by the other presented methods, however, the specificity and accuracy values remain similar. These values are likely skewed due to the difference in the number of detected features; in these cases, regions of false positive are zero while the regions of

Table 1. Average values of sensitivity, specificity, accuracy, and F_1 score calculated across all subjects and lighting conditions. The number of features that went undetected are also shown. The most desirable values for each metric are presented in boldface.

	Viola [22]	Jobson [14]	Elad [5]	Ours	Viola [22]	Jobson [14]	Elad [5]	Ours
	Face				Eyes			
Sensitivity	80.21 %	93.31 %	90.02 %	**93.92 %**	45.47 %	64.42 %	71.62 %	**76.34 %**
Specificity	98.03 %	97.79 %	**98.52 %**	98.41 %	**99.95 %**	99.92 %	99.90 %	99.92 %
Accuracy	94.30 %	96.85 %	96.74 %	**97.45 %**	98.86 %	99.20 %	99.33 %	**99.44 %**
F_1 Score	85.32 %	92.38 %	91.83 %	**93.82 %**	61.09 %	76.02 %	80.65 %	**84.25 %**
Undetected	73	27	22	**0**	1054	635	478	**358**
	Nose				Mouth			
Sensitivity	52.81 %	65.14 %	61.27 %	**73.01 %**	46.38 %	62.85 %	61.27 %	**64.87 %**
Specificity	99.66 %	99.62 %	**99.78 %**	99.53 %	99.54 %	99.58 %	**99.70 %**	99.64 %
Accuracy	99.19 %	99.28 %	**99.40 %**	99.26 %	98.82 %	99.09 %	**99.18 %**	99.17 %
F_1 Score	55.93 %	63.73 %	**66.12 %**	65.90 %	51.13 %	64.27 %	65.83 %	**67.29 %**
Undetected	443	313	481	**85**	325	84	71	**31**

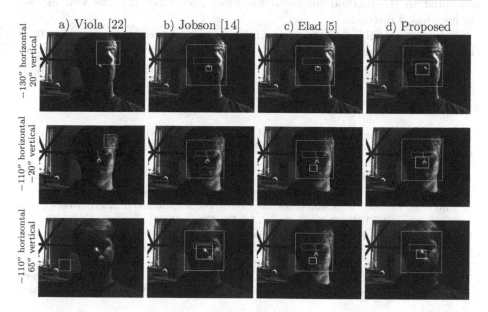

Fig. 3. Examples of facial feature detection performed for the face, eye pair, nose, and mouth. Results from the aforementioned methods are shown in each column, while each row represents a different lighting angle as labelled.

true negative are the entire image, thus leading to large specificity and increased accuracy values as per Eq. 7. The improved sensitivity values and F_1 scores demonstrated by our method suggest that all facial features were detected with greater regions of true positive and smaller regions of false negatives than in the case without illumination compensation.

While all illumination-robust methods resulted in improved performance when compared to the method proposed by Viola and Jones [22], our method results in better performance with the exception of F_1 score for the nose. This suggests that the proposed method is able to better handle complex non-ideal illumination scenarios to facilitate for improved facial feature detection. While Elad [5] and Jobson *et al.* [14] rely on the assumption that L is piece-wise smooth, our method is able to avoid this assumption, leading to better handling of sharp illumination changes (Fig. 3).

5   Conclusions

A method for illumination robust facial feature detection by considering contributions from both the illumination and texture aspects of an image was proposed. Furthermore, it was proposed that the decoupling of illumination and texture be achieved by Bayesian minimization. Results indicate higher sensitivity and F_1 score values while achieving similar specificity and accuracy when compared to the method proposed by Viola and Jones [22], as well as two Retinex-based methods.

Future work will include further validation against a wider variety of state of the art methods. In addition, training of classifiers from illumination compensated features will be explored as a means to achieve improved performance.

References

1. Ahonen, T., Hadid, A., Pietikainen, M.: Face description with local binary patterns: application to face recognition. IEEE Trans. Pattern Anal. Mach. Intel. **28**(12), 2037–2041 (2006)
2. Bartlett, M.S., Littlewort, G., Fasel, I., Movellan, J.R.: Real time face detection and facial expression recognition: Development and applications to human computer interaction. In: Conference on Computer Vision and Pattern Recognition Workshop, CVPRW 2003, vol. 5, pp. 53–53. IEEE (2003)
3. Bradski, G.: Dr. Dobb's Journal of Software Tools (2000)
4. Cristinacce, D., Cootes, T.F.: Facial feature detection using adaboost with shape constraints. In: BMVC, pp. 1–10. British Machine Vision Association (2003)
5. Elad, M.: Retinex by two bilateral filters. In: Kimmel, R., Sochen, N.A., Weickert, J. (eds.) Scale-Space 2005. LNCS, vol. 3459, pp. 217–229. Springer, Heidelberg (2005)
6. Freund, Y., Schapire, R.E.: A decision-theoretic generalization of on-line learning and an application to boosting. J. Comput. Syst. Sci. **55**(1), 119–139 (1997)
7. Frischholz, R.W., Dieckmann, U.: Biold: a multimodal biometric identification system. Computer **33**(2), 64–68 (2000)
8. Georghiades, A., Belhumeur, P., Kriegman, D.: From few to many: Illumination cone models for face recognition under variable lighting and pose. IEEE Trans. Pattern Anal. Mach. Intelligence **23**(6), 643–660 (2001)
9. Gourier, N., Hall, D., Crowley, J.L.: Facial features detection robust to pose, illumination and identity. In: 2004 IEEE International Conference on Systems, Man and Cybernetics, vol. 1, pp. 617–622. IEEE (2004)
10. Hadid, A., Heikkila, J., Silvén, O., Pietikainen, M.: Face and eye detection for person authentication in mobile phones. In: First ACM/IEEE International Conference on Distributed Smart Cameras, ICDSC 2007, pp. 101–108. IEEE (2007)

11. Hadid, A., Pietikainen, M., Ahonen, T.: A discriminative feature space for detecting and recognizing faces. In: Proceedings of the 2004 IEEE Computer Society Conference on Computer Vision and Pattern Recognition, CVPR 2004, vol. 2, pp. II–797. IEEE (2004)

12. Hu, W.C., Yang, C.Y., Huang, D.Y., Huang, C.H.: Feature-based face detection against skin-color like backgrounds with varying illumination. J. Inf. Hiding Multimedia Signal Proces. 2(2), 123–132 (2011)

13. Huang, D., Ardabilian, M., Wang, Y., Chen, L.: 3-D face recognition using elbp-based facial description and local feature hybrid matching. IEEE Trans. Inf. Forensics and Secur. 7(5), 1551–1565 (2012)

14. Jobson, D.J., Rahman, Z.U., Woodell, G.A.: Properties and performance of a center/surround retinex. IEEE Trans. Image Proces. 6(3), 451–462 (1997)

15. Lui, D., Modhafar, A., Glaister, J., Wong, A., Haider, M.: Monte Carlo bias field correction in endorectal diffusion imaging. IEEE Trans. Bio-Med. Eng. 61(2), 368–380 (2014)

16. Morimoto, C.H., Mimica, M.R.: Eye gaze tracking techniques for interactive applications. Comput. Vis. Image Underst. 98(1), 4–24 (2005)

17. Naruniec, J.: A survey on facial features detection. Int. J. Electr. Telecommun. 56(3), 267–272 (2010)

18. Ojala, T., Pietikäinen, M., Harwood, D.: A comparative study of texture measures with classification based on featured distributions. Pattern Recog. 29(1), 51–59 (1996)

19. Papageorgiou, C.P., Oren, M., Poggio, T.: A general framework for object detection. In: Sixth international Conference on Computer Vision, pp. 555–562. IEEE (1998)

20. Roy, A., Marcel, S.: Haar local binary pattern feature for fast illumination invariant face detection. In: British Machine Vision Conference 2009. No. LIDIAP-CONF-2009-048 (2009)

21. Shan, C., Gong, S., McOwan, P.W.: Robust facial expression recognition using local binary patterns. In: IEEE International Conference on Image Processing, ICIP 2005, vol. 2, pp. II–370. IEEE (2005)

22. Viola, P., Jones, M.: Rapid object detection using a boosted cascade of simple features. In: Proceedings of the 2001 IEEE Computer Society Conference on Computer Vision and Pattern Recognition, CVPR 2001, vol. 1, pp. I–511. IEEE (2001)

23. Vukadinovic, D., Pantic, M.: Fully automatic facial feature point detection using gabor feature based boosted classifiers. In: 2005 IEEE International Conference on Systems, Man and Cybernetics, vol. 2, pp. 1692–1698. IEEE (2005)

24. Wilson, P.I., Fernandez, J.: Facial feature detection using haar classifiers. J. Comput. Sci. Coll. 21(4), 127–133 (2006)

25. Wong, A., Clausi, D.A., Fieguth, P.: Adaptive monte carlo retinex method for illumination and reflectance separation and color image enhancement. In: Canadian Conference on Computer and Robot Vision, CRV 2009, pp. 108–115. IEEE (2009)

26. Zhang, H., Gao, W., Chen, X., Zhao, D.: Object detection using spatial histogram features. Image Vis. Comput. 24(4), 327–341 (2006)

27. Zhang, L., Li, S.Z., Yuan, X., Xiang, S.: Real-time object classification in video surveillance based on appearance learning. In: IEEE Conference on Computer Vision and Pattern Recognition, CVPR 2007, pp. 1–8. IEEE (2007)

Posed Facial Expression Detection Using Reflection Symmetry and Structural Similarity

Harish Bhaskar[1]([✉]), Davide La Torre[2,3], and Mohammed Al-Mualla[1]

[1] Visual Signal Analysis and Processing (VSAP) Research Center,
Khalifa University of Science, Technology and Research, P.O.Box 127788,
Abu Dhabi, UAE
harish.bhaskar@kustar.ac.ac
[2] Department of Applied Mathematics and Sciences, Khalifa University of Science,
Technology and Research, P.O.Box 127788, Abu Dhabi, UAE
[3] Department of Economics, Management and Quantitative Methods,
University of Milan, 20122 Milan, Italy

Abstract. In this paper, a method for the detection of posed facial expressions in still images is proposed. The method exploits a combination of geometrical deviations between sets of landmark points together with the difference in quality of visual appearance of patches around these landmark points for accurate and robust detection of posed facial expressions. First, novel descriptors are derived based on the Hausdorff distances between triangulated landmark point sets within a given image satisfying reflective symmetry constraints. Further, the structural similarity of patches around these point sets that are reflection symmetrical is calculated and fused with the geometric features for classification. Experiments using selected examples from publicly available dataset have demonstrated that the proposed method can sufficiently encapsulate the intensity of a facial expression and thus achieve superior accuracy in the separation of posed from spontaneous expressions.

1 Introduction

Non-verbal communication is often dominated by strong facial expression that is considered a reflection of the psychological state of the human mind. Autonomous detection of facial expressions, particularly recognizing posed expression in facial images can contribute to the future in human behaviour analysis in videos. The problem of Spontaneous versus Posed (SVP) expressions recognition has gained increased attention in recent years. Despite initial work in this domain, the problem of posed expression detection is complicated due to factors such as: complementary assumptions in various paradigms for SVP expression analysis, need for encapsulating psycho-physical aspects that makes modelling of SVP expressions difficult, inter-and-intra sample variations of facial expressions, and other extrinsic factors including pose, illumination variations, etc.

In the literature, several methods have been proposed to study posed facial expressions and quantitatively represent its differences from spontaneous expressions. The use of facial action units has been the most familiar approach in facial

© Springer International Publishing Switzerland 2015
M. Kamel and A. Campilho (Eds.): ICIAR 2015, LNCS 9164, pp. 218–228, 2015.
DOI: 10.1007/978-3-319-20801-5_24

expression analysis [12]. However, research in this context has extended into the study of mutually exclusive action units and their contributions towards facial expression analysis. For example, Valstar et al. [16] formulates the SVP problem based on eyebrow movements. The use of geometry and appearance has dominated the research within SVP expression analysis including the work of Cohn and Schmidt [13], who proposed spatio-temporal local texture descriptors, and the work of Bhaskar et al. [15] that explored the combination of Gabor filter banks with geometric morphometric features, among others. SVP expression classification has also been looked from the point-of-view of specific expressions, and smile recognition is the most popular within this category. Posed smile recognition has been addressed in a few recent literature including the work of Valstar et al. [11], Dibeklioglu et al. [14], etc. Since the proposed work focuses on using reflection symmetry to detect posed expressions, some related literature that exploit facial asymmetry for SVP expression analysis include the work of Fasel et al. [22] that demonstrates a technique of estimating facial asymmetry under constrained conditions. Further in the research of Liu et al. [24], an improvement to facial identity recognition is proposed through the combination of facial asymmetry information together with EigenFace and FisherFace. Finally, one of the earliest known work in expression (happy, anger and disgust) analysis by deriving features from facial asymmetry was proposed by Mitra et al. [23].

In this paper, a combination of geometric descriptors based on reflective symmetry and appearance quality indicators using structural similarity is proposed for the detection of posed facial expressions. It is hypothesized that the fusion of geometric descriptors based on reflection symmetry and appearance quality indicators using structural similarity can collectively encapsulate the differential exaggeration of specific facial features that typically characterises that facial expression. The combined features then provide necessary attributes for the accurate classification of posed expressions using a conventional Support Vector Machine (SVM) classifier.

One novelty of the proposed framework is the quantification of exaggeration or intensity in facial expression using fused geometric descriptors and appearance quality indicators for the detection of the posed facial expressions. Furthermore, the assumptions on the reflection symmetry of facial landmark point sets allows determining symmetric point pairs across an autonomously detected line-of-symmetry which further permits measuring differential variations of specific facial features illustrating that posed facial expression. In addition, the extraction of geometric deviations in symmetric shape structures using Hausdorff distance and appearance quality variations in image patches surrounding such symmetric point pairs using structural similarity can also be considered a unique contribution of this research to posed expression analysis. Finally, the joint representation of both the geometric descriptors and appearance indicators into a fused descriptor using form matrices is different from other methods in the literature.

2 Proposed Methodology

A detailed block diagram of the proposed classification model is presented in
Fig. 1. The proposed framework functions in two distinct phases. In phase 1,
(top row in Fig. 1), reflection symmetrization is applied on the original face feature points to obtain the line of symmetry. Further, in the latter phase, the
reflective-symmetry-segmented landmark points are subjected to feature extraction using geometric and appearance constraints to obtain robust descriptors for
classification (bottom row in Fig. 1).

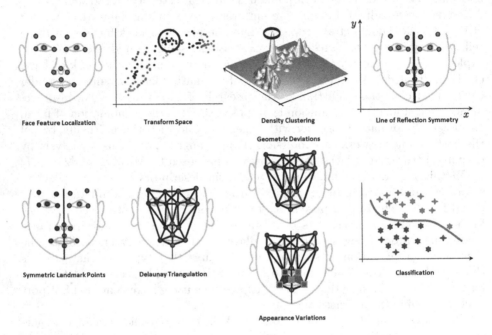

Fig. 1. Block diagram illustrating the process flow of the posed expression detection
framework.

2.1 Facial Feature Localization

The proposed framework begins by representing the face model, after conventional face detection using [29], as a set of N landmark points, $X =
\{x_1, x_2, \ldots, x_N\}$. First, our aim to estimate an optimal set, X^*, that minimizes
the posterior probability,

$$p(X|I) \propto p(I|X)p(X) \tag{1}$$

Several different techniques are available in the literature to solve this
optimization problem including the Active Shape Model (ASM) [25], Active
Appearance Model (AAM) [26], among many others. In the proposed work,

the combined shape models of [17] has been used. According to this method, a restrictive set of optimal candidates for each x_i is chosen, and by making certain assumptions on the conditional independence of features, a Markov Random Field (MRF) is used to derive an approximate solution Y efficiently. In summary, the method begins by initializing the point locations to X_0^* and iteratively over time instants t, candidates solutions are selected as $\text{argmax}_Y\, p(I|Y)p(Y|X)$. Finally, a regularization step is applied to update the land mark points to the optimal set X^*.

2.2 Feature Space

Reflection Symmetry. This work is inspired by the method of Niloy et al. in [28]. The method begins by considering the optimal set of landmark points X^* fitted on image I. Our goal now is to determine the most optimal transformation T^* that maps every point pair in the optimal set $\{x_i^* = (u_i, v_i)\}$ into the transform domain characterized by points $\{\Gamma_j = (m_j, \phi_j)\}$. Suppose p and q are the point-pair under consideration, then there exists a transformation T that maps p to q. Simply, T can be represented by the line that passes through the midpoint $m = \frac{p+q}{2}$ with normal direction $p - q$. The transform space formed by m and ϕ will host each unique pair votes between landmark points in the optimal set X^*. The largest cluster $\Gamma_j^{\hat{c}}$ (identified as the peak of the distribution) in the density plot of this transformation domain is representative of the accumulation of local evidence for the symmetry plane characterised in the spatial domain. These clusters Γ_j^c are generated using the Density Based Clustering algorithm DBSCAN [30]. The underlying principle of the DBSCAN algorithm is the classification of each landmark point in the transform space Γ_j into one of the 3 main types based on the δ-neighbourhood $\eta_\delta(\Gamma_j)$. First, a core point characterised by $\eta_\delta(\Gamma_j) \geq MinPts$, where $MinPts$ is a user-defined threshold. Second, as a noise point that is not density-reachable from any core point and finally, a boundary point, otherwise; where density-reachability of point Γ_k from another point Γ_j is conditioned by: $\Gamma_k \in \eta_\delta(\Gamma_j)$ and there exists points $\Gamma_1, \Gamma_2, \ldots, \Gamma_l$ such that $\Gamma_{j+1} \in \eta_\delta(\Gamma_j)$ and Γ_j is a core point, $j = 1, \ldots, l-1$ with $\Gamma_1 = \Gamma_j$ and $\Gamma_l = \Gamma_k$. A density cluster Γ_j^c is detected when the following two conditions are met: 1) $\forall \Gamma_k, \Gamma_j :$ If $\Gamma_j \in \Gamma_j^c$, and Γ_k is density reachable from Γ_j, then $\Gamma_k \in \Gamma_j^c$ and 2)$\forall \Gamma_k, \Gamma_j : \Gamma_k$ is density connected with Γ_j, iff there exists a point Γ_l where from Γ_k and Γ_j are density reachable.

Thus, the largest cluster is estimated as,

$$\Gamma_j^{\hat{c}} = \max_j \Gamma_j^c \tag{2}$$

Each, $\Gamma_j \in \Gamma_j^{\hat{c}}$ inverse maps to a set of points in the transform space that maps to a unique set of N_s points that represents a subset of landmark points X_s^* falling in the line of symmetry. Thus, the optimal set of landmark points X^* are partitioned into set, $\{X_s^*, X_l^*, X_r^*\}$, where $N = N_s + N_l + N_r$, $N_l = N_r$, X_l^* represents the subset of landmark points representing the landmark points on the left of the line of symmetry and X_l^* is the subset of points representing landmarks on the right of line of symmetry. Note, that there is a one to one mapping between $X_l^* = \Re(X_r^*)$; $\Re$ is a function of reflection symmetry.

Hausdorff Distance. The Hausdorff distance is one among the most common measures of similarity between two point sets. Many properties of the Hausdorff distance and its application to image analysis and processing (including fractal image compression) can be found in [7,8,10]. Using this measure, the set P is considered similar to Q iff every point in P is close to at least one point in Q. That is, the Hausdorff distance is the maximum distance of a set P to the nearest point in the other set Q. Mathematically,

$$H(P, Q) = \max\{h(P, Q), h(Q, P)\} \tag{3}$$

where

$$h(P, Q) = \max_{p \in P}\{\min_{q \in Q}\{d(p, q)\}\} \tag{4}$$

Let us notice that the term h is oriented (or in other words asymmetrical), which means that

$$h(P, Q) \neq h(Q, P) \tag{5}$$

Structural Similarity. Let A and B denote two image patches generated around point pairs that are reflective symmetric. The SSIM measure between A and B was defined originally as follows [5,6],

$$\begin{aligned} S(A, B) &= S_1(A, B)S_2(A, B)S_3(A, B) \\ &= \left[\frac{2\mu_A\mu_B + \gamma_1}{\mu_A{}^2 + \mu_B{}^2 + \gamma_1}\right]\left[\frac{2\sigma_A\sigma_B + \gamma_2}{\sigma_A^2 + \sigma_B^2 + \gamma_2}\right]\left[\frac{\sigma_{AB} + \gamma_3}{\sigma_A\sigma_B + \gamma_3}\right], \end{aligned} \tag{6}$$

where,

$$\mu_A = \frac{1}{N_l}\sum_{i=1}^{N_l} A_i, \quad \sigma_{AB} = \frac{1}{N_l - 1}\sum_{i=1}^{N_l}(A_i - \mu_A)(B_i - \mu_B), \quad \sigma_A = \sqrt{\sigma_{AA}}, \text{ etc..} \tag{7}$$

The small positive constants γ_k are added for numerical stability and can be adjusted to accommodate the perception of the human visual system. Other contributions on the properties of the SSIM measure and its application to image analysis can be found in [1–3,9]. As well described in [4,6], the form of the component S_1 in Eq. (6) was chosen to model Weber's law of perception: it measures the similarity between the means of A and B and it compares local patch luminance or brightness value. The form of S_2 follows the idea of divisive normalization and it measures the similarities of local patch contrasts. The component S_3, if $\gamma_3 = 0$, coincides with the correlation $\Xi(A, B)$ between A and B and measures the similarities of local patch structures. Note that $-1 \leq S(A, B) \leq 1$, and $S(A, B) = 1$ if and only if $A = B$. One main limitation of measuring SSIM in the spatial domain is its increased sensitivity to the translation, scaling, and rotation of image patches which are non-structural distortions [27]. In order to cope with this problem, the complex wavelets SSIM (CW-SSIM) metric was proposed in [27] with the underlying principle that separates phase from magnitude distortion measurement and thereby penalize inconsistent phase distortions. Mathematically, the CW-SSIM is formulated as follows. Given two sets of complex wavelet coefficients $c_u = \{c_{u,i} | i = 1, 2, \ldots, M\}$ and $c_v = \{c_{v,i} | i = 1, 2, \ldots, M\}$ extracted at the same spatial location (u, v) in the same wavelet sub-bands of the two images being compared, the local CW-SSIM index is defined as,

$$\hat{S}(c_u, c_v) = \frac{2 | \sum_{i=1}^{M} c_{u,i} c_{v,i}^{*} | + \kappa}{\sum_{i=1}^{M} |c_{u,i}|^2 + \sum_{i=1}^{M} |c_{v,i}|^2 + \kappa} \tag{8}$$

where c^* denotes the complex conjugate of c and κ is a small positive stabilizing constant. The value of the CW-SSIM index is in the range between 0 to 1, where 1 indicates no structural distortion, invariant to translation, rotation and scale. The global CW-SSIM index $\hat{S}(A, B)$ is computed as the mean of all local CW-SSIM values $\bigcup \hat{S}(c_u, c_v)$ over the entire wavelet sub-band and across all sub-bands.

2.3 Fused Descriptor

According to our research hypothesis, the fusion of the geometrical distances and appearance quality variations into a unified descriptor shall provide essential attributes for posed expression classification. In this paper, the concept of distance matrices, as presented in the study by [15] is extended to incorporate the joint distances in geometry and appearance. In order to accomplish this, Delaunay triangulation is applied the optimal set of landmark points $X^* = \{X_s^*, X_l^*, X_r^*\}$. Further, K triangle pairs satisfying reflective symmetry constraints, and pinned at any landmark point in set X_s^* are denoted as $\{p_1, p_2, ..., p_K\}$ and $\{q_1, q_2, ..., q_K\}$ respectively. Correspondingly, the images patches of specified dimension M, for each triangle pairs are denoted as $\{a_1, a_2, ..., a_K\}$ and $\{b_1, b_2, ..., b_K\}$. In order to compute geometric deviations of triangle (in general, polygon) pairs, the Hausdorff distance metric described in Sect. 2.2 is used. A form matrix representation of the facial expression using K polygon pairs is computed as,

$$FM_H = \begin{bmatrix} H(p_1, q_1) & H(p_1, q_2) & H(p_1, q_3) & .. & H(p_1, q_K) \\ H(p_2, q_1) & H(p_2, q_2) & H(p_2, q_3) & .. & H(p_2, q_K) \\ . & . & . & .. & . \\ . & . & . & .. & . \\ H(p_K, q_1) & H(p_K, q_1) & H(p_K, q_3) & .. & H(p_K, q_K) \end{bmatrix} \tag{9}$$

Similarly, the appearance quality indicators of composite image patch pairs is measured using the SSIM index as in Sect. 2.2. Since, each pair of triangle (in general, polygon) chosen consists of ρ ($= 3$ for triangle) image patches representing the facial feature point, the overall SSIM is factorized as $\prod_{\wp=1}^{\rho} \bar{S}(a_{\wp,.}, \Re(b)_{\wp,.})$, where $\bar{S}$ could represent original SSIM S or the CW-SSIM, $\hat{S}$. Therefore, a similar form matrix for SSIM based appearance quality indicator using K polygon pairs is estimated using,

$$
FM_S = \begin{bmatrix} \prod_{\wp=1}^{\rho} \bar{S}_{(a_{\wp,1},\Re(b)_{\wp,1}))} & \prod_{\wp=1}^{\rho} \bar{S}_{(a_{\wp,1},\Re(b)_{\wp,2})} & \cdots & \prod_{\wp=1}^{\rho} \bar{S}_{(a_{\wp,1},\Re(b)_{\wp,K})} \\ \prod_{\wp=1}^{\rho} \bar{S}_{(a_{\wp,2},\Re(b)_{\wp,1}))} & \prod_{\wp=1}^{\rho} \bar{S}_{(a_{\wp,2},\Re(b)_{\wp,2})} & \cdots & \prod_{\wp=1}^{\rho} \bar{S}_{(a_{\wp,2},\Re(b)_{\wp,K})} \\ \cdot & \cdot & \cdots & \cdot \\ \cdot & \cdot & \cdots & \cdot \\ \prod_{\wp=1}^{\rho} \bar{S}_{(a_{\wp,K},\Re(b)_{\wp,1}))} & \prod_{\wp=1}^{\rho} \bar{S}_{(a_{\wp,K},\Re(b)_{\wp,2})} & \cdots & \prod_{\wp=1}^{\rho} \bar{S}_{(a_{\wp,K},\Re(b)_{\wp,K})} \end{bmatrix}
$$
(10)

Since, form matrices FM_H and FM_S are triangular, the two are composed into,

$$
\zeta = \begin{bmatrix} H(p_1,q_1),\prod_{\wp=1}^{\rho} S_{(a_{\wp,1},\Re(b)_{\wp,1}))} & H(p_1,q_2) & \cdots & H(p_1,q_K) \\ \prod_{\wp=1}^{\rho} S_{(a_{\wp,2},\Re(b)_{\wp,1}))} & H(p_2,q_2),\prod_{\wp=1}^{\rho} S_{(a_{\wp,2},\Re(b)_{\wp,2})} & \cdots & H(p_2,q_K) \\ \cdot & \cdot & \cdots & \cdot \\ \prod_{\wp=1}^{\rho} S_{(a_{\wp,K},\Re(b)_{\wp,1}))} & \prod_{\wp=1}^{\rho} S_{(a_{\wp,K},\Re(b)_{\wp,2})} & \cdots & H(p_K,q_K),\prod_{\wp=1}^{\rho} S_{(a_{\wp,K},\Re(b)_{\wp,K})} \end{bmatrix}
$$
(11)

2.4 Classification

In order to detect posed expressions, the geometric descriptors based on reflective symmetry and form matrix is augmented with the appearance descriptors using structural similarity, forming the combined descriptor ζ that is presented as an input to the two class SVM classification model [31] that separates the posed from spontaneous expression.

3 Results and Analysis

In order to validate the claims of the proposed system, and to benchmark it against competing baseline algorithms, posed smile detection is chosen as an initial case study. Systematic experiments are conducted both evaluating the performance of the proposed framework and measuring the impact of the descriptors on the classification of posed smile expressions. A total of 800 samples from the "happy" expressions category have been chosen from various publicly available databases including, the MUG facial expression dataset [21], the Cohn-Kanade (CK) dataset [19], the extended Cohn-Kanade (CK+) dataset [18] and JAFFE dataset [20] for training and testing purposes. Since, the proposed work relies on asymmetry in the expressions, images where at least 2 out of 3 FACS labellers identified an asymmetric smile were chosen as positive samples and those where none identified an asymmetric smile, were considered negative samples. After appropriate labelling of positive (representing posed smiles) and negative samples (representing spontaneous smiles) using FACS labellers, 300 samples from each category were chosen for training the SVM classifier and 100 samples left for testing. The performance of the detection procedure was evaluated using conventional metrics of precision, recall, accuracy and f-measure.

Results of the proposed method on smile detection demonstrate the superior accuracy and robustness in comparison to the baseline method of [15] as illustrated in Table 1 (row 1). In order to assess the contribution of the individual descriptors towards the overall accuracy, the proposed method was tested using the individual form matrices. Performance, as reported in Table 1 (rows 2 & 3), indicate that the geometric descriptors play a dominating role in posed smile detection. However, the use of appearance quality indicators (in this case using the CW-SSIM) improves the overall accuracy and robustness of the method against outliers. The SSIM metric on its own suffered of higher false positives than its CW-SSIM counterpart. Although not directly comparable, these results are nearly 5 % higher than the nearest counterpart in [16]. We acknowledge that this comparison cannot be direct due the differences in the composition of images chosen between the baseline and ours. However, these results present a general idea of the superiority of the proposed method.

Table 1. Results of posed smile detection using: the fused model [row 1], only the geometric descriptor [row 2], only the appearance variation indicators [row 3] and Baseline Model [row 4].

Method	Precision	Recall	Accuracy	F-Measure
Proposed on smile (Posed class)	0.9529	0.9643	93 %	0.9586
(Other class)	0.8000	0.7500	-	0.7742
Proposed w.o. geometric (Posed class)	0.9176	0.9286	87 %	0.9231
(Other class)	0.6000	0.5625	-	0.5806
Proposed w.o. appearance (Posed class)	0.9014	0.8101	78 %	0.8533
(Other class)	0.4828	0.6667	-	0.5600
Bhaskar et al. [15] (Posed class)	0.9375	0.9494	91 %	0.9434
(Other class)	0.8000	0.7619	-	0.7805

In the second phase of experimental validation, in order to explore the capabilities of the method against other expression, 300 samples of other expressions were collected and tested using the proposed model (230 samples were used for training and 70 for testing). Experimental results in Table 2 indicate that specific expressions such as sadness (row 1), disgust (row 2) are better classified using the proposed strategy as against the others. This is mainly because, the proposed method formulates posed expressions as deviations in landmark points when measured across the perpendicular axes to the plane of symmetry. Therefore, the proposed posed expression detection schema did not work well on other expressions such as anger (row 3), fear (row 4) and surprise (row 5), due to high false positives, where the geometric deformation was found to be in the direction parallel to the plane of symmetry.

Although the experiments so far have focused on individual expressions (trained and tested on individual expressions), facial expressions in the wild

Table 2. Results of posed sad [row 1], disgust [row 2], anger [row 3], fear [row 4], surprise [row 5] and all [row 6] expressions detection

Method	Precision	Recall	Accuracy	F-Measure
Proposed on sad (Posed class)	0.9512	0.9176	90 %	0.9341
(Other class)	0.6111	0.7333	-	0.6667
Proposed on disgust (Posed class)	0.9474	0.8889	87 %	0.9172
(Other class)	0.6250	0.7895	-	0.6977
Proposed on anger (Posed class)	0.9241	0.8795	84 %	0.9012
(Other class)	0.5238	0.6471	-	0.5789
Proposed on fear (Posed class)	0.8974	0.8434	79 %	0.8696
(Other class)	0.4091	0.5294	-	0.4615
Proposed on surprise (Posed class)	0.9873	0.8211	82 %	0.8966
(Other class)	0.1905	0.80003	-	0.3077
Proposed on all (Posed class)	0.8974	0.8861	83 %	0.8917
(Other class)	0.5909	0.6190	-	0.6047

will require posed expression detection to function in an expression-independent manner. Therefore, finally, all posed expressions are submitted as a joint set and classified against its corresponding spontaneous counterpart in an expression-independent manner. The results of this classification in Table 2 (row 6) indicates that there is a marginal improvement in the overall accuracy from any individual expression. This could be because, during training the subtle variations in descriptors across different expressions can be captured better when all the expressions are treated as a whole.

4   Conclusion

In this paper, a framework for posed expression detection combining geometric deviations and appearance variation descriptors, is proposed. The framework has been shown to be more accurate than other baseline methods. However, it is often restricted due to the assumptions of facial asymmetry that is significant for only a subset of expressions. Also, it could be observed that the framework would work compelling better on images captured in the wild (natural images) as against those captured under restrictive constrained conditions. The future work will focus on incorporating the structural texture similarity descriptor and geometric deviations w.r.t. neural expression counterpart for more generic posed facial expression recognition.

References

1. Brunet, D.: A Study of the Structural Similarity Image Quality Measure with Applications to Image Processing, Ph.D. thesis, University of Waterloo (2010)

2. Brunet, D., Vrscay, E.R., Wang, Z.: On the mathematical properties of the structural similarity index. IEEE Trans. Image Process. **21**(4), 1488–1499 (2012)
3. Brunet, D., Vrscay, E.R., Wang, Z.: Structural similarity-based approximation of signals and images using orthogonal bases. In: Campilho, A., Kamel, M. (eds.) ICIAR 2010. LNCS, vol. 6111, pp. 11–22. Springer, Heidelberg (2010)
4. Wainwright, M.J., Schwartz, O., Simoncelli, E.P.: Natural image statistics and divisive normalization: modeling non-linearity and adaptation in cortical neurons. In: Rao, R., Olshausen, B., Lewicki, M. (eds.) Probabilistic Models of the Brain: Perception and Neural Function, pp. 203–222. MIT Press, Cambridge (2002)
5. Wang, Z., Bovik, A.C.: Mean squared error: love it or leave it? A new look at signal fidelity measures. IEEE Signal Processing Magazine **26**(1), 98–117 (2009)
6. Wang, Z., Bovik, A.C., Sheikh, H.R., Simoncelli, E.P.: Image quality assessment: from error visibility to structural similarity. IEEE Trans. Image Process. **13**(4), 600–612 (2004)
7. Ghazel, M., Freeman, G.H., Vrscay, E.R.: Fractal image denoising. IEEE Trans. Image Process. **12**, 1560–1578 (2003)
8. Barnsley, M.F., Hurd, L.: Fractal Image Compression. A.K. Peters, Wellesley (1993)
9. Kowalik-Urbaniak, I.A., Torre, D.L., Vrscay, E.R., Wang, Z.: Some "Weberized" L2-based methods of signal/image approximation. In: Campilho, A., Kamel, M. (eds.) ICIAR 2014, Part I. LNCS, vol. 8814, pp. 20–29. Springer, Heidelberg (2014)
10. Kunze, H., La Torre, D., Mendivil, F., Vrscay, E.R.: Fractal-Based Methods in Analysis. Springer, New York (2014)
11. Valstar, M.F., Pantic, M.: How to distinguish posed from spontaneous smiles using geometric features. In: Proceedings of the International Conference on Multimodal Interfaces (ICMI), vol. 3845 (2007)
12. Tong, Y., Liao, W., Ji, Q.: Facial action unit recognition by exploiting their dynamic and semantic relationships. IEEE Trans. Pattern Anal. Mach. Intell. **29**(10), 1683–1699 (2007)
13. Schmidt, K.L., Ambadar, Z., Cohn, J.F., Reed, L.I.: Movement differences between deliberate and spontaneous facial expressions zygomaticus major action in smiling. J. Nonverbal Behav. **30**, 3752 (2006)
14. Dibeklioğlu, H., Salah, A.A., Gevers, T.: Are you really smiling at me? spontaneous versus posed enjoyment smiles. In: Fitzgibbon, A., Lazebnik, S., Perona, P., Sato, Y., Schmid, C. (eds.) ECCV 2012, Part III. LNCS, vol. 7574, pp. 525–538. Springer, Heidelberg (2012)
15. Bhaskar, H., Al-Mualla, M.: Spontaneous vs. posed facial expression analysis using deformable feature models and aggregated classifiers. In: Proceedings of the International Conference on Information FUSION (2013)
16. Valstar, M.F., Pantic, M.: Automatic analysis of brow actions. In: Proceedings of the ACM International Conference on Multimodal Interfaces (ICMI), pp. 162–170 (2006)
17. Tresadern, P.A., Bhaskar, H., Adeshina, S.A., Taylor, J.C., Cootes, T.F.: Combining Local and Global Shape Models for Deformable Object Matching. In: Proceedings of the British Machine Vision Conference (BMVC), pp. 1–12 (2009)
18. Lucey, P., Cohn, J.F., Kanade, T., Saragih, J., Ambadar, Z., Matthews, I.: The extended Cohn-Kande dataset (CK+) : a complete facial expression dataset for action unit and emotion-specified expression. In: Proceedings of the Third IEEE Workshop on Computer Vision and Pattern Recognition for Human Communicative Behavior Analysis (2010)

19. Kanade, T., Cohn, J.F., Tian, Y.: Comprehensive database for facial expression analysis. In: Proceedings of the Fourth IEEE International Conference on Automatic Face and Gesture Recognition (FG), pp. 46–53 (2000)

20. Dailey, M.N., Joyce, C., Lyons, M.J., Kamachi, M., Ishi, H., Gyoba, J., Cottrell, G.W.: Evidence and a computational explanation of cultural differences in facial expression recognition. Emotion 10(6), 874–893 (2010)

21. Aifanti, N., Papachristou, C., Delopoulos, A.: The MUG facial expression database. In: Proceedings of the 11th International Workshop on Image Analysis for Multimedia Interactive Services (WIAMIS) (2010)

22. Fasel, B., Luettin, J.: Recognition of asymmetric facial action unit activities and intensities. In: Proceedings of the International Conference on Pattern Recognition (ICPR) (2000)

23. Mitra, S., Liu, Y.: Local facial asymmetry for expression classification. In: Proceedings of the IEEE Computer Society Conference on Computer Vision and Pattern Recognition (CVPR), vol. 2, pp. 889–894 (2004)

24. Liu, Y., Schmidt, K.L., Cohn, J.F., Mitra, S.: Facial asymmetry quantification for expression invariant human identification. J. Comput. Vis. Image Underst. 91(1–2), 138–159 (2003)

25. Cootes, T.F., Cooper, D., Taylor, C.J., Graham, J.: Active shape models - their training and application. J. Comput. Vis. Image Underst. 61(1), 38–59 (1995)

26. Cootes, T.F., Edwards, G.J., Taylor, C.J.: Active appearance models. In: Burkhardt, H., Neumann, B. (eds.) ECCV 1998. LNCS, vol. 1407, p. 484. Springer, Heidelberg (1998)

27. Gao, Y., Rehma, A., Wang, Z.: CW-SSIM based image classification. In: Proceedings of the IEEE International Conference on Image Processing (ICIP), pp. 1249–1252 (2011)

28. Mitra, N.J., Guibas, L., Pauly, M.: Symmetrization. ACM Trans. Graphics (SIGGRAPH) 26(3), 1–8 (2007)

29. Viola, P., Jones, M.J.: Robust real-time face detection. Int. J. Comput. Vis. (IJCV) 57(2), 137–154 (2004)

30. Ester, M., Kriegel, H-P., Sander, J., Xu, X.: A density-based algorithm for discovering clusters in large spatial databases with noise. In: Proceedings of the Second International Conference onKnowledge Discovery and Data Mining (KDD), pp. 226–231. AAAI Press (1996)

31. Cristianini, N., Shawe-Taylor, J.: An Introduction to Support Vector Machines. Cambridge University Press, New York (2000)

Improving the Recognition of Occluded Faces by Means of Two-dimensional Orthogonal Projection into Local Subspaces

Paweł Forczmański[✉] and Piotr Łabędź

Faculty of Computer Science and Information Technology,
West Pomeranian University of Technology, Żołnierska Str. 52,
71–210 Szczecin, Poland
{pforczmanski,plabedz}@wi.zut.edu.pl

Abstract. The paper presents a problem of reducing the influence of natural occlusion on face recognition accuracy. It is based on transformation (two-dimensional Karhunen-Loeve Transform) of face parts into local subspaces calculated by means of two-dimensional Principal Component Analysis and two-dimensional Linear Discriminant Analysis. We use a sequence of operations consisting of face scale and orientation normalization and individual facial regions extraction. Independent recognitions are performed on extracted facial regions and their results are combined in order to perform a final classification. The experiments on images taken from publicly available datasets show that such a simple algorithm is able to successfully recognize faces without high computational overhead, in contrast to more sophisticated methods presented recently. In comparison to typical, whole-face-based approach, developed method gives significantly better accuracy.

1 Introduction

1.1 Motivation

An automatic face recognition performed by a computer system is one of the classical problems in pattern recognition. A myriad of methods have been proposed so far and it seems that this problem has already been successfully solved. However, due to its complex characteristic, it is still interesting. Such constant interest is driven by the fact that most of the proposed methods of facial portrait recognition works mainly in the controlled conditions of imaging, with strictly defined illumination, orientation, pose, expression etc. The continuous progress in this field is influenced also by the need of algorithms that are able to work on devices having processing power significantly lower than general-purpose personal computers (e.g. smartphones, tablets, set-top boxes) [5]. Therefore, certain effective, yet simple solutions are still needed.

Despite a large progress in the field of imaging sensors, low quality of input data processed by a typical face recognition algorithm is still one of the issues. Actually, such low quality comes not necessary from the low spatial or dynamic

© Springer International Publishing Switzerland 2015
M. Kamel and A. Campilho (Eds.): ICIAR 2015, LNCS 9164, pp. 229–238, 2015.
DOI: 10.1007/978-3-319-20801-5_25

resolution of images (which is good) but from other distortions observed in the image area, mainly related to physical obstacles like occlusions/incompleteness of face portrait. They often occur as full or partial occlusion of different face areas by an independent object like scarf, dark glasses, hats etc. Such situation highly degrades the performance of FaReS, thus this is the main reason of lasting interest of researchers [20]. We should remember, that in many practical situations we have an access only to a limited training dataset [7], hence we have to perform facial recognition without knowing images having all possible variants of global and/or local distortions (opposite to setups proposed in [20]).

1.2 Related Works

According to the literature review, in order to recognize faces under occlusion we have to select certain invariant features [2]. There are many complex approaches that solve only some of all possible problems, e.g. changing poses [1] or illumination [26]. Except several sophisticated anthropometrical approaches, there are also many straightforward appearance-based methods that combine various elementary features to describe an image. However, as it was mentioned, they lead to the very complex multi-tier algorithms, which are inutile in low-end devices.

An interesting, yet complex algorithm was presented in [14]. It is proposed to detect the presence of scarf or sunglasses and then analyse non-occluded facial regions only. Occluded regions are detected using Gabor wavelets, Principal Component Analysis (PCA) and Support Vector Machines (SVM), while the recognition is done by means of block-based Local Binary Patterns (LBP). The main drawback is related to the assumption about the presence of sunglasses or scarf, without taking into account other occlusion types. Moreover, face recognition by means of LBP is not the most optimal approach.

Most of popular approaches to face recognition employ different kinds of dimensionality reduction techniques [18]. A classical one, namely Eigenfaces [23], works well if images are properly registered, have the same expression, orientation and illumination characteristics. Unfortunately, in case of large image matrices, such an approach is difficult to implement and requires significant memory space. In order to overcome this limitation, taking into account the two-dimensional characteristics of images, many quasi-two-dimensional approaches have been developed, e.g. 2DPCA [15,25] or MatPCA [4]. Unfortunately, most of them are associated with the processing of two-dimensional data by means of data reduction algorithms performed along one dimension only or by dividing an image into smaller parts and treating them with help of classical PCA. The literature survey shows, that even if those methods have been successfully implemented, they operate on fully visible facial portraits not considering a problem of occlusion and local distortions.

The authors of [19] address a problem of reconstructing images using so called Fast-Robust PCA. It was shown that it is possible to recover missing pixels in facial portraits, however it is computationally expensive. An extended method presented in [9] uses a modified (faster) PCA approach, namely Fast Weighted Principal Component Analysis (FW-PCA) and makes it possible to reconstruct distorted pixels in facial portraits. In that approach, occluded regions are detected and recursively updated. Unfortunately, the authors do not address the problem of recognition of reconstructed facial portraits. Another extension of classical PCA, called Lophoscopic PCA, aimed at recognition of occluded faces was presented in [22]. In the experiments single small part of face was synthetically covered with uniform rectangles which hardly represents real-life conditions. Moreover, in that approach a precise face registration and localization of facial parts is required. Since such algorithm is complex and time-consuming (six times slower than a classical PCA) it could not be implemented on low-end devices.

There is another large group of methods employing Local Non-Negative Matrix Factorization (LNMF) [16,27]. In [16] the authors decompose a facial portrait into pre-defined parts. Then the parts with distortions are detected using PCA and Nearest-Neighbor classifier. The final recognition is performed using Selective Local Non-Negative Matrix Factorization with a help of a map of distorted regions.

The common drawback of above methods is the computational complexity associated with an iterative nature of calculating reconstructed images or the need of detecting occluded regions. Hence, it is a general disadvantage when it comes to robust and fast implementation.

In this paper we focus on subspace approaches based on two-dimensional versions of Principal Components Analysis and Linear Discriminant Analysis. They have been proved to be very efficient, yet not very computationally expensive, especially in case of currently available computing power. Further in the paper we present an algorithm of facial recognition under natural occlusion, which is much simpler in comparison to the above presented approaches, yet its efficiency is very similar. It employs a reference database of facial parts that does not include images with local distortions. At the stage of preprocessing it uses fully automatic face normalization and facial regions extraction. At the stage of feature transformation it uses 2DPCA/2DLDA as the only instruments of projection of original data into the low dimensional space [10]. Finally, obtained feature matrices are classified by means of minimum distance classifier with weighting and voting.

2 Algorithm Description

2.1 Algorithm Outline

Developed algorithm is based on an observation that in most situations faces are occluded only to some extent. If an algorithm successfully recognizes *most* of facial parts (like eyes, nose, mouth), then it can lead to the recognition of the whole face. Presented algorithm is a modification and extension of a previously presented work [8]. In comparison to that solution, we introduced three new elements. First, at the preprocessing stage, we add fully automatic facial parts detection and localization [12] by means of two-stage approach. It consists of AdaBoost detection [24] with template matching and does not assume all facial parts to be clearly visible. Second, we eliminated forehead from recognition, since it did not add much discriminative power. Third, we introduced a weighting to the voting stage in order to promote more important (informative) parts of facial portrait. Introduced improvements made it possible to perform experiments on higher number of images then in case of images with manually marked facial features.

2.2 Image Preprocessing

The input image is a grayscale en-face portait of not-assumed spatial resolution. Firstly, it has to be normalized and four characteristic areas have to be extracted. It is done using AdaBoost approach implemented in a Viola-Jones detector [24]. The cascades of V-J detector were learned on respective databases containing gathered facial elements, namely eyes (right and left, independently), noses and mouths [3]. If V-J detector returns more then one candidate (for each class: right eye, left eye, nose and mouth), candidates having dimensions different from expected are eliminated. The rest are compared with templates (averaged images for each class). This same applies to the case, when V-J detector does not find any required facial element. Hence, a fragment closest to the template is returned. It can happen that it is occluded or even a random part, thus its low weight at the final voting stage will decrease its influence.

Above approach is much better then one presented previously [8], since it works in a fully automatic manner. The exemplary results of preprocessing were presented in Fig. 1. The first image (on the left) is an input portrait, which is cropped, using V-J detector. It can successfully detect faces even if they are partially occluded. Detected candidates are verified using simple geometrical criterion (size and orientation). Finally, four above mentioned facial areas are extracted using four dedicated cascades of V-J detector. Further, we use these sub-matrices without any information about geometrical relation between them.

In order to normalize images' dimensions across reference database, they are re-scaled to uniform sizes, in order to comply with different sources (whole face 350×350, left/right eye 40×60, nose 56×68, mouth 63×105 pixels, respectively).

Fig. 1. Results of facial portrait preprocessing

2.3   Projection and Classification

The recognition system works in two modes. The first one is dedicated to database creation (Rdb_k). Actually, there are $k = 4$ independent databases, each one holding images of specific facial element (eyes, nose and mouth). At this offline stage we collect images, preprocess them, calculate transformation matrices and project them into subspaces. The second mode is an actual recognition, when we get an input image, preprocess it (in the same way as reference images), decompose into facial areas and project into respective subspaces (using transformation matrices calculated at the offline stage). Then, each facial element Q_k is recognized independently in its subspace. The recognition is based on minimum distance classifier, namely 1-Nearest Neighbor as it proved many times to be effective in such tasks.

In the experiments presented here, we applied two-dimensional variant of Karhunen-Loeve Transform (2DKLT) [11] employing transformation matrices calculated using two-dimensional Principal Component Analysis (2DPCA) and for comparison, two-dimensional Linear Discriminant Analysis (2DLDA).

The distance of each feature k is calculated using Manhattan distance metric, defined as a sum of absolute values between adequate elements (i, j) of feature matrices R from Rdb_k and query object Q:

$$D_k(R, Q) = \sum_{i,j} |r_{i,j} - q_{i,j}|. \tag{1}$$

For each k-th facial element (facial feature) we get an individual answer (closest class number or individual number) and a calculated distance D_k. This distance is later subject to normalization (weighting). It is performed using predefined weights, calculated for a special calibration probe (a set of facial areas T_k - eyes, noses and mouths, with no distortions/occlusions belonging to n faces). The weights w_1, w_2, w_3, w_4 are the average distances of all images (actually their reduced representations) from a testing probe to all images from reference database Rdb:

$$w_k = \frac{\sum_{l=1}^{n} D_l(R, T)}{n}. \tag{2}$$

The weights calculated independently for 2DPCA/2DKLT and 2DLDA/2DKLT approaches are presented in Table 1. During detection, if a closest match is found for an arbitrary facial part but its distance is higher than a value shown in Table 1, then it is assumed to be wrongly detected or highly occluded. If the distance is lower that above threshold, then the match is useful for recognition. It improves the recognition rate in case of low quality or strongly distorted images.

The final stage is voting. After classification, each individual result points to a specific class (owner of this facial fragment). Associated, normalized distance serves as a sorting criterion. Classes are sorted in an increasing distance order and based on the results, they obtain the following scores: 7, 5, 4, 4. Scores for the same resulting classes are summed. The class with the highest final score is a recognition result.

3   Experiments

3.1   Reference Database

First, it should be noted, that there is no universal benchmark database containing facial portraits under occlusion of variable type [6]. There are several publicly available dataset consisting of image presenting humans wearing glasses, scarfs, hats, but the complex approach to such problem could not be found. In contrast to the database created for the purpose of previous research [8], we have chosen three well-known large databases containing occlusions by different natural objects (e.g. glasses, scarfs, sheets of paper, other body parts or local illumination changes) or heavy changes in grimace and image quality. Thus, we selected the following:

- AR Face Database [13] - 4000 images (135 individuals) taken in two series (different days); resolution 768 × 576;
- Euro Kinect Face Database [17] - 936 images (52 individuals) taken in two series (different days); resolution 256 × 256;
- GTAV Face Database [21] - 653 images (44 individuals), resolution 320 × 240.

The final benchmark database was created using only *en face* portraits with different kinds of occlusions. In effect, it consists of 3793 images of 227 individuals. There are three non-overlapping subsets: the reference subset which includes 1519 images without occlusions, calibration probe for weights calculation - 227 images and testing subset with 2047 images with occlusions. There is a minimum one image per class, maximum 11 images and an average of over 6 images per individual.

3.2   Results

Using a similar experimental setup [8] we tested developed algorithm on images having different distortions. They are divided into 7 subsets (A–G), as follows (see Fig. 2):

(A) All occlusion types with no differentiation (2047 images);
(B) Images from AR database (1529 images);
(C) Images from Euro Kinect database (219 images);
(D) Images from GTAV database (299);
(E) Images with eyes covered (861 images);
(F) Images with occluded lower part of face (741 images);
(G) Additional, not classified occlusions (299 images).

Table 1. Weights calculated for a testing probe associated with two projection methods

Subspace	Left eye	Right eye	Nose	Mouth
2DPCA	17.4771	17.2780	20.1345	27.2012
2DLDA	0.2534	0.2666	0.1016	0.0785

Fig. 2. Sample images belonging to six occlusion categories (in columns): B,C,D,E,F,G

The recognition accuracy, understood as a percentage of correctly recognized portraits for all above subsets and two projection methods is provided in Table 2. The results should be interpreted as follows. For example, if we use only mouth part (M) for experiment E (occluded eyes), then the PCA-based recognition accuracy of whole face is equal to 35.65 %.

An analysis of above table unveils that in most cases LDA-based approach fails. It is probably because of not perfect alignment of facial areas and small number of samples required to form high quality covariance matrices. Moreover, in all cases, the recognition accuracy for individual facial parts is rather low (average 30 % and not more than 60 %). However, we assumed that based on all four individual facial areas we can increase the overall recognition accuracy.

Table 2. Recognition accuracy for individual facial areas compared to whole-face-based and part-based approaches for 7 subsets and two projection methods

Facial part	Subspace	Recognition rate for subset [%]						
		A	B	C	D	E	F	G
Left eye (LE)	2DPCA	31.75	30.01	25.37	41.80	0.81	50.75	27.86
	2DLDA	22.71	23.08	1.82	2.67	0.58	50.20	19.77
Right eye (RE)	2DPCA	34.44	33.55	33.33	42.14	0.58	59.02	37.07
	2DLDA	27.99	22.49	0.45	1.00	0.81	58.56	29.66
Nose (N)	2DPCA	17.20	13.14	34.24	34.11	4.99	26.05	46.29
	2DLDA	1.03	1.43	2.27	1.67	0.11	0.53	3.59
Mouth (M)	2DPCA	17.78	18.70	24.20	22.74	**35.65**	4.8	12.13
	2DLDA	0.68	1.37	2.27	2.34	0.58	0.26	1.57
Whole Face (WF)	2DPCA	29.55	29.43	**58.90**	52.84	18.35	21.05	**65.38**
	2DLDA	23.59	22.04	3.19	12.37	10.34	16.87	56.85
All parts (AP)	2DPCA	**52.61**	**52.84**	47.94	**64.21**	27.78	**68.30**	58.65
	2DLDA	27.01	23.94	1.82	2.00	0.81	53.81	28.54
AP + WF	2DPCA	56.62	56.90	58.45	68.56	23.11	64.64	72.81

In addition, we compared developed algorithm with standard recognition based on whole facial portraits (see Fig. 3). In part-based method each facial area was represented (after projection) by a matrix of 10×10 coefficients, while whole image-based approach, with 20×20 elements. Hence, the dimensionality of feature spaces in both cases was the same (4×100 versus 400). The results are provided in rows marked WF and AP in Table 2. As it can be seen, in most cases our algorithm is better than traditional algorithm based on whole images. It is worth noticing that 2DPCA method is superior to 2DLDA. As it can be seen, the accuracy for experiments C and G is significantly lower. It is caused by parallel occlusion in the eyes and mouth areas.

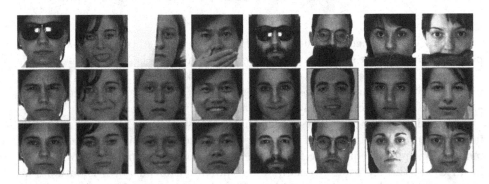

Fig. 3. Exemplary results of recognition: the first row is a query image, the second row - result of whole-face-based recognition and the third row - result of all-parts-based recognition; Four first columns present result where WF and AP are equal, while the last four columns show the superiority of AP approach

In order to further increase the recognition rate it is possible to add a fifth recognition procedure, based on whole face image (facial portrait re-scaled to 70×70 pixels). After that, the recognition accuracy for 2DPCA is further increased. In such case the scores for individual results are as follows: 7,5,4,4,3. The weight for whole face was equal to 36.39.

Further increase in recognition rate may be obtained by fine-tuning spatial positions of nose and mouth. An additional experiment on subset A, when nose and mouth has been cropped manually, showed further increase in recognition accuracy: 62.97 % (for 2DPCA) together with 33.7 % for mouth only and 26.2 % for nose, respectively.

Presented method has some important advantages over the other, recently published approaches. The first one is related to the number of testing images and their origin. In most of works, only one, limited database was used (mostly AR and GTAV). When there were more databases employed, they were taken for independent experiments. In the experiments presented here, we used a large database comprising of a number of images, taken from 3 different origins. Our method was investigated in terms of natural occlusion, as opposite to other works, when a synthetic distortions have been introduced. In such cases (e.g. [22], when e.g. dark rectangle covers face part put in only one of few pre-defined places, the recognition would be much higher. It should be stressed, that it does not represent real-life conditions. The method presented in this paper does not assume a type of occlusion or an object that occludes a face, as opposite to the work [14]. In that paper, the authors constructed individual classifiers for various objects, which increases the computational overhead. In our approach we do not pre-define any facial part position, in contrast ot other methods that depend on exact e.g. eyes positions [14].

4 Summary

Performed experiments confirm advantages of developed method over a traditional approach. The decrease in recognition accuracy comes from not perfect extraction of facial areas like nose and mouth. It leads to high intra-class visual variability of individual features. It is especially true for features that are hard to model (nose) and non-rigid (mouth). Although, single facial areas are not useful for facial recognition (see Table 2), when we join them the final recognition rate is acceptable.

The bottom line is, that LDA-based recognition is not suited for such problems. It is caused by small number of samples having high variability making eigenproblem solution hard to find.

References

1. Asthana, A., Marks, T.K., Jones, M.J., Tieu, K.H., Rohith, M.V.: Fully automatic pose-invariant face recognition via 3d pose normalization. In Proceedings of the IEEE International Conference on Computer Vision, pp. 937–944 (2011)
2. Azeem, A., Sharif, M., Raza, M., Murtaza, M.: A survey: face recognition techniques under partial occlusion. Int. J. Inf. Tech. (IAJIT) **11**(1), 1–10 (2014)
3. Castrillón, M., Déniz, O., Guerra, C., Hernández, M.: ENCARA2: real-time detection of multiple faces at different resolutions in video streams. J. Vis. Commun. Image Represent. **18**(2), 130–140 (2007)
4. Chen, S., Zhu, Y., Zhang, D., Yang, J.-Y.: Feature extraction approaches based on matrix pattern: MatPCA and MatFLDA. PRL **26**, 1157–1167 (2005)
5. Forczmański, P., Kukharev, G.: Comparative analysis of simple facial features extractors. J. Real-Time Image Proc. **4**(1), 239–255 (2007)
6. Forczmański, P., Furman, M.: Comparative analysis of benchmark datasets for face recognition algorithms verification. In: Bolc, L., Tadeusiewicz, R., Chmielewski, L.J., Wojciechowski, K. (eds.) ICCVG 2012. LNCS, vol. 7594, pp. 354–362. Springer, Heidelberg (2012)
7. Forczmański, P., Kukharev, G., Shchegoleva, N.: Simple and robust facial portraits recognition under variable lighting conditions based on two-dimensional orthogonal transformations. In: Petrosino, A. (ed.) ICIAP 2013, Part I. LNCS, vol. 8156, pp. 602–611. Springer, Heidelberg (2013)
8. Forczmański, P., Łabędź, P.: Recognition of occluded faces based on multi-subspace classification. In: Saeed, K., Chaki, R., Cortesi, A., Wierzchoń, S. (eds.) Computer Information Systems and Industrial Management. CISIM 2013, vol. 8104, pp. 148–157. Springer, Heidelberg (2013)

9. Hosoi, T., Nagashima, S., Ito, K., Aoki, T.: Reconstructing occluded regions using fast weighted PCA. In: 19th IEEE Internaternational Conference on Image Processing (ICIP), pp. 1729–1732 (2012)
10. Kukharev, G., Forczmański, P.: Data dimensionality reduction for face recognition. Mach. Graph Vis. **13**(1/2), 99–122 (2004)
11. Kukharev, G., Forczmański, P.: Facial images dimensionality reduction and recognition by means of 2DKLT. Mach. Graph Vis. **16**(3/4), 401–425 (2007)
12. Lienhart, R., Kuranov, A., Pisarevsky, V.: Empirical analysis of detection cascades of boosted classifiers for rapid object detection. MRL Technical report, Intel Labs (2002)
13. Martinez, A.M., Benavente, R.: The AR face database, CVC Technical report #24 (1998)
14. Min, R., Hadid, A., Dugelay, J.: Improving the recognition of faces occluded by facial accessories. In: IEEE International Conference on Automatic Face Gesture Recognition and Workshops (FG 2011), pp. 442–447 (2011)
15. Nagabhushan, P., Guru, D.S., Shekar, B.H.: Visual learning and recognition of 3D objects using two-dimensional principal component analysis: a robust and an efficient approach. Pattern Recogn. **39**(4), 721–725 (2006)
16. Oh, H.J., Lee, K.M., Lee, S.U.: Occlusion invariant face recognition using selective local non-negative matrix factorization basis images. Image Vis. Comput. **26**(11), 1515–1523 (2008)
17. Rui, M., Kose, N., Dugelay, J.-L.: KinectFaceDB: a kinect database for face recognition. IEEE Trans. Syst. Man Cybern. Syst. **44**(11), 1534–1548 (2014)
18. Sirovich, I., Kirby, M.: Low-dimensional procedure for the characterization of human faces. J. Opt. Soc. Am. **4**, 519–524 (1987)
19. Storer, M., Roth, P.M., Urschler, M., Bischof, H.: Fast-robust PCA. In: Salberg, A.-B., Hardeberg, J.Y., Jenssen, R. (eds.) SCIA 2009. LNCS, vol. 5575, pp. 430–439. Springer, Heidelberg (2009)
20. Tan, X., Triggs, B.: Preprocessing and feature sets for robust face recognition. In: IEEE Conference on Computer Vision and Pattern Recognition, CVPR 2007, pp. 1–8 (2007)
21. Tarrés, F., Rama, A.: GTAV Face Database. http://gpstsc.upc.es/GTAV/ResearchAreas/UPCFaceDatabase/GTAVFaceDatabase.htm
22. Tarrés, F., Rama, A., Torres, L.: A novel method for face recognition under partial occlusion or facial expression variations. In: 47th International Symposium ELMAR-2005. Multimedia Systems and Applications, pp. 163–166 (2005)
23. Turk, M., Pentland, A.: Eigenfaces for recognition. J. Cogn. Neurosicence **3**(1), 71–86 (1991)
24. Viola, P., Jones, M.J.: Robust Real-Time Face Detection. International Journal of. Computer Vision **57**(2), 137–154 (2004)
25. Yang, J., Zhang, D., Frangi, A.F., Yang, J.-Y.: Two-dimensional pca: a new approach to appearance-based face representation and recognition. IEEE Trans. Pattern Anal. Mach. Intell. **26**(1), 131–137 (2004)
26. Zhang, T., Fang, B., Tang, Y.Y., Shang, Z., Li, D., Lang, F.: Multiscale facial structure representation for face recognition under varying illumination. Pattern Recogn. **42**(2), 251–258 (2009)
27. Yu-Lian, Z.: Sub-pattern non-negative matrix factorization based on random subspace for face recognition. In: International Conference on Wavelet Analysis and Pattern Recognition, ICWAPR 2007, pp. 1356–1360 (2007)

Hybrid Age Estimation Using Facial Images

Simon Reade and Serestina Viriri[✉]

School of Computing, University of South Africa, Pretoria, South Africa
evirirs1@unisa.ac.za

Abstract. Age estimation determines a person's age or age group using facial images and has many real-world applications. This paper investigates various algorithms used to improve age estimation. A combination of features and classifiers are compared. A database of facial images is trained to extract features using algorithms such as local binary patterns (LBP), active shape models and histogram of oriented gradients (HOG). The age estimation is done using three age groups: child, adult, senior. The ages are classified using support vector machine (SVM), K-nearest neighbour (KNN), gradient boosting tree (GBT). The age estimation model is evaluated using the FG-NET aging database obtaining positive results of 82 % success rate.

1 Introduction

The human face can be described as a *window to the soul* [1], as it reveals personal information relating to an individual, such as identity, gender and age. For humans, it is relatively easy to be able to estimate an individual's age. We have the ability to use facial information to interpret and understand faces and facial gestures as we see them [2]. For computers, the task of estimating an individual's age is much more complex. Computers have to rely on biometric features extracted from facial images and implement algorithms that can allow the age estimation of an individual [3]. Age estimation has numerous real world applications, such as providing internet safety for minors, by preventing access to web pages. It can also be a valuable tool for law enforcement, by providing enhanced security and surveillance measures.

The task of capturing aging variations becomes more difficult with the following challenges [4]:

- *Incomplete aging patterns:* Face aging is uncontrollable.
- *Personalized aging patterns:* Each individual can age in a different way.
- *Temporal aging pattern:* The aging process must follow the order of time.

The aim of this research work is to investigate a variety of algorithms that can be used for efficient age estimation.

2 Literature Review

The topic of face image processing has been active and much interest has been shown. Face image processing is a broad topic and has been active for many years.

© Springer International Publishing Switzerland 2015
M. Kamel and A. Campilho (Eds.): ICIAR 2015, LNCS 9164, pp. 239–246, 2015.
DOI: 10.1007/978-3-319-20801-5_26

There have been various contributions and different approaches that attempt to solve or improve age estimation. Kwon and Lobo [5] discuss anthropomorphic models, which are the measurements and proportions of the face. They proposed calculations for age classification of facial images which is based on craniofacial morphology (the study of shape of face and skull) and wrinkle analysis. They were able to classify face images into three age groups; *babies, young adults, and senior adults*, by combining the analysis of face ratios and wrinkle analysis. The anthropomorphic models only work effectively when distinguishing minors from adults, as an adult human head experiences very little change [6]. Kwon and Lobo [5] failed to address the problem of varying face orientation, as they only concentrated on mugshot viewpoints, which made the ratio calculations easy.

T. Cootes et al. [7] initially proposed the active appearance model (AAM) which is a statistical face model used for coding face images. The AAM depends on *landmark points* in the training set. A statistical shape model and intensity model can be learned separately, with Principle Component Analysis (PCA). AAM can deal with any age and it considers both shape and texture of the face. Lanitis et al. [8] proposed an aging function to explain the variation in age, thus extending the AAMs for face aging. The experiments by Lanitis et al. [8] relied on PCA, which discards local and unsystematic sources of variability. The performance could be improved by incorporating the details of a face with the age estimation procedure. Luu et al. [9] attempted to improve the accuracy of age estimation by focusing on a technique that combined AAMs and Support Vector Machines (SVMs). The AAMs were used for extracting facial features, and the SVMs were used for age estimation. Although there were some incorrect classifications of adults instead of youths, this technique did achieve higher accuracy rates compared to other existing methods.

Geng et al. [10] proposed AGES (**AG**ing patt**E**n **S**ubspace) method, which analyses a sequence of individual images as a whole, not separately. An aging pattern (data structure), defined as a sequence of images from the same person sorted in temporal order, is created [11]. The AGES method has two stages [4]: In the learning stage, the PCA technique is used to create a subspace representation. In the age estimation stage, the most suitable age needs to be found for a single test face image. The preprocess method of AGES relied on many landmark points in the face images, and did not retain information about the outer contour of the face.

3   Methodology

3.1   Preprocessing

Histogram Equalization. Histogram equalization enhances the contrast of images by adjusting their intensities. The probability of an occurrence of a pixel of level i is

$$p_x(i) = p(x = i) = \frac{n_i}{n}, \qquad 0 \leq i \leq L \tag{1}$$

with L being the total number of gray levels, n being the total number of pixels in the image, and $p_x(i)$ being the image's histogram for pixel value i, normalized to $[0,1]$.

The cumulative distribution function corresponding to $p_x(i)$ is:

$$cdf_x(i) = \sum_{j=0}^{i} p_x(j) \tag{2}$$

which is the image's accumulated normalized histogram.

3.2   Region of Interest

The face detection is a haar feature-based classifier proposed by Viola and Jones [12]. A classifier is trained using AdaBoost with hundreds of positive examples and negative examples. Rectangular features are extracted from a sub-window and are compared against facial features.

3.3   Feature Extraction

Principle Component Analysis (PCA). Principle component analysis (PCA) is used to determine the vectors that measure the variation in a set of face images. These vectors, called Eigenfaces, are the set of eigenvectors of the covariance matrix that are extracted from the face image vectors. Eigenfaces extracts important facial information used to determine the variation between face images. By using a small number of parameters used to represent each face image, this reduces the space and time complexity [13].

Active Shape Models (ASMs). The ASMs, introduced by T. Cootes [7], are statistical models of the shape of objects that use 'landmarks' points to describe the location of structures in an image. The facial landmarks can be located using Stasm [14]. Using Stasm 4, the landmarks were extended to 77 points.

Local Binary Patterns (LBP). The Local Binary Pattern operator, introduced by Ojiala et al. [15], is useful in summarizing local gray-level structure. LBP is resistant to lighting effects and they have been shown to be effective for texture classification [15]. The LBP operator labels the pixels of an image by thresholding the 3×3 neighbourhood of each pixel:

$$LBP(x_c, y_c) = \sum_{n=0}^{7} 2^n s(i_n - ic) \tag{3}$$

with n running over 8 neighbours of the central pixel c, i_c and i_n are the gray-level values at c and n, and $s(u) = 1$ if $u \geq 0$ and otherwise 0.

Gabor Filter. The facial wrinkles are important information for age estimation. The Gabor filter is commonly used for segmentation and texture classification

[16], which makes it effective in analysing facial wrinkles. The two dimensional Gabor filter in the spatial domain is:

$$g(x,y) = \left(\frac{1}{2\pi\sigma_x\sigma_y}\right) exp\left[-\frac{1}{2}\left(\frac{x^2}{\sigma_x^2} + \frac{y^2}{\sigma_y^2}\right) + 2\pi jWx\right] \qquad (4)$$

where the standard deviations of the x- and y- axes are σ_x and σ_y, and W is the radial frequency of the sine wave.

Histogram of Oriented Gradients (HOG). Histogram of Oriented Gradients (HOG) are feature descriptors used for object detection. Dalal and Triggs [17] introduced this feature for human detection. The main idea of HOG descriptors is that the distribution of intensity gradients or edge detections can characterize an object's appearance and shape effectively. The image is separated into small regions or cells. The descriptors can be implemented by adding a histogram of gradient orientations to each cell. The descriptor is represented by the combination of the histograms. [18]

Gradient Computation. The calculation of the gradient is done by using a centred point discrete derivative mask either in vertical or horizontal directions or both. The following filter kernels can be used:

$$M_x = [-1, 0, 1] \qquad (5)$$

$$M_y = [-1, 0, 1]^T \qquad (6)$$

3.4   Age Facial Model

The feature vectors extracted from the facial images are used as inputs to the classifier. These extracted feature vectors $f_1=[l_1, ..., l_m]$ and $f_2=[g_1, ..., g_n]$ can be combined into one new vector (m and n are the dimensions of f and g respectively). The new concatenated feature vector is $f_{new}=[l_1, ..., l_m, g_1, ..., g_n]$ with dimension m+n. The combination results in an increased dimension of the feature vector, which means a dimensionality reduction technique (such as PCA) is used.

3.5   Age Estimation Algorithms

Once the model has been created for training and test images, common machine learning algorithms were used to construct a classifier. A supervised learning approach is taken, the classifier is trained with the feature vector of the training images and their corresponding labels/classes. After the classifier is trained, each test image's label is classified/predicted. The machine learning algorithms used are described below:

Support Vector Machines (SVM). Support Vector Machine is a binary linear classifier which finds an optimal hyperplane to separate two classes [9]. Given N training points $d = \{x_i, c_i | x_i \in \mathbb{R}^N, c_i \in \{-1, +1, i = 1, ..., N\}\}$, and suppose the points are linearly separable. We need to maximize the distance to the support vectors, by finding a set of N_S support vectors s_i, coefficient weights α_i, constant b and the linear decision surface:

$$\langle w, x \rangle + b = 0$$

where $\langle .,. \rangle$ is the scalar product and w is the normal vector:

$$w = \sum_{i=1}^{N_S} \alpha_i y_i s_i$$

The basic SVM, which only allows linear classification, can be expanded to become non-linear decision surfaces using a 'kernel trick'. The kernel linearly transforms/maps the original data to a high-dimensional space.

K-Nearest Neighbour (KNN). The K-nearest neighbour (KNN) classifies a test sample based on similarity of known training samples. The KNN works by calculating the distances from the test sample to every known training sample [19]. Then the K-nearest samples are selected and the most common class is used to classify the test sample.

Fisherfaces (LDA). Linear Discriminant Analysis (LDA), introduced by R.A. Fisher [20], is used to find a subspace representation of a set of face images. LDA finds the combination of features that best separate the classes by maximizing the ratio between the between-class and the in-between classes scatter.

Random Forest. A random forest joins a group of randomly selected decision trees at training. It outputs the most frequently occurring class from all the individual trees [21].

Gradient Boosting Trees (GBT). Gradient boosting trees, introduced by Friedman [22], is an ensemble method which uses decision trees as weak learners. A sequence of simple binary trees are computed, where each tree builds on the prediction residuals of the the previous tree. GBT supports both binary and multi-class classification using the deviance loss function. GBT uses the additive model:

$$F(x) = \sum_{m=1}^{M} \gamma_m h_m(x) \tag{7}$$

where h_m are the basis functions.

4   Results and Discussion

The age estimation experiments were performed on the FG-NET Aging Database [23], which contains 1002 colour/gray images of 82 individuals with varying expression, pose and lighting. The ages range from 0 to 69. The experiment performed used 400 training images and 559 test images.

The test results from the experiments performed are shown in Figs. 1 and 2:

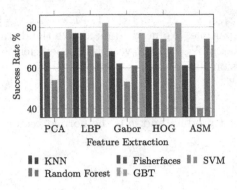

Fig. 1. Age estimation results (Color figure online)

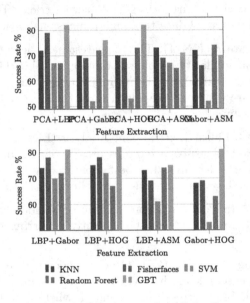

Fig. 2. Hybrid age estimation results (Color figure online)

Figure 1 shows the results for the individual feature vectors. From the results shown, GBT outperforms the other classifiers using the various feature vectors. The GBT uses decision trees and each tree improves on the prediction of the previous tree, which can give better results. LBP achieved the highest average success rate, as it is effective for texture classification. The texture classification is useful for wrinkle analysis, which is important for estimating ages. It was observed that the hybrid age estimation achieved an in-between success rate of the combined feature vectors. Figure 2 shows the results of hybrid age estimation, using a combination of feature vectors.

5   Conclusion

In this paper, methods for efficient age estimation have been investigated using various feature extraction and classification algorithms. The age estimation model proposed, uses a combination of features extracted from facial images. The experimental results achieved a very promising results of an 82 % success rate when the gradient boosting tree (GBT) classifier is used. Further investigation of the effect of the proposed approach by increasing the number of age groups is envisioned.

References

1. Zebrowitz, L.: Reading Faces: Window To The Soul? (2014)
2. Zyga, L.: Researchers hope to build universal human age estimator
3. Esme, B.: On age estimation by using still face images
4. Geng, X., Fu, Y., Smith-Miles, K.: Automatic facial age estimation
5. Kwon, Y.H., da Vitoria Lobo, N.: Age classification from facial images, pp. 762–767. IEEE (1994)
6. El, D., Mohamed, Y., Mohamed, H.: Automatic facial age estimation (2011)
7. Cootes, T.F., Edwards, G.J., Taylor, C.J.: Active appearance models. In: Computer Vision, ECCV 1998, pp. 484–498. Springer (1998)
8. Lanitis, A., Draganova, C., Christodoulou, C.: Comparing different classifiers for automatic age estimation. IEEE Trans. Syst. Man Cybern. Part B Cybern. **34**, 621–628 (2004)
9. Luu, K., Ricanek, K., Bui, T., Suen, C.: Age estimation using active appearance models and support vector machine regression, pp. 1–5 (2009)
10. Geng, X., Zhou, Z.-H.: Automatic age estimation based on facial aging patterns. IEEE Trans. Pattern Anal. Mach. Intell. **29**, 2234–2240 (2007)
11. Petra, G.R.D.: Introduction to human age estimation using face images. faculty of materials science and technology trnavaslovak university of technology in Bratislava (2013)
12. Viola, P., Jones, M.: Rapid object detection using a boosted cascade of simple features. In: Proceedings of the 2001 IEEE Computer Society Conference on Computer Vision and Pattern Recognition, CVPR 2001. Vol. 1, pp. I-511–I-518 (2001)
13. Eigenfaces - scholarpedia
14. Milborrow, S., Nicolls, F.: Active Shape Models with SIFT Descriptors and MARS. VISAPP (2014)
15. Ojala, T., Pietikinen, M., Harwood, D.: A comparative study of texture measures with classification based on featured distributions. Pattern Recogn. **29**, 51–59 (1996)
16. Choi, S.E., Lee, Y.J., Lee, S.J., Park, K.R., Kim, J.: Age estimation using a hierarchical classifier based on global and local facial features. Pattern Recogn. **44**, 1262–1281 (2011)
17. Dalal, N., Triggs, B.: Histograms of oriented gradients for human detection. In: IEEE Computer Society Conference on Computer Vision and Pattern Recognition, CVPR 2005. vol. 1, pp. 886–893. IEEE (2005)
18. Hajizadeh, M., Ebrahimnezhad, H.: Classification of age groups from facial image using histograms of oriented gradients. In: 2011 7th Iranian Machine Vision and Image Processing (MVIP), pp. 1–5 (2011)

19. Patrick, E.A., Fischer III, F.P.: A generalized k-nearest neighbor rule. Inf. Control **16**, 128–152 (1970)
20. Fisher, R.A.: The use of multiple measurements in taxonomic problems. Ann. Eugenics **7**, 179–188 (1936)
21. Bas Pujols, B., Riera Pol, F.: Facial image-based gender and age estimation
22. Friedman, J.H.: Greedy function approximation: a gradient boosting machine. Ann. Stat. 1189–1232 (2001)
23. Face and gesture recognition working group

Unsupervised Sub-graph Selection and Its Application in Face Recognition Techniques

Ahmed ElSayed[✉], Ausif Mahmood, and Tarek Sobh

Department of Computer Science and Engineering, University of Bridgeport,
221 University Avenue, Bridgeport, CT 06604, USA
aelsayed@my.bridgeport.edu

Abstract. One of the limitations of the existing face recognition algorithms is that the recognition rate significantly decreases with the increase in dataset size. In order to eliminate this shortcoming, this paper presents a new training dataset partitioning methodology to improve face recognition for large datasets. This methodology is then applied to the Eigenface algorithm as one of the algorithms that suffer from this problem. The algorithm represents the training face images as a fully connected graph. This graph is then divided into simpler sub-graphs to enhance the overall recognition rate. The sub-graphs are generated dynamically, and a comparison between different sub-graph selection techniques including minimizing edge weight sums, random selection, and maximizing sum of edge weights inside the sub-graph are provided. It is concluded that the optimized hierarchical dynamic technique increased the recognition rate by more than 40 percent in a large benchmark image dataset compared to the original single large graph method. Furthermore, the developed technique is compatible with several other unsupervised face recognition techniques such as ICA, KPCA, RBM, SIFT, and LBP... etc., and other datasets, specially if the number of images per person in the training data are low.

Keywords: Sub-graph selection · Graph theory · Hierarchical recognition · Face recognition

1 Introduction

Identity detection is one of the important problems in the fields of security and intelligence. Face recognition is one of the computer vision fields that is charged with this task. Several face recognition algorithms have been proposed and developed in the last decades including Direct Correlation, Principal Component Analysis (PCA) [9,14], Linear Discriminant Analysis (LDA) [8,16], Independent Component Analysis (ICA) [2,3,9], Kernel methods (i.e. KPCA and SVM) [11,15], and other high dimension features methods such as LBP, SIFT, or 3D methods...etc. Some of these methods are supervised (e.g., LDA and SVM) where the given data is divided into training, testing and validation datasets. The training dataset is then divided into labeled groups (i.e., classes) with each

© Springer International Publishing Switzerland 2015
M. Kamel and A. Campilho (Eds.): ICIAR 2015, LNCS 9164, pp. 247–256, 2015.
DOI: 10.1007/978-3-319-20801-5_27

class containing images of one person. The other methods for face recognition are unsupervised and use extracted features from faces (e.g., PCA, KPCA, ICA, LBP and SIFT) where the given data is separated into training and testing datasets. In this case, the training dataset is unlabeled and the algorithm handles class separation process. Various research and experiments have proven that simple recognition algorithms like Eigenface produce good recognition rates with small sized (typically less than 100 images) datasets with accurately clipped face images. However, when the number of images in the dataset slightly exceeds hundred, the recognition accuracy of these algorithms reduce significantly. One of the ways to handle this problem is to use indexing [13]. However, indexing is only applicable to specific features and techniques, in addition to being very sensitive to image normalization, orientation and features calculation. The hierarchical partitioning technique can be used to improve the recognition rate when large datasets are required. This technique divides the given training dataset into smaller subgroups. This way the input image is compared with the stored images located in relatively smaller sets. The best matches are then selected and fed to the groups that are in the subsequent levels until a single small group remains. Finally, the best result from this final group determines a match or mismatch. Such hierarchical grouping principle on the training dataset has been used in [6,7]. These studies utilize a supervised grouping where the training dataset is divided according to the image class. In other words, the images of the same person are grouped together resulting in a clear separation between groups. One major drawback of this approach is that it implies the group size to be reduced to one when multiple images of the same person are not available. Furthermore, the number of groups increases significantly as the number of different individuals increase, especially when there are few images for each person in the database. The proposed unsupervised grouping technique can solve these problems since it will group images without considering identity. This work distinguishes itself from its counterparts and contributes to the related literature by:

1. Introducing a new unsupervised grouping technique for large training datasets,
2. Applying different grouping criteria in the proposed method,
3. Demonstrating the efficiency of the proposed method by providing a comparative study using multiple databases.

The remaining of the paper is divided into five sections. The following section, Sect. 2 explains the sub-graph selection process. This is followed by a comprehensive description of the proposed hierarchical algorithm (Sect. 3). Section 4 demonstrates how to further improve the recognition rate by optimizing the grouping process. Section 5 depicts the results of the proposed technique. Conclusions and future work are discussed in Sect. 6.

2   Sub-graph Selection Process

The sup-graph selection process requires selecting a sub-graph k_o from a graph G that has a specific criterion. The algorithm assumes that all training face images are a fully connected graph (G) with number of nodes (L) and the edge between every two nodes w_{ij} is the sum of the Euclidean distances between the features of these the nodes i and j. The goal is to obtain the best sub-graphs set $S = \{k_1, k_2, k_3, ..., k_N\}$ where each sup-graph has a number of nodes (l), where k_o is the sub-graph number o, and N is the total number of reconstructed sub-graphs that will be used in the hierarchical technique. Different strategies for this sub-graph selection process are investigated including (1) minimizing the weight of the sum of edges within the entire sub-graph; (2) randomly choosing nodes for the sub-graph and, (3) maximizing the weight of the sum of edges within the entire sub-graph. After sub-graphs are created, regular face recognition technique (Eigenface, in this case) is applied to each fully connected sub-graph to select the top best matches from each group. These sets of matches from the first sub-graphs level form the subsequent level of sub-graphs. This process is repeated until a single small full connected graph of (l) nodes remain. This hierarchical grouping algorithm is presented and different variations are explored by testing it on benchmark datasets to prove the possible improvement in the recognition rate over full connected images graph. Figure 1 shows 2D example for different strategies for the sub-graph selection process.

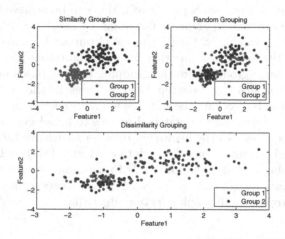

Fig. 1. 2D example for two sub-graphs selection

3   Hierarchical Recognition Technique

Testing various face recognition algorithms proved that recognition rate in unsupervised algorithms such as standard Eigenface technique drops down if the number of images in the dataset is approximately above hundred. In order to understand the impact of smaller subsets generated from the entire training set, the paper proposes the following. As also detailed in the previous sections, assuming that the face images are a fully connected graph (G) with number of nodes (L) with a goal to select the best sub-graphs set $S = \{k_1, k_2, k_3, ..., k_N\}$ each having a number of nodes ($l \leq 100$), where N is the number of reconstructed sub-graphs to improve the recognition rate over the hierarchical technique. With this goal, applying recognition algorithm over each of these sub-graphs (groups), a few top matched nodes from each sub-graph (group) (2 to 5) are selected. Then new groups are generated from these top matches. Depending on the number of images in the dataset, a number of hierarchical levels are created. Recognition algorithm (e.g. Eigenface) is then applied on each level group. As the final step, the top matched images from the final subgroups are collected, and recognition algorithm is re-applied on this final group to select the best-matched image. Figure 3 shows the block diagram of the proposed hierarchical technique with the Eigenface as the recognition method. The main challenge of this technique is to determine the best sub-graphs selection strategy to improve the overall face recognition rate. There are three possible grouping strategies: i) *Similarity* Grouping by minimizing the sum of weights in the entire sub-graph where similar images are added to the same group (the similarity measurement is the distance between faces features, eg. pixels gray level), this can be achieved by using regular clustering techniques, ii) *Random* Grouping by assigning the images to the groups (sub-graphs) randomly, iii) *Dissimilar* Grouping by maximizing sum of weights in the entire sub-graph, in other words, maximizing the standard deviation within the same group where the grouping process based on dissimilarity (Maximizing metric distance between faces features in the same group). An additional challenge is to obtain the suitable number of levels in the hierarchical system along with the number of matched images to be selected from each level to feed into the next level in the hierarchy. In order to achieve these, these three possibilities have been tested on a large dataset (Extended Yale B+) [1] having different positioning and illumination levels to determine the best approach for the hierarchical face recognition technique. Figure 2 shows examples of datasets images for the proposed sub-graph selection algorithm.

Fig. 2. Examples of the dataset images used

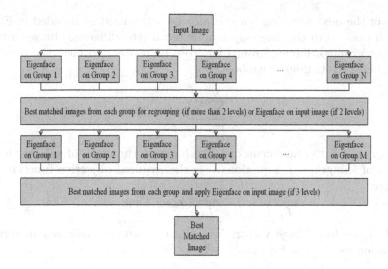

Fig. 3. The proposed hierarchical system for rank 1 recognition

4   Optimized Dissimilarity Sub-graph Selection Technique

As also detailed in the results section, the simple dissimilarity measurement (maximizing distances between in group images by taking the mean image as a reference) performed superior compared to the other two grouping techniques (similarity and random selection). However, this method is not without some drawbacks since these criteria will not guarantee the exact dissimilarity between each group's images. To explain further, consider a 2-D set of (x,y) points. If the training dataset includes {(-2,3),(2,3),(-2,-3),(2,-3)} and is required to group these values into two groups based on dissimilarity, then the mean point will be (0,0) and the Euclidean distance between each one of these points and the total mean will be similar for all four points. This will results in poor grouping. It can easily be observed that the best dissimilarity grouping for this case would be {(-2,3), (2,-3)} as one group, and {(2,3), (-2,-3)} as the second group. Mathematically, stated as the variance between all the sub-graph (group) nodes over all basis should be maximized. Therefore applying this method to a face image dataset sub-graphs selection leads to Eq. (1):

$$\sigma_{total} = \sum_{l=1}^{N} \sum_{k=1}^{m \times n} \sigma_{lk} \tag{1}$$

where m and n are the number of rows and columns of the face image respectively (assuming that the pixels gray level are the image features), N is the number of extracted sub-graphs. σ_{lk} is the standard deviation of image dimension k in the sub-graph l. Equation (1) will be valid if the number of hierarchical grouping levels is 2. If dataset is very large however, a regrouping is required again to the third or higher levels. To ensure this, an additional term guaranteeing that the variance of the next grouping stage is also be maximized is included in Eq. (1). This term deals with the inter-sup-graphs mean (the difference between means of different groups), forcing groups far from each other to have the maximum variance between its group members:

$$\mu_{diff} = \sum_{j=1}^{N} \sum_{i \neq j}^{N} d\left(\mu_i, \mu_j\right) \tag{2}$$

where $d\left(\mu_i, \mu_j\right)$ is the Euclidean distance between the mean of sub-graph i and the mean of sub-graph j. Equation (3) is the required objective function to be maximized:

$$\max_{I_{ij}} g\left(I_{ij}\right) = \max_{I_{ij}} \left(\sigma_{total} + \mu_{diff}\right) \tag{3}$$

where I is the face image vector. Equation (3) can be expressed in terms of minimization as given in Eq. (4).

$$\min_{I_{ij}} g\left(I_{ij}\right) = \min_{I_{ij}} \left(-\sigma_{total} - \mu_{diff}\right) \tag{4}$$

It has been reported in that L1 (absolute difference) metric works better than L2 (Euclidean distance) to measure the distance between two projected images in the Eigen space. Therefore, the effect of both metrics in the grouping process are tested to obtain the best recognition rate. The optimized group generation using Eq. (4) can be done as a separate process through the utilization of meta heuristics such as Simulated Annealing.

5   Results

The results section is divided into two parts for two different datasets. The first section is dedicated to ORL AT&T whereas the rest of the results involve Extended B+ Yale dataset. Each part provides comparisons between the different grouping techniques as well as the difference when using optimum dissimilarity metric. The proposed techniques have been implemented using MATLAB on Ubuntu 12.04 OS.

ORL AT&T Dataset

Total number of images in the dataset is 400. These images have been divided into two sets. A set of 200 images for training, and another set of 200 images for testing. Since the number of images in the dataset is not too large, two level hierarchies have been implemented. The group size is considered as 50 images for the first grouping level. The following table shows the results obtained for rank 1 best match:

Method	Recognition rate
Original Eigenface	92.5 %
Similarity Grouping	94.5 %
Random Grouping	94.0 %
Mean Dissimilarity Grouping	93.5 %
Optimum Dissimilarity L2 Metric	95.0 %
Optimum Dissimilarity L1 Metric	94.0 %

Extended B+ Yale Dataset

The number of images in the dataset is 14,800. Similar to the ORL AT&T dataset the images are divided into two sets. One set of 7,400 images for training, and another set of 7,400 images is for testing. Due to the large number of images, a three level hierarchy has been used (the two levels recognition did not provide significant improvement in recognition rate). The training images have been divided into 140 groups, each with approximately 50 images. Three different grouping strategies have been tested. Following results are obtained for rank 1 best match:

- The original Eigenface algorithm recognition rate is 55 %.

- Similarity Grouping: The recognition rate improves to approximately 77 % - 83.5 % depending on the number of best images selected from each group in the first level, and the number of groups in the regrouping step in the second level. A recognition rate of 83.5 % is achieved when the best 5 matching images are selected from each first level group. A group constructed from these images is regrouped into the next grouping level. Then best 5 matches are selected from each subgroup, and a final Eigenface step is applied on these to obtain the best match. Results are shown in Fig. 4. The main disadvantage of this grouping method is that, the execution time increases when the number of groups in the second level increases. The algorithm used for grouping is the K-means clustering algorithm.

- Random Grouping: The recognition rate improves to a range of 88 % - 88.65 % depending on the number of best matching images selected from the first level groups (from 2 to 5), and the number of groups in the regrouping step in the second level. The recognition rates are noted to be less dependent on the number of best images selected from each group. Further, the execution time is almost independent of the number of best images selected from a group, and the number of regroups.

- Dissimilar Grouping (based on the L2 distance from the mean image on the training set): The recognition rate improves to the range of 89 % - 90.15 % depending on the number of best images selected from each group in the first level, and the number of groups in the regrouping step in the second level. The recognition rates are less dependent on the number of best images selected from first level groups. Further, the execution time is almost similar for any number of best matches selected from a group, and number of regroups.

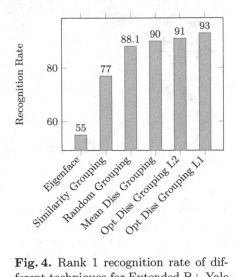
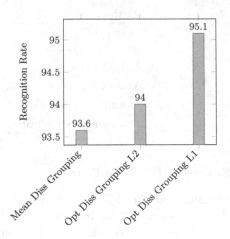

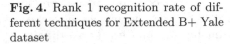

Fig. 4. Rank 1 recognition rate of different techniques for Extended B+ Yale dataset

Fig. 5. Comparison between rank 10 recognition rate of dissimilarity grouping techniques for Extended B+ Yale dataset

- Optimum Dissimilarity (based on L2 metric): Images are grouped based on the stated objective function in three level hierarchy with L2 metric. This method improved rank 1 rate to 91.5 %.

- Optimum Dissimilarity (based on L1 metric): Images are grouped based on stated objective function in three level hierarchy with L1 metric. This method improved rank 1 rate to 93.6 %. Also, for this dataset, the probability that the correct person appears in the best top 10 images is tested (rank 10), as shown in Fig. 5.

The results in Fig. 4 indicate that the recognition rate increased significantly when the hierarchical technique was used, especially for large databases (Extended B+ Yale). The recognition rate has improved further by the proposed optimum dissimilarity grouping criteria. In summary, compared to the results in [4,5,10,12] where the ICA and Boltzmann machines are used on the same datasets (around 82 % for ICA and 83 % for Boltzmann approach), the recognition rate of the proposed algorithm is superior. Further, the proposed optimized dataset grouping technique is compatible with other powerful recognition methods such as ICA or LBP, and not just with the PCA based Eigenface technique. Another advantage of this algorithm is that it uses all the training datasets as one bulk with the unsupervised grouping technique, which is completely independent of the face background and illumination levels.

6   Conclusions

The paper presented a hierarchical sub-graph selection algorithm that aims at overcoming the large dataset limitation of the standard face recognition algorithms. The algorithm is based on creating small sub-graphs, selecting best matches from each sub-graph, and then dynamically creating next-level sub-graphs until a single group remains. The best match from this last group is accepted as the rank 1 final result of face recognition. The study also investigated the best approach for creating sub-graphs by developing an objective function that can be used for best dissimilarity between groups at all levels. Detailed testing on large benchmark datasets indicates that the proposed method produces best results with a sub-graph size of approximately 50 nodes (images) for the Eigenface technique. Compared to the standard Eigenface algorithm, the new hierarchical sub-graph selection algorithm improves the recognition rate by more than 40 % on the original Eigenface algorithm, and by more than 2 % on the mean based dissimilarity method. The future work involves applying the hierarchical technique to additional unsupervised face recognition algorithms such as Independent Component Analysis (ICA), KPCA, LBP, SIFT and other computer vision algorithms that suffer from degradation in recognition rate due to large dataset size.

References

1. http://vision.ucsd.edu/~leekc/ExtYaleDataset/ExtYaleB.html
2. Bach, F.R., Jordan, M.I.: Kernel independent component analysis. J. Mach. Learn. Res. **3**, 1–48 (2003). http://dx.doi.org/10.1162/153244303768966085
3. Bartlett, M., Movellan, J.R., Sejnowski, T.: Face recognition by independent component analysis. IEEE Trans. Neural Networks **13**(6), 1450–1464 (2002)
4. Draper, B.A., Baek, K., Bartlett, M.S., Beveridge, J.R.: Recognizing faces with PCA and ICA. Comput. Vis. Image Underst. **91**(1–2), 115–137 (2003). http://dx.doi.org/10.1016/S1077-3142(03)00077-8
5. Georghiades, A., Belhumeur, P., Kriegman, D.: From few to many: illumination cone models for face recognition under variable lighting and pose. IEEE Trans. Pattern Anal. Mach. Intell. **23**(6), 643–660 (2001)
6. Kyperountas, M., Tefas, A., Pitas, I.: Face recognition via adaptive discriminant clustering. In: 15th IEEE International Conference on Image Processing, 2008. ICIP 2008, pp. 2744–2747, October 2008
7. Lu, J., Plataniotis, K.: Boosting face recognition on a large-scale database. In: Proceedings of the 2002 International Conference on Image Processing, vol. 2, pp. II-109–II-112 (2002)
8. Lu, J., Plataniotis, K.N., Venetsanopoulos, A.N.: Face recognition using lda-based algorithms. Trans. Neur. Netw. **14**(1), 195–200 (2003). http://dx.doi.org/10.s 1109/TNN.2002.806647
9. Moon, H., Phillips, P.J.: Computational and performance aspects of pca-based face-recognition algorithms. Perception **30**(3), 303–321 (2001). http://www.perceptionweb.com/abstract.cgi?id=p2896
10. Naseem, I., Togneri, R., Bennamoun, M.: Linear regression for face recognition. IEEE Trans. Pattern Anal. Mach. Intell. **32**(11), 2106–2112 (2010)
11. Schölkopf, B., Smola, A., Müller, K.R.: Nonlinear component analysis as a kernel eigenvalue problem. Neural Comput. **10**(5), 1299–1319 (1998). http://dx.doi.org/10.1162/089976698300017467

12. Tang, Y., Salakhutdinov, R., Hinton, G.: Robust boltzmann machines for recognition and denoising. In: 2012 IEEE Conference on Computer Vision and Pattern Recognition (CVPR), pp. 2264–2271, June 2012
13. Tse, S.H., Lam, K.M.: Efficient face recognition with a large database. In: 10th International Conference on Control, Automation, Robotics and Vision, ICARCV 2008, pp. 944–949, December 2008
14. Turk, M., Pentland, A.: Face recognition using eigenfaces. In: Proceedings of the IEEE Computer Society Conference on Computer Vision and Pattern Recognition, CVPR 1991, pp. 586–591, June 1991
15. Yang, M.H.: Kernel eigenfaces vs. kernel fisherfaces: face recognition using kernel methods. In: Proceedings of the Fifth IEEE International Conference on Automatic Face and Gesture Recognition, FGR 2002, p. 215. IEEE Computer Society, Washington, DC, USA (2002). http://dl.acm.org/citation.cfm?id=874061.875432
16. Zhao, W., Chellappa, R., Krishnaswamy, A.: Discriminant analysis of principal components for face recognition. In: Proceedings of the Third IEEE International Conference on Automatic Face and Gesture Recognition, 1998, pp. 336–341, April 1998

Human Activity Recognition

Dynamic Perceptual Attribute-Based Hidden Conditional Random Fields for Gesture Recognition

Gang Hu[✉] and Qigang Gao

Faculty of Computer Science, Dalhousie University, Halifax, NS, Canada
{ghu, qggao}@cs.dal.ca

Abstract. The demand for gesture/action recognition technologies has been increased in the recent years. State-of-the-art systems of gesture/action recognition have been using low-level features or intermediate bag-of-features as gesture/action descriptors. Those methods ignore the spatial and temporal information on shape and internal structures of the targets. Dynamic Perceptual Attributes (DPAs) is a set of descriptors of gesture's perceptual properties. Their context relations reveal gestures/actions' intrinsic structures. This paper utilizes the hidden conditional random fields (HCRF) model based on DPAs to describe complex human gestures and facilitate the recognition tasks. Experimental results show our model gains better performance against state-of-the-art methods.

Keywords: Perceptual features · Gesture recognition · Shape extraction · HCRF

1 Introduction

Recently human action/gesture analysis has been drawn increasing research attention due to high demands of emerging applications, including E-healthcare, security system, human computer interface (HCI), video games and so on. 3D gesture recognition is mainly boosted by the developments of the 3D sensor technologies. Human gesture/action understanding is a challenging task as it involves modeling multiple dynamic structural components in 4D spatiotemporal space.

We argue that there are mainly two factors affecting the performance of computer vision-based human action interpretation: low-level spatiotemporal features with less high-level semantics and holistic gesture representations without the description about internal relationships. To deliver more semantics, some state-of-the-art approaches [7, 8] use intermediate gesture features, such as codebook, visual words or bag-of-features based on clustered low-level features. However, they are still far from being able to achieve high-level interpretation. Besides the local and global appearance gesture features, there exist internal structural properties, that are less visually apparent and difficult to describe in terms of visual appearances, in gestures. For example, temporal relationship among multiple gesture features is not as simple as a sequential chain. It could be a fuzzy structure, i.e. a mixture of chain, overlapped and stride modes

© Springer International Publishing Switzerland 2015
M. Kamel and A. Campilho (Eds.): ICIAR 2015, LNCS 9164, pp. 259–268, 2015.
DOI: 10.1007/978-3-319-20801-5_28

with uneven steps. Due to its complexity and uncertainty, many previous approaches model gestures by either ignoring its intrinsic structures or using assumptions to simplify corresponding representations. In fact these intrinsic structural properties reflect the discriminative gestures features, and are able to facilitate recognition tasks. Some research [17] showed that incorporating latent structures into the system can improve the performance.

In this work, we use a set of perceptual gesture descriptors, Dynamic Perceptual Attributes (DPAs) [1] to describe the components of gesture properties. Each DPA is a gesture spatiotemporal segment that represents one type of dynamic changes in 4D spatiotemporal space, and contains rich extrinsic properties, such as duration, change type, change volume, change rate, temporal moment etc. Meanwhile, their intrinsic properties are modeled as the temporal context relations among DPAs, which is governed by hidden conditional random fields (HCRF) (circles in Fig. 1). The proposed gesture modeling method well describes gesture's intrinsic and extrinsic properties, and would be potentially benefit many recognition tasks. In the following parts, we will discuss related work, describe system architecture and HCRF model, and present the evaluation results.

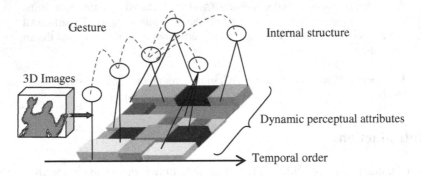

Fig. 1. Gesture representation model.

2 Related Work

Salient points or regions-based representational methodologies have been widely used for human action recognition from RGB data, and they detect salient features, such as space-time interest points (STIP) [2], Cuboids [3] and Hessian [4], then form up feature description using the local information, such as HOG/HOF [5], HOG3D [6] and Extended SURF [3]. Inspired from the text mining area, the intermediate level feature descriptor for RGB videos, Bag-of-Word (BoW) [7, 8], has been popular due to its semantic representation and robustness to noise. Recently, BoW-based methods have been extended to depth data [9]. These intermediate level descriptors have more discriminative powers, but got failures when handling complex gestures/actions, because BoW-based methods ignore the temporal and spatial structural properties. Shotton et al. [10] proposed a Random Forest-based classification method to find body joints from depth images in an efficient way. Real time skeleton data facilitates the human activity analysis research. In [11], visual features for activity recognition are computed based on the 4D differences among joints. This feature set contains static, motion and offset information. Wang et al. [12] described skeleton joints by pairwise and local occupancy patterns, and Fourier Temporal Pyramid is used to model the temporal patterns. Their Actionlet Ensemble model can handle tracking errors and characterize the intra-class variations.

Recognition of complex human activities is challenging as it requires understanding both extrinsic and uncertain intrinsic dynamic properties. Some approaches generate representations of gesture/action videos by using graph [13, 14], attribute list [8], or probabilistic model etc. Among them, graphical models have been used to capture the structure of an activity in terms of the hierarchy and spatiotemporal arrangement of its internal components. Xia et al. [15] used HMMs to model the relationship among visual words, a histogram of 3-D joint locations (HOJ3-D) for body posture representation. Sminchisescu et al. [16] introduced CRF model into the motion recognition tasks. Since the human actions are complex, some internal structure cannot be explicitly observed even by human vision. A hidden CRF (HCRF) model has been applied in some systems [17], where the gesture class is modeled as a root template and a set of hidden labels that are implicitly correlated with feature representation. But their HCRF models either ignore temporal structures, or just use an oversimplified chain structure to model complex dynamic properties. Furthermore, their gesture features are based on global dynamics without the motion information of individual body parts. Our approach recognizes individual body parts and considers the structural relations among them in 4D space.

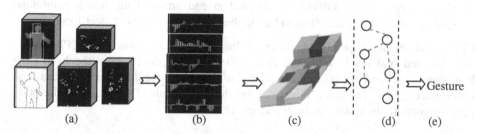

Fig. 2. Overall illustration: (a) 3D Perceptual feature extraction & Body parts estimation, (b) Motion sequences tracking, (c) DPAs, (d) HCRF model, (e) Recognition.

3 Our DPA-Based System

Our approach (Fig. 2) is based on a set of novel perceptual gesture descriptors, Dynamic Perceptual Attributes (DPAs). 3D perceptual shape features are extracted from depth images for body parts classification. Figure 2b shows the motion sequences of tracked body parts where a set of DPAs (Fig. 2c) are extracted. The DPA contain the information about motion trajectory, object shape and orientation, which are represented as a set of 3D blocks with different colors and sizes. These blocks can be viewed as puzzle pieces, and their combination and layout present different view about the gesture properties. We use HCRF to model the temporal context relation of these "puzzle pieces" (Fig. 2d). A gesture representation featured by both extrinsic properties and the intrinsic temporal structure is able to facilitate gesture recognition/classification tasks.

3.1 3D Perceptual Shape Feature for Human Body Part Estimation

Contour features exploit object boundary information and are able to provide shapes in arbitrary view settings. In our approach, each object is represented as a group of generic edge tokens (GETs) and Curve Partitioning Points (CPPs) (Fig. 3(a–b)) defined as PCPG model in [18]. GETs and CPPs are perceptual shape features that are extracted from edge contours. Eight types of segmented edge tokens, GETs, are connected at points (CPPs) along the edge curves. Since each edge pixel from depth images has XYZ values, 3D GETs/CPPs can be derived accordingly. 3D GETs/CPPs can be further clustered into several groups according to their spatial distribution. Each clustered group contains the bottom-up saliency features representing the shapes of a target object (body part), and provides a set of unique visual content descriptors (Fig. 2a).

- *Head*: it is a set of stable GET/CPP primitives with convex hull-like shapes based on the metrics: CPP vertical distribution, location and size.
- *Torso*: it is modeled as a set of 3D GET and CPP primitives with left/right symmetric long vertical GETs.
- *Limbs*: a set of GETs and CPPs that connect to torso.
- *Hands/Feet*: a set of GETs/CPPs located at end areas of the limbs, a minimal spanning tree-based index method is applied to determine hands/feet locations.

CPPs are shape salient points, which reveal shape semantics. In this work, CPP clusters are classified into head, torso and limb CPPs. Figure 3(c–f) show the head-torso boundary boxes, and the red, yellow and green/blue points are the head, torso and limb CPPs respectively. The green boxes are the detected hands. The details of the body parts estimation algorithm can be found in [1].

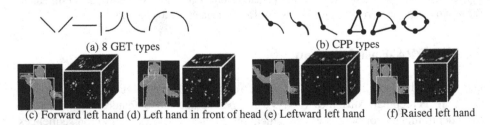

(a) 8 GET types   (b) CPP types

(c) Forward left hand (d) Left hand in front of head (e) Leftward left hand   (f) Raised left hand

Fig. 3. GET/CPP features and body parts classification for different poses.

3.2 Dynamic Perceptual Attributes (DPAs)

DPAs represent the perceptual changes of body parts. Overall there are three types of dynamics: motion trajectory, shape and orientation.

1. *Motion trajectory*: it is measured by the CPP dense trajectories. The trajectory of a body part is collectively determined by all 3D CPP's matches, and can be decomposed into X, Y and Z.
2. *Shape dynamics*: we track the size of the 3D GET clusters to get shape dynamics, which is simple yet effective for shape estimation. The object size is determined by the volume of the 3D boundary box of the target. Besides the object size, other shape properties could be used, such as GET type distribution.
3. *Orientation dynamics*: For some gestures, object orientation is discriminative, e.g. flip palm. It can be measured by the angle between the camera's front panel and the object planes. Figure 4's orientation sequence shows the angel changes.

All these perceptual dynamics have three types of perceptual dynamics: increase (+), decrease (−) and remaining same (0). Then, each sequence can be divided into segments, dynamic perceptual attributes (DPAs) (see red boxes in Fig. 4). Each DPA d, can be viewed as a 3D block whose length and height represent duration and change volume respectively. We define a feature vector as its descriptor:

$$f(d) = \{DPA\ type, Start\ time, Duration, Volume\}. \qquad (1)$$

DPA type of each body part (e.g. hand) has 15 values: 5 dynamic properties (x, y, z, *size* and *orientation*) with 3 possible changes (+, −, 0); *Start time* is related to the sequential order in the video sequence. The value of the *start time* is the moment where the DPA begins. *Duration* is related to the ratio of the DPA respect to the whole sequence. *Volume* is the normalized dynamic change value wrt. the same dynamic type within the video sequence. For instance, a single-hand *Throw* gesture x in Fig. 4 has 6 DPAs:

- d_1: x, with all zeros on the sequence
    $f(d_1) = \{x0, 0, 1, 0\}$
- d_2: y, with positives, 40 % duration, 35 % changes
    $f(d_2) = \{y+, 0, 0.4, 0.35\}$
- d_3: y, with negatives, started at 40 %, 60 % duration, 65 % change
    $f(d_3) = \{y-, 0.4, 0.6, 0.65\}$
- d_4: z, with positives, started at beginning, 100 % duration, 100 % changes
    $f(d_4) = \{z+, 0, 1, 1\}$.
- d_5: *size*, with all zeros, started at beginning, 100 % duration
    $f(d_5) = \{size0, 0, 1, 0\}$.
- d_6: *orientation*, with negatives, 100 % duration, started at 0, 100 % changes
    $f(d_6) = \{ori-, 0, 1, 1\}$.

A gesture can be characterized by a combination of various DPAs, which are a set of perceptual gesture descriptors in the spatiotemporal space. We emphasize that our model is not limited to the above three features and can be generalized to any other dynamics.

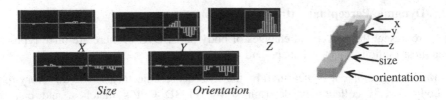

Fig. 4. Five dynamic sequences and a 3D block pattern for a throw gesture.

4 Hidden Conditional Random Field Model

Each DPA reflects one aspect of dynamic properties within the spatiotemporal space. We propose a DPA-based HCRF model for gesture recognition. HCRF well represents the intrinsic properties of complex human gestures. Each video sequence containing a gesture $y_i \in \{y_1, y_2, \ldots, y_n\}$ is a 4D data x that has been segmented into several overlapped DPAs $\{x_1, x_2, \ldots, x_m\}$ for each body part. Each DPA x_i describes one type of dynamic property. The temporal relations among them reflect the discriminative gesture properties, and is governed by a set of hidden labels $\{h_1, h_2, \ldots, h_m\}$, where each h_i takes values from a finite set H of possible labels for each DPA. Intuitively, those hidden labels correspond to the local motion patterns, and their internal structure is able to represent the coherence of any complex gestures. These latent relations are to be learned in training.

We assume that the internal temporal structure is represented by an undirected graph structure $G = (V, E)$, where each vertex $v_i \in V$ corresponds to a hidden variable h_i. We use E to denote the set of edges, and $e(j, k) \in E$ is an edge between variables h_j and h_k. In this paper we assume that E is a tree, which is formed by a minimum spanning tree over the labels. The cost of an edge between is the temporal difference between x_j and x_k within the 4D space. Our choice of E encodes our assumption that latent variables conditioned on DPAs that are temporally close are more likely to be dependent. The gesture x is classified as y^* if $y^* = \mathrm{argmax}_y f_\omega(x, y)$. The pair $<x, y>$ is evaluated by:

$$f_\omega(x, y) = max_h \omega \Phi(x, h, y) \qquad (2)$$

where ω is a vector of parameters and h is a set of hidden variables. $\Phi(x, h, y)$ is a set of potential functions that measure the compatibility among the gesture class y, the configuration of DPAs x, and hidden labels h. The details of the potential functions are:

$\alpha(x_i, h_i)$ gives the measure of the compatibility of the DPA x_i and the hidden label h_i. It is to predict the label h_i for the DPA x_i without considering its gesture class or other DPAs. The parameter $\omega_\alpha(x_i, h_i)$ for predicting is estimated by counting the co-occurrence frequencies of the combinations of $\{x_i, h_i\}$ on the training data.

$$\alpha(x_i, h_i) = I(h_i) \cdot I(x_i) \cdot f(x_i) \qquad (3)$$

where $I(\cdot)$ is the identity function while $f(x_i)$ denotes the feature vector of DPA x_i in (1).

$\beta(y, h_i)$ models the agreement between the class y and a hidden label h_i. It is estimated by counting the co-occurrence frequencies of the pairs of variables on training dataset:

$$\beta(y, h_i) = I(y) \cdot I(h_i) \qquad (4)$$

$\varphi(y, h_i, h_j)$ is a pairwise potential function which models the transition between a pair of hidden labels $e(h_i, h_j)$ for a gesture y. A matrix of transition is built during the training stage. Each element of this matrix is the frequency of the transition between 2 DPAs:

$$\varphi(y, h_i, h_j) = I(y) \cdot I(h_i) \cdot I(h_j) \qquad (5)$$

Putting everything together, the overall model can be computed as

$$\omega\Phi(x, h, y) = \sum_{i \in V} \omega_\alpha \alpha(x_i, h_i) + \sum_{i \in V} \omega_\beta \beta(y, h_i) + \sum_{e(i,j) \in E} \omega_\varphi \varphi(y, h_i, h_j) \qquad (6)$$

where $e(i, j)$ is an edge, h_i is a node, φ_e and $\omega = \{\omega_\alpha, \omega_\beta, \omega_\varphi\}$, ω_e are model parameters.

Our model encodes the temporal relations among multiple gesture properties (trajectory, shape and orientation). Even for a simple gesture, e.g. a dart throw, there are three major dynamics: a hand moving forward, a hand opening and palm orientation changes. Most existing gesture representations only capture the coarse dynamic properties, and ignore the subtle dynamics. In contrast, our model is able to capture those co-occurrence dynamics by exploring the dependence from training data. In this way, the model is able to capture important connections of, for example, hand opening moment and velocity that both affect the throw gesture.

For the model learning and inference, given a set of N gesture training video sequence X with labeled body parts, segmented XYZ change sequences, shape and orientation DPAs, and hidden label number, the goal is to learn a model that can be used to assign the class label Y to a gesture. The learning step needs to estimate parameter to maximize Eq. 2. The output of the learning is a set of models, each representing a set of potential weights $\omega = \{\omega_\alpha, \omega_\beta, \omega_\varphi\}$, ω_e for DPAs and hidden labels in one gesture class. The objective of inference is to classify gestures from a new gesture video sequence according to the trained model. We first extract all DPAs, and then estimate all potential functions for each trained gesture model and find the gesture y^* that corresponds to the maximum likelihood score.

5   Experiments and Evaluation

We recorded 3D videos containing 10 types of human gestures/actions performed several times by 5 subjects individually. The environmental settings for video recording are: a single user in front of a fixed Kinect camera, interacts with a computer by performing gestures/actions including: throw, wave, flip palm, knock and pull-down for one hand, push, drive, expand, clap, climb rope with 2 hands. Currently the dataset contains 506 sequences with one gesture/action for each. Roughly 50 samples per gesture were collected. To obtain a better quality dataset, some constraints and pre-processes were imposed: (i) setting the camera 1.5–2 m far from a subject to get best depth data; (ii) scaling into a grayscale depth image; (iii) smoothing by a 3 × 3 median filter.

To evaluate the performance of the proposed method, we compare our approach with state-of-the-arts local spatio-temproal feature descriptor methods by using a standard BoW SVM approach against our 3D gesture dataset. We take 4 baselines for evaluation: (a) Harris3D detector [2] + HOG/HOF descriptor [5], (b) Dense sampling [19] + HOG3D descriptor [6]; (c) Harris3D detector + HOG3D descriptor; (d) DPA + Histogram [1]. The outputs of first three methods are the list of long feature vectors. The BoW method is applied to get histogram of visual word (V = 200) occurrences as the gesture representation. The DPA-based histogram [1] with 60 bins for 2 hand-gestures is similar to the BoW methods. SVM is used for classification for all 4 baseline methods. Each classifier was trained with a χ^2-RBF-kernel using Leave-One-Out (LOO) cross validation, and one-against-rest approach is applied to select the gesture class with the highest score as the recognized one. Figure 5(a) shows the average classification rates.

Our DPA-based HCRF model gives the best performance on our dataset. The reason is two-fold: first 3 baseline methods only take 2D pixel intensity, but our method derives depth value from pixel intensities; histogram-based methods do not encode intrinsic properties; our DPA-based HCRF reveal more gesture semantics. Dense + HOG3D outperforms DPA + histogram due to its ability to capture useful context information e.g. head, torso etc. Context may be helpful for human gesture recognition. Figure 5(b) shows the confusion matrix for DPA-based HCRF representation. As we can see, there is a clear separation between single hand and 2-hand gestures. The most confusion occurs between the wave and flip gestures because both of them have similar motions and the palm orientation was not able to reflect their differences.

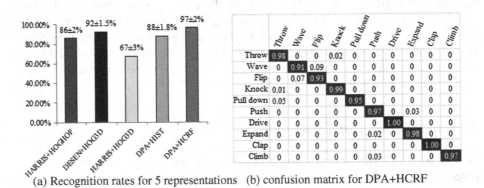

(a) Recognition rates for 5 representations   (b) confusion matrix for DPA+HCRF

Fig. 5. Comparison results on our 3D gesture/action dataset.

6 Conclusion

In this paper, we presented a dynamic perceptual attributes (DPAs)-based HCRF model for gesture modeling. DPAs are the extrinsic gesture descriptors that are able to present high-level semantics. The intrinsic context relations among DPAs reflect the discriminative properties for diverse gestures. Hidden conditional random fields model is applied to capture the internal temporal relations among DPAs. Our model combines both extrinsic and intrinsic properties that contribute gesture classification tasks. The promising results show its potentials for different applications. Though current model is tested on gesture recognition tasks where the related body parts are specified, the method is valid for generic action modeling, and should perform well for any human activities in general.

References

1. Hu, G., Gao, Q.: A 3D gesture recognition framework based on hierarchical visual attention and perceptual organization models. In: ICPR, pp. 1411–1414 (2012)
2. Laptev, I., Lindeberg, T.: Space-time interest points. In: ICCV (2003)
3. Dollar, P., Rabaud, V., Cottrell, G., Belongie, S.: Behavior recognition via sparse spatio-temporal features. In: VS-PETS (2005)
4. Willems, G., Tuytelaars, T., Van Gool, L.: An efficient dense and scale-invariant spatio-temporal interest point detector. In: Forsyth, D., Torr, P., Zisserman, A. (eds.) ECCV 2008, Part II. LNCS, vol. 5303, pp. 650–663. Springer, Heidelberg (2008)
5. Laptev, I., Marszalek, M., Schmid, C., Rozenfeld, B.: Learning realistic human actions from movies. In: CVPR (2008)
6. Klaser, A., Marszalek, M., Schmid, C.: A spatio-temporal descriptor based on 3D gradients. In: BMVC (2008)
7. Niebles, J.C., Chen, C.-W., Fei-Fei, L.: Modeling temporal structure of decomposable motion segments for activity classification. In: Daniilidis, K., Maragos, P., Paragios, N. (eds.) ECCV 2010, Part II. LNCS, vol. 6312, pp. 392–405. Springer, Heidelberg (2010)
8. Liu, J., Kuipers, B., Savarese, S.: Recognizing human actions by attributes. In: IEEE CVPR 2011, pp. 3337–3344 (2011)
9. Hernndez-Vela, A., et al.: Bovdw: Bag-of-visual-anddepth-words for gesture recognition. In: ICPR, pp. 449–452. IEEE (2012)
10. Shotton, J., Fitzgibbon, A., Cook, M., Sharp, T., Finocchio, M., Moore, R., Kipman, A., Blake, A.: Real-time human pose recognition in parts from single depth images. In: IEEE CVPR (2011)
11. Yang, X., Tian, Y.: Eigenjoints-based action recognition using naivebayes-nearest-neighbor. In: CVPR Workshops (CVPRW), pp. pp. 14–19. IEEE (2012)
12. Wang, J., Liu, Z., Wu, Y., Yuan, J.: Mining actionlet ensemble for action recognition with depth cameras. In: CVPR, pp. 1290–1297 (2012)
13. Gaur, U., Zhu, Y., Song, B.: A "String of feature graphs" model for recognition of complex activities in natural videos. In: ICCV (2011)
14. Brendel, W., Todorovic, S.: Learning spatiotemporal graphs of human activities. In: ICCV (2011)

15. Xia, L., Chen, C.-C., Aggarwal, J.: View invariant human action recognition using histograms of 3d joints. In: CVPR Workshops (CVPRW), pp. 20–27 (2012)
16. Sminchisescu, C., Kanaujia, A., Li, Z., Metaxas, D.: Conditional models for contextual human motion recognition. In: ICCV (2005)
17. Wang, Y., Mori, G.: Max-margin hidden conditional random fields for human action recognition. In: CVPR (2009)
18. Hu, G., Gao, Q.: A non-parametric statistics based method for generic curve partition and classification. In: Proceedings of IEEE 17th ICIP, pp. 3041–3044 (2010)
19. Rapantzikos, K., Avrithis, Y., Kollias, S.: Dense saliency-based spatiotemporal feature points for action recognition. In: IEEE CVPR, pp. 1454–1461 (2009)

The Bag of Micro-Movements for Human Activity Recognition

Pejman Habashi$^{(\boxtimes)}$, Boubakeur Boufama, and Imran Shafiq Ahmad

Computer Science Department, University of Windsor, Ontario, Canada
{habashi,boufama,ahmad}@uwindsor.ca

Abstract. The bag of words is a popular and successful method for human activity recognition. This method usually uses visual based sparse features for activity classification. It is also known that movement has useful clues for activity detection, but sparse features usually miss this vital piece of information. Two-dimensional image planar motion information is easy to extract but it is very dependant on depth and calibration parameters. Three-dimensional motion is rich in information and can be calculated from active cameras or multiple passive cameras, but it restricts the applicability of the method. To overcome these issues, we have proposed the use of disparity maps, which are relatively easy to extract from stereo videos and are more informative than 2D image planar motion information. In this work, we have combined the motion information and disparity maps to introduce a new sparse feature descriptor that encodes motion information, instead of visual information.

Keywords: Micro-movements · Feature descriptor · Motion-based descriptor · Human Activity Recognition · Machine vision

1 Introduction

Automated human activity recognition (HAR) is one of the most interesting and challenging areas of machine vision. There are many potential applications for a fully functional HAR system. Human computer interactions, surveillance systems and video content analysis are only few examples of those applications. During last two decades many different approaches have been proposed and tested [1–16], but none of them could fully address all the complexities that exist in a human activity recognition system.

One of the successful methods proposed was the Bag of Features (BOF) [17], which is based on the success of Bag of Words (BOW) assumption in document classification problems. BOW states that the topic (or class) of a document can be determined solely by looking at the words that appeared in that document[1], regardless of their place of appearance. BOF proposed to extract sparse features from input videos and treat them as words in a document.

---

[1] More accurately by the number of times a word appeared in a document compared to the number of times it appeared in other documents.

© Springer International Publishing Switzerland 2015
M. Kamel and A. Campilho (Eds.): ICIAR 2015, LNCS 9164, pp. 269–276, 2015.
DOI: 10.1007/978-3-319-20801-5_29

Different feature point extraction methods have been proposed in the literature [3,9,10,13,14], each of them have their own pros and cons, but almost all of them follow the same approach. First, the points of interest (usually corners) are extracted [3,9,10,17,18]. Then, a descriptor for each interest point is calculated by looking into its neighbourhood [3,9,19]. These descriptors are calculated directly or indirectly from pixel values around a feature point. Here we call them appearance based feature points because these descriptors encode the appearance of their neighbourhood.

The bag of words algorithms try to match two documents based on the words that appear in both documents. In BOF paradigm this translates to matching two videos based on the same words (similar neighbourhoods) appearing in two videos. BOF is a powerful method because it removes complexities related to the duration of an activity or the speed of it. Even though BOF showed promising results, the type of features that was used are barely used by humans for activity recognition.

In the current work we try to find a new descriptor which encodes the motion information in a way that could be effectively used by BOF algorithms. Our work is inspired by [20] which have introduced the motion trajectory descriptors. Our contribution is to combine disparity maps with motion information to improve the motion descriptors that we refer to them as micro-movement descriptors. Disparity maps are relatively easy to extract and they do not need camera calibration and they also provide a depth clue. We believe that disparity maps have enough discriminative information for many applications including HAR. Our descriptor could be used by any sparse recognition method, but bag of features should produce better results.

2   Motivations

The motion is a good clue for activity recognition and many different methods used motion information for activity recognition with different approaches [1,2,4–8,11,15]. Some methods have tracked the location of human joints in 3D space [1,11]. Other methods tried to track joint locations in 2D image plane [4,5]. These methods usually require human skeleton whose extraction, from 2D images, is still prone to errors. Some other methods have used only parts of the body for activity recognition. For example [2] tracked the hand positions of a human and used these trajectories for activity recognition. This method is limited to activities that could be done only by hands. The spatio-temporal space has also been used to obtain a 3D object in that space [6,8]. Other techniques used the compression of the motion into rigid 2D images [7,15].

On the other hand, one of the most successful methods for activity recognition, that showed promising results, is the Bag of Features [17]. This method is based on sparse representation of activities; i.e.; each activity video is represented by a set of isolated feature descriptors. Traditionally, these feature descriptors were directly or indirectly calculated based on the appearance of the neighbourhoods around the feature points [3,9,10]. Most of these descriptors were inspired by their still image counterparts. That explains why most of the sparse feature extractors used appearance based information and completely neglected the motion. One exception is [20] which used dense trajectories and defined a trajectory descriptor. They have also used these trajectories to align feature point neighbourhood frames and made a traditional feature point over aligned neighbourhood. In their experiment, trajectory aligned vision based feature points showed better performance and, later [13,14] they only used motion to align the feature point neighbourhood frames.

It has been suggested in [20] that tracking interest points in 2D image using KLT tracker yields good results. The captured movements happen in x-y image plane and can be expressed in number of pixels. Each image interest point (x, y) represents an space point (X, Y, Z) and the relationship can be expressed by the distance of the space point to the camera and intrinsic and extrinsic parameters of the camera. So the captured movement depend on the depth of scene points movements which is unknown. We believe that combining dense information with 2D motion information could improve the result.

One solution is to capture the depth with the help of active cameras. Even though active cameras are cheap and accessible, their functionality is limited. Since they are using time of flight (TOF) calculation to estimate the depth, they can work in low to moderate resolution and they can cover certain range (between one and three meters depth). Besides, existing active cameras are limited to indoor environments.

Another solution is to use stereo cameras. Let's say a space point P is mapped to P_1 in the first image and to P_2 in the second image. It is possible to calculate the coordinates of P in the scene coordinate system by having the coordinates of P_1 and P_2 in the image plane coordinate systems, using triangulation, assuming the two cameras have the exact same orientation and, the images are horizontally aligned and coplanar. In this situation it can be shown that the depth of point P depends only on the baseline[2] and the focal length[3] of two cameras. In practice, such configuration is hard or impossible to achieve and researchers usually use image rectification [21] to align them, which needs more calculation and camera calibration.

Even though depth information are very useful in transforming motion in image coordinate system to motion in scene coordinate system, this information is hard to extract. Disparities, on the other hand, are much easier to extract and there is no need for camera calibration. In this work we proposed to use disparity instead of depth information to represent motion in a third coordinate system which is similar to scene coordinate system.

3   Micro-Movement Descriptors

Our method captures the motions of interest points as the main clue. First the interest points from both left and right frames are extracted and, for each of them a descriptor is calculated. Here we have used opencv implementations of

---

[2] The distance between two center of projections.
[3] The distance between center of projection and the image plane.

FAST corner detector [22] for interest point detection and SIFT descriptors [19] for feature descriptor calculation. Then this descriptor is used to match feature points between the left and right frames. Having the point correspondences, this descriptor is no longer needed. Each interest point is now represented as $I(x_{li}, y_{li}, d_i)$ in which $P_l(x_{li}, y_{li})$ represents pixel coordinate of interest point i in left image and d_i is the distance between left and right frame calculated as an Euclidean distance:

$$d_i = \sqrt{(x_{ri} - x_{li})^2 + (y_{ri} - y_{li})^2} \tag{1}$$

If we assume the cameras are aligned such that there is no y-displacement, i.e., $y_{ri} - y_{li} = 0$, then the above distance will be reduced to $d_i = |x_{ri} - x_{li}|$ which is x-disparity. Since we are trying to reduce any precondition over camera placements, we have used the 2D Euclidean distance.

We have used KLT tracker to track the interest points in the left and right frames. We tracked the interest points for l consecutive frames before recalculating the interest points for the $l+1$ frame. This way several trajectories of length l have been made.

After extracting trajectories, the displacement vector calculated based on the amount of movement that each point has undergone. For example, if $l = 3$ and a sample trajectory T_i given by:

$$T_i = ([x_1, y_1, d_1], [x_2, y_2, d_2], [x_3, y_3, d_3]) \tag{2}$$

Then the displacement D_i is calculated as:

$$D_i = ([x_2 - x_1, y_2 - y_1, d_2 - d_1], [x_3 - x_2, y_3 - y_2, d_3 - d_2]) \tag{3}$$

Note that each displacement calculated between two consecutive frames (not left and right frames). The displacement contains the motion information that existed in the video. In general case:

$$D_{ij} = I_{i(j+1)} - I_{ij} \tag{4}$$

where D_{ij} represents the component j of trajectory i and I_{ik} represents the interest point triplets (x_{ik}, y_{ik}, d_{ik}) in trajectory i. Note that when the length of T_i is l then the length of D_i would be $l - 1$.

We have defined an energy measurement for each trajectory, given by:

$$e_i = \Sigma_{k=1}^{l-1} |D_{ik}|^2 \text{ Where } |D_{ik}| = \sqrt{x_{ik}^2 + y_{ik}^2 + d_{ik}^2} \tag{5}$$

The energy of a displacement determines the amount of movement of the corresponding trajectory. Low energy trajectories will represent steady feature points in a video. These points are usually background points or points on human body which are steady in l consecutive frames. These points have no or little discriminative information and they are removed by a simple thresholding. This eliminates the trajectories with very low information.

The remaining displacements are mapped onto a three dimensional space which has the characteristics of scene coordinates. From the stereo camera model and triangulation it can be deducted that:

$$Z = fB/d \propto 1/d \tag{6}$$

$$X = uZ/f \propto uZ \propto u/d \tag{7}$$

$$Y = vZ/f \propto vZ \propto v/d \tag{8}$$

In which f is focal length and B is the baseline distance. Assume $D(u, v, d)$ represents a point in displacement coordinate system measured in pixel values. We calculated our micro-movement descriptor by normalizing a displacement as follows:

$$M(X, Y, Z) = (u/d, v/d, 1/d) \tag{9}$$

where $M(X, Y, Z)$ is represented in an independent coordinate system. Movements in this space are similar to movements in the scene coordinate system.

4   Experimental Result

To the best of our knowledge, there is no stereo vision dataset for human activity recognition. Hence, it is hard to compare our proposed method to other methods in the literature. To demonstrate the effectiveness and discriminative power of our proposed micro-movements representation, we have created our own stereo-dataset. The latter contains 12 different simple activities.

Each activity is done several times by two volunteer actors, a male and a female. The videos are recorded with two very low quality and cheap but similar cameras attached to a rigid bar. The videos are captured and recorded in VGA quality. Some sample frames of dataset are also provided on first row of Fig. 1. The second row shows the cameras itself, the left and right images of one sample frame with their corresponding feature points, and the calculated disparity map.

After extracting the micro-movement descriptors, we cluster them using the well known K-Means clustering algorithm. In particular, each cluster represents a word. For each instance of an activity in our dataset, we have counted the

Fig. 1. First row: Sample frames of five different activities, **Second row:** Cameras used, the left and right extracted feature points and their matching result

Table 1. Twelve activity confusion matrix

Activity Name	Class	a	b	c	d	e	f	g	h	i	j	k	l
Walking Right	a	10	0	0	0	0	1	0	0	0	0	0	1
Walking Left	b	0	11	0	0	0	0	0	0	0	0	0	0
Walking (Toward Camera)	c	1	1	2	3	0	0	1	0	0	0	0	0
Walking (Away Camera)	d	0	0	2	8	0	0	0	0	0	0	0	0
Hand Waving (Right)	e	0	0	0	1	5	0	0	0	3	1	0	0
Hand Waving (Left)	f	0	0	0	0	1	4	0	1	1	0	0	0
Jumping	g	0	0	1	0	1	0	10	4	0	0	0	0
Sitting Down (Front View)	h	0	0	0	0	0	0	1	10	4	1	0	0
Standing Up (Front View)	i	0	0	0	0	0	0	0	2	11	0	1	0
Sitting (Side View)	j	0	0	0	0	0	0	0	1	1	13	0	0
Standing (Side View)	k	0	0	0	0	0	0	0	0	1	0	14	0
Jumping Jack	l	0	0	0	0	0	1	0	0	1	1	0	10

Table 2. Six activity confusion matrix

Activity Name	Class	a	b	c	d	e	f
Walking	a	36	1	3	0	0	1
Hand Waving	b	1	11	0	4	1	0
Jumping	c	1	2	13	0	0	0
Sitting Down	d	0	0	2	27	2	0
Standing Up	e	0	0	0	4	25	0
Jumping Jack	f	0	1	0	1	0	10

number of times each word appears in it. Then, we have made a vector of length w words, where w represents the number of clusters. For this experiment we fixed the length of trajectories to $l = 9$ frames and $w = 400$ as a rule of thumb. We have used Bayes Net for classification of activities based on the word count vector. We were able to correctly classify 73.47 % of the activities without any parameter tuning. It is hard to compare this value with other works. The nearest work to ours is the image plane motion descriptors of [20]. They achieved 67.2 % accuracy on YouTube dataset which shows the effectiveness of our descriptor. However, their trajectory aligned descriptor hit 83.9 % which is better than many other descriptors including ours. The confusion matrix of twelve activities are represented in Table 1. We should emphasise that our result is preliminary and we are sure it will be improved during the future research. We proposed several trends for improvement in the next section of this paper.

Our test setting neither designed nor optimized for online processing, however with current setting the extraction of features is done in 8.3 frames per second on a single thread ran on a 2.8 GHz Core i7 CPU. With some improvements one might be able to implement it in real time, but the original BOF algorithm should also be altered to work in online manner.

To further demonstrate the flexibility of our classifier, considering that some of the activities in our dataset are very similar and they typically have the same name in our natural language, we have combined the similar classes to examine the discriminative power of our descriptors. We summarized our activities into six different classes. Using same Bayes Net classification method without parameter tuning we have achieved 83.56 % accuracy. This is a lot better compared to 67.2 % of closest work [20]. The confusion matrix of this experiment is shown in Table 2.

5   Conclusion and Future Work

This paper proposed a new sparse feature descriptor based on movement clues. To the best of our knowledge, this is the first work which take advantage of disparity-maps in stereo-image videos for human activity recognition. We have proposed a new descriptor, that is easily extracted from stereo videos, to be used to discriminate between different activities. Since the proposed descriptor is based on disparity map information, there is no need for camera calibration. Our simple experiments demonstrate the discriminative power of our descriptor. Even though we tested it against a small dataset, we believe it would work well in more sophisticated cases. Our descriptor is not bound to human activity detection by any means. It may be used for many other event detection applications where the movement of interest points seems discriminative.

There are many ways to improve the results, which we consider for future work. (1) The number of actors and activity classes will be significantly increased. Furthermore, because some activities are shorter in time, they might be repeated more often in dataset in order to have enough instances of each activity for learning. (2) Because there are different algorithms/tools for the different stages of our micro-movement descriptor extraction process, we will need to test and compare alternative algorithm/tools for possible improvement of our final results. (3) We will investigate other classifiers, in addition to Bayes Net, used for the classification of bag of features. (4) Another possible improvement would be the combination of appearance-based clues with our descriptor.

References

1. Campbell, L.W., Bobick, A.F.: Recognition of human body motion using phase space constraints. In: Fifth International Conference on Computer Vision, Proceedings, pp. 624–630. IEEE (1995)
2. Rao, C., Shah, M.: View-invariance in action recognition. In: Proceedings of the 2001 IEEE Computer Society Conference on Computer Vision and Pattern Recognition, CVPR 2001, vol. 2, pp. II–316. IEEE (2001)
3. Dollár, P., Rabaud, V., Cottrell, G., Belongie, S.: Behavior recognition via sparse spatio-temporal features. In: 2nd Joint IEEE International Workshop on Visual Surveillance and Performance Evaluation of Tracking and Surveillance 2005, pp. 65–72. IEEE (2005)

4. Sheikh, Y., Sheikh, M., Shah, M.: Exploring the space of a human action. In: Tenth IEEE International Conference on Computer Vision, ICCV 2005, vol. 1, pp. 144–149. IEEE (2005)

5. Yilmaz, A., Shah, M.: Actions sketch: A novel action representation. In: IEEE Computer Society Conference on Computer Vision and Pattern Recognition, CVPR 2005, vol. 1, pp. 984–989. IEEE (2005)

6. Yilmaz, A., Shah, M.: Recognizing human actions in videos acquired by uncalibrated moving cameras. In: Tenth IEEE International Conference on Computer Vision, ICCV 2005, vol. 1, pp. 150–157. IEEE (2005)

7. Bobick, A.F., Davis, J.W.: The recognition of human movement using temporal templates. IEEE Trans. Pattern Anal. Mach. Intel. 23(3), 257–267 (2001)

8. Blank, M., Gorelick, L., Shechtman, E., Irani, M., Basri, R.: Actions as space-time shapes. In: Tenth IEEE International Conference on Computer Vision, ICCV 2005, vol. 2, pp. 1395–1402. IEEE (2005)

9. Laptev, I.: On space-time interest points. Int. J. Comput. Vis. 64(2–3), 107–123 (2005)

10. Laptev, I., Marszalek, M., Schmid, C., Rozenfeld, C.: Learning realistic human actions from movies. In: IEEE Conference on Computer Vision and Pattern Recognition, CVPR 2008, pp. 1–8. IEEE (2008)

11. Uddin, M.Z., Thang, N.D., Kim, J.T., Kim, T.-S.: Human activity recognition using body joint-angle features and hidden markov model. Etri J. 33(4), 569–579 (2011)

12. Barnachon, M., Bouakaz, S., Boufama, B., Guillou, E.: Human actions recognition from streamed motion capture. In: 2012 21st International Conference on Pattern Recognition (ICPR), pp. 3807–3810. IEEE (2012)

13. Wang, H., Kläser, A., Schmid, C., Liu, C.-L.: Dense trajectories and motion boundary descriptors for action recognition. Int. J. Comput. Vis. 103(1), 60–79 (2013)

14. Wang, H., Schmid, C.: Action recognition with improved trajectories. In: 2013 IEEE International Conference on Computer Vision (ICCV), pp. 3551–3558. IEEE (2013)

15. Diaf, A.A.: Eigenvector-based dimensionality reduction for human activity recognition and data classification. Ph.D. thesis, University of Windsor (2013)

16. Barnachon, M., Bouakaz, S., Boufama, B., Guillou, E.: Ongoing human action recognition with motion capture. Pattern Recog. 47(1), 238–247 (2014)

17. Niebles, J.C., Wang, H., Fei-Fei, L.: Unsupervised learning of human action categories using spatial-temporal words. Int. J. Comput. Vis. 79(3), 299–318 (2008)

18. Willems, G., Tuytelaars, T., Van Gool, L.: An efficient dense and scale-invariant spatio-temporal interest point detector. In: Forsyth, D., Torr, P., Zisserman, A. (eds.) ECCV 2008, Part II. LNCS, vol. 5303, pp. 650–663. Springer, Heidelberg (2008)

19. Lowe, D.G.: Distinctive image features from scale-invariant keypoints. Int. J. Comput. Vis. 60(2), 91–110 (2004)

20. Wang, H., Klaser, A., Schmid, C., Liu, C.-L.: Action recognition by dense trajectories. In: 2011 IEEE Conference on Computer Vision and Pattern Recognition (CVPR), pp. 3169–3176. IEEE (2011)

21. Kang, Y.-S., Ho, Y.-S.: Efficient stereo image rectification method using horizontal baseline. In: Ho, Y.-S. (ed.) PSIVT 2011, Part I. LNCS, vol. 7087, pp. 301–310. Springer, Heidelberg (2011)

22. Rosten, E., Drummond, T.W.: Machine learning for high-speed corner detection. In: Leonardis, A., Bischof, H., Pinz, A. (eds.) ECCV 2006, Part I. LNCS, vol. 3951, pp. 430–443. Springer, Heidelberg (2006)

An Efficient Method for Extracting Key-Frames from 3D Human Joint Locations for Action Recognition

Md. Hasanul Kabir, Ferdous Ahmed[✉], and Abdullah-Al-Tariq

Department of Computer Science and Engineering,
Islamic University of Technology, Dhaka, Bangladesh
{hasanul, tariq93}@iut-dhaka.edu,
ferdous.iut.cse@gmail.com

Abstract. Human Action Recognition is one of the intriguing research area of modern Artificial Intelligence and Computer Vision where different techniques are followed to distinguish various human actions. Accuracy of such methods mainly depend on how a sequence of action frames can be represented by a number of most distinguishable frames, otherwise called key frames. In this paper, we have introduced an efficient method to extract key frames by maximizing accumulation of motion between frames for recognizing human actions using the help of 3D skeletal joint locations. Our feature representation is the combination of histogram of joint 3D (HOJ3D) and static posture feature of 3D skeletal joint locations. Then we used Hidden Markov Model (HMM) for human action recognition from the extracted frame sequence.

Keywords: Discriminative patterns · 3D skeletons · 3D depth images · Key frame extraction · Action recognition

1 Introduction

Enabling machines to recognize human actions is a prominent area of studies in computer vision and artificial intelligence. Its application is extended from tracking humans in smart homes, security establishments or video gaming to augmented reality or gesture navigation. To recognize human actions, silhouettes and spatiotemporal interest points are selected as discriminative features. With the invention of novel devices like Microsoft Kinect, new techniques have emerged to extract human joint locations for each frame from action videos [1]. Researchers who used silhouettes have followed one of two major categories to classify actions. One is to extract patterns from silhouette sequence [4, 5, 6, 7, 14, 15] and the other is to create a model from each silhouette [6, 8, 9, 10, 11, 16, 17]. The major challenges for human action recognition using 3D skeletal joint locations are: selection of significant frames, overlapping actions, diversity in actions, representation of temporal sequence, arbitrary viewing angel, discriminative features, noise, subjective interpretation of actions, etc. In [12], an approach-based taxonomy is presented to categorize all the different approaches researches follow to recognize human activities [13, 12]. There are two broad approaches: (a) single-layered

© Springer International Publishing Switzerland 2015
M. Kamel and A. Campilho (Eds.): ICIAR 2015, LNCS 9164, pp. 277–284, 2015.
DOI: 10.1007/978-3-319-20801-5_30

and (b) hierarchical. These approaches are followed to classify human actions where the distinctive features can be of different types. One of the feature is the Histogram of Joints 3D (HOJ3D). In [18], HOJ3D is created from skeleton sequence and then Key frames are extracted from Self Similarity Matrix based on the video summarization method proposed by Huang P. et al. [19]. At last the actions are classified using TF-IDF. Lu Xia et al. [3] used probabilistic voting on HOJ3D to generate the key frames and then used HMM to recognize actions. X. Yang et al. [2] used Eigen Joints, difference between neighboring frames and difference between current frame and initial frame as distinctive features and then used PCA and LDA for dimension reduction.

The objective of this paper is to use efficient algorithm for extracting key frames from a video of action sequence and to classify them. As not all frames in an action sequence are informative, temporal segments of an action can be intuitively approximated by the statuses of neutral, onset, apex, and offset. The discriminative information is not evenly distributed in the four statuses, but concentrates more on the frames from onset and apex statuses. On the other hand, motions of neutral and offset statuses are usually similar across different action categories. So informative frame selection corresponds to extract frames from onset and apex but discard frames from neutral and offset. For this purpose we have proposed a new method where we extract a fixed number of frames that best summarizes the action sequence. In this paper, we at first take 3D human skeleton joint locations from Kinect, combine HOJ3D and static posture of 3D joints together as feature and extract the key frames. Then we use HMM to classify the actions.

Our main contribution in this paper is to device a method for key frame extraction that is both computationally inexpensive and robust. Our work is motivated by the video summarization technique which used a graph based technique to extract significant frames from a video sequence [3]. But since computational complexity of that approach was significantly high we tried to reduce the complexity by devising a simpler but efficient approach.

2 Proposed Method for Key Frame Extraction

Our proposed method starts with extracting 3D human skeletal joints from sequential depth images [1]. After that these 3D joints go through a series of pre-processing steps. Then feature vector is generated by combining 3D joint vector difference as static posture feature [2] and histogram of joint 3D (HOJ3D) [3].

Then we have used our approach to extract key frames from the action sequence. After that codebook is generated and feature vectors are converted to observation symbols. For Action recognition we used discrete HMM. An overview of the proposed system is given in Fig. 1.

2.1 3D Skeletal Joints Pre-processing

3D skeletal joint locations are pre-processed to make these extracted 3D co-ordinate suitable for subsequent operations. In our proposed system the following

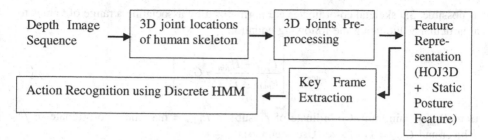

Fig. 1. Overview of the human action recognition system

pre-processing steps are used on the 3D skeletal joints to make the 3D skeletal model view and scale invariant:

i. User to Kinect Sensor Distance Adaptation.
ii. Rotating and aligning the model along the right shoulder.
iii. Normalising each joints with respect to radial distance.
iv. 3D joint position normalization

First problem with the 3D skeletal joints is direction of the camera changes along with the movements of the user. So we need to adapt these changing direction of the camera. To resolve this scenario we used the hip center of the user as the Centre of Gravity (COG) and translate 3D model of human skeleton to the hip center.

$$P^j_{new} = P^j_{old} - P^j_{hp} \tag{1}$$

Here, P^j_{hp} is the coordinate of the hip centre of jth subject. Then 3D skeletal model is rotated and aligned with the right shoulder. This step is performed to reduce variability of data across multiple subjects. Rotation of the 3D skeletal model is done around the Y axis and rotation angle is calculated in spherical co-ordinate system.

$$P^j_{new} = M^j_{\varphi} P^j_{old} \tag{2}$$

Here M^j_{φ} is the transformation matrix for j^{th} subject and φ is the angle of the right shoulder. After the previous step we need to normalize the joints with respect to the radial distance to make the 3D skeletal model scale invariant. We used the following equation for this purpose:

$$R^j_i = \frac{R^j_i}{R^j_{max}} \tag{3}$$

Here R^j_i = Radial distance of ith co-ordinate of jth subject and R^j_{max} = maximum radial distance of the jth subject. As the co-ordinates are only an approximation of the real co-ordinates and also these are subject to noise we need to minimize the error as much as possible. 3D skeletal co-ordinates are normalized by associating a range of values to a particular value using the following equation.

$$P^j_{new} = \left\lfloor \left| \frac{P^j_{old} - P^j_{min}}{P^j_{max} - P^j_{min}} \right| * G_{size} \right\rfloor \tag{4}$$

Here P^j_{min} = minimum Co-ordinate of jth subject P^j_{max} = maximum co-ordinate of jth subject and G_{size} = Grid size (User defined).

2.2 Feature Representation

Human action is modelled as a sequence of frames. So we need to find a suitable feature descriptor for each and every frame of the sequence. In our proposed framework to model human action sequence we have employed vector difference of 3D skeletal joints as static posture feature f_{sp} and histogram of joint 3D skeletal co-ordinate system f_{hoj3d}. We then concatenate these two feature channels as f.

$$f = \begin{pmatrix} f_{hoj3d} \\ f_{sp} \end{pmatrix} \tag{5}$$

Here $f_{sp} = \{ X_i - X_j | i, j = 1, 2, \ldots \ldots, N; i \neq j \}, f_{hoj3d} = \begin{pmatrix} h_{el} \\ h_{az} \end{pmatrix} h_{az}$ = histogram of 3D joints along azimuth (θ) direction and h_{el} = histogram of 3D joints along elevation (φ) direction.

We partition the 3D space into n bins. The azimuth angle θ and elevation angle φ both are divided into 12 bins. With our spherical coordinate, any 3D joint can be localized at a unique bin. The azimuth angle θ has a 30 degree resolution and elevation angle φ has a 15 degree resolution. To make the representation robust against minor errors we have used a Gaussian weight.

For each joint, we only vote over the bin it is in and the two neighboring bins. We calculate the probabilistic voting on θ and φ separately since they are independent. Standard deviation σ is calculated by dividing the corresponding resolution by two [3] (Fig. 2).

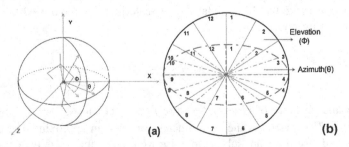

Fig. 2. (a) 3D Human Skeleton in spherical co-ordinate system. (b) Number of bins used for elevation (Φ) and azimuth (θ) in spherical co-ordinate system.

We accumulate these values for each of the 16 joint locations over these two bins. After the accumulation we concatenate these two bins to produce f_{hoj3d}.

2.3 Key Frame Extraction

First self-similarity matrix S is calculated. For any two skeletons i and j, let their feature descriptor be expressed as f_i and f_j where a measure of similarity between the skeletons can be computed using the following distance function:

$$S_{i,j} = d(i,j) = \sqrt{(f_i - f_j)^T (f_i - f_j)} \; where \; (i,j) \{1, 2, \ldots Number \; of \; frames\} \quad (6)$$

Then we have derived a Cost Matrix (C) which is defined by the following equation:

$$C_{i,j} = \sum_{n=i}^{j-1} S_{n,n+1} \quad (7)$$

Here $C_{i,j}$ represents accumulation of motion from frame i to frame j. Let's say significant frames between the first frame, f and the last frame l needs to be calculated. Then we need to split the sequence on frame p such that,

$$p = argmin_i |C_{f,i} - C_{i,l}| \quad (8)$$

On the next iteration using the same approach we further split the frame sequence f to p and frame sequence p to l. This process is iterated k number of times to produce $2^k + 1$ number of significant frames. If the value of k is too small then many discriminative action poses might be lost. Again if the value is set too high then extracted frame sequence might contain too many frames with little discriminative patterns. To test our algorithm to generate key frames, we acquired 3D joint location data used by Lu Xia et al. [3] of 10 subjects performing 10 different actions each performed twice which are spread throughout an arbitrary number of frames. All the actions are performed differently. The joint locations are captured using a static Kinect hardware in an indoor environment with 30 fps speed. Each frame consists of 3D joint locations of twenty joints of a human body (Figs. 3 and 4).

2.4 Action Recognition Using Discrete HMM

Vector quantization on the extracted frame sequence is performed to reduce the number of observation symbol. We clustered the feature vectors into 16 clusters (a 16-word vocabulary) using K-means algorithm. Then each frame is represented by an observation symbol.

Our system used a left to right HMM to model sequential events of human activity. We have used 5 hidden states in our experiment. Each of the human activity is modelled using a HMM model. The maximum likelihood among these trained HMM models are chosen as the recognized human action:

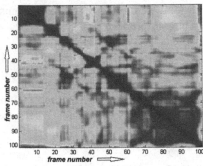

Fig. 3. Self-similarity matrix of 100 frames

Fig. 4. Key Frames extracted from a walking video sequence using our method

$$L_{max} = \arg max_{i=1}^{N}(P(O|H_i)).$$

Here L_{max} is the maximum likelihood of the action sequence based on the observation symbol O and H_i represents HMM model parameters of activity i.

2.5 Experimental Results

In our experiment we used 10-fold cross subject validation technique. Based on the extracted frame sequence we achieved a mean accuracy of 94.9 % and best accuracy of achieved is 95.26 %.

As we can see from Fig. 5 is that our technique performs better than some of the existing methods. This is because extracted frame sequences are quite discriminative. Also our feature representation is quite robust compared to other methods.

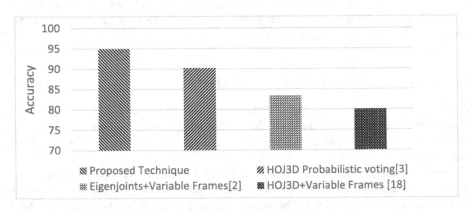

Fig. 5. Comparative analysis of different methods

As frame number is increased accuracy of the recognition is also increased because it allowed the frame sequence to capture more informative frames. But increasing frame number too much might result in a reduced performance because redundant frames are selected with very little discriminative capability. Figure 6 shows how accuracy of the system changes with respect to the changing number of key frames.

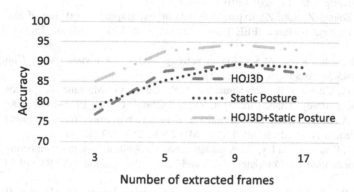

Fig. 6. Action recognition using different number of extracted key frames

3   Conclusion

We have seen how efficiently we can extract key frames from a frame sequence of arbitrary length. The approach discussed has proven to be quite robust. Extracted key frames using the proposed method showed significant discriminative patterns and the feature descriptor is also quite robust. This claim is supported by better action recognition.

References

1. Shotton, J., Fitzgibbon, A., Cook, M., Sharp, T., Finocchio, M., Moore, R., Kipman, A., Blake, A.: Real-time human pose recognition in parts from a single depth image. In: Computer Vision And Pattern Recognition (CVPR) (2011)
2. Yang, X., Tian, Y.: Effective 3D action recognition using eigenjoints. Vis. Commun. Image Represent. **25**(1), 2–11 (2014)
3. Xia, L., Chen, C.-C., Aggarwal, J.K.: View invariant human action recognition using histograms of 3D joints. In: CVPR Workshops, IEEE, pp. 20–27 (2012)
4. Bobick, A., Davis, J.: The recognition of human movement using temporal templates. IEEE Trans. Pattern Anal. Mach. Intell. **23**(3), 257–267 (2001)
5. Meng, H., Pears, N., Bailey, C.: A human action recognition system for embedded computer vision application. In: Proceedings of the CVPR (2007)
6. Davis, J.W., Tyagi, A.: Minimal-latency human action recognition using reliable-inference. Image Vis. Comput. **24**(5), 455–473 (2006)
7. Chen, D.-Y., Liao, H.-Y.M., Shih, S.-W.: Human action recognition using 2-D spatio-temporal templates. In: Proceedings of the ICME, pp. 667–670 (2007)

8. Kellokumpu, V., Pietikainen, M., Heikkila, J.: Human activity recognition using sequences of postures. In: Proceedings of the IAPR Conference on Machine Vision Applications, pp. 570–573 (2005)
9. Sminchisescu, C., Kanaujia, A., Li, Z., Metaxas, D.: Conditional models for contextual human motion recognition. In: Proceedings of the ICCV, vol. 2, pp. 808–815 (2005)
10. Zhang, J., Gong, S.: Action categorization with modified hidden conditional random field. Pattern Recogn. **43**, 197–203 (2010)
11. Li, W., Zhang, Z., Liu, Z.: Expandable data-driven graphical modeling of human actions based on salient postures. IEEE Trans. Circuits Syst. Video Technol. **18**(11), 1499–1510 (2008)
12. Aggarwal, J.K., Ryoo, M.S.: Human activity analysis: a review. ACM Comput. Surv. (CSUR) **43**(3), Article 16, 43p. (2011)
13. Turaga, P., Chellapa, R., Subrahmanian, V.S., Udrea, O.: Machine recognition of human activities: a survey. Trans. Circ. Syst. Video Technol. **18**(11), 1473–1488 (2008)
14. Bobick, A., Davis, J.W.: The recognition of human movement using temporal templates. Trans. Pattern Anal. Mach. Intell. (TPAMI) **23**(3), 257–267 (2001)
15. Meng, H., Pears, N., Bailey, C.: A human action recognition system for embedded computer vision application. In: Computer Vision and Pattern Recognition (CVPR), vol. 2(1), p. 2122 (2007)
16. Davis, J.W., Tyagi, A.: Minimal-latency human action. Image Vis. Comput. (IVC) **24**(5), 455–473 (2006)
17. Kellokumpu, V., Pietikainen, M., Heikkila, J.: Human activity recognition using sequences of postures. In: International Association of Pattern Recognition (IAPR) (2005)
18. Thanh, T.T., FanChen, K.B.: Extraction of discriminative patterns from skeleton sequences for accurate action recognition. Fundamenta Informaticae **XX**, 15 (2012). doi:10.3233/FI-2012-0000. IOS Press
19. Huang, P., Hilton, A., Starck J.: Automatic 3D video summarization: key frame extraction from self similarity. In: 4th International Symposium on 3D Data Processing, Atlanta, GA, USA. pp. 71–78, June 2008

Robotics and 3D Vision

A Simple View-Based Software Architecture for an Autonomous Robot Navigation System

Salvador E. Ayala-Raggi$^{(\boxtimes)}$, Pedro de Jesús González, Susana Sánchez-Urrieta, and Aldrin Barreto-Flores

Facultad de Ciencias de la Electrónica, Benemérita Universidad Autónoma de Puebla, Av. San Claudio Y 18 Sur, Col. Jardines de San Manuel, 72570 Puebla, Puebla, Mexico
{saraggi,surrieta,abarreto}@ece.buap.mx, pedro_dj_g@hotmail.com
http://ece.buap.mx

Abstract. This paper describes the design and implementation of a basic architecture for view-based autonomous navigation of a mobile robot platform. Our system is composed by an interface module which communicates a robotic platform with a decisions module. The system tries to follow a original trained path by calculating a rotation angle using a scene comparison. We implemented this comparison by performing a matching between the current view of the robot and a memorized panoramic image. The matching process is carried out by two methods: NCC-based template matching and SURF-based marching. Our results demonstrate an acceptable performance of the autonomous navigation for both methods when no changes in the environment are present, and a superior performance of the SURF-based method even in the presence of new objects which were not present during the training stage. abstract environment.

Keywords: Robot vision · Autonomous navigation · Template matching · SURF features · RANSAC

1 Introduction

The great necessity of relieving people from monotonous and repetitive tasks has accelerated the evolution of technology by investing many resources aided to design more intelligent robots with the ability to perform their work without any human intervention and automatically within non controlled environments and unforeseen situations. Perhaps, the best example of these kind of robots are those with an autonomous navigation system [1–9]. Probably, the recent need for designing robots with autonomous navigation capability arises from the growing complexity of the human society. This complex society demands much brute workforce which could be accomplished by machines, freeing people for more creative and intellectual work. In this context, autonomous navigation opens a window to a wide range of complex tasks which were reserved just for human beings during a long time.

© Springer International Publishing Switzerland 2015
M. Kamel and A. Campilho (Eds.): ICIAR 2015, LNCS 9164, pp. 287–296, 2015.
DOI: 10.1007/978-3-319-20801-5_31

Several works have been proposed for vision-based autonomous navigation, specifically, those which only use a camera as a single sensor have demanded special attention [5,10,11]. View-based approaches commonly have to deal with many problems like environmental changes between the training stage and the autonomous navigation stage. In indoor environments, those changes can include lighting variation, image noise, and new unknown objects appearing in the scene, like persons and all kind of office or home stuff. Some works which deal with this kind of problems have been proposed and they use SIFT features for view-based autonomous navigation, because its inherent computational speed [9].

Similarly to the SIFT features approach [12], a faster version known as SURF features technique [13,14] has been used in autonomous navigation implementations which use a panoramic camera as primary sensor [6,10]. Except in [9] where the SIFT features method was used, the above works do not face the problem of new objects appearing in the scene. Here, we describe a simple autonomous navigation system which uses a conventional camera and software modules in which we have implemented SURF features detection in combination with $RANSAC$ algorithm in order to compare the current view of the robot during navigation with images of the learned path stored in its memory. We face the problem of navigating in the presence of new obstacles not present during the training stage. Additionally, in a similar way as [1,3], and [15] who uses the SAD (*sum of absolute differences*) distance as a measure to compare images, we implemented an appearance-based navigation which uses NCC (*Normalized Cross Correlation*) template matching. We compare the performance of the both methods proposed.

The overall system is composed by a third-party two-wheeled robot platform equipped with a single conventional camera and two software modules developed in this work. The first module is a software interface programmed in Visual Basic which communicates the physical platform X80SV (from Dr. Robot) with a software module programmed in $MATLAB$ which is actually a *decisions-making* machine. All the computer vision algorithms were programmed in the $MATLAB$ module. The autonomous navigation system described in this work has many useful applications. Particularly, an autonomous navigation system can be implemented in wheelchairs to transfer disabled patients from one place to another without any supervision. This application could take place in home or in public hospital facilities.

2   System Overview

In this work, we developed autonomous navigation software modules for a X80SV robotic platform. The X80SV is a two-wheeled mobile robot [16] which can be controlled by a PC computer via USB serial communications port, or WiFi TCP/IP communications link [17]. An interface module was programmed in Microsoft Visual Basic .Net language and it provides a communication link between sensors data from the robot and a MATLAB function called *decision_maker*. Similarly, movement commands generated by the *decision_maker* function are sent back to the robot via the interface module.

Additionally, the interface module also has a training submodule that was designed in order to perform a training stage as a previous step before autonomous path tracking. The training submodule was programmed in Visual Basic .Net and allows the user to control the robot to follow an arbitrary path. Each time the user gives a command to the robot from the interface, for instance *turn left 30° and go straight* 0.3*m*, the robot performs the following procedure: (1) The robot rotates on its own axis 30° left; (2) Captures three views around before starting its movement; (3) starts an straight movement of 0.3 m towards the next waypoint selected by the user. Internally, the interface program captures three images covering $76° \times 3 = 228°$ of field of view and calls a *MATLAB* function which stores the three images in real time. In this way, a trained path is nothing but n sets of three images where n is the number of waypoints, named from now on as *pathnodes*.

3   Path Tracking by Image Matching

The *decisions_maker* function is the core of our system. When this function determines that the matching process between the current view and the respective three memorized images is successful, then it computes a rotation angle that the robot should perform before moving straight towards the next path node.

Specifically, the current view of the robot is compared with three memorized images belonging to the waypoint where the robot supposes to be there. The comparison is used to compute the angle that the robot should turn (rotate) in order to correct the path towards the following waypoint. Two methods were developed for this purpose: the first one is by template matching and the second one by SURF matching. The template matching approach is the computation of the *NCC* between the current view and a sequence of consecutive regions taken from the panoramic image composed of the three aforementioned images. The horizontal location of the maximum *NCC* value corresponds to the best match, and therefore indicates the magnitude of the angle to rotate.

In the other hand, in the SURF matching approach, SURF features are calculated for the current view and for each one of the three images. The image with the best match of SURF features is selected. We make sure that this is the best match by using *RANSAC* in order to eliminate possible outliers. A good match is considered when there are at least 4 SURF pairs who have survived the stage of outliers elimination. Then, the horizontal translation of the matched SURF features is calculated by Procrustes analysis. Finally, this horizontal translation quantity is transformed to a proper rotation angle value. When the computed rotation angle is very small (< 3 degrees), the robot is commanded to rotate the specified rotation angle and to move straight 0.3m. Conversely, if the angle is greater, the robot is commanded to rotate and stay in the same path node. Then, the next time the function is called, the rotation angle is computed again. When there is not a match between the images a random rotation angle is calculated and a rotation command is sent.

3.1   Path Tracking by NCC Template Matching

We have designed and implemented a path tracking algorithm based in direct image comparison also known as the template matching approach. Here, we take the current view that the robot sees, and we compare it with consecutive sample images taken from a panoramic view. The sample images are taken by shifting one pixel to the right the position of the ROI (Region Of Interest) over the panoramic image (three views merged). In computer vision, there are some known measures of similarity between images: SAD (Sum of Absolute Differences), SSD (Sum of Squared Differences), Euclidean distance, and NCC (Normalized Cross Correlation), see [14]. Although NCC is more complex than the other mentioned measures, we have chosen that because it is invariant to affine intensity changes, typically appearing in real images when illumination changes occur. Once the NCC is calculated between the current view and all the ROI's taken from the panoramic image, we select the position where the NCC value is maximum. This position minus the central position (that corresponding to the first pixel of the central image, remembering that the three images form a panoramic) gives a vector which is proportional to the angle that the robot should rotate in order to be ready to begin its travel towards the next path node. Figure 1 illustrates this technique.

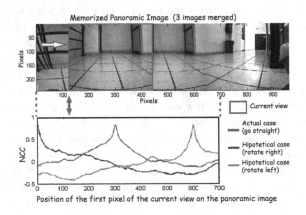

Fig. 1. The rotation angle is obtained by computing NCC between the current view and the panoramic image

3.2   Path Tracking by SURF Features Matching

The SIFT (Scale invariant features transform) method was proposed by Lowe et al. in [12]. It is a technique for finding feature points on the image whose descriptors are invariant to variations in scale, rotation, translation, illumination, and viewpoint of the objects in the scene. In this way, if we have two images containing the same object but perhaps rotated, scaled and with different illumination, the SIFT points found in both images will be located on the same physical points of the object. The descriptors of two corresponding points should be very similar if these points belong to the same location on the object. In order to eliminate possible outliers (false positive matches), we have to keep only the pairs of points with the highest similarity.

On the other hand, SURF, an acronym of Speeded Up Robust Features, was proposed in [13]. This scale-invariant features detector is based on SIFT but it is several times faster. Because its fast processing speed, we have used SURF features. The similarity criterion that we utilized for comparing the $128 - elements$ descriptors was the euclidian distance. Even when an appropriate threshold was used to eliminate outliers in the set of pairs of SURF points, there could be survivors that are outliers. In fact, frequently, inliers are points which have the same relative positions with respect to their neighbors in both images. This configuration of relative positions is preserved in the second image even when changes in scale and rotation have taken place, i.e., the polygon formed by the SURF points in the second image should be a rotated and scaled version of that in the first image. Therefore, in order to reduce even more the quantity of outliers, we have to find and eliminate those pairs of points which do not fit in the aforementioned configuration. We have used the $RANSAC$ (Random Sample Consensus) algorithm for that purpose, see [18].

A set of SURF features is extracted from the current view and each one of the three images in the memorized panoramic. By measuring the Euclidean distance between descriptors from image pairs (current view vs each one of the three the memorized images). In order to eliminate the outliers we execute the $RANSAC$ elimination process. Next, we choose the image in the panoramic with the highest number of SURF matches with respect to the current view. The next step is to determine horizontal translation between the two polygons. We have solved this task by using Procrustes Analysis [19]. Procrustes analysis translates, re-scales, and rotates the points of the polygon in the second image into an optimal superimposition over the points of the first image. This horizontal translation is proportional to the angle that the robot has to rotate in order to be ready to begin its travel towards the next path node. Figure 2 illustrates this process.

4   Results

In the first experiment, the robot learned a path with 81 path nodes. During the training stage, the robot was tele-commanded to follow the desired path and to take 3 pictures in each node. We use the two methods of navigation, NCC and $SURF$, to evaluate their performance in ideal conditions: the same illumination that in the training stage and no new objects in the scene. From Fig. 3, which shows the navigation results, we observe that both methods achieved a very good performance reaching the goal point. In order to obtain a better knowledge about the performance of the both methods, we performed five trials of the autonomous path tracking for each method. Figure 3 shows the position error average that we have measured as an absolute distance between the original path

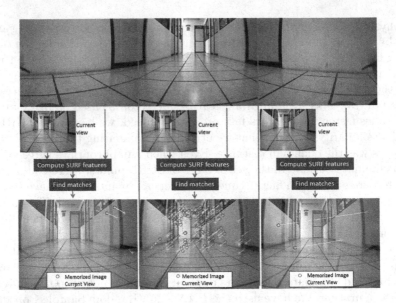

Fig. 2. SURF features are computed for each one of the 3 images in the panoramic stored in memory. Similarly, SURF features are computed in the current view. Best matches are found and possible outliers are eliminated. In this example, the image of the center is considered to be the best match, because it has the highest number of SURF matches

node (marked on the floor) and the actual position of the robot for each path node. We see that the position error is small, some centimeters, in comparison to the path size (several meters) (3).

Subsequently, we have placed new objects along the path in order to evaluate the performance of both methods of autonomous navigation. These objects were placed so that they did not obstruct the way of the learned path. The *NCC* template matching method was unable to reach the goal point. In fact, when the robot approached to the first object, it was unable to determine the correct rotation angle towards the next path node. Figure 4 illustrates this case, where the *NCC* value is higher in a wrong position on the panoramic view.

4.1   Is It a Small Bit of the Scene Enough to Not Getting Lost?

In contrast to the *NCC*-based navigation, in the same experiment with the same new objects along the trajectory, the *SURF*-based navigation method worked correctly and the goal point was reached successfully. We observed that despite the presence of new objects in the scene, a sufficient quantity of SURF matches guarantees the recognition of the scene, and therefore, a successfully navigation towards the goal point is possible. Figure 5 illustrates that when a new object appears in one of the two images to be compared, there are still a sufficient quantity of SURF matches in order to claim that a match exists between the

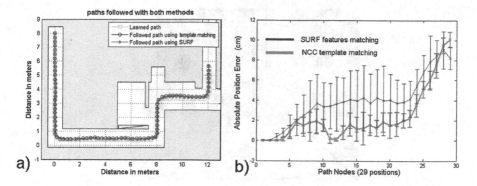

Fig. 3. (a) Two autonomous path trackings. One by using *NCC* template matching (blue) and the other by using SURF features (red). The environmental conditions were the same that those existing during the training stage. (b) Position error average for 5 autonomous navigation rounds using *NCC* template matching and *SURF* features matching. In both cases, vertical segments represent standard deviation (Color figure online).

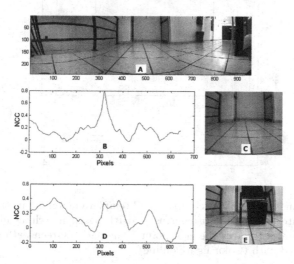

Fig. 4. The presence of a new object in the scene causes a wrong determination of the position of the current view on the panoramic image.

two images. Procrustes analysis gives us the translation distance between both polygons, and that distance is used to calculate the rotation angle of the robot.

Finally, Fig. 6 shows a comparison between the autonomous path tracking of the two methods when new objects were present along the path. We observe that *NCC*-based method was unable to reach the goal point.

Fig. 5. In the approach that uses *SURF*, *RANSAC* and *ProcrustesAnalysis*, we observed that an acceptable number of SURF matches were found always out of the region where the new object lies. This fact ensures that the image can be recognized despite the existence of new objects in the scene.

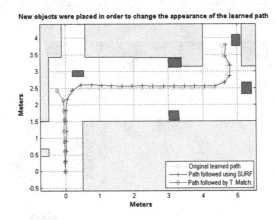

Fig. 6. Two autonomous path trackings. *NCC* template matching method was unable to finish the route (red path). In contrast, SURF-based matching method finished successfully the travel towards the goal point (blue path). Green path corresponds to the original trained path (Color figure online).

5   Conclusions

In this paper, we have described the implementation of a basic autonomous navigation system. Our system is integrated by two software modules: an interface module programmed in Microsoft Visual Basic .Net and a *decisions maker* module programmed in MATLAB. The *decisions maker* module is the heart of our architecture and it is basically a *reactive agent* type function which is iteratively called by a timer control from the interface module. Autonomous path tracking is achieved by the *decisions maker* module by computing a rotation angle that the robot has to move in order to go straight ahead to the next path node. Two approaches for this angle calculation have been proposed for our system.

The first one is based in directly comparing the current view with a panoramic image from a set of stored images captured during the training stage. In this mentioned method, we have selected NCC as a measure for image comparison because its distinctiveness and its robustness to illumination changes. In the second approach, we used SURF features in combination with $RANSAC$ algorithm and Procrustes Analysis in order to compute the rotation angle. Our results show that the NCC matching method is prone to give wrong rotation angles when new objects, absent during the training stage, are present during navigation. In contrast, we found that the proposed approach which uses $SURF$, $RANSAC$ and Procrustes Analysis is tolerant to new objects even if these are as large as one third of the area of the full image. With respect to the position error, we refer the superiority of the NCC-based method over the $SURF$-based one to the inherent tolerance of the SURF features to variations in scale and viewpoint. Nevertheless, and although with a slightly higher position error, we can conclude that the SURF-based method overcomes to the NCC-based approach, because the first one is certainly more robust to appearance changes in the scene. Finally, we estimate that it is possible to improve our results if we take into account the viewpoint differences, i.e., if the implicit linear transformation between the polygon pairs of SURF points in both images is used to correct the position of the robot with respect to the objects in the scene.

References

1. Matsumoto, Y., Inaba, M., Inoue, H.: Visual navigation using view-sequenced route representation. In: Proceedings of the 1996 IEEE International Conference on Robotics and Automation, vol. 1, pp. 83–88. IEEE (1996)
2. Gaspar, J., Winters, N., Santos-Victor, J.: Vision-based navigation and environmental representations with an omnidirectional camera. IEEE Trans. Robot. Autom. **16**, 890–898 (2000)
3. Matsumoto, Y., Sakai, K., Inaba, M., Inoue, H.: View-based approach to robot navigation. In: Proceedings. 2000 IEEE/RSJ International Conference on Intelligent Robots and Systems, (IROS 2000), vol. 3, pp. 1702–1708. IEEE (2000)
4. Zhang, Y., Cao, J., Lou, L., Su, B.: Appearance-based mobile robot navigation using omnidirectional camera. In: 2012 9th International Conference on Fuzzy Systems and Knowledge Discovery (FSKD), pp. 2357–2361. IEEE (2012)
5. Tabuse, M., Nakai, D.: Mobile robot navigation using surf features. ACS **10**, 276–279 (2010)
6. Murillo, A.C., Guerrero, J.J., Sagues, C.: Surf features for efficient robot localization with omnidirectional images. In: 2007 IEEE International Conference on Robotics and Automation, pp. 3901–3907. IEEE (2007)
7. Sharma, K., Jeong, K.y., Kim, S.G.: Vision based autonomous vehicle navigation with self-organizing map feature matching technique. In: 2011 11th International Conference on Control, Automation and Systems (ICCAS), pp. 946–949. IEEE (2011)
8. Wang, H., Mou, W., Ly, M.H., Lau, M.W.S., Seet, G., Wang, D.: Mobile robot ego motion estimation using ransac-based ceiling vision. In: 2012 24th Chinese Control and Decision Conference (CCDC), pp. 1939–1943. IEEE (2012)

9. Booij, O., Terwijn, B., Zivkovic, Z., Krose, B.: Navigation using an appearance based topological map. In: 2007 IEEE International Conference on Robotics and Automation, pp. 3927–3932. IEEE (2007)
10. Tabuse, M., Kitaoka, T., Nakai, D.: Outdoor autonomous navigation using surf features. Artif. Life Robot. **16**, 356–360 (2011)
11. Goedeme, T., Tuytelaars, T., Van Gool, L., Vanacker, G., Nuttin, M.: Feature based omnidirectional sparse visual path following. In: 2005 IEEE/RSJ International Conference on Intelligent Robots and Systems (IROS 2005), pp. 1806–1811 (2005)
12. Lowe, D.G.: Distinctive image features from scale-invariant keypoints. Int. J. Comput. Vis. **60**, 91–110 (2004)
13. Bay, H., Tuytelaars, T., Van Gool, L.: SURF: speeded up robust features. In: Leonardis, A., Bischof, H., Pinz, A. (eds.) ECCV 2006, Part I. LNCS, vol. 3951, pp. 404–417. Springer, Heidelberg (2006)
14. Roland, S., Reza, N.I., Davide, S.: Introduction to autonomous mobile robots. Volume Intelligent robotics and autonomous agents series. MIT Press (2011)
15. Mitchell, T., Labrosse, F.: Visual homing: a purely appearance-based approach. In: University of Essex, pp. 101–108 (2006)
16. Dr Robot Inc.: User manual (2013). http://www.drrobot.com/products/item_downloads/x80sv_1.pdf
17. Dr Robot Inc.: Data sheet (2013). http://www.robotshop.com/media/files/pdf/x80sv-datasheet-x80sv.pdf
18. Fischler, M.A., Bolles, R.C.: Random sample consensus: a paradigm for model fitting with applications to image analysis and automated cartography. Commun. ACM **24**, 381–395 (1981)
19. Ross, A.: Procrustes analysis (2005). http://citeseerx.ist.psu.edu/viewdoc/summary?doi=10.1.1.119.2686

A Comparison of Feature Detectors and Descriptors in RGB-D SLAM Methods

Oguzhan Guclu$^{(\boxtimes)}$ and Ahmet Burak Can

Department of Computer Engineering, Hacettepe University,
Ankara, Turkey
{oguzhanguclu,abc}@hacettepe.edu.tr

Abstract. In RGB-D based SLAM methods, robot motion is generally computed by detecting and matching feature points in image frames obtained from an RGB-D sensor. Thus, feature detectors and descriptors used in a SLAM method significantly affect the performance. In this work, impacts of feature detectors and descriptors on the performance of an RGB-D based SLAM method are studied. SIFT, SURF, BRISK, ORB, FAST, GFTT, STAR feature detectors and SIFT, SURF, BRISK, ORB, BRIEF, FREAK feature descriptors are evaluated in terms of accuracy and speed.

Keywords: SLAM · Feature detector · Feature descriptor

1 Introduction

Simultaneous Localization and Mapping (SLAM) is one of the most fundamental problems in the field of robotics. Determining position in the environment is an important requirement for an autonomous robot. If the robot is in an unknown environment (in other words it does not have map of the environment), it must create map of the environment and determine its position on the map simultaneously. However, position information is needed for creating the map while environment map is needed for obtaining the position information. In this respect, SLAM is similar to chicken and egg problem.

In SLAM systems, laser or sonar range sensor based methods [1–3] are proposed as well as stereo or monocular camera based approaches [4–6]. Estimating the motion of the robot and detecting whether the robot has visited a previously mapped region of the environment (loop closure) are main problems. Solving loop closure problem becomes more difficult in range sensor based methods because only depth information is available. It is possible to develop more successful solutions to the loop closure problem by using color data obtained from the camera. However, operations performed during the transition from 2D to 3D create a serious computational overhead. With the introduction of RGB-D sensors like the Microsoft Kinect, which provide color images and depth maps together in real-time, SLAM approaches using both RGB and depth data have become increasingly popular. By using color and depth data together, more

© Springer International Publishing Switzerland 2015
M. Kamel and A. Campilho (Eds.): ICIAR 2015, LNCS 9164, pp. 297–305, 2015.
DOI: 10.1007/978-3-319-20801-5_32

effective solutions for the loop closure and illumination change problems can be developed.

In SLAM, registration of data frames is an important step to compute the robot's motion. In most SLAM methods, preferred approach for registration is matching feature points detected in image frames. Thus, feature detectors and descriptors have critical importance for SLAM performance. In this work, effects of several feature detectors and descriptors on the accuracy and speed of an RGB-D SLAM method are investigated. The RGB-D SLAM method proposed in [7] is used as a test environment. SIFT [8], SURF [9], BRISK [10], ORB [11], FAST [12], GFTT (*Good Features to Track*) [13], CenSurE based STAR [14] feature detectors and SIFT, SURF, BRISK, ORB, BRIEF [15], FREAK [16] feature descriptors are tested and their effectiveness on the system performance is evaluated.

2   Related Work

Computing the robot's motion and building map with an RGB-D camera is a new research area. Henry et al. [17] developed a SLAM method that uses visual features and shape based alignment together. SIFT feature points are detected in RGB frames and associated with depth data. Then the transformation between matched features is calculated using RANSAC [18] and the set of feature pairs that produce best transformation is obtained. ICP algorithm [19] is applied to minimize odometry error by initialization with the transformation found by RANSAC. In loop closure detection step, RANSAC transformation between related frames is calculated and count of inliers is needed to exceed a predefined threshold. After each loop closure detection, optimization is performed on the graph with TORO [20]. In [21], Henry et al. use FAST detector with Calonder descriptor [22] in their previous approach and improve system performance. When calculating the transformation between frames, ICP algorithm is not applied if inlier count after RANSAC exceeds a threshold. *Sparse Bundle Adjustment* [23] is used for graph optimization. Endres et al. [24] use SIFT, ORB and SURF for feature detection. They calculate transformation with RANSAC and apply *g2o* [25] for graph optimization. Fioraio and Konolige [26] use color and depth features together to perform global adjustment as well as frame registration. Also the effect of noise is reduced by subsampling depth images. *g2o* is preferred for optimization.

3   Method

One of the most popular solutions for SLAM is the graph based approach. Nodes of the graph contain robot positions in time and edges hold constraints between positions connected [27]. In this approach, SLAM problem is described as a least squares optimization of an error function in a graph [25]. For minimizing error, optimization is performed on this graph structure and the most probable values for the robot positions are determined.

In this paper, graph based RGB-D SLAM method of Endres et al. [7] is used. In this method, feature points in RGB frames are detected and descriptor vectors are constructed. 3D coordinates of each feature point are calculated by using depth data in the related depth frame. After matching feature points, transformation between frames is calculated from 3D point correspondences via RANSAC for computing motion. For each new frame from the RGB-D sensor, if a valid transformation can be calculated with candidate frames, an edge is added to the graph between the related nodes. Candidate frames are divided into 3 different groups. First group is the n frames preceding the current frame. Second group consists of k frames chosen from the neighborhood of the previous frame in the graph (candidates in the first group are not considered). Third group contains l frames chosen from keyframes. The candidates in the second and third groups are used for loop closure detection. In this way, the graph grows with the addition of new nodes and edges by arrival of frames from the sensor. $g2o$ method is used for graph optimization. The edges having higher error values than a certain level are pruned. The positions during the movement of the robot are computed to determine the trajectory. Map of the environment is created by combining observations of each position in a common coordinate system.

In this study, effects of feature detectors and descriptors on SLAM performance are studied. SIFT, SURF, BRISK, ORB, FAST, GFTT, GFTT_HARRIS (GFTT with Harris detector [28] enabled) and STAR are used as feature detectors. BRIEF and FREAK feature descriptors are tested with all detectors. SIFT, SURF, BRISK and ORB descriptors are also tested with their own detectors.

4   Experiments and Evaluation

In the experiments, *TUM RGB-D benchmark* [29] dataset and its error metric are used. The dataset contains RGB and depth frames recorded with an RGB-D camera and ground truth camera trajectory obtained with a motion capture system. 9 sequences of the *fr1* dataset containing scenes of an office environment are chosen for the experiments. *Absolute Trajectory Error* (ATE) metric is used for performance evaluation. This error metric represents difference between the ground truth and the estimated trajectory. The experiments are performed on a PC running Ubuntu 12.04 with Intel Core i7-2600 3.40GHz CPU, 8GB RAM and NVIDIA GeForce GTX 550 Ti graphics card. *OpenCV* implementations of the feature detectors and descriptors are used in the experiments.

The maximum number of feature points extracted from a frame is set to 700. The number of RANSAC iterations for the transformation calculation is chosen as 250. These parameters are determined after doing several experiments and observing the results. Candidate frame parameters n, k and l are assigned to equal values of 4, 8, or 12. Thus the candidate value of 4 means that $n = k = l = 4$. The optimization is performed after processing of all data frames. While matching feature points, *Bruteforce-Hamming* method is used for binary descriptors (BRISK, ORB, BRIEF and FREAK) and *FLANN* method is used for floating point descriptors (SIFT and SURF).

Table 1. Accuracy (root mean square error of ATE) results for *fr1* dataset

Feature detector	Feature descriptor	Cand.=4	Cand.=8	Cand.=12	Average
BRISK	BRIEF	0,0461 m	0,0491 m	0,0381 m	0,0444 m
BRISK	FREAK	0,0559 m	0,0430 m	0,0411 m	0,0467 m
BRISK	BRISK	0,0502 m	0,0464 m	0,0460 m	0,0475 m
FAST	BRIEF	0,0680 m	0,0587 m	0,0567 m	0,0611 m
FAST	FREAK	0,0832 m	0,0629 m	0,0584 m	0,0682 m
GFTT	BRIEF	0,0402 m	0,0377 m	0,0383 m	0,0387 m
GFTT	FREAK	0,0396 m	0,0380 m	0,0373 m	0,0383 m
GFTT_HARRIS	BRIEF	0,0404 m	0,0390 m	0,0387 m	0,0394 m
GFTT_HARRIS	FREAK	0,0399 m	0,0392 m	0,0376 m	0,0389 m
ORB	BRIEF	0,1081 m	0,1134 m	0,0824 m	0,1013 m
ORB	FREAK	0,2614 m	0,2181 m	0,2329 m	0,2375 m
ORB	ORB	0,1630 m	0,1601 m	0,1058 m	0,1430 m
SIFT	BRIEF	0,0551 m	0,0521 m	0,0515 m	0,0529 m
SIFT	FREAK	0,0459 m	0,0472 m	0,0436 m	0,0456 m
SIFT	SIFT	0,0426 m	0,0387 m	**0,0372 m**	0,0395 m
STAR	BRIEF	0,0460 m	0,0383 m	0,0381 m	0,0408 m
STAR	FREAK	**0,0395 m**	**0,0365 m**	0,0377 m	**0,0379 m**
SURF	BRIEF	0,0490 m	0,0405 m	0,0396 m	0,0430 m
SURF	FREAK	0,0526 m	0,0492 m	0,0497 m	0,0505 m
SURF	SURF	0,0409 m	0,0389 m	0,0385 m	0,0394 m
Average		0,0684 m	0,0624 m	0,0575 m	0,0627 m

Accuracy results of all test combinations are given in Table 1. Accuracy is expressed as root mean square of ATE. Smaller value means more precise trajectory estimation. STAR+FREAK combination has the best results on average with 3,79 cm root mean square of ATE. Although STAR+FREAK is the most successful choice for 4 and 8 candidates, SIFT+SIFT is the most successful for 12 candidates. GFTT+FREAK and GFTT+BRIEF combinations also have close performance to STAR+FREAK combination in average results. Error rates of the most successful 6 combinations for 9 sequences in *fr1* dataset are analyzed in Fig. 1. Sequences containing loops, such as *360*, *plant*, *room*, and *teddy*, generally produce higher error values except *floor* sequence. The error value for *floor* sequence is relatively lower since camera movements are more stable and angular velocity is low. Ground truths and estimated trajectories for *desk* and *plant* sequences with STAR+FREAK and candidate value of 8 are given in Fig. 2. The estimated trajectory for the *desk* sequence is very close to the ground truth. However, deviation between the ground truth and the estimated trajectory for *plant* sequence is more notable due to the larger error rate.

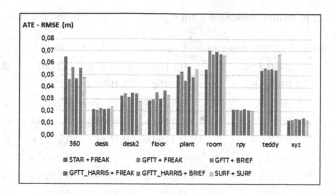

Fig. 1. Detailed error rates of the best 6 combinations for 9 sequences in *fr1* dataset (Average of 4, 8 and 12 candidate value results)

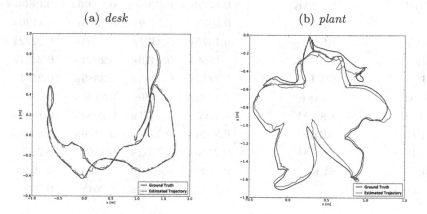

Fig. 2. x-y plane projections of ground truth and estimated trajectory for *desk* and *plant* sequences with STAR+FREAK (Candidate=8)

Besides accuracy, computational complexity is important in SLAM applications. Table 2 shows runtime results of all tested cases. The time spent for optimization is considered when calculating processing time per frame. The fastest method on average is ORB+FREAK with 0,0866 seconds per frame. In our experiments, ORB is the fastest feature detector with all descriptors but its accuracy is worst as it can be seen in Table 1. When accuracy and speed are evaluated together, the most appropriate option is STAR+FREAK with 3,79 cm error and 0,1657 s processing time on average. GFTT+FREAK and GFTT+BRIEF seem to be next best options after STAR+FREAK. Enabling Harris detector with GFTT provides an increase in speed but the error rate grows. Processing time increases with larger candidate values because more frames are compared for loop closure detection. However, larger values of candidates in the loop closure detection generally reduce the error rate as it can be seen in Table 1. On the other hand, accuracy of the system may decrease in some cases, such as

Table 2. Runtime (processing time per frame) results for *fr1* dataset

Feature detector	Feature descriptor	Cand.=4	Cand.=8	Cand.=12	Average
BRISK	BRIEF	0,1182 s	0,1775 s	0,2120 s	0,1692 s
BRISK	FREAK	0,1253 s	0,1902 s	0,2365 s	0,1840 s
BRISK	BRISK	0,1258 s	0,1917 s	0,2567 s	0,1914s
FAST	BRIEF	0,1194 s	0,1806 s	0,1960 s	0,1653 s
FAST	FREAK	0,1194 s	0,1687 s	0,2551 s	0,1811 s
GFTT	BRIEF	0,1354 s	0,1926 s	0,2460 s	0,1913 s
GFTT	FREAK	0,1301 s	0,2132 s	0,2825 s	0,2086 s
GFTT_HARRIS	BRIEF	0,1315 s	0,1762 s	0,2233 s	0,1770 s
GFTT_HARRIS	FREAK	0,1296 s	0,2100 s	0,2757 s	0,2051 s
ORB	BRIEF	0,0915s	0,1193 s	0,1210 s	0,1106 s
ORB	FREAK	**0,0836 s**	**0,0867 s**	**0,0895 s**	**0,0866 s**
ORB	ORB	0,0955 s	0,1089 s	0,1315 s	0,1120 s
SIFT	BRIEF	0,1875 s	0,2337 s	0,2603 s	0,2272 s
SIFT	FREAK	0,1865 s	0,2310 s	0,2909 s	0,2361 s
SIFT	SIFT	0,2815 s	0,3343 s	0,3385 s	0,3181 s
STAR	BRIEF	0,1242 s	0,1680 s	0,2195 s	0,1706 s
STAR	FREAK	0,1205 s	0,1671 s	0,2094 s	0,1657 s
SURF	BRIEF	0,2524 s	0,2941 s	0,3126 s	0,2864 s
SURF	FREAK	0,2360 s	0,2752 s	0,3196 s	0,2769 s
SURF	SURF	0,4349 s	0,4986 s	0,5584 s	0,4973 s
Average		0,1614s	0,2109 s	0,2518 s	0,2080 s

STAR+FREAK, SURF+FREAK, GFTT+BRIEF, etc. This problem may happen due to false detection of loop closures while examining more candidates. In Fig. 3, processing times of the most successful 6 combinations for 9 sequences are given in detail. Except *xyz* and *rpy* sequences, the results are generally close to each other. *xyz* and *rpy* sequences consist of simple and small scale camera movements. Therefore, the number of candidate frames that a valid transformation can be calculated for each new frame increases faster comparing to other sequences. Thus the number of edges added to the graph grows faster and computation time increases for each frame.

BRIEF and FREAK descriptors are tested with all detectors in the experiments. Considering the results in Table 1, BRIEF produces 5,27 cm average error on 8 different combinations while FREAK produces 7,04 cm. According to the runtime results, 0,1872 s are spent for each frame with BRIEF and 0,1930 s with FREAK on average. When BRIEF and FREAK are used with SIFT, SURF, BRISK and ORB detectors, which have their own descriptors, processing time generally decreases. On the other hand, when SIFT and SURF detectors are used with their proposed descriptors, more accurate results are obtained.

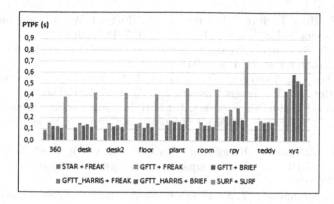

Fig. 3. Frame processing times of the best 6 combinations for 9 sequences in *fr1* dataset (Average of 4, 8, and 12 candidate value results)

5   Conclusion

In this study, effects of various feature detectors and descriptors on performance of an RGB-D SLAM method are analyzed in terms of accuracy and speed. When considering both accuracy and speed, the most efficient option is STAR+FREAK combination with 3,79 cm error and 0,1657 s processing time per frame on average. The best results in terms of speed are reached with ORB+FREAK combination. Experiments have shown that feature detector and feature descriptor selections are important in SLAM performance. The factors such as detecting few feature points in the frame, sudden change of the light level in the environment and noise level of the frame effect performance adversely. Fast movement of the camera and vibration cause to blurring problems and increase error rate. As a future work, filtering techniques can be studied to improve the quality of feature detection and matching.

References

1. Thrun, S., Burgard, W., Fox, D.: A real-time algorithm for mobile robot mapping with applications to multi-robot and 3D mapping. IEEE Int. Conf. Robot. Autom. (ICRA) **1**, 321–328 (2000)
2. Triebel, R., Burgard, W.: Improving simultaneous mapping and localization in 3D using global constraints. Natl. Conf. Artif. Intell. **3**, 1330–1335 (2005)
3. Kang, J.G., An, S.Y., Kim, S., Oh, S.Y.: Sonar based simultaneous localization and mapping using a neuro evolutionary optimization. In: International Joint Conference on Neural Networks, pp. 1516–1523 (2009)
4. Konolige, K., Agrawal, M.: FrameSLAM: from bundle adjustment to real-time visual mapping. IEEE Trans. Robot. **24**(5), 1066–1077 (2008)
5. Clemente, L., Davison, A., Reid, I., Neira, J., Tardos, J.: Mapping large loops with a single hand-held camera. Robotics: Science and Systems (RSS) (2007)
6. Davison, A.: Real-time simultaneous localisation and mapping with a single camera. IEEE Int. Conf. Comput. Vis. **2**, 1403–1410 (2003)

7. Endres, F., Hess, J., Sturm, J., Cremers, D., Burgard, W.: 3-D mapping with an RGB-D camera. IEEE Trans. Robot. **30**(1), 177–187 (2014)
8. Lowe, D.: Discriminative image features from scale-invariant keypoints. Int. J. Comput. Vision **60**(2), 91–110 (2004)
9. Bay, H., Ess, A., Tuytelaars, T., Van Gool, L.: Speeded-Up Robust Features (SURF). Comput. Vis. Image Underst. **110**(3), 346–359 (2008)
10. Leutenegger, S., Chli, M., Siegwart, R.: BRISK: binary robust invariant scalable keypoints. In: IEEE International Conference on Computer Vision, pp. 2548–2555 (2011)
11. Rublee, E., Rabaud, V., Konolige, K., Bradski, G.: ORB: an efficient alternative to SIFT or SURF. In: IEEE International Conference on Computer Vision, pp. 2564–2571 (2011)
12. Rosten, E., Drummond, T.W.: Machine learning for high-speed corner detection. In: Leonardis, A., Bischof, H., Pinz, A. (eds.) ECCV 2006, Part I. LNCS, vol. 3951, pp. 430–443. Springer, Heidelberg (2006)
13. Shi, J., Tomasi, C.: Good features to track. In: IEEE Computer Society Conference on Computer Vision and Pattern Recognition, pp. 593–600 (1994)
14. Agrawal, M., Konolige, K., Blas, M.R.: CenSurE: center surround extremas for realtime feature detection and matching. In: Forsyth, D., Torr, P., Zisserman, A. (eds.) ECCV 2008, Part IV. LNCS, vol. 5305, pp. 102–115. Springer, Heidelberg (2008)
15. Calonder, M., Lepetit, V., Strecha, C., Fua, P.: BRIEF: binary robust independent elementary features. In: Daniilidis, K., Maragos, P., Paragios, N. (eds.) ECCV 2010, Part IV. LNCS, vol. 6314, pp. 778–792. Springer, Heidelberg (2010)
16. Alahi, A., Ortiz, R., Vandergheynst, P.: FREAK: fast retina keypoint. In: IEEE Computer Society Conference on Computer Vision and Pattern Recognition, pp. 510–517 (2012)
17. Henry, P., Krainin, M., Herbst, E., Ren, X., Fox, D.: RGB-D mapping: using depth cameras for dense 3D modeling of indoor environments. In: 12th International Symposium on Experimental Robotics (ISER) (2010)
18. Fischler, M.A., Bolles, R.C.: Random sample consensus: a paradigm for model fitting with applications to image analysis and automated cartography. Commun. ACM **24**(6), 381–395 (1981)
19. Segal, A., Haehnel, D., Thrun, S.: Generalized-ICP. Robotics: Science and Systems (RSS) (2009)
20. Grisetti, G., Grzonka, S., Stachniss, C., Pfaff, P., Burgard, W.: Efficient estimation of accurate maximum likelihood maps in 3D. In: IEEE International Conference on Intelligent Robots and Systems, pp. 3472–3478 (2007)
21. Henry, P., Krainin, M., Herbst, E., Ren, X., Fox, D.: RGB-D mapping: using kinect-style depth cameras for dense 3D modeling of indoor environments. Int. J. Robot. Res. **31**(5), 647–663 (2012)
22. Calonder, M., Lepetit, V., Fua, P.: Keypoint signatures for fast learning and recognition. In: Forsyth, D., Torr, P., Zisserman, A. (eds.) ECCV 2008, Part I. LNCS, vol. 5302, pp. 58–71. Springer, Heidelberg (2008)
23. Konolige, K.: Sparse sparse bundle adjustment. In: British Machine Vision Conference (BMVC) (2010)
24. Endres, F., Hess, J., Engelhard, N., Sturm, J., Cremers, D., Burgard, W.: An evaluation of the RGB-D SLAM system. In: IEEE International Conference on Robotics and Automation, pp. 1691–1696 (2012)

25. Kummerle, R., Grisetti, G., Strasdat, H., Konolige, K., Burgard, W.: g2o: a general framework for graph optimization. In: IEEE International Conference on Robotics and Automation (2011)
26. Fioraio, N., Konolige, K.: Realtime visual and point cloud slam. In: RGB-D Workshop on Advanced Reasoning with Depth Cameras at Robotics: Science and Systems (RSS) (2011)
27. Grisetti, G., Kummerle, R., Stachniss, C., Burgard, W.: A tutorial on graph-based SLAM. IEEE Intell. Transp. Syst. Mag. 2(4), 31–43 (2010)
28. Harris, C., Stephens, M.: A combined corner and edge detector. In: Alvey Vision Conference (1988)
29. Sturm, J., Engelhard, N., Endres, F., Burgard, W., Cremers, D.: A benchmark for the evaluation of RGB-D slam systems. In: IEEE International Conference on Intelligent Robots and Systems, pp. 573–580 (2012)

Accuracy Improvement for Depth from Small Irregular Camera Motions and Its Performance Evaluation

Syouta Tsukada, Yishin Ho, Norio Tagawa$^{(\boxtimes)}$, and Kan Okubo

Graduate School of System Design, Tokyo Metropolitan University,
Hino, Tokyo 191-0065, Japan
tagawa@tmu.ac.jp
http://www.comp.sd.tmu.ac.jp/t-lab/tagawalab/home/Welcome.html

Abstract. We have proposed three-dimensional recovery methods using random camera rotations imitating involuntary eye movements of a human eyeball. Those methods are roughly classified into two types. One is a differential-type using temporal changes of image intensity, and is suitable for coarse textured images relative to the amplitude of the image motion. Another is an integral-type using image blur caused by the camera motions, and is proposed for fine textured images. In this study, we focus on the differential-type method. In this method, it is important that unsuited image pairs for the gradient equation should not be used for computing. We attempt to improve the accuracy by selecting suitable image pairs at each pixel and using only those to recover a depth map. Additionally, we evaluate the performance of the improved method by actually implementing the camera system which can capture images with performing small irregular rotations.

Keywords: Shape from motion · Gradient method · Random camera motions · Fixational eye movements

1 Introduction

Recently, in the field of computer vision, depth reconstruction has gotten high accuracy and a binocular stereopsis [1] has become a mainstream. By the usual binocular stereopsis, we can get relatively large disparities, which enables high accurate depth reconstruction. However, exact point correspondences between two images is difficult, and additionally, occlusions may often occur. To solve these problems, a huge number of studies have been carried out. We focus on a motion stereo vision, i.e. a monocular stereopsis, in which these problems are not severe as compared with a binocular stereo. In a motion stereo vision, to recover a dense depth map with less computations, the analytic solution using spatiotemporal differentials of image intensity called the gradient method has attracted attention. The gradient method is effective for a small motion parallax between two successive images, therefore it cannot get high accurate reconstruction in

© Springer International Publishing Switzerland 2015
M. Kamel and A. Campilho (Eds.): ICIAR 2015, LNCS 9164, pp. 306–315, 2015.
DOI: 10.1007/978-3-319-20801-5_33

general. Accordingly, we expect to increase depth information for each pixel, i.e. each three-dimensional (3-D) point on a target object.

On the other hand, the human vision system has unconscious irregular eye movements called fixational eye movements [2]. Fixational eye movements consist of three components; the drift moving gradually toward a certain direction, the microsaccade generating momentarily a large movement and the tremor indicating random and small vibrations. Because the tremor covers only a small number of visual cells of a retina and hence, it can acquire depth information of the same 3-D point approximately without point tracking on a retina, we have picked up the tremor so far. When we rotate a camera randomly by imitating the rotations of a human eyeball, translational motions occur at the lens center, which enables depth recovery as a motion stereo vision.

Using such an imaging system imitating the tremor, we can use many image pairs obtained simultaneously by the random camera rotations, and already proposed the algorithms based on the gradient method [3,4]. For processing multiple image pairs simultaneously, we constructed the direct method in which depth is defined as a common variable explicitly instead of optical flow regarded as a variable in many gradient based methods [5–7]. The gradient equation, which is a fundamental equation in the gradient method, is defined as a first-order approximation of the invariant constraint of image intensity before and after the camera motion. The equation indicates the relation between spatiotemporal differentials of image intensity and optical flow. Since the effectiveness of the gradient equation highly depends on the adaptability of the first-order approximation, in the case when the optical flow is greatly large as compared with the spatial wavelength of the image intensity, the error in the depth reconstruction can be regarded as a result of the aliases of the optical flow, which are not detected explicitly. Therefore, to improve the accuracy we propose a strategy that only the suitable image pairs expected to have little approximation error are used to recover the depth. In this study, we implement the proposed camera system and carry out the calibration of it [8]. Using this system, we confirm the performance of the proposed method for selecting suitable image pairs and acquire the useful results leading future studies.

The proposed imaging system having random camera rotations is expected to be used to improve the performance of a binocular stereopsis. In a future system which we plan, both camera systems in a binocular stereopsis firstly detect a rough depth map respectively or cooperatively using random camera rotations, which accuracy is not so high but is hard to be affected by occlusions. Using the detected rough depth map, the stereo matching can be done stably with avoiding occlusions. In addition, the rough depth map can be used as a feature amount for the stereo matching together with intensity information.

2   Camera Model Imitating Tremor

In this study, we assume the perspective projection. A camera is fixed in the (X, Y, Z) coordinate system, shown in Fig. 1, and we set the lens center of the

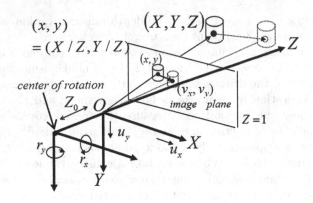

Fig. 1. Camera motion and image projection model.

camera at the origin O, the optical axis along Z axis, the camera focus length as $f = 1$, and the image plane as $Z = 1$. A 3-D vector $X = [X, Y, Z]^T$ indicating a 3-D point on an object is projected onto a point $(x, y, 1)$ in the image using a homogeneous coordinate. We show the camera motion model also in Fig. 1. The translational velocity vector $u = [u_x, u_y, u_z]^T$ and the rotational velocity vector $r = [r_x, r_y, r_z]^T$ are indicated. Optical flow at each pixel satisfies the following equations.

$$v_x = xyr_x - (1 + x^2)r_y + yr_z - (u_x - xu_z)d, \tag{1}$$

$$v_y = (1 + y^2)r_x - xyr_y - xr_z - (u_y - yu_z)d, \tag{2}$$

where d is an inverse of Z, and is unknown at each pixel. On the other hand, (u, r) are unknown parameters for a whole image. On the analogy of a human eyeball, we can set a camera's rotation center at the back of a lens center with Z_0 along an optical axis, and we assume that there is no explicit translational motions of a camera. This rotation with the rotational velocity vector r can also be represented using the coordinate origin as its rotation center with the same rotational vector. On the other hand, this difference between the origin and the rotation center causes a translational velocity vector u implicitly, and is formulated as follows:

$$u = r \times \begin{bmatrix} 0 \\ 0 \\ Z_0 \end{bmatrix} = Z_0 \begin{bmatrix} r_y \\ -r_x \\ 0 \end{bmatrix}. \tag{3}$$

Using this representation, we can formulate optical flow specially for the tremor-like camera motions as follows:

$$v_x = xyr_x - (1 + x^2)r_y - Z_0 r_y d \equiv v_x^r - r_y Z_0 d, \tag{4}$$

$$v_y = (1 + y^2)r_x - xyr_y + Z_0 r_x d \equiv v_y^r + r_x Z_0 d. \tag{5}$$

3 Outline of Depth Recovery Method Using Tremor

We represent image intensity as $f(x, y, t)$, and a first-order approximation of the intensity invariant constraint before and after the camera motion is derived as follows and is called the gradient equation.

$$f_t = -f_x v_x - f_y v_y, \tag{6}$$

where f_t, f_x, f_y are the partial derivatives of f. By substituting Eqs. 4 and 5 into Eq. 6, the gradient equation for rigid motion can be formulated as follows:

$$f_t = -(f_x v_x^r + f_y v_y^r) - (-f_x r_y + f_y r_x) Z_0 d \equiv -f^r - f^u d. \tag{7}$$

Usual gradient method firstly detects optical flow, and next depth is recovered from the detected optical flow. However, to use multiple image pairs simultaneously and efficiently, depth should be defined as a common variable for all images.

We model that $f_t^{(i,j)}$ includes the observation error according to the normal distribution with an average of 0 and a variance of σ_o^2. The pixel position and the frame number are indicated by i and j respectively. In addition, we assume that $r^{(j)}$ is a sample of the 2-D normal distribution with an average of $\mathbf{0}$ and a variance of σ_r^2. Using these probabilistic models, the joint probability of $\{f_t^{(i,j)}\}$ and $\{r^{(j)}\}$ is given as follows, where $\Theta = \{\sigma_o^2, \sigma_r^2\}$ is unknown parameters.

$$p(\{f_t^{(i,j)}\}, \{r^{(j)}\}|\Theta) = \prod_{i=1}^{N} \prod_{j=1}^{M} p(f_t^{(i,j)}|d^{(i)}, r^{(j)}, \sigma_o^2) \prod_{j=1}^{M} p(r^{(j)}|\sigma_r^2)$$

$$= \frac{1}{2\pi^{M(N+1)/2} \sigma_o^{MN} \sigma_r^{2M}} \exp \left\{ -\frac{\sum_{i=1}^{N} \sum_{j=1}^{M} \left(f_t^{(i,j)} + f^{r(i,j)} + f^{u(i,j)} d^{(i)} \right)^2}{2\sigma_o^2} \right.$$

$$\left. -\frac{\sum_{j=1}^{M} r^{(j)\top} r^{(j)}}{2\sigma_r^2} \right\}, \tag{8}$$

where $i = 1, \cdots, N$ and $j = 1, \cdots, M$.

In this study, we use many frames vibrating caused by the random camera rotations, therefore the detected depth should be considered as the average value of the neighboring local area, namely, $d^{(i)}$ has a local correlation as a result. The spatial extension of this correlation also depends on the value of depth, but now, for simplification, we use the prior probability as the next formula.

$$p(d|\sigma_d^2) = \frac{1}{(\sqrt{2\pi}\sigma_d)^N} \exp \left\{ -\frac{d^\top L d}{2\sigma_d^2} \right\}, \tag{9}$$

where d is an N-dimensional vector composed of $\{d^{(i)}\}$ and L indicates the matrix corresponding to the N-dimensional Laplacian operator under a free boundary condition. The variance-covariance matrix of the prior probability is $\sigma_d^2 L^{-1}$, which models succinctly a smooth depth map because of $d^\top L d = \|Dd\|^2$ with a first order differential operator D. σ_d^2 is a control parameter for the depth

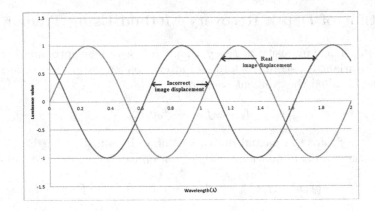

Fig. 2. Illustration of alias using profiles of image intensity of successive image pairs.

smoothness, which is treated as a known value in this method. Based on the above models, we can determine $\{\sigma_o^2, \sigma_r^2\}$ as a maximum likelihood estimate and d and $\{r^{(j)}\}$ are a MAP estimate. To do those stably, we can apply the EM scheme [9], especially the One-Step-Late (OSL)-MAP-EM algorithm [10].

4   Proposed Technique for Accurate Depth Recovery

4.1   Alias in Optical Flow Detection

Aliases are the state caused by a low sampling rate against the maximum frequency of a signal. In our problem, when the image motion is large comparing with the spatial length of image intensity pattern, the direction of the implicitly detected optical flow is opposite to the true direction and causes a large recovery error of depth. We illustrate the example of the image intensity profiles of two successive images, when alias occurs in Fig. 2.

In this figure, the red sine wave has moved toward the right direction from the position shown as the blue sine wave. Since the displacement is larger than $\lambda/2$, where λ means the wavelength of a signal, by the human perception and many methods for detecting optical flow, the incorrect motion directed to the left side is obtained. To avoid such a mistake, the displacement, i.e. the amplitude of optical flow should be sufficiently smaller that $\lambda/2$.

4.2   Selective Use of Image Pairs to Improve Accuracy

As we can use many image pairs for each pixel, we propose a scheme that at each pixel we exclude the gradient equations, i.e. the successive image pairs, having a large approximation error at each pixel. M means the number of images given according to the random camera rotations. An inner product of the spatial gradient vectors of two successive images can be used to select the image pairs causing no alias problems. For each pixel, the image pairs of which the sign of the inner product $\boldsymbol{f}_s^{(i,j)\top} \boldsymbol{f}_s^{(i,j-1)}$ is negative are discarded. It is noted that $\boldsymbol{f}_s^{(i,j)} = [f_x^{(i,j)}, f_y^{(i,j)}]^\top$.

In the next step, from the image pairs remained by the above decision, we additively select the good image pairs for each pixel by estimating the amount of the nonlinear terms included in the observation of f_t. f_t is exactly represented as follows:

$$f_t = -f_x v_x - f_y v_y - \frac{1}{2}\left\{f_{xx}v_x^2 + f_{yy}v_y^2 + 2f_{xy}v_x v_y\right\} + \cdots . \tag{10}$$

After discarding the wrong image pairs, the nonlinear term can be considered small, and in this case the second-order term in Eq. 10 can be estimated at each pixel i as follows:

$$-\frac{1}{2}\left\{(f_x^{(i,j)} - f_x^{(i,j-1)})v_x^{(i,j)} + (f_y^{(i,j)} - f_y^{(i,j-1)})v_y^{(i,j)}\right\}. \tag{11}$$

Spontaneously, we can define the measures as a ratio for the amount of the first-order term for estimating the amount of the equation error.

$$J = \frac{|(f_x^{(i,j)} - f_x^{(i,j-1)})v_x^{(i,j)} + (f_y^{(i,j)} - f_y^{(i,j-1)})v_y^{(i,j)}|}{2|f_x^{(i,j)}v_x^{(i,j)} + f_y^{(i,j)}v_y^{(i,j)}|}. \tag{12}$$

This measure depends on the direction of optical flow but is invariant with respect to the amplitude of optical flow. To use J for estimating the equation error, the true value of optical flow is required to be known. By examining the details of J, even if the difference of the spatial gradient $\boldsymbol{f}_s^{(i,j)} - \boldsymbol{f}_s^{(i,j-1)}$ is large, when the direction of $\boldsymbol{f}_s^{(i,j)} - \boldsymbol{f}_s^{(i,j-1)}$ is perpendicular to that of optical flow, the equation error becomes small. Hence, the value $|\boldsymbol{f}_s^{(i,j)} - \boldsymbol{f}_s^{(i,j-1)}|/|\boldsymbol{f}_s^{(i,j)}|$ can be used as a worst value. In this study, the image pairs for which $|\boldsymbol{f}_s^{(i,j)} - \boldsymbol{f}_s^{(i,j-1)}|/|\boldsymbol{f}_s^{(i,j)}|$ is less than the certain threshold value are selected at each pixel to be used for depth recovery.

5   Performance Evaluation Through Experiments

5.1   Implementation of Camera System

From the past, we have variously improved the depth recovery method based on the camera rotations imitating fixational eye movements through many simulations. Therefore, we attempted to build the camera hardware system for examining the practical performance of our camera model shown in Fig. 1. The implemented camera system which we use in the experiments of this study is shown in Fig. 3(a), and the monitor image of the control software is shown in Fig. 3(b).

The camera system can be rotated around the horizontal axis i.e. X-axis and around the vertical axis, i.e. Y-axis. The rotation around the optical direction, i.e. Z direction, cannot be performed, which is not needed to obtain the depth information. The parameters of the system are shown as follows:

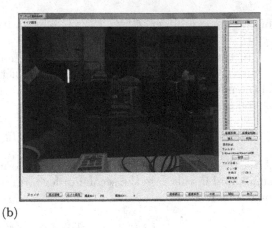

(a)   (b)

Fig. 3. Experiment system: (a) camera system implemented for tremor rotations, (b) monitoring display of software to control camera rotation and capture images.

- Focal length: 2.8 − 5.0 mm
- Image size : 2 million (1200 × 1600) pix.
- Movable width : X-axis 360 deg., Y-axis $(−10, +10)$ deg.
- Drivable minimum unit : X-axis : 1 pulse = 0.01 deg. , Y-axis : 1 pulse = 0.00067 deg.

The 1st and 2nd columns shown in the right side in Fig. 3(b) are the sections to input the rotation values around X-axis and Y-axis respectively. These data can be input by manual operation or loaded from data files by the control software, and then the camera moves according to them. For each rotation angle, an image can be captured continuously.

5.2   Experiments

We refer to the results of the experiments using the real images captured by the developed camera system. Our camera system has the parallel stereo function, namely the camera can move laterally by a slide system. Before experiments, the system was calibrated by the method in [8] and the stereo vision. The images are gray scale and consist of 256×256 pixels with 8 bit digitization. An example is shown in Fig. 4(a). The true inverse depth of the target object is shown in Fig. 4(b). In this figure, the horizontal axis indicates the position in the image plane, and the vertical axis indicates the inverse depth using a focal length as a unit. We captured 100 images. The maximum repetition number of the MAP-EM algorithm was set as 600, within which almost iterations converges. In addition, we determined σ_d^2 heuristically. The average value of $|f_s^{(i,j)} - f_s^{(i,j-1)}|/|f_s^{(i,j)}|$ explained in the previous section with respect to all pixels was defined for each image pair as a standard magnification ($\times 1$) of the threshold for each image pair to select the suitable image pairs for each pixel. Namely, by decreasing the threshold magnification, we can discard more image pairs. Conversely, by increasing

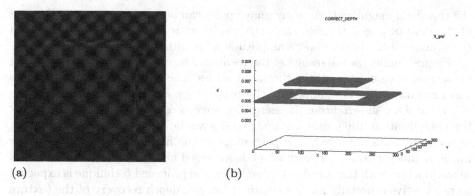

Fig. 4. Data for experiments: (a) example of captured image, (b) true inverse depth of object.

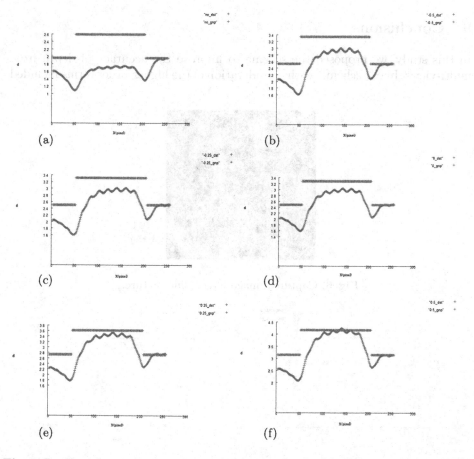

Fig. 5. Profiles of cross-section of recovered inverse depth: (a) all image pairs are used (100%), (b) threshold ×1.5(94% image pairs were used), (c) threshold ×1.25(86%), (d) threshold ×1(68%), (e) threshold ×0.75(62%), (f) threshold ×0.5(62%).

the threshold magnification, many image pairs can be used for recovery. Because of the limit of pages, we only show the results with $\sigma_r^2 = 2.64 \times 10^{-2}$ by which the average of the optical flow's amplitude approximately coincides with $\lambda/4$.

Figure 5 indicates the results of the recovered inverse depth as a cross section for several magnification of the threshold values. The result using all image pairs was examined also. For simplicity, the profile views of the cross-section of the recovered d are shown. From theses results, we can confirmed that by decreasing the magnification, the unsuitable image pairs can be discarded and the accuracy of the recovery is improved. The percentage in the figure captions indicates the image number used for recovery which is averaged about all pixels and is varied in conjunction with the threshold value. Since the proposed technique is expected to be effective especially for fine textured images, depth recovery of the texture shown in Fig. 6 was also carried out. The results under the same condition of Fig. 5 are shown in Fig. 7.

6   Conclusions

In this study, we proposed the scheme to improve the accuracy of depth from multi-views. In our scheme, with consideration of the higher-order terms included

Fig. 6. Captured image having fine texture.

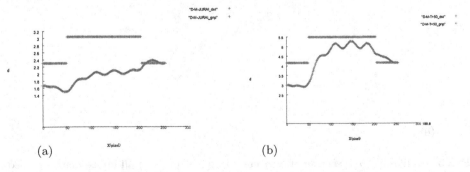

(a)   (b)

Fig. 7. Profiles of cross-section of recovered inverse depth for fine image: (a) all image pairs are used (100 %), (b) threshold ×1.5(45 % image pairs were used).

in the observed temporal differentials, we selected the image pairs having less higher-order terms using the difference of the spatial gradient of the image intensity between two successive images as an estimate. Through the real image experiments using the developed camera system, we confirmed that our scheme is effective for the accuracy. We will perform more actual experiments using objects having general textures and shapes. In the future, we are going to develop the binocular stereo system each camera of which has the function proposed in this study to obtain high performance.

References

1. Lazaros, N., Sirakoulis, G.C., Gasteratos, A.: Review of stereo vision algorithm: from software to hardware. Int. J. Optomechatronics 5(4), 435–462 (2008)
2. Martinez-Conde, S., Macknik, S.L., Hubel, D.: The role of fixational eye movements in visual perception. Nat. Rev. 5, 229–240 (2004)
3. Tagawa, N.: Depth perception model based on fixational eye movements using bayesian statistical inference. In: ICPR 2010, pp. 1662–1665 (2010)
4. Tagawa, N., Alexandrova, T.: Computational model of depth perception based on fixational eye movements. In: VISAPP 2010, pp. 328–333 (2010)
5. Horn, B.K.P., Schunk, B.: Determining optical flow. Artif. Intell. 17, 185–203 (1981)
6. Simoncelli, E.P.: Bayesian multi-scale differential optical flow. In: Jähne, B., Haussecker, H., Geissler, P. (eds.) Handbook of Computer Vision and Applications, vol. 2, pp. 397–422. Academic Press, New York (1999)
7. Bruhn, A., Weickert, J.: Lucas/Kanade meets Horn/Schunk: combining local and global optic flow methods. Int. J. Comput. Vision 61(3), 211–231 (2005)
8. Zhang, Z.: A flexible new technique for camera calibration. IEEE Trans. PAMI 22(11), 1330–1334 (2000)
9. Dempster, A.P., Laird, N.M., Rubin, D.B.: Maximum likelihood from incomplete data. J. Roy. Statist. Soc. B 39, 1–38 (1977)
10. Green, P.J.: On use of the Em algorithm for penalized likelihood estimation. J. Roy. Statist. Soc. B 52, 443–452 (1990)

Fast and Robust Algorithm for Fundamental Matrix Estimation

Ming Zhang[1,2], Guanghui Wang[1(✉)], Haiyang Chao[1], and Fuchao Wu[2]

[1] School of Engineering, University of Kansas, Lawrence, KS 66045, USA
ghwang@ku.edu
[2] National Lab of Pattern Recognition, Chinese Academy of Sciences,
Beijing 100190, China

Abstract. Fundamental matrix estimation from two views plays an important role in 3D computer vision. In this paper, a fast and robust algorithm is proposed for the fundamental matrix estimation in the presence of outliers. Instead of algebra error, the reprojection error is adopted to evaluate the confidence of the fundamental matrix. Assuming Gaussian image noise, it is proved that the reprojection error can be described by a chi-square distribution, and thus, the outliers can be eliminated using the 3-sigma principle. With this strategy, the inlier set is robustly established in only two steps. Compared to classical RANSAC-based strategies, the proposed algorithm is very efficient with higher accuracy. Experimental evaluations and comparisons with previous methods demonstrate the effectiveness and advantages of the proposed approach.

Keywords: Fundamental matrix · Robust estimation · Outlier elimination

1   Introduction

Fundamental matrix plays an important role in epipolar geometry since it contains all geometric information about the relative transformation between two images. Fundamental matrix estimation is based on solving a homogeneous linear system in which each linear equation is formed by a pair of correspondence feature points. When the data is free of outliers, the nonlinear seven-point method [1] or linear eight-point method [2] is used to recover the fundamental matrix from the linear system via least squares. In practice, however, the outliers or large measurement errors are inevitable due to the inconsistency in feature extraction and matching process. Therefore, a robust algorithm that is resilient to outliers is vital for fundamental matrix estimation.

A large number of robust estimation approaches have been proposed to alleviate the influence of outliers to the fundamental matrix estimation. The M-estimator method [1,3] reduces the effect of outliers by applying weight functions to transform the problem to a weighted least squares problem. However, the

© Springer International Publishing Switzerland 2015
M. Kamel and A. Campilho (Eds.): ICIAR 2015, LNCS 9164, pp. 316–322, 2015.
DOI: 10.1007/978-3-319-20801-5_34

approach needs a good initial estimation and only works under low percentages of outliers. LMedS [4,5] evaluate each estimation in terms of the median symmetric epipolar distances of the point correspondences and choose the one which minimizes the median error. The method does not need to know the percentage of outliers, but it is very time-consuming. RANSAC is a very popular robust algorithm for fundamental matrix estimation [6,7]. The algorithm use minimal points set to estimate an initial guess. Then, the confidence of the estimation is established by testing each point correspondence against the hypothesized model; and an inliers set is determined by choosing points that have error below a given threshold. Next, a new fundamental matrix is estimated by the inliers set. Iteratively, the RANSAC algorithm attempts to find a solution that maximize the amount of the inlier set. In the last two decades, several RANSAC based algorithm have been proposed.

PROSAC algorithm [8], by taking into account additional information of the quality of the errors of the point matches, largely reduces the number of iterations. The MLESAC algorithm [9] maximizes a likelihood which is a mixture model of normal distribution for inliers and uniform distribution for outliers. The parameter of the model is estimated by expectation maximization. MAPSAC [10] maximizes the posterior estimation of the fundamental matrix and matches. Feng et al. [11] proposed a robust estimation method that measure the point matches by means of 2D reprojection error. The algorithm uses the mixture models of Gaussian and Uniform distributions. Huang et al. [12] improved the RANSAC algorithm by means of constructing a voting array for all the point correspondence pairs to record the consistency votes for each pair from a number of fundamental matrix estimations to better identify the outliers. Carro et al. [13] proposed a new robust method by combining the PROSAC and LMedS algorithms. All the above RANSAC-based approaches basically concentrate on the evaluation criterion of the estimation instead of the iteration step. Although these methods can achieve a better estimation of the fundamental matrix, the time cost issue is still not solved. The iterations increase greatly with the increase of outlier percentages, as a result, much more computation time is required.

In this paper, we adopt reprojection error, rather than the widely used algebraic error, to evaluate the confidence of the fundamental matrix. By assuming Gaussian image noise, it is shown that the reprojection error of point correspondences can be described by a chi-square distribution, and the outliers usually yield very large reprojection errors. Thus, the outliers can be simply eliminated using the 3-sigma principle. Based on this observation, a fast and robust algorithm is proposed for the fundamental matrix estimation. With this strategy, the inlier set can be robustly established in only two steps. Compared to other robust algorithms, the proposed technique is not only very efficient, but also extremely accurate. The algorithm is validated by extensive experiment using both synthetic and real image data.

2 Robust Fundamental Matrix Estimation

2.1 Eight-Point Linear Algorithm

Fundamental matrix is estimated from a set of point correspondences between two images. Given an image pair I and I′, suppose $\mathbf{x}_i \in$ I and $\mathbf{x}'_i \in$ I′ are a pair of corresponding homogeneous points between the two images. Then, the fundamental matrix $\mathbf{F}$ satisfies the following equation.

$$\mathbf{x}'^T_i \mathbf{F} \mathbf{x}_i = 0 \tag{1}$$

where the fundamental matrix is a 3×3 homogeneous matrix defined up to scale. Each pair of point correspondence yield one linear constraint the entries of $\mathbf{F}$. Thus, the fundamental matrix can be linearly estimated from eight point pairs. When more correspondences are available, the fundamental matrix can be estimated via least squares.

2.2 Algebric Error and Reprojection Error Evaluation

After obtaining an estimation of the fundamental matrix, an error measure can be evaluated for each pair of point correspondence. The most commonly used criterion is the algebraic error defined as $e_a(i) = \mathbf{x}'^T_i \mathbf{F} \mathbf{x}'_i$. This definition is simple, however, it does not have any geometric meaning.

Based on the initially estimated fundamental matrix, a pair of camera matrices can be recovered, and thus, a perspective 3D reconstruction of all corresponding points is obtained via triangulations [14]. Then, the reconstructed 3D points can be reprojected back to the two images via the camera matrices. Suppose $\hat{\mathbf{x}}_i$ and $\hat{\mathbf{x}}'_i$ are the reprojected images of point i, the 2D reprojection error of the corresponding point is defined as

$$e_r(i) = \frac{1}{2}\sum \|\mathbf{x}_i - \hat{\mathbf{x}}_i\|^2_F + \|\mathbf{x}'_i - \hat{\mathbf{x}}'^2_i\|_F, \quad s.t. \quad \hat{\mathbf{x}}'^T_i \mathbf{F} \hat{\mathbf{x}}_i = 0 \quad \forall i \tag{2}$$

The 2D reprojection error is proven to be more superior to other geometric errors. Optimal triangulation [14] is a linear triangulation method which converts the least-square function to a one parameter function and finds a global optimal solution.

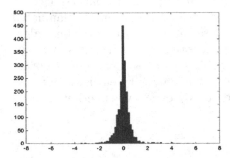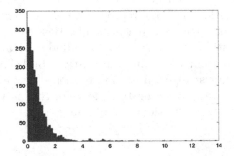

Fig. 1. (left) The histogram distribution of the real added noise and outliers. (right) The histogram distribution of the reprojection errors.

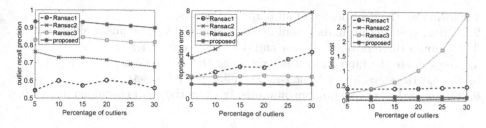

Fig. 2. Evaluation results from synthetic data. (left) Outlier detection rates; (middle) reprojection errors; and (right) computation time (second) by different algorithms.

2.3 Outlier Detection Strategy

The image noise is normally modeled by Gaussian distribution. Under this assumption, it can be verified that the reprojection error should follow chi-square χ^2 distribution, as shown in our simulation result Fig. 1.

In Fig. 1, the added noise is Gaussian, while the added outliers are some random points with large standard deviations. As shown in the figure, the points located at the leftmost and rightmost areas are added outliers. Through extensive simulations, we found that the reprojection errors of outliers are usually greatly larger than those of inliers. This result is also support by our early study on structure from motion [16]. As a result, these outliers can be identified using 3-sigma principle. Points with reprojection errors larger than the triple variance of all the reprojection error can be classified as outliers. Based on robust statistics [15], we can obtain a robust standard deviation of the reprojection errors by the following equation.

$$\sigma = 1.4826 \left(1 + \frac{5}{n-q}\right) \mathrm{median}_i |e_i^r| \tag{3}$$

The above equation is the median absolute deviation (MAD) scale estimate [15]. The first number is obtained from the inverse of the cumulative normal distribution, and the term $(1 + \frac{5}{n-q})$ is the finite sample correction factor with the total number of parameters $q = 8$ and n the total number of features. The details of the derivation can be found in [15]. According to the distribution model, we distinguish the inliers from their reprojection errors of each pair of corresponding points. The points whose reprojection errors are less than 3σ are deemed as inliers, since 99.14% of the data points lies within 3σ under the assumption of the Gaussian distribution error model.

2.4 Outline of the Proposed Approach

Based on the above discussion, the implementation details of proposed approach is summarized as below.

1. Normalize the coordinates of all matching points;
2. Estimate an initial fundamental matrix using eight-point linear algorithm;
3. Compute the reprojection error and determine an outlier threshold;
4. Re-estimate the fundamental matrix using the inliers detected in step 3;
5. Repeat the steps 3 and 4 one time to refine the inlier set;
6. Estimate the optimal fundamental matrix using the inliers obtained in step 5.

3   Evaluations on Synthetic Data

The proposed algorithm was evaluated on synthetic data and compared with previous algorithms. During the simulation, 200 space points were randomly generated with a cube of [10, 10, 10], and two images were produced from these points. The image size is 800×800; and the focal lengths of the two cameras are set at 800. Gaussian noise with zero mean and 2 pixels standard deviation is added to each pixel. Outliers are simulated as Gaussian noise with large standard deviation (greater than 8 pixels in the test); and they are randomly added to part of the image points. The percentage of outliers varies from 5% to 30% in a step of 5%.

We evaluated and compared the performance of the proposed algorithm with three popular previous algorithms proposed in [12,13], and [11], which are named as Ransac1, Ransac2, and Ransac3, respectively. The evaluation criteria include outlier detection rate, final reprojection error, and computational cost. 200 independent trials are carried out under each configuration in order to yield a more meaneaingful statistical result. Figure 2 shows the experimental results, from which we can see that the proposed algorithm obviously outperforms all other three approaches in terms of the outlier recall precision and the reprojection error. The computational cost of the proposed algorithm is also noticeably lower than the Ransac1 and Ransac3 algorithms.

4   Evaluations on Real Images

The proposed algorithm has been evaluated using extensive real images, and only one result is reported here due to limited space. Two images from the "Model House" sequence (http://www.robots.ox.ac.uk/~vgg/data1.html) are used in the experiment, as shown in Fig. 3. The points marked in red circles denote the point correspondences between the two images. We randomly select different ratios of the matched points and add large random noise onto them to simulate the outliers. Figure 4 shows the outlier detection rates, final reprojection errors, and computational cost with respect to different percentage of outliers by different algorithms. We can see from Fig. 4 that the results are similar to those on synthetic data. The proposed algorithm yields obviously better results than other three approaches in the real image test.

Fig. 3. Two images of a model house with matching result shown in red circles.

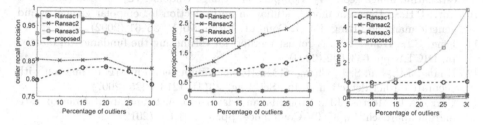

Fig. 4. Evaluation results on model house images. (left) Outlier detection rates; (middle) reprojection errors; and (right) computation time (second) by different algorithms.

5   Conclusion

In this paper, we have proposed a new robust algorithm for fundamental matrix estimation based on reprojection errors. Compared with previous algorithms, we adopted a more meaningful error criterion to evaluate the confidence of the estimated fundamental matrix. With the new outlier detection strategy, the outliers can be identified from all pairs of point correspondences in two steps, leading to a more robust and more accurate estimation of the fundamental matrix. Compared to the RANSAC-based algorithms, the proposed algorithm can find the optimal solution in two steps.

Acknowledgment. The work is partly supported by the Kansas NASA EPSCoR Program, and the NSFC (61273282).

References

1. Zhang, Z.: Determining the epipolar geometry and its uncertainty: a review. Int. J. Comput. Vision **27**, 161–198 (1998)
2. Hartley, R.: In defense of the 8-point algorithm. In: Proceedings of the 8th International Conference on Computer Vision, pp. 1064–1070 (1995)

3. Stewart, C.V.: Robust parameter estimation in computer vision. SIAM Rev. **41**, 513–537 (1999)
4. Armangué, X., Salvi, J.: Overall view regarding fundamental matrix estimation. Image Vis. Comput. **21**, 205–220 (2003)
5. Rousseeuw, P.J., Leroy, A.M.: Robust Regression and Outlier Detection. Wiley, New York (1987)
6. Torr, P.H.S., Murray, D.W.: The development and comparison of robust methods for estimating the fundamental matrix. IJCV **24**, 271–300 (1997)
7. Fischler, M., Bolles, R.: Random sample consensus: a paradigm for model fitting with applications to image analysis and automated cartography. Commun. ACM **24**, 381–385 (1981)
8. Chum, O., Matas, J.: Matching with PROSAC - progressive sample consensus. In: IEEE Conference on Computer Vision and Pattern Recognition, June 2005
9. Torr, P.H.S., Zisserman, A.: MLESAC: a new robust estimator with application to estimating image geometry. Comput. Vis. Image Underst. **78**, 138–156 (2000)
10. Torr, P.H.S.: Bayesian model estimation and selection for epipolar geometry and generic manifold fitting. Int. J. Comput. Vision **50**(1), 35–61 (2002)
11. Feng, C.L., Hung, Y.S.: A robust method for estimating the fundamental matrix. In: DICTA, pp. 633–642 (2003)
12. Huang, J.F., Lai, S.H., Cheng, C.M.: Robust fundamental matrix estimation with accurate outlier detection. J. Inf. Sci. Eng. **23**(4), 1213–1225 (2007)
13. Carro, A.I., Morros, J.R.: Promeds: an adaptive robust fundamental matrix estimation approach. In: 3DTV-Conference, pp. 1–4. IEEE (2012)
14. Hartley, R.I., Sturm, P.: Triangulation. Comput. Vis. Image Underst. **68**(2), 146–157 (1997)
15. Rousseeuw, P., Leroy, A.: Robust Regression and Outlier Detection. Wiley, New York (1987)
16. Wang, G., Zelek, J., Wu, J., Bajcsy, R.: Robust rank-4 affine factorization for structure from motion. In: IEEE WACV, pp. 180–185 (2013)

Medical Image Analysis

Biologically-Inspired Supervised Vasculature Segmentation in SLO Retinal Fundus Images

Samaneh Abbasi-Sureshjani[1]([✉]), Iris Smit-Ockeloen[1], Jiong Zhang[1], and Bart Ter Haar Romeny[1,2]

[1] Eindhoven University of Technology, Eindhoven, The Netherlands
{s.abbasi,j.zhang1,B.M.terhaarRomeny}@tue.nl
[2] Biomedical and Information Engineering, Northeastern University, Shenyang, China

Abstract. We propose a novel Brain-Inspired Multi-Scales and Multi-Orientations (BIMSO) segmentation technique for the retinal images taken with laser ophthalmoscope (SLO) imaging cameras. Conventional retinal segmentation methods have been designed mainly for color RGB images and they often fail in segmenting the SLO images because of the presence of noise in these images. We suppress the noise and enhance the blood vessels by lifting the 2D image to a joint space of positions and orientations ($SE(2)$) using the directional anisotropic wavelets. Then a neural network classifier is trained and tested using several features including the intensity of pixels, filter response to the wavelet and multi-scale left-invariant Gaussian derivatives jet in $SE(2)$. BIMSO is robust against noise, non-uniform luminosity and contrast variability. In addition to preserving the connections, it has higher sensitivity and detects the small vessels better compared to state-of-the-art methods for both RGB and SLO images.

Keywords: Scanning laser ophthalmoscope · Primary visual cortex · Anisotropic wavelets · Multi-scale · Orientation score · Left-invariant Gaussian derivatives · Blood vessel segmentation · Diabetic retinopathy

1 Introduction

Diabetic retinopathy (DR) is the result of progressive damage to the network of tiny blood vessels that supply blood to the retina and it is the leading cause of vision loss in working adult populations. Patients with severe levels of DR are reported to have poorer quality of life and reduced levels of physical, emotional, and social well being [15]. Therefore, it is essential to diagnose and control DR at early stages.

It has been shown that quantitative delineation of morphological attributes of the retinal vasculature is very useful for diagnosis and monitoring of diabetes at early stages [8]. It is also possible to study other early DR signs, such as nerve damage in the cornea with confocal laser microscopy, or changes in retina neural tissue layer thickness with optical coherence tomography (OCT), but these are

© Springer International Publishing Switzerland 2015
M. Kamel and A. Campilho (Eds.): ICIAR 2015, LNCS 9164, pp. 325–334, 2015.
DOI: 10.1007/978-3-319-20801-5_35

less suitable and more costly for large-scale screening. That is why, an extensive research has been investigated on retinal blood vessel segmentation. However, an automated computer-aided diagnostic system is far from being clinically used and still suffers from major difficulties like enhancing and crossing-preserving segmentation of the vessels at low-contrast and noisy images.

Almost all the proposed segmentation techniques in the literature are designed based on RGB color fundus images. Supervised pattern recognition methods often outperform unsupervised ones, because they are based on pre-classified data. Several features were introduced in the literature for discrimination of the vessel from non-vessel pixels e.g. the gray level-based properties [11,13], moment-invariant-based features [11]. Moreover, spatial-frequency techniques (including Gabor wavelets) and also differential descriptors (including Gaussian derivatives and steerable filters) were frequently used in the literature [12,13]. Although. several methods have been proposed, but most of them are not universal and highly dependent on the imaging technology. This requires us to redesign or modify the segmentation algorithms for new images. The scanning laser ophthalmoscope (SLO) camera is one of these technologies. These cameras use laser light instead of bright flash of white light and provide high contrast images with different noise and background profiles, compared to normal color images. Despite the advantage of the new SLO images, very few studies (e.g. [16]) were dedicated to them.

The main purpose of this study is to propose a fully automatic and supervised delineation technique for SLO images. The proposed method (called Brain-Inspired Multi-Scales and Multi-Orientations: BIMSO) is inspired by recent findings about orientation-selective property of receptive fields in primary visual cortex (V1) [7]. Orientation scores are constructed by projecting the 2D images to the joint space of positions and orientations (identified by $SE(2)$) [4], which results in disentanglement of vessels at crossings and differentiating between their features. The contextual information is extracted at several orientations and scales using cake wavelets and left-invariant Gaussian derivatives in rotation-translation group ($SE(2)$) [2,6]. BIMSO is mainly proposed for SLO images, but the performance on RGB images is also as good as state-of-the-art methods. It has a high sensitivity for both types of images and detects the small vessels (clinically important) very well compared to state-of-the-art techniques.

This article is structured as follows: Sect. 2 provides the theory of invertible orientation score, its transformation and reconstruction. The proposed method is explained in detail in Sect. 3. After suppressing noise at individual orientation layers at preprocessing, different intensity-based and contextual features are extracted from the enhanced images. Then a feed-forward neural network is trained using two datasets (RGB and SLO images). The datasets used for validating our method and the performance measurements are all explained in Sect. 4. The article is concluded is Sect. 5.

2 Invertible Orientation Score

The orientation score as a function on $SE(2) \equiv \mathbb{R}^2 \times S^1$ domain is obtained by correlating the input image (f) with an anisotropic wavelet ψ [3]:

$$U_f(x, \theta) = (\overline{R_\theta(\psi)} \star f)(x) = \int_{\mathbb{R}^2} \overline{\psi(R_\theta^{-1}(y - x))} f(y) dy \tag{1}$$

where R_θ is the 2D counter-clockwise rotation matrix over angle θ, the overline denotes the complex conjugate and $\star$ represents the correlation.

Cake Wavelets. The cake wavelets are directional wavelets similar to the Gabor wavelets [2]. They have quadratic property in the direction orthogonal to the structures to be detected, meaning that the real part contains information about the locally even structures, e.g. ridges, and the imaginary part contains information about the locally odd structures, e.g. edges. Despite Gabor wavelets, cake wavelets uniformly cover the entire frequency domain and they ensure that the information at all scales are preserved in transformation; so they allow for a stable inverse transformation. In this case, 2D image reconstruction is achieved by summing over all orientations as $f(x) = \sum_{j=0}^{N_o-1} U_f(x, js_\theta)$ (2) where N_o is the finite number of orientations. By using a symmetric cake wavelet, $s_\theta = \pi/N_o$ where π is the periodicity of the orientation score [3,6].

Left-Invariant Gaussian Derivatives in $SE(2)$. Theoretically, because of the curved geometry of orientation space, it is wrong to take the derivatives in orientation score using $\{\partial_x, \partial_y, \partial_\theta\}$ derivative frame (we use shorthand notation $\partial_i = \frac{\partial}{\partial_i}$) [4]. Therefore, left-invariant differential operators $\{\partial_\xi, \partial_\eta, \partial_\theta\} = \{\cos\theta\partial_x + \sin\theta\partial_y, -\sin\theta\partial_x + \cos\theta\partial_y, \partial_\theta\}$ are used in $SE(2)$. The ∂_ξ and ∂_η are the spatial derivative tangent and orthogonal to the orientation θ. The parameter μ, with unit $1/length$, is also introduced to deal with the different physical dimensions in this domain. It is important to mention that not all the left-invariant derivatives commute e.g. $\partial_\theta\partial_\xi U \neq \partial_\xi\partial_\theta U$ [3,6].

In order to regularize the differential operators in $SE(2)$ the convolution with Gaussian kernel $G_{\sigma_s,\sigma_o}(x, \theta) = G_{\sigma_s}(x)G_{\sigma_o}(\theta)$ is used. The spatial and angular scales are determined by $\frac{1}{2}\sigma_s^2$ and $\frac{1}{2}\sigma_o^2$, and in case of left-invariant operators the spatial Gaussian kernel is isotropic i.e., $\sigma_s = \sigma_\xi = \sigma_\eta$.

3 Proposed Method

The proposed Brain-Inspired Multi-Scales and multi-Orientation segmentation method (BIMSO) has four main steps: preprocessing, feature extraction, classification and post-processing. The green channel from the color fundus photographs and the images taken with green laser of the SLO camera are used at all steps, because they ensure the best contrast between vasculature and background.

3.1   Preprocessing

Retinal images are often affected by noise, non-uniform luminosity and contrast variability, because of non-ideal image acquisition conditions. These imperfections cause low quality images followed by wrong results in analysis. Therefore, before doing any analysis, it is effective to attenuate these effects and enhance the blood vessels. We use the luminosity and contrast normalization method proposed by [5]. This method is preferred to other techniques in the literature, because it is only based on the background part of the image and it does not smooth the vessels or lesions.

In next step, the image is denoised and the vessels get enhanced in a novel approach. By using the directional cake wavelets in orientation score transform the elongated structures (vessels) get high responses in this domain, while non-elongated structures including background and noise get low responses. By considering this characteristic and using an appropriate non-linear filter it is possible to attenuate low orientation score responses (noise) and enhance high values (vessels). We propose to use the gamma transform ($\check{U}_{\tilde{f}} = \alpha |U_{\tilde{f}}|^{\gamma}$) for this purpose. Because of the quadratic property of cake wavelets, absolute value of orientation score ($|U_{\tilde{f}}|$, phase invariant) is used for gamma correction and α is determined by the sign of the real part of orientation score ($Re(U_{\tilde{f}})$). By setting the γ parameter to a value larger than 1 (typically we use $\gamma = 1.5$), the blood vessels get enhanced while the noise is suppressed. The image after applying the gamma correction in $SE(2)$ could be reconstructed ($\check{f}$) based on Eq. (2). Figure 1 shows two sample image patches from SLO and RGB images before and after applying the proposed preprocessing steps. As depicted in this figure, the proposed preprocessing technique is very effective for both RGB and SLO images.

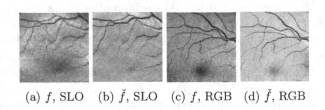

(a) f, SLO   (b) $\check{f}$, SLO   (c) f, RGB   (d) $\check{f}$, RGB

Fig. 1. Results of applying the proposed preprocessing on SLO and RGB images

3.2   Feature Extraction

Next step is to assign a feature vector to each pixel of preprocessed image ($\check{f}$) to be used for training the classifier. Since the blood vessels have different orientations and widths, the feature vector is extracted in different orientations and scales. The feature vector proposed in BIMSO includes the intensity of pixels, the filter response to half-cake wavelet and multi-scale Gaussian derivatives jet of orientation scores. Each of these features is explained in detail.

Gray Level. The blood vessels are normally darker than background in both RGB and SLO images. Therefore, the intensity of preprocessed image ($\check{f}$) is considered as one of the main features for segmentation.

Multi-scale Gaussian Derivatives Jet of Orientation Scores. Different linear and non-linear combinations of first and second order Gaussian derivative operators were used very often in the literature for detection of edges, ridges and contours as local differential structures in images. We propose to use the first and second order regularized left-invariant Gaussian derivatives of the preprocessed orientation score ($\check{U}_{\check{f}}$) instead of normal derivatives of 2D images. Lifting the vessels especially at crossings and junctions makes it possible to take the derivatives in the directions (e_ξ, e_η, e_θ) attached to individual structures in different orientation layers. Since there are three directions for taking the derivatives, it is possible to take 3 first order and 9 second order derivatives at each point in $SE(2)$. As mentioned in Sect. 2 not all the left-invariant derivatives commute, that is why there are only 8 unique second order derivatives and in total 11 (first and second order) derivatives at one scale. The maximum detection of differential structures is obtained when the spatial scale is selected as $\sigma_s = r/\sqrt{2}$, where r stands for the vessel caliber [10]. So in order to detect all the vessels with varying widths, the appropriate range of scales need to be selected according the vessel calibers in each dataset. If we call the number of considered scales and discrete orientations N_s and N_o respectively, there would be $11 \times N_s \times N_o$ derivatives in total. In order to decrease the number of features and make them orientation-invariant, for each of the derivatives at multiple scales, the maximum intensity projection over all orientations is used. So at the end only $11 \times N_s$ derivatives would be obtained at this step. The selected scales for different datasets are explained in Sect. 4.

Second Local Maximum Intensity Projection. The selectiveness of cake wavelets as directional wavelets is π-periodic and the response of the filter is the weighted average over the forward and backward directions. At high curvature points there is a drastic change in orientation. The difference between the forward and backward orientation of the structure of investigation is no longer π, which results in a non-accurate filter response. A similar behavior can also occur at background points nearby high curvature points. This behavior results in streaks in the area around high curvature points after applying maximum over the orientations (see Fig. 2b). Instead, we use half-cake kernels to find the response for forward and backward directions separately. Applying maximum intensity projection using these single-sided wavelets still results in some streaks, as seen in Fig. 2c and that is because of the presence of background noise in pixels near high curvature points. But the second local maximum value over the orientations for every spatial position gives a streak free result (see Fig. 2d). This response (not sensitive to noise) is also included in feature vector.

To conclude, the entire feature vector has the size of $11 \times N_s + 2$. It includes the information about the pixel intensity, the orientation score response to half-cake

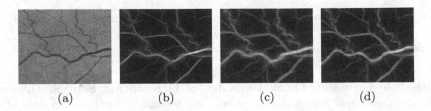

(a)   (b)   (c)   (d)

Fig. 2. (a) Exemplary image patch, (b) maximum intensity projection over the orientations using double-sided cake wavelets, (c) using single-sided cake wavelets, and (d) second highest local maxima projection over the orientations using single cake wavelets.

wavelets and also the Gaussian derivatives jet of orientation scores. At the end, the extracted features are normalized for each image in order to reduce the inter-image variation and the classification error.

3.3   Classification

Next step after extracting the features is training the classifier and preparing it for further classifications. Among different classifiers trained for this purpose, the feed-forward neural network (NN) classifier results in the highest performance. This classifier has been often used and performed well in supervised blood vessel segmentation techniques (e.g. [11]). For each dataset a separate classifier was trained. The configuration of these classifiers is explained in Sect. 4. By classifying the pixels in test images and thresholding the outputs of the classifier (called soft segmentations) final segmentations are obtained. The threshold selection scheme is explained in Sect. 4.

4   Validation and Discussion

4.1   Datasets

The method is trained, validated and tested on two different datasets. The public DRIVE [14] dataset includes 40 RGB color images, acquired with a Canon CR5 non-mydriatic 3CCD camera with a 45° field of view (FOV) and resolution of 565 × 584. The IOSTAR dataset is a private dataset and the images were taken with an EasyScan camera[1] based on SLO technology (using the green and infrared lasers). These high contrast images have a resolution of 1024 × 1024 with 45° FOV. The blood vessels in 24 images have been annotated and corrected by two different experts in order to decrease the inter-user variability. Half of the images in each dataset are considered as the training and other ones as the test images.

---

[1] Provided by i-Optics B.V. company in the Netherlands.

4.2   Performance Evaluation

In order to compare the performance of the BIMSO with state-of-the-art segmentation algorithms, four common parameters are measured: a)true positives (tp), b) false positives (fp), c) true negatives (tn), and d) false negatives (fn), where vessel pixels are positives and non-vessel pixels are negatives. These four measurements are used to obtain the receiver operating characteristics (ROC) curve, area under ROC curve (AUC), sensitivity (Se), specificity (Sp), accuracy (Acc) and Matthews correlation coefficient (Mcc). Two separate threshold values $(t_{acc}$ and $t_{mcc})$ are defined for each dataset. They are the values that maximize the average accuracy $(\overline{Acc})$ and average Mathews correlation coefficient $(\overline{Mcc})$ for the entire dataset respectively. Although, maximizing the average accuracy (which is the proportion of correct predictions) is often used in the literature, it is not a good criterion for blood vessel segmentation as mentioned by [1]. Because in our target images the two classes (vessel and non-vessel) have very different sizes, and assigning every object to the larger set (non-vessel class) achieves a high accuracy but it is not a good and useful classification.

We compare the performance of BIMSO with one of the best supervised segmentation methods (introduced by [13] for color fundus images) for our private dataset (IOSTAR). Therefore, we trained a Gaussian mixture model (GMM) classifier (as proposed in this work) with different parameter settings in order to find the best parameters for this dataset. The performance of our method on the public DRIVE dataset is also compared to the best supervised and unsupervised segmentation methods reported in the literature.

The best configuration of NN for both datasets had 2 hidden layers and rectified linear activation function at each hidden layer. Each layer had 222 and 186 hidden nodes for the IOSTAR and DRIVE datasets respectively. The parameters used for each dataset in both methods (BIMSO and [13]) are reported in Table 1, where n_s denotes the number of randomly selected samples used for training the classifiers. A small and fixed angular scale (σ_θ) is selected for both datasets. The spatial scales are selected according the vessel calibers in each dataset. In all our experiments we set $\mu = \sigma_o/\sigma_s$. As mentioned by [13] $\{a, k_0, \epsilon\}$ are the parameters used for adjusting the shape of Gabor wavelets as directional elongated filters and k is the number of vessel and non-vessel Gaussians modeling each class likelihood of GMM classifier. Similar to BIMSO, N_o is the number of orientations used in this approach.

Table 1. Parameters used in BIMSO and method by [13]

	BIMSO						[13]					
	N_s	N_o	γ	$\sigma_\xi = \sigma_\eta$	σ_o	ns	N_o	a	k_o	ϵ	k	ns
IOSTAR	6	18	2	$\{1, 2, \ldots, 6\}$	$\pi/18$	5.5m	18	$\{1,2,\ldots,9\}$	3	4	20	4m
DRIVE	5	18	1.5	$\{1, 2, \ldots, 5\}$	$\pi/18$	3m	18	$\{1,2,\ldots,5\}$	3	4	20	1m

Table 2. Comparison of segmentation results for the DRIVE and IOSTAR datasets

		t_{acc}	t_{mcc}	$\overline{Mcc}$	$\overline{Se}$	$\overline{Sp}$	$\overline{Acc}$	AUC
DRIVE	**Supervised**							
	BIMSO	0.5	–	0.7590	0.7403	0.9794	**0.9485**	0.9525
	BIMSO	–	0.45	**0.7608**	**0.7695**	0.9742	0.9477	0.9525
	[13]	–	–	–	0.7332	0.9782	0.9466	**0.9614**
	[11]	–	–	–	0.7067	**0.9801**	0.9452	0.9588
	[14]	–	–	–	–	–	0.9441	0.9520
	[12]	–	–	–	–	–	0.9416	0.9229
	Unsupervised							
	[1]	–	–	0.7475	0.7655	0.9704	0.9442	**0.9614**
	[9]	–	–	–	0.7517	0.9741	0.9468	–
IOSTAR	**Supervised**							
	BIMSO	0.54	–	0.7726	0.7523	**0.9805**	**0.9507**	**0.9615**
	BIMSO	–	0.47	**0.7752**	**0.7863**	0.9747	0.9501	**0.9615**
	[13]	0.38	–	0.7502	0.7291	0.9787	0.9461	0.9603
	[13]	–	0.32	0.7535	0.7676	0.9720	0.9453	0.9603

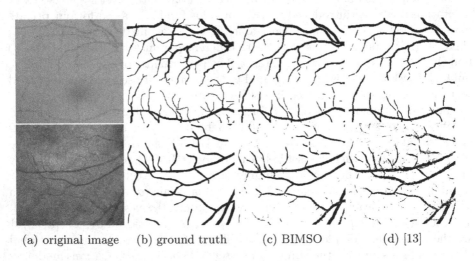

(a) original image   (b) ground truth   (c) BIMSO   (d) [13]

Fig. 3. Comparison between the segmentations obtained by BIMSO and the method proposed by [13] for RGB (first row) and SLO images (second row).

Table 2 represents the performance measurements of BISMO compared to the best results reported in the literature for the DRIVE and obtained for the IOSTAR dataset. In this table, the third and fourth columns specify the threshold value which was used in final step. Based on these results, BIMSO has the highest $\overline{Mcc}$ and $\overline{Se}$ (when using t_{mcc}) for both the DRIVE and IOSTAR datasets compared to state-of-the-art techniques. Because it is able to detect the small vessels in low contrast regions very well. Comparing the quality of segmentations support these quantitative measurements. Figure 3 depicts two sample segmentations obtained for one of the images of the DRIVE (top row) and one of the images of the IOSTAR dataset. As seen in this figure, the number of small detected vessels by BIMSO is higher for both RGB and SLO images compared to the method by [13]. The segmentations obtained by BIMSO are also less sensitive to the noise in SLO images thanks to the proposed enhancement approach. It can be observed as lots of small components in Fig. 3d, which have been falsely considered as vessel pixels but they are created because of noise. In addition, the connectivity of the vessel pixels are preserved better by BIMSO. The reason for this effect is lifting the vessels in rotation-translation space and finding their features separately especially at crossings and bifurcations.

5 Conclusion

We developed a biologically inspired blood vessel segmentation technique (called BIMSO) for SLO retinal images. Although, it was mainly designed for the images taken with SLO cameras (using laser instead of white light), the validation results proved that the performance of this method on RGB images is as good as state-of-the-art methods. The sensitivity of the method for both types of images is high and the smaller vessels are detected well compared to other methods. Small vessels are attractive in a screening setting, because it is expected that just the smaller vessels will show effects of the disease, as diabetic retinopathy, earlier. Moreover, by taking advantage of the extracted features using full and half cake wavelets, the connectivity of the vessels are preserved better especially at crossings and junctions where two elongated structures meet. Although, the detection of small vessels in low contrast regions is very good, but still the connectivity of these vessels is not preserved well (compared to thicker vessels). Therefore, a post-processing step is needed for correcting these missing connections. Moreover, more quantitative experimental validations will be investigated in future works to support the strength of the method in detecting the smaller vessels and robustness against noise.

Acknowledgements. This project has received funding from the European Union's Seventh Framework Programme, Marie Curie Actions- Initial Training Network, under grant agreement $n°607643$ "Metric Analysis For Emergent Technologies (MAnET)".

References

1. Azzopardi, G., Strisciuglio, N., Vento, M., Petkov, N.: Trainable cosfire filters for vessel delineation with application to retinal images. Med. Image Anal. **19**(1), 46–57 (2015)
2. Bekkers, E., Duits, R., Berendschot, T., ter Haar Romeny, B.: A multi-orientation analysis approach to retinal vessel tracking. J. Math. Imaging Vis. **49**(3), 583–610 (2014)
3. Duits, R.: Perceptual organization in image analysis. Ph.D. thesis, Eindhoven University of Technology, Department of Biomedical Engineering, The Netherlands (2005)

4. Duits, R., Felsberg, M., Granlund, G., ter Haar Romeny, B., et al.: Image analysis and reconstruction using a wavelet transform constructed from a reducible representation of the euclidean motion group. Int. J. Comput. Vision **72**(1), 79–102 (2007)

5. Foracchia, M., Grisan, E., Ruggeri, A.: Luminosity and contrast normalization in retinal images. Med. Image Anal. **9**(3), 179–190 (2005)

6. Franken, E.M.: Enhancement of crossing elongated structures in images. Ph.D. thesis, Eindhoven University of Technology. Eindhoven, The Netherlands (2008)

7. Hubel, D.H., Wiesel, T.N.: Receptive fields, binocular interaction and functional architecture in the cat's visual cortex. J. Physiol. **160**(1), 106 (1962)

8. Kanski, J.J., Bowling, B.: Synopsis of Clinical Ophthalmology. Elsevier Health Sciences, Amsterdam (2012)

9. Krause, M., Alles, R.M., Burgeth, B., Weickert, J.: Fast retinal vessel analysis. J. Real-Time Image Proc. 1–10 (2013). http://link.springer.com/article/10.1007%2Fs11554-013-0342-5

10. Lindeberg, T.: Scale-space Theory in Computer Vision. Springer Science & Business Media, New York (1993)

11. Marin, D., Aquino, A., Gegundez-Arias, M., Bravo, J.: A new supervised method for blood vessel segmentation in retinal images by using gray-level and moment invariants-based features. IEEE Trans. Med. Imaging **30**(1), 146–158 (2011)

12. Niemeijer, M., Staal, J., van Ginneken, B., Loog, M., Abramoff, M.D.: Comparative study of retinal vessel segmentation methods on a new publicly available database. In: Medical Imaging 2004, pp. 648–656. International Society for Optics and Photonics (2004)

13. Soares, J.V., Leandro, J.J., Cesar, R.M., Jelinek, H.F., Cree, M.J.: Retinal vessel segmentation using the 2-d gabor wavelet and supervised classification. IEEE Trans. Med. Imaging **25**(9), 1214–1222 (2006)

14. Staal, J., Abràmoff, M.D., Niemeijer, M., Viergever, M.A., van Ginneken, B.: Ridge-based vessel segmentation in color images of the retina. IEEE Trans. Med. Imaging **23**(4), 501–509 (2004)

15. Viswanath, K., McGavin, D.M.: Diabetic retinopathy: clinical findings and management. Community Eye Health **16**(46), 21 (2003)

16. Xu, J., Ishikawa, H., Wollstein, G., Schuman, J.S.: Retinal vessel segmentation on slo image. In: 30th Annual International Conference of the IEEE on Engineering in Medicine and Biology Society, 2008, EMBS 2008, pp. 2258–2261. IEEE (2008)

Assessment of Retinal Vascular Changes Through Arteriolar-to-Venular Ratio Calculation

Behdad Dashtbozorg[1,2]([✉]), Ana Maria Mendonça[2,3], and Aurélio Campilho[2,3]

[1] INEB - Instituto de Engenharia Biomédica, Porto, Portugal
[2] Faculdade de Engenharia, Universidade Do Porto, Porto, Portugal
{behdad.dashtbozorg,amendon,campilho}@fe.up.pt
[3] INESC TEC - INESC Technology and Science, Porto, Portugal

Abstract. The Arteriolar-to-Venular Ratio (AVR) is an index used for the early diagnosis of diseases such as diabetes, hypertension or cardiovascular pathologies. This paper presents three automatic approaches for the estimation of the AVR in retinal images that result from the combination of different methodologies in some of the processing phases used for AVR estimation. Each one of these methods includes vessel segmentation, vessel caliber estimation, optic disc detection or segmentation, region of interest determination, vessel classification into arteries and veins and finally AVR calculation. The values produced by the proposed methods on 40 images of the INSPIRE-AVR dataset were compared with a ground-truth obtained by two medical experts using a semi-automated system. The results showed that the measured AVRs are not statistically different from the reference, with mean errors similar to those achieved by the two experts, thus demonstrating the reliability of the herein proposed approach for AVR estimation.

Keywords: Artery/Vein classification · Arteriolar-to-Venular Ratio · Optic disc detection · Retinal images · Vessel segmentation

1 Introduction

Retinal vessel features play an important role in the early diagnosis of several systemic diseases, namely diabetes, hypertension and vascular disorders. In diabetic retinopathy, the blood vessels often show abnormalities at early stages [11]. Changes in retinal blood vessels, such as significant dilatation and elongation of main arteries, veins, and their branches, are often associated with hypertension and other cardio-vascular pathologies [10].

Among several characteristic signs associated with vascular changes, the Arteriolar-to-Venular Ratio (AVR) is used as an indicator of cardiovascular risk, since it reflects the narrowing of the retinal blood vessels. A lower AVR value is associated with a high blood pressure increasing the risk of stroke, diabetes and hypertension [5]. Manual estimation of AVR is a difficult task and currently most of the medical approaches for computing this index are semi-automatic. Different automatic algorithms for AVR calculation have been presented previously [9,13,14].

© Springer International Publishing Switzerland 2015
M. Kamel and A. Campilho (Eds.): ICIAR 2015, LNCS 9164, pp. 335–343, 2015.
DOI: 10.1007/978-3-319-20801-5_36

In this paper, we propose two new approaches for the estimation AVR, which are alternatives to the one previously described in Dashtbozorg et al. [1]. The methods use automated techniques for vessel segmentation, vessel caliber measurement, optic disc (OD) detection and segmentation, artery/vein (A/V) classification and AVR calculation. For defining the region of interest (ROI) where the index is to be measured, the coordinates of disc center and disc diameter are needed. For A/V classification a graph-based method is used to classify the retinal vessels using a combination of structural information taken from the vasculature graph with intensity features from the original color image. Besides the supervised classification approach described in Dashtbozorg et al. [2], we propose a new unsupervised alternative for integrating the intensity information in the final A/V classes.

2   Methods

The estimation of AVR requires the detection of several retinal landmarks, namely the optic disc and the vessels, followed by vessel caliber measurement and artery/vein classification [5]. For segmenting the vessels, the method previously proposed by Mendonça et al. [8] was chosen and adapted for the segmentation of high resolution images [7]. The segmented vascular structure generated by this method for the image presented in Fig. 1(a) is the binary image shown in Fig. 1(b). Vessel calibers are estimated on the binary vessel image, using the Euclidean distance transform for labelling each pixel (p) on the vessel with its distance to the closest boundary point, d_p. For each vessel centerline pixel, the vessel caliber, $vc(p)$, is simply estimated by $vc = 2d_p - 1$.

2.1   ROI Definition

AVR is calculated from the calibers of vessels inside a ROI, defined as the standard ring area within 0.5 to 1.0 disc diameter from the optic disc margin [5]. As a consequence, both the localization of the optic disc center (ODC) and its diameter are required for automating the AVR calculation. The center of the OD is estimated using an automatic methodology based on the entropy of vascular directions described in Mendonça et al. [6].

Two main options were considered for ROI definition: the first one uses the ODC as the center of the ROI, which is afterwards established considering a fixed disc diameter adapted to the size and field of view (FOV) of the image under analysis; the second approach calculates a disc diameter for each image using a segmentation algorithm for delineating the OD border proposed by Dashtbozorg et al. [3]. In this OD segmentation method, the response of a filter suitable for the enhancement of bright circular regions, the sliding band filter (SBF), is used for estimating both the OD center and the OD boundary. For high resolution images, the SBF is used twice. The first SBF is applied on downsampled images to estimate the initial ODC which is then used for defining a region of interest where the second SBF is afterwards applied for fine boundary extraction.

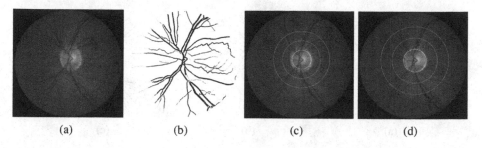

(a)   (b)   (c)   (d)

Fig. 1. (a) Input image; (b) Binary vessel image result; (c) ROI for AVR calculation (delimited by the two green circles) centered on the initial ODC and a fixed OD radius of 180 pixels; (d) ROI for AVR calculation (delimited by the two green circles) and approximation of the extracted OD boundary by a circle (white circle with radius of 215 pixels)(Color figure online).

The ROI defined using a fixed OD radius of 180 pixels is presented in Fig. 1(c), while Fig. 1(d) refers to ROI definition after OD segmentation.

2.2   Artery/Vein Classification

In order to classify a vessel as artery or vein, two alternatives are compared in this work: an improved version of the automatic graph-based A/V classification method previously described in Dashtbozorg et al. [2] and a new proposal that combines the structural information obtained from the retinal vessels and unsupervised classification. Both methods represent the segmented vasculature as a graph whose nodes are extracted from the centerline image by finding the intersection points (pixels with more than two neighbors) and the endpoints or terminal points (pixels with just one neighbor). The graph is afterwards modified for removing some typical errors, such as node splitting and missing or false links. Afterwards, the modified graph is analyzed for deciding on the type of intersection points (graph nodes) and, based on the node types in each separate subgraph, all vessel segments (graph links) that belong to a particular vessel are assigned an identical label. The extracted graph is depicted in Fig. 2(a), while Fig. 2(b) illustrates the result of the labeling procedure.

The two A/V classification approaches mainly differ in the methodology for assigning the final A/V class to each one of the labels resulting from graph analysis. In the method described in Dashtbozorg et al. [2], the structural information provided by the graph is combined with the individual setting of A/V class for each vessel provided by a linear discriminant analysis (LDA) classifier and a set of intensity features extracted from the image. The result of A/V classification is displayed in Fig. 2(c), where the red color is used for representing arteries and veins are shown in blue.

Since images of different datasets have diverse properties, the LDA classifier in the supervised A/V class assignment approach requires a computationally demanding training phase for each dataset. This requirement prevents the

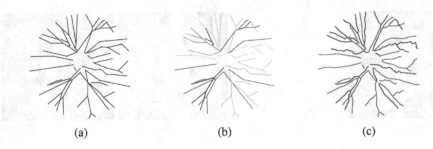

(a)   (b)   (c)

Fig. 2. (a) Graph representing the segmented retinal vasculature after modification; (b) Subgraphs with distinct labels assigned; (c) A/V classification combining the graph and LDA classifier.

method from achieving the expected A/V classification performance when the classifier is trained with images from a different set. In order to overcome this limitation, a new unsupervised approach for the final A/V class assignment is developed using a k-means clustering algorithm. The histogram of artery pixels and vein pixels in different color planes using the manual A/V classification showed that the red intensity is the best discriminator between artery pixels and vein pixels. For this reason, we selected the red component for using in the k-means clustering algorithm.

First from the original color image, a normalized intensity image is obtained from the red plane, and the red intensity for all vessel pixels are extracted and stored in a set, I. The elements of the obtained set are sorted in ascending order which is used for determining three cluster centroids, C_v, C_u and C_a, that allow the initializing of a k-means algorithm for clustering each vessel pixel into one of three classes: (1) Artery; (2) Vein; (3) Unknown.

As retina arteries normally appear thinner and brighter red than the corresponding veins with a normal artery-to-vein caliber ratio of 2:3 [4], to compute the initial centroids the sorted set of intensities is divided into 7 intervals, each one containing the same number of pixels. The first 3 intervals are considered as the initial vein cluster, the 2 last intervals belong to the initial artery cluster and the 2 middle intervals are initially considered as the unknown cluster. The different number of intervals in the artery and vein classes derives from the fact that veins are larger than arteries, so we have more vein pixels than artery pixels. All intensities in the 2 middle intervals are associated with the unknown class for the case of uncertainty. The initial centroids, C_v, C_u and C_a, are set equal to the centers of vein, unknown and artery initial clusters, respectively.

Using the k-means algorithm and the calculated initial centroids all vessel pixels are clustered as artery, vein or unknown as shown in Fig. 3(a). Then, the probability of a label being an artery is calculated based on the relation between the number of pixels in each cluster. Subsequently, in each paired subgraph (Fig. 3(b)), the label with higher artery probability will be considered as an artery, and the other one as a vein, where the result is illustrated in Fig. 3(c).

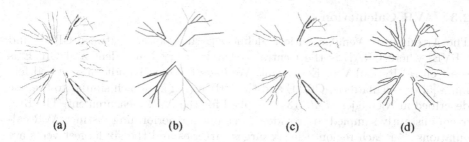

Fig. 3. (a) k-means clustering result (Red: artery, Blue: vein and Green: unknown); (b) Paired subgraphs; (c) Result of assigning A/V classes to paired subgraphs using k-means algorithm; (d) Final result of unsupervised graph-based A/V classification(Color figure online).

In the next step, the two thresholds are recalculated based on the result of A/V assignment in paired-subgraphs. The threshold values for arteries (T_a) and veins (T_v) are set as

$$T_a = \mu_a - \sigma_a \tag{1}$$

$$T_v = \mu_v + \sigma_v \tag{2}$$

where μ_a is the average intensity and σ_a is the standard deviation of all pixels in the artery subgraphs previously classified, respectively, and μ_v and σ_v have identical definition for the vein subgraphs. Afterwards, the classification process is repeated for all vessel pixels based on the obtained threshold. Each pixel (p) with intensity of I_p is classified as following:

$$\text{For each pixel } (P) \begin{cases} \text{if } I_p \leq T_v & \Rightarrow p \in \text{Vein class} \\ \text{if } I_p \geq T_a & \Rightarrow p \in \text{Artery class} \\ \text{if } T_v < I_p < T_a & \Rightarrow p \in \text{Unknown class} \end{cases} \tag{3}$$

For the subgraphs, each vessel pixel is counted as a vein or an artery using the threshold values and the probability of each label to be an artery is calculated. Then for each label in each unpaired subgraph if the probability of being artery is higher than 0.5 then the label will be assigned as artery or otherwise it will be assigned as vein; and for each pair of labels in paired subgraphs, the label with higher artery probability is assigned as an artery class, and the other as a vein class.

Finally, to prevent a wrong classification of a link as a result of an error in the analysis of the graph, the A/V probability for each individual vessel (graph link) is also calculated. If one of these probabilities is higher than 0.8, the vessel is considered as belonging to that class independently of the result derived from the subgraph classification procedure. Final result of unsupervised A/V classification is shown in Fig. 3(d).

2.3   AVR Calculation

The Arteriolar-to-Venular Ratio is defined as the quotient between CRAE and CRVE, where CRAE is the Central Retinal Artery Equivalent and CRVE is the Central Retinal Vein Equivalent. We have followed Knudtson's revised formula [5] to calculate the CRAE and the CRVE. An approach similar to the one described in Niemeijer *et al.* [13] is applied for the AVR measurement. The ROI is equidistantly sampled to provide six regions for performing distinct AVR calculations. For each region, the six largest arteries and the six largest veins are identified, and the CRAEs and CRVEs are obtained for calculating the regional AVRs. The final AVR estimate for the complete image is the average of the six regional values.

3   Results

For validating the proposed AVR calculation methods, we have used the INSPIRE-AVR dataset which contains 40 high resolution color images. This dataset includes two AVR measures that were computed by two ophthalmologists using a semi-automated computer program, IVAN, developed at the University of Wisconsin [12]. The AVR estimates of Observer 1 are used as reference for calculating the errors for the results of both Observer 2 and our methods. Three different methods for AVR calculation are used which mainly differ in the approach for A/V classification and ROI determination.

Method 1: In this method, the results of supervised A/V classification are used and the ROI is determined by defining a ring area within 0.5 to 1.0 disc diameter from the optic disc margin and considering a fixed radius of 180 pixels for the OD.

Method 2: Similar to method 1, the results of supervised A/V classification are used but the ROI is determined using the OD radius obtained from SBF-based OD segmentation method.

Method 3: In this method, the A/V classification result is obtained using the unsupervised technique and the ROI is defined based on the OD radius obtained from the SBF-based OD segmentation method.

Figure 4 shows the arteries and veins found inside the ROI for different methods for AVR calculation. Table 1 summarizes the estimated AVR values for the images of the INSPIRE-AVR dataset, and besides the results achieved by the proposed methods, it includes the values computed by the two human observers and the results produced by the recent approach presented by Niemeijer *et al.* [13]. The analysis of values in Table 1 allow the conclusion that the correlation coefficients and errors produced by proposed methods are similar to those of Observer 2 and of the approach presented in Niemeijer *et al.* [13].

The AVR value can be used as a sign for screening patients in the case of diabetes, hypertension or other cardiovascular diseases. Different values of AVR are considered as a threshold for the differentiation between subjects with or without pathological conditions, depending on the method which is used for the AVR calculation. Here, in order to evaluate the performance of the proposed

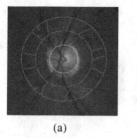 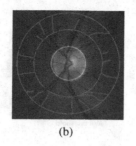 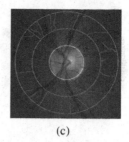

(a)   (b)   (c)

Fig. 4. A/V classification results inside the ROI for (a) Method 1 (supervised AV classification and fixed OD radius); (b) Method 2 (supervised AV classification and OD segmentation); (c) Method 3 (unsupervised AV classification and OD segmentation.

Table 1. AVR values for the 40 images of the INSPIRE-AVR dataset

Image number	Reference AVR	Observer 2		Niemeijer's method		Method 1 (OD location + Fixed OD radius) + supervised A/V classification)		Method 2 (OD segmentation + supervised A/V classification)		Method 3 (OD segmentation + unsupervised A/V classification)	
		AVR	Error	AVR	Error	AVR	Error	AVR	Error	AVR	Error
Mean	0.67	0.66	0.05	0.67	0.06	0.65	0.05	0.68	0.05	0.649	0.05
Stdev	0.08	0.08	0.05	0.07	0.04	0.09	0.04	0.10	0.05	0.07	0.04
Min	0.52	0.45	0.00	0.55	0.01	0.48	0.00	0.55	0.00	0.49	0.00
Max	0.93	0.85	0.29	0.81	0.15	0.86	0.15	0.95	0.17	0.82	0.16
Correlation coefficient	-	0.55	-	0.59	-	0.67	-	0.69	-	0.64	-

methods for clinical applications, the 40 subjects of INSPIRE-AVR dataset are classified based on a threshold as pathological and non-pathological using the obtained AVR values for each method. Since there is no information about the average of AVR values for the normal subjects, several values between the range of 0.63-0.70 are defined as a threshold (T_{AVR}) for the classification of subjects. If the AVR value of a subject is higher than the threshold the subject is considered as non-pathological, otherwise as pathological one. Figure 5 shows the number of subjects with matched classification for different methods when compared with the reference values. As defined in Eq. 4, the matched classification means that the classification result of a subject based on the reference value (R_{AVR}) and the method value (M_{AVR}) is the same, while the mismatched classification represents that the results of classification using reference value and method value are not the same.

$$\begin{cases} M_{AVR} \leq T_{AVR} \text{ and } R_{AVR} \leq T_{AVR} & \Rightarrow \text{ Matched classification} \\ M_{AVR} > T_{AVR} \text{ and } R_{AVR} > T_{AVR} & \Rightarrow \text{ Matched classification} \\ M_{AVR} \leq T_{AVR} \text{ and } R_{AVR} > T_{AVR} & \Rightarrow \text{ Mismatched classification} \\ M_{AVR} > T_{AVR} \text{ and } R_{AVR} \leq T_{AVR} & \Rightarrow \text{ Mismatched classification} \end{cases} \quad (4)$$

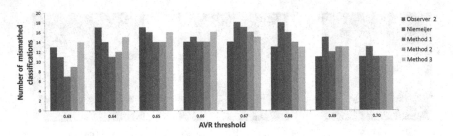

Fig. 5. Number of subjects with matched classification between methods and reference.

As it can be seen in Fig. 5, the number of matched classifications for the proposed approaches are similar to the ones for the second observer when different AVR values are considered as a threshold.

4   Conclusion

We have described two new automatic approaches for the measurement of AVR in retinal images to increase the independence of AVR calculation from the particular characteristics of the images to be evaluated. The proposed new solutions are alternatives to the one previously described in Dashtbozorg *et al.* [1]. One of the methods complements the OD detection algorithm with a segmentation approach that allows the estimation of the actual disc radius of the image under analysis, thus making the definition of the ROI for AVR calculation a fully automated procedure. The other method is an unsupervised classifier using intensity features whose results still needs to be combined with the structural information extracted from the graph representation for A/V classification purposes. This is also an important step towards automation because the classifier is naturally adapted to the intensity characteristics of each particular image.

The obtained AVR values show that the proposed methods have a performance similar to those of human observers. The low errors and good correlation with reference AVR values are promising and demonstrate that described approaches have a high potential for clinical application.

Acknowledgments. This work was financed by the FCT - Fundação para a Ciência e a Tecnologia (Portuguese Foundation for Science and Technology) within project UID/EEA/50014/2013 and research grant SFRH/BD/73376/2010.

References

1. Dashtbozorg, B., Mendonca, A.M., Campilho, A.: Assessment of vascular changes in retinal images. In: 2014 IEEE International Symposium on Medical Measurements and Applications (MeMeA), pp. 1–4. IEEE (2014)

2. Dashtbozorg, B., Mendonça, A.M., Campilho, A.: An automatic graph-based approach for artery/vein classification in retinal images. IEEE Transact. Image Process. **23**(3), 1073–1083 (2014)
3. Dashtbozorg, B., Mendonça, A.M., Campilho, A.: Optic disc segmentation using the sliding band filter. Comput. Biol. Med. **56**, 1–12 (2015)
4. Grosvenor, T., Grosvenor, T.P.: Primary Care Optometry. Elsevier Health Sciences, UK (2007)
5. Knudtson, M.D., Lee, K.E., Hubbard, L.D., Wong, T.Y., Klein, R., Klein, B.E.: Revised formulas for summarizing retinal vessel diameters. Current Eye Res. **27**(3), 143–149 (2003)
6. Mendonça, A.M., Sousa, A., Mendonça, L., Campilho, A.: Automatic localization of the optic disc by combining vascular and intensity information. Comput. Med. Imaging Graph. **37**(5), 409–417 (2013)
7. Mendonça, A., Dashtbozorg, B., Campilho, A.: Segmentation of the vascular network of the retina. In: Ng, E.Y.K., Acharya, U.R., Campilho, A., Suri, J.S. (eds.) Image Analysis and Modeling in Opthalmology, pp. 85–109. CRC Press, Boca Raton (2014)
8. Mendonça, A.M., Campilho, A.: Segmentation of retinal blood vessels by combining the detection of centerlines and morphological reconstruction. IEEE Transact. Med. Imaging **25**(9), 1200–1213 (2006)
9. Muramatsu, C., Hatanaka, Y., Iwase, T., Hara, T., Fujita, H.: Automated selection of major arteries and veins for measurement of arteriolar-to-venular diameter ratio on retinal fundus images. Comput. Med. Imaging Graph. **35**(6), 472–480 (2011)
10. Neubauer, A.S., Luedtke, M., Haritoglou, C., Priglinger, S., Kampik, A.: Retinal vessel analysis reproducibility in assessing cardiovascular disease. Optom. Vis. Sci. **85**(4), E247–E254 (2008)
11. Nguyen, T.T., Wong, T.Y.: Retinal vascular changes and diabetic retinopathy. Curr. Diab. Rep. **9**(4), 277–283 (2009)
12. Niemeijer, M., Xu, X., Dumitrescu, A., Gupta, P., van Ginneken, B., Folk, J., Abramoff, M.: INSPIRE-AVR: Iowa Normative Set for Processing Images of the REtina-Artery Vein Ratio (2011). http://webeye.ophth.uiowa.edu/component/k2/item/270
13. Niemeijer, M., Xu, X., Dumitrescu, A.V., Gupta, P., van Ginneken, B., Folk, J.C., Abramoff, M.D.: Automated measurement of the arteriolar-to-venular width ratio in digital color fundus photographs. IEEE Transact. Med. Imaging **30**(11), 1941–1950 (2011)
14. Ruggeri, A., Grisan, E., De Luca, M.: An automatic system for the estimation of generalized arteriolar narrowing in retinal images. In: 29th Annual International Conference of the IEEE Engineering in Medicine and Biology Society, EMBS 2007, pp. 6463–6466. IEEE (2007)

Automatic Segmentation of Vertebrae in Ultrasound Images

Florian Berton[1]($\boxtimes$), Wassim Azzabi[2], Farida Cheriet[1],
and Catherine Laporte[2]

[1] École Polytechnique de Montréal, Montreal, QC H3T 1J4, Canada
{florian.berton,farida.cheriet}@polymtl.ca
[2] École de Technologie Supérieure, Montreal, QC H3C 1K3, Canada
wassim.azzabi.1@ens.etsmtl.ca, catherine.laporte@etsmtl.ca

Abstract. This paper presents an automatic method for the segmentation of vertebrae in ultrasound images. Its goal is to determine whether each pixel belongs to the bone surface, its acoustic shadow or other tissues. The method is based on the extraction of several image features described in the literature and which we adapted to our problem, and on a random forest classifier. Morphological operations and vertebra-specific constraints are then used in a regularisation step in order to obtain homogeneous regions of both the surface and the acoustic shadow of the vertebra. Experiments on a test database of 9 images show promising results, with average recognition rates for the bone surface and acoustic shadow of 81.87 %, and 91.01 %, respectively.

Keywords: Segmentation · Vertebrae · Ultrasound · Acoustic shadow · Random forests

1 Introduction

Ultrasound is increasingly used for imaging the spine, with applications in image guided epidural needle insertion [8–10] and in the study of spine deformities such as scoliosis [11–14]. The principle of ultrasound imaging is that acoustic waves are sent through the body, and their reflections off the anatomy are detected to form an image. However, when they meet with a highly echogenic bone surface, the acoustic waves are totally reflected, creating an acoustic shadow immediately below the bone surface, and a bright area at the soft tissue-bone interface. When the bone surface is the spinous process, however, the interface is very short and it is difficult to determine exactly where the acoustic shadow begins and ends. Thus, the interpretation of vertebral ultrasound images by non-experts is difficult and not entirely reproducible.

A few algorithms have been developed for the purpose of automatic bone segmentation in ultrasound images. Two different categories of methods can be distinguished. First, there are the methods that try to delineate the bone surface. Foroughi et al. [3] proposed a method that computes a "bone probability

© Springer International Publishing Switzerland 2015
M. Kamel and A. Campilho (Eds.): ICIAR 2015, LNCS 9164, pp. 344–351, 2015.
DOI: 10.1007/978-3-319-20801-5_37

map" based on the quantity of shadow and a local edge detector. Hacihaliloglu et al. [2] used local phase symmetry as a measure for the presence of bone surface. Another method proposed by Daanen et al. [1] consists in a set of heuristics based on the reasoning of a medical expert. The second class of methods is concerned with the detection of acoustic shadows in ultrasound images. For this purpose, an automatic method was developed by Hellier et al. [6] combining the shape of the ultrasound image and a statistical test along each of its lines, providing the boundary between the acoustic shadow and the tissues above it. More recently, Karamalis et al. [7] used random walks to provide an ultrasound data confidence map that highlights acoustic shadows.

In the context of ultrasound guided epidural needle insertion, some vertebra detection methods were also developed. Tran et al. [9] proposed a method for automatic detection of the lamina in ultrasound images based on a ridge detector. Automatic detection of spinous processes in panoramic ultrasound images was proposed by Al-Deen Ashab et al. [10]. Their method uses a bilateral filter followed by Otsu thresholding to extract a wave-like profile in which local maxima correspond to spinous processes.

All these methods were devised either for bone surface or acoustic shadow detection, and most of them were not developed for the specific purpose of segmenting vertebrae. In the context of measuring the quality of the acquired vertebral ultrasound image, it would be useful to detect both the soft tissue-bone interface and the acoustic shadow which reflects the shape of the vertebra, as these are the defining features of a high quality vertebral image [10]. This paper proposes a unique method allowing automatic and simultaneous detection of the acoustic shadow and of the bone surface in vertebral ultrasound images. It is based on the combination of different features from the literature and on the use of random forests [5] for pixel classification. The paper is organized as follows: in Sect. 2, we describe our methodology for feature extraction, pixel classification and regularisation. In Sect. 3, we present our experimental results, which demonstrate the promise of the proposed approach, and conclude in Sect. 4.

2   Proposed Segmentation Algorithm

The segmentation algorithm aims at classifying each pixel into one of three regions: 'Bone surface', 'Acoustic shadow', and 'Other tissues', which corresponds to the other tissues found in the ultrasound image. The proposed approach is illustrated in Fig. 1. First, a set of training data is created using pixels chosen randomly from a learning database of ultrasound images. A feature extraction step is performed to train a random forest classifier. Next, the segmentation of new ultrasound images is performed in three steps: first, the extraction of the different features for each pixel, then their classification using the random forest, and finally the regularisation of the different regions in the image.

2.1   Feature Extraction

Several features such as image gradient [1], Foroughi et al.'s bone probability map [3], phase symmetry [2] and Hellier et al.'s rupture points [6] were already

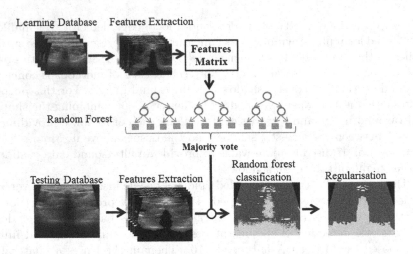

Fig. 1. Block diagram of the proposed image segmentation method in three regions.

shown to be effective in characterizing soft tissue-bone interfaces or acoustic shadows. We exploit all of these, in addition to Local Binary Patterns [4] (LBP), which are successful with texture analysis in medical images. The complete set of extracted features is described below.

Gradient and Intensity Images: The gradient and the intensity (Fig. 2(c), (d)) are considered as features, since the gradient gives information about the transition between the shadow area and the bone surface, and the image itself gives information about the acoustic shadow and the bone surface.

Bone Probability: Foroughi et al. [3] proposed a bone probability map (Fig. 2(a)) based on the high reflection of bones obtained with the Laplacian of Gaussian (LoG) filter and the quantity of shadow (SH) below the bone defined as

$$SH(x,y) = \frac{\sum_{j=y}^{H} G(j-y)I(x,j)}{\sum_{j=y}^{H} G(j-y)}, \tag{1}$$

where x and y correspond to the position of the pixel, $G(.)$ and $I(.)$ represent a Gaussian weighting function and the image intensity, respectively, and H is the number of rows in the image.

Phase Symmetry: Hacihaliloglu et al. [2] used the phase symmetry (Fig. 2(b)) as a ridge detector to describe the bone surface. The phase symmetry feature is based on Log Gabor filters:

$$PS(x,y) = \frac{\sum_r \sum_m \lfloor [|e_{rm}(x,y)| - |o_{rm}(x,y)|] - T_r \rfloor}{\sum_r \sum_m \sqrt{e_{rm}^2(x,y) + o_{rm}^2(x,y)} + \epsilon}, \tag{2}$$

where $e_{rm}(x, y)$ and $o_{rm}(x, y)$ correspond to the responses of quadrature Log Gabor filters [2] with scale r and orientation m.

Local Binary Patterns: The texture of an ultrasound image contains a lot of useful information. LBP are pixel texture descriptors defined as

$$LBP\_Sign_{P,R} = \sum_{p=0}^{P-1} s(g_p - g_c)2^p, \quad s(x) = \begin{cases} 1 & x \geq 0 \\ 0 & < 0 \end{cases} \tag{3}$$

$$LBP\_Mag_{P,R} = \sum_{p=0}^{P-1} m(g_p - g_c)2^p, \quad m(x) = |x| \tag{4}$$

where g_p and g_c correspond to the intensity of the central pixel and the neighbouring pixels, P and R correspond to a neighbourhood size for each pixel and a scale parameter, respectively. LBPs were not only computed on the intensity image, but also on the phase symmetry, bone probability, and the gradient images, thus providing a total of 8 additional features (Fig. 2(e)–(l)).

Rupture Points: This feature is derived from the work of Hellier et al. [6] on acoustic shadow detection. A statistical test based on physical ultrasound properties is performed on each scan line of the image. For each line, the purpose of the test is to detect a rupture in the signal, corresponding to the transition between a region with low signal intensity and a structure with high echogeneicity (Fig. 2(m)).

Each of these features has potential for characterizing a specific region. For instance, the rupture points (Fig. 2(m)) and LBP sign (Fig. 2(i)) provide useful information about the shape of the acoustic shadow but none about the bone surface, whereas the bone probability map (Fig. 2(a)) provides a mediocre outline of the former, but enhances the latter. That is, the ability of each feature to discriminate the three regions is limited, but their combination is promising.

2.2   Random Forest Classification

A random forest [5] is an ensemble of decision trees. As a learning machine method, it is reasonably fast, allows the classification of non linearly-separable elements and does not require much effort on feature selection to attain good performance. In this work, an ensemble of 90 of decision trees is created from a learning database of pixels from 16 ultrasound images. Nine other images were used as the testing database. For all 25 images, the ground truth segmentation was obtained manually by an expert. The learning database contains 2.2×10^4 pixels from acoustic shadows, 4.4×10^3 pixels from bone surfaces and 2.2×10^4 pixels from other tissues. We consider five times more pixels for the acoustic shadow and the other tissues because these regions are larger and more diverse so more data are required to describe them well. Each decision tree is created

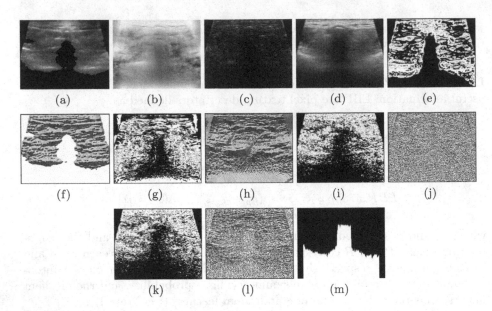

Fig. 2. Normalized feature images used for the classification (a) Bone probability, (b) Phase symmetry, (c) Gradient, (d) Intensity, (e)–(l) LBP features extracted from the bone probability, phase symmetry, gradient and intensity images, respectively, (m) Rupture points.

iteratively, and for each node, the best feature which splits the node into two is selected among 4 features chosen randomly. Additionally, it was determined that each tree should have at least 2 leaves. These optimal parameters for the random forest were obtained by cross-validation within the learning database, with 2/3 of the data used to create the random forest and 1/3 to test it. The new input data from the 9 image test database are classified using all the decision trees. The final decision of the random forest (i.e. the class assigned to each pixel) is based on a majority vote of the ensemble of decision trees.

2.3   Regularisation

Because some artefacts appear in the segmented image due to the misclassification of some pixels, it is important to regularise the segmentation results to reflect our context-specific constraints. First, we expect that a pixel will usually belong to the same class as its neighbour. To enforce this, median filtering, followed by morphological closing and opening operations, are applied to the binarized segmented images of the bone surfaces and of the acoustic shadow. Only connected components larger than a hundred pixels are kept. We also expect the segmentation results to agree with the known geometrical properties of vertebrae. A vertebra casts only one acoustic shadow and has a spinous process as its highest point. The highest pixel of the acoustic shadow is thus taken to represent the spinous process, and all the acoustic shadow regions beneath it in the direction of the wave propagation are merged into a single region. All the bone surface regions above this highest pixel in the direction of wave propagation are also kept. Finally, we obtain one connected component for the acoustic shadow, a few connected components for the bone surface above it, and one connected component for the other tissues.

3   Experiments and Results

We acquired the database of 25 ultrasound images (400×260) of vertebrae in the coronal plane using a Siemens 14L5 linear probe at a depth of 4.5 cm. The images were acquired from healthy adult volunteers (aged 21–24) in prone position. All the algorithms were implemented using Matlab on an Intel Core I5 PC.

Table 1 shows the result of our approach combining all proposed features as a confusion matrix. The average classification rates on 9 images are 81.97 % for the bone surfaces, 91.01 % for the acoustic shadow and 92.30 % for the other tissues. The average standard deviation of the classification rates (Table 2) are 16.33 % for the bone surface, 4.88 % for the acoustic shadow and 3.09 % for the other tissues. The low standard deviation obtained for the acoustic shadow classification rate shows that the proposed method is particularly robust for this class. The bone surface classification rate has a higher standard deviation because this region contains fewer pixels. Each image had an average of only 291 pixels in this region, so, for instance, 10 misclassified pixels alone introduce an error of 3.43 %.

Table 1. Confusion Matrix of the method, averaged over 9 images

Classification rate	Classifier output			
Actual value		Bone	Acoustic shadow	Other
	Bone	81.97 %	0.30 %	0.32 %
	Acoustic shadow	0 %	91.01 %	7.38 %
	Other	18.03 %	8.69 %	92.30 %

Table 2. Standard deviation of the classification rates, averaged over 9 images

	Bones surface	Acoustic shadow	Rest
Standard deviation	16.33 %	4.88 %	3.09 %

Figure 3 shows sample qualitative results for visual inspection. These images are typical vertebral ultrasound images. In Figs. 3(c) and (g), the general shape of the acoustic shadow and bone surface were distinguished clearly by our algorithm, but there are some small regions with misclassified pixels. In the second example (Fig. 3(g)), the acoustic shadow is broken into two distinct regions. Regularisation (Fig. 3(d)) removes many of these artefacts.

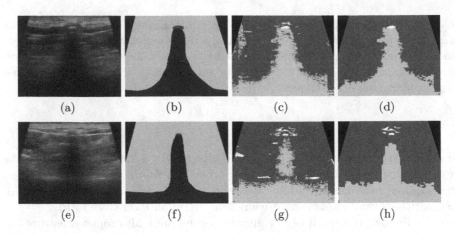

Fig. 3. Automatic segmentation results in two vertebral ultrasound images. (a)&(e) Original image, (b)&(f) Ground truth segmentation. Dark: acoustic shadow, medium: bone surface, light: other tissues. (c)&(g) Segmented image after random forest classification. (d)&(h) Segmented image after regularisation.

Another criterion which has to be considered is the computational efficiency of the method. Feature extraction and pixel classification take an average of 24 seconds per image. The method is fast but not fast enough to be used in real-time. Optimizing our implementation would likely improve its speed to a large extent. Alternative, possibly more computationally efficient classifiers (in combination with feature selection) could also be investigated in future work.

4   Conclusions

In this paper, we presented an automatic method for the segmentation of vertebrae in ultrasound images. In contrast with the methods already proposed in the literature, our method allows accurate detection of both the acoustic shadow and the bone surface. Our method is based on the combination of different features proposed in the literature and the use of random forests as a pixel classification method. A regularisation step which accounts for the properties of vertebrae was introduced to refine the segmentation. We obtained classification rates of 81.97 % for bone surfaces, 91.01 % for acoustic shadows and 92.30 % for other tissues. These results are promising and the method could be used to evaluate the quality of vertebral ultrasound image acquisitions. Other directions for future work include improving the classification rate for bone surfaces. For this purpose, other features will be investigated. We will also diversify our image database (thereby increasing the generalisability of our method) by using a variety of ultrasounds probes and acquiring images on more subjects.

References

1. Daanen, V., Tonetti, J., Troccaz, J.: A fully automated method for the delineation of osseous interface in ultrasound images. In: Barillot, C., Haynor, D.R., Hellier, P. (eds.) MICCAI 2004. LNCS, vol. 3216, pp. 549–557. Springer, Heidelberg (2004)
2. Hacihaliloglu, I., Abugharbieh, R., Hodgson, A., Rohling, R.: Bone surface localization in ultrasound using image phase-based features. Ultrasound Med. Biol. **35**(9), 1475–1487 (2009)
3. Foroughi, P., Boctor, E., Swartz, M., Taylor, R., Fichtinger, G.: Ultrasound bone segmentation using dynamic programming. In: Proceedings of the Ultrasonics Symposium, pp. 2523–2526 (2007)
4. Guo, Z., Zhang, L., Zhang, D.: A completed modeling of local binary pattern operator for texture classification. IEEE Trans. Image Process. **19**(6), 1657–1663 (2010)
5. Breiman, L.: Random forests. Mach. Learn. **45**, 5–32 (2001)
6. Hellier, P., Coup, P., Morandi, X., Collins, D.L.: An automatic geometrical and statistical method to detect acoustic shadows in intraoperative ultrasound brain images. Med. Image Anal. **14**, 195–204 (2010)
7. Karamalis, A., Wein, W., Klein, T., Navab, N.: Ultrasound confidence maps using random walks. Med. Image Anal. **16**, 1101–1112 (2012)
8. Kerby, B., Rohling, R., Nair, V., Abolmaesumi, P.: Automatic identification of lumbar level with ultrasound. In: Proceedings of the IEEE EMBC, pp. 2980–2983 (2008)
9. Tran, D., Rohling, R.N.: Automatic detection of lumbar anatomy in ultrasound images of human subjects. IEEE Trans. Ultrason. Ferroelectr. Freq. Control **57**(9), 2248–2256 (2010)
10. Al-Deen Ashab, H., Lessoway, V.A., Khallaghi, S., Cheng, A., Rohling, R., Abolmaesumi, P.: An augmented reality system for epidural anesthesia (AREA) prepuncture identification of vertebrae. IEEE Trans. Biomed. Eng. **60**(9), 2636–2644 (2013)
11. Chung-Wai, J.C., Guang-Quan, Z. Siu-Yin, L., Tak-Man, M., Ka-Lee, L., Yong-Ping, Z.: Ultrasound volume projection imaging for assessment of scoliosis. IEEE Transactions on Medical Imaging (2015) (in press)
12. Wei, C., Lou, E.H.M., Le, L.H.: Ultrasound imaging of spinal vertebrae to study scoliosis. Open J. Acoust. **2**(3), 95–103 (2012)
13. Cheung, C., Siu-Yin, L., Yong-Ping, Z. : Development of 3-D ultrasound system for assessment of adolescent idiopathic scoliosis (AIS): And system validation. In: Proceedings of the IEEE EMBC, pp. 6474–6477 (2013)
14. Ungi, T., King, F., Kempston, M., Keri, Z., Lasso, A., Mousavi, P., Rudan, J., Borschneck, D.P., Fichtinger, G.: Spinal curvature measurement by tracked ultrasound snapshots. Ultrasound Med. Biol. **40**(2), 447–454 (2014)

Towards an Automatic Clinical Classification
of Age-Related Macular Degeneration

Thanh Vân Phan[1(✉)], Lama Seoud[1,2], and Farida Cheriet[1]

[1] École Polytechnique de Montréal, Montreal, Canada
{thanh-van.phan,lama.seoud,farida.cheriet}@polymtl.ca
[2] DIAGNOS Inc., Brossard, Canada

Abstract. Age-related macular degeneration (AMD) is the leading cause of visual deficiency and irreversible blindness for elderly individuals in Western countries. Its screening relies on human analysis of fundus images which often leads to inter- and intra-expert variability. With the aim of developing an automatic grading system for AMD, this paper focuses on identifying the best features for automatic detection of AMD in fundus images. First, different features based on local binary pattern (LBP), run-length matrix, color or gradient information are computed. Then, a feature selection is applied for dimensionality reduction. Finally, a support vector machine is trained to determine the presence or absence of AMD. Experiments were conducted on a dataset of 140 fundus images. A classification performance with an accuracy of 96 % is achieved on preprocessed images of macula area using LBP features.

Keywords: Age-related macular degeneration · Fundus photography · Automatic grading system · Texture analysis · Support vector machine

1 Introduction

Age-related macular degeneration (AMD) is an eye disease leading to progressive degeneration of the macula. It is the main cause of visual deficiency and irreversible blindness in elderly individuals in Western countries [1]. Although it is asymptomatic in early stages, central vision is gradually lost until legal blindness in advanced stages. Even though there is currently no cure to AMD, treatments for slowing its progression exist and thus, regular eye examination is required.

Fundus photography is a common imaging modality used for eye examination. It is a fast and non-invasive modality that allows direct visualisation of structures of the retina. Based on fundus photography, grading AMD's severity stages, illustrated in Fig. 1, helps in determining specific and optimal treatment. A recommended clinical classification is the simplified AREDS classification [2], dividing AMD cases into four categories: non-AMD, early, moderate and advanced. However, human evaluation of retinal images is time-consuming and leads to inter- and intra-expert variability. To address this problem, automatic grading systems for AMD have been proposed for a faster and reproducible assessment.

Previous work on AMD focuses mostly on drusen segmentation. Drusen are early signs of AMD and depending on their number, size and position, a severity stage can

© Springer International Publishing Switzerland 2015
M. Kamel and A. Campilho (Eds.): ICIAR 2015, LNCS 9164, pp. 352–359, 2015.
DOI: 10.1007/978-3-319-20801-5_38

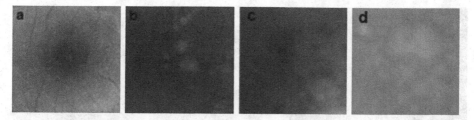

Fig. 1. Macula images of AMD stages: early with hard drusen (a), moderate with soft drusen (b), advanced with hemorrhages (c) and advanced with geographic atrophy (d)

be determined [3]. However, it is not sufficient for a complete AMD grading because drusen are not present in some advanced cases with large hemorrhages or geographic atrophies, which will then not be detected. Thus, methods with features directly computed on fundus images, such as visual context [4] or texture [5], were proposed to characterize the different forms of AMD. Generally, AMD vs. non-AMD classification is performed for AMD screening. Other binary classifications such as non-AMD vs. moderate cases or non-AMD and early cases vs. moderate and advanced cases are also considered in [4] to highlight moderate cases on which we must pay attention, because the patient still has a good visual acuity but there are high risks to progress to an advanced stage. These methods show a good accuracy (> 90 %) for binary classifications of good quality images. However, an automatic system performing AMD screening which is sufficiently robust to image quality does not exist.

The aim of this project is to identify the best set of image features that allows a robust AMD classification. The considered features are based on texture, color and gradient information and a support vector machine (SVM) with Gaussian kernel is used for classification.

2 Materials and Methods

In this method, a classical preprocessing is first applied to assure robustness to image quality, which is highly variable depending on the acquisition system. Features are then extracted from the preprocessed images and are submitted to a procedure of feature selection to use only the most relevant ones for classification.

2.1 Preprocessing

The fundus images come from different acquisition systems via telemedicine. For a non-biased comparison of these images, a classical preprocessing is first applied. For each color channel of the image, a large median filter with a kernel size of one-fourth the image size is applied in order to estimate the background illumination. The median filtered image is subtracted from the original image color channel, and then, the result is multiplied by 2 for contrast enhancement and the mean of the intensity range is added for the sake of visualization. An image with illumination normalization and contrast enhancement is obtained (Fig. 2c).

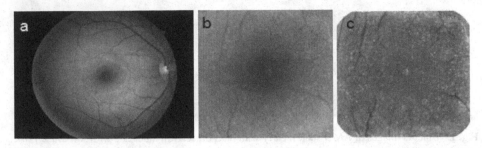

Fig. 2. Image type for each database: retina images (a), macula images (b) and preprocessed macula images (c)

2.2   Feature Extraction

This section presents the different features considered for image classification.

Local Binary Pattern (LBP) Features. Multiresolution information is used to analyze the images on different scales. In this study, it is obtained through Lemarié wavelet transform with four levels of decomposition. For each level, an approximation coefficient containing low resolution information and three detail coefficients containing high resolution information are obtained. With the original image, there are 17 images on which textural information are extracted. LBP is commonly used for texture analysis and shows its efficiency in many classification problems [5]. It consists in measuring the occurrence of local textures primitives, such as corners or edges. To do so, the sign of LBP [6] is computed for each pixel of grey value g_c in a neighborhood of radius R and P neighbors of gray value g_p :

$$LBP_{P,R} = \sum_{p=0}^{P-1} s(g_p - g_c)2^P \tag{1}$$

$$\text{With } s(x) = \begin{cases} 1, & \text{if } x \geq 0 \\ 0, & \text{Otherwise} \end{cases}$$

In this study, the parameters are empirically set to R = 1 and P = 4 or 8. The magnitude of LBP [7] is also computed from the absolute differences of gray intensity between the central pixel and the neighbors $m_p = |g_p - g_c|$:

$$LBPM_{P,R} = \sum_{p=0}^{P-1} t(m_p, c)2^P \tag{2}$$

$$\text{With } t(x, c) = \begin{cases} 1, & \text{if } x \geq c \\ 0, & \text{Otherwise} \end{cases}$$

The threshold c is set to the image mean value. From the sign and magnitude of LBP, two histograms are computed by measuring the occurrence of the different patterns in the image. The features vector is then constructed by their concatenation. This method is applied separately on each color channel (red, green and blue).

Grey Level Run-Length Matrix (GLRLM). GLRLM is another simple method for texture analysis. For a given image and a given direction, the GLRLM $P(i, j)$ measures the number of runs in the image of a grey level i and a run-length j [8]. As there are many zeros in the matrix, it is generally represented by 11 scalars derived from the GLRLM. The features vector is obtained by concatenation of the 11 features computed in the four principal directions ($0°$, $45°$, $90°$ and $135°$). Again, the method is applied separately on each color channel.

Color Histograms. Generally, works on fundus images analysis only use green channel because blood vessels and lesions are more visible on it [3–5]. Because structures characterizing AMD have different colors, the information from the other color channels must also be considered. In this study, red and blue channels are used with the green one. Once all the color plans are extracted, 4 and 8 bins histograms are computed on each channel. The features vector corresponds to the concatenation of the three color histograms.

Histograms of Oriented Gradients. HOG [9] is a feature used for edge detection, but can be used as directional information for classification. Indeed, images with lesions should show more gradient in a specific direction. The method consists in calculating the magnitude and the direction of the gradient for each pixel. The gradient images in horizontal G_x and in vertical G_y are obtained by applying 1D point centered derivatives kernels [1 0 -1], on the image. The gradient's magnitude and direction are computed from G_x and G_y. Then, the image is divided in 16x16 cells and histograms of 4 and 8 directions are locally constructed by measuring the number of pixels in a certain direction, weighted by the gradient's magnitude.

2.3 Feature Selection

Generally, feature extraction leads to a large number of features compared to the number of samples. To avoid the curse of dimensionality and data overfitting, a sequential floating forward selection (SFFS) [10] is used to find the optimal subset of features. It consists in applying iteratively sequential forward selection (SFS) and sequential backward selection (SBS). SFS begins with an empty model of features subset and successively adds the best feature which, when combined to the previously selected features maximizes a criterion function. In this study, we considered a non-optimized Gaussian kernel SVM classification performance, with parameters set on $C = 1$ and $\gamma = 1$, on the validation set as the criterion function. SBS starts with all the features computed on the image and consists in deleting the worst feature at each iteration according to the same criterion function. In SFFS, it starts with an empty model. Then, at each iteration, the SFS algorithm is applied l times and the SBS algorithm is applied r times. The l and r parameters are determined by the system itself and thus they are left floating. The process is repeated until the maximum number of iteration is achieved or until no more improvement of the criterion function, whichever comes first. This method tends to find a close to optimal solution.

2.4   Classifier Modeling

To determine the presence or absence of AMD, an SVM classifier with Gaussian kernel [11] is chosen because it is efficient for small samples and for more complex separation than a linear classifier. The decision boundary function is computed using the elements x_i of a learning set and their label y_i:

$$H(x) = \sum_{i=1}^{l} \alpha_i y_i k(x_i, x) + b \qquad (3)$$

$$\text{With } k(x, y) = \exp(-\gamma \|x - y\|^2)$$

$k(x, y)$ is the Gaussian kernel, l the number of elements in the learning set, α_i and b coefficients from margin optimisation. The classifier is then optimized with γ, the kernel parameter and C, a tolerance parameter for elements to be on the margin. The optimal parameter values are chosen according to the performance assessment using 10 folds cross-validation strategy. In the testing stage, a new element x is classified with a label y depending on its relative position to the decision boundary:

$$y(x) = sign(H(x)) \qquad (4)$$

2.5   Validation Method

Most of the fundus images used in this project is provided by the telemedicine platform of DIAGNOS Inc. (Canada). Because it has been acquired in a real screening context and using various cameras, the images are highly heterogeneous in terms of quality, resolution, illumination and contrast. To complete this private database, images from public databases such as Automated Retinal Image Analysis (ARIA, United Kingdom) and Structured Analysis of Retina (STARE, United States) are added. These databases contain images with low resolution and low quality, such as blurred images or bad illumination. This preliminary study focuses solely on AMD vs. non-AMD classification. All the images have been labelled by a clinical expert. Overall, the considered dataset is composed of 80 images with different stages of AMD and 60 images without AMD. Another dataset is derived from the first one. It is obtained by manually identifying and segmenting the macula area when visible. This second dataset is thus composed of 76 macula images with AMD and 49 without AMD. A third dataset is established from the same macula images with preprocessing.

The three datasets are divided in a learning set for system modeling and in a testing set for performance assessment. The retinal learning set is composed of 115 images, 65 of which are with AMD with a large proportion of advanced cases and some early and moderate cases, and 50 of which are non-AMD images with healthy and other eye diseases cases. The macula learning sets (with and without preprocessing) are composed each of the same 100 macula images, 63 of which are with AMD, and 37 without AMD. The testing datasets are composed of 15 AMD and 10 non-AMD cases for retina images, 13 AMD and 12 non-AMD for macula images and 13 AMD and 12 non-AMD for preprocessed macula images. These images were selected to represent the different AMD severity stages and the different image quality levels.

3   Results and Discussion

For each testing set, the images are represented using each of the features vectors described in Sect. 2.3. Tables 1, 2 and 3 show the features sets that achieved the best classification performance for each testing dataset. The performance assessment is based on the accuracy (proportion of well classified elements), the sensitivity (proportion of well classified AMD elements) and the specificity (proportion of well classified non-AMD elements). For ends of comparison, the last row corresponds to the results obtained for the method proposed in [5] and applied on the same datasets.

Table 1. Best performance on retina images

Features set	Parameters	Sensitivity	Specificity	Accuracy
LBP4 (blue)	C = 10, γ = 1	93.33 %	40 %	72 %
HOG8	C = 10, γ = 0.1	86.67 %	50 %	72 %
LBP4 (red)	C = 10, γ = 1	86,67 %	50 %	72 %
Garnier [5]	LDA	80 %	60 %	72 %

LBP4 = local binary pattern with 4 neighbors, HOG8 = histograms of oriented gradient with 8 directions, LDA = linear discriminant analysis.

Table 2. Best performance on macula images

Features set	Parameters	Sensitivity	Specificity	Accuracy
LBP8 (blue)	C = 1, γ = 1	100 %	75 %	88 %
LBP8 (green)	C = 50, γ = 1	92,31 %	83,33 %	88 %
HOG4	C = 100, γ = 1	100 %	66,67 %	84 %
Garnier [5]	LDA	100 %	66,67 %	84 %

LBP8 = local binary pattern with 8 neighbors, HOG4 = histograms of oriented gradient with 4 directions, LDA = linear discriminant analysis.

Table 3. Best performance on preprocessed macula images

Features set	Parameters	Sensitivity	Specificity	Accuracy
LBP8 (green)	C = 1, γ = 1	100 %	91,67 %	96 %
HOG4	C = 1, γ = 1	100 %	75 %	88 %
Color8	C = 1, γ = 1	92.31 %	83.33 %	88 %
Garnier [5]	LDA	69,23 %	58,33 %	62 %

LBP8 = local binary pattern with 8 neighbors, Color8: Histograms of color with 8 bins, HOG4 = histograms of oriented gradient with 4 directions, LDA = linear discriminant analysis

RETINA   **MACULA**   **PREPROCESSED MACULA**

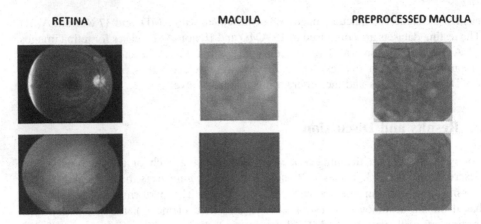

Fig. 3. Examples of misclassification for each testing dataset

In Fig. 3, examples of misclassified images are illustrated. For the retina dataset, the best accuracy achieved is 72 %, which is similar to the one reported in [5]. Misclassifications were noted on images with bad quality, in particular with reflections or with non-visible macula. When the analysis is focused only on the macula area, the results are improved with 88 % accuracy for the best features (LBP applied on blue and green channels). These features combined with an SVM classifier perform better than the method used in [5]. Here, misclassification were noted on advanced AMD images with large hemorrhages and on images with reflections. When the features are extracted on preprocessed macula images, the performance increases significantly. Common misclassification with HOG and color features are noted on early AMD images with visible reflections. The best result, with 96 % accuracy, is obtained with LBP applied on the green channel of the preprocessed images. In this case, the only misclassified image contains exudates, retinal lesions highly similar to drusen.

The method with LBP features on preprocessed images shows robustness to image quality with a good classification of bad quality images, that the method proposed in [5] could not perform. Some examples are illustrated in Fig. 4.

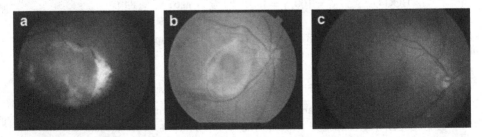

Fig. 4. Examples of good classification of bad quality images: bad illumination (a), low resolution (b) and visible reflections (c)

4 Conclusion

The proposed automatic classification system for AMD showed promising results, with good classification and robustness to image quality. The conducted experiments demonstrate the effectiveness of features based on texture with a Gaussian kernel SVM for this application. The preliminary results highlights the discriminative strength of a local analysis of fundus images using LBP computed on preprocessed images. The proposed method outperforms previous published work applied on the same dataset. In future work, we plan on evaluating a combination of the features sets used in this study. Moreover, an extensive validation with a more complete dataset will be conducted in order to develop an automatic AMD grading system with the four different stages. Once improved and validated, this system should allow a reliable AMD diagnosis.

References

1. Kasuga, D.T., Chen, Y., Zhang, K.: Genetics of age-related degeneration. In: Ho, C.A., Regillo, C.D. (eds.) Age-related Macular Degeneration Diagnosis and Treatment, pp. 1–14 (2011)
2. Davis, M.D., Gangnon, R.E., Lee, L.Y., Hubbard, L.D., Klein, B.E., Klein, R., Ferris, F.L., Bressler, S.B., Milton, R.C.: The age-related eye disease study severity scale for age-related macular degeneration. Arch. Ophtalmol. **123**, 1484–1498 (2005)
3. van Grinsven, M.J., Lechanteur, Y.T., van de Ven, J.P., van Ginneken, B., Hoyng, C.B., Theelen, T., Sánchez, C.I.: Automatic drusen quantification and risk assessment of age-related macular degeneration on color fundus images. Invest. Ophthalmol. Vis. Sci. **54** (4), 3019–3027 (2013)
4. Kankanahalli, S., Burlina, P.M., Wolfson, Y., Freund, D.E., Bressler, N.M.: Automated classification of severity of age-related macular degeneration from fundus photographs. Invest. Ophthalmol. Vis. Sci. **54**(3), 1789–1796 (2013)
5. Garnier, M., Hurtut, T., Tahar, H.B., Cheriet, F.: Automatic multiresolution age-related macular degeneration detection from fundus images. In: SPIE Medical Imaging, International Society for Optics and Photonics. pp. 903532-903532 (2014)
6. Ojala, T., Pietikainen, M., Maenpaa, T.: Multiresolution gray-scale and rotation invariant texture classification with local binary patterns. IEEE Trans. Pattern Anal. Mach. Intell. **24** (7), 971–987 (2002)
7. Guo, Z., Zhang, D.: A completed modeling of local binary pattern operator for texture classification. IEEE Trans. Image Process. **19**(6), 1657–1663 (2010)
8. Tang, X.: Texture information in run-length matrices. IEEE Trans. Image Process. **7**(11), 1602–1609 (1998)
9. Dalal, N., Triggs, B.: Histograms of oriented gradients for human detection. In: IEEE Computer Society Conference on Computer Vision and Pattern Recognition, 2005, vol. 1, pp. 886-893 (2005)
10. Pudil, P., Ferri, F.J., Novovicova, J., Kittler, J.: Floating search methods for feature selection with nonmonotonic criterion functions. In: Proceedings of the Twelveth International Conference on Pattern Recognition, IAPR (1994)
11. Steinwart, I., Christmann, A.: Support Vector Machines. Springer Science & Business Media, New York (2008)

Optical Flow Based Approach for Automatic Cardiac Cycle Estimation in Ultrasound Images of the Carotid

Teresa Araújo[1,2]($\boxtimes$), Guilherme Aresta[1,2], José Rouco[1],
Carmen Ferreira[3], Elsa Azevedo[3], and Aurélio Campilho[1,2]

[1] INESC TEC - INESC Tecnologia e Ciência, Porto, Portugal
{tfaraujo,gmaresta}@inescporto.pt
[2] Faculdade de Engenharia da Universidade do Porto, Porto, Portugal
[3] Faculdade de Medicina da Universidade do Porto, Porto, Portugal

Abstract. This paper proposes a method to detect a reference frame in an ultrasound video of the carotid artery. This reference frame, usually located at the end of the diastole, is used as the location to measure several vascular biomarkers. Our approach is based on the analysis of the movement of the carotid walls in ultrasound images using an optical flow technique. A periodic movement resembling heart beat is observed in the resulting signals. The comparison of these signals with electrocardiograms validates the proposed method for detecting the reference frame.

Keywords: Optical flow · Carotid ultrasound · Electrocardiogram · Heart rate

1 Introduction

Ultrasound (US) imaging techniques are widely used for the diagnosis of cardiovascular diseases. This real-time harmless and usually non-invasive modality allows movement analysis of the vessel walls. Common carotid artery (CCA) US image is commonly used to evaluate the risk of cardiovascular diseases through the analysis of atherosclerosis markers like carotid intima media thickness (IMT) [1] and plaque formation [2].

The IMT is correlated with the adventitia-to-adventitia and intraluminal CCA diameters, which vary along the cardiac cycle. Thus, for comparison purposes, it should be always measured at the same stage of the cardiac cycle [1,3,4]. Despite IMT measurement can be performed manually, several semi-automatic or fully-automatic methods have been proposed [5–7]. These methods rely on segmentation algorithms to locate and delineate the CCA walls from an input US image. It is usually assumed that the reference frame within the cardiac cycle is provided as input image. Likewise, in the standard acquisition protocols, it is recommended to use a clear 3-lead electrocardiographic signal, to define the location of end-diastole frame in US video sequences.

© Springer International Publishing Switzerland 2015
M. Kamel and A. Campilho (Eds.): ICIAR 2015, LNCS 9164, pp. 360–367, 2015.
DOI: 10.1007/978-3-319-20801-5_39

In this work, an alternative method for the location of the standardized frame of measurement from US video sequences is proposed. Unlike previous approaches, the proposed method relies on carotid wall movement analysis to infer the cardiac cycle, so that a synchronized electrocardiographic signal is not required. To that end, Optical Flow (OF), which is a technique that allows to estimate movement on a sequence of frames [8], is used. Movement analysis has been previously used for diagnosis from US sequences. These techniques include block matching with Kalman filters [9–11], OF [9,11] and speckle traking techniques [12]. These methodologies have been sucessfuly used for the estimation of vessel diameter during systole and diastole [9], the assessment of plaque vulnerability [10], the measurement of elasticity of vessel walls [11], and the estimation of the blood movement and velocity [12], demonstrating the correlation of the local movement of image patterns with physiological features of the blood vessels that are relevant to the diagnosis of atherosclerosis. Concretely, optical flow demonstrated higher performance in some of these applications in comparison with other alternative techniques [9,11]. However, to our knowledge, the use of such techniques for the application herein described has not been explored in the bibliography, being the use of a 3-lead ECG the only available method.

This document is structured as follows: Sect. 2 describes the algorithms used for the analysis of the US videos; Sect. 3 presents the description of the experimental setting, and the discussion of the obtained results; finally, Sect. 4 provides a summary of the conclusions derived from the research herein presented.

2 Methods

This section explains each step of our approach to find an optimal reference frame in the US video for the automatic measurement of cardiovascular biomarkers. Briefly, the algorithm is divided in the following two stages. First, a region of interest (ROI) containing the vessel walls is automatically selected, and a set of regions around the wall is detected for each frame. Then, in the second stage, OF is computed, quantized and integrated for each region, in order to allow the characterization of vessel wall movement.

2.1 Selection of the Region of Interest

To apply OF on an US video a ROI is selected, so that only the movement of the vessel walls is taken into account in the analysis. A Canny edge detector [13] with a high sigma is applied to obtain a rough location of the vessel walls. Note that an accurate segmentation is not needed, since the objective is to adjust the selection of the ROI near the CCA walls. The CCA is automatically located using a lumen centerline detection algorithm, based on [14]. From the detected centerline, the nearest upper and lower Canny edges are selected for each image column, and then the largest connected component on each side is selected as the vessel wall. This allows to select a ROI containing the CCA walls as depicted in Fig. 1, along with the identification of the upper and lower wall contours.

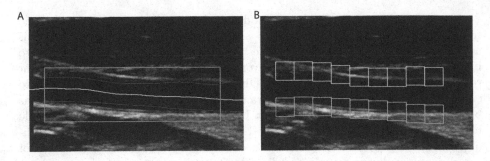

Fig. 1. A - ROI (green rectangle) containing upper and lower walls (red) based on the segmented lumen (yellow). B - Resulting squares along the vessel walls (Color figure online).

After this initial step both upper and lower wall contours are divided in segments of 50 pixels width. For each segment the movement is analyzed inside a set of square regions that contain 20 % lumen and 80 % wall, as shown in Fig. 1B. The square positions are updated on the basis of the Canny results for each frame t, and the union of these small ROIs for each wall w is denoted as $\Omega_w(t)$.

2.2   Optical Flow: Lucas-Kanade Algorithm

The movement analysis is performed using the Lucas-Kanade algorithm with a single frame [8]. With this technique, for each pixel a 2D vector that gives the pixel displacement compared to the previous frame is determined. This method has a good performance for small image displacements, as it is the case in the present study. Also, this approach is based on the brightness constancy constraint, i.e. the intensity of a pixel that has a small motion between two frames that are close in time is the same, as expressed in the following equation:

$$I(x,y,t) = I(x + \delta x, y + \delta y, t + \delta t) \tag{1}$$

where $I(x,y,t)$ denotes the image intensity at the position (x,y) and time t.

Assuming small movement, the development in Taylor series of the image intensity $I(x,y,t)$, leads to the following equation

$$I_x v_x + I_y v_y = -I_t \tag{2}$$

where I_x and I_y denote the x and y derivatives of $I(x,y,t)$; v_x and v_y are the x and y components of the OF velocity vector $v = (v_x, v_y)$ and I_t denotes the time derivative of $I(x,y,t)$. Other equations, imposing additional constraints, are needed to determine the OF. In the case of the Lucas-Kanade method, it is assumed that the OF in a small neighborhood of a pixel is the same for every pixel in that window (smoothness assumption). The OF velocity vector $v(x,y)$ for each pixel is then determined using least squares fit.

After computing the OF on the video sequence, the resulting velocity vectors $v(x,y;t)$ are quantized in disjoint angle intervals, and their magnitudes are

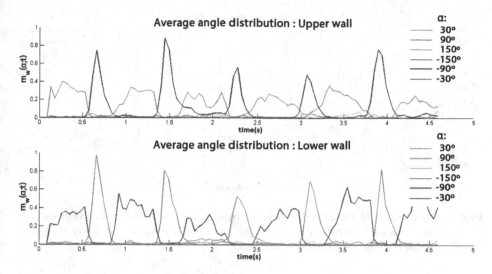

Fig. 2. Distribution of movement in the different directions with time of the upper and lower walls.

integrated for each wall position $\Omega_w(t)$. The amount of movement $m_w(\alpha; t)$ for each angle α, time t and wall w, is given by

$$m_w(\alpha; t) = \sum_{(x,y) \in \Omega_w(t)} \|v(x, y; t)\| \times \Phi_\alpha(v(x, y; t)) \tag{3}$$

where $\Omega_w(t)$ denotes the ROI at the wall w and time t; Φ_α is an indicator function of the vector angle, having value 1 in the interval $[\alpha - 30°, \alpha + 30°]$ and 0 elsewhere; and $\alpha \in \{-150°, -90°, -30°, 30°, 90°, 150°\}$. The amount of movement $m_w(\alpha; t)$ is used to analyse the wall movement through time. An example is shown in Fig. 2. As expected, the main movement is evidenced in the vertical direction $\alpha = \pm 90°$, corresponding to the contraction and dilation movements of the vessel walls.

From the analysis of Fig. 2 it also possible to verify a periodic behavior of the movement, divided into two distinct stages: a faster movement in convergent wall direction, and a noisier and slower movement (approximately two times the duration) on the divergent wall direction. This is related to the cardiac cycle, which is also divided on a strong contraction (systole) followed by a period of rest with twice the systole duration (diastole). The hypothesis validation of the detected movement being related to the cardiac cycle is discussed on the next section.

3   Results and Discussion

The proposed method is evaluated on 3 US video sequences provided by Centro Hospitalar São João. This dataset consists on multiframe DICOM files (frame

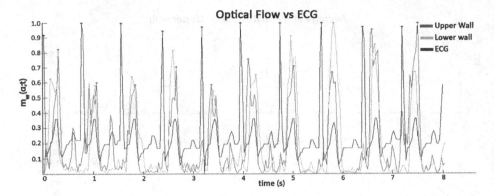

Fig. 3. Comparison of the signal extracted from OF for the down direction on the upper wall, the signal extracted from OF for the up direction on the lower wall and the ECG signal, along with the detected peaks.

rate: 33 Hz; resolution: 800 × 600) recorded using a Philips Healthcare iU22 ultrasound system on healthy individuals, with age of approximately 20 years. The files also contain the synchronized ECG signals.

The ECG and OF signals are compared to evaluate the systole synchronism. To that end, both the R-peaks of the ECG signals (the peak from the QRS segment that corresponds to ventricular depolarization, i.e., heart contraction) and the peaks of the up and down OF signals are detected and compared with each other using a Bland-Altman analysis [15]. In this sense, R-peaks are compared with peaks obtained from the movement signal extracted from OF for the down direction on the upper wall $(m_{upper}(-90; t))$, and for the up direction on the lower wall $(m_{lower}(90; t))$. These signals are depicted in Fig. 3 for comparison purposes.

From the analysis of Fig. 3 it is possible to verify that the systolic movements of the lower and upper wall are synchronous, as expected. It is also possible to verify that this periodic movement resembles the cardiac cycle due to its similarity in frequency with the retrieved ECG waveform. Furthermore, a delay between the ECG and the derived movement is also noticeable.

Figure 4 shows a graphic representation (Bland-Altman plot) of the wall movement obtained for each window, during the systole, and for three US videos. Likewise, Table 1 shows the mean time difference (μ_d) and the standard deviation of the time differences (σ_d) measured for each video and for each wall. Through the analysis of the results, several conclusions can be taken. Firstly, for the top window, it is visible that the mean difference is almost equal for all the three videos, leading to infer that the delay between the wall systole and the cardiac systole is almost constant. It is also noticeable that the differences for videos 1 and 2 are more spread (larger σ_d) than for videos 2 and 3, respectively. This can be due to the fact that video 3 was the video during which the subject had a more constant and lower heart rate: in video 1, the heart rate decreased from 74 bpm to 65 bpm. This can introduce physiological constraints in the results,

Table 1. Mean and standard deviation of the delay (in seconds) between the ECG R-peaks and the OF movement signal peaks for each wall.

	Video 1	Video 2	Video 3
Upper wall	-0.22 ± 0.06	-0.21 ± 0.03	-0.18 ± 0.02
Lower wall	-0.20 ± 0.04	-0.18 ± 0.02	-0.18 ± 0.02

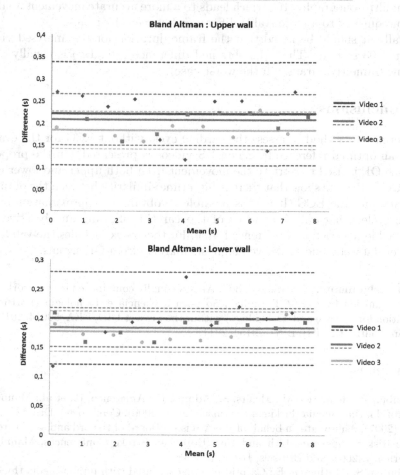

Fig. 4. Bland-Altman plot comparing the systole peaks derived from OF and ECG signals. Full lines represent the mean difference μ_d and dashed lines represent $\mu \pm 2\sigma_d$.

since the response of the vessels to a change in the heart rate can suffer a non linear variation, i.e. the increase in the frequency of the heartbeat may not lead to an immediate and proportional increase in the frequency of contraction of the vessel.

For the bottom window the proximity of the means for the three videos can still be observed, leading to the same conclusions as before. Additionally, the means obtained for the top window are close to those obtained for the bottom window (showing a small difference, in the order of a few milliseconds, being that the bottom window shows a smaller mean). Nevertheless, some differences in the two results can be noticed. The difference spreads σ_d for the bottom windows are also smaller than for the top windows. This can be justified by the fact that lower wall has a higher imaging quality, due to the contrast enhancing effects of fluids in ultrasonography [16], which leads to a more accurate movement analysis and consequently to a more stable difference between the peaks.

Finally, it should be noted that the frame duration for the analysed videos is about 0.03 seconds. Thus, the obtained difference spread σ_d is usually lower than one frame (two frames in the worst case).

4   Conclusions

An alternative method to assess the cardiac cycle without ECG for the evaluation of an optimal reference frame on US videos is presented. On the proposed approach OF is used to retrieve the movement from both upper and lower walls of the CCA. Results show that there is high time similarity between the obtained OF signal and the ECG. It is thus possible to obtain an approximation of the cardiac cycle using only US videos of the carotid, allowing an objective and reproducible selection of a reference frame. Further work includes the validation on larger datasets, and to derive diagnosis markers from OF signals.

Acknowledgements. T. Araújo and G. Aresta equally contributed to this work. This work is financied by the FCT - Fundação para a Ciência e Tecnologia (Portuguese Foundation for Science and Technology) within the project UID/EEA/50014/2013 and the grant contract SFRH/BPD/79154/2011.

References

1. Toubul, P., Hennerici, M., Meairs, S., Adams, H., Amarenco, P., et al.: Mannheim carotid intima-media thickness consensus (2004–2006). Cerebrovasc Dis. 23(1), 75–80 (2007). An update on behalf of the Advisory Board of the 3rd and 4th Watching the Risk Symposium, 13th and 15th European Stroke Conferences, Mannheim, Germany, 2004, and Brussels, Belgium, 2006
2. Johnsen, S., Mathiesen, E.: Carotid plaque compared with intima-media thickness as a predictor of coronary and cerebrovascular disease. Curr. Cardiol. Rep. 11(1), 21–27 (2009)
3. Polak, J., Meisner, A., Pencina, M., Wolf, P., D'agostino, R.: Variations in common carotid artery intima-media thickness during the cardiac cycle: implications for cardiovascular risk assessment. J. Am. Soc. Echocardiogr. 25(9), 1023–1028 (2012)
4. Menees, S., Zhang, D., Le, J., Chen, J., Raghuveer, G.: Variations in carotid artery intima-media thickness during the cardiac cycle in children. J. Am. Soc. Echocardiogr. 23(1), 58–63 (2010)
5. Molinari, F., Zeng, G., Suri, J.: A state of the art review on intima-media thickness (IMT) measurement and wall segmentation techniques for carotid ultrasound. Comput. Methods Programs Biomed. 100(3), 201–221 (2010)

6. Rocha, R., Campilho, A., Silva, J., Azevedo, E., Santos, R.: Segmentation of the carotid intima-media region in B-mode ultrasound images. Image Vis. Comput. **28**, 614–625 (2010)
7. Rocha, R., Silva, J., Campilho, A.: Automatic segmentation of carotid B-mode images using fuzzy classification. Med. Biol. Eng. Comput. **50**, 533–545 (2012)
8. Lucas, B., Kanade, T.: An iterative image registration technique with an application to stereo vision. In: Proceedings of the International Joint Conference on Artificial Intelligence, pp. 674–679 (1981)
9. Gastounioti, A., Golemati, S., Stoitsis, J., Nikita, K.: Comparison of Kalman-filter-based approaches for block matching in arterial wall motion analysis from B-mode ultrasound. Meas. Sci. Technol. **22**, 114008–17 (2011)
10. Gastounioti, A., Golemati, S., Stoitsis, J., Nikita, K.: Carotid artery wall motion analysis from B-mode ultrasound using adaptive block matching: in silico evaluation and in vivo application. Phys. Med. Biol. **58**, 8647–8661 (2013)
11. Golemati, S., Stoitsis, J., Gastounioti, A., Dimopoulos, A., Koropouli, V., Nikita, K.: Comparison of block matching and differential methods for motion analysis of the carotid artery wall from ultrasound images. IEEE Trans. Inf. Technol. Biomed. **16**(5), 852–858 (2012)
12. Swillens, A., Segers, P., Torp, H., Lvstakken, L.: Two-dimensional blood velocity estimation with ultrasound: speckle tracking versus crossed-beam vector doppler based on flow simulations in a carotid bifurcation model. IEEE Trans. Ultrason. Ferroelectr. Freq. Control **57**(2), 327–339 (2010)
13. Canny, J.: A computational approach to edge detection. IEEE Trans. Pattern Anal. Mach. Intell. PAMI **8**(6), 679–698 (1986)
14. Rouco, J., Campilho, A.: Robust common carotid artery lumen detection in B-mode ultrasound images using local phase symmetry. In: International Conference on Acoustics, Speech and Signal Processing, pp. 929–933 (2013)
15. Bland, J., Altman, D.: Statistical methods for assessing agreement between two methods of clinical measurement. Lancet **327**, 307–310 (1986)
16. Wikstrand, J.: Methodological considerations of ultrasound measurement of carotid artery intima-media thickness and lumen diameter. Clin. Physiol. Imaging **27**, 341–345 (2007)

Statistical Textural Distinctiveness in Multi-Parametric Prostate MRI for Suspicious Region Detection

Audrey G. Chung$^{(\boxtimes)}$, Christian Scharfenberger, Farzad Khalvati, Alexander Wong, and Masoom A. Haider

Department of Systems Design Engineering, University of Waterloo, 200 University Ave W, Waterloo, Canada
agchung@uwaterloo.ca

Abstract. Prostate cancer is the most diagnosed form of cancer, but survival rates are relatively high with sufficiently early diagnosis. Current computer-aided image-based cancer detection methods face notable challenges including noise in MRI images, variability between different MRI modalities, weak contrast, and non-homogeneous texture patterns, making it difficult for diagnosticians to identify tumour candidates. We propose a novel saliency-based method for identifying suspicious regions in multi-parametric MR prostate images based on statistical texture distinctiveness. In this approach, a sparse texture model is learned via expectation maximization from features derived from multi-parametric MR prostate images, and the statistical texture distinctiveness-based saliency based on this model is used to identify suspicious regions. The proposed method was evaluated using real clinical prostate MRI data, and results demonstrate a clear improvement in suspicious region detection relative to the state-of-art method.

Keywords: Computer-aided prostate cancer detection · Multi-Parametric Magnetic Resonance Imaging (MP-MRI) · Texture-based saliency · Statistical textural distinctiveness

1 Introduction

Prostate cancer is the most commonly diagnosed cancer in Canadian men (excluding non-melanoma skin cancers), with an estimated 23,600 new cases and 4,000 deaths from it in 2014 [5]. According to the Canadian Cancer Society, prostate cancer is the third leading cause of death from cancer, accounting for 10 % of cancer deaths in Canadian men. Despite these statistics, survival rates

---

A.G. Chung—This research was undertaken, in part, thanks to funding from the Canada Research Chairs program. The study was also funded by the Natural Sciences and Engineering Research Council (NSERC) of Canada and the Ontario Ministry of Economic Development and Innovation.

© Springer International Publishing Switzerland 2015
M. Kamel and A. Campilho (Eds.): ICIAR 2015, LNCS 9164, pp. 368–376, 2015.
DOI: 10.1007/978-3-319-20801-5_40

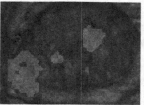

Fig. 1. From left to right: pathology samples, identification results of proposed method (6 texture atoms), identification results for [4].

are relatively high with sufficiently early diagnosis, making the need for fast and reliable detection methods crucial.

The current clinical model uses a digital rectal exam (DRE) or a prostate-specific antigen (PSA) test for initial screening. Men with a positive DRE or elevated PSA require a follow-up transrectal ultrasound (TRUS) guided biopsy to assess malignancy. Recent studies [2,13] indicate that the PSA test has a high risk of overdiagnosis, with an estimated 50 % of screened men being diagnosed with prostate cancer. This oversensitivity results in expensive and painful prostate biopsies, which cause discomfort, possible sexual dysfunction, and may result in increased hospital admission rates due to infectious complications [10]. The challenge diagnosticians face is how to improve prostate cancer diagnosis by reducing the overdiagnosis caused by conventional screening methods while still maintaining a high sensitivity (Fig. 1).

Current imaging-based cancer screening methods (such as the use of magnetic resonance imaging or MRI) require extensive interpretation by an experienced medical professional. One notable challenge is the variability between diagnosticians ("inter-observer variability") and the variability of a single diagnostician over multiple sittings ("intra-observer variability") when evaluating features using multi-parametric MRI (i.e., different MRI modalities) [7]. The European Society of Urogenital Radiology (ESUR) recently introduced PI-RADS, or the Prostate Imaging - Reporting And Diagnosis System [3]. PI-RADS is a set of guidelines for interpreting multiple MRI images, and aims to raise the consistency between diagnosticians through a common set of criteria.

Despite PI-RADS and further development to standardize the interpretation of multi-parametric MRI images [11], there is still a level of subjectiveness that can lead to inconsistent diagnosis. Notable challenges include noise in MR images, variability between different MRI modalities, weak contrast, and non-homogeneous texture patterns, making it difficult for diagnosticians to identify tumour candidates. Computer-aided cancer detection methods are being developed to help the physicians with the process.

One specific area of research is the identification of suspicious regions to aid physicians with performing a more efficient and accurate diagnosis. The current method for identifying suspicious regions is to threshold apparent diffusion coefficient (ADC) maps, as low ADC values are associated with tumorous tissue [6].

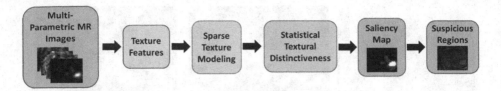

Fig. 2. Proposed framework for identifying suspicious regions using prostate multi-parametric MRI. Unique texture features extracted from different MRI modalities are used to learn a sparse texture model, and suspicious regions are identified via a statistical textural distinctiveness-based saliency map.

Cameron *et al.* [4] proposed a threshold-based approach where tissue associated with ADC values within a threshold range are automatically identified as suspicious. However, this method depends on fixed thresholds, making it susceptible to noisy MR images and ADC variations across different sets of multi-parametric MRI data.

To facilitate a more reliable diagnosis, a novel method for identifying suspicious regions indicative of potential prostate cancer using texture-based saliency in multi-parametric MR images is proposed. The proposed method uses unique texture information from each MRI modality to learn a sparse texture model, and better characterize suspicious tissue within a patient's MRI data.

2   Methods

A novel method is proposed for identifying suspicious regions to better aid physicians with performing more efficient and accurate diagnoses. The proposed method uses multi-parametric MR images and incorporates cross-modality texture features to better identify suspicious regions via statistical textural distinctiveness. Figure 2 shows the general algorithmic framework developed.

2.1   Region-Based Textural Representations

Region-based textural representations are used to allow for the characterization of texture features indicative of suspicious regions in prostate MR images. For region-based textural representations, we incorporate the feature set proposed by Khalvati *et al.* [8], which consists of sets of 19 low-level texture features extracted each from T2-weighted (T2w) images, apparent diffusion coefficient (ADC) maps, computed high-b diffusion-weighted imaging (CHB-DWI) data, and correlated diffusion imaging (CDI) data, to better capture healthy and cancerous tissue characteristics. These MRI modalities were selected based on their potential to separate cancerous from healthy prostate tissue.

The sets of texture features are combined into a single textural representation $h(x)$, and a compact version of the textural representation is produced using principal component analysis (PCA). A compact textural representation $t(x)$ is produced using the u principal components of $h(x)$ with the highest variance:

$$t(x) = \langle \Phi_i(h(x))|1 \leq i \leq u \rangle \tag{1}$$

where Φ_i is the ith principal component of $h(x)$. While u can be selected based on variance compactness, u components of $h(x)$ were selected to represent 90 % of the variance of all the textural representations as determined through extensive empirical testing.

2.2 Sparse Texture Model

To characterize healthy and suspicious tissue for a patient, a sparse texture model is learned using the extracted multi-parametric MRI texture features [8]. The sparse texture model incorporates unique texture features from each MRI modality to learn tissue characteristics via cross-modality texture information. Thus, the sparse texture model can better identify healthy and suspicious tissue.

Using a subset of $t(x)$ as training data, a global texture model is defined to represent the heterogeneous characteristics of healthy and suspicious prostate tissue. As global texture modelling is computationally expensive, we generalize an MRI slice as being composed of a set of regions where a particular texture pattern is repeated over a given area. In addition, the number of areas with unique texture patterns is assumed to be much fewer than the number of individual voxels in the training data.

Using this generalization, we can establish a textural sparsity assumption, and the global textural characteristics of prostate tissue can be well-represented using a small set of distinctive local textural representations. This allows for the use of a sparse texture model, defined as a set of m representative texture atoms:

$$T^r = \{t_i^r|1 \leq i \leq m\} \tag{2}$$

The sparse texture model used in the proposed method is a set of representative texture atoms corresponding to healthy or suspicious tissue, where each texture atom represents the mean and covariance (i.e., $t_i^r = \underline{\mu}_i, \Sigma_i$) of a particular texture pattern characteristic of healthy or suspicious tissue. The representative atoms in the sparse texture model are learned via expectation maximization [1].

2.3 Statistical Textural Distinctiveness

Suspicious regions in prostate MRI data can be characterized as areas that are highly unique and texturally distinct. Using the concept of statistical textural distinctiveness [12], we quantify the distinctiveness of texture patterns and uncover the underlying saliency by using the statistical relationship between texture patterns across different MRI modalities.

To define statistical textural distinctiveness between two representative texture atoms (denoted as t_i^r and t_j^r) in the sparse texture model, we use Kullback-Leibler (KL) divergence [9] to measure the statistical difference between the representative texture atoms in the sparse texture model:

$$\beta_{i,j} = \log \frac{|\Sigma_j|}{|\Sigma_i|} - u + trace(\Sigma_j^{-1}\Sigma_i) + \frac{(\underline{\mu}_j - \underline{\mu}_i)^T \Sigma_j^{-1} (\underline{\mu}_j - \underline{\mu}_i)}{2} \qquad (3)$$

where u is the number of PCA components selected, $\underline{\mu}_i$ and $\underline{\mu}_j$ represent the mean of t_i^r and t_j^r, respectively, and Σ_i and Σ_j represent the covariance of t_i^r and t_j^r, respectively. Thus, the distinctiveness metric $\beta_{i,j}$ increases as the texture patterns become more distinct from one another.

2.4   Suspicious Region Detection via Saliency Map Computation

As the majority of prostate tissue is considered to be healthy, salient regions can be interpreted as suspicious due to the uniqueness and statistical occurrence of the corresponding cross-modality texture characteristics. Given a subset of compact texture features used for testing (denoted as $t(x)_Z$), the saliency map for a given MRI image can be computed using the previously determined statistical textural distinctiveness graphical model. The saliency α_i is defined as:

$$\alpha_i = \sum_{j=1}^{m} \beta_{i,j} P(t_i^r | t(x)_Z) \qquad (4)$$

where $P(t_i^r | Z)$ is the occurrence probability of t_i^r in $t(x)_Z$.

For S_i being the set of texture representations that corresponds to saliency α_i, voxels belonging to salient representative texture atoms S_i (i.e., $\alpha_i > \frac{\alpha_{max}}{2}$) are classified as regions of suspicious tissue, with all other voxels classified as healthy tissue. That is, each voxel x in a given MRI image is assigned a label y:

$$y = \begin{cases} 1 & x \in S_i, \alpha_i > \frac{\alpha_{max}}{2} \\ 0 & otherwise \end{cases} \qquad (5)$$

3   Results

3.1   Experimental Setup

The performance of the proposed method was evaluated using the MRI data of 13 patients acquired using a Philips Achieva 3.0 T machine at Sunnybrook Health Sciences Centre, Toronto, Ontario, Canada. The resolution of the signal acquisitions ranged from 1.36 mm × 1.36 mm to 1.67 mm × 1.67 mm, with a median of 1.56 mm × 1.56 mm. Institutional research ethics board approval and patient informed consent for this study was obtained at Sunnybrook Health Sciences Centre. The patients' ages ranged from 53 to 75. The data set includes segmentation information to isolate the prostate, and ground truth data for tumour size and location. All images were reviewed and marked as healthy and cancerous tissue by a radiologist with 18 and 13 years of experience interpreting body and prostate MRI, respectively.

Each patient dataset had corresponding T2w images, ADC maps, CHB-DWI data, and CDI data. Using the radiologist contour of the prostate, a rectangle cropped around the prostate gland was selected as the region of interest (ROI) for each MRI slice. The performance of each method was evaluated using leave-one-patient-out cross-validation. A subset of the training texture features were randomly selected and used to train the classifier, and the voxels in a single MRI slice were classified as either healthy or cancerous tissue and assigned the saliency value of the nearest texture atom.

In addition, the number of texture atoms used to compute the spare texture model (as described in Subsect. 2.2) was varied to determine the optimal number of representative texture atoms for identifying suspicious regions in prostate MR images. The ADC-based method was compared against the proposed texture distinctiveness method (TD) via sensitivity, specificity, and accuracy metrics.

$$\text{Sensitivity} = \frac{TP}{P} \quad \text{Specificity} = \frac{TN}{N} \quad \text{Accuracy} = \frac{TN + TP}{N + P}$$

where the performance of each method was quantified by the metrics' closeness to one. TP is the number of voxels in the intersection of the identified cancerous tissue and the radiologist's tissue segmentation, TN is the number of voxels not in the identified tissue that are also not in the radiologist's segmentation, N is the number of voxels not in the radiologist segmented tissue, and P is the number of voxels in the radiologist segmented tissue.

3.2   Experimental Results

The proposed textural distinctiveness method (TD) was evaluated using both four-atom and six-atom sparse texture models. Table 1 shows the performance metrics for the ADC-based method [4] and the proposed method. The testing data contained 52 tumours (as identified by an experienced radiologist) across the slices from 13 different patients.

As seen in Table 1, the proposed TD method outperforms the ADC-based method [4] in terms of sensitivity, specificity, and accuracy. While there is only a relatively small increase in sensitivity (approximately 1.5 %), TD shows an increase of at least 10 % in specificity and accuracy relative to the ADC-based method. This is especially beneficial, as a low specificity negatively impacts a

Table 1. Comparison of TD (trained with both 4 and 6 texture atoms) with ADC-based method [4]. TD has similar sensitivity values as the ADC-based method, and improved specificity and accuracy values.

	Sensitivity	Specificity	Accuracy
ADC-based method [4]	0.7911	0.7107	0.7115
TD (4 texture atoms)	0.8088	0.8285	0.8283
TD (6 texture atoms)	0.8103	0.8303	0.8301

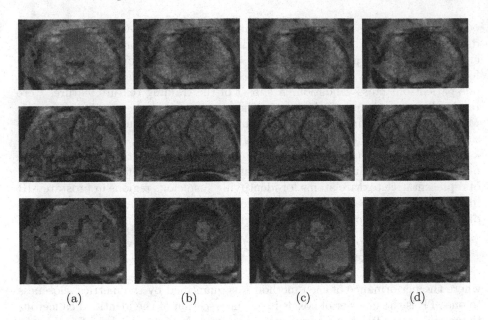

(a)   (b)   (c)   (d)

Fig. 3. Visual comparison of identified suspicious regions (shown in red) between (a) ADC-based method [4], (b) TD using four texture atoms, (c) TD using six texture atoms, and (d) radiologist segmented regions (colour figure online).

diagnostician's ability to perform quick and accurate assessments of MRI data. By increasing specificity, TD minimizes the number of wrongly detected regions that contain no tumour candidates. This is important for procedures such as radical prostatectomy where an extremely high specificity rate is required.

Figure 3 shows the suspicious regions detected using the ADC-based method [4] and the proposed TD method using four and six representative texture atoms. While all methods identify the cancerous regions as suspicious, the ADC-based method in particular has a tendency to be over-sensitive and often identifies a large portion of the prostate tissue as suspicious. A visual inspection of the identified suspicious regions shows that TD consistently produces spatially compact and useful regions regardless of the number of texture atoms.

4   Conclusion

A novel method was proposed to aid physicians in efficiently and accurately diagnosing patients via the identification of suspicious regions in prostate MR images. We extracted unique textural information from different MRI modalities, and used a sparse texture model to learn tissue texture characteristics. As the majority of prostate tissue is considered to be healthy, texturally distinct regions can be interpreted as suspicious due to the uniqueness and statistical occurrence of the corresponding cross-modality texture characteristics.

The proposed statistical textural distinctiveness approach (using four-atom and six-atom sparse texture models) was evaluated against the ADC-based method [4]. In both cases, statistical textural distinctiveness has higher sensitivity, specificity, and accuracy values than the state-of-art ADC-based method. In additional, statistical textural distinctiveness also identifies suspicious regions on a per patient basis, rather than relying on a fixed ADC value characteristic of typical cancerous tissue (as is the case with the ADC-based threshold method). Thus, statistical textural distinctiveness shows potential for more flexible and visually meaningful identification of suspicious tumour regions.

Future work includes the further investigation of additional MRI modalities, and the use of spatial consistency to enforce more compact identified suspicious areas. Applications include identifying suspicious regions for clinicians to better stream-line a patient's diagnosis, and automatically identifying regions of interest for computer-aided tumour detection methods.

References

1. Aitkin, M., Rubin, D.B.: Estimation and hypothesis testing in finite mixture models. J. Roy. Stat. Soc. Ser. B (Methodological) **47**, 67–75 (1985)
2. Andriole, G.L., Crawford, E.D., Grubb, R.L., Buys, S.S., Chia, D., Church, T.R., Fouad, M.N., Gelmann, E.P., Kvale, P.A., Reding, D.J., Weissfeld, J.L., Yokochi, L.A., O'Brien, B., Clapp, J.D., Rathmell, J.M., Riley, T.L., Hayes, R.B., Kramer, B.S., Izmirlian, G., Miller, A.B., Pinsky, P.F., Prorok, P.C., Gohagan, J.K., Berg, C.D.: Mortality results from a randomized prostate-cancer screening trial. N. Engl. J. Med. **360**(13), 1310–1319 (2009)
3. Barentsz, J.O., Richenberg, J., Clements, R., Choyke, P., Verma, S., Villeirs, G., Rouviere, O., Logager, V., Fütterer, J.J.: ESUR prostate MR guidelines 2012. Eur. Radiol. **22**(4), 746–757 (2012)
4. Cameron, A., Modhafar, A., Khalvati, F., Lui, D., Shafiee, M.J., Wong, A., Haider, M.: Multiparametric MRI prostate cancer analysis via a hybrid morphological-textural model. In: 2014 36th Annual International Conference of the IEEE Engineering in Medicine and Biology Society, pp. 3357–3360 (2014)
5. Canadian Cancer Society: Prostate cancer statistics (2014)
6. Haider, M.A., van der Kwast, T.H., Tanguay, J., Evans, A.J., Hashmi, A.T., Lockwood, G., Trachtenberg, J.: Combined T2-weighted and diffusion-weighted MRI for localization of prostate cancer. AJR Am. J. Roentgenol. **189**(2), 323–328 (2007)
7. Khalvati, F.: Automated consensus contour building for prostate MRI. In: 2014 36th Annual International Conference of the IEEE Engineering in Medicine and Biology Society, pp. 5534–5537, August 2014
8. Khalvati, F., Modhafar, A., Cameron, A., Wong, A., Haider, M.A.: A multiparametric diffusion magnetic resonance imaging texture feature model for prostate cancer analysis. In: MICCAI 2014 Workshop on Computational Diffusion MRI, pp. 1–10. Medical Image Computing and Computer Assisted Intervention (2014)
9. Kullback, S., Leibler, R.A.: On information and sufficiency. Ann. Math. Stat. **22**, 79–86 (1951)
10. Loeb, S., Vellekoop, A., Ahmed, H.U., Catto, J., Emberton, M., Nam, R., Rosario, D.J., Scattoni, V., Lotan, Y.: Systematic review of complications of prostate biopsy. Eur. Urol. **64**(6), 876–892 (2013)

11. Röthke, M., Blondin, D., Schlemmer, H.P., Franiel, T.: PI-RADS classification: structured reporting for MRI of the prostate. RöFo : Fortschritte auf dem Gebiete der Röntgenstrahlen und der Nuklearmedizin **185**(3), 253–261 (2013)
12. Scharfenberger, C., Wong, A., Fergani, K., Zelek, J.S., Clausi, D.A.: Statistical textural distinctiveness for salient region detection in natural images. In: 2013 IEEE Conference on Computer Vision and Pattern Recognition (CVPR), pp. 979–986 (2013)
13. Schröder, F.H., Hugosson, J., Roobol, M.J., Tammela, T.L.J., Ciatto, S., Nelen, V., Kwiatkowski, M., Lujan, M., Lilja, H., Zappa, M., Denis, L.J., Recker, F., Berenguer, A., Määttänen, L., Bangma, C.H., Aus, G., Villers, A., Rebillard, X., van der Kwast, T., Blijenberg, B.G., Moss, S.M., de Koning, H.J., Auvinen, A.: Screening and prostate-cancer mortality in a randomized European study. N. Engl. J. Med. **360**(13), 1320–1328 (2009)

Automatic Detection of Immunogold Particles from Electron Microscopy Images

Ricardo Gamelas Sousa[1,2], Tiago Esteves[1,2,4], Sara Rocha[6],
Francisco Figueiredo[1,3], Pedro Quelhas[1,2,7], and Luís M. Silva[1,2,5]([⊠])

[1] Instituto de Investigação e Inovação em Saúde (i3S), Porto, Portugal
rsousa@rsousa.org, dee11017@fe.up.pt,
francisco.figueiredo@ibmc.up.pt, lmas@ua.pt
[2] Instituto de Engenharia Biomédica (INEB), Porto, Portugal
[3] Instituto de Biologia Molecular e Celular (IBMC), Porto, Portugal
[4] Faculdade de Engenharia da Universidade do Porto, Porto, Portugal
[5] Dep. de Matemática, Universidade de Aveiro, Aveiro, Portugal
[6] Centro de Biotecnologia dos Açores (CBA),
Universidade dos Açores, Açores, Portugal
sararocha@uac.pt
[7] Metaio GmbH, Munich, Germany

Abstract. Immunogold particle detection is a time-consuming task where a single image containing almost a thousand particles can take several hours to annotate. In this work we present a framework for the automatic detection of immunogold particles that can leverage significantly the burden of this manual task. Our proposal applies a Laplacian of Gaussian (LoG) filter to provide its detection estimates to a Stacked Denoising Autoencoder (SdA). This learning model endowed with the capability to extract higher order features provides a robust performance to our framework. For the validation of our framework, a new dataset was created. Based on our work, we determined that solely the LoG detector attained more than 74.1 % of accuracy and, when combined with a SdA the accuracy is improved by at most 11.4 %.

1   Introduction

Immunogold electron microscopy is a high-resolution method for the selective localization of biological molecules at the subcellular level. Antibodies coupled to particles of colloidal gold, which are visible in the Transmission Electron Microscopy (TEM), can reveal the localization and distribution of the biological molecules of interest. We have used this technique to determine the composition of cell walls which ultimately differentiate into reticulate and flange ingrowths of maize (*Zea mays* L.) endosperm transfer cells [9]. However, a manual immunogold particle detection is a time-consuming task prone to error [11] (Fig. 1 [6]) and which can increasingly benefit from an automatic detection tool.

In this paper we present a method that permits an automatic detection of immunogold particles. We show that Laplacian of Gaussian (LoG) is tolerant to

© Springer International Publishing Switzerland 2015
M. Kamel and A. Campilho (Eds.): ICIAR 2015, LNCS 9164, pp. 377–384, 2015.
DOI: 10.1007/978-3-319-20801-5_41

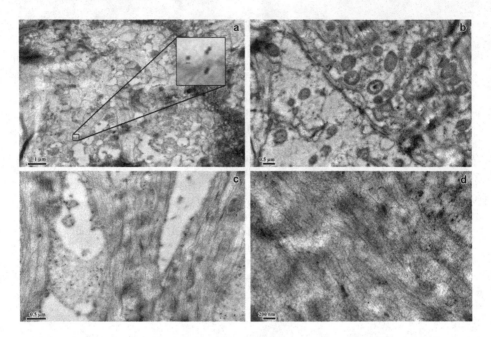

Fig. 1. Representative images of our dataset illustrating different structures that can interfere in the detection of the immunogold particles due to: cellular overlapping, tissues and background noise. Each image has 4000×2600 pixels of dimension with particles *diameter* ranging from 8 to 20 pixels. **(a)** Example of a sample with a magnification of 15000 ($1\,\mu$m, particles with a diameter of 8 pixels—red line); **(b)** magnification of 20000 ($0.5\,\mu$m, 12 pixels diameter particles); **(c)** magnification of 30000 ($0.5\,\mu$m, 15 pixels diameter particles); and, **(d)** magnification of 50000 (200 nm, 20 pixels diameter particles) (Color figure online).

feeble changes of immunogold particles sizes and to noise that may occur during the image acquisition. However, its sole application is insufficient since the recognition solely based on shape and image intensities can induce a higher number of false detections requiring further a-posteriori heuristics. Our proposal consists on coupling the state-of-the-art Stacked Denoising Autoencoder (SdAs) to the detections provided by the LoG filter. This framework explores the capability of SdAs to extract high representative features of our images that lead to the improvement of the recognition rates.

2 Immunogold Particles Detection

Although there is not much work in the automatic analysis of immunogold particle from Electron Microscopy, there is however some previous work for the detection of similar cellular structures. For instance, Fisker *et al.* in [5] explored the possibility to automatically estimate particle sizes in immuno-microscopy imaging. Their approach is based on deformable models that can be fitted to the prior known shape of the particles. As in [5], a different approach was presented by Mallic *et al.* in [8] by using cascade of classifiers. The usage of image filters for image analysis and for organelle detection on cryo-electron microscopy images is not new [14]. However, these methodologies were not tailored neither evaluated on immunogold particles. For the detection of biological structures, there is the publicly available Spot Detector (SD) [10] algorithm that is included in the well-known Icy bioimaging software [3]. Icy (in short) is an open source software with resources to visualize, annotate and quantify bio-imaging data. SD is based on the non-decimated wavelet transform allowing the detection of spots that can be organelles or other biological structures [10]. This approach aggregates a response for each resolution and scale of the image providing detailed information of the objects. As a generic form of spot detection it includes a set of parameters that need to be defined for an appropriate detection. It requires the identification of a trade-off between particles and background; the definition of a scale and sensibility that controls both size of the particles to be detected and a threshold for noise removal.

Our work is distinguished from the aforementioned proposals by addressing different cellular structures that are not irregular (immunogold particles better viewed in Fig. 3) but of difficult detection and quantification. Our work will be focused on the detection of immunogold particles with regular spherical shape, thus avoiding the adoption of a highly parameterized formalism for its detection.

2.1   Immunogold Particles Detection Using LoG Filter

For the task of immunogold particles detection we used the LoG filter, which is based on the image scale-space representation to enhance the blob like structure as introduced by Lindeberg [7]. Given an input image $I(x, y)$, the Gaussian scale space representation at a certain scale t is:

$$L(x,y,t) = g(x,y,t) * I(x,y), \text{ where } g(x,y,t) = \frac{1}{2\pi t} \exp^{-\frac{x^2+y^2}{2t}}, \quad (1)$$

where $*$ is the convolution operation. The scale normalized LoG operator is then defined as: $\nabla^2 L(x,y,t) = t^2(L_{xx}(x,y,t) + L_{yy}(x,y,t))$, where L_{xx} and L_{yy} are the second derivatives of the input image in x and y respectively, and t is the scale parameter so that $t = r/1.5$ for a particle radius r [7]. We set the scale of the filter (t) given the expected range of the immunogold particle radius (Fig. 1). We perform detection of immunogold particles by detecting local maxima of LoG response (Fig. 2 — center) in the input image (Fig. 2 — left). The detected maxima enable us to estimate the position of immunogold particles (Fig. 2 — right). This sole approach however can induce a significant number of false positives or false negatives. Here, we propose a second stage for the immunogold recognition by coupling a SdA to filter the outputs given by the LoG method.

Fig. 2. LoG based cell detection: (left) Original image (crop from an image with magnification of 50000); (center) LoG response; right) Detections overlaid in the original image.

2.2 Immunogold Recognition Through SdAs

An autoencoder is a simple Neural Network (NN) with one hidden layer designed to reconstruct its own input, having, for that reason, an equal number of input and output neurons. The reconstruction accuracy is obtained by minimizing the average reconstruction error between the original (which can be corrupted by some noise [13]) and the reconstructed instances. Hence, these methods are governed by the objective of capturing relevant information of the underlying distribution of the samples [12].

Stacking autoencoders, gives the model the advantage of hierarchical features with low-level features represented at lower layers and higher-level features represented at upper layers [2, Sect. 3]. The unsupervised training of the SdAs is usually referred to as pre-training. On the top of the network a logistic layer is added where the entire network is "fine-tuned" in order to minimize some classification loss function [1,2].

SdA robustness makes it a very promising learning tool for the recognition of the circular shaped immunogold particles. A representative sample of the images that were used to train the SdA is depicted in Fig. 3. Given the similarity of the immunogold particles, it is expected that SdA can capture relevant features from these samples and easily discriminate from the remaining artifacts or cellular structures. A far more complex scenario occurs when multiple immunogold particles are comprised in the same patch (see Fig. 3). In doing so, SdA has also to be robust to the number of particles existing in the same image patch.

3 Experimental Study

Dataset: We have created a new dataset containing 100 images with size of 4000×2600 to assess the performance of our algorithms for the detection of the immunogold particles. This dataset is available upon request to the authors of this work. All images were acquired using a TEM JEOL JEM 1400 with a GATAN Orius SC10000A2 CCD. These images were recorded in four different magnifications: 15, 20, 30 and 50 thousand times from different biological samples (see Fig. 1) whereas manual annotation was conducted with the plugin 'manual counting' within Icy [3].

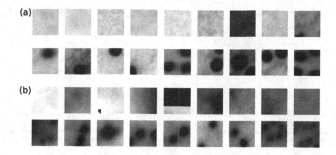

Fig. 3. Different types of patches in the dataset with magnification of 50000 (a): patches of the background and containing artifacts (first row); and, patches containing at least one immunogold particle (second row); and, (b) analogous, but for patches in the dataset with a magnification of 15000.

Parameter and Training Settings for LoG and SdA: For the LoG filter, the scale parameter was set based on the known immunogold particle size varying between 3 to 13 pixels. We also measure the performance for each threshold applied to the filter response with values ranging from 5 to 55. To find the best parameterization we have performed a three-fold cross validation with 60 % (60 images, 15 samples per resolution) for training and 40 % for evaluating the performance of our method. The performance of the LoG is represented by a Precision-Recall curve on the validation set [4].

In order to build (train) the SdA models we proceeded as follows: For a given resolution we used the *same* 60 % of images that were used to train the LoG filter. From this train set we extracted patches with 20×20 pixels containing all immunogold particles and the same amount of patches containing background, (portions of) cellular structures or artifacts. A patch could contain more than one particle or portions of several other particles (see Fig. 3). Finally, patches were labelled as containing at least one immunogold particle if the Euclidean distance between the patch position (on the image) and the annotation position was below the size of the patch. Pixels values from all patches were normalized to be within $[0, 1]$. To find the best SdA model parameterization we have performed a grid search on the pre-training learning rate (0.01 and 0.001), fine-tune learning rate (0.1 and 0.01) and the number of neurons per layer (500, 750 and 1000) by carrying out a three-fold cross-validation in the training set. The number of hidden layers was fixed to 3. Corruption level was set to 0.1 across all hidden layers.

Once we obtained the best parameterization for the LoG and SdA, given a test image, we apply the LoG filter. The filter response give us an estimate of a possible nanoparticle localization. Then, a patch with 20×20 pixels centered at the position of the LoG detection is extracted and evaluated by the SdA. The assessment of the methods performance is described in the following paragraph. Finally, to assess the variability of our methods' performance the experiment was repeated 20 times by randomly shuffling the data.

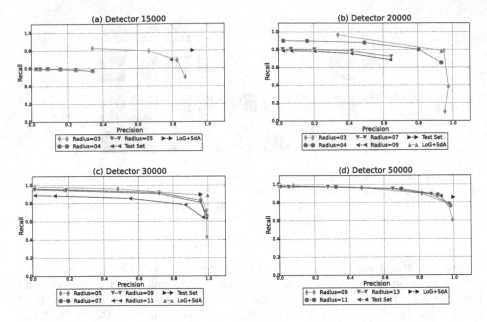

Fig. 4. Illustrates the Precision-Recall curves on the 20 repetitions for the LoG on the validation set by averaging. Isolate points correspond to test results for LoG and LoG+SdA. **(a–d)** results for images with a magnification of 15000, 20000, 30000 and 50000, respectively.

Evaluation: For an objective evaluation each detection is assigned to a ground-truth if the Euclidean distance between them is below the size of the particle radius r. Moreover, we ensure that there is a one-to-one mapping between detection and ground-truth. Based on the assignments we propose the following measures for error counting: (a) True Positive (TP): detected immunogold particle for a corresponding ground-truth; (b) False Positive (FP): detected immunogold particle that does not have a corresponding ground-truth; and (c) False Negative (FN): ground-truth for which no corresponding immunogold particle detection was found.

The performance of both methods was plotted according a Precision-Recall curve as follows: Precision $= \frac{TP}{TP+FP}$, and Recall $= \frac{TP}{TP+FN}$. The final performance is given by the F-measure which combines both precision and recall as: F-measure $= 2\frac{\text{Precision}\times\text{Recall}}{\text{Precision}+\text{Recall}}$.

Results and Discussion: For magnification of 15000—see Fig. 4(a), we observed that the expected immunogold particle radius tested during the detection of immunogold particles attained the best results (*radius* $= 3$). Comparing to the other radius tested, with *radius* $= 3$ it achieved a higher recall, which means a higher number of immunogold particles well detected. A similar analysis can be performed for the remaining figures stating the importance of the size of the radius. As expected, in the majority of our experiments we obtained

Table 1. F-measure performance for the best Precision and Recall for LoG and LoG coupled with SdA (see Fig. 4). Best results are in bold and presented in percentage.

Magnification	LoG			LoG+SdA			
	Precision	Recall	F-measure	Precision	Recall	F-measure	Improvement
15000	79.2	69.6	74.1	91.9	80.0	**85.5**	11.4%
20000	94.2	77.5	85.0	93.9	78.4	85.0	0.0%
30000	95.9	89.8	92.7	99.8	89.0	**94.1**	1.4%
50000	92.6	87.0	89.7	99.9	85.5	**92.1**	2.4%

the best performance for the radius corresponding to the real dimension of the immunogold particle making this an easy method to parameterize.

We can also claim that the best results are achieved for a magnification of 30 and 50 thousand. These results are coherent with the quality of the acquisitions which contain feeble noise and artifacts as well as sparse immunogold particles (see Fig. 1). This could in fact be a desirable setting for the automatic analysis of these images. However, a low magnification (inferior to 30000) can nevertheless be useful to identify important cellular structures and ultra-structures to which immunogold particles can easily bind to.

When we couple the SdA learning models to the results provided by the LoG we can find an interesting result: SdA can efficiently discard detections that correspond to background. Such is confirmed by the increase of the Precision performance. For almost all magnifications SdA was able to discard samples which could be considered as a false immunogold particle. In the overall, LoG coupled with the SdA lead to a noteworthy improvement on the detection of immunogold particles. Towards a better inspection these results we present a table with the F-measure results for the test set on both methods (see Table 1).

4   Conclusion

In this work we have proposed a framework for automatic detection of immunogold particles in different magnifications. We found that solely the LoG filter attained results over 74% of accuracy. When coupled with the state-of-the-art SdA machine learning algorithm it was possible to outperform the LoG filter. These results show that these approaches are also resilient to the presence of noise, artifacts and cluttered background and easy to set-up based on the few parameters of the framework (only dependent on the threshold parameter of the LoG filter response).

Acknowledgements. The work was financed by Portuguese funds through FCT – Fundação para a Ciência e a Tecnologia in the framework of project UID/BIM/04293/2013. This work was also financed by FEDER funds through the Programa Operacional Factores de Competitividade – COMPETE and by Portuguese funds through FCT – in the framework of the project PTDC/EIA-EIA/119004/2010.

We would also like to acknowledge to FCT for funding this research through project SFRH/BD/80508/2011. Sara Rocha was supported by Grant BIIC M3.1.6/F/038/2009 from Direcção Regional de Ciência e Tecnologia and by Grant SFRH/BD/8122/2002 from FCT. We thank Dr. Roberto Salema and Dr. Paulo Monjardino for their insightful comments and to Rui Fernandes from HEMS department, and to Dr. João Relvas for aiding us with the technical knowledge for conducting this work.

References

1. Amaral, T., Silva, L.M., Alexandre, L.A., Kandaswamy, C., Santos, J.M., de Sá, J.M.: Using different cost functions to train stacked auto-encoders. In: 2013 12th Mexican International Conference on Artificial Intelligence (MICAI), pp. 114–120. IEEE (2013)
2. Bengio, Y.: Deep learning of representations for unsupervised and transfer learning. J. Mach. Learn. Res. Proc. Track **27**, 17–36 (2012)
3. de Chaumont, F., Dallongeville, S., Chenouard, N., Hervé, N., Pop, S., Provoost, T., Meas-Yedid, V., Pankajakshan, P., Lecomte, T., Le Montagner, Y., et al.: Icy: an open bioimage informatics platform for extended reproducible research. Nature methods **9**(7), 690–696 (2012)
4. Davis, J., Goadrich, M.: The relationship between precision-recall and ROC curves. In: Proceedings of the 23rd International Conference on Machine Learning, pp. 233–240. ACM (2006)
5. Fisker, R., Carstensen, J.M., Hansen, M.F., Bødker, F., Mørup, S.: Estimation of nanoparticle size distributions by image analysis. J. Nanopart. Res. **2**(3), 267–277 (2000)
6. Sousa, R.G., Esteves, T., Rocha, S., Figueiredo, F., de Sá, J.M., Alexandre, L.A., Santos, J.M., Silva, L.M.: Transfer learning for the recognition of immunogold particles in TEM imaging. In: Rojas, I., Joya, G., Catala, A. (eds.) IWANN 2015. LNCS, vol. 9094, pp. 374–384. Springer, Heidelberg (2015)
7. Lindeberg, T.: Scale-space theory: a basic tool for analyzing structures at different scales. J. Appl. Stat. **21**(2), 224–270 (1994)
8. Mallick, S.P., Zhu, Y., Kriegman, D.: Detecting particles in cryo-em micrographs using learned features. J. Struct. Biol. **145**(1), 52–62 (2004)
9. Monjardino, P., Rocha, S., Tavares, A.C., Fernandes, R., Sampaio, P., Salema, R., da Câmara Machado, A.: Development of flange and reticulate wall ingrowths in maize (Zea mays L.) endosperm transfer cells. Protoplasma **250**(2), 495–503 (2013)
10. Olivo-Marin, J.C.: Extraction of spots in biological images using multiscale products. Pattern Recogn. **35**(9), 1989–1996 (2002)
11. Ribeiro, E., Shah, M.: Computer vision for nanoscale imaging. Mach. Vis. Appl. **17**(3), 147–162 (2006)
12. Rifai, S., Vincent, P., Muller, X., Glorot, X., Bengio, Y.: Contractive auto-encoders: Explicit invariance during feature extraction. In: Proceedings of the 28th International Conference on Machine Learning (ICML 2011), pp. 833–840 (2011)
13. Vincent, P., Larochelle, H., Lajoie, I., Bengio, Y., Manzagol, P.A.: Stacked denoising autoencoders: learning useful representations in a deep network with a local denoising criterion. J. Mach. Learn. Res. **11**, 3371–3408 (2010)
14. Woolford, D., Hankamer, B., Ericksson, G.: The laplacian of gaussian and arbitrary z-crossings approach applied to automated single particle reconstruction. J. Struct. Biol. **159**(1), 122–134 (2007)

Specular Reflectance Suppression in Endoscopic Imagery via Stochastic Bayesian Estimation

Brendan Chwyl$^{(\boxtimes)}$, Audrey G. Chung, Alexander Wong, and David A. Clausi

University of Waterloo, Waterloo, ON N2L3G1, Canada
{bchwyl,agchung,a28wong,dclausi}@uwaterloo.ca
http://vip.uwaterloo.ca/

Abstract. A novel stochastic Bayesian estimation method is introduced for the purpose of suppressing specular reflectance in endoscopic imagery, benefiting both computer aided and manual analysis of endoscopic data. The maximum diffuse chromaticity, which is necessary for the calculation of the specular reflectance, is estimated via Bayesian least-squares minimization, with the posterior probability of maximum diffuse chromaticity given maximum chromaticity constructed via an adaptive Monte Carlo sampling approach. Experimental results using a set of clinical endoscopic imagery showed that the proposed method resulted in lower coefficient of variation values when compared to existing methods in homogeneous regions contaminated by strong specular highlights, which is indicative of improved specular reflectance suppression. These findings are further reinforced by visual assessment of the specular suppressed endoscopic imagery produced by the proposed method.

Keywords: Endoscopy · Specular reflectance suppression · Image processing · Minimally invasive surgery

1 Introduction

Minimally invasive surgery has recently become more widely used in place of classic surgical techniques, with benefits including smaller incision wounds or avoidance of incision wounds entirely, less post-operative pain, faster recovery times, and reduced visible scarring [6]. Minimally invasive surgery is often guided by imagery collected via an endoscope, a flexible tube with a light source and a camera attached at the tip, which is displayed to a surgeon.

Both computer-aided analysis and manual review of endoscopic imagery is beneficial for accurate diagnosis, surgical planning, and surgical assistance. Computerized processing of endoscopic imagery is useful in numerous applications including automated annotation and feature extraction [3], automated classification [4,17], assisted endoscope guidance [7,13], and computer-aided comparison

We would like to thank the Natural Sciences and Engineering Research Council of Canada (NSERC), the Canada Research Chairs Program, and the Ontario Ministry of Research and Innovation for their sponsorship of this research.

M. Kamel and A. Campilho (Eds.): ICIAR 2015, LNCS 9164, pp. 385–393, 2015.
DOI: 10.1007/978-3-319-20801-5_42

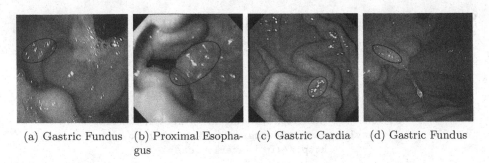

(a) Gastric Fundus   (b) Proximal Esopha-   (c) Gastric Cardia   (d) Gastric Fundus
                      gus

Fig. 1. Examples of specular highlights in endoscopic imagery [2]. Regions of high specular content are circled.

between endoscopic imagery and imaging data obtained through an alternate modality [8,10]. However, image analysis algorithms for endoscopic imagery are often hindered by the presence of strong specular highlights caused by the specular reflectivity of mucous membranes within the human body. Such effects can be seen in Fig. 1, in which specific examples of strong specular highlights have been circled. Furthermore, in a double-blind study conducted by Vogt *et al.* [16] in which physicians were asked to choose between two of the same endoscopic images, one with suppressed specular reflectance and the other unprocessed, it was concluded that physicians preferred to view endoscopy imagery in which specular reflectance has been suppressed. Hence, methods for suppressing strong specular reflectance in endoscopic imagery are highly desired.

Oh *et al.* [11] proposed a method for detecting specular highlights in endoscopy imagery via thresholds on the saturation and value channels in the HSV colour space, as well as on segmented regions of similar texture and colour. However, the threshold values were inflexible and required calibration, and the segmentation algorithm was computationally expensive. Arnold *et al.* [1] used adaptive colour channel thresholds to identify a set of potentially specular pixels, and refined the set via thresholds based on an estimated non-specular colour image for each channel obtained through median filtering. While this has been shown to run faster than [11], the need for manually defined parameters decreases the robustness and reliability of this algorithm in a wide variety of applications.

Tan and Ikeuchi [14] proposed a method for separating the specular and diffuse components of an image by estimating an initial specular-free image and iteratively correcting it to produce a diffuse (specular free) image. This method eliminates the need for thresholds or colour segmentation, but was shown to be very computationally expensive. Yang *et al.* [19] demonstrated an improved method for decoupling the specular and diffuse components of an image which is capable at operating at speeds suitable for real-time applications, and yields more accurate results than [14]. Bilateral filters are used to estimate the maximum diffuse chromaticity which, based on work by Tan *et al.* [15] and Shafer's dichromatic reflectance model [12], can be used to estimate the specular-free diffuse image. While this method resulted in real-time capabilities and improved suppression performance, the use of bilateral filters enforces piecewise smooth reflectance assumptions that may not be well suited for drastic reflectance variations such as those seen in endoscopy imagery. In this work, we propose a novel stochastic Bayesian estimation approach to specular reflectance suppression in endoscopic imagery that extends upon the work of Tan *et al.* [15] to better handle such drastic reflectance variations.

2   Methodology

The proposed method aims to decouple the specular and diffuse components of endoscopic imagery in order to suppress specular reflectance. Building upon work done by Tan *et al.* [14], a stochastic Bayesian estimation approach is introduced to estimate the specular component of endoscopic imagery. Such an approach is better suited for drastic reflectance changes by better use of the underlying image statistics. An overview of the proposed method is shown in Fig. 2.

2.1   Dichromatic Reflection Model

The reflection model used throughout this formulation (Eq. 1) assumes an RGB video endoscope. Based upon Shafer's dichromatic reflection model [12], the light reflected from an object, J, is comprised of two components; the diffuse reflection, J^D, and the specular reflection, J^S:

$$J = J^D + J^S. \tag{1}$$

Furthermore, let chromaticity, σ_c, diffuse chromaticity, Λ_c, and specular chromaticity, Γ_c, be defined as

$$\sigma_c = \frac{J_c}{J_r + J_g + J_b}, \quad \Lambda_c = \frac{J_c^D}{J_r^D + J_g^D + J_b^D}, \quad \Gamma_c = \frac{J_c^S}{J_r^S + J_g^S + J_b^S} \tag{2}$$

where $c \in \{r, g, b\}$, the colour channels captured by an RGB endoscope.

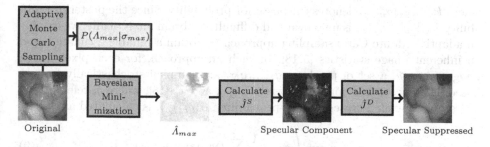

Fig. 2. Overview of the proposed method for specular reflectance suppression in endoscopic imagery

2.2   Specular Reflection Estimation

It was shown by Tan *et al.* [15] that given the estimated illumination chromaticity, the specular colour component of each reflected light can be normalized such that $J_r^S = J_g^S = J_b^S = J^S$ and $\Gamma_r = \Gamma_g = \Gamma_b = \frac{1}{3}$. The diffuse reflection can then be calculated as:

$$J_c^D = J_c - J^S. \tag{3}$$

In addition, Tan and Ikeuchi [14] have shown that J^S can be calculated as a function of the maximum diffuse chromaticity (Λ_{max}) where,

$$\Lambda_{max} = max(\Lambda_r, \Lambda_g, \Lambda_b) \tag{4}$$

and

$$J^S = \frac{max(J_r, J_g, J_b) - (J_r + J_g + J_b)\Lambda_{max}}{1 - 3\Lambda_{max}}. \tag{5}$$

2.3   Stochastic Bayesian Estimation of Λ_{max}

Given Eq. 5, it can be seen that a reliable estimate of the maximum diffuse chromaticity Λ_{max} is critical in the calculation of the specular reflectance J^S. Here, we formulate the problem of obtaining the maximum diffuse chromaticity, denoted by $\hat{\Lambda}_{max}$, as a Bayesian least-squares minimization problem, which can be formulated as follows:

$$\hat{\Lambda}_{max} = \arg \min_{\hat{\Lambda}_{max}} \left(E((\Lambda_{max} - \hat{\Lambda}_{max})^2 | \sigma_{max})) \right) \tag{6}$$

where σ_{max} is formulated as:

$$\sigma_{max} = max(\sigma_r, \sigma_g, \sigma_b). \tag{7}$$

By the same approach as Lui *et al.* [9], the solution of Eq. 6 can be written as:

$$\hat{\Lambda}_{max} = \int P(\Lambda_{max} | \sigma_{max}) \Lambda_{max} d\Lambda_{max}, \tag{8}$$

where $P(\Lambda_{max} | \sigma_{max})$ denotes the posterior probability. Since the posterior probability $P(\Lambda_{max} | \sigma_{max})$ is unknown and difficult to obtain analytically, we employ an adaptive Monte Carlo sampling approach to obtain a reliable estimate based on inherent image statistics [5,18]. In such an approach, for each pixel, x_c, in image space Φ, a set of pixels $q_1, q_2, ..., q_N$, are sampled stochastically from Φ based on an acceptance probability relating q_i and x_c [18], where q_i refers to the ith sampled pixel. The acceptance probability, $\alpha(q_k | x_c)$, is calculated as

$$\alpha(q_k | x_c) = \exp\left(\sigma_1 - \frac{1}{N} \sum_{i=1}^{N} (\aleph_{q_k}(i) - \aleph_{x_c}(i))^2\right), \tag{9}$$

where σ_1 is a constant and $\aleph_{q_k}$ and $\aleph_{x_c}$ represent regions of equal size surrounding q_k and x_c respectively. The set of sampled pixels are used to construct a weighted histogram estimate of $P(\Lambda_{max}|\sigma_{max})$, where the weight of each sampled pixel's contribution, w_k, to the estimate of $P(\Lambda_{max}|\sigma_{max})$ is determined by [18] as

$$w_k = \exp\left(-\frac{\frac{1}{N}\sum_{i=1}^{N}(\aleph_{q_k}(i) - \aleph_{x_c}(i))^2}{\sigma_2}\right) \tag{10}$$

where σ_2 is a constant.

3   Experimental Setup

3.1   Phantom Data Experiment

To validate the effectiveness of the proposed method in general, a simulated phantom model was created. Glossy texture and a simulated light source were then applied to produce the effect of specular highlights. In order to obtain ground truth data, the same object was given a matte texture as to remove the effect of specular highlights. The model's shape is that of a twisted tube with a ridged inner surface to replicate similar reflective qualities as those seen in endoscopy images. The phantom model and ground truth can be seen in Fig. 3. To evaluate the success of the proposed method, the peak signal to noise ratio (PSNR) of the simulated ground truth and the post-processed image were compared.

3.2   Endoscopy Data Experiment

To validate the performance of the proposed method on endoscopic imagery, an experiment was conducted using thirty endoscopy data sets obtained from the Clinical Outcomes Research Initiative [2]. The resolution of each data set ranges from 183×190 to 530×460 pixels and each was captured with an RGB endoscope. Since no ground truth exists for these data sets, the coefficient of variation (COV) was used to quantitatively evaluate the effectiveness of the proposed algorithm.

(a) Specular Phantom Model   (b) Diffuse Phantom Model

Fig. 3. Specular and diffuse phantom models where the diffuse phantom model acts as ground truth for experiments run on this data set.

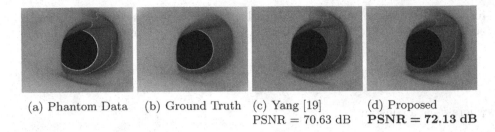

(a) Phantom Data   (b) Ground Truth   (c) Yang [19]   (d) Proposed
                                          PSNR = 70.63 dB   **PSNR = 72.13 dB**

Fig. 4. Results from performing specular highlight suppression on the phantom dataset.
PSNR values are also shown, with the most desirable PSNR value indicated in boldface.

The COV was calculated over a set of selected regions (as shown in Fig. 5)
with largely homogeneous tissue characteristics that have been contaminated by
strong specular reflectance. The COV of a region, X, was calculated as follows:

$$COV = \frac{\sigma_X}{\mu_X} \tag{11}$$

where σ_X and μ_X represent the standard deviation and mean of the region, X,
respectively. COV provides a good indication of intensity homogeneity within a
region, and offers a consistent comparison of variation across all data sets. Since
standard deviations in the selected largely homogeneous regions should be low,

Table 1. Tabulated COV calculated over thirty endoscopic data sets. Lower COV
indicate better performance. The average and standard deviation across the COV for
each method are also displayed. The best results are highlighted in boldface.

Test	Original	[19]	Proposed	Test	Original	[19]	Proposed
1	0.0815	0.0251	**0.0209**	17	0.1415	0.0441	**0.0435**
2	0.1144	0.0275	**0.0262**	18	0.2660	0.0485	**0.0352**
3	0.1124	0.0417	**0.0293**	19	0.1429	**0.0412**	0.0509
4	0.1688	0.0329	**0.0266**	20	0.0984	**0.0232**	0.0266
5	0.1671	0.0526	**0.0413**	21	0.0979	0.0286	**0.0206**
6	0.1136	0.0408	**0.0320**	22	0.0376	0.0262	**0.0132**
7	0.0848	**0.0280**	0.0320	23	0.3211	0.0519	**0.0335**
8	0.1123	**0.0304**	0.0320	24	0.2029	0.0441	**0.0357**
9	0.1224	0.0458	**0.0426**	25	0.0779	0.0291	**0.0253**
10	0.2273	0.0389	**0.0316**	26	0.0680	**0.0385**	0.0409
11	0.0768	0.0406	**0.0337**	27	0.1253	0.0208	**0.0189**
12	0.0671	0.0334	**0.0234**	28	0.0703	0.0307	**0.0250**
13	0.1470	0.0232	**0.0176**	29	0.0684	**0.0277**	0.0289
14	0.2347	**0.0554**	0.0580	30	0.1541	0.0438	**0.0384**
15	0.0889	**0.0370**	0.0416	AVE	0.1240	0.0362	**0.0318**
16	0.0654	0.0252	**0.0205**	STD	0.0525	0.0097	0.0102

a smaller COV is desirable and indicative of specular reflectance suppression performance. For comparison, the method proposed by Yang *et al.* [19] was evaluated as it represents state-of-the-art in specular reflectance suppression. In addition, values of $\sigma_1 = 0.272$ and $\sigma_2 = 0.0172$ were used throughout as they were empirically determined to produce strong results.

4   Experimental Results

4.1   Phantom Data Experiment

The results produced by both Yang *et al.* [19] and the proposed method when applied to the phantom dataset are shown along with the ground truth and specular phantom images in Fig. 4. In addition, PSNR values are indicated beneath each figure where applicable. For the PSNR metric, larger values are desirable as this indicates a lower contribution from noise to the overall signal. By visual inspection, it is clear that both methods perform well to suppress specular highlights, however, PSNR values indicate slight improvements by the proposed method. This can likely be attributed to presence of discontinuous geometry

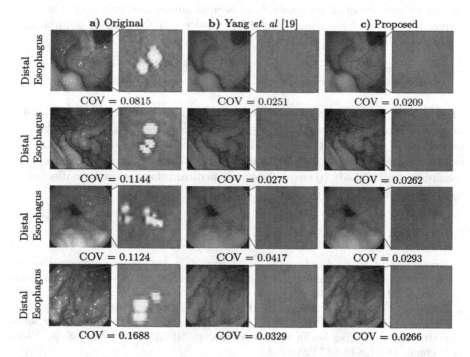

Fig. 5. Visual results from four of the tested endoscopic data sets. The regions used to compute the coefficient of variation are indicated, and the corresponding coefficient of variation is shown below each data set. Column *(a)* contains the unprocessed image, column *(b)* contains the results obtained by [19], and column *(c)* contains the results obtained by the proposed method.

and the ability of the proposed method to handle such scenarios, whereas the method proposed by Yang *et al.* [19] assumes piece-wise smooth geometry.

4.2 Endoscopy Data Experiment

The COV results computed for the thirty endoscopic data sets are tabulated in Table 1. Both of the tested methods resulted in a lower COV than the original endoscopic imagery, indicating that both methods provided specular reflectance suppression. However, the proposed method, on average, produced COV values lower than those produced by [19]. A T-test between the two COV distributions produced a P-value of less than 10 % (0.094), indicating statistical significance. This signifies that within the selected regions, the specular suppressed imagery produced by the proposed method are more homogeneous than those produced by [19] and could be indicative of improved specular reflectance suppression performance. While COV is one way of offering a quantitative comparison, this does not necessarily reflect the benefit to clinicians when visually assessing the specular suppressed endoscopic imagery. As such, a visual comparison for four of the endoscopic data sets is shown in Fig. 5, along with the regions used for the COV calculation. While both methods are effective at suppressing strong specular reflectance in all data sets, the specular suppressed endoscopic imagery produced by the proposed method exhibits fewer artifacts, which is important for both visualization and endoscopic image analysis.

5   Conclusions

A method for suppressing specular reflectance in endoscopic imagery via stochastic Bayesian estimation has been proposed. Experiments show that the proposed method achieved strong specular reflectance suppression with minimal visual artifacts. Future work will include further validation with a more comprehensive clinical study to ensure relevant medical information is unaffected by the proposed method.

References

1. Arnold, M., Ghosh, A., Ameling, S., Lacey, G.: Automatic segmentation and inpainting of specular highlights for endoscopic imaging. EURASIP J. Image Video Process. **2010**, 1–12 (2010)
2. Esophageal and gastric varices (2014). http://digitalcollections.ohsu.edu/
3. Coimbra, M.T., Cunha, J.S.: MPEG-7 visual descriptorscontributions for automated feature extraction in capsule endoscopy. IEEE Trans. Circ. Syst. Video Technol. **16**(5), 628–637 (2006)
4. Esgiar, A., Naguib, R., Sharif, B., Bennett, M., Murray, A.: Fractal analysis in the detection of colonic cancer images. IEEE Trans. Inf. Technol. Biomed. **6**(1), 54–58 (2002)
5. Hastings, W.K.: Monte Carlo sampling methods using Markov chains and their applications. Biometrika **57**(1), 97–109 (1970)

6. Jaffray, B.: Minimally invasive surgery. Arch. Dis. Child. **90**(5), 537–542 (2005)
7. Khan, G., Gillies, D.: Vision based navigation system for an endoscope. Image Vis. Comput. **14**, 763–772 (1996)
8. Liu, J., Subramanian, K., Yoo, T., Van Uitert, R.: A stable optic-flow based method for tracking colonoscopy images. In: IEEE Computer Society Conference on Computer Vision and Pattern Recognition Workshops, CVPRW 2008, pp. 1–8. IEEE (2008)
9. Lui, D., Modhafar, A., Glaister, J., Wong, A., Haider, M.A.: Monte Carlo bias field correction in endorectal diffusion imaging. IEEE Trans. Bio-Med. Eng. **61**(2), 368–380 (2014)
10. Mori, K., Deguchi, D., Sugiyama, J., Suenaga, Y., Toriwaki, J., Maurer, C.R., Takabatake, H., Natori, H.: Tracking of a bronchoscope using epipolar geometry analysis and intensity-based image registration of real and virtual endoscopic images. Med. Image Anal. **6**, 321–336 (2002)
11. Oh, J., Hwang, S., Lee, J., Tavanapong, W., Wong, J., de Groen, P.C.: Informative frame classification for endoscopy video. Med. Image Anal. **11**(2), 110–127 (2007)
12. Shafer, S.A.: Using color to separate reflection components. Color Res. Appl. **10**(4), 210–218 (1985)
13. Song, K.T., Chen, C.J.: Autonomous and stable tracking of endoscope instrument tools with monocular camera. In: 2012 IEEE/ASME International Conference on Advanced Intelligent Mechatronics (AIM), pp. 39–44, July 2012
14. Tan, R.T., Ikeuchi, K.: Separating reflection components of textured surfaces using a single image. IEEE Trans. Pattern Anal. Mach. Intell. **27**(2), 178–193 (2005)
15. Tan, R.T., Nishino, K., Ikeuchi, K.: Illumination chromaticity estimation using inverse-intensity chromaticity space. In: 2003 IEEE Computer Society Conference on Computer Vision and Pattern Recognition, Proceedings, vol. 1, pp. I-673. IEEE (2003)
16. Vogt, F., Paulus, D., Heinrich, N.: Highlight substitution in light fields. In: International Conference on Image Processing, pp. 637–640 (2002)
17. Wang, P., Krishnan, S., Kugean, C., Tjoa, M.: Classification of endoscopic images based on texture and neural network. In: Proceedings of the 23rd Annual International Conference of the IEEE Engineering in Medicine and Biology Society, vol. 4, pp. 3691–3695 (2001)
18. Wong, A., Mishra, A., Zhang, W., Fieguth, P., Clausi, D.A.: Stochastic image denoising based on Markov-chain Monte Carlo sampling. Sig. Process. **91**(8), 2112–2120 (2011)
19. Yang, Q., Wang, S., Ahuja, N.: Real-time specular highlight removal using bilateral filtering. In: Daniilidis, K., Maragos, P., Paragios, N. (eds.) ECCV 2010, Part IV. LNCS, vol. 6314, pp. 87–100. Springer, Heidelberg (2010)

Characterization of Medical Images Using Edge Density and Local Directional Pattern (LDP)

Serestina Viriri[✉]

School of Computing, University of South Africa, Johannesburg, South Africa
evirirsl@unisa.ac.za

Abstract. The use of medical images by medical practitioners has increased to an extent that computers have become a necessity in the image processing and analysis. This research investigates if the Edge density and Local Directional Pattern can be used to characterize medical images. The performance of the Edge density and Local Directional Pattern features is assessed by finding their accuracy to retrieve images of the same group from a database. The combination of the Edge density and Local Directional Pattern features has shown to produce good results in both, classification of medical images and image retrieval. For the classification using the nearest neighbor and 5-nearest neighbor techniques yielded 98.2 % and 99.6 % classification success rates respectively and 99.4 % for image retrieval. The results achieved in this research work are comparable to other approaches used in literature.

1 Introduction

There exist various medical imaging devices which have been used for many years in medicine. Magnetic resonance imaging (MRI), computerized tomography (CT), digital mammography, X-rays and ultrasound images provide effective means for creating images of the human body for the purpose of medical diagnostics. These allow medical professionals to clearly isolate different parts of the human body and determine if disease or injury is present and also improves the decisions made in treatment planning. With the increasing size and number of medical images being produced by various imaging modalities, the use of computers and image processing techniques to facilitate their processing and analysis has become necessary. These medical images can be characterized by the use of image processing techniques to assist medical practitioners with medical diagnostics. Medical images can be characterized by color, texture, shape and region-based descriptors.

In this paper, the Edge density and Local Directional Pattern features are investigated to determine if they can be used to classify medical images. This paper provides an overview of the system used and explains the details of the image enhancement and feature extraction techniques used. And finally assesses the results obtained from using the edge density feature to classify the medical images and to retrieve images from a database.

© Springer International Publishing Switzerland 2015
M. Kamel and A. Campilho (Eds.): ICIAR 2015, LNCS 9164, pp. 394–401, 2015.
DOI: 10.1007/978-3-319-20801-5_43

2   Background and Related Work

Prior to 2005, automatic classification of medical images was often restricted to a small number of classes and has evolved from a task of 57 classes to a task of almost 200 classes in 2009 [1]. Maria et al. [2] proposed a method to characterize mammograms into two categories; normal and abnormal. In their research four features where extracted; mean, variance, skewness and kurtosis, along with these features additional features were added to the training of the classification system, these features are; the type of tissue and the position of the breast. The results obtained where 81.2 % and 69.1 % using neural networks and association rule mining respectively. Yanxi et al. [3] developed a semantic-based image retrieval system centered classification using features that related to size, shape and texture obtained 80 % accuracy on classification and retrieval. Vanitha et al. [4] used the support vector machine (SVM) to characterize medical images and used three approaches for feature extraction, namely, structural, statistical and spectral approaches, with results of 97.5 % during training and 93.33 % during testing.

Edge information can provide essential information of an image, in the universal model for content-based image retrieval done by Nandagopalan et al. [5], edge histogram descriptors were used and compared with other statistical features such as colour and texture. The colour outperformed all other statistical features but the edge histogram descriptor was shown to be successful in precision and recall. In the survey done by Surya et al. [6], the feature proposed by Phung et al. [7], namely edge density, which differentiates objects from non-objects in an image using edge characteristics, was shown to have a good discriminating capability when compared to other features such as Haar-Like features. Phung et al. [7] have also used the concept of edge density to detect people in images and in this work edge density was also found to have stronger discriminating capabilities and can be easily implemented. The work done on texture classification and defect detection by Propescu et al. [8] had used many statistical features including edge density. It was found that edge densities once again had good discriminating capabilities but can achieve better results in texture classification by combining second order type statistical features.

3   Methods and Techniques

The system uses part of the content based image retrieval model proposed by [5]. The system is trained with a set of known images and tested with an unseen image. The feature vectors of both training and unseen images are constructed in exactly the same way. Firstly, the feature vector of every training image is taken and stored in a feature database and, secondly, the Euclidean distance is taken from the feature vector of the unseen image to every image in the feature vector database. The images are ranked and only the images corresponding to the feature vectors that produce the smallest Euclidean distance are retrieved. All images, before undergoing feature extraction, have to be preprocessed.

The medical images characterization system is divided into five processes; image preprocessing, feature extraction, building the feature vector, similarity comparison and image retrieval and classification. The image preprocessing is divided into three steps, finding the edges within the image and creating a new image consisting of these edges, then sharpening of the edges and the image is finally converted to a binary image. The image is then passed to feature extraction where the image is windowed and the edge densities of these windows are computed including the global edge density of the image, as well as computing the Local Directional Pattern features. After feature extraction the feature vector is constructed using these values and used for similarity comparison to finally retrieve images from the database and classifies the query image. The similarity comparison is done using the nearest neighbor method.

3.1 Preprocessing

Image preprocessing involves methods which enhance the quality of the images and prepare the image for feature extraction. Before feature extraction takes place the image is segmented by detecting the edges within the image followed by an enhancement to sharpen the edges. Finally the image is converted to a binary image. In this paper, the feature extraction is performed on the binary image produced by the preprocessing techniques. These preprocessing techniques used ensures that all images provided to the feature extraction mechanism contains pixels that are either black or white and that the edge density is only influenced by pixels that form the main edges of the image. This ensures that noisy edge pixels that have a negative influence on the results are removed.

Image Enhancement. The edges within an image are of primary interest in this process. Image sharpening is performed using the Laplace filter given below.

$$H^L = H_x^L + H_y^L = \begin{bmatrix} 0 & 1 & 0 \\ 1 & -4 & 1 \\ 0 & 1 & 0 \end{bmatrix} \tag{1}$$

Image Segmentation. The segmentation process involves two steps, edge detection and converting to a binary image. The Sobel operator is used to detect the edges and produce a new image with clearly visible edges. The two filters below make up the Sobel operator.

$$H_x^S = \begin{bmatrix} -1 & 0 & 1 \\ -2 & 0 & 2 \\ -1 & 0 & 1 \end{bmatrix} \text{ And } H_y^S = \begin{bmatrix} -1 & -2 & -1 \\ 0 & 0 & 0 \\ 1 & 2 & 1 \end{bmatrix} \tag{2}$$

As with the Prewitt operator the Sobel operator also performs smoothing before computing the gradient with an additional part of assigning a higher weight to the current line and column. H_x^S Performs smoothing over three lines and H_y^S performs smoothing over three columns before computing the x and y gradients respectively.

An adaptive threshold value t is determined from the processed images histogram. The value is used to convert the image to a binary image which will be used for feature extraction.

$$I_t(x,y) = \begin{cases} 0 \; if \; I(x,y) \geq t \\ 1 \; if \; I(x,y) < t \end{cases} \tag{3}$$

Where $I(x, y)$ is the current intensity of pixel (x, y) and $I_t(x, y)$ is the resultant intensity after the threshold is performed. The new intensity value is either 0 or 1 where 0 is black and 1 is white.

3.2 Feature Extraction

The global and local edge densities are extracted from the binary image produced by the preprocessing techniques described. These include one global edge density value and seven local edge density values. The image is subdivided into seven smaller regions to obtain these local edge densities. The global edge density alone is not sufficient to distinguish between two images of different classes hence the use of local edge density to improve results.

Image Windowing. The image is subdivided into seven smaller regions which overlap each other and the entire image region. These regions are given by (x_1, y_1) and (x_2, y_2), these are the two dimensional co-ordinates of the top-left corner and bottom-right corner of the image respectively.

$$TL_0 = (0,0) \; BR_0 = (W,H), \tag{4}$$

$$TL_1 = (0,0) \; BR_1 = \left(\frac{W}{2}, \frac{H}{2}\right), \tag{5}$$

$$TL_2 = \left(0, \frac{H}{2}\right) \; BR_2 = \left(\frac{W}{2}, H\right), \tag{6}$$

$$TL_3 = \left(\frac{W}{2}, 0\right) \; BR_3 = \left(W, \frac{H}{2}\right), \tag{7}$$

$$TL_4 = \left(\frac{W}{2}, \frac{H}{2}\right) \; BR_4 = (W,H), \tag{8}$$

$$TL_5 = \left(\frac{W}{4}, \frac{H}{4}\right) \; BR_5 = \left(\frac{3W}{4}, \frac{3H}{4}\right), \tag{9}$$

$$TL_6 = \left(0, \frac{H}{4}\right) \; BR_6 = \left(\frac{W}{2}, \frac{3H}{4}\right), \tag{10}$$

$$TL_7 = \left(\frac{W}{2}, \frac{H}{4}\right) \quad BR_7 = \left(W, \frac{3H}{4}\right) \tag{11}$$

The regions are described by Eqs. (4)-(11). Where TL_i and BR_i are the top-left and bottom-right corners of each region $i = 0...n, n = 7$. All co-ordinates are taken with the top-left corner of the image being (0, 0) and W, H are the width and height of the image respectively.

Edge Density. For any region r with the top-left and bottom-right corners given by (x_1, y_1) and (x_2, y_2) respectively, and the edge magnitude of the pixels within r given by $e\,(u, v)$, the edge magnitude of the region r is given by Eq. (12).

$$Edge\ density = \frac{1}{A_r} \sum_{u=x_1}^{x_2} \sum_{v=y_1}^{y_2} e(u, v) \tag{12}$$

Where A_r is the area of region r.

$$A_r = (x_2 - x_1 + 1)(y_2 - y_1 + 1) \tag{13}$$

Edge Density Feature Vector. The feature vector is composed of eight components, one component is the edge density of the whole image and the other seven components are the edge densities of the seven sub regions described by Eqs. (5)-(11). Because there is more than one region being used to compute the edge densities for the feature vector a more efficient approach is adopted from [9]. Let $I(x, y)$ be the input image with height H and width W. The edge magnitude $E(x, y)$ is computed using the filters given in Eq. (2) and is given by,

$$E(x, y) = \sqrt{E(x, y)_H^2 + E(x, y)_V^2} \tag{14}$$

The edge magnitude is a combination of the horizontal and vertical edge strengths $E(x, y)_H$ and $E(x, y)_V$ respectively.

From the edge magnitude an integral image $S(x, y)$ is computed by,

$$S(x, y) = \sum_{u=1}^{x} \sum_{v=1}^{y} E(u, v) \tag{15}$$

Where $S(x, y)$ is the sum of edge magnitudes in a rectangular region $\{(1, 1), (x, y)\}$.

$$Edge\ density = \frac{1}{A_r}(S(x_2, y_2) + S(x_1 - 1, y_1 - 1) - S(x_2, y_1 - 1) - S(x_1 - 1, y_2)) \tag{16}$$

With just a single pass over the image to compute the edge magnitudes, given a sub region $r = \{(x_1, y_1), (x_2, y_2)\}$ and the computed edge magnitude integral image, the edge density of region r can be easily computed by Eq. (16).

The feature vector given below will be the final representation after all edge densities of each region within an image is computed.

$$Feature\ vector = \{v_0, v_1, v_2, v_3, v_4, v_5, v_6, v_7\} \tag{17}$$

Where v_0 is the global edge density and v_1 to v_7 are the local edge densities.

Local Directional Pattern (LDP). The Local Directional Pattern (LDP) is an eight bit binary code assigned to each pixel of an input [10, 11]. This pattern is computed by comparing the relative edge response value of a pixel in different directions. The eight directional edge response values of a pixel are calculated using Kirsch masks in eight different orientations (M_0-M_7).

Applying eight masks, eight edge response values are obtained $m_0, m_1, \ldots q_7$, each representing the edge significance in its respective direction. The presence of edge show high response values in particular directions. The k most prominent directions are used to generate the LDP. The computed top k values $|m_i|$ are set to 1 (*in this case* $k = 3$). The other *(8-k)* bit of 8-bit LDP is set to 0 [11].

Local Direction Pattern Feature Vector. The medical image is represented using the LDP operator, I_{LDP}. Then the histogram of LDP, H_{LDP} is computed from the I_{LDP}. Since $k = 3$ (from empirical experiments), the histogram labeled image, H_{LDP} is a 56 bin histogram. H_{LDP} histogram contains detail information of an image, such as edges, corner, spot, and other local texture features. In order to incorporate some degree of location information, the medical images are divided into n number of small regions, $R_0; R_1; \ldots; R_n$, and extracted the $H_{LDP_{R_i}}$ from each region R_n. These n H_{LDP} histograms are concatenated to get a spatially combined global histogram for the global image.

3.3   Feature Normalization

The scales of Edge density features and Local Directional Pattern features are completely different. Firstly, this disparity can be due to the fact that each feature is computed using a formula that can produce various ranges of values. Secondly, the features may have the same approximate scale, but the distribution of their values has different means and standard deviations. A statistical normalization technique is used to transform each feature in such a way that each transformed feature distribution has means equal to 0 and variance of 1.

The similarity between the query image and a training image is given by the Euclidean distance between the two feature vectors. The distances from the query image to all training images are then ordered and images resulting in the smallest distance to the query image are regarded as the relevant images.

$$Distance = \sqrt{\sum_{i=1}^{n}(q_i - t_i)^2} \tag{18}$$

Where the ith entry of the test images feature vector is q_i, t_i is the ith entry of the query images feature vector and n is the dimension of the feature vector.

The classification of the query images uses the nearest neighbor technique. The query image will be classified as an image of the class of the closest image retrieved. The nearest neighbor technique is split into the first nearest neighbor (NN) and the 5-nearest neighbor (5-NN).

4   Results and Discussions

The experiments were carried out using a dataset of 2500 medical images obtained from the medical research centre. The dataset consisted of 125 images of each the researched body region images (hand, pelvis, breast, skull and chest), and other human body images. The researched model is evaluated in two ways, using content based image retrieval and using the nearest neighbor technique for classification. The researched model is used to assess the performance of the edge density feature, LDP features, and the combination of both features. The classification of the query image is based on the first nearest neighbor technique and using the 5-nearest neighbor technique. With the nearest neighbor technique, the class of the closest image to the query image is assigned to the query image, whereas with the 5-nearest neighbor, the class which has the most number of entities within the five closest images is assigned to the query image.

Table 1 shows the results of the classification accuracy along with the image retrieval precision achieved from the characterization of the images. It shows that the Edge density and LDP features complement each other in extraction local distinctive features for global characterization of images. Hence, the combination of the two techniques improved the overall accuracy rate. The 5-NN technique achieved better results than the NN method on all the techniques used. The results obtained show that the edge density and LDP can classify medical images and also be used in content based image retrieval systems for medical applications.

Table 1. Classification and Image Retrieval Accuracy

Method	NN %	5-NN %	Retrieval %
Edge density	90.1	93.3	88.9
LDP	92.4	96.0	98.1
Edge density & LDP	98.2	99.6	99.4

5   Conclusions

An effective approach based on Edge density and LDP for characterizing medical images has been presented. The results obtained were 98.2 % and 99.6 % classification success using the first nearest neighbor and the 5-nearest neighbor respectively. The LDP has also shown to work well in the retrieval of medical images. The results obtained are comparable to the results in the literature. The overall experimental results show that the proposed approach has a high true positive rate. Further investigation of the effect of the proposed approach with image processing in general is envisioned.

References

1. Tommasi, T., Deselaers, T: The medical image classification task, Experimental Evaluation in Visual Information Retrieval Series, vol. 32, 1st Edition (2010)
2. Antonie, M., Osmar, R.Z., Coman, A.: Application of data mining techniques for medical image classification. In: Proceedings of the Second International Workshop on Multimedia Data Mining (2001)
3. Yanxi, L., Deselaers, F., Rotthfus, W.E.: Classification driven semantic based medical image indexing and retrieval, The Robotics Institute, Curnegie Mellon University, Pittsburg
4. Vanitha, L., Venmathie, A.R.: Classification of medical images using support vector machine. Int. Conf. Inform. Netw. Technol. Singapore **4**, 63–67 (2011)
5. Nandagopalan, S., Adigu, B.S., Deepak, N.: A universal model for content based image retrieval. World Academy of Science. Eng. Technol. **46**, 644–647 (2008)
6. Surya, S.R., Sasikala, G.: Survey on content based image retrieval. Indian J. Comput. Sci. Eng. **2**, 691–696 (2011)
7. Phung, S.L., Bouzerdoum, A.: A new image feature for fast detection of people in images. Int. J. Inform. Syst. Sci. **3**(3), 383–391 (2007)
8. Popescu, D., Dobrescu, R., Nicolae, M.: Texture classification and defect detection by statistical features. Int. J. Circ. Syst. Signal Processing **1**, 79–84 (2007)
9. Phung, S.L., Bouzerdoum, A., Detecting people in images: an edge density approach (2007)
10. Jabid, T., Kabir, H., Chae, O.: Gender classification using local directional pattern. In: International Conference on Pattern Recognition (2010)
11. Jabid, T., Kabir, H., Chae, O.: Robust facial expression recognition based on local directional pattern. ETRI J. **32**(5), 784–794 (2010)

Automated Detection of Aortic Root Landmarks in Preprocedure CT Angiography Images for Transcatheter Aortic Valve Implantation Patients

Mustafa Elattar[1](✉), Esther Wiegerinck[2], Floortje van Kesteren[3],
Lucile Dubois[4], Nils Planken[3], Ed vanbavel[1], Jan Baan[2],
and Henk Marquering[1,3]

[1] Biomedical Engineering and Physics, University of Amsterdam,
Amsterdam, Netherlands
mustafa.elattar@gmail.com
[2] Cardiology, University of Amsterdam, Amsterdam, Netherlands
[3] Radiology, Academic Medical Center, University of Amsterdam,
Amsterdam, Netherlands
[4] Biomedical Engineering, Polytech Lyon, Université Claude Bernard Lyon,
Villeurbanne, France

Abstract. Transcatheter aortic valve implantation provides a minimal invasive treatment in patients with severe aortic stenosis. CT Angiography is used for the pre-operative planning, in which the accessibility of the aorta-femoral tract for the catheter and the prosthetic type and size can be determined. Preprocedure planning includes the determination of annulus radius, area and coronary ostia to annulus distance. These measurements use the location of five landmarks; the two coronary ostia and the three hinge points. Automatic landmarks detection is beneficial to speed up the calculation of the sizing parameters. In this paper, we introduce an automated approach to extract the aortic root landmarks and calculate sizing parameters. Our proposed algorithm has a high accuracy in comparison with the manual reference with a mean point-to-point error of 2.47 mm in 20 patients; where the interobserver variation had a mean point to point of 2.30 mm. With the high accuracy shown, the proposed method can be introduced in clinical practice.

Keywords: CTA · TAVI · Landmarks detection · Aortic root · Segmentation

1 Introduction

Aortic stenosis is the most common valvular heart disease [1]. Aortic stenosis occurs mainly due to calcium accumulation on the aortic valve leaflets. The open-heart aortic valve replacement is an effective method to treat severe aortic valve stenosis. Aortic valve replacement (AVR) is the most common heart valve operation, accounting for 60 to 70 percent of all valve surgery performed in the elderly. With a quarter of a million procedures performed annually, it is the most common valvular heart surgery [2].

© Springer International Publishing Switzerland 2015
M. Kamel and A. Campilho (Eds.): ICIAR 2015, LNCS 9164, pp. 402–410, 2015.
DOI: 10.1007/978-3-319-20801-5_44

However, at least 30 % of patients cannot tolerate the surgical trauma due to the advanced age or presence of various comorbidities [3]. Transcatheter aortic valve implantation is a coming up, less invasive procedure to treat severe aortic valve stenosis, where the prosthetic valve is inserted and deployed using a catheter through a small puncture of the femoral artery (the transfemoral approach) or a small incision at the heart apex (the transapical approach) [4]. However, TAVI is associated with a number of adverse effects, such as paravalvular leakage, stroke, coronary obstruction, and conduction disorders [5]. CT Angiography imaging plays an important role in pre-operative surgical planning and patient selection and can be used for post-operative outcome assessment. Planning for this intervention is crucial for assessing the eligibility of the patient and sizing parameters of the aortic root to choose the suitable prosthesis dimensions and type [6]. During the pre-procedure planning, several important sizing parameters of the aortic valve need to be measured. For example, the distance between the coronary ostia and the aortic valve annular plane is a critical parameter for patient selection since a short distance increases the risk of blocking coronary ostia after valve deployment [7]. The diameter and area of aortic valve annulus needs to be measured accurately to select a valve with an appropriate size. These measurements assess the distances of five landmarks that are on the aortic root surface; right coronary ostia, left coronary ostia, right coronary hinge point, left coronary hinge point and the no coronary hinge point. The automated aortic root landmarks detection would speed up the process of measurement and planning and has the potential to reduce interobserver variation.

Two previous studies presented methods for detection of the aortic root landmarks for TAVI purposes. Zheng et al. [8] introduced a fully automatic landmarks detection in C-arm images using a hierarchical approach by first detecting a global object using marginal space learning with subsequent refinement in a small region under the guidance of specific landmark detection. In [9], a model based segmentation was used to locate the coronary ostia and annulus plane. This coronary ostia detection used intensity pattern matching as an extra step for refinement of the ostia location. In their study [9] the accuracy was not compared with manual interobserver variation, which is an important constraint for introduction in clinical practice.

In this work, we introduce a fully automated algorithm to extract the aortic root landmarks, calculate sizing parameters in CTA of patients eligible for TAVI. The accuracy of our approach is assessed by comparison of the interobserver variation.

2 Methods

We propose an image analysis algorithm in which we first segment the aortic root surface [10] which is used as a search span for the required landmarks. These landmarks are used for calculating sizing parameters required for the TAVI procedure. Each landmark was extracted based on landmark specific features combined with a rough estimate of the proximal and distal ends of the aortic root.

In the next sections, we describe the used image data, the aortic root surface segmentation, the landmarks detection methods, and the validation of the detected landmarks by the comparison with the manual delineated landmarks.

2.1 Image Data

We collected a dataset of twenty 3D CT angiography volumes for preprocedure TAVI patients from our institute (Academic Medical Center, The Netherlands). For all patients, ten cardiac phase CTA volumes were acquired. For analysis, we selected the volume at 70 % of the cardiac cycle, which is a phase in which the aortic valve is closed. With the closed valve, there is a separation between the aortic root lumen and the left ventricle outflow tract lumen, which is important for accurate aortic root detection [10]. All image volumes contain about 500–600 slices. The size of each slice in a volume is 512 × 512 pixels with a 16 bit depth. The in plane image resolution is isotropic and varies from 0.44 mm to 0.68 mm. The slice thickness for all data sets is 0.9 mm and the overlap between each two successive slices is 0.45 mm.

2.2 Aortic Root Surface Segmentation

The aortic root in the CTA volumes was automatically segmented by performing the following steps: first, the volume of interest is detected using adaptive thresholding, voxel classification and connected component analysis [10]. The centerline through the ascending aorta and aortic root is determined next. Subsequently, high intensities due to calcifications are masked. Finally, the aortic root is represented in cylindrical coordinates allowing the segmentation of the aortic root using 3D normalized cuts.

2.3 Proximal and Distal Detection of the Aortic Root

To refine the detection of the landmarks, we implemented a technique to locate distal and proximal ends of the aortic root. We exploit the segmented surface and converted this 3D Cartesian surface into 2D radial map. Based on the aorta centerline, CMPRs perpendicular to this centerline are calculated. For every slice, the Fourier transform of the radius of aorta surface is calculated. The elliptical shape of the LVOT is expressed by strong second harmonic contributions; the three sinuses are associated with a strong third harmonic contribution of the Fourier decomposition. We analyzed the ratio of the third harmonic and the second harmonic. This ratio enhances the detection of the three sinuses, minimizing the effect of the elliptical shape at the LVOT. We applied the Laplacian operator on the resulted ratio which produces a signal with two local maxima that represent the proximal and distal extents of the aortic root.

2.4 Coronary Ostia Detection

To locate the coronary ostia on the 3D aorta surface, the relative high intensity in the coronary arteries is used as the main feature. To detect the high intensity contributions, an image of the average value of the volume between the segmented aortic surface and a dilated surface is calculated. Each pixel in this image represents the average intensity along a cylinder starting at the aortic root surface with a length of 2.5 mm. This cylinder has a radius of 0.75 mm. The rows in this image represent the MPR slices and the columns represent the angle around the centerline. The direction of the cylinders is shown as arrows in Fig. 1. The formed image shown in Fig. 1 is weighted using a calculated probability map based on the expected location of the distal extent of the aortic root. We believe that the distal extent represent the sinutubular junction that is generally close to the location of the coronary ostia. The probability map was calculated using Gaussian function centered in the distal slice and had standard deviation of 4 mm in both proximal and distal directions.

Two 1D profiles are created by the projection of the maximum values of the image in both dimensions. The projection in proximal-distal direction (PD) generates a profile as a function of the angle. In this profile, two distinct local maxima represent the angular location of the two coronary ostia. The profile in which the contributions for each angle are projected in as a function of the PD direction, a single maximum is found, which represents the location of the ostia along the centerline.

2.5 Hinge Points Detection

The aortic valve annulus represents the narrowest part of the aortic root and is defined as a virtual ring with three anatomical anchor points at the base of each of the attachments of the aortic leaflets. Often, patients have a heavily calcified annulus, disguising these hinge points. In this section, we are proposing an algorithm to detect the Right Coronary (RC), Left Coronary (LC) and Non Coronary (NC) hinge points. The hinge points are detected using combination of three 2D maps; the Gaussian curvature map (GCM), the minimum intensity inward the aortic wall map (MIIAM), and maximum intensity inward the aortic wall map (MXIAM). These three maps comprehend the usage of intensity and geometrical based features. The Gaussian curvature of the aorta wall is determined by computing the curvature tensor and the principal curvatures at each vertex of the surface mesh.

The MIAAM highlights low intensities representing the leaflets. Each pixel in this map represents the minimum intensity along a cylinder starting at the aortic root surface

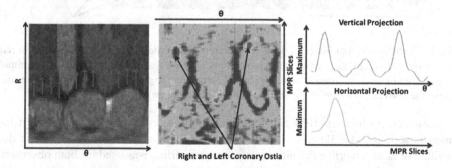

Fig. 1. (Left) Aortic root image in polar coordinates. The aortic root boundary is shown in red. The arrows represent the direction for which an average intensity projection images is created. (Center) The projection image is displayed in the middle showing the two local maxima representing the coronary ostia. Two 1-D maximum projection curves were calculated (Right) to determine the proximal-distal and angular locations of the coronary ostia (Color figure online).

directed inward with a length of 1.5 mm and radius of 0.75 mm. MXIAM is formed in the same manner but only determining the maximum intensity. In the three 2D maps y-axis represent the MPR slices and the x-axis represents the angle around the centerline. We combine the three formed maps by its multiplication forming one map.

The combined image is split into three radial tiles representing the three sinuses and each radial sinus tile represents one sinus and is thresholded using a threshold value of the half of maximum value. The binary pixels are analyzed finding the principal component using Eigen vectors. The principal component for each tile (sinus) is used as a search direction for the hinge points on the combined map.

Figure 2 shows the combined map and the three extracted main Eigen vectors. By resampling the combined map data using each sinus Eigen vector points, An one dimensional profile is provided to locate the first local maximum that represent the hinge point. By applying this on each sinus tile, RC, LC and NC hinge points are detected. RC hinge point is identified as the most anterior point, where LC hinge point is the most posterior and left one.

2.6   Validation

To validate the accuracy of the automatic landmarks detection, we compared these landmarks with manual assessment in 20 CTA image datasets.

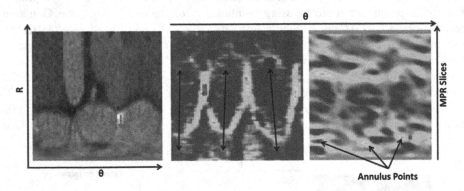

Fig. 2. (Left) Aortic root image in polar coordinates. The aortic root boundary is shown in red. The arrows represent the direction of projections. (Center) a combined image of minimal, maximal, and curvature images shows the leaflet structure. (Right) the Gaussian curvature map shows the convex curvature of the surface (Color figure online).

Two expert observers (EW and FvK) manually selected the five landmarks using 3mensio software in a 3D curved MPR volume. To reduce interobserver variation due to differences in centerline definitions, the same centerline was used for both observers. The software allowed scrolling though different 2D MPR slices to select the landmarks. In the validation, the manually set landmarks were considered the reference values. The differences between the automated method and reference values are compared with the manual interobserver variation. The sizing parameters that are required for the pre-procedure planning of TAVI were calculated. These sizing parameters include the location and orientation of the annulus plane and the perpendicular distance between right and left coronary ostia to the annulus plane.

We calculated common TAVI sizing parameters using the automated extracted and manually set landmarks. The ostia to annulus distances were calculated. The annulus plane was defined as the plane connecting the three hinge points. The difference between the annulus planes using the automated and manually set hinge points is determined by calculating the angle between the two normal vectors of the planes and by calculating the distance between centers of the three points. Furthermore, we calculated the radius of the circle connects the three hinge points.

The accuracy was evaluated for three measurements; Euclidean paired distance between the landmarks, angle difference between annulus planes, Euclidean paired distance between the annulus centers, and the estimated circle radius difference was calculated. The interobserver variation analysis was done based on the same accuracy measurements for the two observers.

3 Results

3.1 Evaluation of Landmark Detection

The aortic root segmentation was successfully applied for all 20 patients. Figure 3 shows the boxplots of the accuracy of each landmark in terms of Euclidean paired distance between landmarks. Table 1 shows the interobserver variation and accuracy for the detection of the location of the landmarks. Our proposed algorithm has shown good performance in comparison with the reference standard with a mean error of 2.47 mm ranging from 2.06 mm to 2.88 mm; where the interobserver variation had a mean paired difference of 2.30 mm ranging from 2.02 mm to 2.59 mm.

3.2 Evaluation of Sizing Parameters for TAVI

In Table 2, the annulus center shift and angle difference are shown, the ostium to annulus distance differences and minimum circle radius that fits the three hinge points differences are shown as well.

The annulus angle mean difference and annulus center mean distance were 6.2 degrees and 1.82 mm when it is compared to the ground truth annulus plane angle and center; where the mean difference and centers distance between observers were 4.4 degrees and 1.56 mm. The mean difference for ostia to annulus distance was 1.58 mm; which is comparable to the interobserver' mean difference of 0.96 mm.

4 Discussion

We have presented a fully automated method for detecting landmarks in the aortic root, which are commonly used in TAVI measurement procedures. Our proposed algorithm has shown good performance in comparison with the reference standard. Since, the accuracy of the proposed algorithm is comparable to the manual interobserver variation this method is suitable in clinical practice.

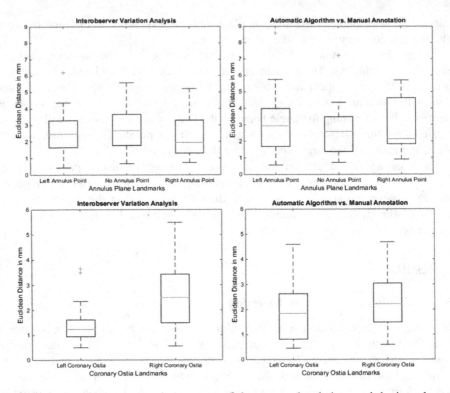

Fig. 3. Four boxplots represent the accuracy of the proposed technique and the interobserver variation for determining the hinge points and coronary ostia.

Table 1. Average, median and standard deviation of the Euclidean distance between points for accuracy and interobserver variation is listed in the table

	Proposed algorithm			Interobserver variation		
Measurement error	*Mean*	*STD*	*Median*	*Mean*	*STD*	*Median*
Hinge points (mm)	2.88	1.69	2.59	2.59	1.40	2.29
Coronary ostia (mm)	2.06	1.13	1.93	2.02	1.24	1.53

Previous studies on aortic root landmarks detection have been reported, based on various imaging modalities. Waechter et al. applied their proposed technique on CT data, where Zheng et al. applied the marginal space learning algorithm on C-arm CT data. These studies have presented similar or less mean error [9] and [8]. Work done in those studies has been validated using reference manual segmentation. In [9], the proposed technique successfully detected 39 ostia out of 40 with root mean square error of 0.9 mm. Evaluation of work done in [8] show accuracy for the ostia to annulus distance of 2.31 ± 1.95 mm. None of the prementioned work has studied the interobserver variability. Since the mean error of the current study with one observer is

Table 2. The average, median and standard deviation of the annulus angle difference, ostia to annulus distance, annulus center error and corresponding annulus radius for the accuracy of the proposed algorithm and interobserver variation.

Measurement error	Proposed algorithm			Interobserver variation		
	Mean	*STD*	*Median*	*Mean*	*STD*	*Median*
Annulus plane (°)	*6.24°*	*3.56°*	*5.31°*	*4.44°*	*3.07°*	*4.43°*
Ostia to annulus distance (mm)	*1.58*	*1.51*	*1.23*	*0.96*	*0.63*	*0.95*
Annulus center (mm)	*1.82*	*0.85*	*1.69*	*1.56*	*0.79*	*1.37*
Corresponding annulus radius (mm)	*0.48*	*0.45*	*0.32*	*0.77*	*0.50*	*0.75*

comparable to interobserver deviations, we believe that the obtained accuracy is sufficient for clinical practice.

The manual annotation of the hinge points was not straight-forward due to the presence of severer calcifications in the region of the annulus plane and the left ventricle outflow tract. These difficulties are reflected in large differences between the manual measurements (up to 2.59 mm for the hinge points in comparison with coronary points with 2.02 mm).

The difference between the accuracy of the proposed algorithm for detecting ostia and hinge points is according the differences for the manual annotations. The accuracy of the detection of the left coronary ostium was higher than for the right coronary ostia. We believe that this improved accuracy is caused by the larger right coronary artery diameter. The large diameter of the right coronary artery [11] make assignment of the ostium is less accurate than left coronary ostium.

For the sizing parameters, the annulus angle mean difference and annulus center mean distance were t is compared to the reference value for the annulus plane angle and center. It is notable that the annulus angle error is not strongly affecting the ostia to annulus distance and the distance error is of the same order as the interobserver accuracy.

This study suffered from a number of limitations. The automatic aortic root surface approach produced over-smoothed surfaces, which affect the accuracy of landmarks. We have used data from only a single medical center and scanner. Although there was a large variety in scanned volumes, image to noise ratio, and anatomy, it could be that different scanning protocols require adjustments of the presented algorithm.

5   Conclusion

We have presented an automated sizing pipeline for sizing in CTAs of patients eligible for TAVI procedures based on the detection of aortic root landmarks. The imaging pipeline starts with segmenting the aortic root, after which the proximal and distal extent of the aortic root were determined. The coronary ostia have been initially identified close to the distal plane and detected based on the average intensity intact with the aortic root surface. The hinge points have been initially identified close to the proximal plane and detected based on the combination of three geometrical and intensity based features. The accuracy of the proposed algorithm was evaluated on 20 CTA datasets and showed that the sizing parameters was comparable to the interobserver variation in terms of ostia to annulus distance, angle error, shift in annulus center, and corresponding annulus radius.

References

1. Nkomo, V.T., Gardin, J.M., Skelton, T.N., Gottdiener, J.S., Scott, C.G., Enriquez-Sarano, M.: Burden of valvular heart diseases: a population-based study. Lancet **368**, 1005–1011 (2006)
2. Billings, F.T., Kodali, S.K., Shanewise, J.S.: Transcatheter aortic valve implantation: anesthetic considerations. Anesth. Analg. **108**, 1453–1462 (2009)
3. Leon, M., Smith, C., Mack, M.: Transcatheter aortic-valve implantation for aortic stenosis in patients who cannot undergo surgery. Engl. J. **363**(17), 1597–1607 (2010)
4. Vahanian, A., Alfieri, O., Al-Attar, N., Antunes, M., Bax, J., Cormier, B., Cribier, A., De Jaegere, P., Fournial, G., Kappetein, A.P., Kovac, J., Ludgate, S., Maisano, F., Moat, N., Mohr, F., Nataf, P., Piérard, L., Pomar, J.L., Schofer, J., Tornos, P., Tuzcu, M., van Hout, B., Von Segesser, L.K., Walther, T.: Transcatheter valve implantation for patients with aortic stenosis: a position statement from the European Association of Cardio-Thoracic Surgery (EACTS) and the European Society of Cardiology (ESC), in collaboration with the European Association of Percu. Eur. Heart J. **29**, 1463–1470 (2008)
5. Baan, J., Yong, Z.Y., Koch, K.T.: Henriques, J.P.S., Bouma, B.J., Vis, M.M., Cocchieri, R., Piek, J.J., de Mol, B. a J.M.: Factors associated with cardiac conduction disorders and permanent pacemaker implantation after percutaneous aortic valve implantation with the CoreValve prosthesis. Am. Heart J. **159**, 497–503 (2010)
6. Tops, L.F., Wood, D.A., Delgado, V., Schuijf, J.D., Mayo, J.R., Pasupati, S., Lamers, F.P.L., van der Wall, E.E., Schalij, M.J., Webb, J.G., Bax, J.J.: Noninvasive evaluation of the aortic root with multislice computed tomography implications for transcatheter aortic valve replacement. JACC Cardiovasc. Imaging. **1**, 321–330 (2008)
7. Okuyama, K., Jilaihawi, H., Makkar, R.R.: Leaflet length and left main coronary artery occlusion following transcatheter aortic valve replacement. Catheter Cardiovasc. Interv. **82**, E754–E759 (2013)
8. Zheng, Y., John, M., Liao, R., Nöttling, A., Boese, J., Kempfert, J., Walther, T., Brockmann, G., Comaniciu, D.: Automatic aorta segmentation and valve landmark detection in C-arm CT for transcatheter aortic valve implantation. IEEE Trans. Med. Imaging **31**, 2307–2321 (2012)
9. Waechter, I., Kneser, R., Korosoglou, G., Peters, J., Bakker, N.H., van der Boomen, R., Weese, J.: Patient specific models for planning and guidance of minimally invasive aortic valve implantation. Med. Image Comput. Comput. Assist. Interv. **13**, 526–533 (2010)
10. Elattar, M.A., Wiegerinck, E.M., Planken, R.N., Vanbavel, E., van Assen, H.C., Baan, J., Marquering, H.A.: Automatic segmentation of the aortic root in CT angiography of candidate patients for transcatheter aortic valve implantation. Med. Biol. Eng. Comput. **52**, 611–618 (2014)
11. Dodge, J.T., Brown, B.G., Bolson, E.L., Dodge, H.T.: Lumen diameter of normal human coronary arteries. Influence of age, sex, anatomic variation, and left ventricular hypertrophy or dilation. Circulation **86**, 232–246 (1992)

Retinal Blood Vessels Differentiation for Calculation of Arterio-Venous Ratio

Samra Irshad[1][(✉)], M. Usman Akram[1], Sara Ayub[1], and Anaum Ayaz[2]

[1] College of Electrical and Mechanical Engineering,
National University of Sciences and Technology, Rawalpindi, Pakistan
sam.ershad@yahoo.com, usmakram@gmail.com,
saraayub71@ee.ceme.edu.pk
[2] Bahira University, Islamabad, Pakistan
anaum.ayaz@gmail.com

Abstract. Hypertensive Retinopathy (HR) is an eye disease occurs due to high blood pressure. This disease primarily damages the blood vessels in retina by altering the vessel caliber. The damage is evaluated by calculation of Arterio-venous Ratio (AVR), which quantifies the change in diameter of retinal blood vessels. It is basically the ratio of arterioles to venules diameter. In order to calculate AVR for an automatic diagnosis of HR, the vascular characterization is an essential step. This paper presents an automatic system for retinal vessel classification which is based on novel combination of intensity and gradient based features. The automated system first segments the retinal vessels, then extracts features and finally classifies the vessels as arteries and veins. The proposed system is tested and validated on locally gathered fundus image database, taken from AFIO, Pakistan. The proposed approach provides an accuracy of 93.49 % and 93.47 % for veins and arteries, respectively.

Keywords: Hypertensive Retinopathy (HR) · Support Vector Machine (SVM) · Arterio-Venous Ratio (AVR) · Optic Disk (OD) · Region Of Interest (ROI)

1 Introduction

Fundus imaging is a technique which allows non-invasive and efficient examination of various retinal anatomical structures [1]. Automated fundus image analysis tools are quite useful as they provide significant assistance to ophthalmologists for an early detection and diagnosis of different complications including hypertension, diabetes, and stroke [2]. Hypertension is a condition which is caused because of high blood pressure. Hypertension mainly affects the blood vessels in the human body. Relevance between increased blood pressure and alteration in retinal vessel calibre has been proved [1]. This alteration in blood vessels causes a complication in retina known as HR.

AVR is an important parameter which is used to quantify the change in vessel diameter and, thus evaluation of disease severity [3]. The classification of retinal vessels into arteries and veins and then measurement of those classified vessels is

© Springer International Publishing Switzerland 2015
M. Kamel and A. Campilho (Eds.): ICIAR 2015, LNCS 9164, pp. 411–418, 2015.
DOI: 10.1007/978-3-319-20801-5_45

essential for the calculation of AVR. The automated differentiation of vessels is also helpful for assessment of other biomarkers of hypertensive retinopathy such as analysis of increase in arteriolar central light reflex [3].

Several methods have been proposed in the past for the automatic classification of retinal vessels. These systems have mainly used intensity features for retinal vasculature differentiation. D. Ortíz et al. [4] developed a system for the diagnosis of HR, in which the retinal vessels are classified using vessel intensity in red channel. A. Ruggeri et al. [5] proposed a system for AVR calculation, which makes use of vessel intensity in hue and red channel to discriminate between arteries and veins. G. Mirsharif et al. [6] presented an automated technique for retinal vessel classification using color features extracted from RGB and HSL color space. Linear Discriminant classifier is used for classification. Profile based features are proposed by M. Saez et al. [7] for retinal vessel differentiation. Profiles across vessels are extracted, which are then classified using k-means clustering algorithm. A. Zampirini et al. [8] developed a system for an automatic labeling of retinal vessels, in which they have used color, structural and spatial information as features. Another system for vessel classification is proposed by C. Muramatsu et al. [9] in which intensity-based features from vessel center-line pixels are used. The system is tested on DRIVE database using LDA classifier and it showed 75 % accuracy.

In our previous work [10], we achieved an overall 81 % accuracy in vessel classification. We extend our research in this paper by developing a larger feature set which is a combination of intensity and gradient based features. With the inclusion of gradient based features, the average accuracy is improved.

The paper is organized in four sections. Flow diagram of our methodology is illustrated in Sect. 2 along with the details of the implementation. Experimental results are given in Sect. 3 followed by conclusion in Sect. 4.

2   Proposed Technique

The proposed system consists of four main modules i.e. background removal, segmentation of blood vessel, determination of Region of Interest (ROI) and classification of vessels lying within this region. Many algorithms proposed previously have classified the complete vessel network for differentiation; however classification of entire retinal vasculature is not necessary for AVR calculation. According to the standards [3], the vessels are measured in a circular zone of twice the radius of Optic Disk (OD), taken some distance away from the OD boundary. Figure 1 shows the flow diagram of proposed system.

2.1   Background Removal

In preprocessing stage, the background mask is segmented from the digital fundus image. Following steps are carried out for the retinal image background segmentation; [11].

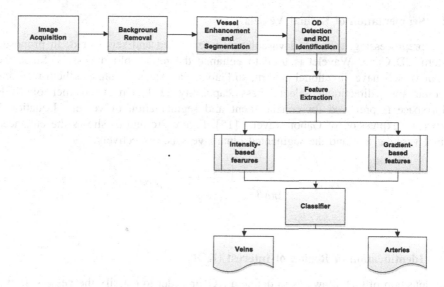

Fig. 1. Flowchart of proposed technique

- An initial threshold ($th = 10$) is applied on the red channel of retinal image and morphological operations are used to remove holes and false regions.
- Then, the objects present in the binary image are labeled using connected component labeling algorithm [12].
- Finally the objects having the largest fundus region is selected [13]. Figure 2(b) shows the result of background segmentation.

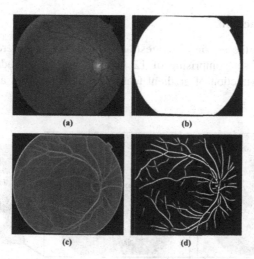

Fig. 2. Background Removal and Blood Vessel Extraction: (a) Original Image, (b) Background Mask, (c) Vessel Enhancement, (d) Segmented Vessels

2.2   Segmentation of Retinal Vessels

After preprocessing, the retinal vasculature is extracted and segmented. In proposed system, 2D Gabor Wavelet is used to enhance the retinal blood vessels. Since the retinal vessels have directional pattern, so Gabor wavelets can enhance them well due to their own directional selectiveness capability [14]. Green channel of RGB color-space is preferred for enhancement and segmentation of vessels. Equation 1 shows the expression of Gabor wavelet [15]. Figure 2(c and d) shows the enhanced retinal vascular tree and the segmented binary vessels, respectively.

$$G(x,y) = \frac{1}{2\pi\sigma\beta} e^{-\pi\left[\frac{(x-x_0)^2}{\sigma^2} + \frac{(y-y_0)^2}{\beta^2}\right]} e^{i[\delta_0 x + \vartheta_0 y]} \tag{1}$$

2.3   Identification of Region of Interest (ROI)

The detection of OD allows us to define a ROI in order to classify the vessels. In this paper, OD is localized using maximum intensity region finding technique [16]. Red channel is chosen for this purpose and an averaging mask of size 31×31 is applied to remove the background artifacts which can cause false localization. The maximum intensity region is detected in the resultant image because the intensity values of optic disk are greater than the background region [16]. After the detection of OD, ROI is defined approximately as an annulus of quarter to twice the radius of optic disk, taken from the OD's margin. Figure 3(a) shows the image with OD position detected and ROI super-imposed on it.

2.4   Feature Extraction

Vessels lying within the region of interest are considered for differentiation. We have developed a feature set comprising of 12 features based on gradient and statistical measures. For the extraction of gradient features, following steps are implemented;

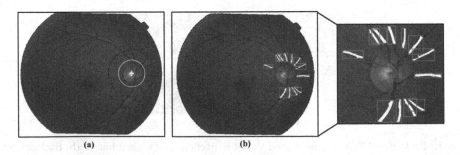

Fig. 3. OD detection and bounding rectangles: (a) OD detection and ROI super-imposed, (b) Vessels lying within ROI shown in bounding rectangles

- First, a minimum bounding rectangle is defined for each vessel segment in ROI and this smallest bounding rectangle contains every pixel of the vessel segment [17]. This step generates sub-images containing vessel segments and their corresponding binary masks. Figure 3(b) shows the bounding rectangles along with their respective sub-images and masks.
- Connected component labeling algorithm [12] is used for discarding those bounding rectangles, which contain more than one binary object. This problem arises due to overlapping bounding boxes. If the features from 'overlapping' bounding boxes are selected, they result in ambiguous features due to presence of more than one vessel in bounding box. Therefore, features from those bounding boxes will not be considered. Figure 4 shows the overlapping bounding rectangles.
- For the bounding rectangle contining only one sub-vessel, gradient $G(x,y)$ [18] of the corresponding sub-imge $I_s(x, y)$ is computed using Sobel masks. Eqs. 2 and 3 show the expression for image gradient and gradient magnitude, respectively [18].

$$G = [I_x I_y]^T = \left[\frac{\partial I}{\partial x} \frac{\partial I}{\partial y}\right]^T \qquad (2)$$

$$\|G\| = \sqrt{(I_x)^2 + (I_y)^2} \qquad (3)$$

The gradient magnitude of sub-vessels is computed for red and green channels of RGB color space. The gradient magnitude values are greater for vein segments due to sharp change in intensity. This feature correlates with clinical characteristic of veins, containing lower intensity values because of less oxygenated content. Arteries are rich in oxygen and therefore gradient magnitude of arteries do not exhibit steep changes.

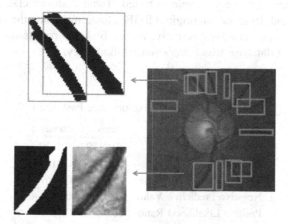

Fig. 4. ROI is shown with bounding rectangles, sub-image at the top shows two over-lapping bounding windows, whereas other sub-images show the sub-vessel and its respective binary mask

Table 1. Description of feature set

Features	Description
1-4	Minimum and maximum of intenity values of vessel pixels in Green ($MinG$, $MaxG$) and Hue ($MinH$, $MaxH$) channel of RGB and HSV color-space
5-8	Mean and standard deviation of intensity values of vessel segmnets in Green ($MeanG$, $StdG$) and Luminance ($MeanL$, $StdL$) channel
9-12	Mean and maximum of gradient magnitude of vessel segments in Green ($Grad_{mean}G$, $Grad_{max}G$) and Red ($Grad_{mean}R$, $Grad_{max}R$) channel

The gradient magnitude of veins and arteries is read into a vector. Other color features are concatenated with the gradient features. Table 1 shows all the features used for classification.

3   Results

The quantitative assessment of the proposed system is done by using a local dataset, collected from AFIO, Pakistan. This dataset contains 25 images with a resolution of 1504×1000. We have considered 233 sub-vessels from 25 retinal images. The vessels in the images are annotated as arteries and veins in red and blue color respectively by our ophthalmologist using a MATLAB based annotation tool. These annotated images are used as ground truth for comparison with the experimental results. Only the vessels that are annotated by our ophthalmologist will be used for classification.

LS-SVM is used for classification. SVM separates arteries and veins from each other with maximum margin by using a separating hyper-plane. We have implemented least squares SVM using LS-SVM toolbox [19] which classifies candidate object into artery or vein. Leave-one-out Cross Validation approach is followed in classification. In this approach, one sample is left for testing and all other samples are used for training. Thus, each and every sample is tested. Table 2 shows classification performance. Figs 5(a) and (b) shows an original RGB retinal image and the vessels classified in ROI as arteries and veins, respectively. Figure 6 shows results on different retinal images from AFIO database using proposed methodology.

Table 2. Classification Performance Parameters

Performance parameter	Veins	Arteries
Sensitivity	0.9130	0.9429
Specificity	0.9565	0.9130
Positive Predictive Value	0.9545	0.9167
Negative Predictive Value	0.9166	0.9544
Positive Likelihood Ratio	20.9885	10.8379
Negative Likelihood Ratio	0.0909	0.0625
Accuracy	0.9349	0.9347

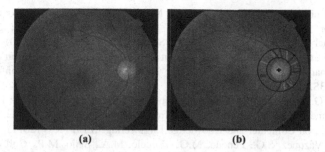

Fig. 5. (a). Original retinal image, (b). Retinal vessels classified inside ROI as arteries and veins

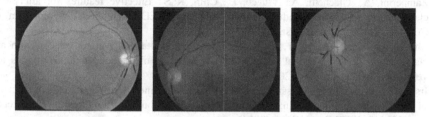

Fig. 6. Retinal images from AFIO database, arteries and veins classified as red and blue, respectively

4 Conclusion

An automated system classification of retinal is proposed in this paper. This system mainly consists of three phases, pre-processing, segmentation of vessels and vessels classification. A new combination of gradient magnitude and color features is presented in this paper for accurate classification of vessels. As compared to our previously proposed system which achieved an average accuracy of 81 %, this classification approach provides an accuracy of 93.49 % and 93.47 % for veins and arteries, respectively. With an addition of gradient magnitude features, this labeling feature set offers high accuracy than those reported in [4–10].

References

1. Yannuzzi, L.A., Ober, M.D., Slakter, J.S., Spaide, R.F., Fisher, Y.L., Flower, R.W., Rosen, R.: Ophthalmic fundus imaging: today and beyond. Am. J. Ophthalmol. **137**, 511–524 (2004)
2. Nguyen, T.T., Wang, J.J., Wong, T.Y.: Retinal vascular changes in pre-diabetes and prehypertension, new findings and their research and clinical implications. Diabetes Care **30**, 2708–2715 (2007)
3. Hubbard, L.D., Brothers, R.J., King, W.N., Clegg, L.X., Klein, R., Cooper, L.S., Sharrett, A.R., Davis, M.D., Cai, J.: Methods for evaluation of retinal microvascular abnormalities associated with hypertension/sclerosis in the atherosclerosis risk in communities study. Ophthalmol. **106**(12), 2269–2280 (1999)

4. Ortíz, D., Cubides, M., Suárez, A., Zequera, M., Quiroga, J., Gómez, J., Arroyo, N.: Support system for the preventive diagnosis of hypertensive retinopathy. In: 32nd Annual International Conference of the IEEE EMBS. IEEE Press, Argentina (2010)

5. Ruggeri, A., Grisan, E., De Luca, M.: An automatic system for the estimation of generalized arteriolar narrowing in retinal images. In: 29th Annual International Conference of the IEEE EMBS. IEEE Press, France (2007)

6. Mirsharif, G., Tajeripour, F., Sobhanmanesh, F., Pourreza, H., Banaee, T.: Developing an automatic method for separation of arteries from veins in retinal Images. In: 1st International eConference on Computer and Knowledge Engineering. IEEE Press (2011)

7. Saez, M., Vázquez, S.G., Penedo, M.G., Barceló, M.A., Seijo, M.P., Coll de Tuero, G., Reino, P.R.: Development of an automated system to classify retinal vessels into arteries and veins. Comput. Methods Programs Biomed. **108**, 367–376 (2012)

8. Zamperini, A., Giachetti, A., Trucco, E., Chin, K.,S.: Effective features for artery-vein classification in digital fundus images. In: 25th IEEE International Symposium on Computer-Based Medical System (2012)

9. Muramatsu, C., Hatanaka, Y., Iwase, T., Hara, T., Fujita, H.: Automated detection and classification of major retinal vessels for determination of diameter ratio of arteries and veins. In: Medical Imaging (2010)

10. Irshad, S., Akram, M.U.: Classification of retinal vessels into arteries and veins for detection of hypertensive retinopathy. In: 7th Cairo International Biomedical Engineering Conference, pp. 133–136. IEEE Press, Cairo (2014)

11. Usman, A., Khitran, S.A., Akram, M.U., Nadeem, Y.: A robust algorithm for optic disc segmentation from colored fundus images. In: Campilho, A., Kamel, M. (eds.) ICIAR 2014. LNCS, vol. 8815, pp. 303–310. Springer, Switzerland (2014)

12. Haralick, R.M., Shapiro, L.G.: Computer and Robot Vision, vol. I, pp. 28–48. Addison-Wesley (1992)

13. Pratt, W.K.: Digital Image Processing, p. 634. Wiley, New York (1991)

14. Akram, M.U., Khan, S.A.: Multilayered thresholding-based blood vessel segmentation for screening of diabetic retinopathy. Eng. Comput. **29**, 165–173 (2013)

15. Lee, T.S.: Image Representation Using 2D Gabor Wavelets. IEEE Trans. Pattern Anal. Mach. Intel. **18**(10), 959–971 (1996)

16. Akram, M.U., Khan, A., Iqbal, K., Butt, W.H.: Retinal images: optic disk localization and detection. In: Campilho, A., Kamel, M. (eds.) ICIAR 2010, Part II. LNCS, vol. 6112, pp. 40–49. Springer, Heidelberg (2010)

17. Freeman, H., Shapira, R.: Determining the minimum-area encasing rectangle for an arbitrary closed curve. Commun. ACM **18**, 409–413 (1975)

18. Gonzalez, R.C., Woods, R.E.: Digital Image Processing, 3rd edn. Prentice Hall (2008)

19. LSSVM MATLAB library. http://www.esat.kuleuven.be/sista/lssvmlab/

Graph Structuring of Skeleton Object for Its High-Level Exploitation

Rabaa Youssef[1,2](✉), Anis Kacem[2], Sylvie Sevestre-Ghalila[2], and Christine Chappard[3]

[1] COSIM, University of Carthage, Cité Technologique des Communications, Tunis, Tunisia
rabaa.youssef@gmail.com
[2] CEA-LIST CEA-LinkLab, Cité Technologique des Communications, Tunis, Tunisia
[3] B2OA, UMR CNRS 7052, Université Paris Diderot, PRES Sorbonne Paris Cité, Paris, France

Abstract. Skeletonization is a morphological operation that summarizes an object by its median lines while preserving the initial image topology. It provides features used in biometric for the matching process, as well as medical imaging for quantification of the bone microarchitecture. We develop a solution for the extraction of structural and morphometric features useful in biometric, character recognition and medical imaging. It aims at storing object descriptors in a re-usable and hierarchical format. We propose graph data structures to identify skeleton nodes and branches, link them and store their corresponding features. This graph structure allows us to generate CSV files for high level analysis and to propose a pruning method that removes spurious branches regarding their length and mean gray level. We illustrate manipulations of the skeleton graph structure on medical image dedicated to bone microarchitecture characterization.

1 Introduction

Skeletonization is used in various applications such as biometrics [1,2], medical imaging [3–5] and character recognition [6] since it provides features that enables user to access high-level analysis of the image objects. In fact, object matching methods based on skeleton features are used in biometric identification through minutiae comparison of hand vein [1] or digital fingerprint [2], in bronchial airway trees monitoring [5], in symbols identification [7] and in character recognition [6]. In addition, classification methods using morphometric features extracted from skeleton helps diagnose osteoporosis [4] and osteoarthritis [3] diseases.

Graph-based representation of the skeleton is widely investigated for matching issues since the correspondence between skeleton branches with graph edges and nodes with its vertices is natural and intuitive. The proposed solutions in the literature are based on shock graphs [7] or attributed relational graphs [9]. These representations based on adjacency matrix can only consider acyclic graphs which restricts the application domains.

© Springer International Publishing Switzerland 2015
M. Kamel and A. Campilho (Eds.): ICIAR 2015, LNCS 9164, pp. 419–426, 2015.
DOI: 10.1007/978-3-319-20801-5_46

Our contribution is to develop a solution for the exploitation of skeleton features in binary and grayscale domain and to save them in a re-usable format easily manipulated. We propose to construct a graph able to represent any skeleton and to store its structural and morphometric features. To this purpose, we identify skeleton with multigraph [10] where multiple edges between nodes and emergence of mass of junctions are permitted. We store the skeleton structural and morphometric features in data structures that link graph vertices to their adjacent edges. This solution allows us to manipulate the skeleton information and to implement a pruning procedure that takes into account not only segments lengths but also their average gray values in order to decide which branches are spurious and thus, delete them. The use of this contribution is illustrated in the context of medical application that cover almost all usable features.

This work is composed of five sections. The first one presents skeleton features for medical application which covers biometric and character recognition structural features. The second section describes the used topological definitions for the graph construction. The third section is devoted to the graph data structures proposed in this work. The fourth section is dedicated to the implemented pruning and the manipulation of the structured graph skeleton on image of subchondral bone in the tibial knee with the aim of characterizing its microarchitecture.

2   Skeleton Features in Medical Imaging

Concerning the characterization of bone microarchitecture, studies has shown that bone changes from a healthy person to a person with osteoporosis [4] or osteoarthritis [3]. These changes are quantified using morphometric parameters of bone microarchitecture such as the number of pixels of the skeleton, the half-width and the length of trabeculae, the number of trabeculae and the number of nodes and ends. These morphometric parameters covers also structural descriptors (detection of nodes and extremities) used in biometric and character recognition applications [1,2,6]. We notice that skeletonization methods used to extract features for applications cited above are binary or gray. Consequently, we choose to make this feature extraction tool applicable on both types of skeleton. Furthermore, we notice that skeleton gray levels are not actually exploited. We propose to consider in the extracted features the segment mean gray level which is useful for the pruning of insignificant skeleton branches.

3   Identification of Topological Configurations

First of all, we need to identify the topological nature of each skeleton point in order to position it in the graph. A skeleton is formed of *ridge*, *junction* and *end* pixels. A *ridge* is a skeleton pixel placed on a crest line that splits the local background in 2 4-connected components. A *junction* splits the local background to 3 or 4 4-connected components and an *end* is a skeleton pixel with a unique skeleton neighbor.

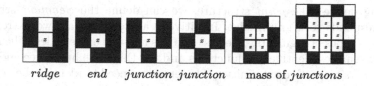

ridge   end   junction junction   mass of junctions

Fig. 1. Topological configurations of skeleton pixels.

Our graph proposal is designed to accept as input any type of skeleton. To do so, it is important to identify critical situations that a conventional graph cannot handle. Indeed, a skeleton could have a mass of junctions that cannot be thinned. In Fig. 1, pixels noted x and identified as mass of *junctions* divide the background in two 4-connected components according to their 8-neighbors. However, these pixels belong to a mass of nodes that should be entirely considered as a unique junction. In the literature, an erosion at nodes is performed before the construction of adjacency matrix in order to eliminate such configurations and to avoid a cyclic graph. A decomposition of the possible mass junctions in 3×3 configurations (with rotations) is made for our proposal in order to identify these pixels when processing the skeleton for graph construction. Once the ambiguous configurations identified, we can proceed with the construction of graph data structures.

4   Graph Construction

Since we intend to conceive a graph that takes into account any kind of skeleton, simple graphs constructed using an adjacency matrix are not appropriate. A graph with multiple edges (multigraph) that manages mass of junctions and stores other morphometric features of skeleton branches is chosen in this work. We detail in the next the data structures used to construct the proposed multigraph and the linking step that permits to connect graph vertices and edges.

4.1   Data Structures for the Graph Construction

First, we define in Table 1 *Point* data structure that differentiates *end*, *junction* and *ridge* pixels and establish a primary link between current pixel and its direct skeleton neighbors.

Table 1. Data structure: *Point*

Structure *Point*	Description		
Identifier	Pixel index in the image (unique)		
flag	(1): *end*	(2): *ridge*	(3): *junction*
neighbors	only one 8-connected neighbor	Table of size [2..4]	Table of size [3..8]

Having defined the *point* structure, we can define the *Segment* structure that corresponds to a graph edge. Intuitively, a *segment* has two extremities. There are 3 types of segments. The first one has two free extremities. The second has its extremities identified as junctions and the third one has a free end and a junction at its respective extremities. Therefore, we need to identify the *segment* extremities in the data structure in order to point out the *segment* type. The data structure *segment* is defined by the attributes listed in Table 2.

Table 2. Data structure: *Segment*

Structure *Segment*	Description
Label	Segment identifier
Head	Table of *point* indentifiers for the segment head (maximum size is 3)
Next to head	Index of the *point* that follows the head in the segment
Tail	Table of *point* indentifiers for the segment tail (maximum size is 3)
Next to tail	Index of the *point* that follows the tail in the segment
Stack	Stack containing segment pixels (index of *ridge points*)
Segment features	Number of pixels, Euclidean length, Mean gray level, Half width

Tail and head attributes correspond to *segment* extremities. These attributes are useful to establish links between graph edges. Since our solution is intended to be general, covering all types of skeleton graph, we consider segments having multiple heads and tails as illustrated by Fig. 2.(a). Hence, we choose for the head attribute (respectively tail) an array of *points* of size 3.

 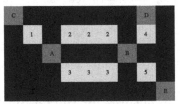

(a): 3 junctions in red   (b): Multiple segments
for the "head" of segment 1   between two junctions

Fig. 2. Particular situations for *segment* structure. In blue: segment *end*. In red: segment head (or tail) labeled as *junction*. In yellow: segment *ridge* point (Color figure online).

Furthermore, and unlike graphs based on adjacency matrix that cannot handle loops, we get our solution to consider a general case that defines more than one segment between two nodes. Consequently, we add two other attributes to the data structure, which are "Next to head" and "Next to queue" in order to distinguish the multiple segments appearing between two junction pixels. Such a case is illustrated by Fig. 2.(b).

4.2 Linking Step for *Segment* Structure

This module enables the implementation to fill *point* data structures and then, create *segment* structures by browsing the skeleton. It proceeds by first searching for graph nodes (*junctions* or *ends*) and second, by monitoring the *ridge* pixels of the same segment structure. Using the "neighbor" attribute stored in the *point* structure, it is possible to follow the segment and fill its remaining attributes. A stop condition of filling a *segment* is the detection of an *end* or other *junction*. This means that the linking step reached the end of the segment, can finally calculate its features and move to the next segment via the "tail" attribute. Figure 3 illustrates an example of segments attributes obtained for the binary skeleton sample of Fig. 2.(b).

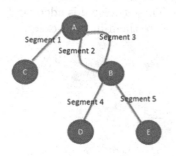

Attributes	Seg 1	Seg 2	Seg 3	Seg 4	Seg 5
Label	1	2	3	4	5
Head	C	A	A	B	B
Next to head	1	2	6	5	9
Tail	A	B	B	D	E
Next to tail	1	4	8	5	9
Stack	1	2, 3, 4	6, 7, 8	5	9
Number of pixels	3	5	5	3	3
Euclidean length	$2 \cdot \sqrt{2}$	$2 + 2 \cdot \sqrt{2}$	$2 + 2 \cdot \sqrt{2}$	$1 + \sqrt{2}$	$2 \cdot \sqrt{2}$
Average gray level	255	255	255	255	255

Fig. 3. Segments data structures for image from Fig. 2.(b).

Finally, the flow chart of Fig. 4 resumes the complete processing stages for the extraction of skeleton features. The graph construction is applicable to gray or binary skeleton resulting from any method of the literature.

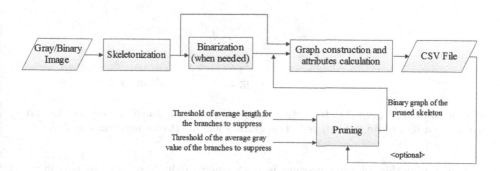

Fig. 4. Flow chart of features extraction tool.

5   Pruning as an Application of Graph Structuring

Skeletonization methods, and especially homotopic thinning are often subject to the emergence of spurious branches. For better reliability of results and pertinence of analysis, a pruning step is performed to eliminate these branches. In some applications, it is the orientation of the segment that indicates its "significance". However, orientation cannot be pertinent for microarchitecture quantification since trabeculae moves in various directions. Through experiments, we notice that the average gray level of spurious branches is informative and generally smaller than the average gray level of significant ones. We propose to implement a pruning procedure based on our graph construction that takes into account not only the length but also the mean gray value of segments to suppress noisy branches. In fact, according to the resulting skeletons of Fig. 5 and their respective features, we can establish an upper threshold for segment lengths and gray values at a fixed percentile (50 % in this case). These thresholds adequately adjusted permit to detect spurious branches and delete them in both cases.

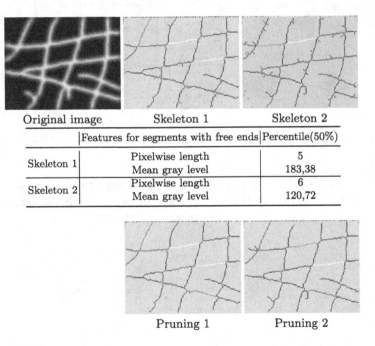

	Features for segments with free ends	Percentile(50%)
Skeleton 1	Pixelwise length	5
	Mean gray level	183,38
Skeleton 2	Pixelwise length	6
	Mean gray level	120,72

Fig. 5. Results of gray skeletonization using methods published in [11] and in [12]. Color intensity (white to blue) reflects segments lengths (Color figure online).

An application of such process is performed on high resolution peripheral computed tomography (HR-pQCT) slice image from Voxelo project[1] as illustrated in Fig. 6. We note respectively $Nb.S$, $Nb.N$, $Nb.E$, $Nb.seg$ the number

---

[1] ANR Voxelo TECS-0018.

of skeleton pixels, nodes, ends and segments, and $\overline{Nb.pix\ seg}$, $\overline{Length\ of\ seg}$, $\overline{Gray\ level\ of\ seg}$ the mean pixelwise length, euclidian length an gray level of segments. We observe in the update of skeleton features a gain in pertinence after pruning spurious branches while preserving significant trabeculae.

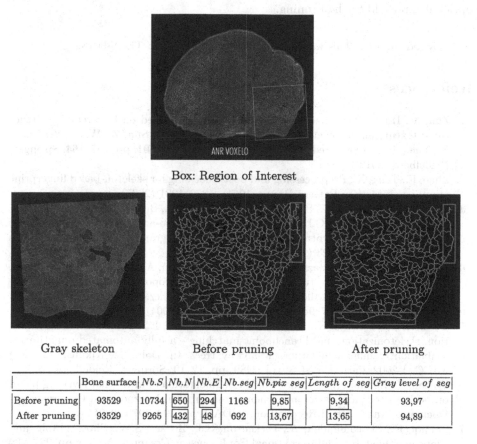

Box: Region of Interest

	Bone surface	Nb.S	Nb.N	Nb.E	Nb.seg	Nb.pix seg	Length of seg	Gray level of seg
Before pruning	93529	10734	650	294	1168	9,85	9,34	93,97
After pruning	93529	9265	432	48	692	13,67	13,65	94,89

Fig. 6. Skeleton pruning of the trabecular microarchitecture in a slice image of suchondral bone in tibial knee: Gain in relevance of features.

6 Conclusion

The proposed graph construction applies to binary and gray skeletons and facilitate a high level manipulation of the skeleton via the structural and morphometric features it stores. The analysis of the trabecular microarchitecture aiming to differentiate normal bone from osteoarthritis is an example of skeleton graph structure usefulness. The pruning procedure exploiting graph and skeleton features eliminates efficiently spurious branches according to thresholds of the mean gray level and length of segments. This high level skeleton manipulation can be used in biometric and character recognition applications in the matching process. Our perspective is to create a GUI for easy handling of the graph: tracking lines, measuring distance between nodes/edges, updating interactively the features. In addition, other features such as branches orientation could be easily added to the data structure *segment* in order to monitor skeleton lines and add another optional threshold to the pruning.

Acknowledgments. This work is financed by ANR Voxelo TECS-0018.

References

1. Zhu, X., Huang, D.: Hand Dorsal Vein recognition based on hierarchically structured texture and geometry features. In: Zheng, W.-S., Sun, Z., Wang, Y., Chen, X., Yuen, P.C., Lai, J. (eds.) CCBR 2012. LNCS, vol. 7701, pp. 157–164. Springer, Heidelberg (2012)
2. Zhao, F., Tang, X.: Preprocessing and postprocessing for skeleton-based fingerprint minutiae extraction. Pattern Recog. **40**(4), 1270–1281 (2007)
3. Chappard, C., Peyrin, F., Bonnassie, A., Lemineur, G., Brunet-Imbault, B., Lespessailles, E., Benhamou, C.L.: Subchondral bone micro-architectural alterations in osteoarthritis: a synchrotron micro-computed tomography study. Osteoarthritis Cartilage **14**(3), 215–223 (2006)
4. Sevestre-Ghalila, S., Benazza-Benyahia, A., Ricordeau, A., Mellouli, N., Chappard, C., Benhamou, C.L.: Texture image analysis for osteoporosis detection with morphological tools. In: Barillot, C., Haynor, D.R., Hellier, P. (eds.) MICCAI 2004. LNCS, vol. 3216, pp. 87–94. Springer, Heidelberg (2004)
5. Tschirren, J., Palágyi, K., Reinhardt, J.M., Hoffman, E.A., Sonka, M.: Segmentation, skeletonization, and branchpoint matching - a fully automated quantitative evaluation of human intrathoracic airway trees. In: Dohi, T., Kikinis, R. (eds.) MICCAI 2002, Part II. LNCS, vol. 2489, pp. 12–19. Springer, Heidelberg (2002)
6. Wshah, S., Zhixin, S., Govindaraju, V.: Segmentation of arabic handwriting based on both contour and skeleton segmentation. In: 10th International Conference on Document Analysis and Recognition, ICDAR, pp. 793–797 (2009)
7. Siddiqi, K., Shokoufandeh, A., Dickenson, S.J., Zucker, S.W.: Shock graphs and shape matching. In: 6th International Conference on Computer Vision, pp. 222–229 (1998)
8. Xiang, B., Latecki, L.J.: Path similarity Skeleton graph matching. IEEE Trans. Pattern Anal. Mach. Intel. **30**(7), 1282–1292 (2008)
9. Di Ruberto, C.: Recognition of shapes by attributed skeletal graphs. Pattern Recog. **37**(1), 21–31 (2004)
10. Gross, J.L., Yellen, J.: Graph Theory and Its Applications, 2nd edn. (Discrete Mathematics and Its Applications). Chapman & Hall/CRC, p. 3 (2005)
11. Youssef, R., Sevestre-Ghalila, S., Ricordeau, A.: Statistical control of thinning algorithm with implementation based on hierarchical queues. In: 6th International Conference of Soft Computing and Pattern Recognition, SoCPaR, pp. 365–370 (2014)
12. Couprie, M., Bezerra, F.N., Bertrand, G.: Grayscale image processing using topological operators. In: SPIE Vis. Geom. VIII vol. 3811, pp. 261–272 (1999)

Applications

Vehicle Detection Using Approximation of Feature Pyramids in the DFT Domain

Mohamed A. Naiel, M. Omair Ahmad[✉], and M.N.S. Swamy

Department of Electrical and Computer Engineering,
Concordia University, Montreal, QC H3G 1M8, Canada
{m_naiel,omair,swamy}@ece.concordia.ca

Abstract. Multi-resolution vehicle detection usually requires extracting a certain kind of features from each scale of an image pyramid to construct a feature pyramid, which is considered as a computational bottleneck for many object detectors. In this paper, a novel technique for the approximation of feature pyramids by using feature resampling in the 2D discrete Fourier transform domain is presented. Experimental results show that the proposed scheme provides higher detection accuracy than that provided by the state-of-the-art techniques on two sequences from LISA 2010 dataset, while maintaining the real-time detection speed.

1 Introduction

Vehicle detection is one of the challenging problems in the field of computer vision. It has many applications such as driver assistance systems, autonomous vehicles and intelligent transportation systems. A review for several methods can be found in [1].

There are several types of image features, such as histogram of oriented gradients (HOG) [2], and Haar-like features [3], that have been used for the purpose of object detection. HOG [2] and its variants have been experimented widely and currently are among the state-of-the-art techniques for object detection [4]. However, neither HOG nor its variants are scale-invariant. Thus, object detectors with multiscale scanning approach usually require extracting certain kind of features at each scale from an image pyramid, which is considered to be computational bottleneck for many object detectors [2,5,6].

In [7,8] Dollár *et al.* proposed a feature approximation technique in the spatial domain, where the gradient histograms and color features extracted at one scale from an image pyramid can be used to approximate feature responses at nearby scales. This method reduces the cost of constructing the feature pyramid and achieves a speedup over other methods, namely, [5,6], with only a small reduction in the detection accuracy. Later, in [9] a classifier pyramid, instead of an image pyramid, has been used, resulting in a speedup over [7]. However, the method in [9] is based on constructing a classifier pyramid that spans different scales (with a scale step of 2), which requires large storage, and training costs.

In this paper, we present a novel feature pyramid approximation technique in the 2DDFT domain for the purpose of vehicle detection. The proposed scheme

© Springer International Publishing Switzerland 2015
M. Kamel and A. Campilho (Eds.): ICIAR 2015, LNCS 9164, pp. 429–436, 2015.
DOI: 10.1007/978-3-319-20801-5_47

is based on 2D feature resampling in the 2DDFT domain. It is shown that by considering the effect of resampling an input image on the feature responses, the exact features extracted at a certain scale from the image pyramid can be used to approximate the features at a lower or higher scale. The proposed technique provides a speedup over the exact method, while maintaining the highest detection accuracy of the state-of-the-art techniques on two sequences from LISA 2010 dataset [10].

2   Feature Approximation in the Spatial Domain

In this section, we present a brief description of the work proposed in [8]. Let s denote a resampling factor, where $s < 1$ represents downsampling, and $s > 1$ represents upsampling. Let I and I_s denote, respectively, an image and its resampled version by a factor s, where $I_s = \mathcal{P}(I, s)$, and $\mathcal{P}$ denotes a function for 2D signal resampling in the spatial domain.

Figures 1 (a) and (b) show the exact and the approximated feature extraction pipelines, respectively. Let Ω denotes a 2D feature extractor in the spatial domain. It has been shown in [8] that the exact features, $g = \Omega(I)$, of size $(N_1 \times M_1 \times \beta)$ where N_1, M_1, and β represent the number of rows, columns, and layers, respectively, computed at the original scale can be used to approximate the features at scale s as

$$g_s^l \approx \bar{g}_s^l = \gamma_s \mathcal{P}(g^l, s) \tag{1}$$

where l denotes the layer number, $l = 1, 2, ..., \beta$, $g_s = \Omega(I_s)$ are the exact features of size $(N_2 \times M_2 \times \beta)$ in the spatial domain, $\bar{g}_s$ are the approximated features of size $(N_2 \times M_2 \times \beta)$ in the spatial domain, γ_s is a multiplicative constant, and the factor $s = N_2/N_1 = M_2/M_1$. It has been shown in [8] that the value of γ_s can be modeled by using the power law as

$$\gamma_s = a_\Omega s^{-\lambda_\Omega} \tag{2}$$

where a_Ω and λ_Ω are constants that can be obtained empirically in the training phase for several types of features, such as color images, gradient magnitude, and gradient histograms.

3   Proposed Algorithm

The proposed scheme is based on approximating the features extracted from the image pyramid by using feature resampling in the 2DDFT domain, and by considering the effect of resampling an input image on the feature responses. Figure 1 (c) illustrates an overview of the proposed feature approximation scheme. First, the exact features $g = \Omega(I)$ of size $(N_1 \times M_1 \times \beta)$ are extracted, where N_1, M_1, and β represent the number of rows, columns, and layers, respectively. The objective is to obtain the approximated features $\tilde{g}_s$ of size $(N_2 \times M_2 \times \beta)$, where $s = N_2/N_1 = M_2/M_1$, and N_1, M_1, N_2 and M_2 are even integers.

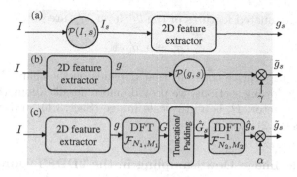

Fig. 1. (a) The exact 2D feature extraction scheme from the image I after resampling by a factor s, (b) 2D feature approximation in the spatial domain proposed by Dollár *et al.* [8], (c) The proposed 2D feature approximation in the 2DDFT domain.

Second, the 2DDFT is employed on the lth layer of the exact features extracted at the original scale, $g^l \in \mathbb{R}^2$, in order to obtain $G^l = \mathcal{F}_{N_1,M_1}(g^l)$, where $l = 1, 2, ..., \beta$, G^l denotes the lth layer of the features in the 2DDFT domain of size $(N_1 \times M_1)$, and $\mathcal{F}_{N_1,M_1}$ denotes $N_1 \times M_1$-point 2DDFT. Next, if $s < 1$, which represents the downsampling case, a truncation process is employed to remove coefficients corresponding to the high frequency components as

$$
\hat{G}_s^l[u, v] = \begin{cases} G^l[u, v], & 0 \le u < \dfrac{N_2}{2}, 0 \le v < \dfrac{M_2}{2} \\[2mm] G^l[u + N_1 - N_2, v], & \dfrac{N_2}{2} \le u < N_2, 0 \le v < \dfrac{M_2}{2} \\[2mm] G^l[u, v + M_1 - M_2], & 0 \le u < \dfrac{N_2}{2}, \dfrac{M_2}{2} \le v < M_2 \\[2mm] G^l[u + N_1 - N_2, v + M_1 - M_2], & \dfrac{N_2}{2} \le u < N_2, \dfrac{M_2}{2} \le v < M_2 \end{cases} \tag{3}
$$

where $\hat{G}_s^l$ of size $(N_2 \times M_2)$, u and v represent the frequency indices. On the other hand, if $s > 1$, which corresponds to the upsampling case, a padding process is utilized as

$$
\hat{G}_s^l[u, v] = \begin{cases} G^l[u, v], & 0 \le u < \dfrac{N_1}{2}, 0 \le v < \dfrac{M_1}{2} \\[2mm] G^l[u + N_1 - N_2, v], & N_2 - \dfrac{N_1}{2} \le u < N_2, 0 \le v < \dfrac{M_1}{2} \\[2mm] G^l[u, v + M_1 - M_2], & 0 \le u < \dfrac{N_1}{2}, M_2 - \dfrac{M_1}{2} \le v < M_2 \\[2mm] G^l[u + N_1 - N_2, v + M_1 - M_2], & N_2 - \dfrac{N_1}{2} \le u < N_2, M_2 - \dfrac{M_1}{2} \le v < M_2 \\[2mm] p, & \text{otherwise} \end{cases} \tag{4}
$$

where $\hat{G}_s^l$ of size $(N_2 \times M_2)$, and p is the value of the padding. It is shown in [11] that the value of p when selected to be the value of the coefficient at half of the spectrum provides higher approximation accuracy than that provided by selecting zero padding. In this paper, we use $p = G^l[N_1/2, M_1/2]$ which provides high detection accuracy. In order to solve the detection problem in the spatial domain, the inverse 2DDFT, $\mathcal{F}_{N_2,M_2}^{-1}$, is performed on the lth layer of $\hat{G}_s^l$, and the features in the spatial domain, $\hat{g}_s^l$, can be obtained as

$$
\hat{g}_s^l = \text{Re}(\mathcal{F}_{N_2,M_2}^{-1}(\hat{G}_s^l)) \tag{5}
$$

Finally, the approximated features of the lth layer, $\tilde{g}_s^l$, are obtained as

$$\tilde{g}_s^l = \alpha_s \hat{g}_s^l \tag{6}$$

where α_s is a multiplicative constant that depends on the channel type and the factor s. In the following sections, we provide more details about the value of α_s if the feature extractor, Ω, is a grayscale image (Sect. 3.1), and other types of 2D features (Sect. 3.2).

3.1   Grayscale Image Downsampling in the 2DDFT Domain

In [11] the effect of resampling a 1D discrete time sequence in the 1DDFT domain has been presented. Let $h_{N_1,M_1} \in \mathbb{R}^2$ represent a grayscale image in the spatial domain of size $(N_1 \times M_1)$, where N_1 and M_1 are even integers. Let $s_x = M_2/M_1$ and $s_y = N_2/N_1$ denote the resampling factors in the x, and y directions, respectively, where N_2 and M_2 are even integers. By employing the $N_1 \times M_1$-point 2DDFT on the image we obtain the 2DDFT coefficients of the original image as $H_{N_1,M_1} = \mathcal{F}_{N_1,M_1}(h_{N_1,M_1})$. Similar to the case of 1DDFT [11], if $s_x < 1$ and $s_y < 1$, the downsampled image in the spatial domain, $\tilde{h}_{N_2,M_2}$, can be obtained from the 2DDFT coefficients of the original image, H_{N_1,M_1}, as

$$\tilde{h}_{N_2,M_2} = s_x s_y \, \mathrm{Re}(\mathcal{F}_{N_2,M_2}^{-1}(\hat{H}_{N_2,M_2})) \tag{7}$$

where $\hat{H}_{N_2,M_2}$ is obtained after applying the truncation process on H_{N_1,M_1}, as seen in (3). From (7) the truncation process, which truncates the coefficients corresponding to the high frequency components, and the multiplicative constant, $\alpha_{s_x,s_y} = s_x s_y$, are used to downsample the image in the 2DDFT domain. Similar relation can be obtained in the case of image upsampling in the 2DDFT domain, where the factor $\alpha_{s_x,s_y} = s_x s_y$. In the next subsection, we derive the relation of the multiplicative constant that is applicable to several types of 2D features.

3.2   Feature Downsampling in the 2DDFT Domain

In this section, we obtain the relation that governs the multiplicative constant, α_s, for several kinds of features in the case of downsampling ($s < 1$). A similar relation can be obtained for the upsampling case. In the object detection framework, our objective is to approximate the features in the 2DDFT domain, such that $\tilde{g}_s$ downsampled in the 2DDFT domain approximates the exact features g_s.

For simplicity, let $s_x = s_y = s$, i.e., the downsampling factor be the same in both the x, and y directions. It can be shown that the multiplicative constant α_s can be modeled as a combination of the power law (2) and 2DDFT domain downsampling (7) effects as follows

$$g_s^l \approx \tilde{g}_s^l = \underbrace{a_\Omega(s)^{-\lambda_\Omega}}_{\text{(Power law effect)}} \underbrace{s^2 \hat{g}_s^l}_{\text{(2DDFT effect)}} = \alpha_s \hat{g}_s^l \tag{8}$$

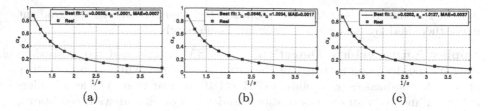

Fig. 2. The multiplicative constant value at different downsampling factor $(1/s)$ and three different features types: (a) color channel, (b) gradient magnitude, and (c) gradient histograms with 6 orientation bins.

$$\alpha_s = a_\Omega(s)^{2-\lambda_\Omega} \tag{9}$$

where l denotes the layer number, $l = 1, 2, ..., \beta$, a_Ω, and λ_Ω are the channel parameters, which can be estimated in the training phase for several types of 2D features as will be shown in the next paragraph. From (6) and (9), the features extracted from the original scale, g, can be used to approximate the features at a lower scale, $\tilde{g}_s$.

In order to estimate the parameters of a certain type of 2D features, we use a training set of N_t training images to infer the value of the multiplicative constant, $\hat{\alpha}_s^i$, for the ith example that solves the following optimization problem

$$\min_{\hat{\alpha}_s^i} \left\| g_s^i - \hat{\alpha}_s^i \hat{g}_s^i \right\|_2^2 \tag{10}$$

where $i = 1, 2, ..., N_t$, $s = 2^{-n/n_0}$, $n \in \{1, 2, ..., N_l - 1\}$, N_l being the number of levels in the feature pyramid and n_0 being the number of scales per octave. By using the mean value of the estimated multiplicative constant $\hat{\alpha}_s = 1/N_t \sum_{i=1}^{N_t} \hat{\alpha}_s^i$, and the model of α_s given by (9), the channel parameters, a_Ω, and λ_Ω, can be estimated by using the least square method.

4   Experimental Results

Channel Parameter Estimation. In this experiment, the channel parameters, a_Ω and λ_Ω, are estimated by using the parameter estimation technique presented in Sect. 3.2, where $N_t = 200$ rear view vehicle images of size 64×64 from KITTI dataset [12] are used. The proposed scheme is tested on three types of channels, namely, color, gradient magnitude, and gradient histograms with 6 orientation bins. Figure 2 shows the value of the estimated multiplicative constant and channel parameters that best fit the curve for the corresponding type of channel, where $s = 2^{-n/n_0}$, $n \in \{1, 2, ..., N_l-1\}$, $N_l = 12$, and $n_0 = 8$. In order to measure the quality of the curve fitting for each channel, the mean absolute error (MAE) defined by $MAE = 1/(N_l - 1) \sum_s |(\alpha_s - \hat{\alpha}_s)|$ is used. For the color channel, Fig. 2(a), $\lambda_\Omega \approx 0$, $a_\Omega \approx 1$, and $MAE \approx 0$; thus by substituting in (9), the power law effect is neglected and the 2DDFT domain effect dominates.

Figures 2(b) and (c) show that the proposed technique can model the gradient magnitude, and gradient histogram channels effectively.

Application to Vehicle Detection. The LISA 2010 dataset [10] is used to measure the detection accuracy of the proposed scheme. This dataset consists of three test sequences of resolution (704×480) for rear view vehicles of different sizes, and the dataset was captured under several illumination conditions. The first sequence (1600 frames) taken on a high density highway during a sunny day (H.-dense), the second (300 frames) on a medium density highway (H.-medium), and the third (300 frames) from a low traffic urban area during a cloudy day (Urban). The dataset does not include training data; therefore, we collect training images of size (64×64) from other datasets as follow: (1) 9013 images of vehicles in rear/front views from KITTI dataset [12], and USC multi-view car dataset [13], and (2) 8415 negative samples from CBCL street scenes dataset[1]. Similar to [10], we collect a number of hard negative samples from the test sequences (229 samples from H.-medium, and 806 samples from H.-dense).

In the training phase, the detector of Dollár et al. [8][2] is trained on the training dataset described above. In this detector, the aggregated channel features (ACF) have been used, and the detector consists of the following channels: LUV color, normalized gradient magnitude, and gradient histograms with 6 orientation bins. Further, these features are used to train boosted decision trees for classification. For more details about ACF, the readers are referred to [8]. In the detection phase, the proposed feature approximation in the 2DDFT domain is used to approximate the feature pyramid (ACF-DFT) instead of using the approximation technique in the spatial domain (ACF-SD) [8] or the exact features (ACF-Exact) [8].

We use the same evaluation metrics as in [10]: true positive rate (TPR) or recall, false detection rate (FDR) or 1-precision, average false positive per frame (AFP/F), average false positive per object (AFP/O), and average true positive per frame (ATP/F). True positive detections are computed by using the PASCAL VOC criterion [14] with overlap threshold 0.5.

Table 1 gives the performance measures by using the proposed scheme[3] and that provided by using various techniques [8,10,15]. The method presented in [10] is based on using Haar-like features and cascade of boosted classifiers, while the method in [15] is based on using a block-partitioned 2DHOG in the 2DDCT domain and multiple support vector machine classifiers with fast histogram intersection kernel (FIKSVM) [6] trained at different vehicle resolutions. It is seen that the proposed scheme yields the highest detection accuracy which is better than that provided by the methods in [10,15] on Urban and H.-medium sequences, while the method itself achieves slightly lower performance than that of the methods in [10] and ACF-Exact on H.-dense sequence. The H.-dense sequence consists of vehicles of various resolutions and several vehicles are in partial occlusion.

---

[1] http://cbcl.mit.edu/software-datasets/streetscenes.

[2] Code: http://vision.ucsd.edu/~pdollar/toolbox/.

[3] Supplementary material shows several detection qualitative results https://www.youtube.com/watch?v=y5-m9c4TJMY.

Table 1. Performance measures of the various techniques using the LISA dataset, where the figures in bold denote the best performance

Sequence	Method	TPR	FDR	AFP/F	ATP/F	AFP/O
H.-dense	Proposed (ACF-DFT)	90.11 %	9.89 %	0.48	**4.4**	0.1
	ACF-Exact	90.14 %	9.86 %	0.48	**4.4**	0.1
	ACF-SD	89.87 %	10.13 %	0.5	4.39	0.1
	[15]	75.97 %	24.03 %	1.05	3.33	0.24
	[10]	**93.50 %**	**7.10 %**	**0.32**	4.2	**0.07**
H.-medium	Proposed (ACF-DFT)	**100.00 %**	**0.00 %**	**0.00**	3.00	**0.00**
	ACF-Exact	**100.00 %**	**0.00 %**	**0.00**	3.00	**0.00**
	ACF-SD	**100.00 %**	**0.00 %**	**0.00**	3.00	**0.00**
	[15]	97.67 %	2.33 %	0.07	2.93	0.02
	[10]	98.80 %	10.30 %	0.37	**3.18**	0.11
Urban	Proposed (ACF-DFT)	**100.00 %**	**0.00 %**	**0.00**	**1.00**	**0.00**
	ACF-Exact	**100.00 %**	**0.00 %**	**0.00**	**1.00**	**0.00**
	ACF-SD	**100.00 %**	**0.00 %**	**0.00**	**1.00**	**0.00**
	[15]	99.33 %	0.67 %	0.01	0.99	0.01
	[10]	80.20 %	41.70 %	0.72	0.98	0.57

Note: higher values of TPR and ATP/F indicate a better performance, whereas lower values of FDR, AFP/F, and AFP/O indicate a better performance.

The average detection speed is computed on 60 images with resolution of 512×512. The average detection speed of the proposed ACF-DFT is 38.46 frames per second (fps), while those of ACF-SD and ACF-Exact are 47.62 fps, and 32.26 fps, respectively, where the scanning window step size is 4 pixels, and the feature pyramid consists of one octave of 8 scales[4]. Thus, the proposed scheme is faster than ACF-Exact by 16.12 %, and lower than ACF-SD. Most of the running time of the proposed technique is spent on computing the forward and inverse transforms of the ACF. In future work, we will explore several methods to improve the running time of the proposed scheme.

5   Conclusions

We have presented a novel technique for the approximation of feature pyramids in the 2DDFT domain for vehicle detection. The proposed method is based on a feature resampling technique in the 2DDFT domain and by considering the effect of resampling an input image on the feature responses. Experimental results have shown that the proposed technique achieves a higher detection accuracy than that of the state-of-the-art techniques on two sequences from LISA 2010 vehicle detection dataset, while maintaining the real-time detection speed.

---

[4] The test is carried out on a PC with 2.9 GHz CPU.

Acknowledgments. This work was supported in part by the Natural Sciences and Engineering Research Council (NSERC) of Canada and in part by the Regroupement Stratégique en Microélectronique du Québec (ReSMiQ).

References

1. Sivaraman, S., Trivedi, M.: Looking at vehicles on the road: A survey of vision-based vehicle detection, tracking, and behavior analysis. IEEE Trans. Intell. Transp. Syst. **14**(4), 1773–1795 (2013)
2. Dalal, N., Triggs, B.: Histograms of oriented gradients for human detection. In: Proceedings of the IEEE Conference on Computer Vision and Pattern Recogn (CVPR), vol. 1, pp. 886–893 (2005)
3. Viola, P., Jones, M.: Rapid object detection using a boosted cascade of simple features. In: Proceedings of the Conference on Computer Vision and Pattern Recogn. (CVPR), vol. 1, pp. 511–518, June 2001
4. Dollár, P., Wojek, C., Schiele, B., Perona, P.: Pedestrian detection: An evaluation of the state of the art. IEEE Trans. Pattern Anal. Mach. Intell. (PAMI) **34**(4), 743–761 (2012)
5. Dollár, P., Tu, Z., Perona, P., Belongie, S.: Integral channel features. In: Proceedings of the British Machine Vision Conference (BMVC), pp. 91.1–91.11 (2009)
6. Maji, S., Berg, A.C., Malik, J.: Classification using intersection kernel support vector machines is efficient. In: Proceedings IEEE Conference on Computer Vision and Pattern Recogn. (CVPR), pp. 1–8 (2008)
7. Dollár, P., Belongie, S., Perona, P.: The fastest pedestrian detector in the west. In: Proceedings of the British Machine Vision Conference (BMVC), pp. 68.1–68.11 (2010)
8. Dollár, P., Appel, R., Belongie, S., Perona, P.: Fast feature pyramids for object detection. IEEE Trans. Pattern Anal. Mach. Intell. (PAMI) **36**(8), 1532–1545 (2014)
9. Benenson, R., Mathias, M., Timofte, R., Gool, L.V.: Pedestrian detection at 100 frames per second. In: Proceedings of IEEE Conference on Comput. Vision and Pattern Recogn. (CVPR), pp. 2903–2910 (2012)
10. Sivaraman, S., Trivedi, M.: A general active-learning framework for on-road vehicle recognition and tracking. IEEE Trans. Intell. Transp. Syst. **11**(2), 267–276 (2010)
11. Bi, G., Mitra, S.K., Li, S.: Sampling rate conversion based on DFT and DCT. Signal Proces. **93**(2), 476–486 (2013)
12. Geiger, A., Lenz, P., Urtasun, R.: Are we ready for autonomous driving? the KITTI vision benchmark suite. In: Proceedings of the Conference on Comput. Vision and Pattern Recogn. (CVPR), pp. 3354–3361 (2012)
13. Kuo, C.H., Nevatia, R.: Robust multi-view car detection using unsupervised sub-categorization. In: Proceedings of the IEEE Workshop on Appl. of Comput. Vision (WACV), pp. 1–8 (2009)
14. Everingham, M., Gool, L.V., Williams, C.K., Winn, J., Zisserman, A.: The pascal visual object classes (VOC) challenge. Int. J. Comput. Vis. **88(2)**, 303–338 (2010)
15. Naiel, M.A., Ahmad, M.O., Swamy, M.N.S.: Vehicle detection using TD2DHOG features. In: Proceedings of the New Circuits and Syst. Conf. (NewCAS), pp. 389–392 (2014)

Real-Time Speed-Limit Sign Detection and Recognition Using Spatial Pyramid Feature and Boosted Random Forest

JaWon Gim, MinCheol Hwang, Byoung Chul Ko[(⊠)],
and Jae-Yeal Nam

Department of Computer Engineering, Keimyung University,
Shindang-Dong Dalseo-Gu, Daegu, South Korea
{jawon,k1321a,niceko,jynam}@kmu.ac.kr

Abstract. Traffic-sign detection and recognition using computer vision is essential for safe driving when using an advanced driver assistance system (ADAS). Among the few types of traffic signs used, in this paper, we focus on the detection and recognition of speed-limit signs because such signs can ensure the safety of drivers and other road users, and facilitate an efficient traffic flow. To detect a speed-limit sign, we first choose the candidate regions for a speed-limit sign using the border color and apply sliding windows to the candidate regions using a two-class boosted random forest (BoostRF) classifier instead of simple random forest. To reduce the computational cost for the image pyramid, the optimal levels of scaling using the search area is adapted. Detected speed-limit signs are fed into the speed-limit sign classifiers based on the multiclass BoostRF. As the feature of the BoostRF, we use spatial pyramid pooling (SPP) based on oriented center symmetric-local binary patterns (OCS-LBP) because SPP is simple and computationally efficient, and maintains the spatial and local information by pooling the local spatial bins. The proposed algorithm was successfully applied to the German Traffic Sign Detection Benchmark (GTSDB) and German Traffic Sign Recognition Benchmark (GTSRB) datasets, and the results show that detection and recognition capabilities of the proposed method are similar or better than those of other methods.

Keywords: Speed-limit sign detection · Speed-limit sign recognition · ADAS · Boosted random forest · Spatial pyramid pooling

1 Introduction

With increasing interest in intelligent vehicles, many researches related to internet and communication technique (ICT) techniques have focused on advanced driver assistance systems (ADASs). In particular, computer vision and machine learning are the most important techniques for implementing an intelligent ADAS. One of the active areas studied in the field of ADAS is automatic traffic-sign detection and recognition. Although a driver can receive traffic-sign information from a navigation system using a geographic database and GPS information, the navigation system used may not give the driver up-to-date information owing to changes in the roads and their traffic signs.

© Springer International Publishing Switzerland 2015
M. Kamel and A. Campilho (Eds.): ICIAR 2015, LNCS 9164, pp. 437–445, 2015.
DOI: 10.1007/978-3-319-20801-5_48

Therefore, camera-based traffic-sign recognition provides significant assistance for safe driving. In particular, speed assistance systems became a new item in car safety testing in European Union's new car assessment program (NCAP) in 2015. In NCAP, recognizing and limiting the vehicle speed are the core functions of car safety because they can ensure the safety of the driver and other road users, facilitate an efficient traffic flow, and promote safe driving conditions [1].

Traffic signs are designed based on specific colors, shapes, and the presence of text or symbols with high contrast with the background, as shown in Fig. 1. Therefore, human drivers can detect and recognize traffic signs easily even when the signs suffer from occlusions, geometric distortion, or variations in illumination [2, 3]. However, under real road conditions, automatic traffic-sign recognition using a camera remains a very challenging problem because of variations in perspective, illumination (from rain, fog, or shadows), motion blur, scaling, rotation, and occlusions [3]. Among the different types of traffic-sign recognition, the recognition of speed-limit signs is more difficult than for other traffic signs because they have similar patterns, such as a round shape, black text, red boundary, and white background.

Fig. 1. Candidate pixel detection using color probability models (a) and five sizes of template model (b) for sign detection

1.1 Related Works

For traffic-sign recognition, the signs should first be detected. Conventional methods use sliding window approaches to detect and recognize traffic signs concurrently. However, because sliding window approaches require a certain amount of computational time, many researches have been using color- [4] or gray-based [5] segmentation to reduce the search space by considering the traffic-sign characteristics. However, chromatic shifts from changes in lighting are the main problem of color- or gray-based segmentation. To overcome the limitations of color-based segmentation, shape information is also used for sign detection. Barnes and Zelinsky [6] used the radial symmetry of traffic signs based on a Hough transform for circular shapes. However, this type of method has a limitation in that it can detect only circular shapes. A Histogram-of-oriented gradient (HOG) is the representative feature for shape-based sign detection because it provides an effective way to capture the shape information [7].

Creusen et al. [8] incorporated HOG to color information and proved that CIE-Lab and YCbCr color spaces achieve the best results.

After traffic-sign detection is applied, classification is subsequently conducted alone or simultaneously with the detection. For classification, neural networks [9] and multi-class support vector machines (MSVM) [3] are widely used owing to their high performance and accuracy. However, these methods are not suitable when the feature used has high-dimensionality and the database contains over 1,000 images, which result in computational complexity. Convolutional networks (ConvNets) and a deep neural net [10] have recently become popular classification methods because of their high classification performance. ConvNets learn the multiple stages of invariant features using a combination of supervised and unsupervised leaning. Sermanet and Le-Cun [11] modified a ConvNet by feeding the first and second stage features into the classifier Cireşan [10] combined various DNNs trained from differently preprocessed data into a Multi-Column DNN (MCDNN) to further boost the recognition performance. Although this method showed a higher classification rate based on the German Traffic Sign Recognition Benchmark (GTSRB) [2], a detailed algorithm for detecting traffic signs on a real road and incorporating the detection into the classifier in real time was not proposed.

In this paper, we introduce algorithms for detecting and recognizing speed-limit signs for supporting an ADAS. We first choose the candidate regions of the traffic signs using the border color and determine the final traffic signs using the sliding window method. To reduce the computational cost for an image pyramid, optimal levels of scaling are applied using the search area. To detect the presence of a traffic sign, we use a two-class boosted random forest [12] with low-dimensional oriented center symmetric-local binary patterns (OCS-LBP) [13]. Detected traffic signs are passed to the speed-limit sign classifiers based on the multiclass BoostRF. For the BoostRF feature, we use OCS-LBP-based spatial pyramid pooling (SPP) [13] owing to its simplicity and computational efficiency, and because it maintains spatial information by pooling the local spatial bins.

2 Speed-Limit Sign Detection

For traffic-sign detection, the detection efficiency and speed are important aspects of a real-time application. Because traffic signs, particularly speed-limit signs, in Asia and Europe commonly have a red border with a white background, in contrast with those in North America, which have a black border with a white background, we first use the color information to segment the candidate speed-limit sign regions. Many types of color spaces (e.g., RGB, HSV, YUV, and L*a*b*) have been used for segmentation, and we use the UV color chrominance channel of a YUV space to reduce the influence of changes in lighting. In general, speed-sign images are highlighted in the U channel on a white background and have a relatively low V value when compared to the background and other signs. Therefore, using these characteristics, we determine candidate pixels based on several threshold values using the following formula:

$$I_i = \begin{cases} 255 & If\,(th_{min_u} < U_i < th_{max_u} \ \& \ th_{min_v} < V_i < th_{max_v}) \\ 0 & otherwise \end{cases} \qquad (1)$$

where U and V is an normalized image of U and V channel, th_{min} and th_{max} is minimum and maximum threshold values for each channel. However, if the border regions of a speed-limit sign are accurately detected, some false regions may also be detected owing to the presence of a color similar to the sign border, as shown in Fig. 1 (a). After the candidate pixels are detected, an additional process is needed to remove these false candidate pixels and detect the exact pixels of the speed-limit sign.

2.1 Optimal Size of Template Model

The main problem of a sliding window method is the computational burden of a multi-scale image pyramid and the dense amount of sliding windows per scale. However, if we know the height of the installed camera, we can limit the size of template model By modifying the work in [14], we conduct an cropping of speed-limit signs for all training images, and generate a Hough Windows Map [14] by voting the frequency according to the size of cropped signs. After accumulating of Hough Windows Map, we decide representative five template sizes for speed-limit sign, such as 24×24, 36×36, 48×48, 64×64, and 100×100, as shown in Fig. 1 (b).

2.2 Boosted Random Forest for Speed-Limit Sign Verification

In this study, we use the OCS-LBP [2] from a detected sign target owing to its simplicity and similar performance when compared to HOG. In OCS-LBP, the gradient orientations are estimated for every pixel within a mask, and a histogram of the neighborhood orientation is formed. Each pixel influences the gradient magnitude of the closest orientation bin ranging from $0°$ to $360°$ in increments of $45°$. A normalized OCS-LBP is represented using eight-component histograms, where the OCS-LBP for the target model is denoted by in 8×8 sub-blocks. Therefore, the total dimension of OCS-LBP for one target region is 512 ($8 \times 8 \times 8$).

For verification of a speed-limit sign, we apply a scanning window with a random forest classifier to only the candidate pixels. The random forest classifier is an ensemble of several weak decision trees, and has the capacity to process large amounts of data at high training and testing speeds owing to its randomized characteristic [15]. Although randomization is an advantage of random forests, it depends heavily on the number of decision trees and requires a certain amount of memory and CPU capacity. Therefore, we apply BoostRF [12] to our verification system to maintain the generality with a small number of decision trees when considering the fact that sequential training constructs complementary decision trees for the training samples. BoostRF adds a bootstrapping phase during the learning step, which is similar to the Adaboost algorithm. BoostRF [12] is trained using Algorithm 1.

Algorithm 1 BoostRF learning

T: number of iterations
D: the maximum depth of trees to extend
M: number of classes
S_n: Training set, including positive and negative samples with their labels and weight, $\{\mathbf{x}_1, y_1, w_1\},...,\{\mathbf{x}_N, y_N, w_N\}; \mathbf{x}_i \in X, y \in M$

Initialize sample weight w_i $w_i^{(1)} = 1/N$
For t to T do

    Select subset s from training set S_n
    Grow an unpruned tree using the s subset samples with their corresponding weights.
      For d to D do
        Each internal node randomly selects p variables and determines the best split function using only these variables.

        Using different p-th variables, the split function $f(v_p)$ iteratively splits the training data into left (l_l) and right (l_r) subsets using equation (2).
$$l_l = \{p \in I_n \mid f(v_p) < \gamma\},$$
$$I_r = I_n \setminus I_l. \tag{2}$$

        Compute information gain ΔG function $f(v_p)$

        If (ΔG = max) then determine the best split function $f(v_p)$ for node d ·

        If (d= D) then store the probability distribution $P(c \mid l)$ in the leaf node
      End For
    Output: A weak decision tree

Estimate class label $\hat{y}_i$ of the training data with the trained decision trees:
$$\hat{y}_i = \underset{c}{\operatorname{argmax}} \, P(c \mid l_t) \tag{3}$$

Calculate the error of decision tree ε_t:
$$\varepsilon_t = \sum_{i: y_i \neq \hat{y}_i}^{N} w_i^{(t)} / \sum_i^N w_i^{(t)} \tag{4}$$

Compute weight of the t-th decision tree α_t:
$$\alpha_t = \frac{1}{2} \log \frac{(M-1)(1-\varepsilon_t)}{\varepsilon_t} \tag{5}$$

If $\alpha > 0$, then

    Update weight of training sample $w_i^{(t+1)}$:
$$w_i^{(t+1)} = \begin{cases} w_i^{(t)} \exp(\alpha_t) & \text{if } y_i \neq \hat{y}_i \\ w_i^{(t)} \exp(-\alpha_t) & \text{otherwise} \end{cases} \tag{6}$$

        else
    Reject the decision tree
End For

After BoostRF training using the positive and negative training data, OCS-LBP feature vectors are extracted from the target region, which are used as input to the learned BoostRF. The detection probability of a speed-limit sign class is computed by ensemble averaging each probability distribution of all trees $L = (l_1, l_2, ..., l_T)$ with their corresponding weights (α_t) for the t-th decision tree as

$$P(c|L) = \frac{1}{T}\sum_{t=1}^{T} \alpha_t P(c|lt).$$ (7)

Then, if the speed-limit sign class has the highest probability and is over the minimum threshold $\tau(0.5)$, we choose the target region as a real speed-limit sign.

$$Speed\_sign = \arg\max_C P(c|L) > \tau$$ (8)

3 Speed-Limit Sign Classification

After speed-limit sign verification, the same BootRF classifier is used to confirm the speed of the region indicated by the speed-limit sign through the use of finer features extracted by SPP [13], which is a collection of order-less feature histograms computed over cells defined through a multi-level recursive image decomposition, as shown in Fig. 2.

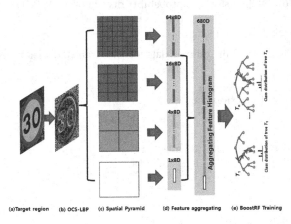

(a)Target region   (b) OCS-LBP   (c) Spatial Pyramid   (d) Feature aggregating   (e) BoostRF Training

Fig. 2. Training steps for sign recognition using a spatial pyramid based on BoostRF and OCS-LBP

SPP partitions the image into cells from finer to coarser levels and aggregates the spatial information by pooling within the local spatial histograms [13]. In this study, we construct a spatial pyramid with three levels and generate eight-dimensional OCS-LBP histograms from each cell. Therefore, the target sign region has 848 dimensions (8 + 32 + 128 + 680).

4 Experimental Results

First, to evaluate the performance of the speed-limit sign detection, we used training and test images from the German Traffic Sign Detection Benchmark (GTSDB) dataset [16], which consists of 900 images in total (divided into 600 training images and 300 evaluation images) with $1,360 \times 860$ pixels. In our experiment, we compared the detection performance for only prohibitive signs because they include speed-limit signs. Figure 3 (a) shows the results as compared with two leading sign-detection algorithms [7, 17] based on the overlapping accuracy. As the figure shows, our proposed method has similar or somewhat higher detection results compared with the other two algorithms. In particular, the other two methods require a longer computation time (at 2.5 and 60 s per image, respectively) than the proposed method (at 0.9 s) because of several processing steps required with high dimensionality.

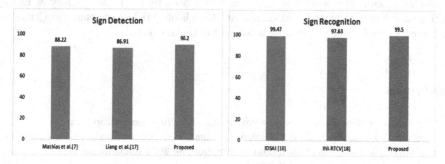

Fig. 3. Comparison of speed-limit sign detection (left) and recognition (right)

Second, to evaluate the speed-limit sign recognition performance, we also used the GTSRB dataset [18], which was created from approximately ten hours of video recorded while driving on different road types in Germany during the daytime. The GTSRB dataset consists of 39,209 training images and 12,630 test images in 43 classes. In fact, although the GTSRB dataset includes lifelike images of more than 12,630 traffic signs in 43 classes, we selected only data on 12,630 images from nine speed-limit sign classes from the available 43 classes because the goal of our study is speed-limit sign recognition. To evaluate the effectiveness of the proposed method, we examined its average correct classification rate (CCR) through a comparison with the IDSIA [10] and INI-RTCV [18] methods, which are known to be the highest traffic-sign recognition methods available. As shown in Fig. 3 (b), our proposed method produces a similar recognition performance as these other methods. The results indicate that a spatial pyramid provides both global and local features when compared to the feature extraction from a whole image, and BoostRF eliminates a large number of false positives using an aggregated spatial pyramid based on the OCS-LBP features.

5   Conclusion

This paper proposed a speed-limit sign detection and recognition algorithm for real-time application. For the sign detection, we used simple color and OCS-LBP features with BoostRF. Using BoostRF, the sign detector can improve the detection performance by utilizing only the optimal number of decision trees. For the speed recognition, we used a spatial pyramid of the OCS-LBP feature to extract both the finer and coarser features from one image at the same time. When we use the same BoostRF with a spatial pyramid, our method shows a similar or somewhat higher recognition result than other deep neural network based methods [10, 18]. For future works, we intend to focus on a reduction in the detection time for speed-limit signs and improving the recognition time and accuracy by combining the convolutional neural network concept with BoostRF.

Acknowledgement. This work was supported by the Ministry Of Trade, Industry & Energy (MOTIE) and Korea Institute for Advancement of Technology(KIAT) through the Center for Mechatronics Parts(CAMP)(B0008866) at Keimyung University.

References

1. The European New Car Assessment Programme. http://www.euroncap.com
2. Stallkamp, J., Schlipsing, M., Salmen, J., Igel, C.: German traffic sign recognition benchmark: A multiclass classification competition. In: 2011 International Joint Conference on Neural Networks, pp. 1453–1460 (2011)
3. Greenhalgh, J., Mirmehdi, M.: Real-time detection and recognition of road traffic signs. IEEE Trans. On Intell. Transp. Syst. **13**, 1498–1506 (2012)
4. Broggi, A., Cerri, P., Medici, P., Porta, P. P., Ghisio, G.: Real time road signs recognition. In: 2007 IEEE Intelligent Vehicles Symposium, pp. 981–986 (2007)
5. Matas, J., Chum, O., Urban, M., Pajdla, T.: Robust wide-baseline stereo from maximally stable extremal regions. Image Vision Comput. **22**, 761–767 (2004)
6. Barnes, N., Zelinsky, A.: Real-time radial symmetry for speed sign detection. In: IEEE Intelligent Vehicles Symposium, pp. 566–571 (2004)
7. Mathias, M., Timofte, R., Benenson, R., Gool, L. V.: Traffic sign recognition - how far are we from the solution?. In: IEEE International Joint Conference on Neural Networks, pp. 1–8 (2013)
8. Creusen, I.M., Wijnhoven, R.G.J., Herbschleb, E., De With, P.H.N.: Color exploitation in hog-based traffic sign detection. In: 17th IEEE International Conference on Image Processing, pp. 2669–2672 (2010)
9. Nguwi, Y.Y., Kouzani, A.Z.: Detection and classification of road signs in natural environments. Neural Comput. Appl. **2**, 265–289 (2008)
10. Cireşan, D., Meier, U., Masci, J., Schmidhuber, J.: Multi-column deep neural network for traffic sign classification. Neural Networks **32**, 333–338 (2012)
11. Sermanet, P., LeCun, Y.: Traffic sign recognition with multi-scale Convolutional Networks. In: 2011 International Joint Conference on Neural Networks, pp. 2809–2813 (2011)
12. Mishina, Y., Tsuchiya, M., Fujiyoshi, H.: Boosted Random Forest. In: International Conference on Computer Vision Theory and Applications, pp. 594–598 (2014)

13. He, K., Zhang, X., Ren, S., Sun, J.: Spatial pyramid pooling in deep convolutional networks for visual recognition. IEEE Transactions on Pattern Analysis and Machine Intelligence, arXiv:1406.4729, pp. 1–14 (Accepted 2015)
14. Ko, B.C., Jeong, M., Nam, J.Y.: Fast human detection for intelligent monitoring using surveillance visible sensors. Sensors **14**, 21247–21257 (2014)
15. Breiman, L.: Random forests. Mach. Learn. **45**, 5–32 (2001)
16. Houben, S., Stallkamp, J., Salmen, J., Schlipsing, M., Igel, C. : Detection of traffic signs in real-world images: the German traffic sign detection benchmark. In: International Joint Conference on Neural Networks, pp.1–8 (2013)
17. Liang, M., Yuan, M., Hu, X., Li, J., Liu, H.: Traffic sign detection by ROI extraction and histogram features-based recognition. In: International Joint Conference on Neural Networks, pp. 1–8 (2013)
18. Stallkamp, J., Schlipsing, M., Salmena, J., Igel, C.: Man vs. computer: Benchmarking machine learning algorithms for traffic sign recognition. Neural Networks **32**, 323–332 (2012)

Automatic Nacre Thickness Measurement of Tahitian Pearls

Martin Loesdau[✉], Sébastien Chabrier, and Alban Gabillon

Laboratoire d'Excellence CORAIL Géopôle du Pacifique Sud EA4238,
Université de la Polynésie Française, FAA, Tahiti, French Polynesia
{martin.loesdau,sebastien.chabrier,
alban.gabillon}@upf.pf

Abstract. In this paper a methodology for an automatized measurement of the nacre thickness of Tahitian pearls is presented. An adapted snake approach as well as our own developed circle detection algorithm are implemented to extract the nacre boundaries out of X-ray images. The results are validated by experts currently performing manually the obligatory nacre thickness control for millions of Tahitian pearls that are exported each year. Equivalent articles propose methods suitable for round pearls, whereas this paper contains methods to evaluate the nacre profile of pearls independently of their shape. As the algorithms are not specifically parametrized for Tahitian pearls, the methods can be adapted for quality assessment of other pearls as well.

Keywords: Pearl classification · X-ray image analysis · Active contours · Circle detection

1 Introduction

The Tahitian pearl is a precious natural gem that is cultivated in the clear warm la-goons of French Polynesia. On the international market the pearl is known under the name 'Queen of Pearls', due to its high quality and the large diversity of different color nuances. To keep its high reputation, the French Polynesian government introduced an obligatory quality control for each pearl that is supposed to be exported. This obligatory control is conducted by the administration of marine and mining resources (*Direction des Ressources Marines et Minières*, DRMM), where the quality of a pearl is evaluated by its form, size, color, luster, surface quality and nacre thickness. The evaluation is done manually by experts, which is a time consuming process, especially seeing the large amount of pearls that are exported each year (over 11 million in 2014, tendency increasing). As the pearl is the first source of export income in French Polynesia (export volume of over 70 million Euro in 2014), one goal of our project is to support this important branch by implementing a computer vision based quality control. An automatized quality assessment can help to guarantee a fast and stable export procedure, which is in the interest of the local pearl farmers as well as the French Polynesian government.

The Tahitian pearl is cultivated by inserting an artificially formed sphere, the nucleus, into a Black-Lip Pearl Oyster (*Pinctada margaritifera*). The pearl grows

M. Kamel and A. Campilho (Eds.): ICIAR 2015, LNCS 9164, pp. 446–455, 2015.
DOI: 10.1007/978-3-319-20801-5_49

Fig. 1. A cut through three Tahitian pearls (left), a Tahitian pearl positioned in a borehole of a wooden plate for X-raying (middle) and the resulting X-ray image (right).

afterwards as a result of a biological defense mechanism of the oyster that 'neutralizes' this foreign substance by building layers of nacre around it (see Fig. 1 on the left for a cut through 3 Tahitian pearls). One of the quality parameters to control is the minimal nacre thickness, a parameter that has to be evaluated by imaging the internal structure of the pearl. For this purpose the DRMM uses X-ray machines. The pearls are stored in boreholes of a wooden plate that is placed in the machine for image capturing (Fig. 1 in the middle). Afterwards an employee evaluates manually the numeric image taken separately for each pearl (Fig. 1 on the right). An obligatory export criterion for a Tahitian pearl is that its minimal nacre thickness has to exceed 0.8 mm. The manual evaluation of the X-ray images serves accordingly the purpose of rejecting pearls with a minimal nacre thickness lower than 0.8 mm from exportation.

In this paper our methodology to automatize the measure of the nacre profile out of X-ray images is presented. The crucial regions to detect to automatize this measurement are visualized in Fig. 2. The example in the left column shows a round pearl situated completely in the plates borehole (green circle). The outer boundary of the pearl (blue line) and the nucleus (red circle) have to be detected and the distance between both describes the nacre thickness profile. The second column shows a pearl with a cavity inside. As the cavity must not contribute to the thickness measurement, the inner boundary of the nacre has to be extracted additionally (cyan line). The distance between the inner and the outer boundary describes the nacre thickness. The third example shows a pearl, whose outer boundary surpasses completely the borehole, leading to superposed gradients of the borehole and the inner structure of the pearl, a complication that will be discussed in section four.

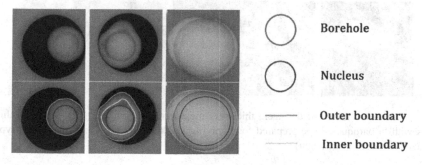

Fig. 2. Three example images (first row) and the crucial regions to detect (second row).

In the next section, related work concerning pearl quality assessment based on nacre thickness, color and shape is described. Section three contains our methods to measure the nacre thickness of Tahitian pearls. In three subsections the stages of extracting the inner and outer boundary of the nacre with active contours, as well as extracting the nucleus with circle detection are described. The fourth subsection contains the final measurement of the nacre profile out of the previously extracted information. In section four perspectives concerning the improvement and further validation of our methods as well as suggestions to improve the image configuration can be found, followed by the conclusion in section five.

2   Related Work

Even though the international pearl market yields large profit in several countries, scientific work in the domain of computer science to improve this industry is rare. An article proposing a method for an automatized nacre thickness measurement can be found under [1]. Optical coherence tomography (OCT), a shallow-depths laser imaging technique, is used to generate greylevel images of the internal structure of a pearl. The OCT images undergo denoising, edge detection and median filtering, to detect the edges of the outer boundary of the nacre. According to the assumption that the outer boundary of the nacre is round, the final boundary is obtained by fitting a circle to the obtained edges using the least-square method. The edge pixels for the inner boundary are identified with Support Vector Machine and the results are treated the same way as for the outer boundary. Further developments of this method are described in [2, 3]. The approaches are based on the assumption that the nacres' boundaries are round, which covers only one of several classes concerning the Tahitian pearl. The left image in Fig. 3, taken from [1], shows two circles in blue that approximate the inner and the outer boundary of a pearl, as a result of the described algorithm. In the middle an image of Tahitian pearls that are controlled for export at the DRMM can be seen, most of them with a 'baroque' shape that cannot be approximated by circles. On the right a typical X-ray image of a pearl with a 'baroque' shape is shown to further illustrate the need for another approach to automatically measure the nacre thickness of Tahitian pearls independently of its shape.

Fig. 3. One result image of the nacre thickness measurement from [1] (left), several Tahitian pearls with 'a baroque' shape prepared for X-raying (middle) and an X-ray image of a typical Tahitian 'baroque' pearl (right).

Further related articles concern the quality assessment of pearls based on color and shape. In [4–7] the relation between the physical properties of a pearl and its human evaluation are investigated. A model is built which aims to support automated inspection systems in regards of for example the spectrum, diffusion and position of a light source. In [8] the pearls shape is described with Zernike moments and afterwards classified with a fuzzy membership function, while an approach to classify the pearls color is presented in [9].

3   Measuring the Nacre Thickness

To measure the nacre thickness out of X-ray images the outer and the inner boundary of the nacre have to be extracted. Our methodology consists of three stages: (i) detecting the outer boundary of the nacre, (ii) detecting the nucleus, and (iii) detecting the inner boundary of the nacre. The methods for these stages will be presented in the following three sections. In the fourth section the final measurement of the nacre thickness out of the obtained information is described.

3.1   Detecting the Outer Boundary

As the intensity and the gradient of the outer boundary of the pearls in X-ray images vary largely, classical edge detection (such as Canny, Sobel or Prewitt) for the detection of the outer boundary failed in first tests. A more efficient approach is to use the active contour approach 'snakes' [10]. This advanced edge integrator consists of a curve that is moved by image-dependent external forces while its form keeps a certain degree of 'smoothness'. The mathematical idea is to maintain equilibrium between internal and external energy defined over the whole curve at each iteration. The according formula is described as:

$$\int \left(\alpha(s) \left(\frac{d(x(s))}{ds} \right)^2 + \beta(s) \left(\frac{d^2(x(s))}{ds^2} \right)^2 + F(s) \right) ds = 0. \tag{1}$$

The first two terms contain the first two derivatives of the curve that describe the smoothness of its contour (internal energy). The third term is the force that moves the curve (external energy), usually a gradient calculated over the whole image. This integral describes an optimization problem that can be solved with the Euler-Lagrange formalism. A simple numeric implementation of the solution can be described by

$$\vec{X}_{t+1} = \left(\bar{\bar{I}} - \bar{\bar{A}} \right)^{-1} \left(\bar{F} + \vec{X}_t \right). \tag{2}$$

In this formula $\bar{\bar{I}}$ is the identity matrix, $\bar{\bar{A}}$ is a matrix that contains the weighted second and fourth derivative of the curve at time t, $\bar{F}$ is a force vector that moves the curve and $\vec{X}$ is a vector that contains the x-coordinates of the curve at time t, respectively, as the algorithm is iterative at time $t + 1$. The algorithm (executed for the x- and y-coordinates) results in a moving curve that stops moving when the external and internal energy at each point are in equilibrium.

The implementation for detecting the outer boundary of the nacre is the following: the initial contour is set to the outer boundary of the image, assuring that the pearl is situated inside the contour (Fig. 4 first row in blue color for three example images). The normal vectors at each point of the curve point to the inside of the curve. The moving force is a negative 'balloon' force, meaning the curve is constantly shrinking in direction of its normal vectors (for a description of the balloon force please see [11]). This force is diminished if the curve touches positive image gradients (dark pixel to light pixel) in direction of its normal vectors. The effect of this configuration can be seen in Fig. 4 second and third row: while the curve in each image passes the strong gradient between the light and the dark background (negative gradient) it stops at the positive gradient that describes the outer boundary of the pearl. These three examples contain different possibilities of pearl position. While the pearl on the right is situated completely in the borehole of the plate on which the pearls are positioned (see as well Fig. 1), the image on the left shows a pearl whose boundary surpasses partially the hole. The image in the middle is an example of a pearl whose boundary surpasses completely the hole. Even though the local gradients of the pearl boundaries are different, no case differentiation has to be done, as for all three configurations the same algorithm with the same parametrization was used.

After obtaining the outer boundary of the pearl, the second stage consists of detecting the nucleus within the pearl.

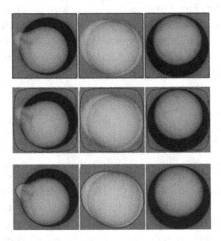

Fig. 4. The initial snake contour for the outer boundary detection in blue (top), after several iterations (middle) and the final result (bottom).

3.2 Detecting the Nucleus

As described in the introduction, the nucleus is an artificially formed sphere, which appears as a circle in X-ray images. The goal of this stage is accordingly classical circle detection. One of the most popular approaches is the circular Hough transform [12]. Even though with high performance, this 'brute force' approach is time and memory consuming. As center and radius of the nucleus are a priori unknown, each pixel within the outer boundary has to be considered as potential center pixel for all radii in this approach. The low gradients and the nacre thickness dependent intensity makes pixel preselection with edge detection difficult. Using the snake approach instead does not guarantee that the result will be a circle, especially if the boundary of the nucleus is only partially visible. For the purpose of the nucleus detection we developed a heuristic approach that consists of an artificial circle with a variable radius that is moved by image gradient forces. The basic idea is: if an artificial circle stays all time in a circular object to detect, while its radius is increased, it will at one time fully cover the outer boundary of the circular object. For this application it means that an initial artificial circle has to move into the nucleus and stay in it while its radius is constantly increased. At a certain moment the artificial circle will fully cover the outer boundary of the nucleus. The mathematical formula satisfying this movement can be denoted as

$$\vec{F} = \sum_{i=1}^{m} f_i \vec{n}_i. \tag{3}$$

In this formula $\vec{n}_i$ denotes the inside pointing normal vector of point i of the artificial circle and f_i the local gradient force at this point (positive from dark to light pixels in direction of the normal vector). The sum over all m points of the circle determines its moving direction $\vec{F}$. Each time the center of the moving circle touches the same pixel for the second time its radius is increased. The implementation for one of the example images is visualized in Fig. 5. On the top left the initial circle is shown with its normal vectors at each point weighted by the local gradient (blue arrows). Due to the spherical form of the nucleus, the gradients at the border are stronger, resulting according to Eq. 3 in a moving direction (black arrow) pointing to the center of the nucleus. As the border between the nucleus and the nacre is barely visible, a red arrow points for clarification at the partial border. The bigger circle with strong gradients in this image belongs to the borehole of the plate where the pearl is placed for X-raying (see as well Figs. 1 and 2). At the bottom of Fig. 5 is the average of all local gradients of all circle points over each movement visualized in blue. Each time the radius is increased is marked by a vertical black line.

After the first two radius increases, the circle moved further inside the nucleus close to its center (second image on the top). The third image shows the circle and its weighted normal vectors at the moment it fully covers the boundary of the nucleus. Almost all gradients are positive and at a local maximum. A few movements later the circle surpasses this boundary, resulting in an abrupt change of gradient directions in this area (fourth image), due to the beginning of the nacre area. This moment, even though the boundary of the nucleus is only partially visible, can be clearly detected in the trend of the average gradients (on the bottom of Fig. 5). The automatically detected nuclei of all three example pearls with this algorithm are shown in Fig. 6. On the top are the circles initialized at the geometric center of the previously detected outer boundary and the results are on the bottom. For the two example pearls in the right two columns, all necessary information to calculate the nacre thickness is obtained (the inner nacre boundary is equivalent to the boundary of the nucleus). The pearl on the left

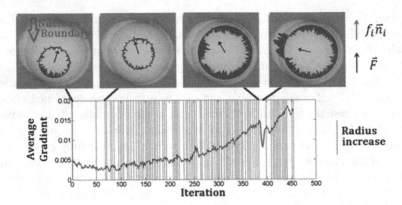

Fig. 5. Four different iteration stages of our circle detection algorithm (top) and the average gradient of each circle point at each iteration (bottom).

however, has a cavity inside the nacre which must not contribute to the nacre thickness measurement. Therefor a third stage of detecting the inner boundary has to be executed.

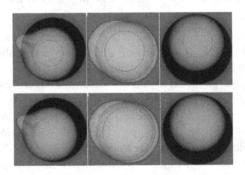

Fig. 6. The initial artificial circle of the implemented algorithm for the nucleus detection in red (top) and the detected nucleus (bottom).

3.3 Detecting the Inner Boundary

In Fig. 7 on the left the result of the first two stages for one of the example images of the previous sections is shown. Within the nacre a slightly darker region can be identified. This region is a cavity within the pearl. Accordingly this region must not contribute to the nacre thickness measurement. For the same reasons as before, the active contour approach 'snakes' can as well be used for this stage.

In this implementation the initial contour is set identical to the detected outer boundary of the pearl. The moving force is like previously a negative 'balloon' force, resulting in a constant shrinking of the curve. This time the shrinking is diminished if the curve touches *negative* gradients or the detected nucleus. The right three images in Fig. 7 visualize the execution of the algorithm. The final result approximates the inner boundary of the nacre. For the other two pearls seen in the previous section, the inner

Fig. 7. Different stages for the detection of the inner boundary of the nacre in case of a cavity within the pearl. The final result is on the right.

boundary is equivalent to the detected boundary of the nucleus, as their inner structure possesses no cavities. As by now all necessary information for the three pearls are extracted, the actual nacre thickness can be evaluated.

3.4   Measuring the Thickness

To evaluate the nacre thickness the distance between the outer and inner boundary is calculated at every point, which describes the nacre thickness profile of the whole pearl (Fig. 8 in the middle). The last step is to identify the regions of the nacre profile that are thinner than the minimal authorized nacre thickness of 0.8 mm for Tahitian pearls to be exported. The areas of the nacre greater than this margin are colored in green while the thinner areas are colored in red (Fig. 8 on the bottom). The results were validated by employees of the DRMM.

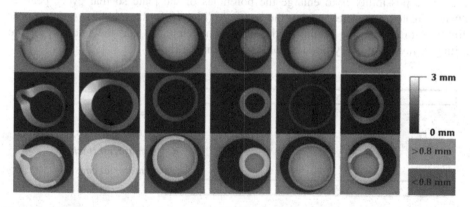

Fig. 8. Original images (top), automatically calculated nacre profiles (middle) and a visualization of areas lower than the minimal allowed nacre thickness for exporting a Tahitian pearl (bottom, areas lower than 0.8 mm in red).

4   Perspectives

As by this case study the used methods are generally validated as suitable, the next step is to acquire a large amount of test images to further improve and adapt the used algorithms. We are currently in contact with the DRMM to obtain a set of several hundred X-ray images together with manual evaluation results. Furthermore several special cases exist as shown in Fig. 9. The image on the left shows a pearl with two inner boundaries, while the image in the middle shows a pearl whose inner structure does not allow a visual discrimination between nucleus and nacre.

Fig. 9. Special cases of inner nacre structure: two inner boundaries (left), inner boundary not visible (middle) and complex inner structure (right).

The image on the right shows a pearl whose inner structure is highly complex. The goal is to automatically identify the special cases to at least, if an automatic detection is impossible, avoid false detections.

Another perspective concerns the plate that is used to position the pearls for X-raying. Currently the pearls are placed in boreholes of a wooden plate (see Figs. 2 and 3).

These additional gradients superposed on the internal structure of the nacre complicate and decelerate the automatic analysis, as well as the manual evaluation by experts. We proposed two possibilities to the DRMM how to avoid these constellations. One possibility is to enlarge the boreholes of the plate so that every pearl is always situated completely within the borehole (Fig. 10 in the middle). Another possibility is to change the profile of the plate completely, so that the intensity of the exiting X-rays is at every point equal (Fig. 10 on the right).

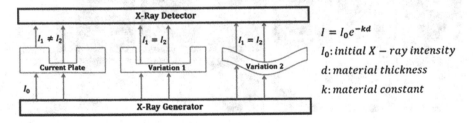

$$I = I_0 e^{-kd}$$

I_0: initial $X - ray$ intensity

d: material thickness

k: material constant

Fig. 10. Profile schema of the currently used wooden plate (left) and variations with enlarged boreholes (middle) and a complete profile change (right) to avoid superposed gradients.

5   Conclusion

In this paper we presented a methodology to automatically measure the nacre thickness of Tahitian pearls out of X-ray images. This work aims to support and improve the French Polynesian pearl business by automatizing an obligatory measurement that is currently done manually. Equivalent articles cover only one particular case of round pearls, whereas this paper contains a more general approach for pearls of different shape. An adapted snake approach as well as our own developed circle detection algorithm are used to extract the necessary information from the X-ray images. Our results were validated by employees of the administration of marine and mining resources of French Polynesia, a governmental institution that is in charge of the obligatory nacre thickness control of Tahitian pearls that are exported. The automatic detection is performed in real-time, a necessary requirement for the quality assessment.

Acknowledgements. We thank Cedrik Lo and Vaihere Mooria from the DRMM for providing us access to their facilities and for the supply of manually classified X-ray images. We thank as well all involved employees of the DRMM for their help and for sharing their knowledge and professional experience to support our work.

References

1. Lei, M., et al.: Automated thickness measurements of pearl from optical coherence tomography images. In: Ninth International Conference on Hybrid Intelligent Systems (HIS 2009), vol. 1. IEEE (2009)
2. Sun, Y., Ming, L.: Automated thickness measurements of nacre from optical coherence tomography using polar transform and probability density projection. In: International Symposium on Intelligent Signal Processing and Communication Systems (ISPACS), IEEE (2010)
3. Liu, J., Tian, X.L., Kui Sun, Y.: Pearl thickness measurements from optical coherence tomography images. Appl. Mech. Mater. **421**, 415–420 (2013)
4. Toshimasa, D. et al.: Implementation of a pearl visual simulator based on blurring and interference. In: Second International Conference on Knowledge-Based Intelligent Electronic Systems Proceedings (KES 1998). vol. 3. IEEE (1998)
5. Nagata, N. et al.: Modeling and visualization for a pearl-quality evaluation simulator. In: IEEE Transactions on 3.4 Visualization and Computer Graphics, pp. 307–315 (1997)
6. Nagata, N., Kamei, M., Usami, T.: Transferring human sensibilities to machines-sensitivity analysis of layered neural networks and its application to pearl color Evaluation. In: MVA (1994)
7. Nagata, N., Dobashi, T., Manabe, Y., Usami, T., Inokuchi, S.: Image analysis and synthesis using physics-based-modeling for pearl quality evaluation system In: Bimbo, A., (Eds.) Image Analysis and Processing. LNCS, vol 1311, pp. 697–704. Springer, Heidelberg (1997)
8. Bin, L., et al.: A classification method of pearl shape based on Zernike moment. In: International Conference on Wavelet Analysis and Pattern Recognition (ICWAPR 2007), vol. 3. IEEE (2007)
9. Tian, C.: A computer vision-based classification method for pearl quality assessment. In: International Conference on Computer Technology and Development (ICCTD 2009), vol. 2. IEEE (2009)
10. Kass, M., Witkin, A., Terzopoulos, D.: Snakes: Active contour models. Int. J. Comput. Vis. **1**(4), 321–331 (1988)
11. Cohen, L.D.: On active contour models and balloons. CVGIP: Image underst. **53**(2), 211–218 (1991)
12. Duda, R.O., Hart, P.E.: Use of the hough transformation to detect lines and curves in pictures. Commun. ACM **15**(1), 11–15 (1972)

Automated Wheat Disease Classification Under Controlled and Uncontrolled Image Acquisition

Punnarai Siricharoen$^{(\boxtimes)}$, Bryan Scotney, Philip Morrow,
and Gerard Parr

School of Computing and Information Engineering,
University of Ulster, Coleraine, UK
siricharoen-p@email.ulster.ac.uk,
{bw.scotney,pj.morrow,gp.parr}@ulster.ac.uk

Abstract. This paper presents a practical classification system for recognising diseased wheat leaves and consists of a number of components. Pre-processing is performed to adjust the orientation of the primary leaf in the image using a Fourier Transform. A Wavelet Transform is then applied to partially remove low frequency information or background in the image. Subsequently, the diseased regions of the primary leaf are segmented out as blobs using Otsu's thresholding. The disease blobs are normalised and then radially partitioned into sub-regions (using a Radial Pyramid) representing radial development of many diseases. Finally, global features are computed for different pyramid layers and combined to create a feature descriptor for training a linear SVM classifier. The system is evaluated by classifying three types of wheat leaf disease: non-diseased, Yellow Rust and Septoria. The classification accuracies are slightly over 95 % and 79 % for images captured under controlled and uncontrolled conditions, respectively.

Keywords: Wheat disease recognition · Radial pyramid · Rotation using Fourier

1 Introduction

With the rapid development of technologies for camera devices, especially on smartphones, the use of image processing algorithms now play an important role for a number of applications; for example, face and object recognition and biomedical applications are important topics in computer vision. Another application area which could benefit significantly from the use of image processing techniques is that of agriculture. For example, plant disease can cause serious damage with regard to the loss of agricultural products and can thus contribute to the problems of world economy and human health. This paper proposes an automated classification system for preliminary recognition of different wheat diseases to assist farmers in crop management (example images can be seen later in Fig. 2). Our study is initially focused on three commonly seen types of foliar wheat disease, which differ in visual appearance [1]. The paper is divided into four main sections. Literature review is detailed in Sect. 2. Section 3

© Springer International Publishing Switzerland 2015
M. Kamel and A. Campilho (Eds.): ICIAR 2015, LNCS 9164, pp. 456–464, 2015.
DOI: 10.1007/978-3-319-20801-5_50

explains the details of the proposed system. The experimentation and results are discussed in Sect. 4. Finally conclusions are presented in Sect. 5.

2 Literature Review

In machine vision Histogram of Oriented Gradients (HOG) and Scale-Invariant Feature Transform (SIFT) algorithms have been shown to be potential local feature descriptors, especially for object classification or detection. Considering the challenges of computer vision for a plant pathology application, disease shapes or distribution patterns can appear differently within the same type of disease depending on their severity levels. Additionally, the colours and the distributions can exhibit similarly but with slight differences between different types of diseases. Other challenges generally include the effects of illumination change and background clutter.

The use of imaging techniques in plant pathology applications has been conducted over the past decade. In 2003, El-Helly et al. [2] implemented Fuzzy c-means to segment diseases from a leaf and then applied various shape characteristics, such as principal axis length, eccentricity, and compactness on three types of cucumber diseases. Amongst the studies in this area, the combination of global colour, texture and shape features are the most frequently applied features which have been shown to be accurate in classifying various diseases [3–5]. Wang et al. [5] applied this combination of features in an expensive classifier based on Neural Networks to discriminate wheat stripe rust from leaf brown rust completely. Tian et al. [4] constructed multiple SVM classifiers for each feature set of colour, texture and shape which achieved 95 % accuracy for classifying four wheat diseases. In general, the feature combination approach considers global properties of an interesting area, to use all features from each feature set is time consuming and can also decrease the classification accuracy (over-fitting). Combinations of features within each feature set were investigated in our previous work [6] to ensure that a selected feature subset contributes significant information representing disease/non-disease area. Moreover, most of the recent studies initially experimented on several diseases whose images were acquired under controlled conditions or required a manual process to reduce the effect of the background. This paper proposes a practical system that is partially tolerant to background clutter and changes in lighting conditions using previously selected feature sets and an extended version of the features which models how a disease develops.

3 Methodology and Proposed Classification System

Our proposed system is illustrated in Fig. 1 and consists of four main components: pre-processing, segmentation, feature extraction and classification. Images are initially scaled and rotated to standardise image size and to adjust the leaf orientation for consistency. Then the background is partially removed and diseased regions are extracted from the leaf during the segmentation process. Each disease region is normalised to a square patch representing a disease texton. Inspired by the Spatial Pyramid method [7] which divided an image into sub-regions for different levels, our disease texton is radially partitioned into layers for different levels regarding the natural characteristics of diseases. Then global features based on texture, colour and visual perception are calculated for sub-regions of the radial pyramid. Finally, the features are combined to create a feature descriptor which is later used as an input for training a multiclass SVM model. Details of the processes are described below.

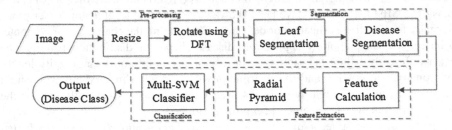

Fig. 1. Our proposed system for wheat disease classification

3.1   Leaf Rotation Using Discrete Fourier Transform

As the visual pattern associated with a wheat disease often aligns with the direction of the leaf's major axis, the extracted features rely on disease orientation on the leaf. Hence rotation is performed to promote the consistency of the leaf alignment. Firstly, we calculate the image gradient using a Canny edge detector to provide information on the alignment of the leaf and leaf veins; this operator is also reasonably invariant to different light conditions. Then, a two-dimensional discrete Fourier transform (DFT) is applied to compute major frequency components in the edge image. The Fourier spectrum shows a major dominant line that is orthogonal to the leaf orientation, and the computed direction of the line is used to determine the rotation required for leaf alignment (see example in Fig. 8(b)). The approach is also robust to rotate leaves that reside in a cluttered background.

3.2   Leaf Segmentation Using Multi-resolution Discrete Wavelet Transform

To remove the effect of the image background, we deployed a single-level two-dimensional Wavelet transform (DWT), which is exploited to decompose an image into coefficients of four different components: an approximation component (cA), and horizontal, vertical, and diagonal details (cH, cV, and cD). We combined horizontal, vertical and diagonal detail information based on Daubechies wavelets and then thresholded out the low coefficient values to remove part of the background from consideration in the subsequent stages of our process; a segmentation mask $M(i, j)_{leaf}$ is computed as shown in (1) at pixels (i, j) using the three detail components; μ_{cH}, μ_{cV}, μ_{cD}, σ_{cH}, σ_{cV} and σ_{cD} are means and standard deviations of horizontal, vertical and diagonal coefficients respectively. An example of a segmented leaf is shown in Fig. 8(d).

$$M(i,j)_{leaf} = \begin{cases} 1 & \text{if } cH_{i,j} > \mu_{cH} + \sigma_{cH}, cV_{i,j} > \mu_{cV} + \sigma_{cV} \text{ and } cD_{i,j} > \mu_{cD} + \sigma_{cD} \\ 0 & \text{Otherwise} \end{cases} \quad (1)$$

3.3 Disease Segmentation Using Otsu's Threshold

Provided that the non-disease area is consistently greenish, Otsu's threshold is used to maximize between-class variance of the diseased leaf to segment out the disease regions. However, to eliminate the effects of lighting conditions we empirically selected thresholds from Cb and Cr colour components.

3.4 Feature Extraction

Radial Pyramid. Our radial Pyramid is inspired by a spatial pyramid, an extended version of local feature descriptors such as SIFT for scene classification (Lazebnik et al. [7]). The radial pyramid structure aligns with the typical radial development of many diseases. The Septoria disease develops from a small brown-spot surrounded by a yellow halo; yellow rust disease (stripe rust) usually develops on leaf veins; leaf rust usually has a brown or yellow circular shape [1]. Figure 2 displays examples of different wheat diseases exhibiting different characteristics.

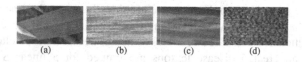

(a)   (b)   (c)   (d)

Fig. 2. Nature of different diseases (a) Non-disease (b) Yellow rust (c) Septoria (d) Leaf rust (Color figure online)

Assuming we have segmented disease blobs from the previous stages of our process, these blobs are normalized into square patches or disease textons [8] representing fundamental disease structures. Two types of texton normalization are explored. A nearest neighbour method is used to normalize a patch with a selection of the nearest neighbouring pixels alternating to maintain the disease scale or to scale a texton into a square patch; eleven normalized patches using this approach are illustrated in Fig. 9(a). Figure 10(a) displays another method, a bicubic normalization that creates a patch by averaging the neighbouring pixels to give a smoother texture in the patch.

Global Feature Descriptor. We deployed three different types of features based on textures, colours and visual perception investigated in [6]. Textural features (F_H) is developed through a spatial grey-level matrix [9]. Colour features (F_C) are based on statistical information of each disease patch, such as mean, variance, skewness and kurtosis of a colour component distribution. Lastly, Tamura [10] proposed a set of features (F_T) describing image patterns more visually, such as coarseness, contrast and

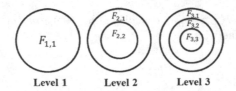

Level 1   Level 2   Level 3

Fig. 3. Example of three-level radial pyramid. There are 1, 2 and 3 layers for levels 1, 2 and 3.

directionality. These features are calculated for each level (k) and layer (l) of a radial pyramid (see Fig. 3 and disease examples in Fig. 9(b-g)). A final feature descriptor (F_K) is constructed from the concatenation of the combined features ($F(k, l)$) from the lower levels ($k = 1, ..., K - 1$) and the current level (K) (K is also equal to the number of layers (L) of the current level). The concatenation process is shown in (2) and (3). Different feature characteristics are computed for different pyramid layers and each descriptor represents a variety of diseases.

$$F(k, l) = [F_H(k, l)\ F_C(k, l)\ F_T(k, l)] \tag{2}$$

$$F_K = [F(1, 1)\ F(2, 1)\ F(2, 2)...F(K, 1)...F(K, L)] \tag{3}$$

3.5 Multiclass SVM Classification

In order to create a practical application, we empirically selected a linear SVM as our classifier as it has been shown to obtain high accuracy, good generalisation and computational efficiency compared to k-NN or neural network-based classifiers. In the learning phase, all created disease textons are trained for a linear SVM classifier. Assuming that all the patches are equally important, the output class of the image is the group that has the most frequently displayed results from the classified textons.

4 Experimentation and Results

We experimented with two types of datasets: data obtained under controlled conditions and uncontrolled conditions. Each dataset contains three types of wheat leaf (50 images each for non-disease, yellow rust and Septoria diseases). The controlled data some of which are shown in Fig. 4 were obtained from the Food and Environmental Research Agency (FERA [11]) and the leaves are manually segmented out from the background

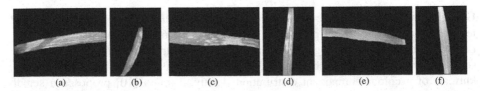

(a)   (b)   (c)   (d)   (e)   (f)

Fig. 4. Controlled images (FERA) (a)–(b) yellow rust, (c)–(d) Septoria, (e)–(f) non-disease (Color figure online)

before being used as inputs for the system. Uncontrolled data (from the Internet) were obtained from more than 50 different online sources that were collected from different farms and at different times using different capture devices, providing various illumination effects and colour tones. Additionally these images are also challenging due to background clutter and different image resolutions (see some examples in Figs. 5, 6 and 7 for yellow rust, Septoria and non-disease images, respectively.

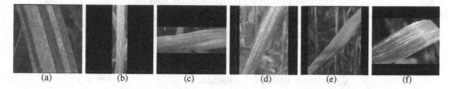

(a)   (b)   (c)   (d)   (e)   (f)

Fig. 5. Uncontrolled images – Yellow rust from (a)-(c) Washington State University, (d) Plant Management Network, (e) A Global Wheat Rust Monitoring System, (f) Bayer Group (Color figure online)

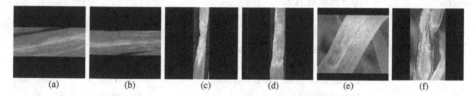

(a)   (b)   (c)   (d)   (e)   (f)

Fig. 6. Uncontrolled images – Septoria from (a)-(b) Rothamsted Research, (c)-(d) The American Phytopathological Society, (e) Biotechnology and Biological Sciences Research Council (BBSRC), (f) Government of Western Australia

(a)   (b)   (c)   (d)   (e)   (f)

Fig. 7. Uncontrolled images - non-disease from (a)–(d) The Food and Research Agency, (e) Mississippi State University, (f) International Maize and Wheat Improvement Center

The system was evaluated using MATLAB 2014b. During pre-processing, the images are resized to 300 × 300 pixels. Four radial pyramid levels and four different patch sizes (15, 20, 25, and 30) are investigated in the experimentation. The best results are based on 15 × 15 texton patch size using the nearest neighbour normalisation method. The colour representation was empirically selected as the YCbCr colour space. The testing scheme is based on 5-fold cross-validation testing.

Table 1. Classification accuracies of the proposed system compared to previous works [4–6]

Dataset	Feature		Accuracy (%)
4 wheat diseases (Controlled)	Colour + Shape + Texture using 2-stage SVM multi-classifier [4]		95.16
2 wheat disease (Controlled)	Colour + Shape + Texture using PCA and BP networks [5]		100
FERA (Controlled)	Top Textural Features [6] (rectangular rotation)[1]		90
	Top Textural Features + Haralick Correlation		91.87
	Top Textural Features with DFT rotation and pyramid level = 4		**95**
	Top Textural Features + Haralick Correlation with DFT rotation, segmentation	Pyramid level = 1	95.73
		Pyramid level = 2	**95.78**
		Pyramid level = 4	95.5
Internet (Uncontrolled)	Top Textural Features [6]		72.33
	Top Textural Features + Haralick Correlation		72.67
	Top Textural Features + Haralick Correlation with DFT rotation and segmentation		**80.13**
	Top Textural Features + Haralick Correlation with DFT rotation, segmentation	Pyramid level = 3	78.27
		Pyramid level = 4	**79**

[1]Accuracy is lower than in [6] due to a different value of the box constraint being used to allow the model to be more flexible and converge when constructing an SVM model.

The results are summarised in Table 1 and are compared with the previous works [4–6]. The wheat disease identification systems [4, 5] which deployed colour, texture and shape features on high quality data of two and four types of wheat diseases and obtained the classification accuracies of 100 % and 95.16 % for [4] and [5], respectively. Our previous work [6] applied sets of global features on the whole image only. The classification accuracy is about 90 %; adding correlation in the system [6] slightly increased the overall performance by 0.5-2.0 % for uncontrolled and controlled data. Although, the results from the literature [4–6] show high classification accuracies, the systems [4, 6] are limited to work with only pre-manually segmented data. The flexibility of [6] is improved in our system to promote more practical application and cope with a variety of data and background clutter. Even though the datasets are different, our proposed system with the data acquired under controlled conditions produced comparable results with the previous works [4–6]. Also, our current system shows improvements of the original system [6] from 91.78 % to 95.78 % when applying the radial pyramid method (level size = 2). However, the classification is not improved further by increasing the level size. Considering the uncontrolled data from the Internet, the use of the previous system [6] obtained classification accuracy of 72.33 %. Including rotation and segmentation from this paper, the results rise to 80.13 % as

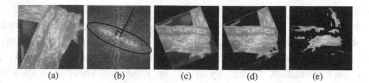

Fig. 8. Uncontrolled image processing in the system (a) original image, (b) DFT on Canny edge, (c) rotated image, (d) partially segmented image, (e) segmented disease.

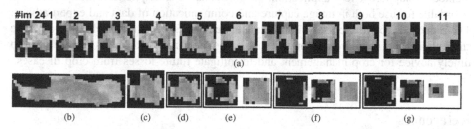

Fig. 9. Normalized textons of diseases in using nearest neighbour technique (a) constructed disease patches, (b) original disease blob (#5), (c) normalised disease patch (d) 1-level (e) 2-level (f) 3-level (g) 4-level radial pyramid patches.

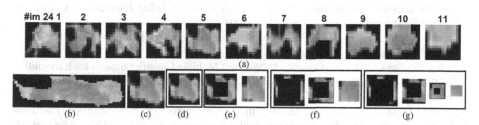

Fig. 10. Normalized textons in using bicubic technique (a) constructed disease patches, (b) original disease blob (#5), (c) normalised disease patch (d) 1-level (e) 2-level (f) 3-level (g) 4-level radial pyramid patches

accurate feature extraction relies on the consistency of the leaf alignment and the diseased leaf patterns. Our system with a 3-level pyramid produces slightly lower accuracy of 78.27 %, but the accuracy rises to 79 % by increasing the level size to 4. The investigation shows that the effect of the background remaining after the segmentation phase has an impact on creating accurate disease textons, especially for non-disease patches, most of which are built from the background.

5 Conclusion

Human-in-the-loop advisory systems for crop management have emerged to assist remote famers in acquiring advice to prevent or mitigate agriculture losses from crop diseases. To enable such systems to cope with the demands at scale, an automated and practical classification system is proposed in this paper initially for classifying three types of wheat diseases. Consistency of leaf alignment is achieved by rotating the primary leaf based on the orthogonal direction of the frequency spectrum from a Fourier transform, and a 2-D Wavelet transform is used to partially remove low frequencies or background. A Radial Pyramid, an extended version of global feature descriptors, is established to model the nature of disease development. We have demonstrated the robustness of our system using controlled and uncontrolled images and the classification accuracies obtained show that this initial system can be implemented to support a real application. In particular, a smartphone is ubiquitous and affordable for use both in image capture and communication of data and expert advice. The proposed crop image analysis system can be integrated with the technologies of the smartphone and cloud computing to enable remote farmers to have online access to timely advice for crop management and to mitigate future losses from crop diseases.

References

1. Agriculture and Horticulture Development Board: HGCA Wheat Disease Management Guide (2012)
2. El-Helly, M., Ahmed, R., El-Gammal, S.: An integrated image processing system for leaf disease detection and diagnosis. In: Proceedings of the 1st Indian International Conference on Artificial Intelligence, pp. 1182–1195 (2003)
3. Barbedo, J.G.A.: Digital image processing techniques for detecting, quantifying and classifying plant diseases. SpringerPlus. **2**, 660 (2013)
4. Tian, Y., Zhao, C., Lu, S., Guo, X.: SVM-based Multiple Classifier System for Recognition of Wheat Leaf Diseases. In: Conference on Dependable Computing, Yichang, China, pp. 2–6 (2010)
5. Wang, H., Li, G., Ma, Z., Li, X.: Image recognition of plant diseases based on backpropagation networks. In: Fifth International Congress on Image and Signal Processing, pp. 894–900 (2012)
6. Siricharoen, P., Scotney, B., Morrow, P., Parr, G.: Effects of different mixtures of features, colours and svm kernels on wheat disease classification. In: Proceedings of the Irish Machine Vision and Image Processing Conference. pp. 43–48 (2014)
7. Lazebnik, S., Schmid, C., Ponce, J.: Beyond bags of features: spatial pyramid matching for recognizing natural scene categories. In: IEEE Computer Society Conference on Computer Vision and Pattern Recognition, pp. 2169–2178 (2006)
8. Zhu, S.C., Guo, C.E., Wu, Y., Wang, Y.: What Are Textons? Int. J. Comput. Vision **62**, 101–143 (2005)
9. Haralick, R.M., Shanmugam, K.: DinsteinIts'shak: textural features for image classification. IEEE Trans. Syst. Man Cybern. **SMC-3**, 613–621 (1973)
10. Tamura, H., Mori, S., Yamawaki, T.: Textural features corresponding to visual perception. IEEE Trans. Syst. Man Cybern. **8**, 460–473 (1978)
11. Food & Environment Research Agency (FERA): Wheat Diseases: Non-disease, Septoria, and Yellow Rust. http://fera.co.uk/

Color Space Identification for Image Display

Martin Vezina[1], Djemel Ziou[1]([✉]), and Fatma Kerouh[2]

[1] Dept. Informatique, Univ. de Sherbrooke, Québec, Canada
`Djemel.Ziou@usherbrooke.ca`
[2] IGEE, Univ. M'Hamed Bougara de Boumerdès, Algiers, Algeria

Abstract. Available color images can be encoded in any color space. However, according to the image display model, it is assumed that the color image is encoded in a specific color space belonging to the RGB family. Displaying an encoded image in a color space by using a system designed for the display of encoded images in another color space leads to a poor reproduction of colors. To overcome this problem, the encoded image in a color space must be converted to the color space used by the display system. Unfortunately, the image color space can be not included in the image metadata and therefore it is unknown. Even if the display systems are massively used, this issue does not seem to be tackled before. In this paper, we propose the identification of the image color space from its colors. First, the Gamut of color spaces is estimated by using a collection of images. Then, the image color histogram is compared to the estimated Gamuts. The obtained identification scores using four color spaces and a collection of 2106 images are encouraging.

Keywords: Color image · Display system · Color space · Gamut

1 Introduction

The trichromatic and opponent color theories lead to the representation of the color in 3D space. Based on those theories, many 3D color spaces such as the RGB, LMS, XYZ, Lab, and HSI have been proposed. Some of them such as Lab and LMS are used to explain perceptual phenomena, while others such as RGB and XYZ are used in color reproduction systems. Requirements of the textile, display, cameras, and other industries requiring of high fidelity of colors lead to the design of various RGB color spaces such as ISO RGB, ROMM RGB, RGB adobe, Apple RGB, and sRGB. The printing have brought higher dimensional color space such as CMYK and RGBY. Note that beyond technology, animals color vision varies between the monochromacy and pentachromacy [1]. One important issue is the choice of a color space for a specific image processing or computer vision task. The answer involves knowing how scene features are represented in each color space. For example, how the distance difference in a given space is and how it is related to the color difference perceived by the human visual system. Knowing that the set of color spaces can be infinite (obviously, all are not physically realizable), the suitable color space selection

© Springer International Publishing Switzerland 2015
M. Kamel and A. Campilho (Eds.): ICIAR 2015, LNCS 9164, pp. 465–472, 2015.
DOI: 10.1007/978-3-319-20801-5_51

for any given task is not easy to implement. There exists some works about the selection and the evaluation of the color spaces in the case of chromatic adaptation, color matching, skin detection, and image segmentation. In chromatic adaptation, an encoded image in RGB color space is successively transformed to the LMS color space, and then to von Kries space, and finally to the RGB color space [2]. The scheme was revisited in order to replace LMS color space by a color space providing a better color adaptation [3,11,16]. Time and accuracy of color matching have been compared in five color spaces [4]. It has been shown theoretically that, the performance of skin detectors cannot be affected by the color space [6]. However, the experimentation has shown the opposite [5,7,9,10].

In this paper, we are interested in a different issue which is the identification of a given image color space. When acquiring the image, most cameras will save the color space name in the image file header. According to their life cycle, the output images are converted to other color spaces in order to be stored, displayed, exchanged, or processed. The color space of these images must be known before carrying out the conversion. For example, the display softwares are designed to display an encoded image in a specific RGB color space such as sRGB. Unfortunately, the color space in which an image is coded cannot be known because of the earlier manipulation operations it undergone. For example, many available conversion operations of image file format do not necessarily keep the metadata. It follows that, the identification of an image color space is necessary in order to faithfully reproduce colors. Figure 1 shows the same image encoded in six color spaces, saved in JPEG, and then displayed by using IrfanView. The first row is the encoded image in sRGB and the image of the difference between sRGB and AdobeRGB. This last image has been scaled in order to make explicit the differences between the two RGB-like color spaces. The differences between the other colors spaces is obvious. The identification of the color space is straightforward when the color space is a part of the image header. Unfortunately, as we mentioned before, sometimes the image metadata is lost. This is why, we propose to identify an image color space from its colors. The dimension, the white coordinates, the structure, the uniformity as well as the Gamut shape and volume of a color space can be relevant features for the identification. The estimation of some of these features is not so accurate to allow the discrimination. We then propose to use the Gamuts of color spaces estimated from a collection of images. The histogram of a given image is compared to the estimated Gamuts by using histogram intersection. The obtained identification scores using four color spaces and a collection of 2106 images are encouraging. Note that, the automatic identification of a given image color space does not seem to be tackled in the state of art. The next section is devoted to the proposed method. The experimental results are described in Sect. 3.

2   Proposed Model

A color space can be characterized by a set of attributes including the dimension, the range, the structure (i.e., linear, non-linear), the Gamut and the white

Fig. 1. The same image encoded in six different colors spaces, saved in JPEG, and displayed by using IrfanView. In the first row, the image in sRGB and the scaled difference image between sRGB and AdobeRGB, HSV and HLS (second row), and Lab and XYZ (third row)(Color figure online).

object seen under a standard light. For the color spaces like RGB and XYZ, primaries are also attributes. For example, the attributes of Adobe 98 RGB are 3D, 8 bits/dimension, linear, extended CRT, D65 while those of sRGB are 3D, 8 bits/dimension, CRT, D65. The reader can find the attributes of the standard RGB color spaces in [8]. One can think to estimate all these attributes from an image and use them for the color space identification. Unfortunately, to the best of our knowledge, there is no available algorithm for the estimation of primaries from real images. However, according to color matching paradigm, the estimation of the primaries from a given image can be achieved by the resolution of the following linear system: for the ith pixel, the color $c_i = M_i e$ where both the 3x3 matrix M_i and the primaries e are unknown. The estimation of the color space white can be carried out by using the illuminant estimation algorithm such as color by correlation [12]. The accuracy estimation lack of some of these attributes is not enough to discriminate between spaces. Algorithms for the estimation of the Gamut and related features have been already proposed [13]. However, most of them were not designed for the Gamut estimation from real images but from a set of predefined colors.

We argue that, the discrimination between color spaces of different families (e.g., RGB, Lab) does not require an accurate estimation of both the shape and the volume. We propose to use the shape of the three-dimensional color space Gamut. As our goal is to estimate the color space from a given image, we need to estimate the Gamut from real images, which is no other but the histogram of colors of image collection. In Fig. 3, we present the histograms of each band collected from a collection of 382 images encoded in four color spaces, that are sRGB, HSV, HLS, and Lab. It should be noted that, there is a difference between the histograms of any two color spaces. Moreover, the non interchangeability of bands can be of a great help for their identification. For example, the second band of HSV color space is the third band of the HLS color space. It follows that, in order to derive an efficient algorithm, the three bands are considered in the order defined by the standards and independent from each other. For the sake of reducing the computational complexity of the proposed algorithm, we opted for the assumption of independence. The image color space identification is seen as that of recovering the similarity between the color space of this image and the Gamuts estimated from a collection of images encoded in different color spaces.

Let us consider a set of color spaces C and a collection of images encoded in a color space $c \in C$. As we mentioned before, we consider that the histogram $h(b_1, b_2, b_3, c)$ of collection images is separable; that is $h(b_1, b_2, b_3, c) = h_1(b_1, c)h_2(b_2, c)h_3(b_3, c)$, where

$$h_k(b, c) = \frac{1}{|\mathcal{I}|} \sum_{n,m,i \in \mathcal{I}} \delta(I_{ic}(n, m) - b) \tag{1}$$

where $\mathcal{I}$ is a set of pixels of the image collection, $|\mathcal{I}|$ its size, I_{ic} the image encoded in the color space c, and δ the Kronecker delta. The histogram $h_k(b, s)$ of the test image is built using this equation where the set $\mathcal{I}$ is its pixels. The goal is then to find the unknown variable s which can take any value of the set C. Two important observations have to be noted. First, the collection size influences the identification accuracy. If $|\mathcal{I}|$ is too small the shape of the estimated Gamut will be too different from the shape of the true gamut and therefore the estimation error will be high. In Fig. 4, we present the histogram of the third band of each of the four color spaces (sRGB, HSV, HLS, Lab) build by using 67000, 1.0 million, 1.6 million pixels drawn randomly from the image collection. The collection size is therefore considered as a parameter which needs to be set by trial and error. Second, we assume that the shape of the Gamut estimated from a single image is relevant. This is one of the main outcomes of the paper, because we will show experimentally how valid is this assumption.

The identification is carried out by sorting the candidate Gamuts according to their similarity to the observed color space. The color space having the highest similarity is chosen. Several similarity measures between histograms have been already proposed. Among them, the histogram intersection was used with some success for image retrieval [15]. It can be written as:

$$s = argmin_c \sum_{k=1}^{3} sim(h_k(x, c), q_k(x, s))) \tag{2}$$

Where q_k is the histogram of the kth band of the test image, sim is the intersection between the two 1D histograms. Even if it seems simple, this rule needs

Fig. 2. A subset of images used for the experimentation.

further explanation. A classifier is associated with each band, where the normalized output is between 0 and 1. The three classifiers output mean is used for ranking. Note that, many classifier fusion rules exist. However, it was proven that the mean rule minimizes the misclassification error [14].

To summarize, the algorithm consists on building three 1D histograms of each color space by using an image collection. This operation is performed offline by using Eq. 1. Given a test image, its histogram is built by using the same equation. The identification of its color space is carried out by using Eq. 2. The computational complexity of the identification algorithm is $O(N \times M + 2^b)$, where b is the number of bits required to encode the largest intensity of the three bands.

3   Experimental Results

To validate the proposed method, we use two collections of real images; Col1 contains 382 images and Col2 1724 images. Example images from the two considered collections are presented in Fig. 2. The collection Col1 is used for the estimation of the Gamuts while Col2 is used for the test. Initially, both Col1 and Col2 are encoded in the sRGB color space. They are converted to HLS, HSV, and LAB by using the open source library OpenCV. As we explained earlier, an histogram per converted collection is computed by using one million pixels drawn at random from the set of all pixels of Col1. For the test purpose, the histogram of each image band of Col2 encoded in each of the color space is built. The identification of each test image color space is carried out as explained earlier. As the ground truth is available, the confusion matrix between color spaces is used as a measure of the algorithm accuracy. The four first columns and the four rows of the Table 1 presents the confusion matrix between the color spaces. The percentage of the correct identification is given in the last column. For example, 59 confusions between sRGB and HLS are noted and the percentage of correct identification of sRGB is 83.06 %. The easiest space to identify is the Lab and the most difficult one is the HLS. Note that, the proposed method is simple, efficient, and the obtained scores are promising. The computational time is 3.71 millisecond Pentium processor with 6 Gig memory for an image of 4000 × 3000 pixels using Matlab software.

Table 1. Confusion matrix

	sRGB	HSV	HLS	Lab	Percentage
sRGB	1432	191	59	42	83.06 %
HSV	149	1470	96	9	85.27 %
HLS	67	366	1275	16	73.96 %
Lab	25	0	0	1699	98.55 %

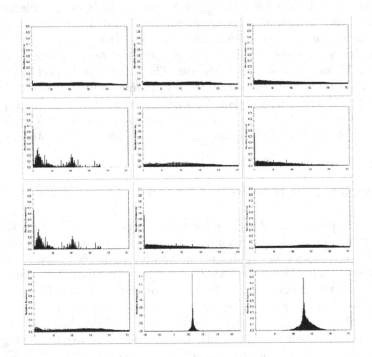

Fig. 3. The histogram of each band of the color spaces sRGB, HLS, HSV, and Lab.

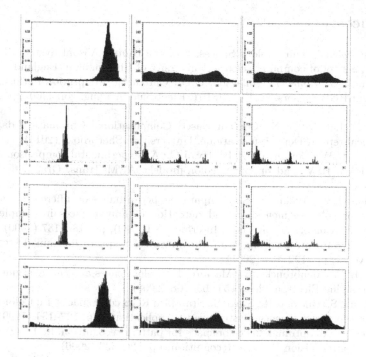

Fig. 4. The histogram of the third band of the four color spaces (sRGB, HSV, HLS, Lab) built by using 67000, 1.0 million, 1.6 million pixels drawn randomly from the image collection

4   Conclusion

Several color spaces exists and they are massively used. Available images can be encoded in any of these color spaces. Unfortunately, the color space of an image may not be in the metadata saved in the image header. However, the display systems are designed for the display of an encoded image in some specific color space. It follows that, improving the image quality display requires the identification of an image color space and its conversion to the display system color space. In this paper, we focus on the content based identification of the color space of a given image. The main idea is to compare the image histogram to the Gamuts of existing color spaces. The proposed method is simple, efficient, and promising in the case of color spaces of different families. However, the Gamut as we implemented seems to be insufficient for the discrimination between RGB-like spaces. These spaces may share several attributes such as the number of bits and the white. The consequences is that, the shape of Gamuts and the distribution of colors within the Gamuts are close. In further work, we will refine the Gamut estimation in 3D space without using the separability properties.

References

1. Cotton, S.D.: Colour, Colour Spaces, and the Human Visual System. Technical report, School of computer science, University of Birmingham, England (1995)
2. Süsstrunk, S., Holm, J., Finlayson, G.D.: Chromatic Adaptation Performance of Different RGB Sensors. In: IS&T/SPIE Electronic Imaging, vol. 4300, pp. 172–183 (2001)
3. Ziou, D., Lahmar, K.N.: Content Based Computational Chromatic Adaptation, Technical report, Dept. Informatique, Universit de Sherbrooke (2014)
4. Schwarz, M.W., Cowan, W.B., Beatty, J.C.: An experimental comparison of RGB, YIQ, LAB, HSV, and opponent color models. ACM Trans. Graph. **6**, 123–158 (1987)
5. Terrillon, J.-C., Akamatsu, S.: Comparative performance of different chrominance spaces for color segmentation and detection of human faces in complex scene images. In: Conference on Vision Interface (VI 1999), pp. 180–187 (2000)
6. Albiol, A., Torres, L., Delp, E.J.: Optimum color spaces for skin detection. In: ICIP, vol. 1, pp. 122–124 (2001)
7. Busin, L., Vandenbroucke, N., Macaire, L.: Color spaces and image segmentation. Adv. Imaging Electron Phys. **151**, 65–168 (2008)
8. Süsstrunk, S., Buckley, R., Swen, S.: Standard RGB color spaces. In: Color Imaging Conference: Color Science, Systems, and Applications, pp. 127–134 (1999)
9. Neagoe, V.: An optimum 2D color space for pattern recognition. In: Image Processing Computer Vision Pattern Recognition, pp. 526–532 (2006)
10. Filali, I., Ziou, D., Benblidia, N.: Multinomial bayesian kernel logistic discriminant based method for skin detection. In: SITIS, pp. 420–425 (2012)
11. Finlayson, G.D., Drew, M.S., Funt, B.V.: Spectral sharpening: sensor transformations for improved color constancy. JOSA A **11**, 1553–1563 (1994)
12. Finlayson, G.D., Hordley, S.D., Hubel, P.M.: Color by correlation: a simple, unifying framework for color constancy. IEEE TPAMI **23**, 1209–1221 (2001)
13. Morovic, J., Luo, M.R.: Calculating medium and image gamut boundaries for gamut mapping. Color Res. Appl. **25**, 394–401 (2000)
14. Terrades, O.R., Valveny, E., Tabbone, S.: Optimal classifier fusion in a non-bayesian probabilistic framework. IEEE TPAMI **31**, 1630–1644 (2009)
15. Lee, S.M., Xin, J.H., Westland, S.: Evaluation of image similarity by histogram intersection. Color Res. Appl. **30**(4), 265–274 (2005)
16. Madi, A., Ziou, D.: Color constancy for visual compensation of projector displayed image. Displays **36**, 6–17 (2014)

Application of the General Shape Analysis in Determining the Class of Binary Object Silhouettes in the Video Surveillance System

Katarzyna Gościewska[1,2]([✉]), Dariusz Frejlichowski[1], and Radosław Hofman[2]

[1] Szczecin, Faculty of Computer Science, West Pomeranian University of Technology, Żołnierska 52, 71-210 Szczecin, Poland
dfrejlichowski@wi.zut.edu.pl
[2] Smart Monitor sp. Z o.o., Niemierzyńska 17a, 71-441 Szczecin, Poland
{katarzyna.gosciewska,radekh}@smartmonitor.pl

Abstract. The paper discusses the problem of the General Shape Analysis (GSA) and considers an attempt to adapt this approach for binary silhouette analysis in the 'SM4Public' system. In the GSA, for a particular test shape, one or a few most similar, general templates are indicated. Shapes are represented using shape descriptors and representations are matched using similarity or dissimilarity measure. In the paper the GSA is explained and the application of the GSA in the 'SM4Public' system is investigated. Using a test dataset containing binary silhouettes of various objects (extracted from the 'SM4Public' video database) and selected shape description algorithms, an experiment was carried out. The aim of the experiment was to verify whether the GSA can be applied in the 'SM4Public' system as a solution for determining the class of binary silhouettes (as a preliminary classification).

1 Introduction

Shape of an object extracted from a digital image is considered as the most characteristic and distinguishable feature among other appearance-based features such as colour or texture. Information about a shape is low-dimensional what decreases the computational complexity of the shape analysis. It has to be taken into account that an object's silhouette on the video sequence can be deformed, occluded or distorted by noise [1]. Nevertheless, minor changes resulted from noise should not influence the possibility of shape recognition—affine transformations (i.e. scaling, translation or rotation) may occur, since they do not influence the original shape [2].

Depending on the task, the shape analysis can be very detailed, like in case of the identification, or more coarse, what is a base of the General Shape Analysis. In this approach shapes are processed similarly to the traditional recognition or retrieval, but at the more general level. The exact recognition or identification are not performed, but for each of the processed objects a general class is indicated. Each general class is represented by one general shape, e.g. a triangle, circle or

© Springer International Publishing Switzerland 2015
M. Kamel and A. Campilho (Eds.): ICIAR 2015, LNCS 9164, pp. 473–480, 2015.
DOI: 10.1007/978-3-319-20801-5_52

rectangle. Originally ten classes are used, each represented by one general template, and a larger group of test objects which are more diversified shapes. In the GSA each test object is matched with all templates in order to indicate one or a few most similar general templates. For matching purposes the similarity or dissimilarity measure is employed. Moreover, shapes are matched based on their representations—shape descriptors—obtained using a particular shape description algorithm. The GSA process results in the extraction of predominant shape features which can enable simple separation or reduction of the data subjected e.g. to an exact identification at a later stage.

Besides GSA there is another approach to the analysis of an objects' general shape. It was introduced by Paul Rosin and uses global shape measures which describe a region using a single value [2–4]. Global shape measures are based on the deviation of a processed shape from the best matching perfect instance of this shape. Additionally, if a region is described by a significantly large combination of shape measures, then it would enable to discriminate one shape from another. The main goal of a global shape measure is to capture a general shape class, therefore the similarity of this idea to the GSA is obvious.

In the paper we discuss an attempt to introduce the General Shape Analysis procedure in the 'SM4Public' system for the purpose of distinguishing between several classes based on object silhouettes. The main goal of the research is to find out which general shapes can be used to represent a particular test object class and to verify if, by using sets of general shapes, the class separation can be performed. The mentioned 'SM4Public' system is now being developed within the framework of the EU co-founded project and is aimed at the creation and implementation of an innovative system prototype that will enable automatic analysis of public spaces where busy environments with multiple objects are observed.

The rest of the paper is organized as follows. The second section describes the GSA and shape description algorithms that have been employed so far. The third section explains the idea of the experiments and discusses the obtained results, while the last section concludes the paper.

2   The General Shape Analysis: Definition, Applications and Employed Shape Descriptors

The General Shape Analysis is a problem similar to the traditional recognition or retrieval of shapes but with some significant differences. In the GSA a small group of templates (simple shapes, e.g. triangle or rectangle) and a larger group of more complicated test shapes are analysed. By finding one or few most similar templates for each test object it is possible to determine the general information about it, e.g. how rectangular or triangular it is. In order to estimate the similarity between particular objects, their representations obtained using shape description algorithms are matched by means of the template matching approach—the idea is to represent all shapes in the same way and to compare each test object with every template using similarity or dissimilarity measure.

The GSA problem has been discussed in the literature repeatedly and a variety of shape description algorithms have been investigated. For instance in [5] the Two-Dimensional Fourier Descriptor, UNL-Fourier Descriptor and Point Distance Histogram were employed. The first mentioned benefits from frequency domain, whereas the latter two are polar transform-based shape description algorithms. These two methods—similarly to the Generic Fourier Descriptor that has also been employed in the GSA—produce shape representations invariant to translation within an image plane, and changeable object scale if normalization is performed. Another group of applied methods are moment-based descriptors, namely Moment Invariants, Contour Sequence Moments and Zernike Moments.

Originally in the GSA shapes were matched using the Euclidean distance. Moreover, a specific method for the estimation of experimental effectiveness was employed, namely the results of the experiments were compared with human benchmark results, collected by means of inquiry forms, and the percentage coincidence between benchmark and experimental results gave the final effectiveness value. Thanks to that the best solution could be indicated.

Further publications concerned the experimental investigation of other solutions to the GSA problem or modifications of the original approach. For example in [6] the use of the correlation coefficient instead of the Euclidean distance was proposed. In [7] three Fourier Transform-based shape description algorithms were investigated and used to produce multiple shape descriptors of different size. In turn in [8] the possibility of using various measurements and shape factors based on the Minimum Bounding Rectangle method was studied. The original GSA test dataset is presented in Fig. 1. There are 50 various shapes stored as 200×200 binary images—10 templates (first row) and 40 test objects. For the purpose of our experiment we utilized the same template set. These templates have always been used in the GSA problem and are considered as a basic standard.

There are some practical applications of the GSA given in the literature. For instance in [9] it was used for the recognition of stamp types. The proposed solution included the detection, localisation and extraction of stamps from scanned documents stored in digital form. The aim of stamp recognition is to avoid printing the falsified document copies and can be considered as a coarse classification

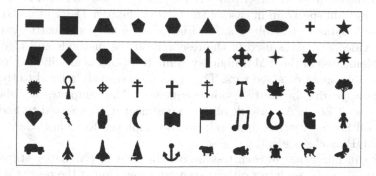

Fig. 1. The original GSA test data set—templates are given in the first row.

preceding the detailed analysis of the text on the stamp. Another application is the coarse separation of the data to initially reduce the number of shapes subjected to more detailed recognition or identification. The GSA can also be applied to iteratively search multimedia databases using voice commands, e.g. 'find yellow circular object' [5].

The use of the General Shape Analysis in the 'SM4Public' system can cover the analysis of foreground objects, extraction of general features, preliminary separation or coarse classification of silhouettes to four main classes: people, cats, dogs and cars. As can be seen, the General Shape Analysis utilizes various shape description algorithms which are popular in the image analysis and shape recognition tasks. Based on the literature review we have decided to experimentally investigate six shape description algorithms, namely Two-Dimensional Fourier Descriptor [5], Generic Fourier Descriptor [10], UNL-Fourier Descriptor [11], Zernike Moments [12], Point Distance Histogram [13] and Moment Invariants [14], along with the Euclidean distance as a dissimilarity measure. If possible, several shape descriptor versions were prepared using a particular algorithm. More detailed explanation of the selected methods along with the appropriate formulas can be found in the given literature sources.

3   Experimental Conditions and Results

In order to verify the possibility of incorporating the General Shape Analysis approach into the 'SM4Public' system we have prepared an experiment divided into several tests. In each case one variant of the shape description algorithm was used and representations of all test objects and templates were obtained. Then each test object representation was matched with all template representations using Euclidean distance. Finally, as an experimental result, three most similar (less distant) templates were indicated for each test object. The following variants of shape description algorithms were used: original Moment Invariants (MI, 7 values); full representation of the UNL-Fourier Descriptor (UNL-F); 2nd, 5th and 10th order of Zernike Moments (ZM); 2, 5 and 10 histogram bins in Point Distance Histogram (PDH); 2×2, 5×5 and 10×10 spectrum subparts for the Two-Dimensional Fourier Descriptor (2DFD); 2×2, 5×5 and 10×10 spectrum subparts and full spectrum in case of the Generic Fourier Descriptor (GFD).

The test dataset (test objects, see Fig. 2) are binary silhouettes extracted from the video sequences used in the research on the methods and algorithms to be implemented in the 'SM4Public' system. Test objects are divided into four classes: people, dogs, cats and cars. The classes are directly related to the types of objects appearing in the test video sequences. The templates are shown in the first row of Fig. 1. As a result of the experiment it is expected to find out if the General Shape Analysis approach can be employed for coarse classification in the 'SM4Public' system.

Having in mind that in each test we obtain a set of templates—three most similar templates for each test object—the interpretation of the results is a little problematic. Due to the fact that the proposed approach is atypical and there

Fig. 2. Test objects—95 object silhouettes used in the experiments.

is no benchmark for comparison, some elements have to be analysed jointly. Therefore, three aspects have to be taken into consideration: test shapes, classes and shape descriptors (where a shape descriptor is a variant of the representation obtained using a particular shape description algorithm). According to that, and by choosing the most frequently occurring template, the results can be analysed in three ways:

1. For all shape descriptors jointly and each test object separately, what gives information about percentage similarity of a test object to all templates (see Fig. 3 for examples);
2. For all shape descriptors, for all test objects and for each class separately, what gives information about percentage similarity of templates to all objects in a particular class (Fig. 4);
3. For all test objects, for each class separately and for each shape descriptor separately, what gives information about a possibility of class separation based on a set of templates resulted from the particular test (Fig. 5; in three cases it was impossible to extract the most frequent template due to the fact that at least two templates have the same percentage frequency of occurrences).

Several conclusions can be made based on the first and second interpretation, and the results given in Figs. 3 and 4:

- Human silhouettes are most similar to a star, cross and rectangle;
- Star and cross templates are common in case of people, dogs and cats;
- Car silhouettes are most frequently considered similar to ellipse, trapeze and rectangle;

	—	■	▲	⬟	⬟	△	●	⬬	+	★
(object)	0%	7%	29%	7%	11%	2%	9%	29%	2%	4%
(object)	18%	0%	2%	11%	2%	7%	2%	2%	27%	29%
(object)	20%	0%	2%	9%	7%	2%	2%	4%	24%	29%

Fig. 3. Percentage similarity of exemplary test objects to all templates.

	—	■	▲	⬟	⬟	△	●	⬬	+	★
Cars	14%	4%	15%	8%	6%	8%	5%	19%	8%	12%
Cats	18%	0%	5%	11%	3%	8%	3%	4%	23%	25%
Dogs	20%	0%	8%	12%	5%	15%	2%	7%	11%	18%
People	19%	2%	5%	9%	4%	8%	2%	8%	20%	24%

Fig. 4. The occurrence frequency of templates in each class.

- Objects with protruding elements, like legs, arms or paws are mostly considered similar to a star or cross;
- The most frequently indicated templates for dogs are ellipse, trapeze and rectangle.

Figure 5 contains a table with the pictorial interpretation of the results according to the third approach. Three most frequently occurring templates were indicated. It can be seen that in most cases the resulted templates in each class are common with the templates indicated in the table illustrated in Fig. 4. We can also observe significant discrepancies between sets of templates, depending on the applied shape descriptor. This may result from the fact that various shape description algorithms are based on different shape characteristics. However, in case of shape descriptors, there are also some similarities. For example, considering a class of cats, all variants of 2DFD and GFD indicated almost the same templates. Moreover, if a set of templates with preserved order will be used, then, in case of the full representation of the GFD, cats and dogs could be distinguished. In addition, some predominant characteristics of object classes can be concluded.

Ultimately, considering all tests, it is not possible to classify objects based only on the selected templates. However, there is a possibility that if some changes in the pre-assumed conditions will be made, then the results would be more unambiguous and useful. For instance, we can eliminate some less frequently occurring templates or increase the number of test objects in the dataset, or employ other set of shape descriptors. The potential in this type of analysis can be seen, but some improvements could be implemented.

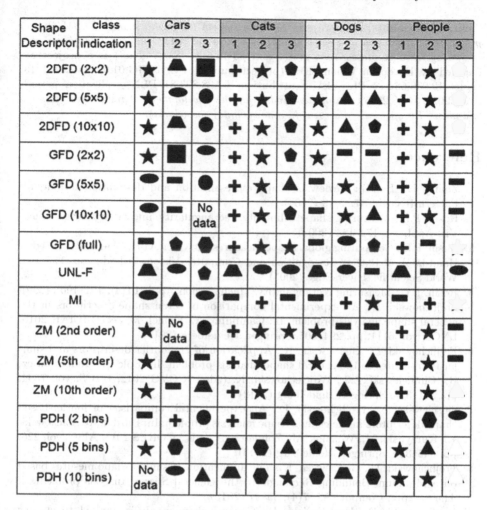

Fig. 5. The most frequently occurring templates in each class.

4   Summary and Conclusions

In the paper, the problem of the General Shape Analysis was discussed and an attempt to introduce this approach to the 'SM4Public' system has been made. It was proposed that the GSA can be applied as a method for the indication of the object's general class or extraction of predominant features. The initial results give us some general rules, however more effective solution is needed. Hence, future work on the problem is necessary. It is possible that after some modifications the analysis of general shape can be introduced to some extent to the system.

Acknowledgments. The project *"Security system for public spaces — 'SM4Public'*
prototype construction and implementation" (original title: *Budowa i wdrożenie pro-*
totypu systemu bezpieczeństwa przestrzeni publicznej 'SM4Public') is a project co-
founded by European Union (EU) (project number PL: POIG.01.04.00-32-244/13,
value: 12.936.684,77 PLN, EU contribution: 6.528.823,81 PLN, realization period:
01.06.2014–31.10.2015). *European Funds—for the development of innovative economy*
(*Fundusze Europejskie—dla rozwoju innowacyjnej gospodarki*).

References

1. Zhang, D., Lu, G.: Review of shape representation and description techniques.
   Pattern Recogn. **37**, 1–19 (2004)
2. Rosin, P.L.: Measuring shape: ellipticity, rectangularity, and triangularity. Mach.
   Vis. Appl. **14**, 172–184 (2003)
3. Rosin, P.L.: Computing global shape measures. In: Chen, C.H., Wang, P.S.P. (eds.)
   Hand-book of Pattern Recognition and Computer Vision, 3rd edn, pp. 177–196.
   World Scientific, River Edge (2005)
4. Rosin, P.L.: Measuring rectangularity. Mach. Vision Appl. **11**(4), 191–196 (1999)
5. Frejlichowski, D.: An experimental comparison of seven shape descriptors in the
   general shape analysis problem. In: Campilho, A., Kamel, M. (eds.) ICIAR 2010.
   LNCS, vol. 6111, pp. 294–305. Springer, Heidelberg (2010)
6. Frejlichowski, D., Gościewska, K.: Application of 2D fourier descriptors and similarity measures to the general shape analysis problem. In: Bolc, L., Tadeusiewicz,
   R., Chmielewski, L.J., Wojciechowski, K. (eds.) ICCVG 2012. LNCS, vol. 7594,
   pp. 371–378. Springer, Heidelberg (2012)
7. Gościewska, K., Frejlichowski, D.: An experimental comparison of fourier-based
   shape descriptors in the general shape analysis problem. In: Burduk, R., Jackowski,
   K., Kurzynski, M., Wozniak, M., Zolnierek, A. (eds.) CORES 2013. AISC, vol. 226,
   pp. 345–354. Springer, Heidelberg (2013)
8. Frejlichowski, D., Gościewska, K.: The application of simple shape mesures based
   on a Minimum Bounding Rectangle to the General Shape Analysis problem. J.
   Theor. Appl. Comput. Sci. **7**(4), 35–41 (2013)
9. Frejlichowski, D., Forczmański, P.: General shape analysis applied to stamps
   retrieval from scanned documents. In: Dicheva, D., Dochev, D. (eds.) AIMSA 2010.
   LNCS, vol. 6304, pp. 251–260. Springer, Heidelberg (2010)
10. Zhang, D., Lu, G.: Shape-based image retrieval using generic fourier descriptor.
    Sig. Process. Image **17**(10), 825–848 (2002)
11. Rauber, T.W.: Two-dimensional shape description. Technical report: GR
    UNINOVA-RT-10-94, Universidade Nova de Lisboa (1994)
12. Wee, C.-Y., Paramesran, R.: On the computational aspects of Zernike moments.
    Image Vis. Comput. **25**(6), 967–980 (2007)
13. Frejlichowski, D.: Trademark recognition using PDH shape descriptor. Ann. Univ.
    Mariae Curie-Sklodowska, Sectio: Informatica **8**(1), 67–73 (2008)
14. Hu, M.K.: Visual pattern recognition by moment invariants. IRE Trans. Inf. Theor.
    8, 179–187 (1962)

Speedy Character Line Detection Algorithm Using Image Block-Based Histogram Analysis

Chinthaka Premachandra[1]([✉]), Katsunari Goto[2], Shinji Tsuruoka[2],
Hiroharu Kawanaka[3], and Haruhiko Takase[3]

[1] Department of Electrical Engineering, Graduate School of Engineering,
Tokyo University of Science, 6-3-1 Niijuku,
Katsushika-ku, Tokyo 125-8585, Japan
chinthaka@ee.kagu.tus.ac.jp
[2] Graduate School of Regional Innovation Studies, Mie University,
Tsu, Mie, Japan
[3] Graduate School of Engineering, Mie University, Tsu, Mie, Japan

Abstract. Academic institutions such as universities and technical colleges usually employ paper-based examinations and reports to evaluate the academic performance of students. Consequently, teachers expend considerable time and energy in the marking of such paper-based examinations. We are developing an automatic paper marking system geared towards reducing this paper-marking burden on teachers. To execute paper marking, handwritten character lines are extracted from examination papers, and then characters on those lines are recognized. In this paper, we primarily discuss how the character line is extracted from handwritten examination papers without ruled lines. The extraction of character lines from non-ruled papers is difficult because of the writing characteristic of students. Further, extraction accuracy is an important factor in character recognition performance. Conventional character line extraction algorithms for printed documents perform poorly on this problem. Furthermore, most proposed methods conduct tests using document images that include only character lines. In this paper we develop a less time-consuming algorithm for this task.

Keywords: Examination paper · Character line · Document image analysis · Figure detection

1 Introduction

Various kinds of paper-based examinations are employed in academic institutions such as universities and technical colleges to evaluate the academic performance of students. In Japan, examinees are provided with answer sheets in most of these kinds of examinations. The answer sheets provided are of two types: marking sheets and writing sheets. The former is a special mark sheet or OCR sheet and can be marked automatically by current automatic marking systems. For example, these marking sheets are used in most university entrance examinations under the auspices of the National Center for University Entrance Examinations in Japan. In such examinations, examinees mark on the paper and grading is conducted automatically. The latter type of sheet

M. Kamel and A. Campilho (Eds.): ICIAR 2015, LNCS 9164, pp. 481–488, 2015.
DOI: 10.1007/978-3-319-20801-5_53

requires handwritten answers and cannot be marked automatically by current character recognition software. Current character recognition software can recognize most printed characters with high accuracy; however, their accuracy with handwritten characters is inadequate. Consequently, handwritten document recognition is a significant problem in Japanese document analysis. A very important factor that can help to achieve accurate character recognition of handwritten documents such as examination sheets is character line extraction.

Figure 1 shows a sample image of a handwritten examination sheet. The sheet comprises multiple character lines, but those lines are not straight. The complexity of the structure of the document varies according to the writing style of the examinee. An automatic marking system that is able to accurately process these kinds of handwritten examination papers is one of the most desired practical applications in the Japanese education system.

Currently, most teachers expend considerable time and energy marking examination papers. The development of an automatic marking system for such handwritten examination papers would reduce the burden on these teachers. The results of surveys conducted indicate that most teachers desire automatic marking of non-ruled paper-based examination papers. Consequently, we are currently conducting studies on automatic marking of non-ruled handwritten examination papers. As stated above, character line detection is an important stage in this project. As a consequence, this paper focuses on the problems besetting handwritten character line extraction. Conventional methods found in the literature for character line extraction [1–7] are very

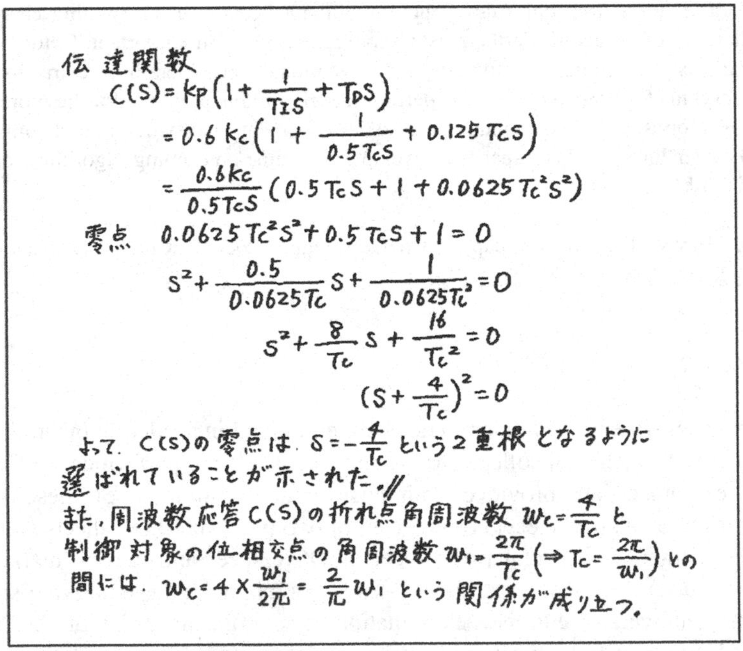

伝達関数
$$C(S) = K_P \left(1 + \frac{1}{T_I S} + T_D S\right)$$
$$= 0.6 k_c \left(1 + \frac{1}{0.5 T_c S} + 0.125 T_c S\right)$$
$$= \frac{0.6 k_c}{0.5 T_c S} \left(0.5 T_c S + 1 + 0.0625 T_c^2 S^2\right)$$

零点 $0.0625 T_c^2 S^2 + 0.5 T_c S + 1 = 0$
$$S^2 + \frac{0.5}{0.0625 T_c} S + \frac{1}{0.0625 T_c^2} = 0$$
$$S^2 + \frac{8}{T_c} S + \frac{16}{T_c^2} = 0$$
$$\left(S + \frac{4}{T_c}\right)^2 = 0$$

よって、$C(S)$の零点は、$S = -\frac{4}{T_c}$ という2重根となるように
選ばれていることが示された。//
また、周波数応答 $C(S)$ の折れ点角周波数 $w_c = \frac{4}{T_c}$ と
制御対象の位相交点の角周波数 $w_1 = \frac{2\pi}{T_c}$ $\left(\Rightarrow T_c = \frac{2\pi}{w_1}\right)$ との
間には、$w_c = 4 \times \frac{w_1}{2\pi} = \frac{2}{\pi} w_1$ という関係が成り立つ。

Fig. 1. Handwritten examination paper image

time-consuming. Furthermore, they are usually tested using only document images with character lines and figure, and no consideration is given to character line classification. In this paper, figure extraction is first conducted using one of our previously proposed methods [3]. Then, a simple and less time-consuming algorithm is proposed for character line extraction. The proposed algorithm extracts character lines via image block-based horizontal histogram analysis. Tests conducted of the proposed algorithm using appropriate handwritten examination papers indicate that its computational time is faster than that of conventional methods. Furthermore, it exhibits good character line extraction performance.

The remainder of this paper is organized as follows. Section 2 discusses previous approaches to handwritten character line extraction. Section 3 presents the details of our proposed approach. Section 4 presents and discusses experimental results obtained. Finally, Sect. 5 concludes and outlines plans for further work in this project.

2   Previous Studies on Character Line Detection

Several studies have been conducted on character line extraction of printed documents and blackboard images.

Adachi et al. [1] and Tsuruoka et al. [2] proposed a method that uses a thinning approach to detect character lines. In their proposed method, all characters are thinned and their gravity points then used to detect character lines. Unfortunately, experience has taught us that these methods require more than 40 s to process a single image. Consequently, they are not appropriate for real time applications. Hirabayashi et al. [3] proposed an interesting method that detects character lines via the Hough Transform (HT). In the proposed method, the gravity points of characters are detected and then HT is used to detect the character lines. However, this method is very time-consuming because of the voting-based processing utilized by HT. In addition, it cannot be used to detect handwritten curved character lines because classical HT cannot detect randomly curved lines. However, it exhibits good performance in the detection of printed character lines. Louloudisa et al. [4] proposed a multi-step method: The first step in the proposed method comprises image binarization and enhancement, connected component extraction, partitioning of the connected component domain into three spatial sub-domains, and average character height estimation. In the second step, a block-based HT is then used to detect potential text lines. A third step is employed to correct possible splitting, detect text lines that the previous step did not reveal, and finally, to separate vertically connected characters and assign them to text lines. This method is also very time-consuming because connected component detection and HT typically require considerable time for computation. Chaudhuri et al. [5] proposed a method that detects character lines by following the gap between two lines. The method is interesting; however, it has difficulty detecting character lines with high accuracy when the gap between two lines is very small. Yin and Liu [7] proposed an approach to character line detection based on minimum spanning tree (MST) clustering with new distance measures. First, the connected components of the document image are grouped into a tree by MST clustering with a new distance measure. The edges of the tree are then dynamically cut to form text lines using a new objective function to find the number of clusters. This method also includes time-consuming connected component analysis. In particular, connected component analysis takes time to process large document images. More recently, Khayya et al. [8] proposed detection of handwritten text lines by applying an adaptive mask to morphological dilation. This method first identifies the characteristics of the document and its connected components to set the parameters and thresholds of the algorithm. The final smearing of the document is then decided by the dynamic mask. The recursive function *separateLines(blob)* plays an important role in the method as it breaks up blobs according to the attraction and repulsion of the text within those blobs. This is also an interesting idea; however, it is also time-consuming because of the connected component analysis process.

The approaches cited above consider character line detection of documents that include only characters. In addition, they require at least 20 s to process a 744 × 1053 pixel document image. This paper proposes a method that reduces the character line detection time by analyzing block-based histograms because histogram calculation is a very simple process.

3   Proposed Method

3.1   Figure Extraction

In the method proposed in this paper, we extract figures from the image before conducting character line extraction. We use a simple method [3] in which the maximum rectangle of each object in the image is generated in accordance with their aspects, as illustrated in Fig. 2. Figure 2(a) and (b) are the original image and its maximum rectangle calculation image, respectively. Following this calculation, the rectangles larger than a certain threshold are extracted as figures, as depicted in Fig. 2(c).

3.2   Character Line Extraction Algorithm

We propose a new, less time-consuming algorithm that is completely different from that of previous methods. In the new algorithm, character lines are extracted by

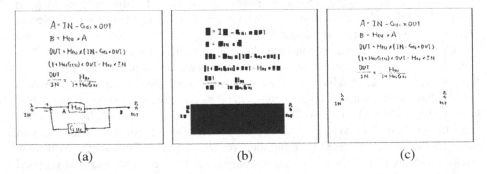

(a)   (b)   (c)

Fig. 2. Figure extraction: (a) original image, (b) maximum rectangle calculation, and (c) result of figure extraction.

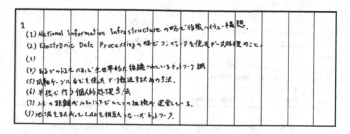

Fig. 3. Examination paper divided into blocks

calculating the horizontal histograms of vertical image blocks. The details of the proposed algorithm are as follows.

First, the examination paper image is divided into n ($n = 12$) vertical image blocks (Fig. 3). The process then counts the number of black pixels in the horizontal direction (horizontal distribution of the pixel) in each domain and a histogram is generated, as shown in Fig. 4. The horizontal pixel counting of a single line $h_{c,1}$ is summarized in Eq. 1. In the equation, w indicates the width of a domain while f_i indicates the scanning pixel.

$$h_{c,1} = \sum_{i=0}^{w} f_i \quad \begin{cases} f_i = 1\,(black\ pixels) \\ f_i = 0\,(white\ pixels) \end{cases} \tag{1}$$

As Fig. 4 illustrates, the histogram appears with horizontal mountains. The peak of each mountain is determined and all peaks are plotted on image domain borders, as illustrated in Fig. 5—in which the vertical coordinate of the peak values are plotted.

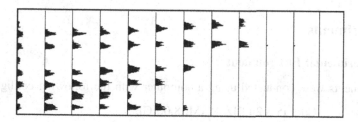

Fig. 4. Counting the number of black pixels

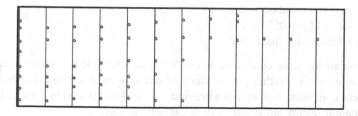

Fig. 5. Extracting the maximum value of the number of black pixels

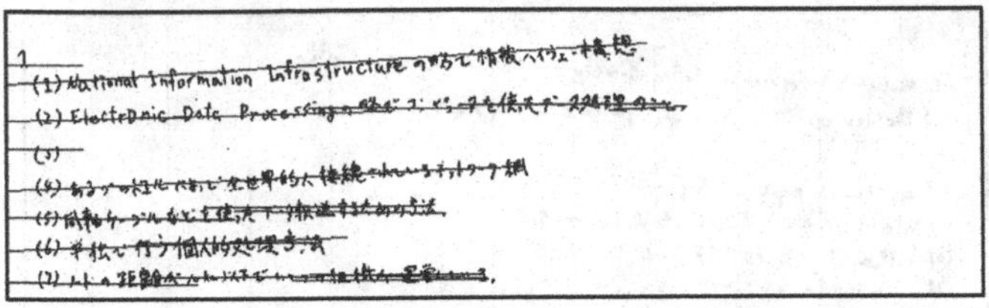

Fig. 6. Extracted straight line from the character line

Horizontal straight lines are then determined by using the plotted coordinates. The plotted coordinates are tracked from left to right keeping an almost constant direction. The initial direction is determined using the first two points tracked. After completing a vertical tracking, a straight line equation is determined by using the first and last points in the tracking. A point pair is indicated as (x_1, y_1), (x_2, y_2). Then, determination of a straight line equation can be conducted following Eqs. (2), (3), and (4). The character area is extracted by detecting the corresponding pixels to create the histogram peak of each image block. Figure 6 illustrates the detected lines of the image shown in Fig. 3.

$$y = ax + b \tag{2}$$

$$a = \frac{y_2 - y_1}{x_2 - x_1} \tag{3}$$

$$b = \frac{x_1 y_2 - y_1 x_2}{1 - x_2} \tag{4}$$

4   Experiments

4.1   Experimental Environment

All experiments were conducted using a computer with the following configuration:

Windows 8.1, Core i5 3.2 GHz, RAM: 8.00 GB
Programing Language: C#

The images used in the tests had the following specifications:

Handwritten examination papers: 34
Image Size: 744 × 1053 pixels
Number of character lines: 802

The experiments were conducted to confirm character line extraction performance and processing time reduction performance of our proposed method. Further, its performance was compared with that of a previous method mentioned in Sect. 2. Details of the experimental results are given in the next sub-section.

4.2   Experimental Results

Figures 7 and 8 show the character line extraction results obtained using the proposed method. The left side image in each figure is the original image while the image on the right denotes the extracted character lines.

Table 1 shows the character line extraction rate of the proposed method and the method proposed by Yin and Liu [6]. The average processing time of the proposed method is 2.7 s. The results indicate that our proposed method has better character line extraction and processing time performance than that of Yin and Liu.

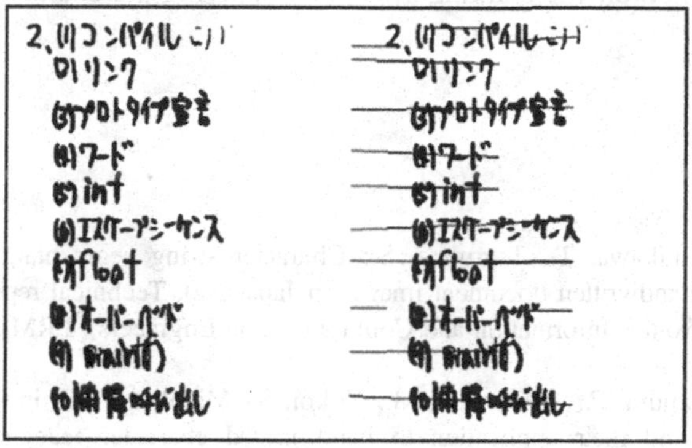

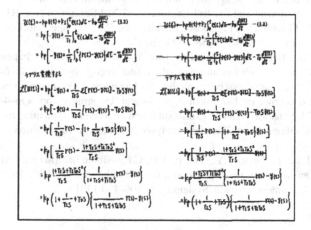

Fig. 7. Character line extraction result

Fig. 8. Character line extraction result

Table 1. Comparison of Extracted Character Lines

Method	Character line extraction rate [%]	False positive rate [%]	Average processing time [s]
Yin and Liu [6]	89.1	10.0	41.6
Proposed method	91.1	1.2	2.7

5 Conclusions

In this paper, we proposed a new and simple method that utilizes image block histogram analysis to conduct character line extraction from handwritten examination papers. Evaluations conducted of the proposed method using appropriate images of paper-based handwritten reports and examination documents indicate that it has a better processing time performance than a previously proposed method. It also showed better character line extraction performance than that of the previous method.

In the future, we plan to further improve the character line extraction rate. We also plan to develop an automatic marking system by applying the character line extraction approach.

References

1. Adachi, Y., Yoshikawa, T., Tsuruoka, S.: Character string segmentation using thinning algorithm from handwritten document image (in Japanese), Technical report of IEICE (The Institute of Electronics Information and Communication Engineers), PRMU98-208, pp. 121–126 (1999)
2. Tsuruoka, S., Kimura, F., Yoshimura, M., Yokoi, S., Miyake, Y.: Thinning algorithms for digital pictures and their application to hand-printed character recognition. Trans. Inst. Electron. Inf. Commun. Eng. (IEICE) Inf. Syst. **J66-D**(5), 525–532 (1983)
3. Hirabayashi, K., Tsuruoka, S., Kawanaka, H., Takase, H., Ozaki, T.: Character line segmentation from blackboard image using hough transform. In: Proceedings of Mie Section of the Society of Instrument and Control Engineers (SICE-Mie), pp. B11-1–B11-4 (2008)
4. Louloudisa, G., Gatosb, B., Pratikakisb, I., Halatsisa, C.: Text line detection in handwritten documents. Pattern Recogn. **41**, 3758–3772 (2008)
5. Chaudhuri, B.B., Bera, S.: Handwritten text line identification In: Indian Scripts, 10th International Conference on Document Analysis and Recognition, pp. 636–640 (2009)
6. Yin, F., Liu, C.L.: A variational bayes method for handwritten text line segmentation. In: 10th International Conference on Document Analysis and Recognition, pp. 436–440 (2009)
7. Yin, F., Liu, C.L.: Handwritten text extraction based on minimum spanning tree clustering. In: International Conference on Wavelet Analysis and Pattern Recognition, pp. 1123–1128 (2007)
8. Khayyat, M., Lam, L., Suen, C.Y., Yin, F., Liu, C.L.: Arabic handwritten text line extraction by applying an adaptive mask to morphological dilation. In: 10th IAPR International Workshop on Document Analysis Systems, pp. 100–104 (2012)

Detecting Parked Vehicles in Static Images Using Simple Spectral Features in the 'SM4Public' System

Dariusz Frejlichowski[1]([⊠]), Katarzyna Gościewska[1,2], Adam Nowosielski[1], Paweł Forczmański[1], and Radosław Hofman[2]

[1] Faculty of Computer Science and Information Technology, West Pomeranian University of Technology, Szczecin, Żołnierska 52, 71-210 Szczecin, Poland
{dfrejlichowski,anowosielski,pforczmanski}@wi.zut.edu.pl
[2] Smart Monitor Sp. Z o.o., Niemierzynska 17a,
71-441 Szczecin, Poland
{katarzyna.gosciewska,radekh}@smartmonitor.pl

Abstract. In the paper, the use of selected algorithms for the detection of specific objects and extraction of their characteristics from static images is presented. The problem concerns the selection of algorithms to be implemented in the 'SM4Public' security system for public spaces and is focused on specific system working scenario: detecting vehicles parked in restricted areas. Two popular feature extractors based on the Discrete Cosine Transform and Discrete Fourier Transform were experimentally tested. The paper contains the description of the 'SM4Public' system, explanation of the problem and presentation of similar solutions given in the literature. The stress is put on the definition of the employed feature extractors and the description of the experimental results.

1 Introduction

This paper concerns the scientific research on the algorithms to be implemented in the prototype 'SM4Public' system. The system is now being developed within the framework of EU co-founded project and is aimed at construction and implementation of innovative video content analysis-based system prototype that will ensure the safety of various public spaces using real-time solutions and typical computer components. The idea of the project was risen during the development of the previous system entitled 'SmartMonitor' [1–4]—an intelligent security system based on image analysis, created for individual customers and home use. The analysis of alternative system applications has shown that there is a need to build other solution for public space video surveillance to effectively detect events threatening public safety, especially in places characterized by simultaneous movement of large number of people.

The complexity of captured scenes along with a variety of places, events and objects under video surveillance make it impossible to create a universal solution that would be equally effective in all cases. For this reason such system should be

M. Kamel and A. Campilho (Eds.): ICIAR 2015, LNCS 9164, pp. 489–498, 2015.
DOI: 10.1007/978-3-319-20801-5_54

highly customizable and offer features enabling adaptation of system operation. In other words, it should be possible to implement different working scenarios. According to that, 'SM4Public' system will be able to work under scenarios specific for public spaces, such as scenarios associated with vehicle traffic (e.g. failing to stop at the red light, accident detection), infrastructure protection (e.g. devastation or theft detection), breaking the law (e.g. drinking alcohol in public spaces, prohibited in many countries) or treats to life or health (e.g. a fall). In the paper we propose an algorithmic solution to be implemented for the another scenario concerning the detection of vehicles parked in restricted areas.

In the paper, the problem of object detection in static scenes is investigated using two popular feature extractors, based on the Discrete Cosine Transform and Discrete Fourier Transform. The second section contains the description of the problem and lists some related publications. The third section briefly presents employed algorithms. In the fourth section the experimental conditions and results are given, and the last section concludes the paper.

2   Problem Statement

In some public areas, i.e. pavements, roads or parking, we can observe diverse movements of people and vehicles. In such places it is important that the movement should comply with the traffic regulations in order to avoid accidents, traffic congestion and impeding the movement of other people and vehicles. Nowadays, one can often encounter problems with parking spaces, which can lead people to stop vehicles improperly or on restricted areas, and simultaneously breaking the law. By using a system with a scenario detecting improperly parked vehicles we can facilitate the work of the police and the movement of the other road users.

Despite the need for real-time complex solutions we should not forget about the capabilities of those less complicated. The type of monitored scene can determine the occurrence probability of specific objects or the limitation of the scene area under analysis. By employing Visual Content Analysis algorithms we aim at automatic detection and differentiation of vehicles in restricted areas. The considered scenario do not require complex calculations and high computational power, and is characterized by a high detection rate and a small error probability. Therefore, it is possible to perform static image analysis with a time interval of a few or more seconds—the analysis of static scenes with given time interval may enable the analysis of even tens of frames on a single central unit.

The task of extracting specific objects from a static scene involves the determination of the image part containing the searched object. This process has two steps: object detection and object localization. The main problem with the detection of objects from static images is an appropriate selection of characteristic features (i.e. building an object model), the mechanism of feature matching and the method for scanning the source image. The detection problem presented in the literature assumes the absence of information about the object under detection—the probable object size and location are unknown. Additional difficulties result from changes in scene lighting and appearance of objects (e.g. various vehicle silhouettes shape and colour, see Fig. 1). When scanning a source image using the sliding window approach, the detection of object refers to an appropriate scanning of the image and matching the selected image parts with templates from the training set. In case of the lack of information about an object, the object detection from static images requires to perform search process in all possible locations and using all probable object scales, which increases the computational complexity. In some of the planned scenarios the mentioned problems can be omitted. It is important to take into account certain clues associated with a scenario and camera location—this concept was presented also in [5]. System calibration is the key—in the video surveillance system it is possible to determine the approximate size of the object, e.g. the size of vehicles appearing in different parts of the scene.

Fig. 1. Variation in appearance of the vehicle silhouettes.

The analysis of images containing parking areas can be associated with several issues. Depending on the needs it can be a vehicle detection, free parking space detection and parking lot occupation detection. Therefore various objects/regions would be under analysis—a car or a single parking space—as well as the aim of the detection process would vary, e.g. detecting 'no parking' area violation or free parking lot. For instance in [6] an unsupervised system based on image analysis for the evaluation of parking place status is presented. For every rectangular image of parking place a related weight map is obtained and quad tree decomposition can be used to evaluate uniform image segments. If the resulting segments overpass a defined threshold value, parking space is evaluated as occupied. Another video-based parking space detection system was proposed in [7]. In turn authors of [8] adopt a self-organizing model based on the scene background and foreground analysis to detect vehicles stopped in 'no parking' areas. In [9] a real-time method for illegally parked vehicles is presented. The proposed methodology uses a novel one dimensional image projection for 'no parking' zones representation. Other methodology using Fourier transform for vehicle detection can be found in [10].

3   Feature Extraction Algorithms Applied for the Object Detection in the Considered Scenario

Discrete Cosine Transform (DCT) of the two-dimensional signal (an image containing rows and columns) decomposes it to a weighted sum of cosine functions oscillating at different frequencies. The base of this transform is a set of orthonormal cosine functions, which are the modified real part of the Fourier Transform. The Two-Dimensional DCT for an input image $X_{M \times N}$ can be calculated as follows [11]:

$$C(p,q) = \alpha_p \alpha_q \sum_{m=0}^{M-1} \sum_{n=0}^{N-1} X(m,n) \cos \frac{(2m+1)\pi p}{2M} \cos \frac{(2n+1)\pi q}{2N} , \qquad (1)$$

$$\alpha_p = \begin{cases} \frac{1}{\sqrt{M}}, for\ p = 0 \\ \frac{2}{\sqrt{M}}, for\ 1 \leq p \leq M-1 \end{cases}, \quad \alpha_q = \begin{cases} \frac{1}{\sqrt{N}}, for\ q = 0 \\ \frac{2}{\sqrt{N}}, for\ 1 \leq q \leq N-1 \end{cases},$$

where the C matrix contains a set of coefficients, has a size equal to the size of the input image and is called a spectrum. The use of the two-dimensional DCT as a feature extractor results from the characteristics of the transform coefficients and their spatial arrangement. Low frequencies with large values are located in the left top part of the coefficient matrix and correspond to the image regions containing similar pixels (low variability), while in the right bottom corner of the matrix the high frequency values are found, which correspond to high variability of pixel values, e.g. the image regions containing object edges. According to that, a small amount of low frequency coefficients carry a substantial part of image energy. The most important coefficients are selected from the top left corner of the transformation matrix using the triangle method, i.e. a triangular part of the matrix is composed of consecutive diagonals: diagonal 1 and the corresponding point $(0,0)$; diagonal 2 and the corresponding points $(1,0)$, $(0,1)$; diagonal 3 and the corresponding points $(2,0)$, $(1,1)$, $(0,2)$; etc. Selected coefficients, from tens to a hundred of features, are transformed into a vector, which is used in the recognition process. However, there is another issue to be solved—DCT is not invariant to the size of the object. Feature vectors extracted for images or their parts having various scales would be proportional to each other but not equal. Therefore the additional normalization step is introduced.

Based on the above explanations the DCT feature extractor has been implemented and experimentally verified due to two aspects: scale problem and object differentiation. Figure 2 shows the analysis results of the scene observed by the pan-tilt-zoom camera. For various focal lengths, three images of the same scene were obtained and one particular object in different scales was extracted from each image. For all selected images' subparts, containing the extracted object, the DCT feature vectors were obtained. Each feature vector consisted of 50 coefficients, wherein the first coefficient was omitted. The number of coefficients has been arbitrarily selected, and an optimal number of coefficients can be accurately determined for each particular training set. The graph demonstrates that all vectors are similar. In turn Fig. 3 shows the results of the ability of the DCT feature extractor to differentiate various objects—it can be seen from the graph (right part of Fig. 3) that different objects are characterized by various feature vectors.

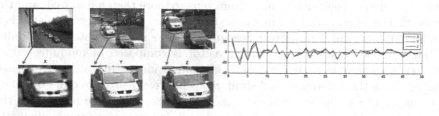

Fig. 2. An example of the effective operation of the DCT feature extractor for an object of different scales.

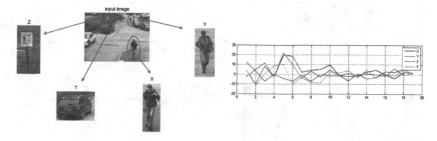

Fig. 3. An example of the effective operation of the DCT feature extractor for various objects.

The second feature extractor uses the Two-Dimensional Discrete Fourier Transform (DFT) which, for an input image $X_{M \times N}$, can be calculated using the following formula:

$$C(p,q) = \frac{1}{MN} \sum_{m=0}^{M-1} \sum_{n=0}^{N-1} X(m,n) \cdot \exp^{-i2\pi\left(\frac{pm}{M} + \frac{qn}{N}\right)} \cdot \exp^{-i2\pi\left(\frac{pm}{M} + \frac{qn}{N}\right)}$$

$$= \cos\left(2\pi\left(\frac{pm}{M} + \frac{qn}{N}\right)\right) - i\sin\left(2\pi\left(\frac{pm}{M} + \frac{qn}{N}\right)\right), \quad (2)$$

where the C matrix contains a set of coefficients, has a size equal to the size of an input image and is called a spectrum. The Two-Dimensional DFT is based on the set of sine and cosine features which are symmetrical to one another due to the phase shift. Therefore, the spectrum is symmetrical as well. Coefficient values located in the four corners of the original spectrum have high values and correspond to low frequencies in the image, and simultaneously carry the most information. For high frequencies the reverse is true. For simple calculation of the Two Dimensional DFT, the Fast Fourier Transform algorithm is used.

Object recognition is performed using a part of the original spectrum—$a \times a$ square subparts are taken from the left and right corners of the coefficient matrix. In the case of the shifted spectrum a rectangular block of the coefficient matrix located in the central part under the horizontal symmetry axis is used [12]. The number of selected coefficients varies from tens to more than a hundred, and the first coefficient is not included in the feature vector. Each spectrum value is a complex number, which in pattern recognition tasks is represented as modulus and phase angle. Therefore, a feature vector is composed of modulus values and thanks to that is invariant to object translation within an image plane. Figure 4 shows the differences and similarities between feature vectors obtained for various parts of the single scene image. The selected image parts have the same size but different content. Two of them contain the same person's silhouette but in different locations. Despite this, corresponding X and Y feature vectors presented on the graph are very similar—this results from translation invariance.

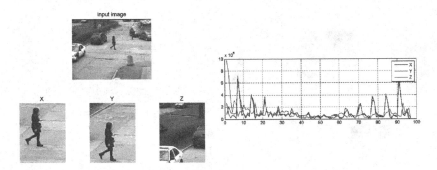

Fig. 4. An example of the effective operation of the DFT feature extractor for various objects.

4   Experimental Conditions and Results

Several experiments have been carried out in order to verify the effectiveness of the implemented feature extractors in the task of detecting vehicles parked in the restricted areas. The proposed solution is very specific and specially designed for the implementation in the video-based security system, where small, key areas have to be protected. This can be considered as opposite to the solutions presented in the literature, where the occupancy of all parking lots is verified. In the experiments, three video sequences from the project database were used. The sequences were recorded with the resolution of 1440×1080 pixels, and 25 frames per second. Each video sequence contained a scene in which a parking area and a lawn are visible. The scene is observed in perspective view—for a video surveillance purposes it is better to look down on objects than to see them from the side.

Figure 5 shows the analysed static scene with the quadrangular region reflecting the restricted area (a parking place for people with disabilities) and its corresponding binary mask, marked manually at the calibration stage. In the video sequences we can observe moving objects—cars and people. However, a person in restricted area, unlike the car, should not induce the alarm. In the experiments, DCT and DFT feature extractors were tested in the process of static image analysis. The restricted area shown in Fig. 5 was used as a template. The template was matched with the frames extracted from three video sequences—every 25th frame was under analysis. Only features corresponding to pixels under the masked area were used for detection.

Fig. 5. The analysed scene with the selected restricted area and the corresponding binary mask (first row), and the analysed scene with objects on restricted area—a walking person and a parked car.

Figure 6 shows the results for the first video sequence and the DCT feature extractor. The first graph presents two feature vectors, one for the template and one for the test image—both feature vector plots overlap. The second graph is a cumulative graph of differences calculated using the Euclidean distance between the template and consecutive frames from the video sequence (treated as test images). The Euclidean distance is sufficient since recognition is not performed. Large temporary differences (high peaks) correspond to the situation when a person passes through the protected area repeatedly.

Another two video sequences were tested using the same template and the DCT feature extractor. These sequences contain a scene in which a vehicle parks in the restricted area and drives away after a while. Moreover, these two sequences were analysed together with the first, previously processed video sequence. The experimental results are shown in Fig. 7. The graph on the right contains two types of distance increase—smaller, singular peaks correspond to

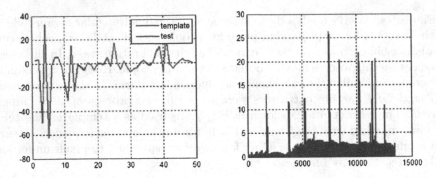

Fig. 6. The results of the analysis of the consecutive static images extracted from the first video sequence.

a person passing through the restricted area without stopping (a short change), while the larger group of high peaks reflects the situation in which a vehicle parks in the restricted area. Changes caused by a vehicle last significantly longer. It can also be concluded that a group of people would generate high peaks, similarly to a car, however the change would be short and dynamic due to small movements of people. Moreover, the detection of a significant change can precede a more complex object recognition module for the verification of alarm activation.

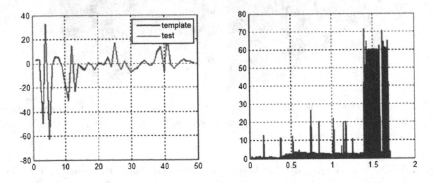

Fig. 7. The results of the analysis of the consecutive static images for three combined sequences and the DCT feature extractor.

The same experiment was repeated using the DFT feature extractor and the results are shown in Fig. 8. In this case the effective event detection was observed as well. Therefore, it can be concluded that changes in restricted area can be successfully detected using a threshold value for the distance between a test image and the template as well as by determining the tolerance time for the change.

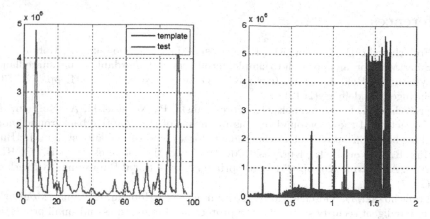

Fig. 8. The results of the analysis of the consecutive static images for three combined sequences and the DFT feature extractor.

5 Conclusions

In the paper, the problem of object detection and feature extraction using static images was investigated. Firstly, some general information about the 'SM4Public' project and the considered problem were given. Secondly, two selected algorithms for feature extraction were presented and evaluated, namely the Two Dimensional DCT and DFT feature extractors. Then, the experiments using three video sequences and both algorithms were performed. Static image analysis can have practical importance in the part of the planned scenarios of the 'SM4Public' system, because these scenarios are characterized by a low computational complexity and high event detection rate. Moreover, there is a low probability of error. The theoretical analysis enabled an appropriate preparation of the two feature extractors based on DCT and DFT which proved out to be effective. The future work would include the implementation of dynamic image analysis which takes into account background modelling, tracking and object recognition, and can be helpful in the detection of complex events in the other scenarios.

Acknowledgments. The project *"Security system for public spaces—'SM4Public' prototype construction and implementation"* (original title: *Budowa i wdrożenie prototypu systemu bezpieczeństwa przestrzeni publicznej 'SM4Public'*) is a project co-founded by European Union (EU) (project number PL: POIG.01.04.00-32-244/13, value: 12.936.684,77 PLN, EU contribution: 6.528.823,81 PLN, realization period: 01.06.2014–31.10.2015). *European Funds—for the development of innovative economy (Fundusze Europejskie—dla rozwoju innowacyjnej gospodarki).*

References

1. Frejlichowski, D., Forczmański, P., Nowosielski, A., Gościewska, K., Hofman, R.: SmartMonitor: an approach to simple, intelligent and affordable visual surveillance system. In: Bolc, L., et al. (eds.) ICCVG 2012. LNCS, vol. 7594, pp. 726–734. Springer, Heidelberg (2012)
2. Frejlichowski, D., Gościewska, K., Forczmański, P., Nowosielski, A., Hofman, R.: Extraction of the foreground regions by means of the adaptive background modelling based on various colour components for a visual surveillance system. In: Burduk, R., Jackowski, K., Kurzynski, M., Wozniak, M., Zolnierek, A. (eds.) CORES 2013. AISC, vol. 226, pp. 351–360. Springer International Publishing, Switzerland (2013)
3. Frejlichowski, D., Gościewska, K., Forczmański, P., Hofman, R.: 'SmartMonitor' – an intelligent security system for the protection of individuals and small properties with the possibility of home automation. Sensors 14, 9922–9948 (2014)
4. Frejlichowski, D., Gościewska, K., Forczmański, P., Hofman, R.: Application of foreground object patterns analysis for event detection in an innovative video surveillance system. Pattern Anal. Appl., 1–12 (2014)
5. Pantrigo, J., Hernández, J., Sánchez, A.: Multiple and variable target visual tracking for video surveillance applications. Pattern Recogn. Lett. 31(12), 1577–1590 (2010)
6. Fabian, T.: An algorithm for parking lot occupation detection. In: Proceedings of the 7th Computer Information Systems and Industrial Management Applications, pp. 165–170 (2008)
7. Bin, Z., Dalin, J., Fang, W., Tingting, W.: A design of parking space detector based on video image. In: 9th International Conference on Electronic Measurement & Instruments, pp. 2-253–2-256 (2009)
8. Maddalena, L., Petrosino, A.: Self organizing and fuzzy modelling for parked vehicles detection. In: Blanc-Talon, J., Philips, W., Popescu, D., Scheunders, P. (eds.) ACIVS 2009. LNCS, vol. 5807, pp. 422–433. Springer, Heidelberg (2009)
9. Lee, J.T., Ryoo, M.S., Riley, M., Aggarwal, J.K.: Real-time detection of illegally parked vehicles using 1-D transformation. In: IEEE Conference on Advanced Video and Signal Based Surveillance, pp. 254–259 (2007)
10. Pamuła, W.: Detection of vehicles in a video stream using spatial frequency domain features. In: Chmielewski, L.J., Kozera, R., Shin, B.-S., Wojciechowski, K. (eds.) ICCVG 2014. LNCS, vol. 8671, pp. 494–501. Springer International Publishing, Switzerland (2014)
11. Pratt, W.K.: Digital Image Processing: PIKS Inside, 3rd edn. John Wiley & Sons Inc, Hoboken (2001)
12. Kukharev, G., Nowosielski, A.: Face recognition using simple feature extractors. multimedia and intelligent techniques. Spec. Issue Live Biometrics Secur. 1(1), 87–98 (2005)
13. Han, F., Shan, Y., Cekander, R., Sawhney, H., Kumar, R.: A two-stage approach to people and vehicle detection with HOG-based SVM. In: Performance Metrics for Intelligent Systems Workshop, pp. 133–140 (2006)

Road Detection in Urban Areas Using Random Forest Tree-Based Ensemble Classification

Safaa M. Bedawi[1,2(✉)] and Mohamed S. Kamel[2]

[1] National Authority for Remote Sensing and Space Sciences, Cairo, Egypt
[2] Center of Pattern Analysis and Machine Intelligence, Waterloo, ON, Canada
{sbedawi,mkamel}@pami.uwaterloo.ca

Abstract. The rapid growth in using remote sensing data highlights the need to have computationally efficient geospatial analysis available in order to semantically interpret and rapidly update current geospatial databases. Object identification and extraction in urban areas is a challenging problem and it becomes even more so when very high-resolution data, such as aerial images, are used. In this paper, we use Random Forest Classifier tree based ensemble to enhance the extracting accuracy for roads from very dense urban areas from aerial images. Both the spatial and the spectral features of the data are used for pre-classification and classification. Comparisons are made between the RF ensemble and other ensembles of statistic classifiers and neural networks.

The proposed method is tested to aerial and satellite imagery of an urban area. The result shows that the RF ensemble enhances the overall classification accuracy for roads by 8 %. Also, it demonstrates that the approach is viable for large datasets due to its faster computational time performance in comparison to other ensembles.

Keywords: Random forest classifier · Ensemble of classifiers · Remote sensing · Very high resolution · Aerial images · Road extraction

1 Introduction

Objects extracted from very high resolution Remote Sensing (RS) imagery [1] have numerous applications in urban planning, forest monitoring, disaster management, and climate modeling. Urban land-cover/land-use maps are still generated by human experts, which makes the process both expensive and time consuming. Human experts tend to favor higher spatial resolution to higher spectral ones as higher spatial resolution increases the visibility of terrestrial features. This is the case especially with urban objects through reducing per-pixel spectral heterogeneity and thereby improving land cover identification. This explains why aerial imagery has traditionally been the primary source used for urban planning. Recent developments in sensor technology demonstrate a shift from aerial imagery to satellite based images for urban applications, as a new high spatial resolution multispectral satellite has recently been launched (e.g., GeoEye and WorldView). However, increase in resolution has also lead to augmentation of manual costs. This has also lowered accuracy, particularly in urban image classification, as urban areas are dense objects that become visible with the use of very high resolution. This visibility leads to displaying complex urban features [2], which

© Springer International Publishing Switzerland 2015
M. Kamel and A. Campilho (Eds.): ICIAR 2015, LNCS 9164, pp. 499–505, 2015.
DOI: 10.1007/978-3-319-20801-5_55

may not be the case for other non-man made land covers and land uses such as forests, wetland, desert landscape, and agriculture.

Various classifiers have been used in extracting land-cover/land-use from RS imagery. Typical methods include multivariate regression models, spectral mixture models, machine learning models and integration with geographical information systems [3] among others. It is desirable to use spectral-spatial data in order to extract as much information as possible concerning the area being classified. The superiority of one technique over the others cannot be claimed [4]. In contrast to standard classifiers, which are based solely on the decision of a single classifier, the ensemble approach combines several different classifier outputs. In doing so the overall accuracy usually increases. Random Forest classifiers (RF) are one example of such a classifier system [5]. Ensembles of Multiple Classifiers/Multiple Classifier Systems have proved to be the most remarkable applications for over two decades in RS applications [6–10, 12].

In this paper, the RF Tree Based ensemble is used for the classification of urban data when using aerial images. Motivated by its relatively low computation requirement, robustness to outliers and because of reported good results with other RS in literature, we choose the RF Tree Based Ensemble. To the best of our knowledge, few researchers have exploited the use of RF in very high-resolution aerial images for dense urban areas [10, 11], especially when there is no height information available. In our experiment we use both the spatial and spectral features when performing classification. We compare the performance of RF ensemble with three types of ensembles of neural network and three ensemble based ones on statistical classifiers.

The paper is organized as follows. Section 2 briefly introduces the Random Forest Classifier while Sect. 3 describes ensembles of multiple classifiers. In Sect. 4, we present the results and finally, our conclusion is drawn in Sect. 5.

2   Random Forests (RF)

Random Forest [13] is a tree-based ensemble machine- learning technique that is increasingly used in RS image classification. A Random Forest Classifier consists of a number of decision trees whose predictions are typically combined using majority voting. The goal of the training procedure is to reduce the variance of the ensemble by attempting to produce de-correlated trees. This is achieved by learning each tree on a random subset of the dataset and by using a random subset of the input variables. We selected each trained sample from the original training sample by the bootstrapped method.

Gini Index is used as a based for construction of RF classifier. This targets locating the biggest homogeneous subclass within the training set to differentiate the rest of the train sample [14].

We can reduce the computational complexity and reduce the correlation between trees by limiting the number used in split. This makes it possible for RF to handle the complexities found in very high resolution RS imagery for urban areas.

3   Ensemble of Multiple Classifiers

The concept of ensemble of multiple classifiers can be described concisely as: The final classification decision is taken by the fusion of the output of multiple learning machines based on a certain decision fusion scheme [4]. Multiple classifiers are commonly structured in 2 schemes: parallel and serial connection. The parallel combination is typically used in remote sensing applications.

The performance of an ensemble is highly correlated with individual classifiers and their combination scheme. For this reason, it is imperative to make a decision about how to choose classifiers from a classifier ensemble and how to combine them [15]. In classifier ensemble approaches, two approaches have been commonly applliled in literature: (1) the static selection, where the best classifier (or a subset of classifiers) for all samples is selected from the individual classifiers pool. (2) Dynamic selection, where for each unclassified pixel is a specific classifier (or a subset of classifiers) that appears to be more suitable to be selected [16].

This study focuses on the Static Classifier Selection. In this method, a classifier ensemble is addressed that use a variant of the base classifier that is known to be a weak base classifier where the classifier is not tuned to performs its best. We distributed the feature space randomly among the ensemble. As a combination scheme we used majority voting.

4   Experiment Setup and Outcomes

In this part, we investigate the ability of RF Tree Based Ensemble to extract land-use classes in dense urban areas. Its average performance is also compared to other classifier based ensemble such as three ensembles of neural networks: FFNN based classifiers, radial basis neural network base classifiers and three ensembles of statically based classifiers: Linear Classifier, K-nearest Neighbour Classifier and Parzen Window Classifiers.

4.1   Data Set

One important point of using machine learning for very high resolution aerial/satellite image analysis is the size of the data used in the analysis. In literature, most studies rely on ground truth data that were manually labeled for both training and testing purposes [11, 17]. However, this is not only time consuming but also results in small datasets in aerial image analysis. Usually, very high resolution datasets cover a fairly small area of a city, ranging from 1 km^2 to 10 km^2 [11]. Good results on a small dataset do not necessarily indicate good performance regarding a whole urban area, specifically if that area differs from the scene observed while training. Consequently, acquiring labeled data that are highly accurate is essential for both evaluating present approaches and training new algorithms.

In our experiments, hand-labeling data is not necessary as the ground truth information is provided by the city. The wealth of correctly labeled data for roads makes it an excellent land-use/land-cover where one can apply machine-learning algorithm for road extraction. In our experiment we detect roads from a large dataset for the city of Kitchener-Waterloo (K-W) and the city of Toronto Ontario, Canada. The Geospatial Centre of the University of Waterloo [18] had made the dataset available for this research. We used three datasets: two aerial datasets for the city of KW and one QuickBird satellite for the city of Toronto. The ortho-rectified aerial mosaic images for the KW dataset are 12 cm in pixel resolution and were taken by a digital color airborne camera with 8-bit radiometric resolution as well as infrared (CIR) mosaic images. We divided the ortho-mosaic into 280 images to be input into the classifiers while the ortho-rectified aerial mosaic images for the Toronto greater area dataset 19 is available in RGB bands only and was taken in April 2007. The QuickBird satellite dataset [20] is of 60 cm resolution and was taken in 2006. The main land-cover/land-uses of interests in our study are roads, buildings and green areas such as parks.

4.2 Experiment Setup

The data is segmented first as in [21] where both the spatial and spectral features were used in the clustering based segmentation process.

We used standard MATLAB classifiers that were trained with 50 % of the input data, validated over 20 % of the input data tested over 30 % of the data. The divided datasets have the same classes' distribution as the originally input data set in each of the three dataset used. The input features of the ensemble are the colour (RGB, Lab and HIS) and texture (Gray-level Co-occurrence Matrix) of the segmented parts. Using the 3 multispectral bands of the image for a window of 5 by 5 pixel size, the input feature vector is 261 dimensional image features.

For the RF tree based ensemble we investigated the effect of the number of individual trees. We conducted an experiment were the number of trees was varied from 10–100 trees and used the default values in Matlab for the rest of the variables. We found that 30 trees give the best performance in our case.

We are comparing our results to those of neural network and statically based ensembles. Each ensemble has 9 base classifiers and each classifier in the ensemble was fed with an input feature vector of 29 sub-features. All classifiers were trained/validated separately applying the training/validation sets. The classification results were averaged over forty runs. As we targeted a set of weak classifiers, no parameter optimization was done for the ensemble.

4.3 Experiment Results

The training and test accuracies for the different approaches are demonstrated in Table 1. The results are averaged over the three datasets. The table clearly indicates the advantages of the RF tree based ensemble. The accuracy increased up to 89 % for road class, which is 14 %, enhanced over the best ensemble method and 8 % enhanced over the average ensemble performance. The computation time of RF- tree is almost 1/3 less

Table 1. Comparison of the averaged classification accuracies of road using: Random forest tree based ensemble, and ensembles of Linear Classifiers, KNN Classifiers, Parzen Window Classifiers and Neural Networks Classifiers, applied on the three datasets training, validation and test sets images.

Ensemble of classifier	Training accuracy	Validation accuracy	Test accuracy
Linear classifier	76.155	75.021	74.814
KNN	100	81.514	80.831
Parzen Window	81.121	81.051	80.571
FFNN	80.112	79.552	79.588
RBN	81.522	82.017	87.536
PNN	81.561	82.451	82.019
RF tree base ensemble	90.612	89.691	89.301

(a) A sample of a test scene from the KW aerial image dataset

(b) The extracted roads are overlaid the original test scene

Fig. 1. Road classification and extraction using a RF tree based ensemble for KW aerial dataset.

than the neural network compared ensemble approaches. Qualitative result is shown in Fig. 1 for KW aerial dataset.

5 Conclusion

Road classification in dense urban areas from aerial data has been investigated. Experimental results indicate that the RF tree based ensemble yielded excellent accuracies: 89 % for classification of complex dense urban scenes, and it outperformed the highest accuracies for the other compared ensemble by 14 %. These results are obtained using a large dataset which are expected to get close results when applied to other urban datasets.

In addition, RF computational time is normally 55 % less than that of other ensemble methods used in our experiments. This should encourage the use of RF classifiers for large datasets of very high-resolution images and when updating geo-spatial databases.

Acknowledgement. We would to express our gratitude to the Geospatial Centre at the University of Waterloo for providing the datasets.

References

1. Mayer, H.: Object extraction in photogrammetric computer vision. ISPRS J. Photogram. Remote Sens. **63**(2), 213–222 (2008)
2. Campbell, J.: Introduction to Remote Sensing, 4th edn. The Guilford Press, New York (2007)
3. Lu, D., Weng, Q.: A survey of image classification methods and techniques for improving classification performance. Int. J. Remote Sens. **28**, 823–870 (2007)
4. Kuncheva, L.I.: Combining Pattern Classifiers: Methods and Algorithms. Wiley, Chichester (2004)
5. Bo, Y.C., Wang, J.F.: Combining multiple classifiers for thematic classification of remotely sensed data. J. Remote Sens. **5**, 555–564 (2005)
6. Benediktsson, J.A., Chanussot, J., Fauvel, M.: Multiple classifier systems in remote sensing: from basics to recent developments. In: Haindl, M., Kittler, J., Roli, F. (eds.) MCS 2007. LNCS, vol. 4472, pp. 501–512. Springer, Heidelberg (2007)
7. Del Frate, F., Pacifici, F., Schiavon, G., Solimini, C.: Use of neural networks for automatic classification from high-resolution images. IEEE Trans. Geosci. Remote Sens. **45**, 800–809 (2007)
8. Du, P., Zhang, W., Sun, H.: Multiple classifier combination for hyperspectral remote sensing image classification. In: Benediktsson, J.A., Kittler, J., Roli, F. (eds.) MCS 2009. LNCS, vol. 5519, pp. 52–61. Springer, Heidelberg (2009)
9. Giacinto, G., Roli, F.: Design of effective neural network ensembles for image classification processes. Image Vis. Comput. J. **19**(9/10), 699–707 (2001)
10. Baltsavias, E.P.: Object extraction and revision by image analysis using existing geodata and knowledge: current status and steps towards operational systems. ISPRS J. Photogram. Remote Sens. **58**(3–4), 129–151 (2004)
11. Kluckner, S., Mauthner, T., Roth, P.M., Bischof, H.: Semantic classification in aerial imagery by integrating appearance and height information. In: Zha, H., Taniguchi, R.-i., Maybank, S. (eds.) ACCV 2009, Part II. LNCS, vol. 5995, pp. 477–488. Springer, Heidelberg (2010)
12. Yu-Chang, T., Kun-Shan, C.: An adaptive thresholding multiple classifiers system for remote sensing image classification. Photogram. Eng. Remote Sens. **75**, 679–687 (2009)
13. Breiman, L.: Random forest. Mach. Learn. **45**(1), 5–32 (2001)
14. Waske, B., Benediktsson, J.A., Arnason, K., Sveinsson, J.R.: Mapping of hyperspectral aviris data using machine learning algorithms. Can. J. Remote Sens. **35**(S1), 106–116 (2009)
15. Kang, H.J., Doermann, D.: Selection of classifiers for the construction of multiple classifier systems. In: Proceedings of the Eight International Conference on Document Analysis and Recognition, pp. 263–268 (2005)
16. Smits, P.C.: Multiple classifier systems for supervised remote sensing image classification based on dynamic classifier selection. IEEE Trans. Geosci. Remote Sens. **40**(4), 801–813 (2002)
17. Nguyen, T., Kluckner, S., Bischof, H., Leberl, F.: Aerial photo building classification by stacking appearance and elevation measurements. In: Proceedings ISPRS, 100 Years ISPRS-Advancing Remote Sensing Science on CDROM (2010)

18. Tri-Cities and Surrounding Communities Orthomosaics [computer file]. Waterloo, Ontario: The Regional Municipality of Waterloo (2014)
19. Greater Toronto Area Orthoimagery 2007 [computer file]. Ontario Ministry of Natural Resources (2007)
20. QuickBird Satellite Imagery {computer file}, Digital Globe, Longmont, Colorado, USA (2006)
21. Bedawi, S.M., Kamel, M.S.: Segmentation of very high resolution remote sensing imagery of urban areas using particle swarm optimization algorithm. In: Campilho, A., Kamel, M. (eds.) ICIAR 2010. LNCS, vol. 6111, pp. 81–88. Springer, Heidelberg (2010)

Application of the Polar–Fourier Greyscale Descriptor to the Automatic Traffic Sign Recognition

Dariusz Frejlichowski[✉]

Faculty of Computer Science and Information Technology,
West Pomeranian University of Technology,
Żołnierska 52, 71-210 Szczecin, Poland
dfrejlichowski@wi.zut.edu.pl

Abstract. An object extracted from a digital image has to be represented using particular features, e.g. shape, colour, texture. In the paper the Polar–Fourier Greyscale Descriptor is employed for this purpose, which applies the information about silhouette and intensity of an object. Its properties are experimentally analysed using the images of traffic signs extracted from real video sequences. These objects were selected, because in many cases the images of traffic signs are strongly distorted, which hampers the proper recognition. During the experiments 500 images were used for each of the 20 classes, which resulted in 10000 instances. The average recognition rate was above 89 %.

1 Introduction

In computer vision tasks, the object extracted from the digital image for further analysis or recognition has to be properly represented. So called descriptors are applied for this purpose. The algorithms work on particular features, e.g. luminance, colour, texture, shape, context of the information, etc. [1]. The selection of a feature is crucial, strongly depends on the application, and influences the obtained results. For example, shape descriptors perform better for rigid objects, e.g. machine parts, car license plates, airplanes, while they are worse for the recognition of living beings, like animals or humans. It does not mean that they cannot be used for those types of silhouettes, but usually more sophisticated algorithms or more numerous template database have to be used in such cases. The colour would be applicable for the analysis of art images, e.g. the classification of paintings made by an artist [2]. The texture is better for the analysis of aerial images. Many other examples could be easily recalled. The combination of various features is becoming very popular nowadays and is effective in some applications [3,4].

In this paper the usage of greyscale information for object representation and further recognition is analysed. Such an approach was applied for example in [5], where the moment theory is applied for shapes with greyscale attributes. The described algorithm is experimentally investigated using signatures and hand

M. Kamel and A. Campilho (Eds.): ICIAR 2015, LNCS 9164, pp. 506–513, 2015.
DOI: 10.1007/978-3-319-20801-5_56

gestures. Another example is described in [6], where the gradient and curvature of the greyscale is applied for the recognition of handwritten numerals. A very similar application (character recognition) is described in [7]. The detection of three types of objects in an image, based on greyscale information was described in [8]. These are only few exemplary applications of the greyscale as a feature for various computer vision tasks. In this paper the Polar–Fourier Greyscale Descriptor is applied for the automatic recognition of traffic signs. The main goal is the experimental analysis of the algorithm's parameters, when applied for greyscale objects that are significantly distorted by various factors. In [9] the most typical problems occurring when recognising road signs were identified: color fading, similarity among various classes, varying standardization for particular countries, weather conditions (e.g. rain, snow, fog, sunlight), objects visible in the scene that are similar to signs, disorientation, occlusion, damage, car vibration and motion blur, variations in illumination, shadows, highlights. Several distorted traffic signs images are provided in Fig. 1.

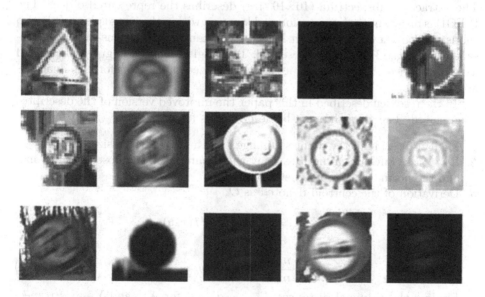

Fig. 1. Examples of distorted images containing traffic signs.

Recently the automatic road signs recognition has become popular. Many car producers have applied the system assisting the driver this way, which is a result of many years of research on the problem. In this paper only the last stage is considered, namely the description and classification of the previously located and extracted traffic signs, since the stress is put on the distortions hampering the recognition. Several approaches were applied for the description of the extracted road signs so far, e.g. Scale-Invariant Feature Transform (SIFT) [10], Haar-like features [11], Error Correcting Output Codes (ECOC) [12], FOveal System for Traffic Signs (FOSTS) [13], fractal reconstruction [14], Fourier Descriptors [15], genetic algorithms [16], HOG features [17], Colour DistanceTransform (CDT) [18], blob signature [19], Gabor wavelets [20], Zernike moments [21]. In the paper the Polar–Fourier Greyscale Descriptor (P-FGD) is applied to the problem.

The rest of the paper is organised as follows. The second section describes the applied algorithm. The third section provides the experimental conditions and results, and finally, the last section concludes the paper.

2 The Polar–Fourier Greyscale Descriptor

The descriptor under consideration (Polar–Fourier Greyscale Descriptor, P–FGD) was introduced in [22]. So far it has been applied for the identification of ery-throcyte types for the automatic diagnosis of some diseases [22], the biometric identification based on ear images [23], and the recognition of objects similar in shape [24]. The algorithm is composed of several stages, however, the most important is the usage of polar and 2D Fourier transforms for greyscale object. The extracted subspectrum (10×10 size) describes the represented object. The P-FGD is invariant to size, rotation and location within the image plane. It is also robust to some level of noise. In Fig. 2 some examples of various objects repre-sented using the P-FGD are presented. The original images in greyscale as well as the obtained representation — the normalized polar–transformed images – are provided.

In the research described in this paper the improved version of the descriptor is employed. The algorithm can be described as follows:

1. Median filtering of the input subimage I with the kernel of size 3.
2. Low–pass convolution filtering using the square mask composed of nine ones and the normalization parameter of 9.
3. Derivation of the centroid denoted as O:

$$m_{pq} = \sum_x \sum_y x^p y^q I(x, y), \tag{1}$$

$$x_c = \frac{m_{10}}{m_{00}}, \qquad y_c = \frac{m_{01}}{m_{00}}. \tag{2}$$

4. Finding the maximal distances d_{maxX}, d_{maxY} for $X-$ and $Y-$axis respec-tively from the boundaries of I to the centroid O.
5. Expanding the image into both directions by $d_{maxX} - x_c$ and $d_{maxY} - y_c$ and filling in the occurring new parts using greyscale level 127.
6. Derivation of the polar coordinates and insertion in the image P:

$$\rho_i = \sqrt{(x_i - x_c)^2 + (y_i - y_c)^2}, \qquad \theta_i = atan\left(\frac{y_i - y_c}{x_i - x_c}\right). \tag{3}$$

7. Resizing the image P into square size, e.g. 128×128.
8. Derivation of the absolute two-dimensional Fourier transform [25]:

$$C(k,l) = \frac{1}{HW} \left| \sum_{h=1}^{H} \sum_{w=1}^{W} P(h, w) \cdot e^{(-i\frac{2\pi}{H}(k-1)(h-1))} \cdot e^{(-i\frac{2\pi}{W}(l-1)(w-1))} \right|, \tag{4}$$

where:

H, W — height and width of P,

k — sampling rate in vertical direction ($k \geq 1$ and $k \leq H$),

l — sampling rate in horizontal direction ($l \geq 1$ and $l \leq W$),

$C(k, l)$ — the coefficient of discrete Fourier transform in $k - th$ row and $l - th$ column,

$P(h, w)$ — value in the image plane with coordinates h, w.

9. Selection of the spectrum subpart, e.g. $10 \ldots 10$ size and concatenation into vector V.

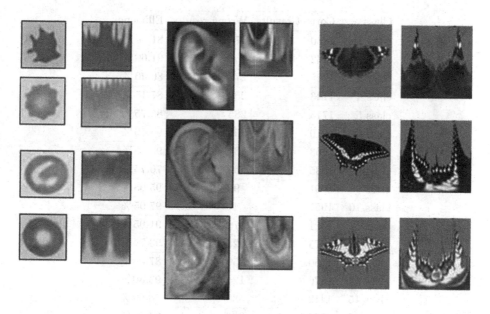

Fig. 2. Examples of various objects represented using the Polar–Fourier Greyscale Descriptor — the normalised polar–transformed images are presented, before the application of two–dimensional Fourier transform.

3   Conditions and Results of the Experiment

As it was already mentioned, the main goal of the performed experiment was to investigate the efficiency of the Polar–Fourier Greyscale Descriptor when applied to strongly deformed and distorted objects extracted from the digital images. For this purpose the traffic signs were selected as they sometimes are very difficult to recognise in real world conditions. Amongst several publicly available databases one of the most popular is The German Traffic Sign Recognition Benchmark [26], hence it was used as the source of the images for the described experiments. The extracted road signs were used. In total, 10000 images were applied and 20 different classes were used. The examples of images employed in the experiment were presented in Fig. 1. For each class 50 instances were randomly selected from the 500 images and used as the learning examples (i.e. they were the templates) and 200 random images were employed as the test data. This procedure was repeated ten times and the average recognition rate was obtained. The Polar–Fourier Greyscale Descriptor was employed for the representation of the objects and the Euclidean distance was used for the selection of the template closest to a test instance. As a result, the recognised class was established. The average efficiency for particular classes is provided in Table 1.

Table 1. The average efficiency obtained for particular classes.

Class	Correct results	Wrong results	Efficiency
class 1	1630	370	81.50 %
class 2	1832	168	91.60 %
class 3	1728	272	86.40 %
class 4	1743	257	87.15 %
class 5	1715	285	85.75 %
class 6	1910	90	95.50 %
class 7	1863	137	93.15 %
class 8	1535	465	76.75 %
class 9	1901	99	95.05 %
class 10	1959	41	97.95 %
class 11	1821	179	91.05 %
class 12	1875	125	93.75 %
class 13	1750	250	87.50 %
class 14	1876	124	93.80 %
class 15	1412	588	70.60 %
class 16	1694	306	84.70 %
class 17	1945	55	97.25 %
class 18	1837	163	91.85 %
class 19	1712	288	85.60 %
class 20	1954	46	97.70 %
TOTAL	**35692**	**4308**	**89.23 %**

The obtained average efficiency exceeds 89 %. It seems not perfect, however it has to be stressed that the images used in the experiments were in many cases difficult to recognise even for humans. Several examples are presented in Fig. 1. The analysis of the results brings the conclusion that the most difficult are blurred images (resulting from the fast movement of the car with installed recording camera) and unusual light conditions, when the images are too dark or too bright. In those cases the evaluated descriptor failed. The examples of wrongly recognised traffic signs are provided in Fig. 3.

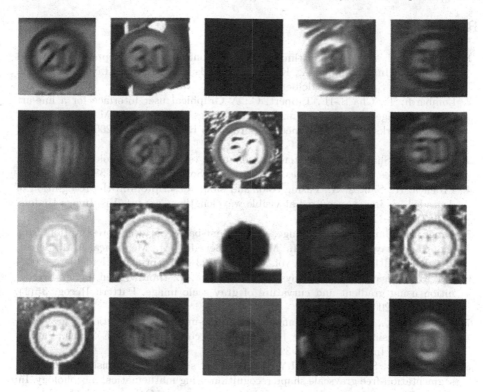

Fig. 3. Examples of wrongly recognised speed limit traffic signs.

4   Concluding Remarks

In the paper the experimental results on the application of the Polar–Fourier Greyscale Descriptor to the recognition of traffic signs were described. The algorithm is based on the combination of the polar and Fourier transforms. The usage of greyscale gives more information than when using only the shape. In case of the analysed descriptor the method of its derivation allows for the consideration of the object's silhouette as well. However, above all the greyscale is taken into account. It is assumed that this makes the final representation more effective.

For the experiments the images from The German Traffic Sign Recognition Benchmark [26] were applied. The selection of the traffic signs for the experiments was based on the strong distortions and deformations of the real data for this case. The main goal was the analysis of the efficiency of the P–FGD in this difficult case. In total, 10000 images were employed and the average efficiency above 89 % was obtained, which can be considered as a good result, considering the strong distortions of the experimental data (some examples can be seen in Figs. 1 and 3).

References

1. Frejlichowski, D.: An algorithm for binary contour objects representation and recognition. In: Campilho, A., Kamel, M.S. (eds.) ICIAR 2008. LNCS, vol. 5112, pp. 537–546. Springer, Heidelberg (2008)
2. Lombardi, T., Cha S.-H., Tappert, C.: A Graphical user interface for a fine-art painting image retrieval system. In: Proceedings of the 6th ACM SIGMM International Workshop On Multimedia Information Retrieval, MIR 2004, pp. 107–112 (2004)
3. Verma, A., Sharma, D.: Content based image retrieval using color, texture and shape features. Int. J. Adv. Res. Comput. Sci. Softw. Eng. 4(5), 383–389 (2014)
4. Proença, H., Santos, G.: Fusing color and shape descriptors in the recognition of degraded iris images scquired at visible wavelengths. Comput. Vis. Image Unders. 116(2), 167–178 (2012)
5. Lange, M., Ganebnykh, S., Lange, A.: Moment-based pattern representation using shape and grayscale features. In: Martí, J., Benedí, J.M., Mendonça, A.M., Serrat, J. (eds.) IbPRIA 2007. LNCS, vol. 4477, pp. 523–530. Springer, Heidelberg (2007)
6. Shi, M., Fujisawa, Y., Wakabayashi, T., Kimura, F.: Handwritten numeral recognition using gradient and curvature of gray scale image. Pattern Recog. 35(1), 2051–2059 (2002)
7. Wakahara, T., Kimura, Y., Tomono, A.: Affine-invariant recognition of gray-scale characters using global affine transformation correlation. IEEE Trans. Pattern Anal. Mach. Intel. 23(4), 384–395 (2001)
8. de Araujo, S.A., Kim, H.Y.: Rotation, scale and translation-invariant segmentation-free grayscale shape recognition using mathematical morphology. In: Proceedings of the 8th International Symposium on Mathematical Morphology, October 10–13, 2007, Rio de Janeiro, Brazil, vol. 2, pp. 61–62 (2007)
9. Gudigar, A., Chokkadi, S., Raghavendra, U.: A review on automatic detection and recognition of traffic sign. Multimedia Tools and Appl. 71, 1363–1380 (2014). doi:10.1007/s11042-014-2293-7
10. Hazelhoff, L., Creusen, I.M., de With, P.H.N.: Exploiting street-level panoramic images for large-scale automated surveying of traffic signs. Mach. Vis. Appl. 25, 1893–1911 (2014)
11. Timofte, R., Zimmermann, K., van Gool, L.: Multi-view traffic sign detection, recognition, and 3D localisation. Mach. Vis. Appl. 25, 633–647 (2014)
12. Escalera, S., Pujol, O., Radeva, P.: Traffic sign recognition system with β - correction. Mach. Vis. Appl. 21, 99–111 (2010)
13. Gao, X.W., Podladchikova, L., Shaposhnikov, D., Hong, K., Shevtsova, N.: Recognition of traffic signs based on their colour and shape features extracted using human vision models. J. Vis. Commun. Image Repres. 17, 675–685 (2006)
14. Pazhoumand-dar, H., Yaghoobi, M.: A new approach in road sign recognition based on fast fractal coding. Neural Computing and Applications 22, 615–625 (2013)
15. Lillo-Castellano, J.M., Mora-Jimenez, I., Figuera-Pozuelo, C., Rojo-Alvarez, J.L.: Traffic Sign segmentation and classification using statistical learning methods. Neurocomputing 153, 286–299 (2015)
16. de la Escalera, A., Armingol, J.M., Mata, M.: Traffic sign recognition and analysis for intelligent vehicles. Image Vis. Comput. 21, 247–258 (2003)
17. Zaklouta, F., Stanciulescu, B.: Real-time traffic sign recognition in three stages. Robot. Autonom. Syst. 62, 16–24 (2014)

18. Ruta, A., Li, Y., Liu, X.: Real-time traffic sign recognition from video by class-specific discriminative features. Pattern Recog. **43**, 416–430 (2010)
19. Jimenez, P.G., Bascon, S.M., Moreno, H.G., Arroyo, S.L., Ferreras, F.L.: Traffic sign shape classification and localization based on the normalized fft of the signature of blobs and 2D homographies. Sig. Proces. **88**(18), 2943–2955 (2008)
20. Koncar, A., Janssen, H., Halgamuge, S.: Gabor wavelet similarity maps for optimising hierarchical road sign classifiers. Pattern Recog. Lett. **28**, 260–267 (2007)
21. Fleyeh, H., Dougherty, M., Aenugula, D., Baddam, S.: Invariant road sign recognition with fuzzy artmap and zernike moments. In: Proceedings of the IEEE Intelligent Vehicles Symposium, pp. 31–36 (2007)
22. Frejlichowski, D.: Identification of erythrocyte types in greyscale MGG images for computer-assisted diagnosis. In: Vitrià, J., Sanches, J.M., Hernández, M. (eds.) IbPRIA 2011. LNCS, vol. 6669, pp. 636–643. Springer, Heidelberg (2011)
23. Frejlichowski, D.: Application of the polar-fourier greyscale descriptor to the problem of identification of persons based on ear images. In: Choraś, R.S. (ed.) Image Processing and Communications Challenges 3. AISC, vol. 102, pp. 5–12. Springer, Heidelberg (2011)
24. Frejlichowski, D.: An experimental evaluation of the polar-fourier greyscale descriptor in the recognition of objects with similar silhouettes. In: Bolc, L., Tadeusiewicz, R., Chmielewski, L.J., Wojciechowski, K. (eds.) ICCVG 2012. LNCS, vol. 7594, pp. 363–370. Springer, Heidelberg (2012)
25. Kukharev, G.: Digital Image Processing and Analysis. Szczecin University of Technology Press (1998)
26. Stallkamp, J., V, M., Salmen, J., Igel, C.: The German traffic sign recognition benchmark: a multi-class classification competition. In: Proceedings of the IEEE International Joint Conference on Neural Networks, pp. 1453–1460 (2011)

Camera-Based Lane Marking Detection
for ADAS and Autonomous Driving

Yasamin Alkhorshid[1]([✉]), Kamelia Aryafar[2], Gerd Wanielik[1],
and Ali Shokoufandeh[2]

[1] Professorship of Communications Engineering,
Chemnitz University of Technology, Chemnitz, Germany
{yasamin.alkhorshid,gerd.wanielik}@etit.tu-chemnitz.de
[2] Computer Science Department, Drexel University,
Philadelphia, PA, USA
{kca26,ashokouf}@cs.drexel.edu

Abstract. Advanced driver assistance systems (ADAS) and autonomous
driving (AD) have increasingly gained more attention in automotive industries and road safety research. Several sensors such as Radar, LiDAR, GPS,
ultrasonic sensors and cameras are often embedded in modern vehicles
to facilitate ADAS and AD applications. The data obtained from these
sensors can often be used in combination with machine learning models
to create an empirical approach for ADAS vision tasks such as lane detection (LD). In this paper we survey recent techniques and approaches in
vision-based lane marking detection for ADAS systems. We introduce
a benchmark dataset and initial lane marking detection results using
probabilistic Hough transform.

Keywords: ADAS · Lane Detection (LD) · Hough transform · Machine
learning

1   Introduction

Lane detection and estimation is a crucial task for controlling vehicle's lat-
eral position in road safety applications such as lane change assistance systems
(LCAs) [1], vehicle localization [2], lane departure warning [3], and lane keeping
assistance (LKA) [4]. Lane marking detection in urban and high traffic roads,
faded lane markings, illumination variation and harsh weather conditions make
LD applications challenging. Monocular camera, GPS, RGB camera, stereo camera, LiDAR sensors are often utilized to facilitate data collection for LD tasks.
Availability, cost and human perception make cameras an invaluable source of
sensory information in LD applications. In this paper, we adopt camera as primary source of data.

Lane detection and road understanding algorithms are composed of multiple modules: image pre-processing, feature extraction and model-fitting. Image
(frame) pre-processing reduces noise and disturbing imaging artifacts, enhances

© Springer International Publishing Switzerland 2015
M. Kamel and A. Campilho (Eds.): ICIAR 2015, LNCS 9164, pp. 514–519, 2015.
DOI: 10.1007/978-3-319-20801-5_57

Fig. 1. LD challenges in different lane types is illustrated. From the left: unknown curve and illumination variation, shadow, high traffic roads are main challenges in lane detection applications.

image quality using appropriate filters and defines the region of interest (ROI)[1]. Illumination variations often make pre-processing an important step for LD applications. Figure 1 illustrates existing challenges in LD such as illumination variations, shadow, high traffic road conditions and various lane types. Various methods have been proposed in the literature to address illumination variation such as vanishing point detection using a voting map [5] and pixel classification [6]. Inverse perspective mapping method (IPM) maps the image to a bird's eye-view and makes the lane markers appear straight and parallel to eliminate the perspective effect in model fitting [7].

Hough Transform (HT) is the most popular line detection method which is mainly suitable for detecting straight lines on the edge image. Canny along with Sobel are the most popular edge detectors [5]. Conventional HT is computationally expensive in illumination processing due to voting on the pixel level in the edge map [8]. Parallelizing the processing hierarchical HT is also computationally expensive due to re-computing the HT at each level. Various models have been proposed in the literature to describe cost effective features for LD such as accumulator-based method [8], Oriented Distance Transform (ODT) [9] and band-pass filters [10].

A wide range of lane structures can be modeled as straight line model, Hyperbola [11], least square method, B-Snake, B-Spline [3] and RANSAC (RANdom SAmple Consensus) model fitting [12]. Kang et al. [13] uses RANSAC method for extracting lane features. Lane fitting can then be achieved via RANSAC parabolic model and RANSAC straight lines' histogram [10]. To deal with curves on the road model a combination of four algorithms is proposed [14]: segmentation of curves into several Hough lines, separating curves (lanes) based on their slope, clustering Hough lines, and applying a feedback algorithm to continuously compare parameters of consecutive frames. The Tracking part of LD is mainly performed using Kalman filters [3], particle filters, or meanshift with assumption of constant velocity or acceleration for the vehicle as motion models. LD applications have also been tested in virtual scenes [3]. Using a single camera on a virtual and real dataset, Li et al. [3] performed detection and tracking of lane marks for highway and urban scenarios.

---

[1] The ROI is often in front of the vehicle which contain fallacious information and mostly occurs in the bottom half of image.

2   Hurdles and Gaps

Hillel et al. [15] provided well-researched information in the road and lane detection field. While for a short distance ahead, HT algorithm solves the problem of detection in 90 % of the highway cases, urban scenarios remain a challenge. Diverse road shapes and lane marking types, image clarity problem (too much illumination or shadow or snow on the road), and poor visibility situations (heavy rain, fog, reflection on the road in night) are the most challenging parts of LD [15]. Traditional machine learning models such as convolutional neural networks (CNNs) and SVM for lane marking detection suffer from broad variations in learning data with lane markings and the assumption of a pre-specified motion model of the vehicle [16]. LD studies also suffer from two fundamental weakness in terms of evaluation of results [9]: first, the lack of a benchmark dataset to compare various models using the same data, and second, the lack of a defined performance measure for automatic evaluation of the results. Son et al. [5] and Li et al. [3] have reported their experimental result for various datasets such as DIML-dataset1 (vehicular camera), SLD-2011 and Caltech Lanes Dataset using different evaluation techniques. This presents a need for a benchmark dataset. In this paper, we introduce a benchmark dataset to create a baseline for LD research in Germany's road. We present two initial lane marking detection based on HT and IPM that can be used in combination with machine learning models to perform LD under various road and illumination conditions.

Fig. 2. Conventional Lane-Mark detection based on the search for maximum gradient magnitude is illustrated. Detected vehicle regions were removed from the thresholding. Top left: edge image, top right: searching for gradient magnitude, bottom left: model fitting, bottom right: lane-mark detection results.

3   Benchmark Dataset

In this section we introduce our benchmark dataset along with canny edge detection and IPM-Hough as baseline feature extraction and pre-processing methods for LD applications. Our dataset consists of more than 5400 min of 640×480, 30 Hz video captured from our test vehicle Carai-1[2] [17]. The videos were taken in 60 different daylight and weather conditions for the same predefined path in Chemnitz urban environment and autobahn. The data were taken from a calibrated monocular camera, mounted on the top-inner of windscreen of Carai-1. Image data along with data captured from other integrated sensors are stored in a common stream file format to facilitate the offline access and processing steps. The BASELABS Connect[3] is used for accessing the raw data captured during the test drive and visualization of results with precise time stamps.

As a benchmark approach, gradient magnitude in the edge image is used in combination with Kalman filters to achieve a robust lane detection and tracking. Figure 2 illustrates conventional lane marking detection and estimation result in a sample frame of the benchmark dataset. In this method, lane markings are detected based on the changes in gradient magnitude in the edge image. The idea behind lane detection via gradient magnitude changes is that there should be a brightness gradient near every point along the lane edges. The larger the magnitude of that gradient, the more likely it is to correspond to a lane edge. Unscented Kalman Filter (UKF) is then employed for the tracking over the next frames. In this approach the vehicles offset with respect to the right and left lane markings are modeled as a function of time (assuming a set of frames over time is available). The UKF is then used to predict the future values of these offset parameters, based on observations in preceding frames. Our initial results show that while this approach is robust in LD given ideal lane marking conditions, constant range of illumination, and autobahn scenarios, the results are not satisfactory for urban roads and complicated traffic situations. The detection result also does not fulfill our requirement of determining lane markings types such as dashed-line or continuous-line.

The next approach as shown in Fig. 3, is based on IPM transform and Hough line detection and is tested as a baseline model to address the shortcomings of UKF modeling. Figure 3 shows an original frame, IPM image, Canny edge image and detected Hough lines on a sample frame from the benchmark dataset. As discussed before, IPM removes the perspective effect from the acquired image from the road and remaps it into a new 2-dimensional domain. Thus, the distribution of information in the new 2D domain is homogeneous among all pixels. Gaussian smoothing filter of OpenCV[4] is used on the image and subtracted from the original image to sharpen the edges and to remove the blur from the image. Afterwards, probabilistic Hough transform (PHT) is applied on the Canny edge image as an efficient line detection method. PHT minimizes the portion of points used

---

[2] http://www.carai.de.

[3] http://www.baselabs.de.

[4] http://opencv.org.

Fig. 3. IPM-Hough method (feature extraction) and line detection process is illustrated. Top left: original image, top right: IPM image, bottom left: Canny edge image, bottom right: Hough lines.

for voting process and returns in line segments represented by starting and ending points. Experimental results are visually tested for 45300 frames in daytime and show acceptable performance in an initial testing of lane markers in urban roads. This model generates a viable candidate for lane marking detection which can be used in combination with classifiers such as SVM and CNNs to create a real-time lane marking classifier. We anticipate that the lane detection and tracking classifier will be able to deal with challenging scenarios such as a lane curvature, worn lane markings, lane changes, and emerging, ending, merging, and splitting lanes.The information captured from GPS sensor could also be integrated in order to derive a ground truth for the detection results in future studies.

4   Conclusion and Future Work

This work represents an initial study on understanding lane-marking detection in urban roads through various models presented in the state-of-the-art. We surveyed the state-of-the-art in lane marking detection. We introduced the urge of lane marking detection in ADAS and different possible sensory information for LD and enumerated the components of a typical LD algorithm. We introduced a benchmark dataset and two sets of LD models: Hough transform and IPM. In the future we intend to apply machine learning models such as convolutional neural networks to boost the performance of real-time lane detection applications in challenging environments. We believe a calibrated model can enhance the accuracy of detection on the benchmark dataset and deal with challenging scenarios such as a lane curvature, worn lane markings, lane changes, and emerging, ending, merging, and splitting lanes.

References

1. Schubert, R., Wanielik, G.: Empirical evaluation of a unified bayesian object and situation assessment approach for lane change assistance. In: 2011 14th International IEEE Conference on Intelligent Transportation Systems (ITSC), pp. 1471–1476, October 2011
2. Chandakkar, P.S., Wang, Y., Li, B.: Improving vision-based self-positioning in intelligent transportation systems via integrated lane and vehicle detection. In: 2015 IEEE Winter Conference on Applications of Computer Vision (WACV), pp. 404–411, January 2015
3. Li, W., Gong, X., Wang, Y., Liu, P.: A lane marking detection and tracking algorithm based on sub-regions. In: 2014 International Conference on Informative and Cybernetics for Computational Social Systems (ICCSS), pp. 68–73, October 2014
4. Jung, H.G., Lee, Y.H., Kang, H.J., Kim, J.: Sensor fusion-based lane detection for lks+acc system. Int. J. Aut. Technol. 10(2), 219–228 (2009)
5. Son, J., Yoo, H., Kim, S., Sohn, K.: Real-time illumination invariant lane detection for lane departure warning system. Expert Syst. Appl. 42(4), 1816–1824 (2015)
6. Batista, M.P., Shinzato, P.Y., Wolf, D.F., Gomes, D.: Lane detection and estimation using perspective image. In 2014 Joint Conference on Robotics: SBR-LARS Robotics Symposium and Robocontrol (SBR LARS Robocontrol), pp. 25–30, October 2014
7. Ding, D., Yoo, J., Jung, J., Kwon, S.: An urban lane detection method based on inverse perspective mapping. Adv. Sci. Technol. Lett. 63, 53–58 (2015)
8. Yi, S.-C., Chen, Y.-C., Chang, C.-H.: A lane detection approach based on intelligent vision. Comput. Elec. Eng. 42, 23–29 (2015)
9. Shin, B.-S., Tao, J., Klette, R.: A superparticle filter for lane detection. Pattern Recognition (2014). http://www.sciencedirect.com/science/article/pii/S0031320314004282
10. Kwon, S., Ding, D., Yoo, J., Jung, J., Jin, S.: Multi-lane dection and tracking using dual parabolic model. Bulletin of Networking, Computing, Systems, and Software 4(1), 65–68 (2015). http://bncss.org/index.php/bncss/article/view/60
11. Chen, C., Zhang, B., Gao, S.: A lane detection algorithm based on hyperbola model. In: Eric Wong, W., Zhu, T. (eds.) Computer Engineering and Networking. LNEE, vol. 277, pp. 609–616. Springer, Heidelberg (2014)
12. Aly, M.: Real time detection of lane markers in urban streets. In: 2008 IEEE Intelligent Vehicles Symposium, pp. 7–12, June 2008
13. Kang, S.-N., Lee, S., Hur, J., Seo, S.-W.: Multi-lane detection based on accurate geometric lane estimation in highway scenarios. In: 2014 IEEE Intelligent Vehicles Symposium Proceedings, pp. 221–226, June 2014
14. Dubey, A., Bhurchandi, K.M.: Robust and real time detection of curvy lanes (curves) with desired slopes for driving assistance and autonomous vehicles. CoRR, abs/1501.03124 (2015)
15. Bar Hillel, A., Lerner, R., Levi, D., Raz, G.: Recent progress in road and lane detection: a survey. Mach. Vis. Appl. 25(3), 727–745 (2014)
16. Gopalan, R., Hong, T., Shneier, M., Chellappa, R.: A learning approach towards detection and tracking of lane markings. IEEE Trans. Intel. Transp. Syst. 13(3), 1088–1098 (2012)
17. Schubert, R., Richter, E., Mattern, N., Lindner, P., Wanielik, G.: A concept vehicle for rapid prototyping of advanced driver assistance systems. In: Advanced Microsystems for Automotive Applications 2010, pp. 211–219. Springer, Heidelberg (2010)

Handling Inter-object Occlusion for Multi-object Tracking Based on Attraction Force Constraint

Yuke Li[(⊠)], Isabelle Bloch, and Weiming Shen

State Key Laboratory of LIESMARS, Wuhan University,
Wuhan, China
{leesunfreshing,wmshen66}@gmail.com, isabelle.bloch@telecom-paristech.fr

Abstract. This paper presents a novel social interaction relation, attraction (interaction that would lead to occlusion for inter-object) for multi-object tracking to handle occlusion issue. We propose to build attraction by utilizing spatial-temporal information from 2D image plane, such as decomposed distance between objects. Then pairwise attraction force is obtained by the modeled attraction. Lastly, the attraction force is used to improve tracking when hierarchical data association performs. To meet requirements of practical application, we have our method evaluated on widely used PETS 2009 datasets. Experimental results show that our method achieves results on par with, or better than state-of-the-art methods.

Keywords: Attraction force · Occlusion handling · Multi-object tracking

1 Introduction

Inter-object occlusion is one of the most difficult task to deal with in object tracking field. This issue could be explained by the spatial-temporal information for the objects, that are involving occlusion is quite different from those are not. However, most of these approaches ignore that spatial-temporal information is not exploited sufficiently.

Many research have been accomplished great achievement w.r.t. occlusion handling. In [1,7,17], the authors focus on focus on the appearance change while occlusion happens. [12] propose to utilize scene knowledge to solve objects missing caused by occlusion. Nevertheless, most of them neglect the spatial-temporal information when occlusion happens. By contrast, the social force interaction among multi-object [6], which is based on exploring spatial-temporal information, provides a different perspective for multi-object tracking. Whereas none of the research in such a field considers that, inter-object occlusion is caused by social force interaction. For example, [11] and [13] use the interaction to predict objects location, without considering occlusion between objects.

Intuitively, the spatial-temporal information for objects that are involving occlusion is different from those are not. For instance, the distance for those

© Springer International Publishing Switzerland 2015
M. Kamel and A. Campilho (Eds.): ICIAR 2015, LNCS 9164, pp. 520–527, 2015.
DOI: 10.1007/978-3-319-20801-5_58

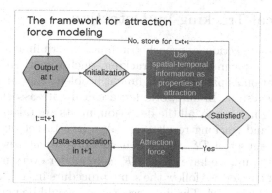

Fig. 1. Our framework of attraction force modeling. After initialization, the spatial-temporal information, such as distance, is utilized to decide whether there is attraction. The final step would be to integrate the attraction force into the tracking scheme.

occluded objects would be relative closer. Similar rationale has been employed lately for scene understanding [4]. The idea of considering the global scene spatial-temporal information has been receiving great attention in the field of more complex activity recognition [3] as well. Motivated by this intuition and based on the observation above, in this work we present a framework of inter-object occlusion handling for multi-object tracking based on attraction force (social force that may lead to occlusion between objects). The framework of our attraction force modeling is shown in Fig. 1.

The contributions of our work[1] are summarized as follows: 1. We extend the concept of social force by building attraction force. Attraction force is particular for the situations that would lead to inter-object occlusion. This model is completely based on 2D image plane information without any scene knowledge, such as camera calibration, etc. By utilizing change of distance between objects, the relative velocity as well, we propose that attraction force suggests information of occlusion between objects in next frame. 2. A novel occlusion handling method is proposed. Our approach focus on dealing with occlusion in data-association level. Attraction force is used as penalty to optimize final association score. The authors in [2] utilizes a similar rationale, But our method differs in occlusion modeling and data association framework

The reminder of this paper is organized as follows: Firstly, hierarchical tracking-by-detection framework is discussed in Sect. 2. Section 3 focus on modeling attraction force utilizing spatial-temporal information, and handling occlusion based on attraction force in hierarchical data-associations, followed by a set of detailed experimental results and analysis in Sect. 4. Finally, we conclude in Sect. 5.

---

[1] This work is performed when the first author was with Institut Mines Télécom, Paris. The author would like to thank Prof. Isabelle Bloch, Dr. Ling Wang and Dr. Henrique Morimits for meaningful discussion and very helpful suggestions.

2   Hierarchical Tracking-by-Detection

Online tracking-by-detection approach combines discriminative [14] and generative methods [10] for multi-object tracking. Such a method treats frame by frame data association as pair-wise assignment problem, that matches the detection with tracking results. In our work, hierarchical data-association method is adopted. Assuming in t frame, all the detection inputs are taken as one of detection division $\mathcal{DE}$, and tracking results are taken into target division $\mathcal{TR}$. Candidates $\mathcal{CA}$ is the subset of $\mathcal{DE}$, which is used to represent new objects appear in the scene. To sum up, we have $\mathcal{DE} + \mathcal{TR}$ as input for every frame. Regarding birth and death of tracker, we follow the same procedure in [16], which is the new tracker is generated from $\mathcal{CA}$. The data-association would be performed between $\mathcal{DE}$ and $\mathcal{TR}$. Noted that since the $\mathcal{CA}$ may contain false positive, we follow the procedure by [2], tracker will be generated when one candidate is matched for at least 2 consecutive frames.

To assign correct detection to correct tracking result, one matching score by computing likelihood between detections and tracking results is used. The matching score (M) includes several components, in our case, we use

$$M = Pos \cdot Size \cdot App \tag{1}$$

where $Pos = \mathcal{N}(0, dis(P_{de} - P_t r))$, with (P_*) is position of detector and tracker in current frame, $Size = \mathcal{N}(0, \frac{size_{de} - size_{tr}}{size_{tr}})$ with $(size_*)$ is the size of detector and tracker. $\mathcal{N}$ is Gaussian distribution with zero mean. For the appearance, we employ Hellinger distance the HSV color histogram. It consists on computing the histogram of both detector and tracker on the HSV color space. In order to deal with situation such as illumination changing and occlusion, we keep the color histogram information of first frame and last frame that object has correctly tracked . After having those matching score, Hungarian algorithm [9] provides the best match.

For each object, the tracking result and its matched detection is output, if there is one; otherwise, only the tracking result is used as output instead.

3   Inter-object Occlusion Handling Strategy Based on Attraction Force

Even hierarchical tracking-by-detection tackles occlusion implicitly by using color histogram from first and last frame. The matching score cannot always give the best result when inter-object occlusion occurs, since detector may not always find the right object under occlusion. In this section, we will present our method to handle occlusion by detailedly analysis and model attraction force.

3.1   Initialization of Attraction Force

We manually set search region as square shape to eliminate the objects that are too far away to have attraction. The size of one side of the search region is considered as twice as the height of the object. Euclidean distance between center point of bounding boxes of objects is employed to estimate the distance among objects. Only the objects are within the search region of other objects, and without any occlusion are initialized for attraction force. Additionally, If the overlapping area of two bounding boxes is more than 40%, we consider the spatial information is invalid in order to avoid potential errors. Furthermore, the example that to deal with size of the object may lead to information lost. For instance, x^1 and x^2 is object with bigger and smaller size respectively. When we consider attraction of x^2, besides of all the objects within the search region, we need enumerate attraction of x^1. If we find out attraction between x^1 and x^2 for x^1, this information is stored and taken into account for x^2.

3.2 Attraction Analysis

Intuitively, inter-object occlusion would only happen for objects moving towards each other from at least one axis from image plane. Let us start with the situation such that two objects annotated as x^i and x^j walk towards each other, and there is an attraction between them. The following equation is used to describe this situation:

$$\begin{cases} D^X_{t-1}(x^i, x^j) - D^X_t(x^i, x^j) > 0 \\ D^Y_{t-1}(x^i, x^j) - D^Y_t(x^i, x^j) > 0 \end{cases} \tag{2}$$

where $D^X_{t-1}(x^i, x^j)$ and $D^Y_{t-1}(x^i, x^j)$ is the Euclidean distance between x^i and x^j in X and Y axis, at time $t-1$ and t. In order to avoid some confused ambiguities lead by general distance, decomposed distance in X and Y axis is employed. For instance, when two pedestrian are passing by each other from image plane, no occlusion will be observed. Nevertheless utilizing the general distance is hard to distinguish whether these two objects are passing by or having occlusion. This reason remains in the following.

Equation 2 implies two things: firstly, x^i and x^j are closer; besides, the relative displacement of x^i and x^j between two subsequent frame could present as relative velocity between these two objects, and Eq. 2 indicates that they tend to meet each other.

Two objects are moving towards from only one axis, X axis is used as paradigm. Two cased is considered for this situation. The first one is no distance change in Y axis, and the second one is repelling from Y axis. To asses if there is attraction, we still rely on the distance information, with aiding by the size of the object. First case could be described by

$$\begin{cases} D^X_{t-1}(x^i, x^j) - D^X_t(x^i, x^j) > 0 \\ D^Y_{t-1}(x^i, x^j) - D^Y_t(x^i, x^j) = 0 \\ D^Y_t(x^i, x^j) < 0.5(H_{x^i} + H_{x^j}) \end{cases} \tag{3}$$

and second case is

$$\begin{cases} D^X_{t-1}(x^i, x^j) - D^X_t(x^i, x^j) > 0 \\ D^Y_{t-1}(x^i, x^j) - D^Y_t(x^i, x^j) < 0 \\ \dfrac{0.5(H_{x^i} + H_{x^j}) - D^Y_{t,x^i}(x^j)}{VY_{t,x^i}(x^j)} > \dfrac{-0.5(W_{x^i} + W_{x^j}) + D^X_{t,x^i}(x^j)}{VX_{t,x^i}(x^j)} \end{cases} \tag{4}$$

where H_{x^*} and W_{x^*} is height and width of the x^i and x^j respectively. and $V^*{}_{t,x^i}(x^j)$ is the relative velocity between x^i and x^j..

Two objects have attraction or not judging by the size information.

Similar situation for Y axis is symmetrical to the situation described by Eq. 3 and Eq. 4 (simply switch X and Y, height and width).

3.3 Attraction Force

Attraction modeled previously is utilized as properties for attraction force. Noted only objects satisfy one of these properties, will be taken into account for attraction force.

The attraction force is modeled as:

$$\begin{cases} F^{X,t}_{att}(x^i, x^j) = I \cdot \left(1 - exp^{-\left|V^X{}_{t,x^i}(x^j)\right| \cdot (\alpha - D^X{}_t(x^i,x^j))}\right) \\ F^{Y,t}_{att}(x^i, x^j) = I \cdot \left(1 - exp^{-\left|V^Y{}_{t,x^i}(x^j)\right| \cdot (\alpha - D^Y{}_t(x^i,x^j))}\right) \end{cases} \tag{5}$$

I is indicator function that equals one if there is attraction between x^i and x^j based on the explanation of previous sections, equals zeros if otherwise. α equals to the height of x^i. $\alpha - D^X{}_t(x^i, x^j) > 0$ makes sure x^j is within the search region of x^i. $\left|V^X{}_{t,x^i}(x^j)\right|$ is the absolute of relative velocity of x^i and x^j, which is defined by object state (Subsect. 4.3).

3.4 Occlusion Handling Strategy

In this work, all inter-object occlusion relation (only the matching score $> \tau$ is taken as occlusion, where τ is the threshold manually set) between objects will be enumerated within the same division, only the matching score of at least two detections and two targets are considered connected, are treated as occlusion group. As we have already pointed in previous subsection, attraction force based occlusion rationale is to predict occlusion for $t+1$. Therefore the data-association in this section performs in $t + 1$ as well. Assuming that d_m, tr_n are within the same occlusion group, we propose

$$\hat{M} = \arg\max_{m,n} \sum_{m,n} M(d_m, tr_n) - \hat{F_{att}^t} \tag{6}$$

for optimizing matching score. Where $\hat{F}$ is overall attraction force in this occlusion group, and used to penalize the occlusion. $\hat{F_{att}^t}$ is only considered once for each pair. For example, if attraction force $F_{att}^t(x^h, x^k)$ exists between occlusion group which is comprised of object x^h and x^j, $\hat{F_{att}^t} = F_{att}^t(x^h, x^k)$.

4   Experiments

4.1 Datasets

To better evaluate the capability of our method, We have our approach tested on widely used PETS2009 benchmark provided by [15].

The most challenges of this dataset is frequently occlusion caused by dynamic pedestrians movement. We also run experiments on more challenged S2L2 datasets, which more pedestrian presents in the scene.

To achieve fair comparison score, we use the goundtruth provided by [15], where all the person occurring in the scene have been annotated.

4.2   Metrics

To measure performance, the CLEAR MOT metrics [8] is adopted. The metrics include: 1. Multiple Object Tracking Accuracy (MOTA, higher value is better) returns a accuracy score; 2. Multiple Object Tracking Precision (MOTP, lower value is better), which consider intersection union of bounding boxes; 3. Mostly Tracker (MT) and 4. Mostly lost (ML). MT and ML is not used for our evaluation for PETS2009 S2L2 dataset, because most of the methods in our comparison do not provide such a value. The procedure provided by [9] is adopted, in which the results will be re-evaluated by 2D matching protocol.

4.3   Experiment Settings

Performing tracking, Kalman filter is employed. The entire object state is defined as $\{\mathcal{X}, \mathcal{Y}, \mathcal{H}, \mathcal{W}, V^X{}_t, V^Y{}_t\}$, where $\mathcal{X}, \mathcal{Y}$ is the position in X axis and Y axis respectively, $\mathcal{H}, \mathcal{W}$ is the height and width of x^i, $V^X{}_t, V^Y{}_t$ is the velocity w.r.t each axis. The noise of them are manually set as $\mathcal{N}(0,10)$ and $\mathcal{N}(0,5)$ respectively, Δt is the time between 2 consecutive frames.

The noises of them are both manually set as $\mathcal{N}(0,10)$ and $\mathcal{N}(0,5)$ respectively. $V^X = V^Y = 0$ at the frame that tracker is initialized.

Similar to [12], DPM (Deformable Part based Model detector)[5] is utilized to generate detection input. In additional, following the settings presented in [16], the false positives of detection is removed by the size.

4.4   Results and Analysis

Figure 2 depicts our results for exemplar two consecutive frames. Table 1 illustrates the quantitative comparison of our method and state-of-the-art online tracking approaches.

Table 1 compares the performance of the tracker on PETS2009 S2L1 dataset. Utilizing scene knowledge, camera calibration for instance, makes the approach of [12] outperforms to other methods, however, our approach performs favorably compared to most of online trackers. Our novel occlusion handling improves the capability to deal with occlusion of the tracker. For the tracking method employ similar hierarchical data-association scheme [16], our occlusion handling makes the tracker more robust. Thus, we achieve better MOTA score and significant improved MOTP score.

Considering more challenged PETS2009 S2L2 sequences, our method provides better scores in both MOTA and MOTP than most of other approaches.

Fig. 2. The experimental results of our method for exemplar two consecutive frames, on PETS2009-S2L1 (the first and the second on the left) and PETS2009-S2L2 (the first and the second on the right) respectively. Our method shows good capability to handle occlusion. The details of experiments presents in Sect. 4.

Both datasets confirm that the proposed method are beneficial by employing occlusion handling method. Comparing with other methods only consider appearance under occlusion [2,12,16], spatial-temporal information could be more reliable. Furthermore, the experimental results suggest that, employing scene knowledge [12] may lead to further improvement of tracking performance.

Table 1. Comparison of different online tracking methods.

PETS2009-S2L1	MOTA [%]	MOTP [%]	MT [%]	ML [%]	PETS2009-S2L2	MOTA [%]	MOTP [%]
Proposed method	93.6	71.3	100.0	0.0	Proposed method	68.2	60.7
Breitenstein et al. [2]	79.7	56.3	-	-	Breitenstein et al. [2]	50.0	56.3
Possegger et al. [12]	98.1	80.5	100.0	0.0	Possegger et al. [12]	66.0	64.8
Jianming et al. [16]	93.4	68.2	100.0	0.0	Jianming et al. [16]	66.7	58.6

5   Conclusion

A novel occlusion handling method based on attraction force is proposed.By detailed analysis every possible situation would lead to attraction, occlusion handling is performed in data-association level. The experimental results show that our method could be comparable with, even better than state-of-the-art.

References

1. Andriyenko, A., Roth, S., Schindler, K.: An analytical formulation of global occlusion reasoning for multi-target tracking. In: 2011 IEEE International Conference on Computer Vision Workshops (ICCV Workshops), pp. 1839–1846. IEEE (2011)

2. Breitenstein, M.D., Reichlin, F., Leibe, B., Koller-Meier, E., Van Gool, L.: Online multiperson tracking-by-detection from a single, uncalibrated camera. IEEE Trans. Pattern Anal. Mach. Intel. **33**(9), 1820–1833 (2011)
3. Chang, X., Zheng, W.S., Zhang, J.: Learning Person-Person interaction in collective activity recognition. IEEE Trans. Image Proces. **24**(6), 1905–1918 (2015)
4. Choi, W., Chao, Y.W., Pantofaru, C., Savarese, S.: Understanding indoor scenes using 3d geometric phrases. In: 2013 IEEE Conference on Computer Vision and Pattern Recognition (CVPR), pp. 33–40. IEEE (2013)
5. Felzenszwalb, P.F., Girshick, R.B., McAllester, D., Ramanan, D.: Object detection with discriminatively trained part based models. IEEE Trans. Pattern Anal. Mach. Intel. **32**(9), 1627–1645 (2010)
6. Helbing, D., Molnar, P.: Social force model for pedestrian dynamics. Phys. Rev. E **51**(5), 4282 (1995)
7. Hua, Y., Alahari, K., Schmid, C.: Occlusion and motion reasoning for long-term tracking. In: Fleet, D., Pajdla, T., Schiele, B., Tuytelaars, T. (eds.) ECCV 2014, Part VI. LNCS, vol. 8694, pp. 172–187. Springer, Heidelberg (2014)
8. Kasturi, R., Goldgof, D., Soundararajan, P., Manohar, V., Garofolo, J., Bowers, R., Boonstra, M., Korzhova, V., Zhang, J.: Framework for performance evaluation of face, text, and vehicle detection and tracking in video: Data, metrics, and protocol. IEEE Trans. Pattern Anal. Mach. Intel. **31**(2), 319–336 (2009)
9. Kuhn, H.W.: The hungarian method for the assignment problem. In: 50 Years of Integer Programming 1958–2008, pp. 29–47. Springer, Heidelberg (2010)
10. Nummiaro, K., Koller-Meier, E., Van Gool, L.: An adaptive color-based particle filter. Image Vis. Comput. **21**(1), 99–110 (2003)
11. Pellegrini, S., Ess, A., Schindler, K., Van Gool, L.: You'll never walk alone: Modeling social behavior for multi-target tracking. In: 2009 IEEE 12th International Conference on Computer Vision, pp. 261–268. IEEE (2009)
12. Possegger, H., Mauthner, T., Roth, P.M., Bischof, H.: Occlusion geodesics for online multi-object tracking. In: Proceedings of the IEEE Conference on Computer Vision and Pattern Recognition (CVPR) (2014)
13. Ramanathan, V., Yao, B., Fei-Fei, L.: Social role discovery in human events. In: 2013 IEEE Conference on Computer Vision and Pattern Recognition (CVPR), pp. 2475–2482. IEEE (2013)
14. Tang, S., Andriluka, M., Milan, A., Schindler, K., Roth, S., Schiele, B.: Learning people detectors for tracking in crowded scenes. In: 2013 IEEE International Conference on Computer Vision (ICCV), pp. 1049–1056. IEEE (2013)
15. Yang, B., Nevatia, R.: Multi-target tracking by online learning of non-linear motion patterns and robust appearance models. In: 2012 IEEE Conference on Computer Vision and Pattern Recognition (CVPR), pp. 1918–1925. IEEE (2012)
16. Zhang, J., Presti, L., Sclaroff, S.: Online Multi-person Tracking by Tracker Hierarchy. In: 2012 IEEE Ninth International Conference on Advanced Video and Signal-Based Surveillance (AVSS), pp. 379–385, September 2012
17. Zhang, T., Jia, K., Xu, C., Ma, Y., Ahuja, N.: Partial occlusion handling for visual tracking via robust part matching. In: 2014 IEEE Conference on Computer Vision and Pattern Recognition (CVPR), pp. 1258–1265. IEEE (2014)

Indian Sign Language Recognition
Using Kinect Sensor

Kapil Mehrotra[✉], Atul Godbole, and Swapnil Belhe

Centre for Development of Advanced Computing (C-DAC), Pune, India
{kapilm,atulg,swapnilb}@cdac.in

Abstract. There has been a lot of research on automatic recognition of
Sign languages and is an effective means of transferring information for
Deaf and Hard of Hearing (HoH) community. Here we propose a system
for Indian Sign Language recognition, which uses Microsoft Kinect sensor and Machine learning for effectively recognizing some signs used in
Indian Sign Language. Kinect generates the skeleton of a human body
and detects 20 joints in it. We use 11 out of 20 joints and extract 34
novel features per frame, based on distances and angles involving upper
body joints. These features are trained with a multi-class Support Vector
Machine achieving an accuracy of 100 % and 86.16 % on train and test
data respectively. Proposed system recognizes 37 signs in real time. The
data is used in the proposed system is generated by the Deaf and Hard
of Hearing (HoH) persons in our lab.

1 Introduction

Sign Language recognition has been a popular topic of research for some years
now. A sign is a form of non-verbal communication made with some part of
the body, mainly involving facial expressions and hand movements. Most people
use signs and body movements in addition to words when they speak. Sign
Language recognition can be seen as a way for computers to begin to understand
human body language. Sign recognition enables humans to communicate with
the machine and interact naturally without any mechanical devices. This can
be a promising medium for man-machine communication without any intrusive
mechanical device. The ability of Kinect, to capture scene depth information and
generate 3D skeletal data for body movements has made them highly popular
among researchers. The major use is in Sign language Recognition and Gesture
Recognition. The classifier used for recognition task is a multi-class Support
Vector Machine(SVM). It is basically a binary classifier but it can also be used
for multi-class problems. The SVM has been effectively used in many pattern
recognition applications.

Vast number of research has been done on the Sign Language Recognition
which is described in Sect. 2, Sect. 3 explains the proposed approach, Sect. 4
discusses the experimental results, and Sect. 5 concludes the work with a word
about the future direction of research.

© Springer International Publishing Switzerland 2015
M. Kamel and A. Campilho (Eds.): ICIAR 2015, LNCS 9164, pp. 528–535, 2015.
DOI: 10.1007/978-3-319-20801-5_59

2   Literature Review

In the past, human gesture recognition has been based on color image processing as explained by Chua et al. [7]. For hand detection which is an essential component for sign recognition, Bretzner et al. [6] and Pavlovic et al. [12] use color or motion information. For these approaches tracking hand motion is non-trivial task under challenging light conditions. Above methods worked with a single camera, which may lead to self occlusion in subjects resulting in low performance. Further research introduced multi-camera systems to solve occlusion. The attempt was to track a particular body part as done by Madabhushi et al. [11] or to track the joints as done by Ali et al. [4] and Uddin et al. [15].

Since the introduction of Kinect by Microsoft in 2010 and release of Kinect SDK in 2011, lots of work is happening using Kinect sensor for gesture recognition [2]. Depth information from kinect sensor is used by Biswas et al. [5] to recognize signs in Japanese Sign Language (JSL). They use low level features and achieve more than 90 % accuracy on 8 signs. Agarwal et al. [3] use Depth and Motion profile for sign language recognition. Rajam et al. [13] and Ghotkar et al. [10] have only hands gestures for alphabet recognition in Indian sign language.

With the introduction of skeleton tracking feature in kinect, research in gesture recognition has received further boost. Zahoor et al. [17] used the kinect sensor for educational games for deaf children. Recently, Saha et al. [14] use the skeleton information for Indian Classical Dance Gesture recognition for classifying 5 dance gestures. Also, Geetha et al. [9] and Agarwal et al. [3] are recognizing 10 Indian gestures using Kinect for words and numerals respectively. Comparatively, proposed approach has attempted to increase the number of gestures to 37 Indian langauge signs (for recognition).

The Kinect provides us with two type of output feeds i.e. Depth and Skeleton. In case of depth information, it is always a challenge to separate the hands from other body parts, if the hands are too close to the body, then it will not be clear enough to segment the body parts. Also the depth information very much depends on the illumination. In Skeleton Information, it tracks the skeleton of a human standing in front of the camera at a finite distance. The skeleton gives us 20 joints in $\mathbb{R}^3$, out of which we have used 11 joints in our approach. The Fig. 1c shows the skeleton as detected by Kinect.

3   Proposed System

In this paper, we present our work for recognizing a set of commonly used 37 Non-Continuous Indian Signs as shown in Table 1. These signs depicts different festivals, objects, cities, and are also part of Indian Sign Language, one of the gestures for "computer" is shown in Fig. 2a. We have used 11 joints per frame from 3-D Skeleton of the human, standing in front of kinect as shown in Fig. 2. We have extracted the features from joints based on angles and distances. Support Vector machine is trained for building the model out of these features. Finally, SVM classifies the signs done by the presenter.

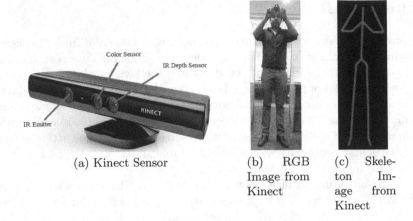

(a) Kinect Sensor

(b) RGB Image from Kinect

(c) Skeleton Image from Kinect

Fig. 1. Kinect sensor and its output components

Table 1. List of signs

Agra (City)	Airport	Bank	Bengali (Language)
Christmas	Cinema	Computer	Dhobi (Laundry person)
Diwali (Festival)	Dosa (Food Dish)	Farmer	Film
Flute	Ganpati (Hindu God)	Guitar	Holi (Festival)
Kite	Leather	Magnet	Marathi (Language)
Milk	Police	Pune (City)	Poster
Ramzan (Festival)	Shooting	Video Camera	Shimla (City)
Urdu (Language)	World	Karate	Pooja (Worship)
Buddha Poornima (Festival)	Dhol (Drum)	Mechanic	Floppy
Tea			

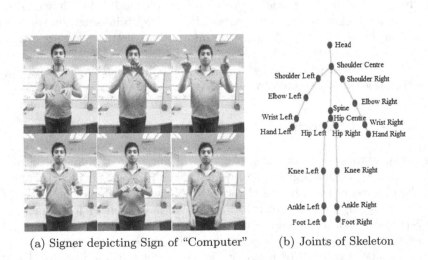

(a) Signer depicting Sign of "Computer"

(b) Joints of Skeleton

Fig. 2. Gestures and joints

3.1 Data Acquisition

The skeleton data from the Kinect SDK is extracted for each frame. To record the sign, performer stands in front of kinect. Each sign starts by raising the hands above hip level and ends once both hands are below hip level. In between these actions, the sign is performed. Since only the co-ordinates of skeleton joints are used, we store the co-ordinates given by Kinect SDK for feature extraction discussed in Sect. 3.2.

Sign data is collected using kinect from 15 different users. Each user performs a sign 5 times, thus a total of 2775 samples are collected. Further we divide the data into train and test sets of 1943 and 832 samples respectively. The signs are taken from FDMSE [1].

3.2 Feature Extraction

All the discussed 37 signs are done using upper body parts. So, we have only considered 11 out of 20 joints (covers upper body parts) per frame for feature extraction. The red dots in the skeleton in Fig. 3 shows these 11 joints which is in $\mathbb{R}^3$.

Fig. 3. Red joints used for feature extraction

In our approach, features are extracted from 11 different joints by calculating angles and distances.

Joint Angle. The Joint Angle is an essential feature as all the signs listed above are done primarily by hands and the angle changes a lot. We have calculated various such angles considering different joints. These angles are calculated between 3 joints on all 3 planes, making 3 features per joint angle. Also, when those joints are considered which have both left and right joints as shown in Fig. 4, features count goes to 6 per joint angle. Joint Angle can be calculated as described below:

A(x1,y1,z1), B(x2,y2,z2) and C(x3,y3,z3) are 3 joints for which we have to calculate joint angle in XY plane.

Step 1: Calculate Euclidean Distance between all three joints:

$$D_1^{xy} = \sqrt{(x2 - x1)^2 + (y2 - y1)^2} \tag{1}$$

$$D_2^{xy} = \sqrt{(x3 - x2)^2 + (y3 - y2)^2} \tag{2}$$

$$D_3^{xy} = \sqrt{(x3 - x1)^2 + (y3 - y1)^2} \tag{3}$$

Similar distances can be calculated using Eqs. 1, 2 and 3 for YZ and XZ plane.

Step 2: Calculating angle by using Law of Cosines which relates the lengths of the sides of a triangle to the cosine of one of its angles:

$$\alpha = \arccos\left(\frac{(D_1^{xy})^2 + (D_2^{xy})^2 - (D_3^{xy})^2}{2 * D_1^{xy} * D_2^{xy}}\right) * \frac{180}{\pi} \tag{4}$$

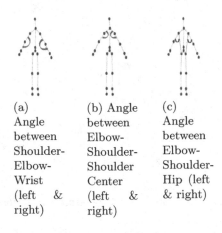

(a) Angle between Shoulder-Elbow-Wrist (left & right)

(b) Angle between Elbow-Shoulder-Shoulder Center (left & right)

(c) Angle between Elbow-Shoulder-Hip (left & right)

Fig. 4. Angle between joints

In Eq. 4, angle α on B made by A and C in XY plane. Similarly, we calculated the angle β and γ in YZ and XZ plane respectively.

Following features are extracted via Joint Angle:

1. Shoulder-Elbow-Wrist: The angle is made on Elbow by Shoulder and Wrist joints as shown in Fig. 4a. This angle is calculated for left and right and on all the three planes making it 6 features.
2. Elbow-Shoulder-Shoulder Center: The angle is made on Shoulder by Elbow and Shoulder Center joints as shown in Fig. 4b. Similarly, this angle is also calculated for left and right and on all the three planes making it 6 features.

3. Elbow-Shoulder-Hip: The angle is made on Shoulder by Elbow and Hip joints as shown in Fig. 4c. This angle is too calculated for left and right both the sides and on all the three planes making it as 6 features.
4. Wrist, Head and Shoulder Center: The angle is made on Head by Wrist and Shoulder joints. This angle is calculated for left and right both the sides and on all the three planes making it as 6 features.

Euclidean Distance. The distance between two joints varies for every gesture and is different for different performers. The Euclidean Distance between Joint A(x1,y1,z1) and B(x2,y2,z2) is

$$D = \sqrt{(x2 - x1)^2 + (y2 - y1)^2 + (z2 - z1)^2} \tag{5}$$

Following features are extracted via Euclidean distance. The joint combinations for calculating the distance using Eq. 5 are as follows:

1. Shoulder-Wrist: Distance between Shoulder and Wrist joints for left and right as shown in Fig. 5a.
2. Elbow-Hip Center: Distance between Elbow and Hip center joints for left and right as shown in Fig. 5b.
3. Elbow-Hip: Distance between Elbow and Hip joints for left and right.
4. Wrist-Hip: Distance between Wrist and Hip joints for left and right.
5. Ratio of Distances:
   (a.) A ratio of distances between Wrist Left and Wrist Right to Shoulder Center and Hip Center as shown in Fig. 5c.
   (b.) A ratio of distances between Elbow Left and Elbow Right to Shoulder Left and Shoulder Right as shown in Fig. 5d.

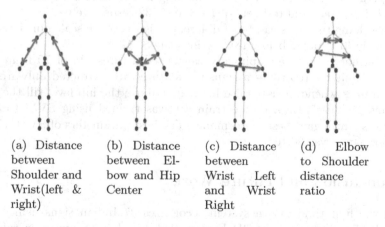

(a) Distance between Shoulder and Wrist(left & right)

(b) Distance between Elbow and Hip Center

(c) Distance between Wrist Left and Wrist Right

(d) Elbow to Shoulder distance ratio

Fig. 5. Distance between joints

Features like Ratio of Distances are calculated so that features are independent of signer's height. Thus, we have selected novel features, which uniquely represents 37 signs considered in this paper.

Total of 34 features are extracted per frame using above mentioned joint angle and euclidean distances.

3.3 Classification

The data in the train sets was used to build the Support Vector machine model [8], and data in the test sets was used to evaluate the performance of the classifier. The SVM classifier aims to identify a handful of points called the support vectors from the entire data-set which allow us to draw a linear or a non-linear separating surface in the input space of the data-set. SVM models are typically built with the help of kernel functions which allow us to transform the data into n-dimensional space where a hyper plane can be easily constructed to partition the data. We used RBF kernel with cross validation and grid search [16] for selecting the best parameters value in checking the performance of SVM classifier.

4 Experimental Results

For the purpose of our study, we collected signs data on our own as described in Sect. 3.1. To demonstrate the experiment, a signer stands in front of the kinect with his/her hands below hip level. Once the signer raises his/her hands above hip level, 11 skeleton joints are collected for each frame and features are extracted as described in Sect. 3.2. This continues till the signer's both hands are below hip level which signifies sign completion. Then feature vector is formed by appending features recorded from each frame. This process is then repeated for all 37 gestures, for all 15 users. Thus, making it a total of 2775 samples which we divide into train and test sets of 1943 and 832 respectively.

Signer doing the signs can be of different heights, so we scale our data-set to normalize in [0,1] range before feeding into the SVM.

Furthermore, we have empirically calculated a threshold of 70 frames as a maximum limit for recording a sign, i.e. features are extracted only from the first 70 frames whenever user raise his hands above the hip level till the hands are below hip level. Data in the train set was trained using SVM to obtain parameters which gave best performance. For best parameters of SVM, the test set performance was 86.16 %.

5 Conclusion and Future Work

This is the first time that a system recognizes 37 Indian signs using Kinect sensor. While extracting the 3D human skeleton, Kinect sensor is robust to performer's height, weight, and dress. Consequently, the proposed system also shows robustness to the above variations. We have experimented with a minimal set of features to distinguish between the given signs with practical accuracies.

Presently, we have worked on non-continuous gestures. For each sign, the performer needs to lift his hands above the hips to start a sign and again bring them below the hips to end. The future scope of our work will be to recognize continuous gestures. This will require non-trivial segmentation. Also, we aim to extend our system to a wider set of practical gestures by adding advanced features. Latest kinect sensor with more accurate and robust functioning will push our work towards the said goals.

References

1. http://indiansignlanguage.org
2. (2012). http://gesture.chalearn.org/dissemination/cvpr2012
3. Agarwal, A., Thakur, M.K.: Sign language recognition using microsoft kinect, August 2013
4. Ali, A., Aggarwal, J.K.: Segmentation and recognition of continuous human activity (2001)
5. Biswas, K.K., Basu, S.K.: Gesture recognition using microsoft kinect x00ae, December 2011
6. Bretzner, L., Laptev, I., Lindeberg, T.: Hand gesture recognition using multi-scale colour features, hierarchical models and particle filtering, May 2002
7. Chua, C.-S., Guan, H., Ho, Y.-K.: Model-based 3D hand posture estimation from a single 2D image. Image Vis. Comput. **20**(3), 191–202 (2002)
8. Cristianini, N., Shawe-Taylor, J.: An introduction to support vector machines: and other kernel-based learning methods (2000)
9. Geetha, M., Manjusha, C., Unnikrishnan, P., Harikrishnan, R.: A vision based dynamic gesture recognition of indian sign language on kinect based depth images. In: 2013 International Conference on Emerging Trends in Communication, Control, Signal Processing Computing Applications (C2SPCA), pp. 1–7, October 2013
10. Ghotkar, A.S., Khatal, R., Khupase, S., Asati, S., Hadap, M.: Hand gesture recognition for indian sign language. In: 2012 International Conference on Computer Communication and Informatics (ICCCI), pp. 1–4, January 2012
11. Madabhushi, A., Aggarwal, J.K.: Using head movement to recognize activity (2000)
12. Pavlovic, V.I., Sharma, R., Huang, T.S.: Visual interpretation of hand gestures for human-computer interaction: A review. IEEE Trans. Pattern Anal. Mach. Intell. **19**(7), 677–695 (1997)
13. Rajam, P.S., Balakrishnan, G.: Real time indian sign language recognition system to aid deaf-dumb people. In: 2011 IEEE 13th International Conference on Communication Technology (ICCT), pp. 737–742, September 2011
14. Saha, S., Ghosh, S., Konar, A., Nagar, A.K.: Gesture recognition from indian classical dance using kinect sensor, June 2013
15. Uddin, M.Z., Duc Thang, N., Kim, T.-S.: Human activity recognition via 3-D joint angle features and hidden markov models, September 2010
16. Wei Hsu, C., Chung Chang, C., Jen Lin, C.: A practical guide to support vector classification (2010)
17. Zafrulla, Z., Brashear, H., Starner, T., Hamilton, H., Presti, P.: American sign language recognition with the kinect (2011)

Automatic Planning of Minimally Invasive Aortic Valve Replacement Surgery

Mustafa Elattar[1]([✉]), Floortje van Kesteren[2,4], Esther Wiegerinck[2],
Ed van Bavel[1], Jan Baan[2], Riccardo Cocchieri[3], Nils Planken[4],
and Henk Marquering[1,4]

[1] Biomedical Engineering and Physics Department, Academic Medical Center,
University of Amsterdam, Amsterdam, The Netherlands
mustafa.elattar@gmail.com
[2] Heart Center, Academic Medical Center, University of Amsterdam,
Amsterdam, The Netherlands
[3] Cardiothoracic Surgery Department, Academic Medical Center,
University of Amsterdam, Amsterdam, The Netherlands
[4] Radiology Department, Academic Medical Center, University of Amsterdam,
Amsterdam, The Netherlands

Abstract. The minimally invasive aortic valve replacement procedure provides
a good alternative to conventional open heart surgery. Currently, Planning of the
mini-AVR is supported by the selection of closest intercostal space to the sinutubular junction manually. In this work, we automate and standardize this
planning by automatically detecting the intercostal spaces and the sinutubular
junction, from which we calculate the closest incision location. The proposed
algorithm provides qualitatively and quantitatively accurate results; where the
sinutubular junction detection has mean error of 3.4 mm. This work has the
potential to be implemented in the clinical practice for reproducible and accurate
mini-AVR planning.

Keywords: CT angiography · Mini-AVR · Segmentation · Sinutubular
junction · Intercostal spaces

1 Introduction

Aortic stenosis is the most common form of valvular heart disease. Aortic stenosis
occurs mainly due to calcium accumulation on the aortic valve leaflets. Severe aortic
stenosis usually requires aortic valve replacement (AVR). During AVR the aortic valve
is replaced with a new prosthesis. The standard procedure to replace the aortic valve is
conventional open heart surgery (full sternotomy) [1]. Recently, minimally invasive
aortic valve replacement (mini-AVR) was introduced to reduce the recovery time after
the surgery and produce smaller scars in comparison with conventional open heart
surgery [2] (Fig. 1). Minimally invasive AVR has shown excellent results in terms of
mortality, morbidity, and patient satisfaction, providing less pain, faster recovery, and a
shorter hospital stay [3]. As intraoperative trans-esophageal echocardiography became

© Springer International Publishing Switzerland 2015
M. Kamel and A. Campilho (Eds.): ICIAR 2015, LNCS 9164, pp. 536–540, 2015.
DOI: 10.1007/978-3-319-20801-5_60

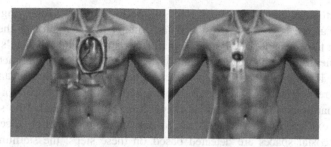

Fig. 1. Schematic figure showing open heart surgery (Left) Mini-AVR (Right)

the standard imaging modality to use during the procedure, 3D CTA has much to offer in the preoperative planning and supports the decision making system.

Usage of 3D CTA is helpful in assessing the required measurements for the surgery [4]. Preoperative evaluation is performed with the aid of CT angiography images, assessing the amount of the calcification in the ascending aorta in addition for measuring the closest distance between the sinutubular junction and the different intercostal spaces as shown in Fig. 2.

Currently, these preoperative measures are performed manually, which makes it prone to interobserver variation. Therefore we propose the usage of image analysis to standardize and automate the preoperative planning. In this work, we introduce a fully automated algorithm detecting the sinutubular junction, intercostal spaces, and finding the closest intercostal space to propose the incision location. The accuracy of the algorithm was assessed quantitatively and qualitatively.

2   Methods

To determine the closest intercostal space to the sinutubular junction, we automatically extract the sinutubular junction, and 2nd, 3rd and 4th intercostal spaces. We implemented the aortic root segmentation technique by Elattar et al. [5] to segment the surface of the aortic root.

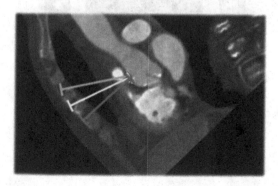

Fig. 2. Reconstructed hyper plane shows the three intercostal spaces and the ascending aorta. The three colored lines showing the three distances to the sinutubular junction

The sinutubular junction is detected by performing the following steps: the 2segmented surface is converted to the polar domain for each slice of the shape and perpendicular to centerline. The Fourier transform is applied on each slice's radius. The second and the third harmonic component of the radius function are extracted per slice forming two 1D signals representing the contribution of the elliptical and the three cusps shapes respectively. Subsequently, we applied the Laplacian operator on the ratio of the third harmonic to the second harmonic contributions. Finally, the second local maximum is extracted which corresponds to the sinutubular junction slice.

The intercostal spaces are detected based on these steps: the sternum is located using thresholding and morphological operators resulting in a set of seed points, which are used to apply a region growing extracting only the bone marrow of the sternum. The resulted volume is dilated, and subsequently the surface of the dilated volume is used to generate a multi-planar reconstructed image.

Figure 3 shows the reconstructed images which intersect with the cross sections of the ribs cartilages. K-means clustering is used to segment each cartilage cross section appearing in the formed reconstructed image. Finally, the centroids of the segmented cartilages clusters are calculated from which the intercostal spaces are estimated.

The distance between the 2nd, 3rd and 4th intercostal space and the sinutubular junction of the aortic root was calculated and the minimum distance was presented.

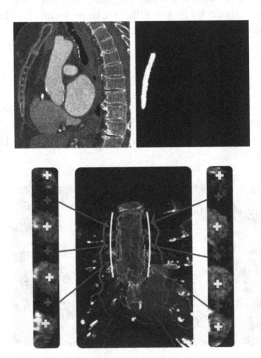

Fig. 3. Sagittal view for the sternum with located seed points and the binary region growing result is shown (upper) coronal view for the sternum and the cartilages cross section image is shown on both sides with detected centroids in red and intercostal spaces in green (Bottom)

The evaluation of the detection of the intercostal spaces was done visually by giving a score of Good, Bad, or Reject for each detected intercostal space. The sinutubular junction detection error was evaluated by measuring the 3D Euclidean distance between the center of the detected sinutubular junction contour and the manual annotated contour center.

3 Results

The developed algorithms were applied on 20 severe aortic stenosis patients for validation purposes. The sternum has been detected successfully in 19 patients. The intercostal spaces were extracted successfully in 18 out of 19 patient datasets. Visual inspection of the detected intercostal spaces showed high accuracy. The sinutubular junction was detected successfully in the 20 patient datasets with mean error of 3.4 ± 2.4 mm; where the error between observers was 1.9 ± 1.0 mm (Table 1).

Table 1. Accuracy of the sinutubular junction detection for the proposed technique and the interobserver analysis.

Sinutubular junction detection	Mean	Median	STD
Proposed algorithm	3.4 mm	2.6 mm	2.4 mm
Interobserver variation	1.9 mm	2.8 mm	1.0 mm

4 Discussion

We present a fully automatic algorithm detecting the sinutubular junction, the three intercostal spaces on both sternum sides which were used for calculating their distances to present the optimal incision location. The proposed algorithm showed quantitatively good accuracy for sinutubular junction detection. The visual assessment of the intercostal spaces showed good accuracy as well. Sternum detection failed in a single case because of high levels of noise in this image data. Another case suffered from incomplete volume of interest which led to incorrect detection of intercostal spaces. Further quantitative analysis and validation for the detection of the sinutubular junction is in progress.

5 Conclusion

In this work, we proposed an automated method, which is composed of two techniques to extract the sinutubular junction and the intercostal spaces to evaluate the minimum distance for optimal ascending aorta access. The whole workflow was evaluated and showed good accuracy. We believe that this is the first solution to be developed. This work has the potential to be implemented in the clinical practice tool for supporting mini-AVR planning.

References

1. Rosengart, T.K., Feldman, T., Borger, M.A., Vassiliades, T.A., Gillinov, A.M., Hoercher, K.J., Vahanian, A., Bonow, R.O., O'Neill, W.: Percutaneous and minimally invasive valve procedures: a scientific statement from the american heart association council on cardiovascular surgery and anesthesia, council on clinical cardiology, functional genomics and translational biology interdisciplinary working group, and quality of care and outcomes research interdisciplinary working group. Circulation **117**, 1750–1767 (2008)
2. Cohn, L., Adams, D.: Minimally invasive aortic valve replacement. Semin. Thorac. Cardiovasc Surg **9**, 293–297 (1997)
3. ElBardissi, A.W., Shekar, P., Couper, G.S., Cohn, L.H.: Minimally invasive aortic valve replacement in octogenarian, high-risk, transcatheter aortic valve implantation candidates. J. Thorac. Cardiovasc. Surg. **141**(2), 328–335 (2011)
4. Stelzer, P.: 3D thinking for mini-AVR. JACC Cardiovasc. Imag. **6**(2), 272–273 (2013)
5. Elattar, M.A., Wiegerinck, E.M., Planken, R.N., Vanbavel, E., van Assen, H.C., Baan, J., Marquering, H.A.: Automatic segmentation of the aortic root in CT angiography of candidate patients for transcatheter aortic valve implantation. Med. Biol. Eng. Comput. **52**(7), 611–618 (2014)

Author Index

Abbasi-Sureshjani, Samaneh 325
Abdullah-Al-Tariq, 277
Adithya, V. 71
Ahmad, Foysal 178, 194
Ahmad, Imran Shafiq 269
Ahmed, Ferdous 277
Akter, Nasreen 90
Aljohani, Nawaf 194
Alkhorshid, Yasamin 514
Alkinani, Monagi H. 51
Almarashda, Khalfan 109
Al-Mualla, Mohammed 109, 218
Araújo, Teresa 360
Aresta, Guilherme 360
Arias, Pablo A. 178
Aryafar, Kamelia 514
Ayala-Raggi, Salvador E. 287
Ayaz, Anaum 411
Ayub, Sara 411
Azevedo, Elsa 360
Azzabi, Wassim 344

Baan, Jan 402, 536
Balamuralidhar, P. 71
Barreto-Flores, Aldrin 287
Bedawi, Safaa M. 499
Belacel, Nabil 150
Belhe, Swapnil 528
Berton, Florian 344
Bhaskar, Harish 109, 218
Bloch, Isabelle 520
Boufama, Boubakeur 269
Bouguila, Nizar 141, 159

Campilho, Aurélio 335, 360
Can, Ahmet Burak 297
Castelli, Jane 3
Chabrier, Sébastien 446
Chao, Haiyang 316
Chappard, Christine 419
Cheriet, Farida 344, 352
Chung, Audrey G. 368, 385

Chwyl, Brendan 210, 385
Clausi, David A. 82, 210, 385
Cocchieri, Riccardo 536

Dashtbozorg, Behdad 335
Dawood, Ali 109
Dozier, Gerry V. 178
Dubois, Lucile 402
Dutta, Tanima 71

Elattar, Mustafa 402, 536
Elguebaly, Tarek 159
El-Sakka, Mahmoud R. 43, 51, 60, 129
ElSayed, Ahmed 247
Esteves, Tiago 377

Ferreira, Carmen 360
Fieguth, Paul 82
Figueiredo, Francisco 377
Forczmański, Paweł 119, 229, 489
Frejlichowski, Dariusz 169, 473, 489, 506

Gabillon, Alban 446
Gao, Qigang 259
Gim, JaWon 437
Godbole, Atul 528
Gondra, Iker 90
González, Pedro de Jesús 287
Gościewska, Katarzyna 169, 473, 489
Goto, Katsunari 481
Guclu, Oguzhan 297

Habashi, Pejman 269
Haider, Masoom A. 368
Hasan, Mahmud 60
Hemmati, Nasim 3
Ho, Yishin 306
Hofman, Radosław 473, 489
Hu, Gang 259
Huo, Jie 100
Hwang, MinCheol 437

542   Author Index

Irshad, Samra   411

Jenadeleh, Mohsen   14

Kabani, AbdulWahab   129
Kabir, Md. Hasanul   277
Kacem, Anis   419
Kamel, Mohamed S.   499
Kardouchi, Mustapha   150
Kasiri, Keyvan   82
Kawanaka, Hiroharu   481
Kerouh, Fatma   465
Khalvati, Farzad   368
Ko, Byoung Chul   437
Koff, David   3
Kowalik-Urbaniak, Ilona A.   3

La Torre, Davide   33, 218
Łabędź, Piotr   229
LaPlante, François   150
Laporte, Catherine   344
Li, Yuke   520
Liu, Jizhong   186
Loesdau, Martin   446

Mahmood, Ausif   247
Maleika, Wojciech   119
Marquering, Henk   402, 536
Martin, Thomas   109
Maruf, Golam M.   43
Masoudimansour, Walid   141
McFadden, Steven B.   22
Mehrotra, Kapil   528
Mendonça, Ana Maria   335
Moghaddam, Mohsen Ebrahimi   14
Morrow, Philip   456

Nacereddine, Nafaa   203
Naiel, Mohamed A.   429
Nam, Jae-Yeal   437
Nowosielski, Adam   489

Okubo, Kan   306
Omair Ahmad, M.   429
Otero, Daniel   33

Parr, Gerard   456
Phan, Thanh Vân   352

Planken, Nils   402, 536
Premachandra, Chinthaka   481

Quelhas, Pedro   377

Reade, Simon   239
Rizo-Rodriguez, Dayron   203
Rocha, Sara   377
Rouco, José   360
Roy, Kaushik   178, 194

Sánchez-Urrieta, Susana   287
Sarkar, Soumyajit   186
Scharfenberger, Christian   368
Scotney, Bryan   456
Seoud, Lama   352
Sevestre-Ghalila, Sylvie   419
Sharma, Hrishikesh   71
Shelton, Joseph   178, 194
Shen, Weiming   520
Shokoufandeh, Ali   514
Silva, Luís M.   377
Siricharoen, Punnarai   456
Smit-Ockeloen, Iris   325
Smolarski-Koff, Nadine   3
Sobh, Tarek   247
Sousa, Ricardo Gamelas   377
Swamy, M.N.S.   429

Tabbone, Antoine   203
Tagawa, Norio   306
Takase, Haruhiko   481
Ter Haar Romeny, Bart   325
Thangarajah, Akilan   100
Tsukada, Syouta   306
Tsuruoka, Shinji   481

Usman Akram, M.   411

van Bavel, Ed   536
van Kesteren, Floortje   402, 536
vanbavel, Ed   402
Vezina, Martin   465
Viriri, Serestina   239, 394
Vrscay, Edward R.   3, 33

Wang, Guanghui   100, 186, 316
Wang, Jiheng   3
Wang, Zhou   3
Wanielik, Gerd   514

Ward, Paul A.S.   22
Wiegerinck, Esther   402, 536
Wong, Alexander   210, 368, 385
Wu, Fuchao   316
Wu, Q.M. Jonathan   100

Youssef, Rabaa   419

Zhang, Jiong   325
Zhang, Ming   316
Ziou, Djemel   203, 465

Printed in the United States
By Bookmasters

Printed in the United States
By Bookmasters